# Advances in Internal Medicine®
Volume 37

# Advances in Internal Medicine®

Volumes 1 through 33 (Out of Print)

## Volume 34

The Molecular Biology of Interleukin 1 and Acute Phase Response, by Jean D. Sipe

Campylobacters and Gastroduodenal Inflammation, by Martin J. Blaser and William R. Brown

Intestinal and Hepatic Manifestations of AIDS, by Donald P. Kotler

Special Health Problems of Mexican-Americans: Obesity, Gallbladder Disease, Diabetes Mellitus, and Cardiovascular Disease, by Andrew K. Diehl and Michael P. Stern

Liver Transplantation, by David H. Van Thiel, Vincents J. Dindzans, Judith S. Gavaler, Ralph E. Tarter, and Robert R. Schade

Early Diagnosis and Treatment of Hemochromatosis, by Paul C. Adams, June W. Halliday, and Lawrie W. Powell

Medical and Surgical Management of Obesity, by Robert H. Lerman and David R. Cave

Disorders of Micturition in the Aging Patient, by Joseph G. Ouslander and Reginald Bruskewitz

The Role of Androgens in the Treatment of Hematologic Disorders, by Sharhabil S. Ammus

Non-Hodgkin's Lymphoma, by Arthur T. Sharin

Carcinogen Monitoring by DNA Adduct Methodology in Humans: Clinical Perspectives for the 1990s, by Howard K. Koh, Marianne N. Prout, and John D. Groopman

Effects of Radiation on the Thyroid Gland, by Lester Van Middlesworth

The Risks and Benefits of Oral Contraceptives, by Karen H. Brown and Charles B. Hammond

Aluminum-Related Osteodystrophy, by Donald J. Sherrard and Dennis L. Andress

Paraendocrine Syndromes of Cancer, by William D. Odell

The Endothelium, Platelets, and Coronary Vasospasm, by John C. Hoak

Silent Myocardial Ischemia, An Update, by Peter F. Cohn

The Exercise Test: Evolution of an Old Form, by Milton Hollenberg

Current Concepts in the Use of Digitalis, by Elliot M. Antman and Thomas W. Smith

## Volume 35

Rheumatogenic Group A Streptococci and the Return of Rheumatic Fever, by Gene H. Stollerman

Topical Respiratory Therapy, by Ira D. Lawrence and Roy Patterson

# Advances in
# Internal Medicine®

## Editor
### Gene H. Stollerman, M.D.
Professor of Medicine, Boston University School of Medicine, Boston,
Massachusetts; Veterans Administration Distinguished Physician, Veterans
Administration Medical Center, Bedford, Massachusetts

## Associate Editors
### J. Thomas LaMont, M.D.
Chief, Section of Gastroenterology, Boston University Medical School, University
Hospital, Boston, Massachusetts

### James J. Leonard, M.D.
Chairman, Department of Medicine, Uniformed Services University of the Health
Sciences, Department of Defense, Bethesda, Maryland

### Marvin D. Siperstein, M.D., Ph.D.
Professor of Medicine, University of California, San Francisco; Chief, Metabolism
Service, Veterans Administration Medical Center, San Francisco, California

**Volume 37 • 1992**

Mosby
Year Book

St. Louis   Baltimore   Boston   Chicago   London   Philadelphia   Sydney   Toronto

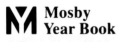

# Mosby
# Year Book

Dedicated to Publishing Excellence

*Sponsoring Editor:* Nancy G. Puckett
*Associate Managing Editor, Manuscript Services:* Denise Dungey
*Assistant Director, Manuscript Services:* Frances M. Perveiler
*Production Coordinator:* Timothy A. Phillips
*Proofroom Manager:* Barbara M. Kelly

Editorial Office:
Mosby–Year Book, Inc.
200 North LaSalle St.
Chicago, IL 60601

International Standard Serial Number: 0065-2822
International Standard Book Number: 0-8151-8307-0

# Contributors

**William B. Applegate, M.D., M.P.H.**
Professor of Medicine and Preventive Medicine, University of Tennessee, Memphis, School of Medicine, Memphis, Tennessee

**Stanley P. Ballou, M.D.**
Associate Professor of Medicine, Case Western Reserve University at MetroHealth Medical Center, Cleveland, Ohio

**John D. Brunzell, M.D.**
Professor of Medicine, Department of Medicine, Division of Metabolism. Endocrinology and Nutrition, University of Washington School of Medicine, Seattle, Washington

**David P. Carbone, M.D., Ph.D.**
Assistant Professor of Medical Oncology, University of Texas Southwestern Medical Center, Dallas, Texas

**Alan Chait, M.D.**
Professor of Medicine, Department of Medicine, Division of Metabolism, Endocrinology and Nutrition, University of Washington School of Medicine, Seattle, Washington

**Irun R. Cohen, M.D.**
Mauerberger Chair of Immunology, Department of Cell Biology, The Weizmann Institute of Science, Rehovot, Israel

**Mitchell B. Cohen, M.D.**
Associate Professor of Pediatrics, Division of Pediatric Gastroenterology, University of Cincinnati College of Medicine, Children's Hospital Medical Center, Cincinnati, Ohio

**Catherine E. DuBeau, M.D.**
Instructor in Medicine, Division on Aging, Harvard Medical School; Geriatric Research Education and Clinical Center, Brockton/West Roxbury Department of Veterans Affairs Medical Center; Geriatric Division, Brigham and Women's Hospital, The Hebrew Rehabilitation Center for Aged, Boston, Massachusetts

**Ralph A. Giannella, M.D.**
Mark Brown Professor of Medicine and Director, Division of Gastroenterology, University of Cincinnati College of Medicine, Veterans Administration Medical Center, Cincinnati, Ohio

## Carl Grunfeld, M.D., Ph.D.

Associate Professor of Medicine, Co-Director Special Diagnostic and Treatment Unit, Department of Medicine, University of California, San Francisco, School of Medicine, Metabolism Section, Medical Service, Department of Veterans Affairs Medical Center, San Francisco, California

## Hunter Heath III, M.D.

Professor of Medicine, Endocrine Research Unit, Mayo Medical School, Consultant in Endocrinology, Metabolism, and Internal Medicine, Mayo Foundation and Clinic, Rochester, Minnesota

## Ahvie Herskowitz, M.D.

Assistant Professor of Medicine, Department of Medicine, Department of Immunology and Infectious Diseases, The Johns Hopkins Medical Institutions, Baltimore, Maryland

## John C. Hoefs, M.D.

Associate Professor, Department of Medicine, University of California, Irvine, School of Medicine, Orange County, California

## David R. Holmes, Jr., M.D.

Consultant, Division of Cardiovascular Diseases and Internal Medicine, Mayo Clinic and Mayo Foundation; Professor of Medicine, Mayo Medical School, Rochester, Minnesota

## Patricia C. Hsia, M.D.

Fellow in Gastroenterology and Hepatology, Veterans Affairs Medical Center, Georgetown University School of Medicine, Washington, D.C.

## Gavin M. Jonas, M.D.

Clinical Instructor, Gastroenterology, Southern California Permanente Medical Group, Anaheim, California

## Irving Kushner, M.D.

Professor of Medicine and Pathology, Case Western Reserve University at Metro-Health Medical Center, Cleveland, Ohio

## Scott A. Mackler, M.D., Ph.D.

Section of General Internal Medicine, Department of Pharmacology, University of Pennsylvania School of Medicine, Philadelphia, Pennsylvania

## John D. Minna, M.D.

Director, Simmons Cancer Center, University of Texas Southwestern Medical Center, Dallas, Texas

## David A. Neumann, Ph.D.

Research Associate, Department of Immunology and Infectious Diseases, The Johns Hopkins Medical Institutions, Baltimore, Maryland

## Rick A. Nishimura, M.D.

Consultant, Division of Cardiovascular Diseases and Internal Medicine, Mayo Clinic and Mayo Foundation; Associate Professor of Medicine, Mayo Medical School, Rochester, Minnesota

## Charles P. O'Brien, M.D., Ph.D.

Department of Psychiatry, University of Pennsylvania School of Medicine, Philadelphia, Pennsylvania

## Mark A. Perrella, M.D.

Fellow, Division of Internal Medicine and Thoracic Diseases, The Mayo Foundation and Clinic, Rochester, Minnesota

## Neil M. Resnick, M.D.

Chief of Geriatrics and Director of the Continence Center, Brigham and Women's Hospital; Geriatric Research Education and Clinical Center, Brockton/West Roxbury Department of Veterans Affairs Medical Center; The Hebrew Rehabilitation Center for Aged, Division on Aging; Harvard Medical School, Boston, Massachusetts

## Noel R. Rose, M.D., Ph.D.

Professor and Chairman, Department of Immunology and Infectious Diseases; Professor, Department of Medicine, The Johns Hopkins Medical Institutions, Baltimore, Maryland

## Edward C. Rosenow, III, M.D.

Arthur M. and Gladys D. Gray Professor of Medicine, Division of Internal Medicine and Thoracic Diseases, The Mayo Foundation and Clinic, Rochester, Minnesota

## Sharon Safrin, M.D.

Assistant Clinical Professor of Medicine and Epidemiology and Biostatistics, University of California, San Francisco, School of Medicine, Division of Infectious Diseases, San Francisco General Hospital, San Francisco, California

## Susan Savage, M.D.

Assistant Professor, Department of Medicine, University of Colorado School of Medicine, Denver, Colorado

## Clark T. Sawin, M.D.

Professor of Medicine, Tufts University School of Medicine, Chief, Endocrine-Diabetes Section, Medical Service, Boston Veterans Affairs Medical Center, Boston, Massachusetts

## Robert C. Schlant, M.D.

Professor of Medicine (Cardiology), Emory University School of Medicine; Chief of Cardiology, Grady Memorial Hospital, Atlanta, Georgia

## Robert W. Schrier, M.D.

Professor and Chairman, Department of Medicine, University of Colorado School of Medicine, Denver, Colorado

## Leonard B. Seeff, M.D.
Chief, Gastroenterology and Hepatology, Veterans Affairs Medical Center, Georgetown University School of Medicine, Washington, D.C.

## Thomas J. Török, M.D.
Chief, Epidemiology Section, Respiratory and Enterovirus Branch, Division of Viral and Rickettsial Diseases, National Center for Infectious Diseases, Centers for Disease Control, Atlanta, Georgia

## James P. Utz, M.D.
Consultant, Division of Internal Medicine and Thoracic Diseases, The Mayo Foundation and Clinic, Rochester, Minnesota

## Paul Volberding, M.D.
Professor, Department of Medicine, University of California, San Francisco, School of Medicine; Chief, Division of AIDS Oncology, Director, AIDS Program, San Francisco General Hospital, San Francisco, California

# Preface

The selection of topics for volume 37 by the editors of *Advances in Internal Medicine®* follows our usual policy of spotting new and timely information of importance to medical practice, regardless of whether the subject matter is at the subcellular or the global epidemiologic level. It is not easy, therefore, to group our topics except by the specific choices proposed by each of the editors. These choices reflect, of course, each of their special interests. To gain a place in the table of contents, however, each choice must win a unanimous endorsement and then survive a priority listing and the cut-off of page restrictions. This process that we have used for many past volumes results in an assemblage of reviews of remarkable range and diversity.

The list of infections flagged this year for the reader's attention is rather long. HIV, coxsackievirus myocarditis, parvoviruses in marrow aplasia, hepatitis C, and hemolytic-uremic *E. coli* range through a variety of organ systems and are augmented by immunologic topics in acute phase host defenses and autoimmunity. Neurobehavioral effects of cocaine outweighed most other competitors. The geriatric topics carved out their usual big niche with such unavoidables as the successful treatment of systolic hypertension in the elderly, the issues of benign prostatic hypertrophy and bladder dysfunction, thyroid and hyperparathyroid dysfunction, among others. Diabetes got its foot in the door again and the use of ACE inhibitors in renal failure couldn't be avoided either. The lung and its oncogenetics captured this year's oncology niche, and the "hyperlipidemic syndrome" topped the choices for this year's "lipidology." Nor were technical procedures neglected: Open lung biopsy, diagnostic paracentesis, balloon valvuloplasty and TURP come in for their fair share of medical critique. Finally, the numerous (too numerous?) options for the current management of uncomplicated myocardial infarction are addressed evenhandedly and in masterful fashion by a master of the subject.

What have we omitted? Plenty! But what we've included should keep our readers busy, well-informed and, we hope, interested for another year.

*Gene H. Stollerman, M.D.*

# Contents

# The Current Management of the Patient With Uncomplicated Myocardial Infarction

## Robert C. Schlant, M.D.

Professor of Medicine (Cardiology), Emory University School of Medicine; Chief of Cardiology, Grady Memorial Hospital, Atlanta, Georgia

## Editor's Introduction

The management of the patient with uncomplicated acute myocardial infarction has changed dramatically in recent years.

Although the mortality in uncomplicated myocardial infarction, especially the original such episode, may be considered relatively low, a number of agents each used separately have definitely improved mortality figures.

Nevertheless, as Dr. Schlant points out, the precise effect of various combinations of these therapeutic interventions is difficult to assess. Dr. Schlant offers his best advice on management of the individual patient in view of the variables involved and stresses the importance of early recognition of the event and prompt initiation of therapy.

*James J. Leonard, M.D.*

In the last 3 decades, the management of patients with acute myocardial infarction (AMI) has changed markedly.[1-13] This is true for patients with both uncomplicated and complicated infarctions. There is evidence that the decline in mortality rates from coronary artery disease is due, in part, to a decrease in both out-of-hospital and in-hospital coronary deaths of patients with AMI.[14] Because of the rapid changes that have taken place in therapy as well as the many different therapies employed in management, there are only limited accurate data regarding the results of current "conventional" treatment of patients with AMI, particularly since virtually all large series utilize selected or biased samples. In addition, in view of the multiple individual factors that influence acute and long-term prognosis, the many therapies that physicians may employ, and the significant decrease in acute and chronic mortality following AMI, it is becoming more and more difficult to document conclusively the additional beneficial effect of a single change in treatment. This is especially true since the overall mortality of patients admitted to coronary care units (CCUs) with AMIs is now relatively low.

The following discussion will cover the management of patients with uncomplicated AMIs. As a basic principle, management should be individualized to each patient. The optimal therapy to be utilized depends upon many variables, including the patient's age; the presence of other medical problems; how soon after the onset of symptoms the patient is seen; the size, location, and potential complications of the possible or probable myocardial infarction; and the local medical facilities available. In the United States, it also is increasingly apparent that there should be a greater emphasis on two special areas: public education regarding the early manifestations of AMI and the development of rapid and effective emergency care, transportation, and triage facilities.

## General Measures

The patient with suspected AMI should be seen by medical personnel as early as possible. In some preliminary studies, therapy (at times including thrombolytic agents) has been started in either the patient's home or the fully equipped emergency transportation vehicle; obviously, the extent of such therapy depends upon the individual patient and the capabilities and experience of the local system. The patient with suspected AMI should be evaluated as soon as possible for thrombolytic therapy (as discussed later) and aspirin therapy. Aspirin usually can be administered very early after contraindications such as pericarditis, aortic dissection, esophagitis, and peptic ulcer disease have been reasonably ruled out. Initially, aspirin may be given either by a single 325-mg tablet orally or by 2 to 4 chewable 81-mg tablets. Enteric-coated aspirin should not be used in this situation.

Pain is best relieved by morphine given at a dose of 2 to 4 mg intravenously every 5 to 20 minutes until relief is provided. In addition to alleviating pain, morphine produces venous and arterial vasodilation and is helpful in allaying anxiety.[15] Atropine, 0.5 mg intravenously, is given for nausea and vomiting due to morphine unless the patient has tachycardia. Meperidine, which has a mild vagolytic effect, also can be used to relieve pain, especially in patients who have atrioventricular block on their electrocardiogram. The usual dose is 25 to 50 mg intravenously, repeated in 15 minutes, if necessary.

Since most patients with AMI have some degree of arterial hypoxemia, oxygen, 3 to 4 L/min, should be given by nasal prongs for 1 to 2 days.

In view of the importance of initiating thrombolytic therapy (see later) promptly, it usually is best begun after the patient is evaluated in the emergency ward. The patient then should be admitted to a CCU. The electrocardiogram of a patient with suspected AMI should be monitored continuously soon after the patient is first seen. In the CCU, the patient should rest in a comfortable, attractive, and quiet environment. Loud talking and other sounds should be minimized. Patients who are loud or agitated or whose management requires considerable activity should be attended in a distant area whenever possible. Patients with uncomplicated AMIs do not require either direct monitoring of arterial blood pressure or balloon-flotation right heart catheter monitoring of right heart pressures.

After 2 to 3 days in the CCU, patients with uncomplicated myocardial infarctions may be moved to an adjacent step-down unit (if available), where the electrocardiogram should be monitored by telemetry for an additional 2 to 3 days prior to transfer to the general medical ward. These patients usually can be discharged safely after 7 to 14 days. Currently, the longer periods are used primarily for older patients or those with other medical problems. Patients with uncomplicated AMIs do not require transfer to a tertiary care facility.

A clear liquid diet is given for the first 24 hours, followed by a 2 g sodium (5 g salt), low-cholesterol, low-fat diet. Most patients are given a stool softener such as dioctyl sodium sulfosuccinate at a dose of 100 mg daily for the first few days. Patients with anxiety are treated with diazepam, 2 to 5 mg three or four times a day. To help sleep, flurazepam, 15 to 30 mg, or triazolam, 0.125 to 0.250 mg, may be given. The nurses, attending physicians, and other personnel should provide psychological support.

## Nitrates

Patients who have chest pain or discomfort when first seen should initially be given sublingual nitroglycerin, 0.3 to 0.4 mg, two or three times. Those with AMI who have continued or intermittent chest pain should be treated with intravenous nitroglycerin (5 to 200 μg/min).[16, 17] In most instances, continued nitrates are better given intravenously rather than orally or percutaneously, since their effects can be controlled more carefully and rapidly by this route. In this situation, intravenous nitroglycerin, begun with a 15-μg bolus and followed by a pump-controlled infusion of 5 to 10 μg/min with dosage increases of 5 to 10 μg/min every 5 to 10 minutes, not only relieves pain, but also may lessen the extent of infarction and decrease mortality.[16, 17] The endpoints of dose titration with intravenous nitroglycerin include the following: the relief of pain, a decrease in mean blood pressure of 10% in normotensive patients or 30% in hypertensive patients, an increase in heart rate of more than 10 beats per minute, intolerable headache, or a decrease in systolic blood pressure to below 90 mm Hg in normotensive patients or higher levels in chronically hypertensive patients. Nitrate tolerance with diminished responsiveness can begin to occur after 12 to 24 hours of intravenous therapy. Nitrates should be used for about 48 hours after thrombolytic therapy. In patients with a right ventricular infarction, nitrates may produce abrupt or marked hypotension, at times with bradycardia, and must be used with great caution, if at all. If these side effects do develop, the patient should be treated by raising the legs and administering intravenous fluids. Intravenous atropine, 0.5 to 1.0 mg, also can be useful.

## Thrombolytic Agents

Most patients who are seen within 6 hours of the onset of their chest discomfort, have the appropriate electrocardiographic changes and clinical indications (Table 1), and do not have a contraindication (Table 2) are treated with a thrombolytic agent.[18-40] Although many studies of thrombolytic agents to date have not included patients over 70 or 75 years of age, such therapy may be appropriate for many older individuals, who have a higher mortality rate from AMI, particularly those who are thought to be otherwise in good health and to have an infarction of at least moderate size.[41] In addition, some patients may benefit from thrombolytic therapy given even more than 4 to 6 hours and up to 24 hours after the onset of chest pain, particularly if the pain persists or is present intermittently for more than 6 hours.[26, 42] Currently in the United States, only about 15% to 25% of patients with AMI are treated with intravenous thrombolytic therapy, most often recombinant tissue plasminogen activator (rt-PA) followed by streptokinase (SK), anisoylated plasminogen streptokinase activator complex (APSAC), and urokinase (UK). A number of newer thrombolytic agents are under development.

There is good evidence that early thrombolytic therapy results in reperfusion of the infarct-related blood vessel in a significant number of patients,[12, 18, 29-32, 36] and improved ventricular function[12, 27-32, 35] and decreased mortality, both acutely and up to 4 years.[12, 18-40] There is still controversy, however, regarding the relative benefits of rt-PA, SK, APSAC, and UK on coronary patency, ventricular function, and patient survival. Furthermore, the dosage and rate of administration of rt-PA is under continued investigation, as are treatments with adjunctive therapies such as heparin and β-blockers (see later).

In the study done by the Gruppo Italiano per lo Studio della Sopra-

**TABLE 1.**
**General Indications for Thrombolytic Therapy**

Characteristic chest pain of myocardial ischemia or equivalent for at least 30 minutes

Electrocardiographic changes with new ST segment elevations in at least two contiguous precordial leads of at least 2 mm in suspected anterior infarction or of at least 1 mm in at least two leads (II, III, or aVF) in suspected inferior infarction; Q waves may be present

Ability to have therapy instituted within 4 to 6 hours of the onset of chest discomfort

Clinically apparent reinfarction within a few days of apparently successful thrombolytic therapy

## TABLE 2.
## Contraindications to Thrombolytic Therapy

Absolute contraindications.
  Active internal bleeding.
  Recent (within 2 months) intracranial or intraspinal surgery or trauma.
  Intracranial neoplasm, arteriovenous malformation, or aneurysm.
  Prolonged or traumatic cardiopulmonary resuscitation.
  Recent serious gastrointestinal or genitourinary bleeding.
  Recent (within 10 days) major surgery, organ biopsy, or puncture of a
    noncompressible vessel.
  Known bleeding diathesis.
  Diabetic hemorrhagic retinopathy or other hemorrhagic ophthalmic condition.
  Previous allergic reaction to the thrombolytic agent (streptokinase or
    anisoylated plasminogen streptokinase activator complex).
  History of cerebrovascular accident.
  Blood pressure over 200/120 mm Hg that cannot be quickly lowered with
    medications.
  Suspected aortic dissection or acute pancreatitis.
  Pregnancy.
Relative contraindications.
  History of intracranial or intraspinal surgery or trauma.
  History of gastrointestinal or genitourinary bleeding.
  History of recent trauma, including brief cardiopulmonary resuscitation.
  Cerebrovascular disease.
  Recent (within 2 months) major surgery or trauma.
  Chronic severe hypertension with or without drug therapy.
  Hemostatic defects including severe renal or hepatic disease.
  Acute pericarditis, infective endocarditis.
  Concurrent anticoagulant therapy.
  Recent therapy (especially within 9 months) with streptokinase or anisoylated
    plasminogen streptokinase activator complex if repeat therapy is
    contemplated with these agents (not a contraindication to tissue plasminogen
    activator or urokinase).

vivenza nell'Infarto Miocardico (GISSI-II) and the International t-PA/SK Mortality Trial, the in-hospital, 2-week mortality of patients treated wtih either t-PA or SK was 8.7%, with no difference between those receiving rt-PA (8.9%) and those receiving SK (8.5%).[38, 39] There also was no significant difference in mortality between those who received heparin (8.5%) and those who did not (8.9%). Unfortunately, the study design employed subcutaneous heparin, 12,500 units every 12 hours, beginning 12 hours after the end of the infusion of the lytic agent. Since heparin administered subcutaneously may not result in a significant prolongation of the partial prothrombin time for at least 12 hours, it may have produced little effect during the first 24 hours. This may have been more important in patients receiving t-PA than in those receiving SK, which produces high levels of fibrin degradation products that inhibit platelet aggregation. Most patients in the GISSI-II study and the International t-PA/SK Mortality Study also received aspirin, 325 mg/day.

Numerous regimens of rt-PA have been employed.[43-46] These have differed in several important aspects, including the total dose, the adjustment of dosage by weight, the duration of administration, and the amount of "front-loading." One conventional regimen of intravenous rt-PA consists of 100 mg infused over 3 hours, with a 10-mg bolus, followed by 50 mg infused over 1 hour, and then 20 mg/hr for 2 hours. Some of the other regimens of rt-PA that have been employed include the following: 100 mg of rt-PA given over 6 hours with 60 mg in the first hour, 20 mg in the second hour, and 5 mg/hr over the next 4 hours; 2 mg/kg over 3 hours, with 1.8 mg/kg (10% as a bolus injection) over 1 hour, followed by 0.8 mg/kg over the next 2 hours (median dose approximately 145 mg[45]; 1.25 mg/kg given over 3 hours, with 0.75 mg/kg (10% as a bolus injection) over 1 hour, followed by 0.5 mg/kg over the next 2 hours (median dose approximately 100 mg[45]); and an accelerated regimen of up to 100 mg given over 90 minutes, with a 15-mg bolus, followed by a 50 mg infusion over 30 minutes and 35 mg over the ensuing 60 minutes.[43] The use of combination therapy employing either intravenous rt-PA (1 mg/kg over 60 minutes with 10% given as a bolus) and SK (1.0 to 1.5 million units over 60 minutes) or intravenous rt-PA and UK currently is being evaluated in large, multicenter studies. Some studies of combination therapy have used smaller doses of t-PA (50 mg), which decreases the cost of this therapy.

Intravenous SK usually is given as 1.5 million units over 1 hour. APSAC may be given intravenously at a dose of 30 units over 5 minutes. UK has been given both as an intravenous bolus of 2.0 million units and as an intravenous infusion of 3.0 million units over 60 or 90 minutes.

At present, we use the standard regimen of 100 mg of t-PA administered over 3 hours as described previously, with some decrease in dosage for weight. It appears likely, however, that future studies will indicate the advisability of alternate regimens or combination therapy. Patients with uncomplicated myocardial infarction who receive thrombolytic therapy do not require either emergency or routine cardiac catheterization and possible coronary angioplasty.[47-50] These procedures are best performed selectively on patients following AMI who have evidence of myocardial ischemia either subjectively or objectively at rest or during specialized testing prior to discharge.

## Heparin

Heparin is an important adjunct to t-PA as a thrombolytic agent.[51] It is initiated at the start of t-PA infusion (or no later than at the end of t-PA infusion) as a 5,000-unit bolus, followed by 1,000 units hr, with the infusion rate titrated to maintain the partial prothrombin time at 1.5 to 2.0 times control for the duration of the patient's stay in the hospital. The early concurrent use of heparin helps to maintain the relatively high patency rates achieved with t-PA, particularly in the first 24 hours following thrombolysis.[52, 53]

Full-dose intravenous heparin also is given to most patients with anterior AMI, whether or not they are treated with thrombolytic therapy, to decrease the likelihood of left ventricular thrombus.[54] In such patients, warfarin (Coumadin) usually is started about the same time, and the heparin is discontinued when the prothrombin time is in the therapeutic range of 1.3 to 1.5 times control. If the echocardiogram prior to discharge shows any evidence of left ventricular thrombus, warfarin is continued for 3 to 6 months at a dose that will maintain a therapeutic prothrombin time together with aspirin, 80 to 160 mg per day.

Acute anticoagulation with intravenous heparin followed by warfarin also is employed prophylactically in other groups of high-risk patients, including those with congestive heart failure, atrial fibrillation, a history of pulmonary embolus or venous thrombophlebitis, significant varicose veins, or marked obesity.[55–57] Prophylactic anticoagulation with low-dose subcutaneous heparin (5,000 to 16,000 units/12 hr) is easier to administer, but not as effective as full-dose intravenous heparin. In addition, when subcutaneous heparin is used alone, therapeutic levels may not be reached for 12 to 24 hours.

## Warfarin

The routine use of chronic oral anticoagulant therapy in patients with uncomplicated AMI is still controversial, despite the promising results of several clinical trials.[58–61] At present, this therapy is not employed routinely, but is used only in patients thought to be at higher risk (as described earlier). In many such patients, low-dose therapy with warfarin is continued indefinitely. In this situation, concurrent chronic therapy with aspirin is given in very low dosage, i.e., 80 to 160 mg per day.

## Aspirin

Aspirin is given to most patients with suspected AMI as soon as conditions such as aortic dissection, acute pericarditis, and acute peptic ulcer disease are reasonably excluded.[51, 62, 63] In most patients, therapy is initiated with 162 to 325 mg by mouth, given as either a single tablet or 2 or 4 81-mg chewable tablets. In older patients or those with a remote history of peptic ulcer disease, 162 mg may be used rather than 325 mg. In most patients, long-term aspirin therapy (preferably 325-mg enteric-coated tablets) is continued indefinitely after recovery from AMI, only 80 to 160 mg if they are on long-term warfarin therapy.

## β-Blockers

The use of intravenous β-blockers early in the treatment of patients with AMI may decrease infarct size, cardiac arrhythmias, and acute mortality. This has been demonstrated in studies employing metoprolol,[64-66] timolol,[67, 68] and atenolol.[69-71] On the basis of these studies, β-blockers currently are administered to most patients during the acute phase of myocardial infarction if there are no contraindications such as evidence of severe chronic obstructive pulmonary disease, atrioventricular heart block, bradycardia below 60 beats per minute, severe heart failure, or a systolic blood pressure below 100 mm of Hg. β-Blockers should be used very cautiously in patients with a history of asthma, concurrent use of β-blockers or calcium channel blockers, severe peripheral vascular disease, or insulin-dependent diabetes mellitus. They are of particular benefit in patients with hypertension and sinus tachycardia. Currently, β-blockers are given to about 50% to 60% of patients with AMI; treatment preferably is initiated within the first few hours of the onset of symptoms. Meta-analysis of trials of β-blockers in AMI suggests that such therapy may decrease mortality by approximately 13%.[32, 72, 73]

Patients also have been shown to benefit from continued, chronic therapy with oral β-blockers after recovery from AMI. This has been demonstrated in studies employing propranolol,[74] metoprolol,[64-66] and timolol.[67] In these trials, ventricular ectopy, sudden death, and total mortality were decreased, especially in patients at higher risk because of ventricular ectopy or decreased left ventricular function.[72, 74, 75] The benefits of chronic β-blocker therapy, which appear to persist for at least 6 to 7 years, are less clear in patients who have sustained their first myocardial infarction without any complications, have no evidence of ventricular dysfunction or electrical instability, and have a normal exercise test or 201-thallium exercise reperfusion scan. In such patients, who have a very good prognosis for the next 1 to 2 years, the cost-benefit ratio of chronic β-blocker therapy is rather high. Accordingly, such very low-risk individuals are not given chronic β-blocker therapy routinely after discharge.

## Calcium Channel Blockers

Although the three most widely used calcium channel blockers, nifedipine, verapamil, and diltiazem, have been shown to protect ischemic myocardium and are very useful in treating exertional and vasospastic angina pectoris and hypertension, as a group they have not been shown to be effective in the routine treatment of patients with acute or suspected myocardial infarction.[12] Studies of nifedipine in patients with threatened AMI have not shown any benefit.[76] Similarly, most studies of the use of verapamil in patients with AMI have not shown any benefit, although one recent study[77] suggested a possible benefit in selected patients. On the other hand, in patients with non–Q-wave AMI, diltiazem has been shown to decrease the incidence of recurrent infarction, refractory angina pectoris, and angina pectoris with electrocardiographic changes over the next several weeks.[78] Most long-term studies of calcium antagonists in patients after recovery from AMI generally have failed to demonstrate a clear benefit. In the Multicenter Diltiazem Post-Infarction Trial, the routine use of diltiazem did not decrease the 2- or 3-year mortality of patients who had sustained myocardial infarction.[79] In the approximately 20% of patients in this study who had pulmonary congestion on a chest x-ray or a left ventricular ejection fraction below 40% soon after their infarction, the use of diltiazem was associated with an increase in mortality. Patients with a reduced ejection fraction below 40% soon after their infarction who were given diltiazem also had an increased incidence of congestive heart failure during follow-up.[80] On the other hand, the use of diltiazem in the remaining 80% of patients, who did not have either of these findings, was associated with decresed mortality. This benefit was also apparent in a post hoc analysis of patients who sustained their first non–Q-wave or inferior infarction.[81]

## Percutaneous Transluminal Coronary Angioplasty and Coronary Artery Bypass Grafting

Although percutaneous coronary angioplasty and emergency coronary artery bypass grafting have been shown to be effective forms of therapy for AMI in a number of nonrandomized studies,[82–86] logistical problems prevent their use in most patients. On the other hand, if the patient is in a facility where such therapies can be employed successfully and rapidly, angioplasty or bypass grafting can be acceptable alternatives to thrombolytic treatment. These therapies are also of use in selected patients who have contraindications or appear to fail thrombolytic treatment and have continued or recurrent chest discomfort with electrocardiographic changes. In selected patients with unsuccessful angioplasty, emergent bypass grafting can be extremely useful.

## Antiarrhythmic Therapy

Although the routine administration of lidocaine has been advocated sometimes as prophylaxis against ventricular tachycardia or fibrillation, this is not recommended currently.[87–89] Rather, lidocaine is used selectively in patients who develop a significant amount of ventricular ectopy with premature ventricular complexes that are frequent (more than six per minute), closely coupled (R on T), multiform in configuration, or occur in runs of three or more.[12, 88]

## Non–Q-Wave Infarction

Approximately one fourth to one third of patients diagnosed as having AMI sustain non–Q-wave infarctions. In general, patients with non–Q-wave infarctions have an acute mortality lower than that of patients with Q-wave infarctions, although the total mortality of the two groups is essentially equal after 2 to 3 years.[90-92] Thus, it is important to evaluate most patients with non−Q-wave infarction for any evidence of myocardial ischemia that is apparent either spontaneously at rest or during an exercise thallium-201 imaging test. Although routine coronary arteriography of all patients who sustain a non−Q-wave myocardial infarction is not recommended at this time, any evidence of ischemia, either subjective or objective, is an indication for coronary arteriography and consideration for possible revascularization by either coronary artery bypass grafting or percutaneous transluminal coronary angioplasty.

At present, patients with non−Q-wave AMI are treated with aspirin (325 mg/day) and diltiazem (240 to 360 mg/day).[78, 92-94] Most studies examining β-blockers in the treatment of AMI have not prospectively evaluated their use in patients with non−Q-wave infarction. In contrast to the results obtained in patients with Q-wave AMI, most such studies have not demonstrated a clear benefit in the subset of patients diagnosed as having non-Q-wave infarction,[92, 95] although one study with timolol suggested a benefit. Similarly, there is still no clear evidence of any overall benefit of thrombolytic therapy in patients with non−Q-wave myocardial infarction, many of whom probably have undergone spontaneous thrombolysis.

## Risk Stratification

Most patients who sustain an uncomplicated myocardial infarction should undergo some form of risk stratification to evaluate two major determinants of prognosis[12, 97-99]: left ventricular function and evidence of myocardial ischemia. In the majority of such individuals, this is accomplished prior to discharge by performing an exercise treadmill test, often in combination with a thallium-201 perfusion scan. If the patient is receiving a β-blocker or calcium channel blocker, therapy is not stopped. In most instances, a symptom-limited exercise test with thallium is performed just prior to discharge at 10 to 14 days after AMI. Patients who are discharged earlier than 10 days should have a limited, submaximal test prior to their release. This test usually is limited either by heart rate (120 beats per minute) or by the level of exercise (i.e., 5 METS). In these patients, a symptom-limited exercise test with thallium is performed at 4 to 8 weeks. Ambulatory 24-hour continuous electrocardiographic recordings to detect cardiac arrhythmias or silent ischemia, and signal-averaged electrocardiography to detect abnormal late potentials are not performed routinely in patients with uncomplicated myocardial infarction.

## Postinfarction Care

Most patients with uncomplicated myocardial infarction can be instructed successfully by the physician in a program of progressive increased physical activity. In selected patients, particularly those who may be slightly depressed, who smoke, or who are very unconditioned, participation in a structured group program of cardiac rehabilitation and instruction in risk reduction several times a week for 8 to 12 weeks is useful.

Major components of postinfarction management include continued medical management, cessation of tobacco exposure, early recognition and evaluation of recurrent myocardial ischemia, and evaluation and management of blood lipids.

For most patients, follow-up medical management involves continued aspirin (one 325-mg enteric-coated tablet daily) and, especially for those who have sustained a Q-wave infarction, regular use of a β-blocker, unless contraindicated because of pulmonary disease, atrioventricular block, or insulin-requiring diabetes. For patients who have sustained an uncomplicated non–Q-wave AMI, diltiazem (120 or 180 mg in sustained release form twice daily) is used in place of the β-blocker. Patients with an anterior myocardial infarction and evidence of left ventricular thrombus are maintained on warfarin for 3 to 6 months. Patients who are demonstrated to have an extensive thrombus partially occluding the infarct-related vessel on coronary arteriorgraphy also are given low-dose warfarin (either 5 mg/day or enough to prolong the prothrombin time to 1.3 to 1.5 times control) for 3 to 6 months, although there have not yet been any clinical trials specifically designed to evaluate such therapy.[100]

Patients who have occasional asymptomatic ventricular ectopy with more than six premature ventricular complexes per hour are at some increased risk over the next several years.[97, 98] At present, however, such individuals should not be treated with agents such as flecainide or encainide, which have been shown in the Cardiac Arrhythmia Suppression Trial to be associated with increased mortality.[101] Currently, such patients are best managed with either no specific treatment for the ventricular ectopy other than β-blocker therapy, or, if the opportunity is still available locally, by enrollment in the continuation of the aforementioned trial, which is comparing the effects of moricizine vs. placebo.

A preliminary report has suggested that the use of captopril in patients with diminished left ventricular function after recovery from AMI may result in long-term benefit on left ventricular function.[102] If these results are confirmed in larger long-term studies, such therapy may be a valuable adjunct in the future.

Exposure to all forms of tobacco (cigarettes, cigars, snuff, or chewing tobacco) is strongly forbidden. In selected patients, the temporary use of nicotine-containing chewing gum[103] or transcutaneous nicotine patches[104] may assist patients who wish to give up tobacco. Clonidine has been reported to be of use also.[105]

The patient should be examined usually at least every 3 to 4 months to detect any symptoms or signs of myocardial ischemia, decreased ventricular function, or ventricular ectopy. A repeat exercise test, often with thallium scintigraphy, is performed approximately every year.

There is now reasonable evidence that patients with coronary artery disease who have serum cholesterol levels above ideal have a decreased rate of coronary artery disease progression (and perhaps, occasionally, even regression) if their blood lipids are lowered significantly by any of several regimens, including diet and lipid-lowering drugs,[106-112] marked dietary and life-style changes,[113] or ileal bypass surgery.[114] Currently, most patients with known coronary artery disease are managed initially by placing them on the step-I diet of the American Heart Association. It is best if a dietitian or nutritionist instructs both the patient and the spouse in this regimen. A fasting lipid profile (total cholesterol, high-density lipoprotein cholesterol, triglyceride, and calculated low-density lipoprotein cholesterol) is obtained prior to hospital discharge and repeated 1 month later. In selected patients with hyperlipidemia that does not respond adequately to dietary therapy, pharmacologic treatment utilizing a hydroxymethylglutaryl coenzyme A (HMG CoA) reductase inhibitor, (lovastatin, 20 to 80 mg/day), and/or a bile-sequestrating resin (colestipol, 5 to 30 g/day or cholestyramine, 4 to 24 g/day) is used. Nicotinic acid (2 to 6 g/day) is also useful, particularly in patients with persistently low high-density lipoprotein levels. For maximum lowering of total and low-density lipoprotein cholesterol, it frequently is necessary to use a combination of a bile-sequestrating resin and either lovastatin or nicotinic acid. Occasionally, all three may be employed. Gemfibrozil, 300 to 600 mg twice daily, may be useful in patients with moderate hypercholesterolemia, particularly in association with elevated triglyceride and decreased high-density lipoprotein levels.

## Family Management

The family should be educated about coronary artery disease and the factors known to be associated with increased risk. Often, it is appropriate to obtain blood lipid levels on family members at this time and to instruct them on the importance of diet, weight and blood pressure control, and the avoidance of tobacco. When possible, members of the immediate family should be instructed in basic life support cardiopulmonary resuscitation.

## References

1. Gersh B, Chesebro JH, Clements IP: Acute myocardial infarction. B. Management and complications, in Brandenburg R, Fuster V, Giulani ER, et al (eds): *Cardiology: Fundamentals and Practice*. Chicago, Year Book Medical Publishers, Inc, 1987, pp 1153–1219.
2. Anderson JL (ed): *Acute Myocardial Infarction: New Management Strategies*. Rockville, Maryland, Aspen, 1987.
3. Pasternak RC, Braunwald E, Sobel BE: Acute myocardial infarction, in Braunwald E (ed): *Heart Disease*, 3rd ed. Philadelphia, WB Saunders, 1988, pp 1222–1313.
4. Gregoratos G: Management of uncomplicated acute myocardial infarction, in Parmley WW, Chatterjee K (eds): *Cardiology. Volume 2. Cardiovascular Disease*. Philadelphia, JB Lippincott, 1988, pp 1–25.

5. Califf RM, Mark DB, Wagner GS (eds): *Acute Coronary Care in the Thrombolytic Era.* Chicago, Year Book Medical Publishers, 1988.
6. Topol EJ (Ed): *Acute Coronary Intervention.* New York, Alan R Liss, 1988.
7. Cabin HS: Management of acute myocardial infarction, in Cabin HS (ed): *Cardiology Clinics.* Philadelphia, WB Saunders, 1988, pp 1–184.
8. Hlatky MA, Cotugno HE, Mark DB, et al: Trends in physician management of uncomplicated acute myocardial infarction, 1970 to 1987. *Am J Cardiol* 1988; 61:515–518.
9. Frye RL, Gibbons RJ, Schaff HV, et al: Treatment of coronary artery disease. *J Am Coll Cardiol* 1989; 13:957–968.
10. Morris DC, Walter PF, Hurst JW: The recognition and treatment of myocardial infarction and its complications, in Hurst JW, Schlant RC, Rackley CE, et al (eds): *The Heart,* 7th ed. New York, McGraw-Hill, 1990, pp 1054–1078.
11. Francis GS, Alpert JS (eds): *Modern Coronary Care.* Boston, Little, Brown & Co, 1990.
12. Gersh BJ, Rahimtoola SH (eds): *Acute Myocardial Infarction.* New York, Elsevier, 1990.
13. ACC/AHA Task Force Report: Guidelines for the early management of patients with acute myocardial infarction. *J Am Coll Cardiol* 1990; 16:249–292.
14. Goldberg RJ, Gore JM, Alpert JS, et al: Recent changes in attack and survival rates of acute myocardial infarction (1975 through 1981). *JAMA* 1986; 255:2774–2779.
15. Remetz MS, Cabin HS: Analgesic therapy in acute myocardial infarction. *Cardiol Clin* 1988; 6:29–36.
16. Jugdutt BI, Warnica JW: Intravenous nitroglycerin therapy to limit myocardial infarct size, expansion, and complications: Effect of timing, dosage, and infarct location. *Circulation* 1988; 78:906–919.
17. Yusuf S, Collins R, MacMahon S, et al: Effect of intravenous nitrates on mortality in acute myocardial infarction: An overview of the randomized trials. *Lancet* 1988; 1:1088–1092.
18. Yusuf S, Collins R, Peto R, et al: Intravenous and intracoronary fibrinolytic therapy in acute myocardial infarction: Overview of results on mortality, reinfarction and side-effects from 33 randomized controlled trials. *Eur Heart J* 1985; 6:556–585.
19. ISAM (Intravenous Streptokinase in Acute Myocardial Infarction) Study Group: A prospective trial of intravenous streptokinase in acute myocardial infarction (I.S.A.M.): Mortality, morbidity, and infarct size at 21 days. *N Engl J Med* 1986; 314:1465–1471.
20. Gruppo Italiano per lo Studio Della Streptochinasi Nell'Infarto Miocardico (GISSI): Effectiveness of intravenous thrombolytic treatment in acute myocardial infarction. *Lancet* 1986; 1:397–401.
21. Williams DO, Borer J, Braunwald E, et al: Intravenous recombinant tissue-type plasminogen activator in patients with acute myocardial infarction: A report from the NHLBI thrombolysis in myocardial infarction trial. *Circulation* 1986; 73:338–346.
22. Schroder F, Neuhaus KI, Leizorovicz A, et al: Trial of Intravenous Streptokinase in Acute Myocardial Infarction (ISAM): Long-term mortality and morbidity. *J Am Coll Cardiol* 1987; 9:197–203.
23. Yusef S: Interventions that potentially limit myocardial infarct size: Overview of the clinical trials. *Am J Cardiol* 1987; 60:11A–17A.

24. Gruppo Italiano Per Lo Studio Della Streptochi-nasi nell'infarto miocardico (GISSI): Long-term effects of intravenous thrombolysis in acute myocardial infarction: Final report of the GISSI study. *Lancet* 1987; 2:871–874.
25. AIMS Trial Study Group: Effect of intravenous APSAC on mortality after acute myocardial infarction: Preliminary report of a placebo-controlled clinical trial. *Lancet* 1988; 1:545–549.
26. ISIS-2 (Second International Study of Infarct Survival) Collaborative Group: Randomized trial of intravenous streptokinase, oral aspirin, both, or neither among 17,187 cases of suspected acute myocardial infarction. *Lancet* 1988; 2:349–360.
27. Braunwald E: Thrombolytic reperfusion of acute myocardial infarction: Resolved and unresolved issues. *J Am Coll Cardiol* 1988; 12:85A–95A.
28. Van de Werf F, Arnold AER, and the European Cooperative Study Group for Recombinant Tissue-Type Plasminogen Activator (rt-PA): Intravenous tissue plasminogen activator and size of infarct, left ventricular function, and survival in acute myocardial infarction. *Br Med J [Clin Res]* 1988; 297:1374–1379.
29. Chesebro JH, Holmes DR, Mock MB, et al: Thrombolysis in acute myocardial infarction. *Cardiol Clinics* 1988; 6:119–137.
30. Collen D, Stump DC, Gold HK: Thrombolytic therapy. *Annu Rev Med* 1988; 39:405–423.
31. O'Neill WW, Pitt B: Reperfusion therapy of acute myocardial infarction. *Prog Cardiovasc Dis* 1988; 30:235–266.
32. Yusuf S, Wittes J, Friedman L: Overview of results of randomized clinical trials in heart disease. I. Treatments following myocardial infarction. *JAMA* 1988; 260:2088–2093.
33. Wilcox RG, von der Lippe G, Olsson CB, et al: Trial of tissue plasminogen activator for mortality reduction in acute myocardial infarction. Anglo-Scandinavian Study of Early Thrombolysis (ASSET). *Lancet* 1988; 2:525–530.
34. Magnani B: Plasminogen Activator Italian Multicenter Study (PAIMS): Comparison of intravenous recombinant single-chain human tissue-type plasminogen activator (rt-PA) with intravenous streptokinase in acute myocardial infarction. *J Am Coll Cardiol* 1989; 13:19–26.
35. Bassand J-P, Machecourt J, Cassagnes J, et al: Multicenter trial of intravenous anisoylated plasminogen streptokinase activator complex (APSAC) in acute myocardial infarction: Effects on infarct size and left ventricular function. *J Am Coll Cardiol* 1989; 13:988–997.
36. Simoons ML: Thrombolytic therapy in acute myocardial infarction. *Annu Rev Med* 1989; 40:181–200.
37. AIMS Trial Study Group: Long-term effects of intravenous anistreplase in acute myocardial infarction: Final report of the AIMS study. *Lancet* 1990; 335:427–431.
38. Gruppo Italiano per lo Studio della Sopravivenza nell'Infarto Miocardico. GISSI-II: A factorial randomized trial of alteplase versus streptokinase and heparin versus no heparin among 12,490 patients with acute myocardial infarction. *Lancet* 1990; 336:65–70.
39. International Study Group: In-hospital mortality and clinical course of 20,891 patients with suspected acute myocardial infarction randomized between alteplase and streptokinase with or without heparin. *Lancet* 1990; 336:71–75.
40. Collen D: Coronary thrombolysis: Streptokinase or recombinant tissue-type plasminogen activator? *Ann Intern Med* 1990; 112:529–538.
41. Lew AS, Hod H, Cerrek B, et al: Mortality and morbidity rates of patients

older than 75 years with acute myocardial infarction treated with intravenous streptokinase. *Am J Cardiol* 1987; 59:1–5.

42. Schroeder R, Linderer T, Brueggemann T, et al: Controversial indications. Rationale for thrombolysis: Later than 4–6 h from symptom onset, and in patients with smaller infarctions. *Eur Heart J* 1990; 11(suppl F):19–28.

43. Neuhaus K-L, Feuerer W, Jeep-Tebbe S, et al: Improved thrombolysis with a modified dose regimen of recombinant tissue-type plasminogen activator. *J Am Coll Cardiol* 1989; 14:1566–1569.

44. Braunwald E: Enhancing thrombolytic efficacy by means of "front-loaded" administration of tissue plasminogem activator. *J Am Coll Cardiol* 1989; 14:1570–1571.

45. Smalling RW, Schumacher R, Morris D, et al: Improved infarct-related arterial patency after high dose, weight-adjusted, rapid infusion of tissue-type plasminogen activator in myocardial infarction: Results of a multicenter randomized trial of two dosage regimens. *J Am Coll Cardiol* 1990; 15:915–921.

46. Topol EJ: Ultrathrombolysis. *J Am Coll Cardiol* 1990; 15:922–924.

47. Topol EJ, Califf RM, and the Thrombolysis and Angioplasty in Myocardial Infarction Study Group: A randomized trial of immediate versus delayed elective angioplasty after intravenous tissue plasminogen activator in acute myocardial infarction. *N Engl J Med* 1987; 317:581–588.

48. The TIMI Research Group: Immediate vs. delayed catheterization and angioplasty following thrombolytic therapy for acute myocardial infarction. TIMI II A results. *JAMA* 1988; 260:2849–2858.

49. Simoons ML, Arnold AER, Betriu A, et al: Thrombolysis with tissue plasminogen activator in acute myocardial infarction: No additional benefit from immediate coronary angioplasty. *Lancet* 1988; 1:197–203.

50. de Bono DP: The European cooperative study group trial of intravenous recombinant tissue-type plasminogen activator (rt-PA) and conservative therapy versus rt-PA and immediate coronary angioplasty. *J Am Coll Cardiol* 1988; 12:20A–23A.

51. Fuster V, Stein B, Badimon L, et al: Antithrombotic therapy after myocardial reperfusion in acute myocardial infarction. *J Am Coll Cardiol* 1988; 121:78A–84A.

52. Kaplan K, Davison R, Parker M, et al: Role of heparin after intravenous thrombolytic therapy for acute myocardial infarction. *Am J Cardiol* 1987; 59:241–244.

53. Hsia J, Hamilton WP, Kleiman N, et al: A comparison between heparin and low-dose aspirin as adjunctive therapy with tissue plasminogen activator for acute myocardial infarction. *N Engl J Med* 1990; 21:1433–1437.

54. Turpie AGG, Robinson JG, Doyle DJ, et al: Comparison of high-dose with low-dose subcutaneous heparin to prevent left ventricular mural thrombosis in patients with acute transmural anterior myocardial infarction. *N Engl J Med* 1989; 320:352–357.

55. Chalmers TC, Matta RJ, Smith H Jr, et al: Evidence favoring the use of anticoagulants in the hospital phase of acute myocardial infarction. *N Engl J Med* 1977; 297:1091–1096.

56. Goldman L, Feinstein A: Anticoagulants and myocardial infarction: The problems of pooling, drowning and floating. *Ann Intern Med* 1979; 90:92–94.

57. Mitchell JRA: Anticoagulants in coronary heart disease: Retrospect and prospect. *Lancet* 1981; 1:257–262.

58. Report of the Working Party on Anticoagulant Therapy in Coronary Thrombosis to the Medical Research Council: Assessment of short-term anticoagu-

lant administration after cardiac infarction. *Br Med J [Clin Res]* 1969; 1:335–342.

59. Veterans Administration Cooperative Investigators: Anticoagulants in acute myocardial infarction: Results of a cooperative clinical trial. *JAMA* 1973; 225:724–729.
60. Chalmers TC, Matta RJ, Smith H Jr, et al: Evidence favoring the use of anticoagulants in the hospital phase of acute myocardial infarction. *N Engl J Med* 1977; 297:1091–1096.
61. Smith PM, Arnesan H, Holme I: The effect of warfarin on mortality and reinfarction after myocardial infarction. *N Engl J Med* 1990; 323:147–152.
62. Penny WJ, Chesebro JH, Heras M, et al: Antithrombotic therapy for patients with cardiac disease. *Curr Probl Cardiol* 1988; 13:425–513.
63. Antiplatelet Trialists Collaboration: Secondary prevention of vascular disease by prolonged antiplatelet treatment. *Br Med J [Clin Res]* 1988; 296:320–331.
64. Hjalmarson A, Elmfeldt D, Herlitz J, et al: Effect on mortality of metoprolol in acute myocardial infarction. *Lancet* 1981; 2:823–827.
65. Hjalmarson A, Herlitz J, Holmberg S, et al: The Goteborg Metoprolol Trial: Effects of mortality and morbidity in acute myocardial infarction. *Circulation* 1983; 67(suppl):I25–I32.
66. The MIAMI Trial Research Group: Metoprolol in acute myocardial infarction (MIAMI): A randomized placebo-controlled international trial. *Eur Heart J* 1985; 6:199–226.
67. Norwegian Multicenter Study Group: Timolol-induced reduction in mortality and reinfarction in patients surviving acute myocardial infarction. *N Engl J Med* 1981; 304:801–807.
68. The International Collaboration Study Group: Reduction of infarct size with the early use of timolol in acute myocardial infarction. *N Engl J Med* 1984; 310:9–15.
69. Rossi PRF, Yusuf S, Ramsdale D, et al: Reduction of ventricular arrhythmias with early intravenous atenolol in suspected acute myocardial infarction. *Br Med J [Clin Res]* 1983; 286:506–510.
70. ISIS-1 Collaborative Group: A randomized trial of intravenous atenolol among 16,027 cases of suspected acute myocardial infarction. *Lancet* 1986; 2:57–66.
71. ISIS-1 (First International Study of Infarct Survival) Collaborative Group: Mechanisms for the early mortality reduction produced by beta-blockade started early in acute myocardial infarction. *Lancet* 1988; 1:921–923.
72. Yusuf S, Peto R, Lewis J, et al: Beta blockade during and after myocardial infarction: An overview of the randomized trials. *Prog Cardiovasc Dis* 1985; 27:335–371.
73. Yusuf S, Sleight P, Rossi PRF, et al: Reduction in infarct size, arrhythmias and chest pain by early intravenous beta blockade in suspected acute myocardial infarction. *Circulation* 1987; 67:32–41.
74. Beta-Blocker Heart Attack Trial Research Group: A randomized trial of propranolol in patients with acute myocardial infarction. I. Mortality results. *JAMA* 1982; 247:1707–1714.
75. The MIAMI Trial Research Group: Metoprolol in Acute Myocardial Infarction (MIAMI). *Am J Cardiol* 1985; 56:1G–57G.
76. Muller JE, Morrison J, Stone PH, et al: Nifedipine therapy for patients with threatened and acute myocardial infarction: A randomized, double-blind, placebo-controlled comparison. *Circulation* 1984; 69:740–747.

77. The Danish Study Group on Verapamil in Myocardial Infarction: Effect of verapamil on mortality and major events after acute myocardial infarction (the Danish Verapamil Infarction Trial II—DAVIT II). *Am J Cardiol* 1990; 66:779–785.

78. Gibson RS, Boden WE, Theroux P, et al: Diltiazem and reinfarction in patients with non–Q-wave myocardial infarction. *N Engl J Med* 1986; 315:423–429.

79. Multicenter Diltiazem Post-Infarction Research Group: The effect of diltiazem on mortality and reinfarction after acute myocardial infarction. *N Engl J Med* 1983; 319:385–392.

80. Goldstein RE, Boccuzzi SJ, Cruess D, et al: Diltiazem increases late-onset congestive heart failure in postinfarction patients with early reduction in ejection fraction. *Circulation* 1991; 83:52–60.

81. Boden WE, Krone RJ, Kleiger RE, et al: Electrocardiographic subset analysis of diltiazem administration on long-term outcome after myocardial infarction. *Am J Cardiol* 1991; 67:335–342.

82. O'Neill W, Timmis GC, Bourdillon PD, et al: A prospective randomized clinical trial of intracoronary streptokinase versus coronary angioplasty for acute myocardial infarction. *N Engl J Med* 1986; 314:812–818.

83. Rothbaum DA, Linnemeir TJ, Landin RJ, et al: Emergency percutaneous transluminal coronary angioplasty in acute myocardial infarction: A 3 year experience. *J Am Coll Cardiol* 1987; 10:264–272.

84. O'Neill WW: Primary percutaneous coronary angioplasty: A protagonist's view. *Am J Cardiol* 1988; 62:15K–20K.

85. Ellis SG, O'Neill WW, Bates ER, et al: Coronary angioplasty as primary therapy for acute myocardial infarction 6 to 48 hours after symptom onset: Report of an initial experience. *J Am Coll Cardiol* 13:1122–1126.

86. Topol EJ: Coronary angioplasty for acute myocardial infarction. *Ann Intern Med* 1988; 109:970–980.

87. McMahon S, Collins R, Peto K, et al: Effects of prophylactic lidocaine in suspected acute myocardial infarction: An overview of results from the randomized, controlled trials. *JAMA* 1988; 260:1910–1916.

88. Wyse DG, Kellen J, Rademaker AW: Prophylactic versus selective lidocaine for early ventricular arrhythmias of myocardial infarction. *J Am Coll Cardiol* 1988; 12:507–513.

89. Hine LK, Laird N, Hewitt P, et al: Meta-analytic evidence against prophylactic use of lidocaine in acute myocardial infarction. *Arch Intern Med* 1989; 149:2694–2698.

90. Hutter AM, DeSanctis RW, Flynn T, et al: Non-transmural myocardial infarction: A comparison of hospital and late clinical course of patients with that of matched patients with transmural anterior and transmural inferior myocardial infarction. *Am J Cardiol* 1981; 48:595–602.

91. Goldberg RJ, Gore JM, Alpert JS, et al: Non-Q-wave myocardial infarction: Recent changes in occurrence and prognosis—a community-wide perspective. *Am Heart J* 1987; 113:273–279.

92. Gibson RS: Non–Q-wave myocardial infarction: Diagnosis, prognosis and management. *Curr Probl Cardiol* 1988; 13:1–72.

93. Gibson RS, Young PM, Boden WE, et al: Prognostic significance and beneficial effect of diltiazem on the incidence of early recurrent ischemia after non–Q wave myocardial infarction: Results form the Multicenter Diltiazem Reinfarction Study. *Am J Cardiol* 1987; 60:203–209.

94. Gibson RS: Current status of calcium channel-blocking drugs after Q wave

and non-Q wave myocardial infarction. *Circulation* 1989; 80(suppl IV):IV107-IV119.

95. Gheorghiade M, Schultz L, Tillet B, et al: Effects of propranolol in non-Q-wave acute myocardial infarction in the beta blocker heart attack trial. *Am J Cardiol* 1990; 66:129-133.

96. Pederson TR: The Norwegian multicenter study of timolol after myocardial infarction. *Circulation* 1983; 67(suppl I):49-53.

97. The Multicenter Postinfarction Research Group: Risk stratification and survival after myocardial infarction. *N Engl J Med* 1983; 309:331-336.

98. Bigger JT Jr, Fleiss JL, Kleiger R, et al: The Multicenter Post-infarction Research Group. The relationship among ventricular arrhythmias, left ventricular dysfunction, and mortality in the two years after myocardial infarction. *Circulation* 1984; 69:250-258.

99. Dwyer EM: After the myocardial infarction: A review and approach to risk stratification. *Cardiol Clin* 1988; 6:153-163.

100. Nakagawa S, Hanada Y, Koiwaya Y, et al: Angiographic features in the infarct-related artery after intracoronary urokinase followed by prolonged anticoagulation: Role of ruptured atheromatous plaque and adherent thrombus in acute myocardial infarction in vivo. *Circulation* 1988; 78:1335-1344.

101. The Cardiac Arrhythmia Suppression Trial (CAST) Investigators: Preliminary report: Effect of encainide and flecainide on mortality in a randomized trial of arrhythmia suppression after myocardial infarction. *N Engl J Med* 1989; 321:406-412.

102. Pfeffer MA, Lamas GA, Vaughan DE, et al: Effect of captopril on progressive ventricular dilatation after anterior myocardial infarction. *N Engl J Med* 1988; 319:80-86.

103. Hughes JR, Gust GW, Keenan RM, et al: Nicotine vs. placebo gum in general medical practice. *JAMA* 1989; 261:1300-1305.

104. Hurt RD, Lauger GG, Offord KP, et al: Nicotine-replacement therapy with use of a transdermal nicotine patch—a randomized double-blind placebo-controlled trial. *Mayo Clin Proc* 1990; 65:1529-1537.

105. Franks P, Harp J, Bell B: Randomized controlled trial of clonidine for smoking cessation in a primary care setting. *JAMA* 1989; 262:3011-3013.

106. Brensike JF, Levy RI, Kelsey SF, et al: Effects of therapy with cholestyramine on progression of arteriosclerosis: Results of NHLBI Type II Coronary Intervention Study. *Circulation* 1984; 69:313-324.

107. Levy RI, Brensike JF, Epstein SE, et al: The influence of changes in lipid values induced by cholestyramine and diet on progression of coronary artery disease: Results of NHLBI Type II Coronary Intervention Study. *Circulation* 1984; 69:325-337.

108. Artzenius AC, Kromhout D, Barth JD, et al: Diet, lipoproteins, and the progression of coronary atherosclerosis: The Leiden Intervention Trial. *N Engl J Med* 1985; 312:805-811.

109. Blankenhorn DH, Nessim SA, Johnson RL, et al: Beneficial effects of combined colestipol-niacin therapy on coronary atherosclerosis and coronary venous bypass grafts. *JAMA* 1987; 257:3233-3240.

110. Cashin-Hemphill L, Mack WJ, Pogoda J, et al: Beneficial effects of colestipol-niacin on coronary atherosclerosis: A 4-year follow-up. *JAMA* 1990; 264:3013-3017.

111. Brown G, Albers JJ, Fisher LD, et al: Progression of coronary artery disease as a result of intensive lipid-lowering therapy in men with high levels of apolipoprotein B. *N Engl J Med* 1990; 323:1289-1298.

112. Kane JP, Malloy MJ, Ports TA, et al: Regression of coronary atherosclerosis during treatment of familial hypercholesterolemia with combined drug regimens. *JAMA* 1990; 264:3007–3012.
113. Ornish D, Brown SE, Scherwitz LW, et al: Can lifestyle changes reverse coronary heart disease? The Lifestyle Heart Trial. *Lancet* 1990; 336:129–133.
114. Buchwald H, Varco RL, Matts JP, et al: Effect of partial ileal bypass surgery on mortality and morbidity from coronary heart disease on patients with hypercholesterolemia: Report of the Program on Surgical Control of the Hyperlipidemias (POSCH). *N Engl J Med* 1990; 323:946–955.

# Cocaine Abuse

## Scott A. Mackler, M.D., Ph.D.

Section of General Internal Medicine, Department of Pharmacology, University of
Pennsylvania School of Medicine, Philadelphia, Pennsylvania

## Charles P. O'Brien, M.D., Ph.D.

Department of Psychiatry, University of Pennsylvania School of Medicine,
Philadelphia, Pennsylvania

## Editor's Introduction

The epidemic of cocaine abuse has stimulated much study about addiction in
general because for so long cocaine was thought to be a non-addicting drug. The
psychological aftermath of profound anhedonia that follows prolonged cocaine
abuse, however, has now made it clear that the physical symptoms of withdrawal
are a minor problem compared to the neurobehavioral pathophysiology resulting
from prolonged overstimulation of the "pleasure center." The positive side of the
cocaine epidemic has been its stimulation of the intense study of this pleasure center, whose power over men and animals can reduce them to a fatal slavery, or
even to a kind of living death. Drs. Mackler and O'Brien combine their expertise in
internal medicine, pharmacology, and psychiatry to review one of the fastest moving fields of progress in current medical practice.

*Gene H. Stollerman, M.D.*

The recreational use of cocaine has exploded into a national epidemic in
the past decade. Cocaine use has resulted in several complications, including medical, economic, and other societal problems.[1] The number of
adults who use cocaine on a regular basis has increased over 1,000-fold
since the 1960s. In addition, the population of cocaine addicts (estimated
at more than 2 million) now exceeds that of heroin addicts. Internal medicine physicians, whether they are practicing as primary care providers or as
specialists, must be able to recognize the sequelae of acute and chronic cocaine use and to initiate appropriate treatment plans. This review will discuss the pharmacology of cocaine, medical complications caused by cocaine use, treatment during cocaine withdrawal, and relapse prevention.

## The Pharmacology of Cocaine

Andean Indians have chewed coca leaves for over 5,000 years in order to
increase their sense of well-being and reduce fatigue.[2] Interestingly, this
route of drug delivery has not been associated with the many problems

connected with cocaine addiction today. Initial experiences with cocaine use in the United States were accompanied by an aura of innocence, with no expectation of serious complications. However, both the availability of cocaine in purer, less expensive forms and drug delivery by methods that rapidly achieve maximal serum concentrations can be linked directly to the recent increase in cocaine-related problems. An understanding of the pharmacokinetics and pharmacodynamics of cocaine use explain many, but not all, of the observed medical complications. The majority of the described medical complications consist of individual case reports or retrospective studies representing small sample sizes. However, even in the absence of a direct cause-and-effect relationship, it is clear that the rise in cocaine use has been associated with an increase in medical illnesses not normally observed in young and previously healthy adults.

## The Pharmacokinetics of Cocaine

Cocaine (benzoylmethylecognine) occurs in high concentrations in the leaves of the coca shrubs (Erythroxylum coca and Erythroxylum novogranatense) located in the northwestern regions of South America.[2] The chemical structure of cocaine is similar to that of other local anesthetics, consisting of an amine residue linked to an aromatic group.[3] The half-life of cocaine is approximately 30 to 45 minutes after entering the bloodstream, and it is degraded by plasma esterases and in the liver. People with a deficiency of pseudocholinesterase activity may be at a greater risk for life-threatening complications following cocaine use[4] (Table 1). The major metabolite of cocaine is benzoylecognine, and this has been detected in urine (using gas chromatography and mass spectroscopy) as long as 10 days after the last dose of a cocaine binge.[5] During this period, the presence of benzoylecognine in the urine may go up and down, suggesting sequestration and release from different body compartments. A demethylated metabolite of benzoylecognine is norcocaine, which can cross the blood-brain barrier and has cocainelike activities in vitro. A small percentage of cocaine (1% to 10%) is eliminated unchanged in the urine.

Cocaine hydrochloride may be injected intravenously or absorbed through any mucous membranes following direct application. Alkalinization and extraction of the cocaine base results in a heat-stable, pure form of cocaine that can be smoked (known as free base or crack, because of the popping noises made while heating the crystals). Smoking the free base form results in the rapid development of extremely high serum concentrations, similar to levels attained following intravenous injection of cocaine hydrochloride.

## Complications Attributable to the Pharmacokinetics of Cocaine

The various routes of cocaine administration are associated with specific complications (see Table 1). Intranasal application ("snorting") may result

**TABLE 1.**
**Complications Attributable to the Pharmacokinetics of Cocaine**

I. Cocaine administration.
  A. Intranasal application ("snorting").
    1. Chronic rhinitis/sinusitis.
    2. Septal perforation/necrosis.
    3. Local infection with possible intracranial extension.
  B. Gastrointestinal absorption.
    1. Intestinal ischemia.
    2. Gangrene of the gut.
    3. Intestinal obstruction (body packing).
  C. Smoking ("crack").
    1. Barotrauma (pneumothorax, pneumomediastinum, pneumopericardium, and pneumoperitoneum).
    2. Impaired diffusing capacity.
    3. Reactive airways disease.
    4. Pulmonary edema (noncardiogenic).
    5. Passive inhalation of volatilized cocaine.
  D. Intraurethral.
    1. Priapism/paraphimosis.
  E. Intravenous injection.
    1. Several infectious illnesses (including acquired immunodeficiency syndrome (AIDS) and AIDS-related illnesses).
  F. Adulterants used to "cut" cocaine.
    1. Local anesthetics.
    2. Other psychostimulants.
    3. Strychnine.
    4. Arsenic.
II. Cocaine metabolism.
  A. Pseudocholinesterase deficiency.
III. Cocaine distribution.
  A. Rapid rise and fall of serum levels following smoking free base cocaine or intravenous injection (resulting in an intense craving for repeated drug use).
  B. In utero effects.
    1. Uterine artery vasospasm (fetal hypoxia).
    2. Transplacental passage (?effects of cocaine on the fetus).

in necrosis or perforation of the nasal septum,[6] chronic sinusitis, osteitis, extension of an infection into the brain,[7] and botulism.[8] The young patient with chronic rhinitis of unclear etiology should be questioned about cocaine use and the nasal septum examined carefully.

Cocaine introduced into the gastrointestinal tract is absorbed and may be as effective as intranasal cocaine in achieving the desired euphoria (although the onset is delayed). A common form of cocaine smuggling involves the ingestion or rectal insertion of plastic bags containing cocaine.

These wrappers may deteriorate and release their contents into the gut with subsequent absorption (some "mules," as these smugglers are called, may carry more than 100 packets). The majority of these patients can be managed by careful observation.[9] However, a small percentage require surgery because of intestinal obstruction. Cocaine in the gut can lead to intestinal ischemia and gangrene.[10]

The widespread smoking of free base cocaine has been associated with several pulmonary complications not observed with other forms of cocaine use. Spontaneous pneumomediastinum, pneumothorax, pneumopericardium, and pneumoperitoneum may occur because of barotrauma caused by forced Valsalva maneuvers. Conservative management usually is all that is required with the development of either pneumomedioastinum or pneumothorax.[11] However, an impairment in carbon monoxide diffusing capacity[12] and a possible association with reactive airways disease[13] may contribute to a group of patients who develop dyspnea or a chronic cough. Radiologic findings of pulmonary edema without hemodynamic evidence for a cardiac etiology have been observed in several free base smokers.[14] The passive inhalation of cocaine by children in the presence of adults smoking the drug reportedly has resulted in untoward neurologic effects.[15]

Intravenous cocaine injection is associated with the many complications of unsterile injections and needle sharing.[16] These transmitted illnesses include the acquired immunodeficiency syndrome (AIDS); hepatitis B and delta hepatitis superinfection; non-A, non-B hepatitis; endocarditis; systemic abscesses; and local wound infections (notably tetanus). The increasing proportion of AIDS cases related to intravenous drug use has been contributed to by the greater number of cocaine addicts.[17] Cocaine has been speculated to act directly as an immunosuppressant (observed only in intravenous cocaine users,[18] although these results have not been demonstrated conclusively).

Cocaine has been administered intraurethrally[19] and intravaginally[20] with hopes of increased sexual excitement. A case report described the development of priapism and paraphimosis after intraurethral application. This was followed by the development of disseminated intravascular coagulation, resulting in bilateral leg amputations. People using cocaine are more likely to have multiple sexual partners or engage in compulsive sexual behavior. These practices increase the risk of sexually transmitted diseases[21] (and, most importantly, AIDS-related illnesses).

The developing fetus is at risk for several adverse outcomes when the pregnant mother uses cocaine. Reductions in uterine blood flow and the transplacental transport of cocaine are possible mechanisms of insult. Esterase activity in fetal serum is less when compared to adults, and this possible diminution in the metabolism of cocaine may contribute to fetal damage. Complications include preterm labor; abruptio placentae;[22] the delivery of infants who weigh less, are shorter, and have a smaller head circumference than matched controls; and children with demonstrable neurobehavioral defects.[23] Harmful effects on neonatal brain stem and auditory system development, as well as an increased incidence of neural tube defects and deep brain cysts also have been described. Cocaine-exposed infants also have been reported to have seizures in the neonatal period, when they have had cocaine or its metabolites present in their urine at the time of delivery.[24, 25] A problem with these clinical reports is that it is not possible to establish causality because of the many other factors involved (including poor prenatal care, poor maternal nutrition, other drug use, and lack of normal maternal behavior).

Adulterants found in cocaine available on the street include local anesthetics, sugars and other inert substances, psychostimulants, quinine, arsenic, or strychnine.[26] The local anesthetics may lead to similar episodes of seizures and acute psychosis. The several stimulants used to "cut" cocaine also have profound cardiovascular effects. Strychnine, usually obtained from rodenticides, results in excessive stimulation of the central nervous system and may be indistinguishable from tetanus.

The intense euphoria achieved with cocaine use and the symptoms of dysphoria, hypersomnolence, and food cravings that occur after cocaine use contribute to the addictive potential of this agent. The symptoms of euphoria and dysphoria appear to be more profound with either intravenous injection of cocaine or smoking of the free base form. The peak feelings of pleasure can be linked to the rapid rise of the serum concentration of cocaine resulting from these two forms of administration.[2] The agitation, anxiety, and fatigue that contribute to the dysphoria begin as the serum concentration falls. The rapid change from feelings of euphoria to those of dysphoria may be the most important reason for an intense desire for more cocaine and the resultant addiction.

## The Pharmacodynamics of Cocaine

Cocaine is a psychostimulant that results in euphoria, an increase in clarity of thought processes, sympathetic nervous system stimulation, and appetite reduction. In larger quantities, a person may become garrulous and confused, demonstrate hyperexcitability of the motor system, experience a generalized tonic-clonic seizure, and possibly die. These several desired and undesired effects of cocaine use are directly attributable to the two major actions of cocaine on neurons. Cocaine exerts an effect upon both conduction (by interfering with action potential propagation) and transmission (by altering the re-uptake after synaptic release of several neurotransmitters) within the nervous system.

Cocaine binds to the voltage-sensitive sodium channel and leads to a reduction in the influx of sodium ions[27] normally seen after membrane depolarization. This prevents initiation of an action potential. The local anesthetics (and the related type IA antidysrhythmics) available today also bind to the sodium channel and were developed to avoid the central nervous system effects observed with cocaine use.

Cocaine blocks the re-uptake of dopamine, norepinephrine, and serotonin into the presynaptic terminal[28] after these neurotransmitters are released into the synaptic cleft by a presynaptic neuron. Cocaine is classified as an indirect sympathetic agonist in the nervous system, resulting in an effect similar to that of the psychostimulant amphetamine. Interference with re-uptake of these monoamines eliminates a major mechanism of removal of a neurotransmitter and prolongs stimulation of the postsynaptic receptor. This may result in excessive synaptic activation in the short term (a time sale of seconds to minutes) and alter receptor numbers in the long term (hours to days). The effects on the behaviors that are mediated by these synaptic connections are multiple and complex (as demonstrated by receptor imaging studies in human volunteers).[29]

Demands on the cardiovascular system increase in laboratory animals and human subjects after cocaine use.[30] The heart rate and peripheral vascular resistance increase because of catecholamine re-uptake inhibition in the sympathetic nervous system. These two effects contribute to an increase in the systemic blood pressure. Intense vasoconstriction may occur in several regions of the arterial circulation. In addition, cocaine use increases heat production (by increasing skeletal muscle activity via central nervous system stimulation) and decreases heat loss (from the vasoconstrictor effects), resulting in an elevation in body temperature.

Animals given a choice between cocaine or food for unlimited time periods will demonstrate a preference for cocaine. These animals will neglect self-care, stop eating, and oftentimes die.[31] The use of cocaine in rats leads to a reduction in the threshold for electrical stimulation of the brain in regions associated with pleasure.[32] The anatomic pathways underlying cocaine-related behaviors reside in the limbic portion of the brain. Connections into and out of the limbic region are necessary for repeated self-administration and reduction in the thresholds for reward.[28] The ability of cocaine to interfere with neurotransmitter re-uptake (and, specifically, dopamine re-uptake) correlates most closely with these behaviors in rats and monkeys.[33]

## Complications Attributable to the Pharmacodynamics of Cocaine

Patients who use cocaine wish to attain the feelings of euphoria that occur with an increase in the serum levels of this drug. Nearly all users describe pleasurable experiences, sexual arousal, and bursts of energy. Unfortunately, there exists a narrow therapeutic "window" with cocaine use, and the majority of people eventually will describe dysphoria and more serious psychiatric symptoms. Initally, this may present as reduced energy levels, decreased attentiveness, apathy, and a loss of appetite. These feelings of dysphoria in concert with the initial pleasurable experiences lead to an intense craving for repeat use. This has been described as the severe psychologic dependence that many cocaine users experience. The intense desire to repeat cocaine use dramatically interferes with an individual's ability to function in society and may lead to criminal activities. Finally, a significant percentage of cocaine users report hallucinations, either auditory or tactile. Some also will develop an acute psychosis requiring emergency psychiatric care. These symptoms may lead to violent behavior, and possibly homicide or suicide.

The recent increase in reports of cardiovascular and neurologic complications associated with cocaine use are explained best by the effects of cocaine on conduction and transmission within the nervous system (Table 2). Several other medical complications also result from these actions of cocaine.

The local anesthetic property of cocaine may contribute to many of the

**TABLE 2.**
**Complications Attributable to the Pharmacodynamics of Cocaine**

I. Sodium channel blockade.
   A. Cardiac dysrhythmias.
   B. Seizures.
   C. Psychosis and other psychiatric symptoms.
   D. Neurotransmitter re-uptake inhibition (?).
II. Neurotransmitter re-uptake inhibiton (blockage of monoamine(s) transporter).
   A. Vasoconstriction/increased vascular resistance.
      1. Intestinal ischemia/infarction.
      2. Skin infarction.
      3. Muscle infarction.
      4. Rhabdomyolysis (leading to acute renal failure).
      5. Disseminated intravascular coagulopathy.
      6. Cerebrovascular accidents.
      7. Headaches.
      8. Transient, focal neurologic deficits.
      9. Reduction in heat loss, hyperthermia.
      10. Rupture of the aorta.
      11. Myocardial ischemia and infarctions.
   B. Increased heart rate.
      1. Increased myocardial oxygen demand, myocardial ischemia.
      2. Atrial/ventricular tachycardias.
   C. Increased heat production, hyperthermia.
III. Unclear mechanism.
   A. Myocarditis.
   B. Dilated cardiomyopathy.
   C. Seizures (?).
   D. Psychiatric symptoms (?).
   E. Neuroleptic malignant-like syndrome.
   F. Cerebrovascular angiitis.
   G. Sexual dysfunction.

cardiac dysrhythmias observed in patients. These include supraventricular and ventricular tachycardias in their most dangerous form. Sudden death (which most likely is a consequence of a dysrhythmia) has been reported following cocaine use in any form.[34] Generalized tonic-clonic seizures occurred during 27 of 989 hospital visits directly attributable to cocaine use in one large, retrospective study.[35] Psychiatric symptoms contributed to nearly 10% of these emergency room visits (the design of the study most likely underrepresented these symptoms) and consisted of anxiety, psychosis, or suicidal thoughts. The frequent occurrence of seizures and psychiatric symptoms are similar to the adverse effects observed with lidocaine and other local anesthetics when present in toxic blood concentrations.

The effects of cocaine as a sympathomimetic in the autonomic nervous system cause several complications. Reductions in blood flow have been associated with skin,[36] muscle,[37] and gut[10] infarction. Intense vasoconstriction may underlie the several reported cases of rhabdomyolysis[38] (which have resulted in acute renal failure, hepatic dysfunction, or death) and disseminated intravascular coagulation.[39] The rapid rise in the systemic blood pressure may cause rupture of the aorta[40] (reflected in one case report) and intracerebral hemorrhage.[41] The differential diagnosis of hyperthermia now must include cocaine as one cause, because of its effect on body temperature. In addition, cocaine use may lead to a predisposition for the development of a neuroleptic malignant-like syndrome.[42]

Neurologic complications of cocaine use, in addition to seizures, include strokes, headaches, transient focal signs, and toxic encephalopathy. All varieties of seizures have been documented, including tonic-clonic and partial-complex seizures. The majority of seizures, however, are usually single, generalized, and induced by intravenous or crack cocaine and are not associated with any lasting neurologic effects.[43] Seizure activity induced by cocaine usually begins in the temporal lobe region.

The drug smugglers who accidentally overdose on cocaine when a cocaine-filled condom ruptures in their colon may have multiple seizures. Diazepam and phenobarbital have been found to be useful in seizures of this type.[44] Phenytoin has been found to be ineffective in animal studies of cocaine-induced seizures and carbamazepine has not been tested systematically. In the management of patients with cocaine-induced seizures, a thorough evaluation to rule out other causes of seizures should be conducted. The evaluation of suspected cocaine-induced seizures should include toxicology, with a urine screen for cocaine, cocaine metabolites, and other drugs. Anticonvulsants have not been effective in preventing subsequent seizures if the patient again uses cocaine. While cocaine-kindled seizures have been demonstrated in rats, there is no evidence that they lead to spontaneous seizure disorders in humans.[45] Thus, if no cause for the seizure other than drug abuse is found, anticonvulsant medication is not indicated, though the patient should be placed in a treatment program leading to abstinence from cocaine. The electroencephalogram should be normal soon after a cocaine-induced seizure. If a second seizure is observed, however, a standard seizure treatment protocol should be followed. If status epilepticus develops, phenobarbital loading should be accomplished and the protocol for pentobarbital anesthesia may need to be followed. However, this procedure will require intubation, continuous electroencephalographic monitoring, and admission to an intensive care unit.[46]

Cocaine has been associated with several types of cerebrovascular problems, including intracerebral hemorrhages, cerebral infarction (either embolic or thrombotic), and subarachnoid hemorrhages (occurring in patients with an aneurysm or vascular malformation).[41, 47] Migrainelike headaches have been temporally related to binge use of cocaine.[48] A variety of other neurologic problems include transient symptoms, such as hemisensory loss or visual impairment. Cocaine and other stimulants also can enhance preexisting neurologic abnormalities, including tremor, vertigo, nonspecific dizziness, blurred vision, ataxia, and tinnitus. Tourette's syndrome also has been documented to be exacerbated with cocaine use.[49]

The mechanisms for development of the acute neurologic complications from cocaine use are unclear. One hypothesis proposes that the central sympathomimetic effects of cocaine induce systemic hypertension, tachycardia, and vascular spasms.[50] Another proposed mechanism for both cocaine and amphetamine strokes is a form of necrotizing angiitis.[51] Microaneurysms often can be documented angiographically, but if none are present, necrotizing angiitis cannot necessarily be ruled out. Other features confirming angiitis are stenosis, vessel irregularity, infarction, and thrombosis.

The final major category of the neurologic complications of cocaine use is the variety of psychiatric disorders produced by these drugs. These psychiatric episodes are seen in both acute stimulant overdose and chronic stimulant use. The acute phase manifestations include agitation, dysphoria, assaultiveness, paranoia, hallucinations, and psychosis. Although the exact mechanisms of these syndromes are unknown, these psychiatric disturbances probably are related to cocaine's effects on various neurotransmitter systems (especially dopamine and serotonin).[33] There also is evidence from animal studies that cocaine produces limbic kindling, and this may be related to the increased risk of psychosis with chronic use.[45] In addition, cocaine-dependent patients may present with depressive symptoms that may be accompanied by suicidal ideation.

The cardiovascular effects of cocaine have resulted in serious illnesses. In addition to several dysrhythmias and sudden cardiac death, cocaine use now represents a major risk factor for the development of a myocardial infarction.[52-54] A young patient who suffers a myocardial infarction must be questioned about cocaine use, and all patients should be warned of its cardiovascular risks.

Several facts about patients who have experienced cocaine-related myocardial infarctions deserve comment. The majority of patients who undergo cardiac catheterization soon after the infarction have either a thrombus, stenosis, or occlusion in the infarct-related vessel. Patients have responded well to thrombolytic therapy and should be considered candidates for this intervention. An overwhelming number of these patients smoke cigarettes, also contributing to their risk for coronary artery disease and possibly increasing the vasoconstrictor response of the coronary arteries. Finally, the intranasal application of cocaine (in doses commonly used for rhinolaryngologic procedures) in a controlled setting resulted in a reduction in the intraluminal diameter of the coronary artery and in coronary blood flow.[55] These changes were demonstrated in patients both with and without coronary artery disease. The reduction in coronary blood flow occurred despite an increase in myocardial oxygen demand (resulting from the increase in heart rate and afterload). Interestingly, these episodes of blood flow reduction were not associated with symptoms or electrocardiographic changes of ischemia. Myocardial infarction associated with cocaine use most likely is caused by a combination of an increase in myocardial oxygen demand and a decrease in myocardial oxygen supply (secondary to vasospasm and/or thrombus formation).

Cocaine use also has been linked to myocarditis[56] and the development of congestive heart failure[57] in a few case reports. The heart failure is a dilated, nonischemic cardiomyopathy and appears similar to a rare type of catecholamine-induced cardiomyopathy. In one patient, the clinical course improved and left ventricular function returned to normal during the cocaine-free hospitalization. Adulterants with cardiotoxic properties contained in the cocaine also may have contributed to nonischemic myocardial damage.

Finally, sexual dysfunction can be caused by heavy cocaine use. Cocaine can enhance sexual performance, especially at low doses. It delays ejaculation and orgasm, while producing elevated mood and heightened sensory awareness. When used chronically at high doses, cocaine can impair potency and ejaculation. Chronic cocaine users of both sexes may lose sexual interest or exhibit aberrant sexual behavior, such as compulsive masturbation, and some women may experience difficulty achieving orgasm.[58]

## Treatment of Cocaine Dependence

Each of the complications of cocaine use described above may require specific treatment. However, in the care of any cocaine-abusing patient, it is important to address the underlying disorder in order to prevent a recurrence of the same or different complications. In the case of cocaine, any use is illegal, but occasional use may not be medically harmful for most people. The drug has such potent addicting properties, however, that any use can get out of control quickly, and the effects and risks of cocaine are strongly dose-related. Until the 1980s, cocaine use was self-limiting due to high cost and low availability. Thus, few users could obtain sufficient regular supplies to get into trouble. Snorting of cocaine produced some problems, including dependence, but as supplies increased throughout the 1980s, dependence on nasal cocaine and the new intravenous crack cocaine became a serious problem.

All patients treated for the complications of cocaine use should be referred for treatment of cocaine dependence. The success of the referral for dependence on cocaine or any other substance will depend on four factors. First, the patient needs to acknowledge that there is a problem with drug use. If the patient admits that there is a problem or is willing to go into treatment, he or she must enter into the second, or detoxification, stage of treatment. The withdrawal syndrome for cocaine consists of feelings of fatigue, weakness, somnolence, and depression.[59] In the case of cocaine, no specific medication is required, because the withdrawal syndrome is quite variable and usually mild. The symptoms oftentimes disappear in several days without medication. When depression is severe and persistent, antidepressant medication may be indicated. The craving to return to cocaine use persists beyond the period of withdrawal symptoms and may result in part from conditioned responses in the drug user's environment.[60]

The third important factor in drug treatment, once the detoxification phase is completed, is to evaluate the patient for pharmacotherapy to aid in the prevention of relapse. If there are persistent symptoms of depression, antidepressant medication may be administered. Even in the absence of depression, desipramine has been found to be useful in reducing the return to cocaine use during the first 6 weeks of treatment.[61] This medication is most likely to be of benefit in the context of an overall rehabilitation program as described following. Other drugs currently are being investigated for usefulness in relapse prevention, including carbamazepine,[62] buprenorphine,[63] bromocriptine,[64] and others. These trials have resulted from several animal studies and are still in progress. They require careful double-blind methodology, because clinical impressions are often misleading.

The fourth factor is counseling or psychotherapy, which is essential to any substance abuse treatment program. Of course, all patients should be encouraged to participate in self-help groups such as Alcoholics Anonymous, Cocaine Anonymous, and others. Many patients find these group experiences to be most meaningful and completely compatible with medically oriented therapy. Although an internist or general physician may be able to manage counseling techniques with a very motivated patient, the more severe forms of cocaine dependence are managed best by a treatment team specially trained in drug abuse. Studies of the outcome of treatment show that detoxification alone results in a large majority of patients returning to cocaine use with weeks of leaving treatment. However, results from rehabilitation programs are showing 6-month success rates in the range of 60%.[65] In these trials of more than 100 patients enrolled in either inpatient or outpatient therapy, there is no evidence (from both patient reports and urine analyses) to support continued cocaine use. These results indicate that the goal of abstinence from cocaine use is realistic and, by extrapolation from previous work with other forms of drug abuse,[66] should lead to an improvement in a patient's ability to function in society. Furthermore, efforts to cause extinction of the overwhelming craving for cocaine use in response to environmental cues may be helpful.[60] The widespread use of cocaine in the United States has resulted in enormous costs to society during the past 10 years. The intense craving for repeated ingestion of cocaine leads an individual to obtain and administer cocaine without regard to his or her own safety or that of others around them. An increased incidence of illnesses normally not observed in young people demands that all health care workers recognize the many symptoms of cocaine addiction and initiate appropriate care. In addition, recent advances in studies of the mechanisms of action of cocaine and multiple randomized clinical trials (designed to demonstrate efficacious therapies) will contribute to a reduction in the complications of cocaine use. Most importantly, a significant lowering in the demand for cocaine must occur simultaneously. This will require increased funding in the areas of education, research, and clinical treatment.[67]

## References

1. Goldstein A, Kalant H: Drug policy: Striking the right balance. *Science* 1990; 249:1513–1522.
2. Van Dyke C, Byck R: Cocaine. *Sci Am* 1982; 246:108–122.
3. Ritchie JM, Geene NM: Local anesthetics, in Gilman A, Rall TN, Nies AS, et al (eds): *The Pharmacological Basis of Therapeutics,* seventh ed. New York, Pergamon Press, 1985, pp 319–320.
4. Devenyi P: Cocaine complications and pseudocholinesterase. *Ann Intern Med* 1989; 110:167.
5. Foltz RL, Fentiman AF, Foltz RB: A collection of methods for quantitative analysis of several important drugs of abuse by gas chromatography-mass spectroscopy. *NIDA Res Monogr* 1980; 32:1–198.
6. Vilensky W: Illicit and licit drugs causing perforation of the nasal septum. *J Forensic Sci* 1982; 27:958–962.
7. Rao AN: Brain abcess: A complication of cocaine inhalation. *N Y State J Med* 1988; 10:548–550.
8. Kudrwo DB, Henry DA, Haake DA, et al: Botulism associated with Clostridium botulinum sinusitis after intranasal cocaine use. *Ann Intern Med* 1988; 109:984–985.
9. Caruana DS, Weinbach B, Goerg D, et al: Cocaine packet-ingestion-diagnosis, management, and natural history. *Ann Intern Med* 1984; 100:73–74.
10. Nalbandian H, Sheth N, Dietrich R, et al: Intestinal ischemia caused by cocaine ingestion: Report of two cases. *Surgery* 1985; 97:374–376.
11. Shesser R, Davis C, Edelstein S: Pneumomediastinum and pneumothorax after inhaling alkaloidal cocaine. *Ann Emerg Med* 1981; 10:213–215.
12. Itkonen J, Schnoll S, Glassroth J: Pulmonary dysfunction in freebase cocaine users. *Arch Int Med* 1984; 144:2195–2197.
13. Gordon K: Freebased cocaine smoking and reactive airway disease. *J Emerg Med* 1989; 7:145–147.
14. Hoffman CK, Goodman PC: Pulmonary edema in cocaine smokers. *Radiology* 1989; 172:463–465.

15. Bateman DA, Hegarty ME: Passive inhalation of cocaine. *Am J Dis Child* 1989; 143:25–27.
16. Stein MD: Medical complications of intravenous drug use. *J Gen Intern Med* 1990; 5:249–257.
17. Acquired immunodeficiency syndrome associated with intravenous drug use—United States 1988. *MMWR* 1989; 38:165–170.
18. Chaisson RE, Bacchetti P, Osmond D, et al: Cocaine use and HIV infection in intravenous drug users in San Francisco. *JAMA* 1989; 262:561–565.
19. Mahler JC, Perry S, Sutton B: Intraurethral cocaine administration. *JAMA* 1988; 259:3126.
20. Ettinger TB, Stine RJ: Sudden death temporally related to vaginal cocaine abuse. *Am J Emerg Med* 1989; 7:129–131.
21. Fullilove RE, Fullilove MT, Bowser BP, et al: Risk of sexually transmitted diseases among black adolescent crack users in Oakland and San Francisco, Calif. *JAMA* 1990; 263:851–855.
22. Little BB, Snell LM, Klein VR, et al: Cocaine abuse during pregnancy: Maternal and fetal complications. *Obstet Gynecol* 1989; 73:157–160.
23. Chasnoff IJ, Griffith DR, MacGregor S, et al: Temporal patterns of cocaine use in pregnancy. *JAMA* 1989; 261:1741–1744.
24. Chasnoff IJ, Griffith DR: Cocaine: Clinical studies of pregnancy and the newborn. *Ann N Y Acad Sci* 1989; 562:260–266.
25. Feinman BN: Neurologic sequelae of cocaine. *Hosp Pract [Off]* 1989; 24:97–104.
26. Shannon M: Clinical toxicity of cocaine adulterants. *Ann Emerg Med* 1988; 17:1243–1247.
27. Hille B: Local anesthetics; hydrophilic and hydrophobic pathways for the drug-receptor interaction. *J Gen Physiol* 1967; 69:497–515.
28. Koob GF, Bloom FE: Cellular and molecular mechanisms of drug dependence. *Science* 1988; 242:715–723.
29. Volkow ND, Fowler JS, Wolf AP: Effects of chronic cocaine abuse on postsynaptic dopamine receptors. *Am J Psychol* 1990; 147:719–723.
30. Cregler LL, Mark H: Medical complications of cocaine abuse. *N Engl J Med* 1986; 315:1495–1500.
31. Aigner TG, Balster RL: Choice behavior in rhesus monkeys: Cocaine versus food. *Science* 1978; 201:534–535.
32. Kornetsky C, Esposito RE: Reward and detection thresholds for brain stimulation: Dissociative effects of cocaines. *Brain Res* 1981; 209:496–500.
33. Ritz MC, Lamb RJ, Goldberg SR, et al: Cocaine receptors on dopamine transporters are related to self-administration of cocaine. *Science* 1987; 237:1219–1223.
34. Nanjii AA, Filipenko JD: Asystole and ventricular fibrillation associated with cocaine intoxication. *Chest* 1984; 85:132–133.
35. Lowenstein DH, Massa SM, Rowbotham MC, et al: Acute neurologic and psychiatric complications associated with cocaine abuse. *Am J Med* 1987; 83:841–846.
36. Zamora-Quezada JC, Dinerman H, Stadecker MJ, et al: Muscle and skin infarction after free-basing cocaine (crack). *Ann Intern Med* 1988; 108:564–565.
37. Reinhart WH, Stricker H: Rhabdomyolysis after intravenous cocaine. *Am J Med* 1988; 85:579.

38. Howard R, Kaehny WD: Cocaine and rhabdomyolysis. *Ann Intern Med* 1989; 110:90–91.
39. Roth D, Alarcon FJ, Fernandez JA, et al: Acute rhabdomyolysis and cocaine intoxication. *N Engl J Med* 1988; 319:673–677.
40. Barth CW, Bray M, Roberts WC: Rupture of the ascending aorta during cocaine intoxication. *Am J Cardiol* 1986; 57:496.
41. Caplan LR, Hier DB, Banks G: Current concepts of cerebrovascular disease-stroke: Stroke and drug abuse. *Stroke* 1982; 13:869–872.
42. Kosten TR, Kleber HD: Rapid death during cocaine abuse: A variant of the neuroleptic malignant syndrome? *Am J Drug Alcohol Abuse* 1988; 14:335–346.
43. Alldredge BK, Lowenstein DH, Simon RP: Seizures associated with recreational drug abuse. *Neurology* 1989; 39:1037–1039.
44. Pacual-Leone A, Dhuna A, Altafullah I, et al: Cocaine-induced seizures. *Neurology* 1990; 40:404–407.
45. Post RM, Kopanda RT: Cocaine, kindling, and psychosis. *Am J Psychol* 1976; 133:627–634.
46. Lowenstein DH, Aminoff M, Simon R: Barbiturate anesthesia in the treatment of status epilepticus: Clinical experience with 14 patients. *Neurology* 1988; 38:395–400.
47. Levine SR, Brust JCM, Futrell N, et al: Cerebrovascular complications of the use of the "crack" form of alkaloidal cocaine. *N Engl J Med* 1990; 323:699–704.
48. Satel SL, Gawin FH: Migrainelike headache and cocaine use. *JAMA* 1989; 261:2995–2996.
49. Factor SA, Sawchex-Ramos JR, Weiner WJ: Cocaine and Tourette's syndrome. *Ann Neurol* 1988; 23:423–424.
50. Levine SR, Welch KMA: Cocaine and stroke. *Stroke* 1988; 19:779–783.
51. Rowbotham MC, Lowenstein DH: Neurologic aspects of cocaine abuse. *West J Med* 1988; 149:442–448.
52. Isner JM, Estes NAM, Thompson PD, et al: Acute cardiac events temporally related to cocaine abuse. *N Engl J Med* 1986; 315:1438–1443.
53. Smith HWB, Liberman HA, Brody SL, et al: Acute myocardial infarction temporally related to cocaine use. *Ann Intern Med* 1987; 107:13–18.
54. Frishman WH, Karpenos A, Molloy TJ: Cocaine-induced coronary artery disease: Recognition and treatment. *Med Clin North Am* 1989; 73:475–485.
55. Lange RA, Cigarroa RG, Yancy CW, et al: Cocaine-induced coronary artery vasoconstriction. *N Engl J Med* 1989; 321:1557–1562.
56. Jentzen JM: Cocaine-induced myocarditis. *Am Heart J* 1989; 117:1398–1399.
57. Chokshi SK, Moore R, Pandian NG, et al: Reversible cardiomyopathy associated with cocaine intoxication. *Ann Intern Med* 1989; 111:1039–1040.
58. Cregler LL: Adverse health consequences of cocaine abuse. *J Natl Med Assoc* 1989; 81:27–38.
59. Gawin FH, Ellinwood EH: Cocaine dependence. *Annu Rev Med* 1989; 40:149–161.
60. O'Brien CP, Childress AR, McLellan AT, et al: Integrating systematic cue exposure with standard treatment in recovering drug dependent patients. *Addict Behav* 1990; 15:355–365.
61. Gawin FH, Ellinwood EH: Cocaine and other stimulants. *N Engl J Med* 1988; 318:1173–1182.
62. Gawin FH: Chronic neuropharmacology of cocaine abuse. *J Clin Psychol* 1988; 49:S11–17.

63. Mello NK, Mendelson JH, Bree MP, et al: Buprenorphine suppresses cocaine self-administration by rhesus monkeys. *Science* 1989; 245:859–861.
64. Dackis CA, Gold MS: Bromocriptine for cocaine withdrawal. *Lancet* 1985; 1:1151–1152.
65. O'Brien CP, Alterman A, Walter D, et al: Evaluation of treatment for cocaine dependence. *NIDA Res Monogr* 1989; 95:78–83.
66. McLellan AT, Luborsky L, O'Brien CP, et al: Is treatment for substance abuse effective? *JAMA* 1982; 247:1423–1428.
67. Jarvik ME: The drug dilemma: Manipulating the demand. *Science* 1990; 250:387–392.

# Systolic Hypertension in Older Persons*

## William B. Applegate, M.D., M.P.H.

Professor of Medicine and Preventive Medicine, University of Tennessee, Memphis, School of Medicine, Memphis, Tennessee

### Editor's Introduction

The completion of the 5-year double-blind placebo-controlled trial of the treatment of systolic hypertension in the elderly (SHEP) could hardly have come at a more propitious time for this splendid review of the subject by Dr. William Applegate. Not only is treatment highly effective in preventing cerebrovascular and cardiovascular complications of hypertension, but relatively inexpensive old antihypertensive drugs, such as chlorthalidone, do the job very well and with infrequent side effects. As a long-time student of this subject and leader of the multicenter SHEP study group, Dr. Applegate is just the authority to guide us through the complexities of this important issue in geriatric medical management.

*Gene H. Stollerman, M.D.*

Reports on the prevalence of hypertension in the elderly indicate that between 30% and 50% of persons over the age of 65 years may have chronic hypertension.[1] Since the risk of future cardiovascular morbid and mortal events rises in a continuous fashion as either systolic blood pressure (SBP) or diastolic blood pressure (DBP) rises, there is really no threshold of either that can be described definitively as hypertensive.[2] Clinical convention usually defines isolated systolic hypertension (ISH) as an SBP of 160 mm Hg or more and a DBP of less than 90 mm Hg. Systolic-diastolic hypertension (SDH) is usually defined based on a DBP of 90 mm Hg or more.

Recent reviews have indicated that SDH should be treated in older persons up to at least the age of 80 years.[1, 3] Although a great deal is known about the epidemiology of ISH, the impact of treatment of this condition on subsequent morbid and mortal events has just recently been established by the main systolic hypertension in the elderly program (SHEP) main trial.[3a] The focus of this chapter will be to describe the epidemiology, pathophysiology, and available treatment data with regard to elevations of SBP in older persons.

*Adapted from Applegate WB: *Ann Intern Med* 1989; 110:901-915. Used by permission.

*Advances in Internal Medicine®*, vol. 37.
Copyright 1991, Mosby–Year Book, Inc.

## Epidemiology

Several epidemiologic studies have indicated that average SBP increases throughout the life span, while average DBP rises until the age of 55 to 60 years and then levels off.[4, 5] This increase in blood pressure occurs both in persons previously classified as hypertensive and in those previously considered normotensive. However, data from Framingham and other studies indicate that not all individuals experience the aging-related increase in SBP.[4] In addition, population studies from nonindustrialized societies indicate that average blood pressure does not tend to rise with age.[6]

Estimates of the true prevalence of hypertension vary greatly depending on the age and race of the population, the blood pressure cutpoint used for the definition of hypertension, and the number of measurements made.[7] The prevalence of both SDH and ISH is considerable in persons over the age of 65 years. Since DBP tends to level off around 55 years of age, the prevalence of SDH tends to be constant after that point.[8] Therefore, although some authors speak in general terms of the rise in prevalence of hypertension with age, the prevalence of SDH rises little.[8] Actually, it is the rise in ISH that comprises most of the overall increase in the prevalence of hypertension with advancing age.[5] When one accounts for the effect of multiple measures of blood pressure, it appears that the prevalence of SDH in persons over 65 years of age is about 15% in whites and 25% in blacks.[9] The prevalence of ISH varies with increasing age from 1% to 2% at 50 years of age to greater than 20% over 80 years of age,[9-11] and does not appear to differ much according to race.

Unfortunately, only limited data are available to estimate the rate of onset of new-incidence cases of hypertension in the elderly. Analysis of Framingham data (based on one reading, but biennial measures) indicates that the cumulative incidence of ISH is about 418:1,000 in men and 533:1,000 in women over a 24-year period.[11] Although the clinical treatment of hypertension classically has focused on DBP levels, epidemiologic data indicate that for middle-aged and older adults, the SBP level is more predictive of future cardiovascular morbidity.[12, 13] For men 45 years and older, SBP is a better discriminator of cardiovascular risk than is DBP.[13] Also, for persons with elevations of DBP (greater than or equal to 90 mm Hg), at any level of DBP, SBP gives additional information on risk. For persons with DBP less than 85 mm Hg (including middle-aged individuals as well as the elderly), risk is primarily a function of SBP. However, both SBP and DBP remain independently predictive of future vascular events in the elderly. Analysis of Framingham data indicates that 42% of strokes in elderly men and 70% of strokes in elderly women are directly attributable to hypertension.[13] Shekelle has shown that increasing levels of SBP are associated with a rising incidence of stroke when DBP is normal or constant.[14] In comparison with persons whose SBP is less than 139 mm Hg, persons with an SBP greater than 160 mm Hg have a 2.5 times greater incidence of stroke. There are insufficient data currently available to determine if elevation of SBP or DBP in persons over 80 years of age carries the same risk found in persons aged 65 to 80 years.

When all cardiovascular risk factors are taken into account in the elderly, it is clear that an increased level of SBP is the single greatest risk factor (other than age itself) for increased cardiovascular disease in persons over the age of 65 years.[4] It is also clear that increased blood pressure does interact with other cardiovascular risk factors to compound the risk. For instance, although serum cholesterol declines somewhat as a cardiovascular risk factor in the elderly, it still confers some element of risk (especially when fractionated into the low-density lipoprotein/high-density lipoprotein ratio) and compounds the risk for hypertensives.[4] Also, it has been known for some years that the development of left ventricular hypertrophy is itself an independent cardiovascular risk factor.[15] Recent reports from the Framingham study indicate that left ventricular hypertrophy is more prevalent in older persons and highly correlated with increased SBP.[16] Also, this condition in hypertensives confers an increased risk of ventricular arrhythmias and is an independent risk factor for cardiovascular mortality.[17]

## Pathophysiology

The exact causal mechanisms for the development of hypertension in the elderly and whether they are different from the mechanisms involved in younger persons remains to be fully determined. Since most cases of SDH occur by 55 years of age, it is unlikely that the pathophysiology of SDH is much different in the elderly than it is in the middle-aged. It is known, however, that older hypertensives tend to have lower renin levels and to be somewhat more sensitive to sodium repletion or depletion than are younger hypertensives.[18, 19] It is probable that structural changes in the large vessels play a predominant role in the rise of SBP levels with age.[20] Both a decrease in connective tissue elasticity and an increase in the prevalence of atherosclerosis result in an increase in peripheral vascular resistance and aortic impedance with age.[20–23] Simon has found a strong negative correlation between large-vessel compliance and systolic pressure in older patients.[24] It has been shown that a decrease in aortic compliance results in greater resistance to systolic ejection and, frequently, in disproportionate elevations of SBP.[23] It is fairly clear that the hemodynamic characteristics of ISH are different in patients under 40 years of age (and also fairly rare) than in patients over 65 years of age.[25] Younger patients with ISH usually demonstrate a hyperkinetic circulation manifested by a significantly increased heart rate, elevated left ventricular ejection rate and cardiac indices, and normal vascular resistance. On the other hand, older patients with ISH tend to have a normal heart rate, significantly reduced cardiac and left ventricular ejection rate indices, and increased vascular resistance. Also, plasma volume tends to be reduced in older patients with ISH.

It is unclear whether alterations in the renin-angiotensin system or functional changes in vascular smooth muscle have any impact in terms of raising SBP in older persons. Since renin levels tend to be lower in older patients, it is unlikely that the renin-angiotensin system is involved in the pathogenesis of ISH. It is possible, however, that functional changes in vascular smooth muscle may have some impact on the increased peripheral resistance seen in elderly patients with ISH. Studies in animals indicate that α-adrenergic responsiveness of vascular smooth muscle is not changed greatly with age.[26] However, β-adrenergic responsiveness does decline with age,[27, 28] with a consequent decrease in the relaxation of vascular smooth muscle.[29] Therefore, it has been postulated that the increase in peripheral resistance in elderly hypertensives with ISH may be due in part to diminished β-adrenergic–mediated vasodilation, while α-adrenergic–mediated vasoconstriction continues unabated.[26]

## Data on Treatment

There is ample evidence that treating SDH in older persons, at least up to the age of 80 years, is generally beneficial, and this has been outlined in a recent review.[1] In general, treatment of patients over 60 years of age with SDH results in a relative or percent reduction in cardiovascular morbidity and mortality similar to that seen in patients under 50 years of age. However, when these data are analyzed by the absolute number of events prevented per 1,000 person-years of treatment, it is also clear that more total events are prevented in patients over 60 years of age.[1, 3] Actually, the amount of attributable benefit from the treatment of diastolic hypertension increases both with age and severity. The absolute benefit from drug treatment of diastolic hypertension in persons over 60 years of age varies from 10 events prevented per 1,000 person-years for persons with mild diastolic hypertension (90 to 104 mm Hg) up to 100 events per 1,000 person-years of treatment for persons with moderate diastolic hypertension (105 to 115 mm Hg).[1, 3]

Before the publication of the recent SHEP study,[3a] there were limited data available on the potential benefits of the treatment of ISH. One early descriptive study of a large cohort of elderly black patients with SDH treated over an extensive period of time indicated that even if the DBP was well controlled, continued elevation of SBP was associated with greater subsequent cardiovascular morbidity and mortality.[30] In this study, 503 elderly (over 60 years of age) black hypertensive patients were followed for up to 9 years in a community public health chronic disease clinic system. Only those patients whose DBP was always under 90 mm Hg were studied. The study cohort was divided into the following subgroups: those whose SBP was greater than 160 mm Hg at each visit (mean SBP = 184 mm Hg, mean DBP = 88 mm Hg); those whose SBP was at times greater than 160 mm Hg (mean SBP = 151 mm Hg, mean DBP = 84 mm Hg); and those whose SBP was less than 160 mm Hg at every visit (mean SBP = 137 mm Hg, mean DBP = 78 mm Hg). Although cardiovascular morbidity and mortality rates were highest in the first subgroup (compared to either of the other two subgroups), cardiovascular morbidity and mortality rates were 50% higher in the subgroup with the greatest control (lowest levels) of SBP and DBP, as compared to the intermediate subgroup. Therefore, this study raised some question as to whether too aggressive treatment of hypertension could be harmful.

In the pilot study for the Systolic Hypertension in the Elderly Program, 551 elderly subjects with ISH (SBP greater than or equal to 160 mm Hg and DBP less than 90 mm Hg) were randomized to treatment with chlorthalidone, and a step 2 drug if needed, vs. placebo.[31] Seventy-five percent of the patients in the treatment group had their SBP lowered to the treatment goal with the diuretic alone. Mean blood pressure declined by 30/7 mm Hg in the treatment group and 11/4 mm Hg in the control group (Table 1). As can be seen in Table 1, approximately the same amount of blood pressure reduction was seen across the various age, gender, and race subgroups.[31] Therefore, adequate lowering of SBP occurred primarily through the use of the diuretic and was relatively easy to accomplish without an undue decline in DBP. This pilot study was not designed with sufficient sample size to provide a definitive answer on the impact of treatment on cardiovascular morbidity and mortality. However, it did demonstrate a nonsignificant trend toward a lower stroke rate (9.0 vs. 19.2 per 1,000 participant-years) in the drug-treatment group.[32] There were no other striking differences in event rates between the drug-treatment or placebo groups in the pilot study, except for a nonsignificant trend toward lower rates of all cardiovascular events combined in the drug-treatment group (Table 2). The definitive data on impact of drug treatment of ISH on subsequent cardiovascular and cerebrovascular endpoints from the main SHEP[3a] trial are published in the addendum at the end of this article and in Table 2.

---

**Diagnostic Evaluation of the Patient With Isolated Systolic Hypertension**

The basic approach to the evaluation of the elderly patient with ISH involves accurate determination of the baseline blood pressure, assessment of any possible end-organ damage, and (only in rare cases) ruling out of any underlying conditions that may have caused the blood pressure to rise. Since blood pressure is highly variable, it is important that an average of three readings on two or three occasions of measurement be used to define the baseline blood pressure.[33] High blood pressure readings show regression to the mean, so high initial readings often are lower on the second and third follow-up visits. Also, elderly hypertensive patients should have baseline (and periodic) evaluation of both supine and standing blood pressure, since the prevalence of postural hypotension increases with age, can be especially severe after meals, and can be aggravated seriously by treatment with antihypertensive medications.[34]

## TABLE 1.
### Blood Pressure After 1 Year of Follow-Up by Age, Sex, Race, and Study Group—Intention-To-Treat Analysis Adjusted for Missing Data*

| | Number of Participants† | | Systolic Blood Pressure (mm Hg)‡ | | | Diastolic Blood Pressure (mm Hg)‡ | | |
|---|---|---|---|---|---|---|---|---|
| | Chlorthalidone | Placebo | Chlorthalidone | Placebo | Difference | Chlorthalidone | Placebo | Difference |
| Age | | | | | | | | |
| 60–69 years | 176 | 38 | 140 | 159 | 19§ | 70 | 78 | 8 |
| 70–79 years | 200 | 56 | 142 | 158 | 16§ | 67 | 72 | 5 |
| 80 years | 67 | 14 | 142 | 160 | 18§ | 63 | 70 | 7 |
| Women | 279 | 70 | 142 | 158 | 16§ | 66 | 72 | 6 |
| Men | 164 | 38 | 139 | 158 | 19§ | 69 | 76 | 7 |
| White | 365 | 87 | 141 | 157 | 16§ | 68 | 74 | 6 |
| Nonwhite | 78 | 21 | 142 | 165 | 23§ | 67 | 71 | 4 |
| Overall | 443 | 108 | 141 | 158 | 17§ | 68 | 74 | 6 |

*From Hulley SB, Furberg CD, Gurland B, et al: *Am J Cardiol* 1985; 56:917. Used by permission.

†All statistics are computed by study group assignment, regardless of whether the participant continued to take Systolic Hypertension in the Elderly Program medications.

‡The measured blood pressure was used for those attending the annual visit (n = 401 in chlorthalidone and n = 104 in placebo groups), and the closest preceding value was substituted for those who did not attend.

§P < .01 (one-tailed, not adjusted for multiple comparisons).

**TABLE 2.**
**Death, Stroke, and Combined Major Events by Treatment Groups, Systolic Hypertension in the Elderly Program, Main Trail**

| Event | Drug-treated Group (n = 2,365) Number | Placebo-treated Group (n = 2,371) Number | Relative Risk (drug/placebo) Point Estimate | 95% Confidence Interval |
|---|---|---|---|---|
| Death (all-cause) | 213 | 242 | 0.87 | 0.73–1.05 |
| Definite first stroke (fatal and nonfatal) | 106 | 161 | 0.66 | 0.49–0.82 |
| Coronary heart disease* | 140 | 184 | 0.75 | 0.60–0.94 |
| Total cardiovascular events† | 289 | 414 | 0.68 | 0.58–0.79 |

*Coronary heart disease = definite nonfatal or fatal myocardial infarction, sudden cardiac death, rapid cardiac death, coronary artery bypass graft, and angioplasty.
†Total cardiovascular includes all coronary disease, fatal and nonfatal stroke, transient ischemic attack, aneurysm, and endarterectomy.

Several recent studies have noted that pseudohypertension may be an important condition in the elderly, causing overestimation of the real blood pressure.[35, 36] Pseudohypertension occurs in older persons with thickened or calcified arteries that are not easily compressed by the standard blood pressure cuff. If the arterial wall itself is hardened or calcified, there is a tendency for indirect measurement of the blood pressure with the standard sphygmomanometer to overestimate the level, as compared to the "true" pressure obtained through direct intra-arterial measurement.

However, several scientific limitations of the studies of pseudohypertension reduce the overall importance of this issue. First, some of the studies that initially described pseudophypertension in the elderly only evaluated selected patients already suspected of having the condition.[35, 36] Also, while most of these studies describe the intra-arterial pressure measurement in great detail, none do so for the indirect measurement, leaving its precision and reliability in question.[35, 36] Most of the studies to date indicate that, in these highly selected samples, indirect cuff measurement of blood pressure tends to overestimate the intra-arterial reading of DBP significantly in some cases, but that direct and indirect measures of SBP correlate fairly closely.[35, 37] Recent studies indicate that pseudohypertension is not a very prevalent condition, but one that does occur in some elderly patients with very rigid or calcified vessels. In fact, these are the very patients who are most likely to have ISH. Elderly patients with substantial elevations of SBP who have no evidence of hypertension-related end-organ damage are one group in whom this entity should be suspected. The Osler maneuver can aid the clinician in determining if pseudohypertension might be a problem.[36] To perform this maneuver, the blood pressure cuff is inflated above SBP and the brachial and radial arteries are palpated to determine if the pulseless artery is still palpable. If it is, the patient has rigid arteries and could have pseudohypertension, although the sensitivity and specificity of this maneuver is not really known.

The assessment for end-organ damage should include examination of the retina for hypertensive changes, examination of the peripheral pulses, and examination of the electrocardiogram for signs of left ventricular hypertrophy. It appears that adequate treatment of hypertension may result in regression of left ventricular hypertrophy.[38] The presence of signs of end-organ damage should sway the clinician toward treatment in cases where the blood pressure elevation is borderline.

Most elderly patients with ISH have no underlying reversible disorder that, if treated, will result in a reversal of their hypertension. Therefore, work-up for secondary causes is rarely indicated. One potential (but infrequent) cause of ISH in the elderly is hemodynamically significant aortic insufficiency.

The accuracy and utility of the use of ambulatory blood pressure monitoring devices in older patients with ISH is still under question. Recent studies have indicated that office measurement of blood pressure, at times, consistently overestimates the real blood pressure in certain persons who appear to have "white-coat hypertension."[39] In addition, ambulatory blood pressure measurements in middle-aged persons may be more predictive of end-organ damage than are casual measures of office blood pressure.[40] Ambulatory blood pressure monitoring may be most useful in older patients with ISH who have mild elevations of SBP and no evidence of end-organ damage, since decisions regarding the necessity of treating these individuals (given the probable marginal impact on subsequent cardiovascular events) are most difficult.

## Management

Once an elderly patient has been classified as having ISH, treatment is indicated given the results of the main SHEP trial.[3a] It is recommended that nonpharmacologic therapy be the first step in treatment of ISH.[41] Although there are limited data on the efficacy of nonpharmacologic therapy in these patients, most experts believe that consistent and continued weight loss and sodium restriction are effective.[42] In fact, recent data indicate that elderly patients with ISH may be more sensitive to sodium restriction than are younger hypertensives.[19] Many elderly persons tend to purchase substantial quantities of prepackaged or canned foods, which are higher in sodium, and clinicians frequently find that these patients would rather take a diuretic than severely restrict their salt. The limited data currently available on the impact of aerobic exercise on hypertension indicate that it may have modest benefit in lowering DBP. There are virtually no data on the effect of exercise on ISH.

If nonpharmocologic therapy fails or is not appropriate, the clinician is left with pharmacologic therapy. The pathophysiology of ISH in the elderly, as described earlier, may include high peripheral resistance, low renin levels, and a tendency to a low cardiac output.[18] In addition, it is known that the aging cardiovascular system is less sensitive to both β-adrenergic stimulation and blockade.[43] Based on these physiologic patterns, some experts have predicted that medications that work directly on peripheral resistance, such as diuretics, vasodilators, calcium channel blockers, or angiotensin-converting enzyme inhibitors, will prove to be the most effective antihypertensive agents in the elderly. However, treatment decisions based solely on pathophysiologic considerations have not always proved the most clinically useful in the field of hypertension.

There is currently only a modest amount of clinical data available comparing the efficacy of various antihypertensive regimens in lowering SBP in patients with ISH. To date, diuretics are the only class of agents that have been shown to lower SBP more than DBP in patients with ISH.[31] Calcium channel blockers have been shown to lower SBP by about the same percent as DBP in patients with ISH.[44] Most studies that compare different antihypertensive regimens in elderly patients with ISH do not have adequate sample sizes to allow a definitive statement to be made. The clinician should be aware that many of the newer antihypertensive agents are frequently 10 to 30 times more expensive than a generic prescription for a diuretic. Although these differences in cost may not be meaningful to some individuals, the aggregate impact of more expensive treatment strategies, if used in most elderly hypertensive patients, could well add $500 million to $1 billion in extra charges to the nation's health care bill each year. The drug regimen used in the SHEP main trial (first step low dose diuretic; second step low dose beta blocker) has now been shown to have substantial benefit in reducing both total cardiovascular disease and coronary heart disease events.[3a] Although clinicians may appropriately prefer other regimens for a variety of individual patient-related issues, it is unlikely that any other regimen would have a *better* impact on cardiovascular events than the one used in SHEP.

## Adverse Effects

Concerns about the toxicity of antihypertensive therapy in the elderly have caused clinicians to use restraint, or even to practice therapeutic nihilism with regard to this patient population.[45] Theoretically, there are reasons why the risk-to-benefit ratio for the treatment of either systolic or diastolic hypertension might increase with age. It is thought that the elderly are particularly susceptible to many of the side effects of antihypertensive medication.[45, 46] For instance, it has been shown that elderly patients are more likely to develop hyponatremia and hypokalemia when treated with standard doses of diuretics.[47] It also is thought that older patients are more likely to develop side effects such as depression and confusion when treated with antihypertensive medications that have effects on the central nervous system.[48] There is good evidence that the baroreceptor reflex becomes less sensitive with age and also less active as SBP increases.[34, 49] As a result, elderly patients with ISH could be more sensitive to the postural hypotensive effects of antihypertensive medications, with a consequent propensity for falls and fractures.[50] Although some have argued that elderly persons with ISH actually need the higher SBP to perfuse vital organs such as the brain and kidney adequately,[51] most studies have not shown that judicious use of antihypertensive medications in these patients has a significant adverse effect on either renal or cerebral perfusion.[52–54]

It is surprising that there are few data from large-scale clinical trials to answer definitively the issue of the degree of toxicity of antihypertensive regimens in the elderly. A group of investigators from the Hypertension Detection and Follow-up Program have reported that the total rate of adverse effects in this trial in the treatment of mild-to-moderate SDH was less for the subgroup aged 60 to 69 years at entry than for those under the age of 50 years.[55] While these data are helpful, it should be remembered that persons in the age range of 60 to 69 years really should be classified as "young-old" and may not be as susceptible to side effects as the "old-old" (age 75 years and older). The two largest data sets available on the toxicity of antihypertensive therapy in the elderly comes from the European Working Party on Hypertension in the Elderly (EWPHE) randomized study and the SHEP study. Early reports from EWPHE indicate that treatment with a thiazide-triamterene combination resulted in mild increases in glucose intolerance, serum creatinine, and uric acid, and a mild decrease in serum potassium in the treatment group.[56] Treatment does not appear to have a significant long-term effect on serum cholesterol levels.[57] In the SHEP main trial, 28% of the treatment group and 20% of the placebo group repeated troublesome or intolerable side effects.[3a] Although these differences are not large, clinicians should carefully monitor for side effects and, if necessary, change medications or reduce dosage.

Another area of major concern focuses on the fact that, in middle-aged persons, hypertension treatment trials have tended to show that treatment reduces subsequent rates of stroke and congestive heart failure, but has either a neutral or a negative effect on rates of coronary heart disease. The first concern here is that too vigorous lowering of blood pressure actually may result in impaired coronary artery blood flow, particularly to the subendocardial layer during diastole.[58] In recent years, several studies have raised the question whether too vigorous lowering of SBP or DBP might increase rates of myocardial infarction. Cruickshank recently has reported on a prospective, descriptive 10-year follow-up study of 902 treated patients (mean age 54 years) with diastolic hypertension.[59] Although treated SBP was strongly correlated with subsequent death from myocardial infarction and treated DBP was weakly correlated, there appeared to be a

J-shaped relationship between the level of treated DBP and mortality from myocardial infarction. In other words, mortality rates declined as treated DBP levels declined down to a DBP of 85 mm Hg, but rose again as DBP fell further. The authors noted that this pattern was true only for patients with overt ischemic heart disease at the time of entry into the study.

Similar data reporting a J-shaped relationship between DBP and cardiovascular mortality have been reported by two other prospective, descriptive studies. In fact, a recent study of 686 middle-aged treated hypertensive males (treated with either a β-blocker or thiazide diuretic) appears to show that there is a threshold below which the lowering of blood pressure is harmful (an SBP of 150 mm Hg or a DBP of 90 mm Hg).[60] Applegate also conducted a large prospective study (described earlier) which indicated that elderly persons with SDH treated with medications had higher mortality rates if their SBP was either always above or always below the treatment goal.[30] Neither of these studies was designed to prove cause and effect, but it is possible that excessively vigorous blood pressure lowering could be harmful. On the other hand, some epidemiologic data show a J-shaped relationship between DBP and mortality regardless of treatment.[61] A recent randomized, controlled trial of the treatment of hypertension in an elderly cohort sheds particular light on this subject.[62, 63] Coope performed a randomized trial of drug treatment (atenolol and bendrofluazide) vs. observation for 884 elderly patients with an SBP of more than 170 mm Hg or a DBP of more than 105 mm Hg.[62] Patients were followed for up to 8 years and there was a significantly greater reduction in both SBP and DBP in the treatment group. The treatment group experienced a 30% reduction in the rate of fatal strokes, but there were no differences in the rates of fatal myocardial infarction or total mortality. Further analysis of these data revealed that there was indeed a J-shaped relationship between entry DBP and subsequent rates of fatal and nonfatal myocardial infarction, but this relationship was true for both the treatment and control groups.[63] In light of these findings and the fact that some epidemiologic studies also have demonstrated a J-shaped relationship between SBP and DBP and coronary artery mortality, the most likely explanation is that these epidemiologic and descriptive results are confounded by the fact that the subjects with the lowest blood pressure have a higher prevalence of serious prior cardiovascular disease with a consequent reduction of the heart's ability to generate a higher blood pressure. Nonetheless, caution about overly vigorous treatment of hypertension in the elderly is warranted. The conservative approach would be to avoid lowering SBP much below 140 mm Hg or DBP below 85 mm Hg in elderly patients.

Another possible explanation for the failure of hypertension clinical trials to show that medication reduces the rate of subsequent development of coronary heart disease is that the diuretics most frequently used as the first-step medication in these trials partially offset the beneficial impact of blood pressure lowering by adversely affecting other cardiovascular risk factors, particularly serum lipids, glucose homeostasis, and serum potassium. Recent hypertension studies have tended to reemphasize the fact that an interaction between two or more cardiovascular risk factors is a powerful predictor of subsequent coronary heart disease mortality.[60] In fact, a recent prospective study has shown that a reduction of SBP or DBP unaccompanied by a reduction in cholesterol (if elevated) has less impact.[60] Unfortunately, it has not been established definitely whether lipid lowering in elderly patients really lowers subsequent cardiovascular morbidity and mortality. Results of the European Working Party on High Blood Pressure in the Elderly study seem to indicate that diuretic treatment of elderly hypertensives may not have a prolonged significant impact on serum lipids.[57] In this trial, at the end of 3 years the placebo group had experienced an average fall in total serum cholesterol of 5.9 mg/100 mL/yr, while the treatment group experienced an average decline in total serum cholesterol of 5.0 mg/100 mL/yr.[57] Attributing the lack of impact of antihypertensive treatment on subsequent coronary heart disease (CHD) to the lipid effects of the diuretics alone is problematic. Reaven recently has pointed out that impairment of glucose homeostasis with subsequent increases in serum insulin levels may play a more significant deleterious role than has been appreciated, but data to substantiate this point currently are lacking.[64] The main SHEP trial definitely shows that a treatment regimen with a diuretic as the first step *does* lower coronary heart disease events and, in the author's view, virtually eliminates any validity to the hypothesis that adverse effects of the diuretics are responsible for the fact that many studies have not shown an effect on CHD. On balance, there are not enough incriminating data to negate the use of diuretics in the elderly (particularly in light of their efficacy). However, patients who develop significant and persistent alterations of lipid levels or glucose homeostasis should be placed on other agents.

As stated previously, clinicians are generally concerned that elderly patients may be particularly susceptible to hypokalemia from diuretics. The results of the Multiple Risk Factor Intervention Trial have caused many to question whether diuretic-induced adverse effects led to the study finding that hypertensive males who had electrocardiographic abnormalities at baseline and were treated with a diuretic had a higher coronary heart disease death rate.[65] Certainly diuretics can induce hypokalemia, which in turn can lead to cardiac arrhythmias.[66] However, analysis of the study data shows no relationship between either the participant's most recent potassium level or the presence of ventricular premature beats and coronary heart disease mortality.[67] Also, it is curious that the increased mortality attributed to diuretic treatment occurred only in the subset of participants treated with hydrochlorothiazide rather than chlorthalidone.[68] Further doubts about the significance of these findings include the fact that this analysis was post hoc and the results could well be due to chance alone. In fact, when the study data are reviewed, the striking finding is not that hypertensive males with baseline electrocardiographic abnormalities treated with drugs had such a high coronary heart disease mortality, but that the corresponding usual care group had such a low rate.[65] Finally, although the intervention group in the SHEP main study experienced some lowering of serum potassium, the treatment did reduce CHD events both in those with and without baseline ECG abnormalities. Questions still remain about the possible degree of negative impact that antihypertensive therapy may have on the quality of life of elderly patients. Two recent multicenter trials, however, have shown that the judicious use of common antihypertensive regimens tended to have minimal negative impact on quality of life. A recent Veterans Administration collaborative trial compared the impact of high- and low-dose diuretics as first-step agents and alphamethyldopa, reserpine, hydralazine, and metoprolol as second-step drugs in the treatment of elderly persons with SDH.[70] Basically, there were no differences in any of these treatments with regard to overall impact on quality of life.[71] In another randomized, multicenter trial conducted by Applegate and colleagues, atenolol, diltiazem, and enalapril were compared in elderly women with SDH.[72] Although there were more drug withdrawals due to side effects in the atenolol group, there were no differences in the impact of the three treatment regimens on overall quality of life.

## Summary

In summary, elevated levels of SBP are the single greatest cardiovascular risk factor in patients over 65 years of age. Adequate clinical data exist to indicate that ISH can be treated effectively with a minimum amount of side effects in most elderly patients. The SHEP main trial has now definitely proved that treating ISH lowers cerebrovascular coronary heart disease, and total cardiovascular morbidity and mortality. See Table 3 for antihypertensive treatment recommendations in elderly patients.

## Addendum

The Systolic Hypertension in the Elderly Program (SHEP)[3a], a five-year double-blind placebo-controlled trial with 4,736 participants with isolated systolic hypertension (SBP 160 to 219 mm Hg, DBP < 90 mm Hg) demonstrated clear-cut benefits of pharmacologic treatment (a stepped care regimen including chlorthalidone, 12.5 to 25 mg, and atenolol, 25 to 50 mg, or reserpine, 0.05 to 0.1 mg) on stroke (35% reduction) and cardiovascular events (31% reduction). Overall, the treatment group experienced a reduction of 30 cerebrovascular and 55 cardiovascular morbid and mortal events (over the 5-year study) per 1,000 person years of treatment (Table 2). The observed unambiguous benefit of pharmacologic treatment of isolated systolic hypertension (SBP 160 to 219 mm Hg) suggests that all patients with SBP in that range should be treated. Despite the fact that the first-step drug was a diuretic, the intervention group experienced an impressive and significant 25% reduction in combined fatal and nonfatal coronary heart disease events with a 5-year absolute benefit of 16 such events

**TABLE 3.**
**Treatment Recommendations for Isolated Systolic Hypertension in the Elderly**

Isolated systolic hypertension (systolic blood pressure >160 mm Hg and diastolic blood pressure <90 mm Hg) should be treated. Nonpharmacologic measures should be tried first.

For elderly persons with modest isolated systolic hypertension (systolic blood pressure 160–180 mm Hg), the absolute benefit of drug treatment is reasonably good but not so great that individual patients need be treated in the face of disabling side effects from antihypertensive medications.

For pharmacologic therapy, the initial daily dose should be half that recommended as the starting dose for middle-aged patients.

Judicious lowering of systolic blood pressure to about 135–140 mm Hg is indicated.

A diuretic is the drug of first choice for the treatment of isolated systolic hypertension in older patients; diuretic dosages equivalent to 12.5–25 mg/day of chlorthalidone appear to be most effective with the least toxicity.

The choice of an alternative first-step drug or a second-step drug should be based on individual patient characteristics.

After blood pressure has been controlled for 6 months, the dosage of the drug should be stepped down if possible.

In the future, clinicians should place at least as much emphasis on setting target goals for SBP as for DBP.

---

prevented per 1,000 person years. Subgroup analysis showed that benefit from treatment was seen in persons over age 80 at entry, and in persons with and without baseline electrocardiogram abnormalities. Finally, the magnitude of the benefit from treatment seen in this trial is actually somewhat greater than that seen in trials treating systolic and diastolic hypertension. As a result of the SHEP trial, it is no longer tenable for clinicians to focus exclusively on DBP when treating elderly patients with hypertension. It is clear that treatment goals should target both SBP and DBP, and that SBP treatment goals are the more important of the two.

## References

1. Applegate WB: Hypertension in elderly patients. *Ann Intern Med* 1989; 110:901–915.
2. Kannel WB: Some lessons in cardiovascular epidemiology from Framingham. *Am J Cardiol* 1976; 37:269–282.
3. Amery A, Birkenhager W, Brixko P, et al: Mortality and morbidity results from the European Working Party on High Blood Pressure in the Elderly Trial. *Lancet* 1985; 2:1349–1354.

3a. The Systolic Hypertension in the Elderly Program (SHEP) Cooperative Research Group: Prevention of stroke by antihypertensive drug treatment in older persons with isolated systolic hypertension: Final results of SHEP. *JAMA* 1991; 265:3255–3264.

4. Kannel WB, Gordon T: Evaluation of cardiovascular risk in the elderly; the Framingham Study. *Bull N Y Acad Med* 1978; 54:573–591.

5. Drizd T, Dannenberg A, Engel A: Blood pressure levels in persons 18–74 years of age in 1976–80 and trends in blood pressure from 1960–1980 in the United States. *Vital Health Statistics 1986*. US Department of Health and Human Services, DHHS Publication No (PHS) 86–1684.

6. Page LB, Friedlander J: Blood pressure, age, and cultural change, in Horan MJ, Steinberg GM, Dunbar JB, et al (eds): *Blood Pressure Regulation and Aging, Proceedings from an NIH Symposium*. New York, Biomedical Information Corporation, 1986.

7. Colleandrea MA, Friedman GD, Nickman MZ, et al: Systolic hypertension in the elderly. *Circulation* 1970; 41:239–245.

8. Ostfeld AM: Epidemiologic overview, in Horan MJ, Steinberg GM, Dunbar JB, et al (eds): *Blood Pressure Regulation and Aging, Proceedings from a NIH Symposium*. New York, Biomedical Information Corporation, 1986, pp 3–10.

9. Hypertension Detection and Follow-up Program Cooperative Group: Blood pressures studies in 14 communities. *JAMA* 1977; 237:2385–2391.

10. Rutan G, Kuller LH, Neaton JD, et al: Mortality associated with diastolic hypertension and isolated systolic hypertension among men screened for the Multiple Risk Factor Intervention Trial. *Circulation* 1988; 77:504–514.

11. Wilking SVB, Belanger A, Kannel WB, et al: Determinants of isolated systolic hypertension. *JAMA* 1988; 260:3451–3455.

12. *Build and Blood Pressure Study*. Chicago, Society of Actuaries, 1959.

13. Kannel WB, Gordon T, Schwartz MJ: Systolic vs diastolic blood pressure and risk of coronary heart disease. *Am J Cardiol* 1971; 27:335–346.

14. Shekelle RB, Ostfeld AM, Kiawans HL: Hypertension and risk of stroke in an elderly population. *Stroke* 1974; 5:71–75.

15. Kannel WB, Gordon T, Castelli WB, et al: Electro-cardiographic left ventricular hypertrophy and risk of coronary heart disease. *Ann Intern Med* 1970; 72:813–822.

16. Savage DD, Garrison RJ, Kannel WB, et al: The spectrum of left ventricular hypertrophy in a general population sample: The Framingham Study. *Circulation* 1987; 75(suppl 1):126–133.

17. McLenachan JM, Henderson E, Morris KI, et al: Ventricular arrhythmia in patients with hypertensive left ventricular hypertrophy. *N Engl J Med* 1987; 317:787–792.

18. Messerli FH, Sundgaard-Riise K, Ventura HO, et al: Essential hypertension in the elderly: Hemodynamics. *Lancet* 1983; 2:983–986.

19. Zemel MB, Sowers JR: Salt sensitivity and systemic hypertension in the elderly. *Am J Cardiol* 1988; 61:7h–12h.

20. Hallock P, Benson IC: Studies of the elastic properties of human isolated aorta. *J Clin Invest* 1937; 16:595–602.

21. Chobanian AV: Pathophysiologic considerations in the treatment of the elderly hypertension patients. *Am J Cardiol* 1983; 52:49D–53D.

22. Kannel WB, Wolf PA, McGee DL, et al: Systolic blood pressure, arterial rigidity, and risks of stroke. *JAMA* 1981; 245:1225–1229.

23. Tarazi RC, Martini F, Dustan HP: The role of aortic distensibility in hypertension, in Sasar MP (ed): *International Symposium on Hypertension*. (Milliez P. Sasar M, Ed). Monaco, Boehringer Ingleheim, 1975, pp 143–145.

24. Simon AC, Safar MA, Levenson JA, et al: Systolic hypertension: Hemodynamic mechanism and choice of antihypertensive treatment. *Am J Cardiol* 1979; 44:505–511.

25. Adampoulous PN, Chrysanthakapoulis SG, Frolich ED: Systolic hypertension: Nonhomogeneous diseases. *Am J Cardiol* 1975; 36:697–701.

26. Abrass IB: Catecholamine levels and vascular responsiveness in aging, in Horan MJ, Steinberg GM, Dunbar JB, et al (eds): *Blood Pressure Relation and Aging, an NIH Symposium*. New York, Biomedical Information Corporation, 1986, pp 123–130.

27. Fleich JH, Malin HM, Brodie BB: Beta-receptor activity in a order. Variations with age and species. *Circ Res* 1970; 26:151–162.

28. Fleich JH, Hooker CS: The relationship between age and relaxation of vascular smooth muscle in the rabbit and rat. *Circ Res* 1976; 38:243–249.

29. Van Brummelen P, Buhler FR, Kiowski W, et al: Age-related increase in cardiac and peripheral vascular responses to isoproterenol, studies in normal subjects. *Clin Sci* 1981; 60:571–577.

30. Applegate WB, Vander Zwaag R, Dismuke SE, et al: Control of systolic blood pressure in elderly black patients. *J Am Geriatr Soc* 1982; 30:391–396.

31. Hulley SB, Furberg CD, Gurland B, et al: Systolic hypertension in the elderly program: Antihypertensive efficacy of chlorthalidone. *Am J Cardiol* 1985; 56:913–920.

32. Perry HM, Smith WM, McDonald RH, et al: Morbidity and mortality in the systolic hypertension in the elderly program (SHEP) pilot study. *Stroke* 1989; 20:4–13.

33. The Final Report of the Sub-Committee on Hypertension Definition and Prevalence of the 1984 Joint National Committee: Hypertension prevalence and status of awareness, treatment and control in the United States. *Hypertension* 1985; 7:457–468.

34. Lipsitz LA: Abnormalities in blood pressure hemostasis associated with aging and hypertension, in Horan MJ, Steinberg M, Dunbar JB, et al (eds): *Blood Pressure Regulation and Aging. Proceedings from an NIH Symposium*. New York, Biomedical Information Corporation, 1986, pp 201–211.

35. Spence JD, Sibbald WJ, Cape RD: Pseudohypertension in the elderly. *Clin Sci* 1978; 55:399–402.

36. Messerli FH, Ventura HO, Amodeo C: Osler's maneuver and pseudohypertension. *N Engl J Med* 1985; 312:1548–1551.

37. Vardan S, Mookherjee S, Warner R, et al: Systolic hypertension: Direct and indirect blood pressure measurements. *Arch Intern Med* 1983; 143: 935–938.

38. Dzau BJ: Evolution of the clinical management of hypertension. *Am J Med* 1987; 82:36–43.

39. Pickering TG, James GD, Boddie C, et al: How common is white coat hypertension? *JAMA* 1988; 259:225–228.

40. White WB, Schulman P, McCabe EJ, et al: Average daily blood pressure, not office pressure, determines cardiac function in patients with hypertension. *JAMA* 1989; 261:873–877.

41. Working Group on Hypertension in the Elderly: Statement on hypertension in the elderly. *JAMA* 1986; 256:70–74.

42. Kaplan NM: Non-drug treatment of hypertension. *Ann Intern Med* 1985; 102:359–373.
43. Vestal RE, Wood AZ, Schand DG: Reduced beta-adrenoceptor sensitivity in the elderly. *Clin Pharmacol Ther* 1979; 26:181–186.
44. Pool PE, Massie BM, Venkataram AN, et al: Diltiazem as a model therapy for systemic hypertension. *Am J Cardiol* 1986; 57:212–217.
45. Williamson J, Chopin JM: Adverse reactions to prescribed drugs in the elderly, a multicenter investigation. *Aging* 1980; 9:73–80.
46. Jackson G, Piersoianouski TA, Mohon W, et al: Inappropriate antihypertensive therapy in the elderly. *Lancet* 1976; 2:1317–1318.
47. Flanenbaun W: Diuretic use in the elderly; potential for diuretic-induced hypokalemia. *Am J Cardiol* 1986; 57:38A–43A.
48. Avorn J, Everitt DE, Weiss S: Increased antidepressant use in patients prescribed beta-blockers. *JAMA* 1986; 255:357–360.
49. Gribbin B, Pickering TG, Sleigh P, et al: Effect of age and high blood pressure on baroreflex sensitivity in man. *Cardiovasc Res* 1971; 29:424–431.
50. Caird FL, Andrews GR, Kennedy RD: Effect of posture on blood pressure in the elderly. *Br Heart J* 1973; 35:527–530.
51. Jones JV, Graham DI: Hypertension and the cerebral circulation—its relevance to the elderly. *Am Heart J* 1978; 96:270–271.
52. Strandgard S: Cerebral blood flow and antihypertensive drugs in the elderly. *Acta Med Scand* 1983; 676(suppl):103–109.
53. Ram CBS, Meese R, Kaplan NM, et al: Antihypertensive therapy of the elderly: Effects on blood pressure and cerebral blood flow. *Am J Med* 1987; 82(suppl 1A):53–57.
54. Bertel O, Marx BE: Effects of antihypertensive treatment on cerebral perfusion. *Am J Med* 1987; 82(suppl 3B):29–36.
55. Curb JD, Borhani NO, Blaszkowski TP, et al: Long-term surveillance for adverse effects of antihypertensive drugs. *JAMA* 1985; 253:3263–3268.
56. Amery A, Berthaux P, Birkenhager W, et al: Antihypertensive therapy in patients above 60: Third interim report of the European Working Party on High Blood Pressure in the Elderly. *Acta Cardiol (Brux)* 1978; 33:113–134.
57. Amery A, Birkenhager W, Bulpitt C: Influence of antihypertensive therapy on serum cholesterol in elderly hypertensive patients. *Acta Cardiol (Brux)* 1982; 37:235–244.
58. Strandgaard S, Haunso S: Why does anti-hypertensive treatment prevent stroke but not myocardial infarction? *Lancet* 1987; 2:658–661.
59. Cruickshank JM, Thorp JM, Zacharias FJ: Benefits and potential harm of lowering high blood pressure. *Lancet* 1987; 1:581–584.
60. Samuelsson O, Wilhelmsen L, Anderson OK, et al: Cardiovascular morbidity in relation to change in blood pressure and serum cholesterol levels and treated hypertension. *JAMA* 1987; 258:1768–1776.
61. Anderson TW: Re-examination of some of the Framingham blood pressure data. *Lancet* 1978; 2:1139–1141.
62. Coope J, Warrender TS: Randomized trial of treatment of hypertension in elderly patients in primary care. *Br Med J* 1986; 293:1145–1148.
63. Coope J, Warrender TS: Lowering blood pressure (letter). *Lancet* 1987; 1:1380.
64. Reaven GM, Hoffman BB: A role for insulin in the aetiology and course of hypertension? *Lancet* 1987; 2:435–437.

65. Multiple Risk Factor Intervention Trial Research Group: Multiple risk factor intervention trial. JAMA 1982; 248:1465–1472.
66. Whelton PK, Watson AJ: Diuretic-induced hypokalemia and cardiac arrhythmias. Am J Cardiol 1986; 58:5A–10A.
67. Kuller LH, Hulley SB, Cohen JD, et al: Unexpected effects of treating hypertension in men with electrocardiographic abnormalities: A critical analysis. Circulation 1987; 73:114–123.
68. The Hypertension Detection and Follow-up Cooperative Research Group: The effect of antihypertensive drug treatment on mortality in the presence of resting electrocardiographic abnormalities at baseline. Circulation 1984; 70:996–1003.
69. Holme I, Helgeland A, Hjermann I, et al: Treatment of mild hypertension with diuretics: The importance of ECG abnormalities in the Oslo studies and in MRFIT. JAMA 1984; 251:1298–1299.
70. Matterson BJ, Cushman WC, Goldstein G, et al: Treatment of hypertension in the elderly: I. Blood pressure and clinical changes. Results of a Department of Veterans Affairs cooperative study. Hypertension 1990; 15:348–360.
71. Goldstein G, Matterson BJ, Cushman WC, et al: Treatment of hypertension in the elderly: II. Cognitive and behavioral function. Results of a Department of Veterans Affairs cooperative study. Hypertension 1990; 15:361–369.
72. Applegate WB, Phillips HL, Schnaper H, et al: A randomized, controlled trial of the effects of three antihypertensive agents on blood pressure control and quality of life in elderly females. Arch Intern Med, in press.

# Controversies in the Diagnosis and Management of Benign Prostatic Hypertrophy

## Catherine E. DuBeau, M.D.

Instructor in Medicine, Division on Aging, Harvard Medical School; Geriatric Research Education and Clinical Center, Brockton/West Roxbury Department of Veterans Affairs Medical Center; Geriatric Division, Brigham and Women's Hospital; The Hebrew Rehabilitation Center for Aged, Boston, Massachusetts

## Neil M. Resnick, M.D.

Chief of Geriatrics and Director of the Continence Center, Brigham and Women's Hospital; Geriatric Research Education and Clinical Center, Brockton/West Roxbury Department of Veterans Affairs Medical Center; The Hebrew Rehabilitation Center for Aged, Division on Aging; Harvard Medical School, Boston, Massachusetts

## Editor's Introduction

With the intense interest of geriatricians in urinary dysfunction as a major and growing problem of the elderly, the true contribution of prostatic hypertrophy to the symptoms of "prostatism" has come under close scrutiny. A symptomatic "quick fix" by transurethral prostatectomy (TURP) may not be more than a partial, if not ineffectual, solution for many patients, especially those with less severe symptoms, relapsing symptoms, serious cc-morbidities that reduce surgical success rates, and age-related physiological bladder dysfunction. The intensive studies of Dr. Neil Resnick and his colleagues at Boston's Brigham and Women's Hospital have raised basic questions regarding the role of bladder outlet obstruction in the development of symptoms and in predicting outcomes of surgery. Studies of the natural history of prostatism show serious complications in but a minority of patients so that many medical and surgical alternatives to TURP are being studied. Dr. Catherine DuBeau and Dr. Resnick present an incisive and authoritative analysis of the difficult diagnostic and management issues raised by the aging man with dysfunctional urination in whom benign prostatic hypertrophy is diagnosed.

*Gene H. Stollerman, M.D.*

Prostatism,[1] the complex of obstructive and irritative symptoms associated with adenomatous benign prostatic hypertrophy (BPH), is remarkably prevalent among middle-aged and elderly men: almost one fifth of men over 50 years of age are afflicted, and men living to 80 years of age have a 40% chance of undergoing transurethral prostatectomy (TURP).[2, 3] As a result, 400,000 prostatectomies (TURP) are performed annually, making TURP the most common genitourinary operation in America[4] and the second largest Medicare disbursement for surgery[5] with annual costs of $1.5 billion.[6] And the rate of TURP is increasing, even after adjustment for the aging of the population.[4]

TURP is considered the "gold standard" therapy for BPH, with symptomatic success rates ranging from 84% to 92%.[7-9] However, recent work raises significant concerns regarding the surgical treatment of BPH. First, quality of life following TURP may be significantly improved only for those with the most severe symptoms.[10] Second, symptom improvement following prostatectomy may not be durable. Bruskewitz and colleagues have shown that the success rate declines from 87% at 3 months to 75% at 7 years.[11, 12] Third, success rates are lower in the elderly (less than 80%) and the associated morbidity is higher (up to 71%).[9, 13] Fourth, previous TURP is associated with an increase in abnormal voiding symptoms in elderly institutionalized men.[14] Fifth, in the past decade alternative treatment options have expanded greatly. These include: limited surgery, such as prostate incision,[15] prostatic stents,[16] and balloon dilation[17]; and pharmacologic therapy with $\alpha$-adrenergic blockers,[18] antiandrogens,[19] and luteinizing hormone-releasing-hormone agonists.[20] Finally, although a subset of men with BPH do present with urinary retention, bladder decompensation, and renal insufficiency—suggesting that earlier surgery could prevent such sequelae of obstruction—the time course of decompensation and the true proportion of patients at risk is unknown. These concerns regarding prostatectomy outcomes and alternatives have refocused attention on the indications for surgery in BPH and have fueled the surprising but growing controversy.[6] Emblematic of the present situation are the data from a study of "second opinions" obtained before TURP: in 28% of patients in whom the second physician concurred with the need for surgery, surgery was deferred, while in 33% of patients in whom the second physician recommended against surgery, it was performed anyway.[21]

Since most men with symptoms of BPH present initially to their primary caregiver, it becomes increasingly important for internists to familiarize themselves with the issues raised by BPH. This is especially true for those who care for older men, because of the increased confounding of the clinical situation by comorbid disease, age-related physiologic changes, and medications, and (especially for frail or institutionalized men) the need to redefine therapeutic goals. This review will analyze the presentation and evaluation of BPH, emphasize the existing controversies, and suggest an approach to prostatism appropriate for the primary caregiver.

## Evaluation Considerations

Before considering the existing approaches to the evaluation of prostatism, it is worth reviewing the test characteristics that affect the clinical utility of the various strategies. A test's *predictive value* depends in part on its *sensitivity* (ability to be positive when disease is present) and *specificity* (ability to be negative when disease is absent). Sensitive tests are most useful when the test result is negative, with a resulting high degree of certainty that the condition is not present. Evaluation of sensitivity and specificity generally is based on an accepted "gold standard" test for the disease. Unfortunately, there is no universally accepted standard for prostatic bladder outlet obstruction (BOO), and few data exist on the clinical utility of the commonly used tests (e.g., intravenous pyelography, cystoscopy, voiding cystourethrography). Moreover, data are particularly lacking on the evaluation of elderly men, in whom the sensitivity and especially the specificity of testing for BPH changes because of comorbid diseases, medications, and age-related physiologic changes. In addition, different thresholds of sensitivity may be important in this age group when there is a greater need for therapeutic rather than diagnostic accuracy (e.g., in frail institutionalized patients or the oldest of the old).

The predictive value of a test also depends on the prevalence of the condition: the higher the prevalence, the greater the predictive value. However, while the prevalence of BPH increases with age, the number of confounders for the condition also rises. Urinary flow rate decreases with age, even in the absence of outlet obstruction.[22] Nocturia becomes more prevalent because of the normal age-related delay in excreting a water load and the higher prevalence of pathologic conditions such as congestive heart failure and peripheral edema.[23] Urgency and the uninhibited bladder contractions of detrusor instability also increase in prevalence with age.[24] Similarly, prostatic carcinoma, which may cause obstruction and voiding symptoms, also becomes more prevalent with age. Studies that fail to consider these confounders will overestimate the prevalence of BPH and, therefore, the positive predictive value of tests for BPH and BOO. In addition, the prevalence of BPH is overestimated when prostate size on digital rectal examination or treatment by TURP are used as proxies for the existence of BPH. Digital rectal examination estimates of size are notoriously poor (see later), while the indications for TURP are variable, not well established,[6] and involve subjective symptom tolerances that may vary tremendously among patients and providers.[25] These caveats must be considered in any discussion of the evidence for an optimal assessment strategy for BPH.

## Symptoms and Benign Prostatic Hypertrophy

Symptoms are usually the initial indication of possible prostatic hypertrophy, and they constitute the most common indication for surgical treatment.[9] *Obstructive* symptoms include hesitancy, decreased urinary stream force, interrupted stream, a sense of incomplete emptying, and terminal dribbling. *Irritative* symptoms include frequency, nocturia, and urgency (the sudden, precipitant urge to void that may be difficult to suppress and may result in incontinence). The two main issues regarding symptoms are: (1) What is the relationship between symptoms and the underlying pathophysiology? and (2) What is the clinical utility of symptoms in the diagnosis of BPH and selection for surgery?

The traditional categorization of symptoms has an implicit etiologic differentiation, with obstructive symptoms reflecting mechanical blockage by the adenoma and irritative ones abnormal overactivity of the bladder muscle (detrusor) secondary to an effect of the blockage. However, there are good reasons to question both assumptions.

The association between obstructive symptoms and urodynamic (physiologic) measures of BOO has been poor in several investigations that used a variety of urodynamic criteria for obstruction.[26, 27] For instance, a weak and negative correlation was found between obstructive symptoms and resected weight of the prostate at TURP.[28] Even when one examines men presenting with acute urinary retention—often considered pathognomonic of outlet obstruction from BPH in older men—the correlation is far from perfect. Klarskov[29] prospectively evaluated 228 men presenting with acute urinary retention and found that almost one third of them did not have BPH, including 12% with prostate cancer, 7% with urethral stricture, and 11% with other causes such as neurologic disease and drug effects. Moreover, in elderly men obstructive symptoms are less specific for BPH and BOO[30] due to the higher prevalence of comorbid disease, other urinary tract conditions that mimic BOO (e.g., detrusor hyperactivity with impaired contractility),[31] the use of drugs that affect detrusor function, and perhaps an age-related detrusor weakening.[23]

Another important reason for the lack of correlation between "obstructive" symptoms and BOO is the fact that obstructive symptoms can result from intrinsic detrusor abnormalities alone, as well as in combination with outlet obstruction. When Coolsaet[32] urodynamically investigated 211 men with prostatism, he found that 72 (27%) were not obstructed and were more likely than obstructed men to have impaired detrusor contractility. Turner-Warwick[33] suggested that an increased postvoid residual volume in men with prostatism—often assumed to be a correlate of BOO—reflects abnormal detrusor rather than urethral function. Indeed, Abrams[34] corroborated this when he found no correlation between increased postvoid residual volume and a measure of urethral outlet resistance. Surgical management may not address the underlying problem in patients with obstructive symptoms but underactive bladders. While one may postulate that "improvement" of the bladder outlet by TURP would augment urinary flow when the detrusor is weak, this has not been proven. In fact, the evidence suggests that unobstructed or mildly obstructed patients do not gain significant improvement in peak flow rate or residual urine volume following TURP,[35] while low preoperative voiding pressures (suggestive of detrusor weakness) are associated with poor symptomatic outcome from TURP.[36] Furthermore, surgery in such cases has not been compared with pharmacologic therapy (e.g., $\alpha$-adrenergic blockers) or behavioral approaches (e.g., double-voiding).

Most investigators have found that irritative symptoms are associated with the presence of detrusor instability, i.e., uninhibitied bladder contractions that result in urgency, precipitant voiding, and occasionally urinary incontinence. But while detrusor instability occurs in up to two thirds of men with prostatism,[37] the etiologic relationship between detrusor instability and BPH is unclear. Although an animal model of outlet obstruction demonstrated the de novo development of detrusor instability with acute BOO, the degree of BOO did not predict the development of detrusor instability.[38] In men, no association between the presence of detrusor instability and the degree of BOO has been found using cystoscopic evaluation of prostate size[30, 39] or urodynamic urethral resistance factors[30, 39] or pressure-flow study[40] to quantify obstruction. Cucchi[41] reported a correlation between detrusor instability and the degree of BOO; however, he quantified BOO using a measure of detrusor contractility, which may underestimate obstruction if concomitant detrusor decompensation is present. Moreover, the prevalence of detrusor instability increases with age in both sexes,[23, 24] confounding the relationship between detrusor instability and BPH in the predominantly older group of men affected. Even if BOO can be demonstrated in an elderly man with coexistent detrusor instability, the relationship between the two is often confounded by comorbid conditions that are independently associated with detrusor instability such as diabetes[42] and neurologic disease (e.g., stroke, dementia).[43]

Since the symptoms of BPH may not be due solely to a mechanical effect of the enlarged gland on the urethral outlet, other etiologies have been sought. Hinman[44] suggested that symptoms relate to the compliance of the prostatic capsule, the layer of fibroelastic tissue surrounding the gland. This compliance in turn depends on the elastic and smooth muscle properties of the capsule and the neuromuscular tone affecting its plentiful $\alpha$-adrenergic receptors. Several lines of evidence point toward a significant role for other factors as well. The bladder neck and prostate are richly innervated with $\alpha$-adrenergic receptors that mediate bladder neck and urethral constriction. The number of these receptors increases in BPH nodules,[45] increasing the sensitivity to endogenous and exogenous adrenergic agents (e.g., nonprescription cold tablets). By a different mechanism, altered adrenergic sensitivity may underlie the prevalence of detrusor instability found in BOO, since outlet obstruction has been found in both dogs and men to change the detrusor's response to adrenergic stimulation from predominantly $\beta$-adrenergic (inhibitory) to $\alpha$-adrenergic (stimulatory).[46] BOO also has been associated with increased $\alpha$-adrenergic responsiveness in human detrusor muscle strips.[47] Another mechanism, direct local neurologic influence of the adenoma on the detrusor, was suggested by Chalfin and Bradley,[48] who temporarily abolished detrusor instability in 10 of 11 BPH patients by injecting lidocaine into the prostate and bladder base. On the other hand, BOO may diminish detrusor contractility by an associated decrease in autonomic innervation[49]; however, this finding is confounded by a similar decrease seen with increasing age.[46, 50]

Thus, although symptoms remain the most common indication for surgical treatment of BPH, their diagnostic utility may be limited. Scoring systems, usually weighted toward obstructive symptoms, have been devised to select patients for TURP.[51] However, even in series that examined symptomatic men referred to tertiary centers for TURP, 25% to 33% of patients did not have outlet obstruction on urodynamic testing.[35] While irritative symptoms (particularly urgency) correlate well with detrusor instability, and repeated investigations show that one half to two thirds of men with BPH and detrusor instability will lose the latter postoperatively,[52, 53] there is no reliable way to discriminate preoperatively who will have persistent instability after surgery. Furthermore, patients with persistent detrusor instability often have worse subjective outcomes (see also below). Finally, men may present with severe BOO and partial to complete urinary retention without any voiding symptoms at all. Thus, symptoms are neither necessary, sufficient, nor specific for the diagnosis of BPH and outlet obstruction. Despite their poor diagnostic utility, however, symptom severity and impact on quality of life may prove important predictors of subjective outcome from prostatectomy.[10]

## Physical Findings

Since BPH involves gland enlargement and the prostate is accessible by digital rectal examination, an enlarged gland on examination frequently is considered evidence of obstruction due to BPH in symptomatic men. Both patients and physicians tend to anchor on this finding and therefore may bypass consideration of other causes of symptoms. However, digital rectal examination sizing of the prostate is inaccurate, poorly reproducible, and correlates poorly with the presence or absence of obstruction. Meyhoff[54] found that, although digital rectal examination estimates correlate significantly with resected weights ($r = .664$), 32% of estimates exceeded actual weights by up to 25 g (almost 100% of the average). Since prostates larger than 50 g frequently require an open prostatectomy rather than TURP, 26% of the patients in his series would have been treated with an unnecessary and more extensive procedure based on the digital rectal examination results. Furthermore, digital rectal examination estimates were poorly reproducible (with differences up to 80 g between observers), and estimates by experienced clinicians were no better than those of junior residents. In a second series, this time including only patients with "medium-sized" prostates by digital rectal examination, Meyhoff found no correlation between rectal examination and resected weights.[55] Digital rectal examination estimates also fail to correlate with transrectal ultrasound measurement of prostatic weights.[56] Such lack of correlation is not surprising considering prostate anatomy, since BPH adenomas may occur in the anterior portion and median lobe of the gland, which are inaccessible to rectal palpation. In addition, the volume of the gland is not a proxy for urethral obstruction: patients with small glands may have significant obstruction, those with enlarged glands often are not obstructed, and prostate size does not predict symptomatic outcome after TURP,[26] although patients with smaller glands are more likely to develop bladder neck contractures postoperatively.[11] Nonetheless, digital rectal examination remains a fundamental part of the evaluation of the man with prostatism because of the need to determine which patients have prostates too large to remove transurethrally and the need to screen for prostate adenocarcinoma, which occurs in 10% to 20% of men with BPH.[57]

The digital rectal examination also provides an opportunity to examine the integrity of the sacral innervation supplying the detrusor and the bladder neck. Perineal sensation, anal wink, and the bulbocavernosus reflex reflect the integrity of sacral roots S2 to S5. However, the anal wink in particular may not be a specific test, as up to 10% to 15% of normal healthy elderly in our experience will have an absent wink without demonstrable neurologic disease or peripheral neuropathy.

An increased postvoid residual volume is another physical finding associated with BPH, with the impaired bladder emptying assumed to be secondary to outlet obstruction. But the postvoid residual volume may be normal in men with BPH, and is likely to be increased only with the subsequent onset of detrusor decompensation. Moreover, measurements of postvoid residual volume are quite variable. Two thirds of men demonstrate significant differences in residual volume determinations by ultrasound from different voids on the same day.[58] Catheter determinations of the postvoid residual volume are operator-dependent,[59] and may be especially so with BPH if the catheter is difficult to pass. Intravenous pyelography also is used to assess postvoid residual volume, but it provides only a qualitative measure, with correct estimates occurring as infrequently as 50% of the time.[39] Ultrasound estimations of postvoid residual volume, even when employing three-dimensional formulas to approximate bladder volume, are subject to large degrees of error (up to ± 39%), especially with smaller volumes.[56] Finally, rather than outlet obstruction, an increased postvoid residual volume may be due to detrusor hyperactivity with impaired contractility, detrusor underactivity, fecal impaction, or medications.[23, 33] Thus, the postvoid residual volume determination is not a specific diagnostic test for obstruction and BPH. However, once the diagnosis of obstruction has been established and other causes of an increased residual volume have been excluded, this determination may be useful in deciding on an intervention or predicting surgical outcome.

## Natural History of Benign Prostatic Hypertrophy

Even in the man with prostatism and demonstrable BPH, the need for treatment is predicated in part on the assumed natural history of the condition: the progressive growth of the adenoma with development of worsening symptoms and adverse sequelae including infection, urinary retention, bladder decompensation, hydronephrosis, and renal failure. Cross-sectional studies demonstrate that the prevalence of BPH increases with age,[2, 3] leading to the assumption that the condition is continually progressive beginning in the fourth or fifth decade. However, while it is true that microscopic BPH is nearly universal by the ninth decade, only approximately half of men with microscopic disease have prostate enlargement, and the rate of developing enlargement is slower than that of microscopic disease.[60] Work by Watanabe's group in Japan further challenges the concept of inexorable prostate enlargement with age. Their cross-sectional study using transrectal prostate ultrasound found a decrease in prostate size after a peak in the fifth decade.[61] Using a similar ultrasound evaluation to follow 16 patients longitudinally for 7 years, they found that only 3 had an increase in prostatic weight of over 50%, and that the increase occurred only in the sixth decade.[62] In the remaining patients, the change in prostate size ranged from −24% to +22%. Since only the minority of men had significant prostate growth, the development or worsening of BPH symptoms over time may depend more on factors extrinsic to the gland. Although this work may reflect cultural and genetic factors (e.g., Japanese men also have a lower incidence of prostate cancer[63]), it nonetheless raises important and provocative questions regarding the natural history of BPH.

Several clinical studies also have demonstrated that symptomatic progression is not relentless. In 1937, Clarke[64] described a series of men with prostatism who were deemed surgical candidates but who improved symptomatically for up to 3 years without surgery or other specific therapy. Craigen[65] followed 212 men with prostatism; at follow-up 4 to 7 years later, 48% were symptom-free without having undergone an operation. Life-table analysis showed that the risk of acute urinary retention was 10% over 7 years and that it usually occurred in the first 3 months. Multivariate analysis failed to demonstrate a difference in the type or severity of symptoms between men who "required" surgery and those who did not. Ball[66] followed 107 patients for at least 5 years and found that symptoms increased in only 15% to 20%; 61% had a decreased flow rate, but only 8% of these men were symptomatic. Even in those who felt worse, no parameters (including radiographic evidence of BOO) were associated with the increase in symptoms. The fluctuating nature of prostatism was emphasized further by Birkoff.[67] He found that it took 2 years for symptoms to worsen in half of his 26 patients and, if symptoms remitted, the improvement persisted for the duration of follow-up (3 to 5 years). Like Craigen, he also found that urinary retention was not predictable, and that it was an early rather than a late complication. Castro's early study of spironolactone treatment for BPH[68] demonstrated that 76% of placebo-treated patients had improved symptoms, a significant decrease in postvoid residual, and no worsening of flow rate at 6 months. This work also helped establish the requirement for a control group in the evaluation of any treatment for BPH.

The aforementioned studies provide a rationale for "watchful waiting"[69] of the symptomatic man with prostatism, once coexisting complications such as hydronephrosis and significant urinary retention have been excluded. This approach awaits verification from an ongoing Department of Veterans Affairs randomized cooperative trial of TURP vs. no surgery, but a decision analysis by Barry et al.[69] found that TURP was only marginally better than watchful waiting in terms of number of resulting quality-adjusted life years. While awaiting the results of further studies, it is important to realize that the diagnosis of BPH does not necessarily foreshadow inevitable complications or even the need for therapy. Discussion of patient concerns (regarding diagnosis, symptom interference in activities, fear of malignancy, and postoperative impotence) and treatment preferences (watchful waiting, TURP, medications, newer procedures) need to be fundamental components of the evaluation of the man with prostatism (see later).

## Who Benefits?: Indications for Transurethral Prostatectomy and Treatment

When a patient presents with symptomatic BPH and desires surgical therapy, several questions remain: Will he benefit?, and How can benefit be predicted? A fundamental correlate of this question is: Must the patient have BOO to benefit, and if so, how severe? The following section examines these questions in relation to urodynamic measures of BOO, other correlates of outlet obstruction, and the problem of coexistent detrusor instability.

## Urodynamic Evaluation of Obstruction

**Pressure/Flow Analysis.**—In the presence of BOO, urinary flow rate should be low and simultaneous detrusor pressure should be elevated. Conversely, a low flow rate and normal or low pressure should occur when the detrusor is weak. Therefore, pressure/flow analysis of detrusor pressure and urinary flow rate have been used to detect BOO and evaluate its utility for predicting outcome from TURP.

Abrams[52] used simultaneous pressure/flow analysis to evaluate 152 patients before and after TURP, defining BOO as a urinary flow rate <15 mL/sec and detrusor pressure >100 cm $H_2O$. By contrast with his earlier series,[70] in which the decision to operate was based on clinical grounds alone, the addition of pressure/flow analysis was associated with a symptomatic improvement of 88% compared with 72% in the earlier series. In another study, Jensen[71] employed computer analysis of simultaneous pressure/flow plots to assess BOO before TURP. Unlike the first study, however, the decision to operate was based on traditionally used criteria rather than pressure/flow analysis. While obstructed patients had significantly higher subjective success rates following TURP (93%), unobstructed men still enjoyed substantial improvement (78%, $P <.03$), and there was no difference in mean symptom scores between obstructed and unobstructed men after surgery. Schäfer[35] used a different computer model of pressure/flow results and found that only severely obstructed men had statistically significant improvement in flow rate and residual volume following prostatectomy; his group did not evaluate subjective outcomes. Neal and colleagues[36] examined detrusor voiding pressure at peak flow in a group of men, all of whom had flow rates <15 mL/sec. They found that men with high voiding pressures (greater than 80 cm $H_2O$) were more likely to have good subjective outcomes (80% vs. 65%, $P <.05$), suggesting that obstructed men had better outcomes. However, it is not clear what proportion of men with lower voiding pressures were truly unobstructed or instead had bladder decompensation and BOO. Furthermore, there was no relationship between voiding pressure and subjective outcome in the subgroup of men with coexistent detrusor instability. Finally, George[72] also found a significantly lower success rate after TURP in men with lower voiding pressures, but he also did not specifically look at whether or not the patients were obstructed.

While these studies suggest that men who are obstructed by pressure/flow criteria have better outcomes after TURP, the utility of pressure/flow testing for BOO is mitigated by the findings of substantial improvement in unobstructed men. Since these studies used variable definitions of BOO, did not assess subjective outcome uniformly, and variably considered such confounding issues as detrusor instability, detrusor weakness, and comorbid disease, further work is needed to better assess the utility of pressure/flow evaluation of BOO for predicting outcome from TURP.

Regardless of its utility, however, several considerations related to pressure/flow analysis limit its widespread use in the evaluation of prostatism. First, it is an invasive test that requires specialized equipment and expertise. Second, the patient must be able to both forestall voiding during bladder filling (often difficult for patients with concomitant detrusor instability) and void on command. As a result, even in research urodynamic laboratories dedicated to performing pressure/flow studies, interpretable data are obtained in only 60% to 86% of cases.[73, 74] Third, even when satisfactory tracings are obtained, up to one third of patients are unclassifiable without special computerized post-processing of the data.[34] Finally, there is still considerable disagreement as to when various parameters should be measured during the void.[75, 76] Thus, while pressure/flow testing may provide a precise physiologic assessment of urethral obstruction, these limitations vitiate the likelihood of its widespread application.

**Urethral Resistance Factors.**—Several studies have employed a urethral resistance factor as a measure of BOO. Based on hydrodynamic principles of flow through tubes, urethral resistance is calculated from pressure/flow data as the ratio of the maximum detrusor pressure to the square of the peak urinary flow rate. Values of urethral resistance $\geq 0.5$ are considered evidence of outlet obstruction. However, the urethral resistance factor may offer no marginal benefit over the urinary flow rate for distinguishing obstructed from unobstructed patients.[34] Furthermore, since the urethral resistance factor is based on the hydrodynamics of flow in rigid tubes, it is not truly applicable to the collapsible elastic urethra.[77] Resistance factors, therefore, are no longer considered an accurate or useful measure of BOO by most urodynamicists, although their use persists in the literature.

**Micturitional Urethral Pressure Profile.**—Yalla[78] pioneered the micturitional urethral pressure profile, which examines simultaneous bladder and urethral pressure (from the bladder neck to the bulbous urethra) during voiding. A pressure gradient between the bladder and urethra is used to detect the presence of obstruction and localize its site; in men with BPH, a drop in pressure is seen at the level of the prostatic urethra above the verumontanum.[78] Good correlation has been found between the micturitional urethral pressure profile and pressure-flow studies in men with BOO.[79] Further work is needed to determine whether the profile can quantify obstruction, and whether BOO defined in this way correlates with surgical outcome.

**Passive Urethral Resistance Relation.**—Schäfer[77] used theoretic modeling and computer analysis of pressure/flow data to define urethral resistance by a formula that includes the cross-sectional area of the urethra and the minimal pressure at which flow occurs (Pmuo). The resulting curve, the passive urethral resistance relation, defines BOO by the Pmuo (BOO = Pmuo > 25 cm $H_2O$; the type of BOO can be described further by analysis of the curve shape). Few clinical studies employing the passive urethral resistance relation exist. In a series of 39 men, Schäfer[35] found that only those with severe BOO (Pmuo > 40 cm $H_2O$) had an improvement in flow rate after TURP, while Meyhoff[80] found that postoperative Pmuo was reduced but still high (49 to 75 cm $H_2O$) in 11 men selected for good subjective outcome after TURP. Spangberg[81] found that a modified version of the passive urethral resistance relation discriminated well between normal elderly men and those with BPH. At present, the passive urethral resistance relation and similar methods remain clinically limited by the need for both pressure/flow evaluation and specialized computer postprocessing of the data, as well as the limited data correlating these methods with subjective outcomes.

---

## Evaluation of Correlates of Obstruction in Benign Prostatic Hypertrophy

**Flow Rate.**—Peak urinary flow rate was one of the first urodynamic measures used to assess prostatism. It remains a popular method of evaluation as it is noninvasive and requires relatively simple and inexpensive equipment.

The flow rate is dependent on bladder volume, and several nomograms have been devised to correct for volume voided, expressing flow as a standard deviation from a normal mean.[82–84] Drach's nomogram additionally corrects for patient age, taking into account the age-related decrease in flow rate (although the mean age of his reference population was 35 years[85].) The utility of these nomograms depends on the group used to establish the norm, and how representative it is of the population in which the nomogram will be used in terms of sex, age, site (inpatient or outpatient, community sample, referral group), comorbid disease, and the existence of voiding symptoms. Unfortunately, none of the nomogram studies excluded voiding augmented by straining,[82-84] a phenomenon that may be more common in older patients[86] and that will spuriously elevate peak flow if an obstruction is absent. In addition, most studies of flow rate in BPH have used absolute cutoff levels and not the standard deviation from a norm to define abnormal rates, with results thereby confounded by patient age and the low voided volumes prevalent in the BPH population.

Since flow rate represents the contributions of bladder contraction and outlet opening during voiding, a low flow rate may reflect diminished bladder contractility (due to aging, disease, or medications), as well as outlet obstruction. Thus, a low flow rate is not specific and cannot differentiate BOO from an underactive detrusor, nor does it discriminate well between those who will and those who will not benefit from TURP.[7] Gerstenberg[87] found "normal" flow rates (peak flow >15 mL/sec) in 10% of symptomatic patients, three quarters of whom had outlet obstruction (defined as maximum voiding pressure >100 cm $H_2O$) and experienced symptomatic relief after TURP. Neal[36] found no difference in TURP outcome between those with very low (<10 mL/sec) and marginally low (<15 mL/sec) preoperative peak flow rates; this study corroborated an earlier one by Bruskewitz.[26] On the other hand, not all patients with low flow rates require surgery to improve. Kadow and colleagues[88] randomized 38 patients with peak flows of <10 mL/sec to either TURP or bladder retraining (timed voiding) and medication. They found no significant difference in symptomatic outcome between the two small groups. In addition, although flow rate tends to increase following TURP, there is wide individual variation, and an increased postoperative peak flow does not always correlate with symptom relief.[11]

**Intravenous Pyelography.**—Intravenous pyelography remains a common investigation in prostatism, with the findings of bladder trabeculation, diverticula, prostatic indentation, and increased postvoid residual volume used to diagnose BPH and outlet obstruction. Intravenous pyelography also is used to detect hydronephrosis. However, several lines of evidence now question a continuing role for intravenous pyelography in the routine investigation of prostatism. First, the finding of bladder trabeculation, often considered evidence of long-standing BOO, correlates better with detrusor instability than with obstruction.[89] Although it may be important to rule out severe trabeculation and diverticula before TURP (since prostate chips from the resection can be retained and set up a nidus for infection), the intravenous pyelogram may not be the most efficient or safest way to do so. Second, while the size of a bladder base indentation or filling defect seen on pyelography does correlate with obstruction,[90] the detection of such filling defects is variable and depends on the portion of the prostate predominantly enlarged, the angle of the x-ray beam, and the relative mixing of urine and the radiographic contrast agent.[39] Third, intravenous pyelography does not visualize the bladder outlet during voiding and therefore cannot detect obstruction directly. Fourth, there is no routine need to rule out hydronephrosis in prostatism, as it is uncommon in unselected patients (3% to 10%)[91] and is unsuspected in even fewer (0.1%).[92] Furthermore, when hydronephrosis is a concern, ultrasound is preferable to intravenous pyelography since it does not involve the risk of radiation or a contrast agent, and has a high sensitivity for ureteral dilation.[93] Finally, there is no evidence that the prevalence of asymptomatic renal cancer is increased in men with prostatism; therefore, the cost and risk of routine intravenous pyelography for this indication is unjustified as well.[92] Thus, abandonment of the routine use of pyelography in prostatism is well justified; it also would result in significant cost savings—estimated at $75 million in 1980![94] However, intravenous pyelography is still warranted if hematuria is present.

**Voiding Cystourethrography.**—Voiding cystourethrography involves retrograde filling of the bladder with a contrast agent followed by visualization of the bladder and urethra during the resting, voiding, and postvoiding states. While this examination is subject to the same caveats as intravenous pyelography regarding the evaluation of trabeculation, diverticula, and postvoid residual volume, it has the advantage of providing a dynamic evaluation of the urethral outlet during micturition. However, the sensitivity and specificity of voiding cystourethrography for obstruction have not been investigated extensively. Manoliu[95] defined obstruction as a bladder outlet diameter of 6 mm on voiding cystourethrography, and found that 89% of men obstructed by this criteria also had maximum flow rates less than 10 mL/sec. As noted previously, however, a low flow rate is not specific for obstruction, and Manoliu examined no other measures of BOO.

Although voiding cystourethrography is widely available, often it is performed by technicians and read by radiologists who are not well trained in lower urinary tract physiology and who therefore may provide neither sensitive nor specific analyses. Nevertheless, voiding cystourethrography may be underutilized in prostatism, especially since it provides a direct assessment of the outlet during micturition, when obstruction truly matters. Further research is needed to better define its actual predictive value and clinical utility.

**Cystoscopy.**—Cystoscopy is used in prostatism to rule out intravesical pathology such as tumors or stones that also cause voiding symptoms, and to evaluate bladder trabeculation, prostatic length and size, the presence of an enlarged median lobe, and the degree of lateral lobe "coaptation" or obstruction. Since cystoscopy is performed when the patient is not voiding, lateral lobes that appear obstructive by cystoscopy actually may part adequately enough to permit unobstructed flow during micturition. As a prominent urologist editorialized, "One cannot make the diagnosis of obstruction on endoscopic grounds with absolute certainty even though all of us do so."[96] Like the intravenous pyelogram, cystoscopy is required if hematuria is present; it also should be considered whenever there is pelvic pain with voiding.

## Detrusor Instability and Transurethral Prostatectomy Outcome

Two important questions arise regarding detrusor instability and TURP outcome: (1) Does preoperative detrusor instability predict poor outcome? and (2) Is persistent (or de novo) detrusor instability after TURP associated with poor outcome? Jensen[40] showed that preoperative detrusor instability did not affect patients' subjective outcome. On the other hand, Speakman[97] concluded that patients with preoperative detrusor instability were four times more likely to have a poor outcome; however, he included in the unstable group patients who were not obstructed. Excluding these patients reveals that there is no significant difference between the groups, with a good outcome in 92% of stable and 93% of unstable patients. In Neal's study,[36] preoperative detrusor instability was associated with persistent irritative but not obstructive symptoms after surgery. Reuther[98] examined the issue somewhat differently and tried to differentiate preoperative detrusor instability due to prostatic obstruction (which therefore might remit after resection) from instability due to other causes. He instilled an alkaline lignocaine solution into the bladder during cystometry and found that those patients with persistent detrusor instability after instillation had worse outcomes after TURP. This work suggests that it is the coexistent detrusor instability, rather than the instability "secondary" to obstruction, that causes persistent problems after TURP. However, the study included only eight patients, and other investigators have shown that a decrease in detrusor instability may be due to the alkalinity of the infusion, since lignocaine actually increases instability.[99] Although provocative, this work needs further verification.

In contrast to the controversy surrounding preoperative detrusor instability, detrusor instability postoperatively is a proven marker for poor outcome,[36, 52, 100] although no adequate method for predicting persistent instability after TURP has been developed yet. Most investigators have assumed that detrusor instability found in the setting of BPH and BOO is due to the obstuction and have not tried to differentiate patients who have other etiologies for detrusor instability, as Reuther[98] did. Indeed, the question of the management of patients (usually elderly) with neurologic disease, detrusor instability, and obstructing BPH remains unsettled. Will surgical relief of obstruction convert continent detrusor hyperreflexia to urge incontinence? What is the risk of precipitating urinary retention if anticholinergics are used to control detrusor overactivity without an operation? Does surgery alter the efficacy of medication and bladder training in such patients? What is the efficacy of medical therapy for detrusor instability in terms of subjective improvement and quality of life for patients with persistent instability after TURP? Although much further research is required, at present, clinicians can assist their patients by anticipating and weighing possible adverse outcomes if preoperative detrusor instability is present.

## Other Factors Affecting Outcome

Several other physiologic and operative factors may result in poor outcome following TURP. The lack of good voluntary sphincter control preoperatively has been associated with the development of incontinence after TURP in patients with Parkinson's disease.[101] In Jensen's series,[40] patients with low cystometric bladder capacities (<300 mL) were almost twice as likely (21% vs. 12%) to have a poor outcome. Dorflinger[102] examined the role of prostate histology. Of samples obtained from 81 unselected patients treated with TURP, 50% were predominantly stromal, 25% were predominantly glandular, and the remainder were of mixed histology. Although the patients did not differ in terms of age, symptom duration, preoperative symptom scores, postvoid residual volumes, the presence of detrusor instability, or flow rate, those with stromal enlargement had significantly lower flow rates after TURP. However, there was no significant difference between the groups in subjective outcome from TURP. The question remains whether BOO was equally present in all groups.

A recent study by Roos[103] raised significant controversy by suggesting that patients had increased mortality after TURP compared with open prostatectomy. Open procedures usually are done for large glands (greater than 50 to 60 g), and require general rather than spinal anesthesia and longer operating times. Thus, sicker patients would have been more likely to have undergone TURP, resulting in the strong possibility of bias in this retrospective study.[104] Further prospective studies including careful attention to case mix and quality of life outcome measures are needed and are being conducted to clarify these issues.

## New Treatment Options

In the past 10 years, both new surgical and nonoperative treatments for prostatism have been developed, and the list is expanding. Patients may approach their internists with questions regarding new options that have received extensive coverage in the lay press. Internists making urologic referrals should be aware of such treatments for their patients who are resistant to surgery or who may not be surgical candidates; internists additionally should be aware that experience with these treatments is in most instances still limited, particularly in elderly patients. The following is a brief review of the major new developments.

**α-Adrenergic Blockers.**—Since the BPH adenoma and the prostatic capsule have plentiful α-adrenergic receptors, α-adrenergic blockers are used to decrease the neurologic tone of the gland and thereby reduce the "functional" component of urethral constriction and obstruction. Phenoxybenzamine (5 to 20 mg/day) has been approximately 80% effective in increasing flow rates,[105] but its use is hampered in 30% of patients by side effects (including hypotension), which can be exacerbated by the drug's long half-life.[106] In addition, enthusiasm for its use has waned because of its association with malignancy in rodents.[106] Prazosin (2 to 4 mg/day) and terazosin (5 mg/day) are more $\alpha_1$-selective agents that are less likely to cause side effects, but their clinical efficacy may be somewhat less impressive.[105–107] Overall, $\alpha$-blockers reduce symptoms in 50% to 70% of moderately symptomatic men and provide an acceptable first-line therapy for the man without an absolute indication for surgery (such as retention, infection, or hydronephrosis).[105, 106] The safety profile of these agents in the elderly has not been well established, and they should be used with caution.

**Antiandrogens.**—Although the pathogenesis of BPH is incompletely understood, testicular androgens are believed to play a permissive role in the development of adenomas.[57] Antiandrogen treatment of BPH has been investigated using luteinizing hormone releasing hormone agonists (nafarelin,[20] leuprolide,[108] buserelin[109, 110]), androgen receptor inhibitors (cyproterone acetate,[19] flutamide[111]) and 5$\alpha$-reductase inhibitors (finasteride[19]). Overall, these agents result in a 25% to 30% decrease in prostate size, with variable effects on symptoms.[107] Each of these agents must be continued indefinitely to maintain prostate size reduction; many men find this difficult, since the luteinizing hormone releasing hormone agonists and cyproterone acetate cause impotence and flutamide causes gynecomastia. Finasteride, so far, has had no major side effects, but it is not yet available and its clinical efficacy is still under investigation.

**Other Pharmacologic Agents.**—Antifungals (candicidin[112]), cimetidine,[113] spironolactone,[68] and bromocriptine[114] all have failed to show symptomatic benefit over placebo for the treatment of prostatism. The phytosterol curbicin, a plant-derived fatty acid with antiandrogen properties, resulted in significant improvement in symptoms and flow rate compared with placebo,[115] while another phytosterol, permixon, offered no benefit.[116] Based on its success in childhood enuresis, there has been recent interest in the use of 1-desamino-8-D-arginine vasopressin for treating nocturia associated with BPH. In a short-term, double-blind study, this agent produced a variable decrease in total nocturnal urine output, and its clinical usefulness was questionable (decrease of two episodes of nocturia over 3 nights).[117] Moreover, the safety of the drug in the elderly (the group most likely to have nocturia) is not known.

**Prostate Incision.**—Transurethral prostatotomy, or incision of the prostate (TUIP), is a technically simpler alternative to resection. Randomized studies demonstrate similar short-term (12 months) symptomatic success rates for TUIP compared with TURP in patients with small (<30 g) glands.[118–120] Advantages of TUIP include its low rate of postoperative retrograde ejaculation, short operative time, little bleeding, and (in selected cases) ability to be performed using local anesthesia.[121] For the higher-risk patient for whom surgical management of BOO is needed, and perhaps for the younger patient with a small gland for whom the preservation of antegrade ejaculation is important, TUIP may be a safe and effective alternative to TURP, especially in the hands of a surgeon experienced in the technique.

**Balloon Dilation.**—Although initially promising, transurethral balloon dilation of the prostatic urethra has not yet proved an effective treatment for prostatism on either a short- or long-term basis.[17] In a representative group of 62 men who were candidates for TURP, the 1-year symptomatic success rate was 58%,[122] lower than that for TURP or TUIP and representing little marginal benefit over placebo improvement rates. In particular, patients with large glands or predominant median lobe enlargement respond poorly.[122] However, the procedure can be done under local anesthesia and therefore be used in the high-risk patient. In a series of 55 elderly, high-risk patients, 83% had fair to excellent clinical outcomes at 12 months, although the remainder required TURP.[123]

**Prostatic Stents.**—Wire mesh stents and spirals, placed in the prostatic urethra under endoscopic or radiologic guidance, have been used in several small trials as an alternative to surgery for high-risk patients with urinary retention.[16, 124] Use of the spiral has been complicated by migration of the device,[124] infection,[124] and urinary incontinence or retention.[125] The stent remains in place, becomes covered by epithelium in 6 to 8 months, and results in fewer infections, but it is associated with a high rate of urgency and urge incontinence for up to 2 months.[16, 126] These initial reports are provocative, but limited by their small size (less than 20 patients), high degree of selection, and short follow-up (less than 1 year).

**Hyperthermia.**—The ability of hyperthermia to induce regression of some malignant tumors led investigators to try microwave hyperthermia for BPH, but the results have been largely disappointing. The initial favorable reports were uncontrolled[127, 128] and, in one study, 33% of patients required subsequent surgery within 6 months.[128] A recent trial[129] found no effect on prostate size, voiding parameters, or symptoms. Since treatment requires substantial patient commitment (6 to 12 1-hour sessions), widespread acceptability is unlikely.

## Evaluation: The Role of the Internist

Since the majority of men with prostatism present initially to their primary care provider, there is a significant opportunity to initiate evaluation and therapy while remaining aware of the symptoms and findings that require prompt urologic referral. This is particularly true in the care of elderly patients, in whom factors outside the lower urinary tract are more likely to precipitate voiding symptoms.[23] A two- or three-level approach to the man with prostatism seems most appropriate for the internist: level 1 is the basic evaluation, which every internist should be able to complete; levels 2 and

3—for further diagnostic work-up and empiric therapy—will be outlined for those with the interest and expertise to pursue the problem further. Absolute indications for urologic referral are emphasized, and the role of the internist in helping to sort out patient preferences in treatment will be discussed.

## Level 1: Basic Evaluation

**History and Symptom Assessment.**—The initial role of the internist is to establish the nature of the presenting symptoms and to identify coexistent conditions that may contribute to lower urinary tract dysfunction. Serious conditions that can mimic prostatism (e.g., brain or spinal cord lesions, bladder stones, and bladder and prostate cancer) also should be excluded, as described below.

In addition to reviewing obstructive and irritative symptoms, the physician should instruct the patient to complete a voiding diary[130] in order to provide an objective record and to assess the role of fluid intake and urine volume in the etiology of symptoms. The patient keeps a 48-hour diary to record the time and volume of all voidings (continent and incontinent), as well as associated symptoms (urgency, incomplete emptying) and hours of sleep. From the diary, the clinician can determine the total daytime and nighttime urine output, the median volume voided, voiding frequency, and frequency of nocturia, as well as estimate the bladder capacity from the largest volume voided. If nocturia occurs in the setting of excessive nighttime urine output (over one third of the total daily output in middle-aged men or over one half of the daily output in elderly men), then its cause should be sought, including peripheral edema, congestive heart failure, poor diabetic control, and evening ingestion of diuretics, including caffeinated beverages and alcohol. Elderly men may experience nocturia due to an age-related decrease in glomerular filtration and a delayed ability to excrete a fluid load.[131] However, awakening three or more times a night with nocturia should not be ascribed to the physiologic changes of aging alone. Daytime frequency or large urine volumes at particular times of day may be related to diuretic medications, excessive fluid intake, caffeinated beverages, or endocrine abnormalities (see later). Emotional stress also may play a role in increased frequency and possibly in worsening obstructive symptoms, although this has not been well investigated and mechanisms are speculative. In addition to supplying diagnostic information, a voiding diary provides a baseline measure of symptoms to follow over time and with therapy.

**Exclusion of Confounding Factors.**—All prescription and nonprescription medications should be reviewed carefully with the patient, because many common medications affect lower urinary tract function through interaction with detrusor cholinergic receptors or the $\alpha$-adrenergic receptors of the bladder outlet and prostate. The use of nonprescription medications is especially important to review in men with prostatism. Many such preparations (especially combination "cold" tablets and nose drops) contain α-adrenergic agonists that increase outlet resistance and exacerbate otherwise mild obstruction. Antihistamines, also used in "cold" tablets and agents for insomnia, have anticholinergic properties that decrease detrusor function. Both types of agents alone, and certainly in combination, can precipitate urinary retention; in such instances, the only treatment needed is exclusion of the offending medication and catheter decompression of the bladder—not surgery.

Hyperglycemia, hypercalcemia, and diabetes insipidus—the endocrine abnormalities that cause diuresis—should be searched for in patients with frequency and large urinary outputs (i.e., over 2 L/day). All patients should be evaluated for constipation and fecal impaction, as the latter can precipitate urinary retention, especially in the elderly[132]; restoration of bowel function will also reverse the urinary dysfunction.

**Physical Examination.**—The clinician next should exclude other contributing factors through a targeted physical examination. Neurologic disease can cause urinary dysfunction and mimic prostatism by affecting either the cerebral centers that control micturition (e.g., through dementia, stroke, Parkinson's, tumor, hydrocephalus) or the spinal cord or spinal roots innervating the lower urinary tract (e.g., through spinal stenosis, tumor, and peripheral neuropathies including diabetes, pernicious anemia, and heavy alcohol use). A basic neurourologic examination should be done on all men presenting with prostatism. This should include motor, sensory, and deep tendon reflex testing; evaluation of perineal innervation with sensory testing; and assessment of the anal wink and bulbocavernosus reflexes, and the resting and volitional tone of the external anal sphincter. The bulbocavernosus reflex is checked by quickly stroking the glans penis, and should elicit the same contraction of the anal sphincter as is seen with the anal wink. When testing the volitional control of the anal sphincter, the examiner should ensure that increased tone is not due to contraction of the abdominal muscles. The finding of neurologic disease in men with prostatism should prompt referral if the patient is a surgical candidate, since many of these patients may require urodynamic testing to determine the adequacy of detrusor and outlet function. The rectal examination is done to assess prostatic nodularity and rectal tone, and to exclude fecal impaction, as discussed previously.

**Testing.**—All patients additionally should be screened with urinalysis and a postvoid residual volume determination. Findings of hematuria or urinary tract infection require urologic referral. Urine cytology should be sent for all patients with hematuria. In elderly men, asymptomatic bacteriuria without pyuria requires no special evaluation or treatment.[131] On the other hand, sterile pyuria in the same population can indicate urinary tuberculosis and should be evaluated further with appropriate urine culture. A postvoid residual volume can be obtained directly by catheterizing a patient immediately after a void (and after antibiotic prophylaxis if valvular heart disease, intravascular graft, or joint prosthesis is present), or by ultrasound. Patients with a high postvoid residual volume will require further evaluation for hydronephrosis (which could be done by ultrasound at the time of postvoid volume assessment), and often require urologic referral, even if hydronephrosis is not present. There are few data from which to derive an absolute cutoff level for a "high" postvoid residual volume; in one study by Neal,[133] a volume >300 mL by ultrasound had a sensitivity of 78% and a specificity of 85% for upper tract dilation. We conservatively consider elevated a postvoid residual volume greater than 150 mL, based on local urologic consensus. Threshold values may differ between practitioners and with different patient situations (e.g., a postvoid residual volume of 100 mL may be more worrisome in a 55-year-old man with a porcine mitral valve because of the serious consequences of potential bacteriuria from retention and infection). One further caveat: serum creatinine is not a sensitive screen for hydronephrosis in elderly men, since normal serum creatinine levels may occur with significant impairment in renal function because of an age-related decrease in lean muscle mass. Nonetheless, the blood urea nitrogen and serum creatinine should be determined in all men with prostatism.

## Level 2: Further Diagnostic Evaluation

After the basic evaluation outlined above, the internist may choose to refer the patient to a urologist. Alternatively, the internist with expertise in lower urinary tract function may consider further testing to determine whether outlet obstruction is present, keeping in mind the caveats and controversy concerning the relationship between obstruction and successful treatment outcome. Tests available to most internists include urinary flowmetry and voiding cystourethrography. The average flow rate is calculated easily by dividing the volume voided by the voiding time in seconds, but the average flow rate may be less useful than the peak flow rate, which requires a machine for measurement. As discussed, flow rate is most useful for excluding outlet obstruction by demonstration of a normal flow rate, although the test is not perfectly sensitive. Voiding cystourethrography offers direct information regarding the outlet, although the sensitivity and specificity may vary with technical and radiologic expertise. There are currently no data either to support or to refute the need to evaluate bladder morphology (trabeculation and diverticula) when deciding whether to treat men with prostatism noninvasively.

## Level 3: Empiric Therapy

After correction of the contributing factors identified in level 1, the internist experienced in treating lower urinary tract dysfunction may decide to initiate empiric noninvasive therapy for a mildly or even moderately symptomatic patient. However, despite the caveats mentioned throughout this discussion, it must be appreciated that no treatment for prostatism has yet proved more efficacious than TURP. Nonetheless, depending on the clinical situation and patient preference, options other than TURP may be tried. Such therapy includes adjustment of urine output (if excessive), pharmacologic treatment with α-adrenergic blockers, and behavioral methods to alleviate voiding symptoms. Behavioral methods include timed voiding and bladder retraining for urinary frequency,[134] double-voiding or Credé methods for incomplete emptying, and instruction for "unhurried voiding" for hesitancy and incomplete emptying.[135] Before discussing any therapeutic option, however, the clinician needs to address with the patient his concerns regarding the severity of symptoms; the degree to which symptoms interfere with daily activity; the desire for immediate treatment and concerns regarding forestalling therapy; fears regarding surgical therapy and its outcomes; and willingness to try alternatives to surgery. Questions regarding quality of life with and without therapy also should be discussed. Patients should be aware that a small but significant proportion of men (probably 5% to 10%, but one study reports a rate of 34%) lose potency after prostatectomy, that the risk is higher in older patients, and that approximately two thirds of men develop retrograde ejaculation following TURP.[136] Preservation of potency may be abetted by providing patients preoperatively with information about surgical outcomes.[136] An interactive video program to assist patients and clinicians in such a discussion is presently under development.[137, 138] Furthermore, the Agency for Health Care Policy and Research and the American Urological Association are both in the process of establishing consensus guidelines for the treatment of prostatism based on an exhaustive literature review.

## Summary

The prevalence of BPH ensures a continuing need for internists to be aware of the issues regarding the evaluation and treatment of prostatism, while the developing role of nonoperative therapy and the growing recognition of the importance of patient preferences have opened the way for an expanded involvement of the primary care practitioner in the management of these patients. Prostatism remains a difficult clinical problem since many of the symptoms and diagnostic tests are nonspecific, especially in the elderly. Basic questions regarding the role of bladder outlet obstruction (BOO) in the development of symptoms and in predicting outcome from surgery await further study. Against this background of uncertainty, however, is the reassurance that the natural history of the process results in serious complications in only the minority of patients. Important work is under way that will incorporate quality of life outcomes, compare surgery with "watchful waiting," and randomize patients to surgical and nonsurgical treatments. In the interim, the internist may help patients with prostatism significantly by appreciating the natural history of the condition, treating the conditions that mimic or exacerbate it, understanding the clinical utility and limitations of current evaluation methods, becoming aware of the growing array of nonsurgical and minimal-surgery options, and assisting patients in weighing therapeutic risks and benefits with their concerns about symptoms.

## Addendum

Since this article was submitted, Catalona[139] has published data suggesting that the combination of serum prostate-specific androgen (PSA) and digital rectal examination provide more accurate screening for carcinoma of the prostate. A PSA level should likely be added to the list of routine tests for evaluating men with prostatism.

## Acknowledgments

The authors thank Dr. Subbaro Yalla, Chief of Urology, Brockton/West Roxbury Veterans Administration Medical Center, for his valuable assistance and kind review of the manuscript.

The authors also wish to acknowledge grant support from the National Institutes of Health (Teaching Nursing Home Award and the Claude Pepper Geriatric Research and Training Center [Dr. Resnick]), as well as the Department of Veterans' Affairs (Special Fellowship in Gerontology [Dr. DuBeau] and Specialized Center for Study of Longterm Disability [Dr. Resnick]).

## References

1. Jensen KM-E, Jorgensen JB, Mogensen P, et al: Some clinical aspects of uroflowometry in elderly males: A population survey. Scand J Urol Nephrol 1986; 20:93–99.
2. Lytton B, Emergy JM, Harvard BM: The incidence of benign prostatic obstruction. J Urol 1968; 99:639–645.
3. Glynn RJ, Campion EW, Bouchard GR, et al: The development of benign prostatic hypertrophy among volunteers in the Normative Aging Study. Am J Epidemiol 1985; 121:78–90.
4. Rutkow IM: Urologic operation in the United States: 1979–1984. J Urol 1986; 135:1206–1208.
5. Holtgrewe HL, Mebust WK, Dowd JB, et al: Transurethral prostatectomy: Practice aspects of the dominant operation in American urology. J Urol 1989; 141:248–253.
6. Graverson PH, Gasser TC, Wasson JH, et al: Controversies about indications for transurethral resection of the prostate. J Urol 1989; 141:475–481.
7. Lepor H, Rigaud G: The efficacy of transurethral resection of the prostate in men with moderate symptoms of prostatism. J Urol 1990; 143:533–537.
8. Chilton CP, Morgan RJ, England HR, et al: A critical evaluation of the results of transurethral resection of the prostate. Br J Urol 1978; 50:542–546.
9. Mebust WK, Holtgrewe HL, Cockett ATK, et al: Transurethral prostatectomy: Immediate and postoperative complications. A cooperative study of 13 participating institutions evaluating 3,885 patients. J Urol 1989; 141:243–247.
10. Fowler FJ Jr, Wennberg JE, Timothy RP, et al: Symptom status and quality of life following prostatectomy. JAMA 1988; 259:3018–3022.
11. Bruskewitz RC, Larsen EH, Madsen PO, et al: 3 year follow-up of urinary

symptoms after transurethral resection of the prostate. *J Urol* 1989; 142:1251–1253.

12. Nielsen KT, Christensen MM, Madsen PO, et al: Symptom analysis and uroflowmetry seven years after transurethral resection of the prostate. *J Urol* 1989; 142:1251–1253.

13. Wyatt MG, Stower MJ, Smith PJB, et al: Prostatectomy in the over 80-year-old. *Br J Urol* 1989; 64:417–419.

14. Barkin M, Dolfin D, Herschorn S, et al: Voiding dysfunction in institutionalized elderly men: The influence of previous prostatectomy. *J Urol* 1983; 130:258–259.

15. Orandi A: Transurethral incision of the prostate (TUIP): 646 cases in 15 years—a chronological appraisal. *Br J Urol* 1985; 57:703–707.

16. Chapple CR, Milroy EJG, Rickards D: Permanently implanted urethral stent for prostatic obstruction in the unfit patient: Preliminary report. *Br J Urol* 1990; 66:58–65.

17. Dowd JB, Smith JJ: Balloon dilation of the prostate. *Urol Clin North Am* 1990; 17:671–677.

18. Caine M: The present role of alpha-adrenergic blockers in the treatment of benign prostatic hypertrophy. *J Urol* 1986; 136:1–4.

19. McConnell JD: Medical management of benign prostatic hyperplasia with androgen suppression. *Prostate [Suppl]* 1990; 3:49–59.

20. Peters CA, Walsh PC: The effect of nafarelin acetate, a luteinizing hormone-releasing-hormone agonist, on benign prostatic hyperplasia. *N Engl J Med* 1987; 317:599–604.

21. Schlossberg SM, Finkel ML, Vaughan ED Jr, et al: Second opinion for urologic surgery. *J Urol* 1984; 131:209–212.

22. Andersen JT: Bladder function in healthy elderly males. *Scand J Urol Nephrol* 1978; 12:123–127.

23. Resnick NM: Voiding dysfunction in the elderly, in Yalla SV, McGuire EJ, Elbadawi A, et al (eds): *Neurourology and Urodynamics: Principles and Practice*. New York, Macmillan Publishing Company, Inc, 1988, pp 303–330.

24. Brocklehurst JC, Dillane JB: Studies of the female bladder in old age. I. Cystometrograms in non-incontinent women. *Geront Clin* 1966; 8:285–305.

25. Wennberg JE, Mulley AG Jr, Hanley D, et al: An assessment of prostatectomy for benign urinary tract obstruction: Geographic variations and the evaluation of medical care outcomes. *JAMA* 1988; 259:3027–3030.

26. Bruskewitz RC, Iverson P, Madsen PO: Urodynamics in the evaluation of benign prostatic hyperplasia: Predictive value. *Surg Forum* 1981; 32:630–632.

27. Katz GP, Blaivas JG: A diagnostic dilemma: When urodynamic findings differ from the clinical impression. *J Urol* 1983; 129:1170–1174.

28. Jensen KM-E, Bruskewitz RC, Iversen P, et al: Significance of prostatic weight in prostatism. *Urol Int* 1983; 38:173–178.

29. Klarskov P, Andersen JT, Asmussen CF, et al: Symptoms and signs predictive of voiding pattern after acute urinary retention. *Scand J Urol Nephrol* 1987; 21:23–28.

30. Simonsen O, Moller-Madsen B, Dorflinger T, et al: The significance of age on symptoms and urodynamic and cystoscopic findings in benign prostatic hypertrophy. *Urol Res* 1987; 15:355–358.

31. Resnick NM, Yalla SV: Detrusor hyperactivity with impaired contractility: An unrecognized but common cause of incontinence in elderly patients. *JAMA* 1987; 257:3076–3081.

32. Coolsaet B, Blok C: Detrusor properties related to prostatism. *Neurourol Urodynam* 1986; 5:435–447.
33. Turner-Warwick R, Whiteside CG, Arnold EP, et al: A urodynamic view of prostatic obstruction and the results of the prostatectomy. *Br J Urol* 1973; 45:631–645.
34. Abrams PH, Griffiths DJ: The assessment of prostatic obstruction from urodynamic measurements and from residual urine. *Br J Urol* 1979; 51:129–134.
35. Schäfer W, Rubben H, Noppeney R, et al: Obstructed and unobstructed prostatic obstruction: A plea for urodynamic objectivation of bladder outflow obstruction in benign prostatic hyperplasia. *World J Urol* 1989; 6:198–203.
36. Neal DE, Ramsden PD, Sharples L, et al: Outcome of elective prostatectomy. *Br Med J [Clin Res]* 1989; 299:762–767.
37. Abrams P: Detrusor instability and bladder outlet obstruction. *Neurourol Urodynam* 1985; 4:317–328.
38. Sibley GNA: An experimental model of detrusor instability in the obstructed pig. *Br J Urol* 1985; 57:292–298.
39. Andersen JT: Prostatism: Clinical, radiological, and urodynamic aspects. *Neurourol Urodynam* 1982; 1:241–293.
40. Jensen KM-E, Jorgensen JB, Mogensen P: Urodynamics in prostatism III: Prognostic value of medium-fill cystometry. *Scand J Urol Nephrol Suppl* 1988; 114:78–83.
41. Cucchi A: Detrusor instability and bladder outflow obstruction: Evidence for a correlation between the severity of obstruction and the presence of instability. *Br J Urol* 1988; 61:420–422.
42. Hochberg E, de Tejada IS, Shebar E, et al: Neurourologic studies in the adult diabetic with voiding symptoms. *J Urol* 1985; 133:273A.
43. Katz PG, Greenstein A: Urinary incontinence associated with neurologic disorders. *Semin Urol* 1989; 7:133–138.
44. Hinman F Jr: Point of view: Capsular influence on benign prostatic hypertrophy. *Urology* 1986; 28:347–350.
45. Lepor H, Shapiro E: Characterization of alpha adrenergic receptors in human benign prostatic hyperplasia. *J Urol* 1984; 132:1226–1229.
46. Rohner TJ Jr: Changes in adrenergic receptors in bladder outlet obstruction, in Hinman F Jr (ed): *Benign Prostatic Hypertrophy*. New York, Springer Publishing Company, 1983, pp 410–413.
47. Perlberg S, Caine M: Adrenergic response of bladder muscle in prostatic obstruction: Its relation to detrusor instability. *Urology* 1982; 20:524–527.
48. Chalfin SA, Bradley WE: The etiology of detrusor hyperreflexia in patients with infravesical obstruction. *J Urol* 1982; 127:938–942.
49. Gosling JA, Gilpin SA, Dixon JS, et al: Decrease in the autonomic innervation of human detrusor muscle in outflow obstruction. *J Urol* 1986; 136:501–504.
50. Gilpin SA, Gilpin CJ, Dixon JS, et al: The effect of age on the autonomic innervation of the urinary bladder. *Br J Urol* 1986; 58:378–381.
51. Madsen PO, Iversen P: A point system for selecting operative candidates, in Hinman F Jr (ed): *Benign Prostatic Hypertrophy*. New York, Springer Publishing Company, 1983, pp 763–765.
52. Abrams PH, Farrar DJ, Turner-Warwick RT, et al: The results of prostatectomy: A symptomatic and urodynamic analysis of 152 patients. *J Urol* 1979; 121:640–642.
53. Cote RJ, Burke H, Schoenberg HW: Prediction of unusual postoperative re-

sults by urodynamic testing in benign prostatic hypertrophy. *J Urol* 1981; 125:690–692.

54. Meyhoff HH, Hald T: Are doctors able to assess prostatic size? *Scand J Urol Nephrol* 1978; 12:219–221.

55. Meyhoff HH, Ingemann L, Nordling J, et al: Accuracy in preoperative estimation of prostatic size. *Scand J Urol Nephrol* 1981; 15:45–51.

56. Ohe H, Ohnishi K, Watanabe H, et al: Accuracy of digital palpation for size assessment of the prostate evaluated by transrectal ultrasound. *Tohoku J Exp Med* 1988; 154:323–328.

57. Walsh PC: Benign prostatic hypertrophy, in Walsh PC, Gittes RF, Perlmutter AD, et al (eds): *Campbell's Urology,* 5th ed. Philadelphia, WB Saunders Company, 1986, pp 1248–1267.

58. Birch NC, Hurst G, Doyle PT: Serial residual volumes in men with prostatic hypertrophy. *J Urol* 1988; 62:571–575.

59. Stoller ML, Millard RJ: The accuracy of a catheterized residual urine. *J Urol* 1989; 141:15–16.

60. Isaacs JT, Coffey DS: Etiology and disease process of benign prostatic hyperplasia. *Prostate [Suppl]* 1989; 2:33–50.

61. Watanabe H: Natural history of benign prostatic hypertrophy. *Ultrasound Med Biol* 1986; 12:567–571.

62. Ohnishi K, Watanabe H, Ohe H: Development benign prostatic hypertrophy estimated from ultrasonic measurement with long-term follow-up. *Tohoku J Exp Med* 1987; 151:51–56.

63. Catalona WJ, Scott WW: Carcinoma of the prostate, in Walsh PC, Gittes RF, Perlmutter AD, et al (eds): *Campbell's Urology,* 5th ed. Philadelphia, WB Saunders Company, 1986, pp 1463–1534.

64. Clarke R: The prostate and the endocrines. A control series. *Br J Urol* 1937; 9:254–271.

65. Craigen AA, Hickling JB, Saunders CRG, et al: Natural history of prostatic hypertrophy. *Roy Coll Gen Pract* 1969; 18:226–232.

66. Ball AJ, Feneley RCL, Abrams PH: The natural history of untreated "prostatism". *Br J Urol* 1981; 53:613–616.

67. Birkoff JD, Wiederhorn AR, Hamilton ML, et al: Natural history of benign prostatic hypertrophy and acute urinary retention. *Urology* 1976; 6:48–52.

68. Castro JE, Griffiths HJL, Edwards DE: A double-blind, controlled, clinical trial of spironolactone for benign prostatic hypertrophy. *Br J Surg* 1971; 58:485–489.

69. Barry MJ, Mulley AG Jr, Fowler FJ, et al: Watchful waiting vs immediate transurethral resection for symptomatic prostatism. *JAMA* 1988; 259: 3010–3017.

70. Abrams PH: Prostatism and prostatectomy: The value of urine flow rate measurement in the preoperative assessment for operation. *J Urol* 1977; 117:70–71.

71. Jensen KM-E, Jorgensen JB, Morgensen P: Urodynamics in prostatism II: Prognostic values of pressure-flow study combined with stop-flow test. *Scand J Urol Nephrol Suppl* 1988; 114:72–77.

72. George NJR, Feneley RC, Roberts JBM: Identification of the poor risk patient with "prostatism" and detrusor failure. *Br J Urol* 1986; 58:290–295.

73. Coolsaet BLRA, van Venrooij GEPM, Blok C: Prostatism: Rationalization of urodynamic testing. *World J Urol* 1984; 2:216–221.

74. Chancellor MB, Griffiths DJ, Kaplan SA, et al: Bladder outlet obstruction and

impaired detrusor contractility: A blinded comparison of the videourodynamic diagnosis versus the diagnosis based on a detrusor contractility parameter (WF), a urethral resistance parameter (URA), and a sustain/fade index (SFI). *Neurourol Urodynam* 1990; 9:209–211.

75. Schafer W, Langen P-H, Thorner M: The real pressure/flow-relation during obstructed voiding. *Neurourol Urodynam* 1990; 9:423–425.

76. Kranse M, van Mastrigt R: Cross correlation of detrusor pressure and flow signals. *Neurourol Urodynam* 1990; 9:387–388.

77. Schafer W: Urethral resistance? Urodynamic concepts of physiological and pathological bladder outlet function during voiding. *Neurourol and Urodynam* 1985; 4:161–201.

78. Yalla SV, Sharma GVRK, Barsamian EM: Micturitional static urethral pressure profile: A method of recording urethral pressure profile during voiding and the implications. *J Urol* 1980; 124:649–656.

79. Desmond AD, Ramayya GR: Comparison of pressure/flow studies with micturitional urethral pressure profiles in the diagnosis of urinary outflow obstruction. *Br J Urol* 1988; 61:224–229.

80. Meyhoff HH, Gleason DM, Bottacini MR: The effects of transurethral resection on the urodynamics of prostatism. *J Urol* 1989; 142:785–789.

81. Spangberg A: Quantification of urethral function during micturition by pressure/flow measurement. Dissertation No. 310, Linkoping University, Linkoping, Sweden, 1990.

82. Siroky MB, Olsson CA, Krane RJ: The flow rate nomogram: I. Development. *J Urol* 1979; 122:665–668.

83. Haylen BT, Ashby D, Sutherst JR, et al: Maximum and average urine flow rates in normal male and female populations: The Liverpool nomograms. *Br J Urol* 1989; 64:30–38.

84. Marshall VR, Ryall RL, Austin ML, et al: The use of urinary flow rates obtained from voided volumes less than 150 ml in the assessment of voiding ability. *Br J Urol* 1983; 55:28–33.

85. Drach GW, Layton TN, Binard WJ: Male peak urinary flow rate: Relationships to volume voided and age. *J Urol* 1979; 122:210–214.

86. Jensen KM-E, Bruskewitz RC, Iversen P, et al: Abdominal straining in benign prostatic hyperplasia. *J Urol* 1983; 129:44–47.

87. Gerstenberg TC, Andersen JT, Klarskov P, et al: High flow infravesical obstruction in men: Symptomatology, urodynamics, and the results of surgery. *J Urol* 1982; 127:943–945.

88. Kadow C, Feneley RCL, Abrams PH: Prostatectomy or conservative management in the treatment of benign prostatic hypertrophy. *Br J Urol* 1988; 61:432–434.

89. Talner LB: Specific causes of obstruction, in Pollack HM (ed): *Clinical Urography*, vol 2. Philadelphia, WB Saunders Company, 1990, p 1629.

90. Abrams PH: Use of the intravenous urogram in diagnosis, in Hinman F Jr (ed): *Benign Prostatic Hypertrophy*. New York, Springer Publishing Company, 1983, pp 605–609.

91. Mushlin AI, Thornbury JR: Intravenous pyelography: The case against its routine use. *Ann Intern Med* 1989; 111:58–70.

92. Wasserman NF, Lapoint S, Eckman DR, et al: Assessment of prostatism: Role of intravenous urography. *Radiology* 1987; 165:831–835.

93. Webb JAW: Ultrasonography in the diagnosis of renal obstruction. Sensitive but not very specific. *Br Med J* 1990; 301:944–946.

94. Bauer DL, Garrison RW, McRoberts JW: The health cost implications of rou-

tine excretory urography before transurethral prostatectomy. *J Urol* 1980; 123:386–389.

95. Manoliu RA: Voiding cystourethrography with synchronous measurements of pressures and flow in the diagnosis of subvesical obstruction in men: A radiological view. *J Urol* 1987; 137:1196–1201.
96. McGuire E: Editorial comment. *J Urol* 1983; 129:1174.
97. Speakman MJ, Sethia KK, Fellows GJ, et al: A study of the pathogenesis, urodynamic assessment, and outcome of detrusor instability associated with bladder outflow obstruction. *Br J Urol* 1987; 57:40–44.
98. Reuther K, Aagaard J, Jensen KS: Lignocaine test and detrusor instability. *Br J Urol* 1983; 55:493–494.
99. Sethia KK, Smith JC: The effect of pH and lignocaine in detrusor instability. *Br J Urol* 1987; 60:516–518.
100. Kimche D, Saar M, Lask D: Evoked response studies in detrusor hyperreflexia due to infravesical obstruction in neurological patients. *J Urol* 1985; 133:641–643.
101. Staskin DS, Vardi Y, Siroky MB: Postprostatectomy continence in the Parkinsonian patient: The significance of poor voluntary sphincter control. *J Urol* 1988; 140:117–118.
102. Dorflinger T, England DM, Madsen PO, et al: Urodynamic and histological correlates of benign prostatic hypertrophy. *J Urol* 1988; 140:1487–1490.
103. Roos NP, Wennberg JE, Malenka DJ, et al: Mortality and recuperation after open and transurethral resection of the prostate for benign prostatic hyperplasia. *N Engl J Med* 1989; 320:1120–1124.
104. Greenfield S: The state of outcome research: Are we on target? *N Engl J Med* 1989; 320:1142–1143.
105. Lepor H: Role of alpha-adrenergic blockers in the treatment of benign prostatic hyperplasia. *Prostate [Suppl]* 1990; 3:75–84.
106. Caine M: The present role of alpha-adrenergic blockers in the treatment of benign prostatic hypertrophy. *J Urol* 1986; 136:1–4.
107. Lepor H: Nonoperative management of benign prostatic hypertrophy. *J Urol* 1989; 141:1283–1289.
108. Gabrilove JL, Levine AC, Kirschenbaum A, et al: Effect of a GNRH analogue (leuprolide) on benign prostatic hypertrophy. *J Clin Endocrinol Metab* 1987; 64:1331–1333.
109. Bosch RJH, Griffiths DJ, Blom JHM, et al: Treatment of benign prostatic hyperplasia by androgen deprivation: Effects on prostate size and urodynamic parameters. *J Urol* 1989; 141:68–72.
110. Keane PF, Timoney AG, Kiely E, et al: Response of the benign hypertrophied prostate to treatment with an LHRH agonist. *Br J Urol* 1988; 62:163–165.
111. Caine M, Perlberg S, Gordon R: The treatment of benign prostatic hypertrophy with flutamide (SCH 13521): A placebo-controlled study. *J Urol* 1975; 114:564–568.
112. Jensen KM-E, Madsen PO: Candicidin treatment of prostatism: A prospective double-blind placebo-controlled study. *Urol Res* 1983; 11:7–10.
113. Lidner A, Ramon J, Brooks ME: Controlled study of cimetidine in the treatment of benign prostatic hypertrophy. *Br J Urol* 1990; 66:55–57.
114. Van Poppel H, Boeckx G, Westelinck KJ, et al: The efficacy of bromocriptine in benign prostatic hypertrophy: A double-blind study. *Br J Urol* 1987; 60:150–152.

115. Carbin B-E, Larsson B, Lindahl O: Treatment of benign prostatic hyperplasia with phytosterols. Br J Urol 1990; 66:639–641.

116. Reece Smith H, Merrion A, Smart CJ, et al: The value of permixon in benign prostatic hypertrophy. Br J Urol 1986; 58:36–40.

117. Mansson W, Sundin T, Goldberg B: Evaluation of synthetic vasopressin analogue for treatment of nocturia in benign prostatic hypertrophy: A double-blind study. Scand J Urol Nephrol 1980; 14:139–141.

118. Nielsen HO: Transurethral prostatotomy versus transurethral prostatectomy in benign prostatic hypertrophy: A prospective randomized study. Br J Urol 1988; 61:435–438.

119. Hellstrom P, Lukkarinen O, Konturri M: Bladder neck incision or transurethral electrosection for the treatment of urinary obstruction caused by a small benign prostate? Scand J Urol Nephrol 1986; 20:187–197.

120. Larsen EH, Dorflinger T, Gasser TC, et al: Transurethral incision versus transurethral resection of the prostate for the treatment of benign prostatic hypertrophy. Scand J Urol Nephrol Suppl 1987; 140:83–86.

121. Loughlin KR, Yalla SV, Belldegrun A, et al: Transurethral incisions and resections under local anesthesia. Br J Urol 1987; 60:185.

122. Reddy PK: Role of balloon dilation in the treatment of benign prostatic hyperplasia. Prostate [Suppl]1990; 3:39–48.

123. Daughtry JD, Rodan BA, Bean WJ: Balloon dilation of prostatic urethra. Urology 1990; 36:203–209.

124. Vicente J, Salvador J, Chechile G: Spiral urethral prosthesis as an alternative to surgery in high risk patients with benign prostatic hyperplasia: Prospective study. J Urol 1989; 142:1504–1506.

125. Nordling J, Holm HH, Klarskov P, et al: The intraprostatic spiral: A new device for insertion with the patient under local anesthesia and with ultrasonic guidance with 3 months of follow-up. J Urol 1989; 142:756–758.

126. McLoughlin J, Williams G: Review: Alternatives to prostatectomy. Br J Urol 1990; 65:313–316.

127. Yerushalmi A, Fishelovitz Y, Singer D, et al: Localized deep microwave hyperthermia in the treatment of poor risk patients with benign prostatic hyperplasia. J Urol 1985; 133:873–876.

128. Servadio C, Lindner A, Lev A, et al: Further observations on the effect of local hyperthermia on benign enlargement of the prostate. World J Urol 1989; 6:204–208.

129. Strohmaier WL, Bichler KH, Fluchter SH, et al: Local microwave hyperthermia of benign prostatic hyperplasia. J Urol 1990; 144:913–917.

130. DuBeau CE, Resnick NM: Evaluation of the causes and severity of geriatric incontinence: A critical appraisal. Urol Clin North Am 1991; 18:243–256.

131. Resnick NM: Urinary incontinence—a treatable disorder, in Rowe JW, Besdine RW (eds); Geriatric Medicine. Boston, Little, Brown & Company, 1988, pp 246–265.

132. Resnick NM, Yalla SV: Management of urinary incontinence in the elderly. N Engl J Med 1985; 313:800–805.

133. Neal DE, Styles RA, Powell PH, et al: Relationship between detrusor function and residual urine in men undergoing prostatectomy. Br J Urol 1987; 60:560–566.

134. Burgio KL, Engel BT: Biofeedback-assisted behavioral training for elderly men and women. J Am Geriat Soc 1990; 38:338–340.

135. Root MT: Living with benign prostatic hypertrophy. N Engl J Med 1979; 301:52.

136. Libman E, Fichten CS: Prostatectomy and sexual function. *Urology* 1987; 29:467–478.
137. Faltermayer E: Medical care's next revolution. *Fortune* 1988; pp:126–133.
138. Barry MJ: Medical outcomes research and benign prostatic hyperplasia. *Prostate [Suppl]* 1990; 3:61–74.
139. Catalona WJ, Smith DS, Ratliff TL, et al: Measurement of prostate-specific antigen in serum as a screening test for prostate cancer. *N Engl J Med* 1991; 324:1156–1161.

# Progressive Renal Insufficiency: The Role of Angiotensin Converting Enzyme Inhibitors

## Susan Savage, M.D.

Assistant Professor, Department of Medicine, University of Colorado School of Medicine, Denver, Colorado

## Robert W. Schrier, M.D.

Professor and Chairman, Department of Medicine, University of Colorado School of Medicine, Denver, Colorado

### Editor's Introduction

Drs. Savage and Schrier outline the various factors which are involved in the pathogenesis of renal injury. They point out that intrarenal hemodynamic factors (such as intraglomerular capillary pressure) may interact with other conditions such as systemic hypertension, single nephron hypermetabolism, and cell proliferation, leading eventually to destruction of a critical mass of kidney tissue which, in turn, results in an inexorable progression to end-stage renal disease.

This paper emphasizes that experimental animal studies demonstrate that ACE-inhibition therapy offers renal protection in diabetes mellitus and the remnant kidney model of chronic renal failure. In addition, the authors point out that there is preliminary clinical evidence that ACE-inhibition may slow the decline of glomerular function in progressive renal insufficiency of many etiologies including diabetes in humans.

The putative mechanisms seems to be the effect of ACE inhibition on intraglomerular capillary pressure; nevertheless, the authors point out that the jury will remain out on these issues until the results of prospective clinical trials are available.

*James J. Leonard, M.D.*

In efforts to delay the progression of renal insufficiency and eventual end-stage renal disease (ESRD), several pharmacologic agents have been utilized in a variety of renal diseases. In this regard, hypertension in the presence of renal insufficiency is known to accelerate the decline to renal failure.[1] Thus, attenuation of hypertension by pharmacologic measures presumably should result in the delay in and possible prevention of ESRD. This hypothesis is supported by several animal studies in which urinary albumin excretion has been decreased and the development of ESRD has been delayed with antihypertensive therapy.[2-4]

It has been suggested, however, that increases in intraglomerular capillary pressure may be more important in potentiating the progression of renal insufficiency than increases in systemic arterial pressure.[5-7] Therefore, angiotensin converting enzyme (ACE) inhibitors, which have been found to have unique effects in lowering intraglomerular capillary pressures, may provide renal protective effects in addition to adequately treating the systemic hypertension associated with renal disease. Although several human clinical studies of short duration involving small numbers of patients support this theory,[8-19] there have been no large, randomized, double-blind clinical trials to compare the renal protective effects of ACE inhibitors to those of conventional antihypertensive agents. Moreover, in addition to ameliorating the role of renal hemodynamics in glomerular injury, ACE inhibitors, as well as other pharmacologic agents, may influence additional mechanisms of renal damage.

## Factors Involved in the Pathogenesis of Renal Injury

### Intraglomerular Capillary Hypertension

Several animal studies have demonstrated that extensive renal ablation leads to progressive glomerular damage and eventual renal failure.[5, 20] These animal models of chronic renal failure generally lead to systemic hypertension, a marked increase in single nephron glomerular filtration rate and renal plasma flow in the residual nephrons, and intraglomerular capillary hypertension.[6, 21, 22] As already noted, several studies in experimental models have attempted to demonstrate that intraglomerular capillary hypertension may be more important than systemic hypertension in promoting the progression of glomerular injury.[7, 21] Purkerson et al. demonstrated that hypertensive rats with minimal renal ablation did not develop glomerular structural damage, while rats with extensive ablation and comparable levels of hypertension developed a significant amount of glomerular damage.[20] These findings have led many investigators to suggest that the progression of renal failure is relentless once a critical mass of functioning renal tissue is lost and glomerular capillary hypertension occurs.[21, 23-25]

Not all observations, however, support the theory that intraglomerular hypertension is the sole cause of glomerulosclerosis and progressive renal insufficiency. Clinical studies of long-standing hyperfiltration on kidney function in 29 subjects with one kidney, 3 of whom had insulin-dependent diabetes, did not demonstrate any detectable harmful effects on kidney function.[26] Long-term studies of kidney donors, in spite of calculated increased single nephron glomerular filtration rates, also have not demonstrated renal insufficiency in the remaining kidney.[27-30] These clinical observations are supported by animal studies in which glomerular sclerotic changes were induced with doxorubicin in the absence of increased intraglomerular capillary pressures.[30] Thus, other mechanisms, in addition to glomerular capillary hypertension, also must be involved in the progression of renal disease.

## Other Potential Factors Involved in Progressive Renal Injury

**Growth Factors and Mesangial Cell Proliferation.**—In several animal models of glomerulosclerosis, glomerular hypertrophy occurs as the earliest histologic change.[31] This observation has been made in some clinical circumstances as well, especially with diabetic nephropathy, as the mesangial cells increase in number and the mesangial matrix expands. The role that mesangial expansion plays in the pathogenesis of progressive renal insufficiency, however, is not yet defined, even though it may precede the development of glomerulosclerosis.

Numerous growth factors may be involved in the process of glomerular mesangial expansion, including platelet-derived growth factor,[32] angiotensin II, and interleukin-1.[31] Moreover, heparin may inhibit mesangial cell growth and proliferation directly, independent of its anticoagulant effects.[33] In this regard, heparin has been shown to reduce glomerulosclerosis without affecting renal hemodynamics in the renal ablation model of chronic renal failure.[34] The mechanism involved in the antiproliferative and protective effect of heparin is unknown at this time.[35]

**Hypermetabolism.**—In the renal ablation model of chronic renal failure, net sodium reabsorption and oxygen consumption are increased per single nephron.[36] The increase in nephron oxygen consumption appears to be due to both increased tubular sodium transport and nonsodium transport pathways. With oxygen consumption increased as much as threefold in the remnant kidney model of experimental renal disease, the enhanced formation of oxygen radicals potentially could lead to renal tissue damage.

Phosphate depletion has been shown to prevent progressive renal failure[36, 37] independent of protein intake.[38] The mechanism of this protective effect may include diminished cellular accumulation of calcium[37] and attenuation of the lipid abnormalities associated with uremia[38]; however, a reduction in cellular energy metabolism occurs also.[36]

Chronic administration of verapamil exerts a protective effect on the remnant kidney, as nephrocalcinosis and ultrastructural abnormalities are decreased.[39] This effect of verapamil to attenuate the deterioration of renal function occurs without an observable effect on proteinuria and act independently of its effects on blood pressure. The protective effect of verapamil in the renal ablation model also has been associated with diminished oxygen consumption per nephron.[36] In addition, hypothyroidism has been shown to protect against the progression of experimental renal failure, thus providing further support for a pathogenic role of nephron hypermetabolism.[40]

**Hyperlipidemia.**—Hyperlipidemia, which almost invariably accompanies the various causes of renal insufficiency, may contribute to progressive renal decline.[41] Several animal studies have demonstrated beneficial effects of lipid-lowering therapy on reducing proteinuria and ameliorating the progression of glomerulosclerosis. In the remnant kidney model, clofibric acid and mevinolin were found to increase insulin clearance and reduce urinary albumin excretion.[42] These agents later were used in the obese Zucker rat, a model of type II diabetes mellitus and hyperlipidemia, and a reduction in urinary albumin excretion was accompanied by a much lower incidence of focal glomerulosclerosis compared to control Zucker rats.[43] These agents did not decrease systemic arterial or intraglomerular capillary pressures in either study. The exact mechanism by which hyperlipidemia contributes to progressive renal decline is unknown, but it is possible that mesangial deposition of cholesterol may stimulate mesangial cell growth, similar to the proposed effect of cholesterol on vascular smooth muscle proliferation in atherosclerosis.[44] In addition to its role in glomerular damage, hyperlipidemia also has been incriminated as a pathogenetic factor in the tubulointerstitial changes associated with the remnant of kidney model of chronic renal failure.[45] Hyperlipidemia may also contribute to platelet and coagulation disorders and thereby contribute to glomerular injury.

**High-Protein Feeding.**—High-protein dietary feeding may contribute to the progression of renal failure, and there have been several animal and human studies to support this observation.[46–49] Restricted protein diets prevent glomerulosclerosis in rats with remnant kidneys[50] and, in human studies, the decline of renal function among persons with various causes of renal insufficiency, including diabetic nephropathy,[51] has been retarded with low-protein diets.[52] Restricted protein feeding is known to decrease nephron hyperfiltration and intraglomerular capillary pressures,[49] in addition to serum lipid levels.[53] Protein restriction also is known to decrease nephron oxygen consumption.[54] In a morphological study by Klenner and associates,[55] the effect of protein restriction on increased survival in rats with remnant kidney was associated with a much greater protection against tubulointerstitial than glomerular abnormalities.

**Systemic Hypertension.**—Systemic hypertension may contribute to the progression of renal failure, at least in part, by increasing intraglomerular capillary pressures, particularly in the setting of renal vasodilation, as occurs with protein feeding, nephron loss, and diabetes. In addition, hypertension may contribute to glomerular damage by increasing the leakage of macromolecules into the mesangium, which then may stimulate mesangial matrix synthesis and mesangial cell proliferation.[56] Hypertension is reported to account for 30% of all ESRD in the United States, and in the black and Hispanic population, it accounts for even more. The effect of hypertension to cause nephrosclerosis appears to be increased in the black population.[57] Overall, however, renal failure secondary to hypertension generally is associated with one or more periods of uncontrolled, accelerated hypertension.

In animal models, increased microvascular pressures lead to vascular hypertrophy and hyperplasia, with eventual vessel occlusion.[58] This phenomenon, known as vascular rarefaction, may result in glomerular ischemia and the histopathologic changes of glomerulosclerosis. It has been proposed that as nephrons are lost in all varieties of renal disease, afferent arteriolar vasodilation occurs and exposes the glomerular capillary to high pressures. The early loss of renal autoregulation in association with the hyperglycemia of diabetes also may contribute to glomerular capillary hypertension.

In summary, many pathogenic factors most likely contribute to progressive renal disease. Intrarenal hemodynamic factors may interact with a complex assortment of other abnormalities, including systemic hypertension, single nephron hypermetabolism, hyperlipidemia, coagulation disorders, growth factors and cellular proliferation, which collectively promote the relentless course of renal functional decline. Once a critical mass of renal tissue is destroyed, irrespective of the initial insult, renal disease progresses to ESRD with a variety of etiologic events. Multiple mechanisms result in the common findings of focal glomerulosclerosis[21, 59] and tubulointerstitial lesions.[38, 55, 60, 61] In attempts to prevent and/or ameliorate the progression to ESRD, several therapeutic strategies have been utilized in various models of renal disease, including the remnant kidney model and the diabetic nephropathy model. These results in experimental renal diseases, and preliminarily in clinical studies, are encouraging. The remainder of this article will focus on the potential role of ACE inhibitors in preventing the progression of chronic renal failure.

## Angiotensin Converting Enzyme Inhibition in Experimental Renal Disease

ACE inhibitors prevent the conversion of angiotensin I to the potent vasoconstrictor angiotensin II. Angiotensin II preferentially constricts the efferent glomerular capillary arteriole and results in increased glomerular capillary hydraulic pressures. Micropuncture studies have demonstrated that ACE inhibition reduces both systemic blood pressure and glomerular capillary hydraulic pressure in the renal ablation model[2, 3] and the streptozotocin-induced diabetes rat model.[4] This effect of ACE inhibitors occurs without a fall in either glomerular plasma flow or filtration. In a study by Zatz et al., rats with streptozotocin-induced diabetes exhibited significant elevations in mean glomerular capillary hydralic pressure, progressive proteinuria, and a high incidence of glomerular structural abnormalities, including mesangial expansion and segmental sclerosis. These changes were virtually normalized by ACE treatment.[4]

In another study, by Anderson et al. when ACE-treated, nondiabetic, remnant kidney rats were compared to a group of animals receiving triple antihypertensive therapy (reserpine, hydralazine, and hydrochlorothiazide), the latter animals demonstrated persistently elevated glomerular capillary hydraulic pressures despite systemic blood pressures equivalent to the

ACE-treated animals. The triple-therapy rats developed progressive proteinuria and glomerular lesions comparable to the untreated group.[3] The conclusion of this study was that the correction of systemic blood pressure alone was insufficient to prevent progressive glomerular damage, and that glomerular capillary hypertension must be reduced with ACE inhibition to prevent progressive renal injury.

Recently, it has been proposed that ACE inhibitors may prevent pathogenic mechanisms of renal damage by some means other than correction of glomerular hemodynamic abnormalities. In an experimental model of nephrotic syndrome induced by the aminonucleoside puromycin, reduction of glomerular injury by the ACE inhibitor captopril occurred without a decrease in glomerular capillary pressure.[62] It has been proposed that angiotensin II may act as a growth factor for glomerular and mesangial cells and thus promote renal injury.[63] It is possible that ACE inhibitors may interfere with this process.

In contrast to the animal studies that substantiate the evidence for the renal protective effects of ACE inhibitors, the results using other antihypertensive agents have been variable. Verapamil, independent of its effects on systemic blood pressure, has been shown to reduce the transcapillary glomerular pressure gradient slightly,[64] and to reduce glomerular and tubular injury in rats with renal ablation.[60] In a preliminary study, a long-acting calcium channel blocker, amipamil, has been shown to decrease the progression of renal failure by both its antihypertensive and its cytoprotective effects.[65] Some investigators have found, however, that calcium channel blockers may not prevent progressive renal damage.[66, 67]

## Clinical Studies Using Angiotensin Converting Enzyme Inhibitors in Patients With Renal Disease

The results in experimental animals supporting the benefits of ACE inhibitors in chronic renal disease have galvanized a host of clinical studies using these agents in a variety of progressive renal disorders in human subjects. Nowhere has this been investigated more extensively than in patients with diabetic nephropathy. ACE therapy has been used in hypertensive and normotensive subjects with diabetes and in those with other underlying causes of chronic renal disease. Although the preliminary results are promising, it must be emphasized that these studies frequently are uncontrolled and involve small numbers of patients studied for short durations of time. To date, no large, prospective, randomized, controlled trials have been completed to compare ACE inhibitors to other antihypertensive agents.

## ACE Inhibition in Diabetic Nephropathy

Among type I diabetic patients, 40% eventually will develop diabetic nephropathy.[68] In type I diabetes, the occurrence of glomerular hyperfiltration with a supranormal glomerular filtration rate[69] may precede the urinary excretion of microalbumin (30–300 mg/24hrs), which is followed by increases in systemic blood pressure.[70] Without intervention, patients with microalbuminuria may develop increases in blood pressure averaging 3 to 4 mm of Hg per year.[71] Glomerular hyperfiltration and microalbuminuria may be reversible with strict metabolic control,[72, 73] but once clinical proteinuria (>500 mg/24 hr) develops, optimized insulin treatment generally produces no significant effects.[74]

In type I diabetes patients, hypertension is usually the result of underlying renal disease. Among type I diabetic patients without renal disease, the prevalence of hypertension is similar to that of the general population.[75] If hypertension is present, patients are at a significantly higher risk of dying from renal and coronary heart disease.[76] In type I patients with long survival, diastolic blood pressure is almost universally low.[77]

Hypertension among type II (non–insulin-dependent) diabetics is much more prevalent, and has been noted to be as high as 57% at the time diabetes is diagnosed.[78] The etiology of hypertension associated with type I and type II diabetes may be different. Increased plasma insulin levels have been proposed as significant in the pathogenesis of hypertension, but the mechanism for such an effect is unknown.[79] Microalbuminuria is much more prevalent among type II patients, and is reported to be as high as 50%.[80] Unlike the situation in type I diabetes, the significance of microalbuminuria among type II patients may be more predictive of cardiovascular mortality than of the development of ESRD.[81]

Irrespective of the etiology of hypertension, its presence probably confers significant risks for the development and progression of renal disease,[82] retinopathy,[83] and cardiovascular disease[84] among all diabetic patients. However, all of the large, controlled clinical trials evaluating the effects of antihypertensive treatment on cardiovascular morbidity and mortality have excluded diabetics. Therefore, it is not possible at this time to determine definitively to what degree antihypertensive therapy will benefit the vascular complications of diabetes mellitus. Nevertheless, given the evidence in the nondiabetic population and the risks associated with hypertension in the diabetic population, it is reasonable to assume that antihypertensive therapy may be of considerable benefit.

Early studies using conventional antihypertensive therapy demonstrated that the progression of diabetic nephropathy could be slowed with adequate treatment of hypertension.[82, 85] Subsequently, the ACE inhibitor captopril was found to decrease proteinuria significantly in a small group of azotemic diabetic patients, independent of blood pressure.[8] Several short-term clinical studies using ACE inhibitors in the treatment of diabetic nephropathy and hypertension have been undertaken; the results are summarized in Table 1.

With the exception of the Taguma study,[8] ACE inhibition therapy universally results in reduction of the systemic blood pressure among diabetic subjects. Even in the three investigations evaluating the effects of ACE therapy on diabetic nephropathy among normotensive diabetic patients, systemic blood pressure was reduced significantly from baseline values.[9–11] In most

**TABLE 1.**
**Summary of Effects of Angiotensin Converting Enzyme Inhibitors in Diabetes Mellitus***

| Study | Year | Number of Patients | Duration of Therapy (mo) | Blood Pressure | Albuminuria | Baseline Hypertension | Controls | Renal Insufficiency Present |
|---|---|---|---|---|---|---|---|---|
| Taguma et al.[8] | 1985 | 10 | 2 | ↔ | → | + | − | + |
| Hommel et al.[14] | 1986 | 16 | 3 | → | → | + | + | − |
| Björck et al.[12] | 1986 | 14 | 24 | → | ↔ | + | − | + |
| Marre[9] | 1987 | 10 | 6 | → | → | − | + | − |
| Parving[13] | 1988 | 18 | 30 | → | → | + | + | − |
| Valvo[86] | 1988 | 12 | 6 | → | ↔ | + | − | + |
| Mimran[10] | 1988 | 22 | 18 | → | → | + | + | − |
| Parving[11] | 1989 | 32 | 12 | → | → | − | + | − |

* ↓ = decreased; ↔ = no change; + = present; − = absent.

studies that measured urinary albumin excretion, there was a notable decrease in blood pressure, with the exception of the studies by Bjorck[12] and Valvo,[86] which evaluated only type II diabetic patients.

Several studies have examined the rate of decline in the glomerular filtration rate in diabetic patients receiving ACE inhibitors. In a prospective study of 14 type I patients, the deterioration of the glomerular filtration rate was slowed significantly by the administration of captopril.[12] Although reductions in systemic blood pressure were noted, with a mean arterial blood pressure decrease of 5 mm of Hg, there was no significant correlation between the fall in blood pressure and the reduction in the deterioration of the glomerular filtration rate.[12] Parving[13] noted that captopril significantly diminished the rate of decline of the glomerular filtration rate among a group of 18 hypertensive diabetic patients compared to a hypertensive diabetic control group that received no therapy. Contrary to the results noted by Björk et al.,[12] the rate of fall in glomerular filtration rate and mean arterial blood pressure were significantly correlated.

Several investigators have completed prospective studies of ACE inhibition on kidney function in normotensive diabetic subjects. In one prospective study of such patients with persistent microalbuminuria (30 to 300 mg/24 hr), patients matched for weight, diet, glycosylated hemoglobin, and median microalbumin excretion were randomized to receive either the ACE inhibitor enalapril or placebo. After 6 months of follow-up, the glomerular filtration rate rose and the median microalbumin excretion rate fell in the enalapril-treated group; both continued to rise in the placebo control group. In addition, the mean arterial pressure fell in the enalapril group (mean 10 mm of Hg) and rose in the placebo group.[9] At 12 months of follow-up in the same study, three of the ten participants receiving placebo went on to develop frank proteinuria (albumin > 300 mg/24 hr). None of the ten patients receiving enalapril developed frank proteinuria, and five reverted their urinary albumin excretion back to normal (<30 mg/24 hr). There also was a significant relationship between the increase in mean arterial pressure and the increase in albumin excretion in the placebo group.[87] Parving et al.[11] reported similar results in a 12-month follow-up study of 32 type I diabetes patients. In this trial, a reduction in the mean arterial blood pressure and a decline in the rate of glomerular filtration rate loss occurred in patients treated with captopril compared to those who received placebo.

Thus, many of the results initially found in animal studies now have been reproduced in clinical human studies. The assumption that the primary effect of ACE inhibition is to decrease glomerular capillary hydraulic pressure in general has been applied to the interpretation of human clinical results. However, since it is impossible to perform micropuncture studies in humans, it is difficult to differentiate the effects of ACE inhibition in lowering systemic blood pressure from its unique effects on glomerular hemodynamics observed in experimental animal models. The possibility also exists that diabetic complications can benefit simply by lowering blood pressure, independent of the specific antihypertensive agent used to do so. Several small studies with few patients and short periods of follow-up comparing

TABLE 2.
Summary of the Effects of Angiotensin Converting Enzyme Inhibitors in Chronic Renal Diseases Other Than Diabetes Mellitus*

| Study | Year | Number of Patients | Duration of Therapy (mo) | Blood Pressure | Albuminuria | Baseline Hypertension | Controls | Renal Insufficiency Present |
|---|---|---|---|---|---|---|---|---|
| Heeg[16] | 1987 | 13 | 3 | → | → | + | + | + |
| Bauer[15] | 1987 | 23 | 36 | → | ↕ | + | – | + |
| Reams[17] | 1986 | 9 | 1 | → | → | + | – | + |
| Abraham[18] | 1988 | 7 | >6 | → | → | + | – | + |
| Ruilope[90] | 1989 | 10 | 12 | → | ↕ | + | – | + |
| Lagrue[19] | 1987 | 18 | 18 | → | → | + | – | + |

* ↓ = decreased; ↔ = no change; + = present; – = absent.

ACE inhibitors to calcium channel blockers have been performed, with conflicting results.[10, 88, 89]

Thus, at present, it is not possible to determine if the beneficial renal effects of ACE inhibitors in diabetic nephropathy are attributable to unique alterations in renal hemodynamics, a reduction in systemic blood pressure, or a combination thereof. A large, randomized, double-blind, prospective trial comparing the effects of ACE inhibitors to the effects of other conventional antihypertensive agents must be performed in order to answer this important question.

## Angiotensin Converting Enzyme Inhibitors in Other Chronic Renal Diseases

In addition to diabetic nephropathy, ACE inhibitors have been used to treat the hypertension and proteinuria associated with chronic renal disease of other causes. These studies have evaluated primarily hypertensive patients, and most have noted significant reductions in albuminuria (Table 2). A long-term study by Bauer revealed that patients initially treated with triple therapy consisting of propranolol, furosemide, and hydralazine stabilized the decline of their glomerular filtration rates when they were crossed over to receive captopril.[15]

Unfortunately, nearly all of the studies evaluating the effects of ACE inhibitors in chronic renal disease suffer from small sample sizes, short durations of follow-up, and lack of controls. Akin to the shortcomings of the clinical studies in diabetic nephropathy, a large, prospective, randomized clinical trial comparing ACE inhibitors to other antihypertensive agents must be performed before adequate conclusions can be reached concerning any unique renal protective effects of ACE inhibitors in chronic renal disease.

## The Use of Angiotensin Converting Enzyme Inhibitors in Clinical Practice

There currently are two generations of ACE inhibitors marketed in the United States. Captopril, usually prescribed as a thrice daily drug, now has been joined by the two most frequently prescribed once-a-day, second-generation ACE inhibitors, enalapril and lisinopril. Other ACE inhibitors are also currently under study by several pharmaceutical companies. All ACE inhibitors decrease total peripheral vascular resistance by blocking angiotensin II and by potentiating bradykinin. The second-generation ACE inhibitors have eliminated the sulfhydryl moiety to which some of the side effects of the first-generation agents have been attributed.[91] In addition to decreasing circulating angiotensin II, ACE inhibition may have direct effects on vascular and arterial central nervous system sites.

In the treatment of hypertension associated with diabetes mellitus and chronic renal disease of various causes, ACE inhibitors have advantages over other antihypertensive agents for several reasons. As discussed earlier, in addition to lowering systemic pressure, ACE inhibitors may offer beneficial renal protective effects. Unlike the β-blockers and diuretics that increase serum cholesterol levels, ACE inhibitors have no effect on lipid metabolism. This may be of particular importance, since hypercholesterolemia and increased rates of atherosclerosis substantially contribute to the high morbidity and mortality of cardiovascular disease in patients with diabetic and other forms of nephropathy. β-Adrenergic blockers also decrease insulin release and delay recovery from hypoglycemic episodes. Diuretic agents are associated with an increased incidence of orthostatic hypotension and hyperglycemia. Potassium-sparing diuretics and β-adrenergic blockers may cause hyperkalemia, particularly in patients who have early renal disease with a subclinical hyporenin-hypoaldosterone syndrome, but this is also true with ACE inhibition. ACE inhibitors actually enhance insulin sensitivity, which is of benefit in insulin-resistant type II diabetic patients.[92-94] In comparison with sympatholytic antihypertensive agents, ACE inhibitors may be preferable, since they do not cause male impotence or orthostatic hypotension unless they are given in combination with diuretics.

In spite of their low–side-effect profile, there are circumstances in which ACE inhibitors should be used with caution. Hypotension with ACE inhibition occurs most frequently in hypovolemic states and conditions resulting in high renin states (e.g., congestive heart failure and cirrhosis). Acute renal insufficiency occurs with ACE treatment in patients with bilateral renal artery stenosis or stenosis in a solitary functioning kidney. This effect is probably secondary to dilation of the efferent arteriole, with a resultant decrease in glomerular pressure.[95] Usually, this azotemia is reversible with discontinuation of the ACE agent. Thus, when initiating ACE therapy, renal function should be monitored closely in high-risk patients with diffuse atherosclerosis and/or a single kidney.[96] Hyperkalemia with ACE inhibition occurs most often in the setting of severe sodium restriction, advanced renal failure, congestive heart failure, diabetes mellitus, and concomitant administration of potassium-sparing diuretics, potassium supplements, or nonsteroidal anti-inflammatory agents. Other infrequent side effects include a dry cough, increased potentiation of bradykinin, and rarely, but potentially fatal, angioedema.[97]

## Summary

Experimental animal studies have demonstrated a renal protective effect of ACE inhibition therapy in diabetes mellitus and the remnant kidney model of chronic renal failure. The mechanism of this effect is secondary, at least in part, to the drugs' effects on glomerular hemodynamics. In addition, there is further evidence to suggest that ACE inhibitors may influence other pathogenic mechanisms of progressive renal insufficiency. Preliminary data in clinical studies suggest that ACE inhibition therapy decreases proteinuria and may ameliorate the decline of the glomerular filtration rate in diabetic nephropathy and progressive renal insufficiency of other etiologies. However, before this conclusion can be definite, a large, prospective, randomized clinical trial is required to compare ACE inhibitors to conventional antihypertensive agents. Since calcium channel blockers are metabolically neutral in that they do not increase serum cholesterol or glucose levels and generally do not cause orthostatic hypotension, they may be ideal agents for such a comparison study.

## References

1. Baldwin DS, Neugarten J: Blood pressure control and progression of renal insufficiency, in Mitch WE, Brenner BM, Stein JH (eds): *Contemporary Issues in Nephrology*, vol 13. New York, Churchill Livingston, Inc, 1986, pp 81–110.
2. Anderson S, Meyer TW, Rennke HG, et al: Control of glomerular hypertension limits glomerular injury in rats with reduced renal mass. *J Clin Invest* 1985; 76:612–619.
3. Anderson S, Rennke HG, Brenner BM: Therapeutic advantage of converting enzyme inhibitors in arresting progressive renal disease associated with systemic hypertension in the rat. *J Clin Invest* 1986; 77:1993–2000.
4. Zatz RB, Dunn R, Meyer TW, et al: Prevention of diabetic glomerulopathy by pharmacological amelioration of glomerular capillary hypertension. *J Clin Invest* 1986; 77:1925–1930.
5. Anderson ST, Weber TW, Reunluard HG, et al: Control of glomerular hypertension limits glomerular injury in rats with reduced renal mass. *J Clin Invest* 1985; 76:612–619.
6. Meyer TW, Anderson S, Rennke HG, et al: Reversing glomerular hypertension stabilizes established glomerular injury. *Kidney Int* 1987; 31:752–759.
7. Anderson S, Diamond JR, Karnovsky MJ, et al: Mechanisms underlying transition from acute glomerular injury to glomerulosclerosis in a rat model of nephrotic syndrome. *J Clin Invest* 1988; 82:1757–1768.
8. Taguma Y, Kitamoto Y, Futaki G, et al: Effect of captopril on heavy proteinuria in azotemic diabetes. *N Engl J Med* 1985; 313:1617–1620.
9. Marre M, Leblanc H, Suarez L, et al: Converting enzyme inhibition and kidney function in normotensive diabetic patients with persistent proteinuria. *Br Med J [Clin Res]* 1987; 294:1448–1452.
10. Mimran A, Insua A, Ribstein J, et al: Comparative effect of captopril and nifedipine in normotensive patients with incipient diabetic nephropathy. *Diabetes Care* 1988; 11:850–853.
11. Parving HH, Hommel E, Nielsen MD, et al: Effect of captopril on blood pressure and kidney function in normotensive insulin dependent diabetics with nephropathy. *Br Med J [Clin Res]* 1989; 299:533–536.
12. Björk S, Nyberg G, Mulec H, et al: Beneficial effects of angiotensin converting enzyme inhibition on renal function in patients with diabetic nephropathy. *Br Med J [Clin Res]* 1986; 293:467–470.
13. Parving HH, Hommel E, Smidt UM: Protection of kidney function and decrease in albuminuria by captopril in insulin dependent diabetics with nephropathy. *Br Med J [Clin Res]* 1988; 297:1086–1091.
14. Hommel E, Parving HH, Mathiesen E, et al: Effect of captopril on kidney function in insulin dependent diabetic patients with nephropathy. *Br Med J [Clin Res]* 1986; 293:467–470.

15. Bauer JH, Reams GP, Lal SM: Renal protective effect of strict blood pressure control with enalapril therapy. Arch Intern Med 1987; 147:1397–1400.
16. Heeg JE, DeJong PE, Gjalt K, et al: Reduction of proteinuria by angiotensin converting enzyme inhibition. Kidney Int 1987; 32:78–83.
17. Reams G, Bauer JH: Effect of enalapril in subjects¹ with hypertension associated with moderate to severe renal dysfunction. Arch Intern Med 1986; 146:2145–2148.
18. Abraham PH, Opsahl JA, Keane WF, et al: Efficacy and renal effects of enalapril therapy for hypertensive patients with chronic renal insufficiency. Arch Intern Med 1988; 148:2358–2362.
19. Lagrue G, Laurent RJ: Antiproteinuric effect of captopril in primary glomerular disease. Nephron 1987; 46:99–100.
20. Purkerson ML, Hoffstenand PE, Klahr S: Pathogenesis of the glomerulopathy associated with renal infection in rats. Kidney Int 1976; 9:407–417.
21. Hostetter TH, Olson JL, Brenner BM: Hyperfiltration in remnant nephrons, a potentially adverse response to renal ablation. Am J Physiol 1981; 241:F85–F93.
22. Deen WM, Maddox DA, Robinson CR, et al: Dynamics of glomerular ultrafiltration in the rat. VII: Response to reduced renal mass. Am J Physiol 1974; 227:556–562.
23. Azar S, Johnson MA, Hertel B, et al: Single nephron pressures, flows and resistances in hypertensive kidneys and nephrosclerosis. Kidney Int 1977; 12:28–40.
24. Cameron JS: Glomerulonephritis: Current problems and understanding. J Lab Clin Med 1982; 9:755–787.
25. Mitch WE, Waber M, Buffington UA, et al: A simple method for estimating progression of chronic renal failure. Lancet 1976; 4:1326–1328.
26. Schmitz A, Christensen CK, Christensen T, et al: No microalbuminuria or other adverse effects of long standing hyperfiltration in humans with one kidney. Am J Kidney Dis 1989; 13:131–136.
27. Hahim RM, Goldszer RC, Brenner BM: Hypertension and proteinuria: Long term sequelae of uninephrectomy in humans. Kidney Int 1984; 25:930–936.
28. Weiland D, Sutherland DM, Chavers B, et al: Information on 628 living-related donors at a single institution with long-term follow-up in 472 cases. Transplant Proc 1984; 16:5–7.
29. Vincenti F, Amend WJ, Haysen G: Long-term renal function in kidney donors. Sustained compensatory hyperfiltration with no adverse effects. Transplantation 1983; 36:626–629.
30. Fogo A, Yoshida Y, Glick AD, et al: Serial micropuncture analysis of glomerular function in two rat models of glomerulosclerosis. J Clin Invest 1991; 87:476–481.
31. Klahr S, Schreiner G, Ichikawa I: The progression of renal disease. N Engl J Med 1988; 318:1657–1666.
32. Williams LT: Stimulation of paracrine and autocrine pathways of cell proliferation by platelet-derived growth factor. Clin Res 1988; 36:97–145.
33. Castellot JJ Jr, Hoover RL, Harper PA, et al: Heparin and glomerular epithelial cell-secreted heparin like species inhibit mesangial-cell proliferation. Am J Pathol 1985; 120:427–435.
34. Ichikawa I, Yoshida Y, Fogo A, et al: Effect of heparin on the glomerular structure and function of remnant nephrons. Kidney Int 1988; 34:638–644.
35. Purkerson ML, Tollefsen DM, Klahr S: N-desulfated/acetylated heparin ame-

liorates the progression of renal disease in rats with subtotal renal ablation. *J Clin Invest* 1988; 81:69–74.

36. Harris DC, Chan L, Schrier RW: Remnant kidney hypermetabolism and progression of chronic renal failure. *Am J Physiol* 1988; 245:F267–F276.
37. Ibel LS, Alfrey AC, Hart L, et al: Preservation of function in experimental renal disease by dietary phosphate restriction. *N Engl J Med* 1978; 298:122–126.
38. Lumtertgul D, Burke TJ, Gillim DM, et al: Phosphate depletion arrests progression of chronic renal failure independent of protein intake. *Kidney Int* 1986; 29:658–666.
39. Harris DC, Hammond WS, Burke TJ, et al: Verapamil protects against progression of experimental chronic renal failure. *Kidney Int* 1987; 31:41–46.
40. Tomford RC, Karlinsky ML, Buddington B, et al: Effect of thyroparathyroidectomy and parathyroidectomy on renal function and nephrotic syndrome in rat nephrotoxic serum nephritis. *J Clin Invest* 1981; 68:655–664.
41. Chan MK, Varghese Z, Moorhead JF: Lipid abnormalities in uremia, dialysis and transplantation. *Kidney Int* 1987; 19:625–637.
42. Kasiske BL, O'Donnell MP, Garvis WJ, et al: Pharmacologic treatment of hyperlipidemia reduces glomerular injury in rat 5/6 nephrectomy model of chronic renal failure. *Circ Res* 1988; 66:367–374.
43. Kasiske BL, O'Donnell M, Cleary MP, et al: Treatment of hyperlipidemia reduces glomerular injury in obese Zucker rats. *Kidney Int* 1988; 33:667–672.
44. Ross R: The pathogenesis of atherosclerosis—an update. *N Engl J Med* 1986; 318:488–500.
45. Moorhead JF, Chan MK, Barghese Z: The role of abnormalities of lipid metabolism in progression of renal disease, in Mitch WG, Brenner BM, Stein JH (eds): *Contemporary Issues in Nephrology 14.* New York, Churchill-Livingston, 1986, pp 1333–1346.
46. Klahr S, Buerkert J, Purkerson ML: Role of dietary factors in the progression of chronic renal disease. *Kidney Int* 1983; 24:579–587.
47. Malay EM, MacKay LL, Addis T: Factors which determine renal weight. V. The protein intake. *Am J Physiol* 1978; 86:459–465.
48. Schoolwerth AC, Sandler RS, Hoffman PM, et al: Effects of nephron reduction and dietary protein content on renal ammoniagenesis in the rat. *Kidney Int* 1975; 7:397–404.
49. Brenner BM, Meyer TW, Hostetter TH: Dietary protein intake and the progressive nature of kidney disease: The role of hemodynamically mediated glomerular injury in the pathogenesis of progressive glomerulosclerosis in aging, renal ablation and intrinsic renal disease. *N Engl J Med* 1982; 307:652–659.
50. Brenner BM: Nephron adaptation to renal injury or ablation. *Am J Physiol* 1985; 249:F324–F337.
51. Walker JD, Dodds RA, Murrells TJ, et al: Restriction of dietary protein and progression of renal failure in diabetic nephropathy. *Lancet* 1989; 2:1411–1415.
52. Ihle BU, Baker GJ, Whitworth JA, et al: The effect of protein restriction on the progression of renal insufficiency. *N Engl J Med* 1989; 321:1773–1777.
53. Klahr S, Tripathy K: Evaluation of renal function in malnutrition. *Arch Intern Med* 1966; 118:322–325.
54. Jarusiripipat C, Shapiro JI, Schrier RW, et al: Reduction of remnant kidney hypermetabolism by protein restriction: A survival, perfusion and P-31 NMR study to examine the potential protective mechanism in chronic renal failure. *Clin Res* 1988; 36:520A.

55. Klenner CH, Eram AP, Blomgren D, et al: Effect of protein intake on renal function and structure in partially nephrectomized rats. Kidney Int 1985; 27:739–750.
56. Schrier RW, Holzgreve H: Hemodynamic factors in the pathogenesis of diabetic nephropathy. Klin Wochenschr 1988; 66:325–331.
57. Rostand SG, Brown G, Dirk KA, et al: Renal insufficiency in treated essential hypertension. N Engl J Med 1989; 320:684–688.
58. Bohlen HG: New directions for microvascular research in hypertension. Hypertension 1990; 15:427–428.
59. Shimamura T, Morrison AB: A progressive glomerulosclerosis occurring in five-sixths nephrectomized rats. Am J Pathol 1975; 79:95–106.
60. Harris DC, Hammond WS, Burke TJ, et al: Verapamil protects against progression of experimental chronic renal failure. Kidney Int 1987; 31:41–46.
61. Schrier RW, Harris DC, Chan L, et al: Tubular hypermetabolism as a factor in the progression of chronic renal failure. Am J Kidney Dis 1988; 12:243–249.
62. Fogo A, Yoshida Y, Glock AD, et al: Serial micropuncture analysis of glomerular function in two rat models of glomerulosclerosis. J Clin Invest 1988; 82:322–330.
63. Yoshida Y, Fogo A, Ichikawa I: Glomerular hypertrophy has a greater impact on glomerulosclerosis than the adaptive hyperfunction in remnant nephrons (abstract). Kidney Int 1988; 33:327.
64. Pelayo JC, Harris DC, Stanley PF, et al: Glomerular hemodynamic adaptations in remnant nephrons effect of verapamil. Am J Physiol 1988; 254:F425–431.
65. Jarusiripipat C, Zhoo HZ, Shiparo JI, et al: Effect of long-acting calcium entry blocker on blood pressure, renal function and survival of uremic rats (abstract). Kidney Int 1990; 37:509.
66. Brunner FP, Thiel G, Hermle M, et al: Long-term enalapril and verapamil in rats with reduced renal mass (abstract). Kidney Int 1987; 31:380.
67. Jackson B, Debrevi L, Whitty M, et al: Progression of renal disease: Effects of different classes of antihypertensive therapy. J Hypertens 1986; 4 (suppl 5):S269–S271.
68. Krolewski AS, Warram JH, Christlieb AR, et al: The changing natural history of nephropathy in type I diabetes. Am J Med 1985; 78:785–794.
69. Mogensen CE: Glomerular filtration rate and renal plasma flow in short-term and long-term juvenile diabetes mellitus. Scand J Clin Lab Invest 1971; 28:91–100.
70. Mathiesen ER, Rønn B, Jensen T, et al: Relationship between blood pressure and urinary albumin excretion in development of microalbuminuria. Diabetes 1990; 39:245–249.
71. Christensen CH, Mogensen CE: The course of incipient diabetic nephropathy: Studies of albumin excretion and blood pressure. Diabetic Med 1985; 2:97–102.
72. Feldt-Rasmussen B, Mathiesen ER, Decker T: Effect of two years of strict metabolic control on the progression of incipient nephropathy in insulin dependent diabetes. Lancet 1986; 2:1300–1304.
73. Dahl-Jørgensen K, Brinchmann-Hansen P, Hanssen F, et al: Effect of near normoglycemia for two years on progression of early diabetic retinopathy, nephropathy and neuropathy. Br Med J [Clin Res] 1986; 293:1195–1199.
74. Viberti GC, Bilous RW, MacKintosh D, et al: Long-term correction of hyperglycemia and progression of renal failure in insulin dependent diabetes. Br Med J [Clin Res] 1983; 286:598–602.

75. Parving HH, Andersen AR, Smidt UM, et al: Diabetic nephropathy and arterial hypertension. *Diabetologia* 1983; 24:10–12.

76. Christlieb AR, Warram JH, Kroleweski AJ, et al: Hypertension: The major risk factor in juvenile onset insulin dependent diabetes. *Diabetes* 1981; 30:90–96.

77. Borch-Johnsen K, Nissen H, Nerup J: Blood pressure after forty years of insulin-dependent diabetes. *Diabetic Nephrop* 1985; 4:11–15.

78. Pell S, D'Alonzo CA: Some aspects of hypertension in diabetes mellitus. *JAMA* 1967; 202:104–110.

79. Ferrannini E, Buzzigoli G, Bonnadonna R, et al: Insulin resistance in essential hypertension. *N Engl J Med* 1987; 317:350–375.

80. Falsne J, Balant LP, Vernet AT: The kidney in maturity onset diabetes: A clinical study of 510 patients. *Kidney Int* 1987; 21:730–738.

81. Nelson RG, Pettit DJ, Carraher MJ, et al: Effect of proteinuria on mortality in NIDDM. *Diabetes* 1988; 37:1499–1504.

82. Mogensen CE: Long-term antihypertensive treatment inhibiting progression of diabetic nephropathy. *Br Med J [Clin Res]* 1982; 285:685–688.

83. Knowler WC, Bennett PH, Ballantine EJ: Increased incidence of retinopathy in diabetes with elevated blood pressure. *N Engl J Med* 1980; 302:645–650.

84. Kannel WB, McGee DL: Diabetes and glucose tolerance as risk factors for cardiovascular disease: The Framingham study. *Diabetes Care* 1979; 2:120–126.

85. Parving HH, Andersen AR, Smidt JM, et al: Early aggressive antihypertensive treatment reduces rate of decline in kidney function in diabetic nephropathy. *Lancet* 1983; 1:1175–1179.

86. Valvo E, Bedogna V, Casagrande P, et al: Captopril in patients with type II diabetes and renal insufficiency: Systemic and renal hemodynamic alterations. *Am J Med* 1988; 85:344–348.

87. Marre M, Chatellier G, Leblanc H, et al: Prevention of diabetic nephropathy with enalapril in normotensive diabetics with microalbuminuria. *Br Med J [Clin Res]* 1988; 297:1092–1095.

88. Bakris G: Effect of diltiazem or lisinopril on massive proteinuria associated with diabetes mellitus. *Ann Intern Med* 1990; 112:707–708.

89. Baba T, Ishizami Y, Ido K, et al: Renal effects of nicardipine, a calcium entry blocker, in hypertensive type II diabetic patients with nephropathy. *Diabetes* 1986; 35:1206–1214.

90. Ruilope LM, Miranda B, Raij L, et al: Converting enzyme inhibition in chronic renal failure. *Am J Kidney Dis* 1989; 13:120–126.

91. Gavras I, Garvas H: Angiotensin converting enzyme inhibitors in hypertension and congestive heart failure. *Adv Intern Med* 1990; 35:249–267.

92. Ferriae M, Lachmka H, Mirouze J, et al: Captopril and insulin sensitivity. *Ann Intern Med* 1985; 102:134–135.

93. McMurray J, Fraser DM: Captopril, enalapril and blood glucose. *Lancet* 1986; 1:1035.

94. Helgeland A, Strommen R, Hagelund CH, et al: Enalapril, atenolol and hydrochlorathiazide in mild to moderate hypertension. *Lancet* 1986; 1:872–875.

95. Williams GH: Converting enzyme inhibitors in the treatment of hypertension. *N Engl J Med* 1988; 319:1517–1525.

96. Keane WH, Anderson S, Povar G, et al: Angiotensin converting enzyme inhibitors and progressive renal insufficiency. *Ann Intern Med* 1989; 111:503–516.

97. Dixon CM, Fuler RW, Barnes PJ: The effect of an angiotensin converting enzyme inhibitor, ramipril, on bronchial responses to inhaled histamine and bradykinin in asthmatic subjects. *Br J Clin Pharmacol* 1987; 23:91–93.

# Diabetic Foot Ulcers: Etiology, Treatment, and Prevention

## Carl Grunfeld, M.D., Ph.D.

Associate Professor of Medicine, Co-Director, Special Diagnostic and Treatment Unit, Department of Medicine, University of California, San Francisco, School of Medicine, Metabolism Section, Medical Service, Department of Veterans Affairs Medical Center, San Francisco, California

## Editor's Introduction

Foot ulcers and the subsequent amputation of a lower extremity are the commonest cause of hospitalization among patients with diabetic mellitus. Despite its clinical importance, the methods of treating this devastating complication of diabetes remain largely the product of subjective impressions rather than of objective studies. There are few areas in the field of diabetes in which there are so many strong opinions regarding therapy supported by so few well controlled studies. As Dr. Grunfeld's review emphasizes, this situation is gradually improving; reliable means of assessing the underlying causes of diabetic ulcers are being developed. This review moreover brings to bear a combination of sound clinical judgment coupled with objective data to address the issues of prevention and treatment of the diabetic foot ulcer. Methods are now at hand to quantify diabetic vascular and neuropathic diseases and, as a result, the relationship of vasculopathy and neuropathy to the development of foot ulcers is more firmly established. The frequently devastating problem of infected foot ulcers likewise can now be approached with sound bacteriologic diagnoses and appropriate antibiotic therapy. While there is no question that avoiding trauma, burns, and ill-fitting shoes represents effective means of preventing diabetic ulcers, the treatment of such ulcers is far more problematic. The value of this review to the clinician is that it represents one of the few critical evaluations of the prevention and treatment of this too-common diabetic complication and presents practical approaches to what the physician can accomplish to save the diabetic foot.

*Marvin D. Siperstein, M.D., Ph.D.*

Among all of the chronic complications of diabetes mellitus, ulceration in the feet is probably the least well studied. Yet foot ulcers in diabetic patients take a staggering personal and financial toll. Ulceration of the foot is the major precursor lesion leading to amputation. The amputation rate is 59.7 per 10,000 people with diabetes per year.[1] It was estimated that in 1985, approximately 50,000 lower extremity amputations were performed in patients with diabetes.[2] With the cost averaging $10,000 per hospitalization for amputation (including surgery and anesthesia), this means that approximately half of a billion dollars was spent in 1985 for the amputation of lower extremities in diabetes. The cost for successful treatment of diabetic foot ulcers is harder to estimate. The average admission for a foot infection in diabetic patients was 22 days, suggesting a yearly expenditure in excess of $200,000,000 on direct costs.[3] One in five patients with diabetes who is admitted to the hospital has a foot ulcer as the primary diagnosis, but because of the long length of stay for amputation or even successful treatment, foot complications account for more hospital days than all other diabetic complications combined.[4] Outside of specialized centers, the recurrence rate for ulceration remains high, as does the short-term mortality.[2, 5, 6] Nevertheless, the National Diabetes Advisory Board has suggested that more than 50% of lower extremity amputations could be prevented by instituting adequate foot care in the diabetic population.[7]

## Separating the Wheat From the Chaff

The sections that follow will review the status of our current knowledge in the field of foot ulcerations in diabetes. An attempt will be made to distinguish between principles that are based firmly on research and those that are commonly accepted, often appear in prestigious textbooks, but are as yet unsupported by data. For example, every textbook on diabetes or the diabetic foot offers its own approach to the topical care of foot ulcers. A review of these approaches is quite informative. Take the issue of foot soaks. Many feel these are contraindicated. One prominent textbook states:

> Foot soaks should never be done. Soaking macerates and spreads infection. The heat of the water may burn and literally cook the vulnerable ischemic foot or be too hot for the insensitive neuropathic foot. Foot soaks lead to more complications in diabetes than any other common form of treatment. Foot soaks contribute to the development of gangrene with ultimate amputation more than any other home remedy. Feet should be washed with tepid water and gentle handsoap but washing is *not* soaking them. *Foot soaks should never be done!*[8]

In an equally prominent textbook, the director of another major clinical program for diabetic foot ulcers advocates the routine use of foot soaks in nearly all of his patients as follows:

> If non-sweating skin is kept moist, keratin cracks will not occur. The problem is to prevent dryness without producing maceration from too much moisture. This is a skill and a discipline that must be developed and accepted by every patient who has dry skin, and it is a problem for life.
> So-called moisturizing creams are not the answer or are only part of the an-

swer. The skin needs water. The best way to get water into the keratin layer of the skin is to soak the feet in a basin or bucket of water for 15–20 min/day.[9]

Why this contradiction? How can a large clinic with an impressive success rate for healing foot ulcers routinely use foot soaks, while another group of physicians sees a startling morbidity from this treatment and inveighs against it? Doctors at the National Hansen's Disease Center intensively educate their patients on what they see as the proper way to soak feet; in their view, it is "a skill and a discipline that must be developed." However, other practitioners have seen patients who have suffered thermal injury from placing their feet in water that is too hot or have developed infection between their toes, perhaps from leaving the area too moist. There is no doubt that patients with sensory neuropathy should be instructed in determining the temperature of water and that those at risk for foot complications should dry their feet properly. However, is it necessary to prohibit foot soaks because some patients use the modality improperly? If this is an effective therapy, should the mistakes of a few who use it cause it to be abandoned?

In the days before home blood glucose monitoring was possible, insulin-induced hypoglycemia accounted for between 2% and 13% of all deaths in patients with insulin-dependent diabetes mellitus (IDDM).[10, 11] Of course, no one proposed abandoning insulin therapy, since it is absolutely required for IDDM. Instead, careful education programs were initiated to prevent unnecessary hypoglycemia. Although everyone has anecdotal reports of patients who have burned their feet, this is as likely to occur from a heating pad as from a hot foot soak. Other than anecdotal reports, no published research documents that such treatment is deleterious or proves that "foot soaks lead to more complications in diabetes than any other common form of treatment." However, there also is no evidence that foot soaks are helpful. For instance, the efficacy of this therapy in treating anhidrotic skin has not been tested directly in controlled clinical trials against any other form of therapy, including "so-called moisturing creams."

Similar controversies surround other topical treatments. Several uncontrolled series have proposed that povidone-iodine or povidone-iodine plus sugar enhances the healing of diabetic foot ulcers.[12, 13] In contrast, others argue that "all iodine preparations should be avoided as they kill granulation tissue and interfere with the healing process."[14] Unfortunately, there are no randomized controlled trials in a given clinic that compare povidone-iodine to any other topical agent in patients receiving similar supportive care. Their effect on the healing process is not known. However, there are some studies on experimentally infected wounds in animals. These reveal that povidine-iodine does not offer any advantage over saline in the healing of infected experimental wounds, and that the addition of detergents to povidone-iodine results in an increased rate of infection.[15] While it is logical that an antibacterial agent might decrease the rate of infection, evidence of a sustained antiseptic effect has never been found experimentally. To date, no topical anti-infective agent has been documented to prevent infections in or aid the healing of diabetic foot ulcers. One must be wary about dogmatically backing a therapy because it seems logical in the absence of controlled clinical trials.

The logic of unsupported theories is only a step away from the logic of advertising. In the 1960s, millions of consumers bought chlorophyll breath fresheners because advertisements argued logically that they would work. To counter this, the authors of the "Antiseptics and Disinfectants" chapter of the third edition of Goodman and Gillman's classic *Textbook of Pharmacology* presented a fascinating evaluation of chlorophyll as a breath freshener[16]:

CHLOROPHYLL
Why reeks the goat
On yonder hill
Who dotes so much
On chlorophyll?

Much of what is written in textbooks about diabetic foot ulcers is the result of the personal clinical experience of talented clinician/teachers who feel strongly about their views. Yet, one group may state dogmatically that a procedure is contraindicated and dangerous, while another views it as the treatment of choice. There are two detrimental effects of such contradictory and strongly held opinions. First, the credibility of the whole field is put at risk by the glaring contradictions in the relevant literature. Second, since many of these postulates are promulgated so strongly, the net result is that further work that might advance a scientific understanding of the etiology and treatment of foot ulcers is discouraged.

## Etiology of Foot Ulcers

Despite the paucity of adequately controlled *therapeutic* clinical trials for foot ulcers (also see below), there is a fascinating and growing body of epidemiologic and experimental data that demonstrates the etiologic basis for ulceration in the feet of patients with diabetes. Unlike the anecdotally based clinical chapters that are frequently in disagreement with each other, in the primary research papers, multiple groups have come to similar conclusions independently with regard to the etiology of this complication. The pathologic states that contribute to ulceration include neuropathy, structural changes, abnormal biomechanics, vascular disease, and infection.

## Neuropathy

It is important first to distinguish between neuropathic and ischemic ulcers. Classic neuropathic ulcers occur most frequently on the plantar surfaces of the foot, but also may occur on the medial or lateral surfaces. In contrast, ischemic ulcers often begin as distal gangrenous lesions. Identical neuropathic ulcers are seen in Hansen's disease (leprosy), in which there is also a similar profound neuropathy, but no significant incidence of vasculopathy.

In the past, it has been difficult to distinguish between patients with mild neuropathy and those at risk of neuropathic ulceration using the standard clinical neurologic examination.[17] Quantitative techniques are now available that can assess whether neuropathy is advanced enough to predispose patients to foot ulcers. The simplest, least expensive, and best-documented of these is Semmes-Weinstein aesthesiometry, which utilizes handheld nylon monofilament probes of different diameters; the force generated by the probes is proportional to the diameter of their filament. This method is highly reproducible. Three widely separated groups, at the University of California, San Francisco, the National Hansen's Disease Center in Louisiana, and Washington University in Missouri have found independently that the 5.07 probe ($\log_{10}$ of force in milligrams times 10) cannot be felt by patients with neuropathic foot ulcers.[18–20] Another group at the University of Miami in Florida used multiple probes at smaller increments and set a more sensitive threshold of 4.21.[21] A limited set of probes is available from the Hansen's Disease Center in Carville, Louisiana.

Similar discrimination can be made using vibration. Patients with foot ulcers are unable to feel vibration at less than 20 V using a Biomedical Instruments hand-held electronic biothesiometer; in contrast, normal individuals feel vibration at less than 15 V.[22] A variation on the standard tuning fork method of testing vibration uses a graduated tuning fork (Reidel Seiffert, Germany); all foot ulcer patients scored <2.[23] The Vibration II vibration sensitivity tester (Sensortek, Clifton, New Jersey) can be used in a similar manner.[21] Unfortunately, the threshold for vibration devices varies with the pressure applied during testing, leading to potential errors in measurement.[24]

Thermal sensation (the ability to sense temperature differences) also can be utilized to discriminate those patients at risk for ulceration. Of course, lack of the ability to feel temperature in the feet is the reason why some patients accidentally burn their feet in hot water or with heating pads. The Marstock stimulator utilizes a Peltier heating block that can be programmed to change rapidly between hot and cold; more than a 10°C change in temperature is required for patients with foot ulcers to detect a difference, whereas all normal individuals can detect a difference when the block varies between 3°C and 10°C.[22] The Sensortek thermal sensitivity tester[17] shows somewhat less discrimination.[21]

The combination of multiple electrophysiologic tests may provide a level of risk.[25] Autonomic neuropathy is less discriminating.[25] A new technique tests current perception thresholds, which also are decreased in diabetic neuropathy, but a level that predicts risk for ulceration has not been defined yet.[26, 27] There is good, although not perfect, correlation between different modalities of sensory testing.[21, 22, 27, 28] When several tests were compared directly, the inexpensive hand-held Semmes-Weinstein probes show better sensitivity and specificity than did the more expensive electronic testers.[21, 27]

It is important to screen diabetic individuals for neuropathy. We found that one third of the patients in our diabetes clinic were already insensate using Semmes-Weinstein aesthesiometry and therefore at risk for foot ulcers, although only 16% of clinical patients had a previous history of ulceration.[29] More important, a surprising number of patients were not aware that they had lost feeling in their feet, including some who had experienced ulcers already. Education plays a key role in the prevention of ulcers and must be an ongoing process (see later). Despite ulcer healing, each patient continues to remain at risk, because the neuropathy is permanent.

## Pressure-Induced Necrosis

How does a neuropathic foot become ulcerated? Dr. Paul Brand has investigated the mechanism for pressure-induced ulcers of the skin using animal models.[9, 30] Excessive pressure results in the feeling of pain in normal feet, but patients who have enough neuropathy to be at risk for ulceration feel no pain and continue to allow pressure to occur, eventually inducing necrosis. The risk of ulceration is proportional to both the amount and timing of the pressure applied. Thus, continuous pressure (e.g., that which occurs on the side or top of the feet due to ill-fitting shoes) can induce ulceration in lesser amounts than intermittent pressure (e.g., that which occurs on the bottom of the feet during walking).

One common cause of ulceration is an object inadvertently left in a shoe; the object cannot be felt during walking and produces localized pressure in small areas. We have found nails, screws, toys, stones, needles, glass, and even cigarette lighters embedded in both shoes and foot ulcers. X-rays may be necessary to detect such objects. Other patients have unknowingly worn holes through the soles of their shoes, so that the ground itself induced an ulceration.

In addition, new data indicate that increased pressure occurs during the normal course of walking in patients with severe diabetic neuropathy. Multiple laboratories have used a variety of pressure-measuring devices to document increases ranging from severalfold to nearly 100-fold higher than normal on the plantar surface of diabetic neuropathic feet.[9, 31–34]

## Structural and Biomechanical Factors

The factors thought to contribute to increased pressure in the foot are listed in Table 1. Diabetic patients with neuropathy and ulceration have thinner muscle and fat pads on the plantar surface of their feet, as can be seen with ultrasound.[35] The net result is a lack of cushioning at this site.

Changes in the bony structure of the foot also may contribute to increased pressure. For example, hammer toes and, in particular, the claw-toe deformity, with the combined elevation of the toes and depression of the metatarsal heads, also facilitate ulceration.[29] Recent data indicate that hammer toes are the major factor, other than neuropathy per se, predis-

**TABLE 1.
Structural and Biomechanical
Factors Increasing Pressures in
the At-Risk Diabetic Foot**

Thinning of muscle and fat pads
Hammer toe and claw foot deformities
Charcot joints
Bunions
Decreased ankle and subtalar range of
  motion
Callus, a response that aggravates the
  problem
Inability to sense pain and change gait

posing to ulceration (Grunfeld et al., in preparation). The high frequency of ulceration under the metatarsal heads, therefore, can be explained by the combination of these factors producing increased pressure during walking.

The Charcot joint, or neuro-osteoarthropathy, is a progressive destruction of joint bones that can occur in any disease with severe neuropathy. The resulting change in bone alignment can produce protrusions that lead to pressure-induced ulceration. However, Charcot joints are not common; only 1 out of 94 patients surveyed in our clinic had a Charcot foot.[29]

Bunions make the fitting of shoes difficult and can lead to ulceration in neuropathic feet. Callus is one of the body's responses to repeated increased pressure. Because callus is firm and unyielding compared to muscle and fat, its presence actually worsens the pressure problem. In addition, the callus can cause shear forces with lateral displacement. Signs of blood (hematoma) under a callus indicate that a potential space has been created by the shear; such changes frequently progress to ulceration. Another factor that contributes to increased pressure is decreased range of motion, which is found in the ankles and subtalar joints of diabetic patients with neuropathic ulcers.[21, 29, 36] This rigidity changes the kinetics of walking, increasing the amount of time that a given force is applied to the plantar surface.

Finally, it should be remembered that neuropathy prevents patients from detecting pain; therefore, they are unable to adjust their gait to avoid walking on an area where pressure is inducing necrosis. Patients with diseases other than diabetes that cause similar abnormally high pressures, such as rheumatoid arthritis, can alter their gait and avoid this complication.[37] The rigidity of the higher joints in the feet of patients with diabetes also limits changes in gait.

## Vascular Disease

Although classic ischemic gangrene is obvious, adequate clinical criteria to determine at what level a patient is at risk for ulceration from vascular disease have not been established. Nevertheless, when data from our group and other groups are analyzed, it is estimated that 60% to 70% of diabetics with foot ulcers have neuropathy without vascular disease, 15% to 20% have some signs of vascular disease, and 15% to 20% have both neuropathy and vascular disease.[29, 38] Thus, even with an overly generous definition of vascular disease, most diabetic foot ulcers are due to neuropathy. However while there is no doubt that the presence of vascular disease contributes to poor healing rates in diabetes, ischemia is only one of many causes of amputation[39] (see later).

It is important to recognize that, in the absence of other risk factors, the incidence of peripheral macrovascular disease is increased only slightly in diabetics compared to controls.[40] As is the case with coronary vascular disease, the three risk factors of hypertension, hypercholesterolemia, and cigarette smoking lead to major and additive increases in the incidence of peripheral vascular disease.[40] In one study of occlusive vascular disease in diabetic subjects, 90% had a history of smoking.[41] Although the relationship between macrovascular disease and blood glucose control is not clear, insulin-treated patients with non–insulin-dependent diabetes mellitus (NIDDM) appear to have less peripheral vascular disease than those treated with either diet alone or oral hypoglycemic agents.[41] It is not known whether this difference is secondary to the nature of the therapy, the degree of control, or the severity of the diabetes. Among patients with IDDM or insulin-treated NIDDM, both low-density lipoprotein cholesterol and very-low-density lipoprotein triglycerides are risk factors.[42] In diet-treated NIDDM, high-density lipoprotein cholesterol inversely correlates with occlusive vascular disease. Of course, obesity and poor glycemic control may worsen the lipoprotein profile.

In one study of classic gangrenous lesions, 64% occurred on the digits, 16% on the heel, 10% on the dorsa of the feet, and 10% at the metatarsal heads.[43] Surprisingly, in two thirds of the patients, edema was felt to be the precipitating cause, rather than pure arterial insufficiency. The cause of edema was frequently cardiac decompensation (50%), with some cases due to nephrotic syndrome (5%) and some idiopathic. Cardiac decompensaton without edema was as likely to be a precipitating cause as was peripheral arterial occlusive disease.[43] As with all risk factors, the presence of multiple precipitating events makes the situation worse. Decreased perfusion from cardiac failure, fixed atherosclerotic lesions decreasing flow, and peripheral edema requiring a higher perfusion pressure to penetrate the tissues combine to precipitate ischemia. Edema also may worsen the fit of shoes, thereby increasing surface pressure. Grossly and microscopically, the atherosclerosis seen in the peripheral vessels of patients with diabetes is no different than that seen in the vessels of other patients.[44] However, the prevalence of aortoiliac disease is lower, while distal disease is more widespread and rapidly progressive, particularly in the metatarsal arch and digital vessels.[44, 45]

The role of microangiopathy is not understood. While nearly all patients with diabetes have capillary basement membrane thickening, this does not lead to occlusive microvascular lesions.[46] However, there is additional vascular pathology in the feet of diabetic patients that is not secondary to macrovascular disease, but has been attributed to either microvascular disease or neuropathy. (In fact, there is a debate over whether neuropathy itself is the product of microvascular-induced ischemia or metabolic changes.) The vascular bed shows decreased distensibility in diabetes.[47] Significant arteriovenous shunting may be present in the diabetic foot, robbing critical tissues of oxygen.[48] Blood flow abnormalities consistent with reduced peripheral vascular resistance are found.[49] If anything, there is increased leaking from the capillaries and more diffusion into the tissues of patients with long-term diabetes. Increased amounts of fluorescein rapidly leak out of diabetic capillaries, then spread further away from the pericapillary space compared to controls.[50] As a result of increased leakage, there is greater transcapillary escape of albumin in patients with microvascular disease,[51] which no doubt compounds the problem of tissue edema. Finally, physical training leads to increased muscle capillary formation in controls, but not in patients with diabetes.[52]

## Microbiology of Infected Ulcers

Infection may complicate an ulcer caused by either neuropathy or ischemia. Alternatively, infection starting through breaks in the skin, such as those caused by anhidrosis or aggressive fungal infections (athlete's foot), can be the primary cause of ulceration. The range of bacteria found in diabetic foot ulcers is complex and dependent on the severity of the underlying lesion. An important advance in understanding this microbiology was made by Sapico et al., who found that the method used to culture a foot ulcer can produce a bias in the bacterial flora that are found.[53] These investigators examined infected feet that went to amputation and compared bacterial cultures obtained by three different methods used in the clinical patient setting, with cultures that were made by sterile dissection in the amputated limb. Swabbing the surface of ulcers resulted in the culture of increased amounts of skin contaminants that were not really present in deep infection. Needle aspiration cultured fewer species than actually were present. However, débridement using gauze, followed by curettage and immediate culture, accurately reflected the bacterial mixture found in the infected tissue. The curettage form of culture should be the standard method for studies of the effectiveness of antibiotic therapy in the treatment of diabetic foot infections. It is equally applicable to milder outpatient infections.[54] Although the success of an antibiotic trial could be determined without full and proper culture information, an understanding of the mechanisms for success and failure is dependent upon knowledge of the bacteria as well as other characteristics of the ulcer.

## TABLE 2.
## Common Flora of Infected Foot Ulcers

Penicillinase-producing staphylococci
Drug-resistant gram-negative rods
Anaerobes of varying antibiotic resistance
Enterococci with narrow antibiotic
susceptibility

Life-threatening infections of diabetic foot ulcers contain an amazing array of bacteria.[53, 55] These usually are polymicrobial infections, averaging 4.8 bacterial species per lesion. More important, they can contain types of bacteria for which the appropriate antibiotic therapy is quite divergent (Table 2). Staphylococci that produce penicillinase, gram-negative rods that are drug-resistant, and anaerobes of varying susceptibility frequently are present. It is being recognized increasingly that many infections include enterococci that are resistant to the first-line drugs used for each of the three foregoing types of bacteria. In fact, enterococci appear to play an unusually prominent role in osteomyelitis in diabetic feet.[56]

On the other hand, milder infections, such as those frequently seen in the outpatient setting, have fewer species of bacteria,[54, 57] even when cultured by the curettage technique. Lipsky et al. found that such mild infections averaged 2.1 microorganisms per lesion. Aerobic gram-positive cocci were cultured in 89% of infections and often were the sole pathogen. One third of the infections contained aerobic gram-negative bacilli, and 13% contained anaerobes; the latter almost always occurred in the setting of polymicrobial infections. From a clinical point of view, an infection that is malodorous is more likely to contain anaerobes. Enterococcus was seen even in the less complicated infections.[54]

## Treatment of Foot Ulcers

### Treatment of Infection

The first step in the treatment of diabetic foot ulcers is prompt control of infection when present. Nonviable tissue, which, if necrotic, can serve as a culture medium for microorganisms, must be removed. While all patients with infection are placed on antibiotic therapy, the extent to which such treatment is effective and the causes for failure remain to be determined. When the microbial flora of infected feet that failed antibiotic therapy and required amputation have been examined retrospectively, a surprising number of patients have been found to have been on apparently appropriate antimicrobial therapy.[53] Multiple factors contribute to the failure to control infection in the face of apparently appropriate antibiotic coverage, including local tissue changes, and not just poor vascular supply.[39]

Studies have not yet determined whether it is necessary to cover all bacteria in a mixed infection with specific antibiotics. Despite the wide-based flora, bacteremia in these patients usually is due to a few species, namely staphylococci and bacteroides.[58] Enterococci are a prominent pathogen in deep tissue infections such as osteomyelitis, which requires long-term antibiotic therapy.[56] However, some have disputed the need to cover enterococci in mixed infections.[54, 59]

To date, only two comparative trials of antibiotic therapies have focused on diabetic foot ulcers. In one paper, the authors examined the immediate response and long-term follow-up of foot infections in a randomized, double-blind study of cefoxitin vs. ceftizoxime.[59] However, only 54% of their patients had diabetes; the others had significant peripheral vascular disease. Unfortunately, these authors did not analyze the results of the response to antibiotics specifically within their population of diabetic patients. They did not use curettage for culture, but relied on a variety of techniques, including aspiration, swab, and bone biopsy. The spectrum of the two antibiotics is different: ceftizoxime has superior activity against *Enterobacteriaceae* and *Pseudomonas*, while cefoxitin is superior against *Bacteroides fragilis*. Neither is effective against enterococci. The immediate clinical response was not statistically different; 82% of the patients on ceftizoxime and 68% on cefoxitin had a satisfactory response. Ceftizoxime showed slight superiority in treating soft-tissue infection compared to cefoxitin (93% vs. 69%). The two drugs were equally effective in patients with osteomyelitis. Unfortunately, the diagnostic criteria used to identify soft-tissue infection and osteomyelitis were not presented. It was not possible to show a statistically significant difference between the two drugs in the treatment of particular microorganisms. Ironically, the difference that came closest to statistical significance was that obtained with enterococcus, a bacteria that is not very susceptible to either antibiotic; 88% of these infections responded to ceftizoxime, while only 44% responded to cefoxitin. Of equal interest, *Bacteroides fragilis* was present in four patients treated with cefoxitin, yet only one responded clinically, despite documented susceptibility of all four isolates to that drug. Once again, this study highlights the fact that we do not understand the factors behind the failure of antibiotic therapy.

Another randomized study involved the group of patients described above with non-life-threatening infections.[54] Gram-positive cocci predominated in these patients, while anaerobic organisms were much rarer. The study compared treatment using cephalexin, which has some gram-negative coverage, with clindamycin, which has good anaerobic coverage. Ninety percent of the infections responded to therapy, and there was no significant difference between the two drugs. In the patients failing cephalexin therapy, the infecting organism in each case was susceptible to this agent. Only one of the clindamycin treatment failures had microorganisms that were clindamycin-resistant.

Diagnosing osteomyelitis is difficult in the presence of a diabetic foot ulcer. Periosteal bone resorption, the classic sign of hematogenous osteomyelitis, can be induced by a foot ulcer overlying bone without direct extension into bone. As a result, there is a high false-positive rate in plain x-rays, with specificity averaging 60%.[60, 61] Even multiphasic bone scans show an unacceptable percentage of false-positive results, with a specificity of 77%.[60, 61] Evidence of progressive destruction of bone on x-rays or scans in which the complete bone is illuminated may be more diagnostic, but these changes have not been studied systematically. In addition, both conventional x-rays and bone scans may be negative in the presence of osteomyelitis that is diagnosed on pathology. The sensitivity for conventional x-rays averages 77%; multiphasic bone scans are somewhat better, with sensitivity averaging 89%.[60, 61] The most definitive means of diagnosing osteomyelitis is during débridement; if dissection reaches bone and the texture is abnormal, the bone should be biopsied. Patients should not be committed to long-term parenteral antibiotics[56] unless a definitive diagnosis is made.

As indicated previously, appropriate antibiotic coverage may not treat life-threatening infections. Therefore, supplemental treatment modalities often are considered. In a recent report, hyperbaric oxygen was shown to increase the salvage of gangrenous feet in diabetic patients.[62] However, this was not a randomized study and the patients were characterized inadequately. Although it is not yet possible to define the role of total body hyperbaric oxygen in the therapy of gangrene, larger studies clearly are warranted and long-term follow-up is needed. In contrast, topical oxygen or topical "hyperbaric" oxygen applied to the extremity shows no ability to accelerate healing or increase the percentage of diabetic foot ulcers that heal.[57]

What, then, is the most prudent course for the treatment of infection in diabetic foot ulcers? The best approach is to begin by obtaining a proper culture by the curettage technique.[53] The physician needs to determine whether the infection is mild or life-threatening. Mild infections may not require comprehensive antibiotics, while life-threatening infections definitely do. The studies cited raise the possibility that all bacteria need not be treated. Until our understanding of foot infections in diabetes increases, the best course is to initiate antibiotics based upon the seriousness of the infection and the predicted spectrum of bacteria. By the time cultures come back (24 to 48 hours), a response may be obvious. If there is dramatic improvement, then it may not be necessary to change the antibiotic coverage, even if one of the many organisms is not properly covered. If a single dominant organism is recovered that is not sensitive to the antibiotics being used, or if the infection has not responded to them, then it is appropriate to adjust the antibiotics based on the culture results.

Further trials of antibiotic therapy in diabetic foot infections clearly are needed. The complex nature of these infections should not be a deterrent to investigation, because the study of similar infections has yielded critical information. For example, lung abscesses are polymicrobial and very often anaerobic, despite their obvious location at the organ of oxygen exchange.[63, 64] Just as with diabetic foot infections, authors previously have questioned whether antibiotics adequately penetrate such abscesses and whether all bacteria need to be covered. For many years, the treatment of choice for lung abscesses was penicillin, but with the emergence of increasing proportions of penicillin-resistant bacteroides species (which are also present in diabetic foot ulcers), questions arose as to the efficacy of this agent. Therefore, penicillin was compared to clindamycin in a randomized trial. Randomization in this study was appropriate, which is important, because lung abscesses vary in etiology, with such causes as alcoholism, neurologic disease, drug abuse, and immunosuppression, conditions that could bias results if not evenly distributed between the two therapeutic interventions. Clindamycin was more effective than penicillin at both primary cure and preventing extension, relapse, and the development of empyema.[64]

Similar criteria should be used in studying diabetic foot ulcers. It is important to assure that each group of patients has similar predisposing factors on entry (Table 3). The ulcer should be characterized locally by mea-

---

**TABLE 3.**
**Factors That Need to Be Considered to Demonstrate Adequate Randomization in Trials of Antibiotic Therapy for Diabetic Foot Infection**

---

Area of ulcer
Depth of ulcer
Wound grade
Necrotic tissue
Gangrene
Edema
Cellulitis
Lymphangitis
Osteomyelitis
Fever, chills
White blood cell count
Ankle pressure index
Plethysmography
Transcutaneous partial oxygen tension
Neuropathy
Glucose control
Albumin
Blood urea nitrogen
Creatinine

---

**TABLE 4.**
**Evaluation of Treatment Response in Diabetic Foot Infections**

Duration of induration
Duration of fever
Duration of elevated white blood cell count
Number of débridements
Patients with failed treatment
  Progressive necrosis
  Progressive cellulitis
  Persistent fever
  Persistent drainage
Patients with relapse of infection (<2 mo)
Patients with early amputation (<2 mo)

suring its size and depth and noting the presence of necrotic tissue or gangrene. The surrounding tissue should be evaluated for the presence of edema, cellulitis, lymphangitis, or osteomyelitis. The systemic signs of infection should be documented, including fever, chills, and elevated white cell count. It should be noted that systemic signs can be absent, even in life-threatening infections. The presence of vascular disease should be evaluated by techniques such as ankle/brachial or toe/brachial pressure indices, plethysmography, or transcutaneous partial oxygen tension. The degree of neuropathy should be recorded. Finally, the metabolic status of the patient should be followed, including plasma glucose, albumin, blood urea nitrogen, and creatinine levels.

There are a variety of parameters that can be used to assess the effectiveness of therapy (Table 4). Early response can be determined by the eradication of local symptoms, such as induration, or systemic signs, such as fever and elevated white count. The number of débridements required may be another marker. Patients can fail treatment due to progressive necrosis or cellulitis, as well as persistent fever or drainage. Progression to amputation is the ultimate evidence of failure. Finally, it is necessary to assess short-term relapse of infections that initially appeared to be treated successfully.

The studies described previously suggest that it is important to determine whether it is truly critical to have complete antibiotic coverage for cure of infection. Indeed, markers for failure may include other parameters, such as bacteria per milligram, number of bacterial species, presence of local or systemic signs of infection, and degree of vascular disease, rather than antibiotic susceptibility.

## Local Surgery at the Ulcer Site

As discussed previously, the first therapy of infected foot ulcers should be surgical débridement to remove necrotic or nonviable infected tissue. Failure of an infection to respond to appropriate antibiotics is a sign that further surgical débridement is urgently necessary. In addition, local surgery may continue to play a role, despite the containment of infection. Although most authorities follow this approach, no controlled studies are available to verify it. For instance, fibrin that accumulates at the base of an ulcer may retard granulation, but neither the necessity of removal nor the best method of doing so (e.g., débridement vs. saline wet-to-dry dressings) has been documented. Callus may grow around a healing ulcer, despite relative immobilization. It can grow over the ulcer, giving the appearance of healing, but potentially leaving a space and preventing full granulation or epithelialization of the base. Thus, callus and, particularly, callus with underlying hematoma need to be removed. Skin grafting can speed recovery from a foot ulcer successfully,[65, 66] but technique is critical and the level of blood flow needed is not known. Adequate series on skin grafting of diabetic foot ulcers have not yet been published.

Failure to heal or progress of infection does not always necessitate below-the-knee amputation. Digital (toe only), ray (including the accompanying metatarsal), or transmetatarsal amputations can provide a functional foot. The success of these procedures is dependent on the vascular supply, which can be difficult to assess.

## Role of Vascular Intervention in Therapy of Diabetic Foot Ulcers

As mentioned earlier, while it is easy to show decreased blood flow in the limbs of diabetic patients, there are no clear-cut definitions of the level at which ischemia occurs. This is seen most clearly in attempts to define a level at which ischemia would prevent an ulcer from healing. The ankle/brachial pressure index, the ratio of ankle to brachial blood pressure, is the most common first-line method for assessing vascular flow after palpating the pulses. While criteria of absolute flow in the ankle (<70 mm Hg) or an ankle/brachial pressure index (<.45) that would impede healing are often promulgated, careful studies reveal that there is no clear-cut discriminating level that can predict healing.[67] It should come as no surprise that a significant number of ulcers do not heal, despite normal blood flow. However, ulcers can heal even at the lowest levels of blood flow; therefore, measurements of flow can give only a general guide to the probability of healing.[67]

Calcification of ankle blood vessels leads to poor compressibility and artifactually high ankle/brachial pressure indices. Therefore, the use of toe pressures or ankle/toe pressure indices has been advocated.[68] However, toe measurements still do not allow definition of the level at which ischemia prevents healing; in one study, 9% of patients with the lowest flow still healed.[67] Other variations include analysis of wave forms or measurement of pulse reappearance time after reactive hyperemia.[69, 70]

Finally, tissue oxygenation can be assessed by measuring transcutaneous oxygen tension, the equipment for which is becoming more reliable.[71-75] This technique has theoretic appeal, as it is more sensitive to local factors than the ankle/brachial pressure index, which measures only vessel flow. However, some patients with low transcutaneous oxygen tension still heal.

Vascular measurements can serve as a guide to further diagnostic work-up. If an ulcer is healing rapidly, no major intervention is warranted. If an ulcer is making slow progress and pulses are not bounding, a vascular laboratory work-up should be done. Patients with indices indicative of ischemia are candidates for angiography to determine whether remediable lesions are present. Care should be taken to avoid contrast-induced renal failure, by adequate prehydration or digital angiography.[76-78]

Although lesions in diabetes are more often distal, those that are proximal can be treated with percutaneous transluminal angioplasty.[79] The success rate in patients with diabetes is good, but somewhat less than in those without diabetes (55% vs. 75%, $P < .05$). The limb salvage rate for surgery has improved greatly with the introduction of the distal bypass.[80-85] With increasing experience, reversed vein bypass may be as good as in situ saphenous vein bypass.[85] Regardless of the technique used, the effect of reversal of structural lesions can be seen with improved ankle/brachial pressure indices and transcutaneous oxygen tensions.[75, 79]

The role for pharmacologic intervention in vascular disease is limited. Preliminary data indicate that prostacyclin analogues may increase healing rates, but current drugs require intravenous infusion.[86] Current data do not support the use of antiplatelet drugs to prevent further vascular events (peripheral or cardiovascular) in patients with diabetes.[87] There are no existing data to support the use of oral vasodilators or hemorrheologic agents such as pentoxifylline.

## Local Care: Attempts to Accelerate Wound Healing

Although numerous techniques appear in papers, reviews, and chapters for the local care of diabetic foot ulcers after infection is resolved, they rarely have been subjected to scientific scrutiny. In fact, the first (and, as yet, to my knowledge, the only) randomized trial that adequately demonstrates the effectiveness of one form of ulcer care over another was published in June 1989.[88] This paper could be used as a model for designing other trials.

Because of the role that pressure plays in producing ulceration, several groups have used "total contact casting" to heal long-standing ulcers.[89-93] This technique involves immobilizing the foot in a knee-to-toe cast with a walking heel that directs pressure more evenly over the foot and away from the ulcer. Such casts are used after infection is cleared and the wound begins to granulate. They usually are not used in ischemic feet.

Most practitioners change the cast weekly in the beginning and less frequently over time if it appears to be doing no harm. Mueller et al.[88] randomized their patients to either total contact casts or a "traditional dressing treatment" consisting of saline wet-to-dry dressings. No patient had gangrene, osteomyelitis, or residual infection. Ambulation was limited by asking patients to use crutches or walkers. Randomization was demonstrated to be effective, as there was no significant difference between the two groups in sex, prevalence of IDDM or NIDDM, neuropathy, vascular disease, or ulcer grade, size, or previous duration. As summarized in Table 5, Mueller et al. demonstrated that a significantly higher percentage of ulcers healed and fewer became infected in the total contact cast cohort. There was a trend toward a decrease in the amputation rate, but it was not significant at this sample size. Likewise, because of the large range in the number of days needed to heal such ulcers, it was not possible to show a significant decrease in the time to healing.

It is important to understand the limitations of this study.[88] From a mathematic viewpoint, they found a striking threefold increase in healing in the casted group, which allowed a demonstration of significance despite the small sample size. However, the difference was not due merely to the high rate of healing in patients with total contact casts (90%); it was due also to the low rate of healing in those treated with a traditional dressing (32%). Unfortunately, healing in the traditional group was also lower than the 81% reported by Edmonds et al. in a multidisciplinary clinic setting emphasizing treatment of infection, intensive podiatric care, and provision of specialized footwear, but without use of total contact casts.[38] Our clinic

---

**TABLE 5.**
**Results of the First Adequate Randomized Study of Foot Ulcer Healing***

| Result of Treatment | Type of Treatment | | |
|---|---|---|---|
| | **Total Contact Cast** | **Traditional Dressing (saline wet-to-dry)** | |
| Healed (%) | 19/21 (90%) | 6/19 (32%) | $P < .005$ by chi$^2$ |
| Days to heal (range) | 42 +/- 29 (8–91) | 65 +/- 29 (12–92) | Not significant by t-test |
| Serious infection (%) | 0/21 (0%) | 5/19 (26%) | $P < .05$ by chi$^2$ |
| Amputation | 0/21 | 2/19 | Not significant by chi$^2$ |

*Adapted from Mueller MJ, Diamond JE, Sinacore DR, et al: *Diabetes Care* 1989; 12:384–387.

achieved a 75% healing rate in a recent study (Grunfeld, et al., in preparation). If a 75% healing rate had been achieved in their traditional dressing group, Mueller et al. would have needed a sample size of more than 60 patients in each group to show a significant difference. The question must be raised as to why their traditional dressing group had such a low percentage of healing. Mueller et al. used saline wet-to-dry dressings, which previously had not been studied independently and were not used by Edmonds et al. One must consider the possibility that these dressings prevented healing. Could placing a moist piece of gauze on an ulcer "macerate and spread infection," as the antisoakers would say?

Despite the limitations of this study, it is tempting to accept their reported trend toward acceleration in the rate of healing (days to heal) and link it to the decreased prevalence of infection. Saline wet-to-dry dressings could have caused the infections, or perhaps accelerated healing per se prevents infection (i.e., the shorter time an ulcer is large or open, the less the risk of infection). In this light, it should be pointed out that there are other ways to analyze for accelerated healing. First, given the wide range of healing (8 to 92 days in Mueller's study and even longer in some of our patients), it is highly likely that this parameter is not normally distributed, hence the $t$-test should not have been used. A nonparameteric test such as Kruskal-Wallis, Mann-Whitney, or Wilcoxon rank sum would have been more appropriate. Second, progress in decreasing ulcer size can be monitored. The shape of the ulcer is traced on clear acetate at each visit, then the area is calculated using a graphics tablet and a personal computer. This technique was used in a study discussed earlier in which no significant differences were found in the ability of two modalities to accelerate healing expressed as percent of original wound size at a given time.[57]

Given the interest in accelerated healing, it is not surprising that a variety of topical agents have been proposed for this purpose. A partial list of these therapies appears in Table 6. As discussed before, many of these agents have vociferous proponents, but the literature consists primarily of anecdotal series, not valid randomized studies. (One agent has become a major component at "for-profit" centers for healing diabetic foot ulcers before publication of its efficacy.) As a consequence, the Committee on Standards of Care of the Council on Foot Care of the American Diabetes Association neither endorsed nor condemned any topical agent in their recently published guidelines.[94] Several trials are in progress or in planning that use a new generation of topical agents such as platelet-derived wound-healing factor, platelet-derived growth factor, basic fibroblast growth factor, epidermal growth factor, insulin-like growth factor-1, and transforming growth factor-β (see Table 6). The first agent is a partially purified protein mixture from the supernatants of stimulated platelets and contains multiple factors, while the rest are single pure proteins prepared by recombinant DNA technology. A preliminary report using a small number of subjects has been published and proposes that autologous platelet-derived wound-healing factor may accelerate epithelialization.[95] However, despite randomization, entry data suggested that the populations were not

## TABLE 6.
## Topical Agents Proposed to Accelerate Ulcer Healing*

| | |
|---|---|
| Povidone-iodine | Tegaderm |
| Povidone-iodine plus sugar | Debrisan |
| Dakin's solution | Transcutaneous electrical nerve stimulation |
| Hydrogen peroxide | Saline (wet-to-dry) |
| Silver sulfadiazine | Salcoseryl |
| Sweitzer solution | Insulin |
| Hexylresorcinol (S. T. 37) | Growth hormone |
| Zinc | Platelet-derived wound-healing factor |
| Vitamins A, C, and E | |
| Bacitracin | Platelet-derived growth factor |
| Benzoyl peroxide | Epidermal growth factor |
| Semipermeable hydrogels | Basic fibroblast growth factor |
| Duoderm | Insulin-like growth factor-1 |
| Op-Site | Transforming growth factor-β |

*None of these topical agents has been proven clearly to be more effective than simple local wound care.

## TABLE 7.
## Factors That Need to Be Considered to Assure Adequate Randomization in Trials of Agents That Accelerate Ulcer Healing

Area of ulcer
Depth of ulcer
Wound grade
Prior duration of wound
History of infection
Ankle pressure index
Phethysmography
Transcutaneous partial oxygen tension
Neuropathy
Glucose control
Albumin
Blood urea nitrogen
Creatinine

**TABLE 8.**
**Factors Useful in Assessing the**
**Success of Agents That**
**Accelerate Ulcer Healing**

Percentage healed
Time to epithelialization or closure
Interim rate of healing
Number of débridements required
Occurrence of infection
Percentage requiring skin grafts
Percentage progressing to amputation

similar. When patients treated with this agent were compared to controls, they had trends toward smaller wounds (11.6 ± 24.5 [SD] cm$^2$ vs. 22 ± 19.2 [SD] cm$^2$), wounds that had undergone longer previous treatment (119 ± 114 [SD] weeks vs. 47 ± 63 [SD] weeks), and a lower prevalence of renal failure (creatinine 1.4 ± .76 [SD] mg/dL vs. 2.6 ± 4.0 [SD] mg/dL). Although these differences were reported by the authors as not significant, a student's $t$-test was used and, as discussed before, such data may not be normally distributed, necessitating analysis with nonparametric statistics. More important, special care must be taken before accepting the "null" hypothesis (i.e., that there is no difference) under these circumstances. More recent studies have not found an effect of platelet-derived wound-healing factor (Grunfeld et al., unpublished). However, further studies clearly are warranted on all of the agents listed in Table 6.

It is essential that future studies of agents used to accelerate ulcer healing be large enough to assure adequate randomization of known contributing factors (Table 7). At this time, such studies must be initiated after infections have been treated successfully. It also is not known whether these agents need to be restricted to wounds of certain depth or whether they work in the presence of ischemia.

Criteria demonstrating the success of topical agents are similar to those discussed previously for the treatment of infection and include percentage of ulcers healed, time to epithelialization or wound closure, and rate of healing (Table 8). Such agents may decrease the number of débridements required and prevent secondary infection. The necessity of a skin graft could be viewed as failure of a wound healing agent, despite eventual cure of the ulcer. Again, amputation is the ultimate evidence of failure.

## Prevention of Future Ulceration and Amputation

Successful healing of a foot ulcer or even amputation does not put an end to the problem. Because neuropathy is not reversible, patients remain at risk. Vascular reconstruction unaccompanied by reduction in risk factors leads to reocclusion. The rate of recurrence is unfortunately high. In the long-term follow-up of one of the antibiotic trials, two thirds of the patients experienced recurrence within 1 year.[59] Vascular disease in diabetes is rapidly progressive.[44, 45] Minor amputation is followed, within 6 months, by progressive amputation in 19% of patients.[6] Several studies reveal high rates of amputation of the contralateral limb within a few years of the first amputation.[5, 6] Amputation also is followed by high short-term mortality.[2] Therefore, all patients with a history of ulceration and those at risk from neuropathy or vascular disease should be entered into intensive education and examination programs.

## Multidisciplinary Clinics

Unfortunately, even clinics specializing in diabetes do not examine feet adequately. In one study, only 12% of clinic visits included examination of the feet.[96] As a consequence, many institutions have set up multidisciplinary clinics to which high-risk patients are referred or have transformed their normal diabetes clinics with the addition of trained personnel.[38, 97–99] The results are an impressive 44% to 85% reduction in amputation rates, despite the fact that many of these clinics serve a poor, inner-city population. As discussed earlier, a primary healing rate of 81% was achieved by one of these clinics.[38]

## Education for Patients

In addition to training staff members, the patient, the family, or a friend needs to learn the basics of foot care and the signs of impending problems. When patients have significant retinopathy or blindness, the role of family and friends becomes critical. The American Diabetes Association guidelines for physicians also include instructions for patients at risk due to neuropathy.[94] These are summarized in Table 9. The major features include avoiding situations that could lead to burns or trauma (e.g., hot water, heating pads, walking with bare feet), obtaining correctly fitted shoes, properly breaking shoes in, and checking shoes for foreign objects before putting them on. Most important, daily inspection of the feet can detect a problem early and prevent progression to the point at which a limb is threatened.

## The Pathways to Amputation

It is critical to cure foot ulcers in order to prevent amputation. Pecoraro et al. analyzed the cause of amputation in 80 consecutive diabetic patients.[39] Most were due to multiple factors, with the exception of 4% due to pure ischemia and 8% caused by ischemia and gangrene. The most common pathway leading to amputation included a triad of minor trauma, ulceration, and faulty wound healing. Each of these components was found in more than 80% of patients. This pathway was especially common in pa-

## TABLE 9.
## Instructions for Patients Who Are Insensate and at Risk for Diabetic Foot Ulcers*

Foot care
  Inspect the inside of your shoes for foreign objects before putting the shoes on.
  Inspect your feet daily for blisters, cuts, scratches, redness, dryness, hot spots, or infection.
  Wash feet daily and dry carefully, especially between the toes.
  Avoid hot temperatures; test water with elbow before bathing.
  If your feet are cold, wear socks. Do not use hot water bottles or heating pads.
  Do not cut corns or calluses or use chemical removal agents.
  Do not use adhesive tape on your feet.
  Cut nails in contour with the toes; do not cut deep down the sides or corners.
  Consult your physician before soaking feet or using lubricating creams or oils.
  If your vision is impaired, a family member or friend should be trained in these items.
Footwear
  Shoes should be measured properly at the time of purchase; do not depend on them to stretch out.
  Break shoes in slowly, wearing them for no more than a few hours at a time in the beginning.
  Do not wear the same pair of shoes every day; try to change your shoes within the same day.
  Wear shoes of material that breathes.
  Avoid pointed toes or high heels.
  Do not walk barefoot; particularly avoid hot surfaces in the sun, on beaches or around swimming pools. At night, turn on the lights and do not walk barefoot to the bathroom.
  Wear shoes appropriate to the weather: avoid wearing wet shoes; use thick socks or lined boots in the winter.
  Avoid sandals or thongs.
  Avoid garters, tight elastic bands on socks, or rolling hose. Always wear socks or stockings with shoes, but avoid thick seams or mended areas.
Professional care
  See your physician regularly and be sure that your feet are examined at each visit.
  Notify your physician at once if you develop a blister, sore, or crack in the skin of your feet.

*Adapted from Committee on Standards of Care, Council on Foot Care, American Diabetes Association: *Diabetic Foot Care.* Alexandria, Virginia, American Diabetes Association, 1990, pp 1–12.

tients over 62 years of age. Infection was present in 59% of patients. Ischemia, defined liberally by an ankle/brachial pressure index of <.70 or a transcutaneous partial oxygen tension of >20 mm Hg, was found in 46% of cases. Curiously, 9% had gangrene secondary to local factors rather than vascular disease per se; edema was present in many. Decreases in nutritional parameters and weight were found before amputation. Thus, although ischemia is prevalent in patients who progress to amputation, faulty wound healing plays a prominent role. Research on wound healing should be a high priority in the future.

## Footwear

Because of the obvious link between poorly fitting footwear and foot ulceration, the provision of proper footwear is a cornerstone of any ulcer prevention program. A wide variety of footwear has been proposed to prevent ulceration, ranging from standard running shoes to custom-molded shoes.[100–103] While it is logical that patients with severely deformed feet require custom-molded shoes to match the shape of their feet, there are no comparative data establishing the absolute or relative efficacy of a particular design of shoe for a given foot problem.

The paper most often cited as proof of the efficacy of special shoes in healing diabetic foot ulcers or preventing re-ulceration comes from the multidisciplinary clinic of Edmonds et al.[38] In their clinic, patients who wore special shoes had an ulcer recurrence rate of only 26%, whereas those who did not wear special shoes had a rate of 80%. However, this was not a randomized study; all patients were given "healing shoes" and then custom-molded shoes. Of course, any patient who was given free shoes and chose not to wear them obviously was noncompliant; ulcer recurrence in such a patient may have been more a product of lack of compliance with the total program recommended by Edmonds et al. and cannot be attributed solely to failure to wear specific shoes.

As a consequence of the lack of controlled studies on this topic, it is difficult to obtain a reimbursement for special footwear for patients with diabetes. There is a Medicare demonstration project ongoing in three states that seeks to determine whether patients randomized to custom-molded shoes will have fewer or less extended hospitalizations. However, as currently constructed, the amount of money provided may not be adequate to obtain optimal molded shoes, and only one pair of shoes is provided per patient, contrary to the recommendation of many experts (see Table 9). In addition, the criteria for entry are overly vague. Patients must be certified as at risk by their physician, but no objective documentation at risk is required. There may be serious limits to the power of this study.

Nevertheless, there is reason to suspect that proper footwear fitted correctly will reduce ulceration. From a mechanistic viewpoint, the increased pressure found on the plantar surface of a diabetic foot can be reduced by the use of simple insoles made of sorbothane, a new viscoelastic pressure-absorbent polymer,[104] or experimental acrylic padded hoisery.[105] It should be emphasized that reduction in these pressures was achieved with simple padding and did not require the use of custom-molded shoes or inserts. Many other materials that could reduce pressure similarly are available, but have not yet been studied. No data are available on pressure reduction using custom-molded shoes, but the effect of total contact casting has been studied. Trials using thin, flexible transducers to measure pressures within casts demonstrate that total contact casting can decrease pressure at the site of ulceration. However, a similar reduction was seen with conventional padded casts.[106] While the support and stability of total contact casts is thought to exceed that of conventional padded casts,[88-93] the two types have not been compared directly for efficacy. Total contact casts are known to weaken or loosen; as a consequence, it is recommended that they be removed and evaluated on a weekly basis in the beginning.[88] Conventional padded casts are at least as likely to have padding compress or break down.

Comparative studies obviously are needed to determine which types of specialized footwear will prevent ulceration most effectively. In the interim, recommendations can be based upon the degree of risk. Patients with neuropathy but reasonably normal foot structure should be placed in shoes of breathable material that are fitted carefully by professionals. When a patient who is insensate with neuropathy to the point of risk feels that a pair of shoes "fits well," they are undoubtedly too tight. Patients with mild structural abnormalities of the foot, such as hammer toes or bunions, need special attention to ensure that the toe box is high or wide enough to accommodate these deformities. The presence of a full claw-toe deformity, severe bunions, Charcot joints, or partial amputations most likely necessitates a custom-molded shoe, although reimbursement may not be possible at this time.

## Summary

The role of neuropathy, structural changes, and ischemia in the development of foot ulcerations in diabetic patients is well established. As a result, it is now possible to determine which patients are at risk for ulceration and to place them in education programs or clinics with multidisciplinary care. In such situations, a high rate of ulcer healing and a decrease in amputation can be achieved.

However, the roles of specific therapeutic interventions, particularly local wound healing agents and antibiotics, are not yet understood. Well-characterized patients need to be studied in comparative antibiotic trials for infection and in double-blind, placebo-controlled trials of wound-healing agents. Until such trials are completed, dogmatic advocacy or condemnation of a given therapy should be avoided.

# References

1. Most RS, Sinnock P: The epidemiology of lower extremity amputations in diabetic individuals. *Diabetes Care* 1983; 6:87–91.
2. Bild DE, Selby JV, Sinnock P, et al: Lower-extremity amputation in people with diabetes: Epidemiology and prevention. *Diabetes Care* 1989; 12:24–31.
3. Wheat LJ, Allen SD, Henry M, et al: Diabetic foot infections, bacteriologic analysis. *Arch Intern Med* 1986; 146:1935–1940.
4. Malins JM: *Clinical Diabetes Mellitus*. London, Eyre & Spottiswoode, 1968.
5. Goldner MG: The fate of the second leg in the diabetic amputee. *Diabetes* 1960; 9:100–103.
6. Ebskov B, Josephsen P: Incidence of reamputation and death after gangrene of the lower extremity. *Prosthet Orthot Int* 1980; 4:77–80.
7. National Diabetes Advisory Board: The prevention and treatment of five complications of diabetes: A guide for primary care practitioners. Atlanta, Georgia, Centers for Disease Control, 1983.
8. Rowbotham JL, Gibbons GW, Kozak GP: The diabetic foot, in Kozak GP (ed): *Clinical Diabetes Mellitus*. Philadelphia, WB Saunders, 1982, p 221.
9. Brand PW: The diabetic foot, in Ellenberg M, Rifkin H (eds): *Diabetes Mellitus Theory and Practice*, 3rd ed. Medical Examination Publishing Co Inc, 1983, pp 829–849.
10. Paz-Guevara AT, Hsu TH, White P: Juvenile diabetes mellitus after 40 years. *Diabetes* 1975; 24:559–565.
11. Feingold KR: Hypoglycemia: A pitfall of insulin therapy. *West J Med* 1983; 139:688–695.
12. Knutson RA, Merbitz LA, Creekmore MA, et al: Use of sugar and povidone-iodine to enhance wound healing: Five years' experience. *South Med J* 1981; 74:1329–1335.
13. Anania WC, Rosen RC, Wallace JA, et al: Treatment of diabetic skin ulcerations with povidone-iodine and sugar: Two case reports. *J Am Podiatr Med Assoc* 1985; 75:472–474.
14. Kahan M: The diabetic foot. *Practical Diabetology* 1986; pp 13–15.
15. Rodeheaver G, Bellamy W, Kody M, et al: Bactericidal activity and toxicity of iodine-containing solutions in wounds. *Arch Surg* 1982; 117:181–186.
16. Esplin DW: Antiseptics and disinfectants; fungicides; ecto parasiticides, in Goodman LS, Gilman A (eds): *The Pharmacological Basis of Therapeutics*, 3rd ed. New York, The McMillian Co, 1965, p 1049.
17. Maser RE, Nielsen VK, Bass EB, et al: Measuring diabetic neuropathy: Assessment and comparison of clinical examination and quantitative sensory testing. *Diabetes Care* 1989; 12:270–275.
18. Birke JA, Sims DS: Plantar sensory threshold in the ulcerative foot. *Lepr Rev* 1986; 57:261–267.
19. Holewski JJ, Stess RM, Graf PM, et al: Aesthesiometry: Quantification of cutaneous pressure sensation in diabetic peripheral neuropathy. *J Rehabil Res Dev* 1988; 25:1–10.
20. Mueller MJ, Diamond JE, Delitto A, et al: Insensitivity, limited joint mobility and plantar ulcers in patients with diabetes mellitus. *Phys Ther* 1989; 69:453–462.
21. Sosenko JM, Kato M, Soto R, et al: Comparison of quantitative sensory-

threshold measure for their association with foot ulceration in diabetic patients. *Diabetes Care* 1990; 13:1057–1061.

22. Guy RJC, Clark CA, Malcolm PN, et al: Evaluation of thermal and vibration sensation in diabetic neuropathy. *Diabetologia* 1985; 28:131–137.

23. Thivolet C, El Farkh J, Petiot A, et al: Measuring vibration sensations with graduated tuning fork. *Diabetes Care* 1990; 13:1077–1080.

24. Lowenthal LM, Hockaday TDR: Vibration sensory thresholds depend on pressure of applied stimulus. *Diabetes Care* 1987; 10:100–102.

25. Young RJ, Zhou YQ, Rodriguez E, et al: Variable relationship between peripheral somatic and autonomic neuropathy in patients with different syndromes of diabetic polyneuropathy. *Diabetes* 1986; 35:192–197.

26. Rendell MS, Dovgan DJ, Bergman TF, et al: Mapping diabetic sensory neuropathy by current perception threshold testing. *Diabetes Care* 1989; 12:636–640.

27. Moss K, Holewski JJ, Adams S, et al: Comparison of aesthesiometry, biothesiometry and neuroselective current perception threshold test to quantify sensory deficit in diabetic peripheral neuropathy. *Diabetes* 1989; 38:136A.

28. Dyck PJ, Bushek W, Spring EM, et al: Vibratory and cooling detection thresholds compared with other tests in diagnosing and staging diabetic neuropathy. *Diabetes Care* 1987; 10:432–440.

29. Holewski JJ, Moss KM, Stess RM, et al: Prevalence of foot pathology and lower extremity complications in a diabetic outpatient clinic. *J Rehabil Res Dev* 1989; 26:35–44.

30. Brand PW: Management of the insensitive limb. *Phys Ther* 1979; 59:8–12.

31. Stokes IAF, Faris IB, Hutton WC: The neuropathic ulcer and loads on the foot in diabetic patients. *Acta Orthop Scand* 1975; 46:839–847.

32. Cterceko GC, Dhanendran M, Hutton WC, et al: Vertical forces acting on the feet of diabetic patients with neuropathic ulceration. *Br J Surg* 1981; 68:608–614.

33. Boulton AJM, Hardisty CA, Betts RP, et al: Dynamic foot pressure and other studies as diagnostic and management aids in diabetic neuropathy. *Diabetes Care* 1983; 6:26–33.

34. Rodgers MM, Cavanagh PR, Sanders LJ: Plantar pressure distribution of diabetic feet, in Johnson B (ed): *Biomechanics*. Champaign, Illinois, Human Kinetics Publishers, 1986, pp 343–347.

35. Gooding GAW, Stess RM, Graf PM, et al: Sonography of the sole of the foot: Evidence for loss of foot pad thickness in diabetes and its relationship to ulceration of the foot. *Invest Radiol* 1986; 21:45–48.

36. Delbridge L, Perry P, Marr S, et al: Limited joint mobility in the diabetic foot: Relationship to neuropathic ulceration. *Diabetic Med* 1988; 5:333–337.

37. Masson EA, Hay EM, Stockley I, et al: Abnormal foot pressures alone may not cause ulceration. *Diabetic Med* 1989; 6:426–428.

38. Edmonds ME, Blundell MP, Morris HE, et al: The diabetic foot: Impact of a foot clinic. *Q J Med* 1986; 232:763–771.

39. Pecoraro RE, Reiber GE, Burgess EM: Pathways to diabetic limb amputation. *Diabetes Care* 1990; 13:513–521.

40. Feingold KR, Siperstein MD: Diabetic vascular disease. *Adv Intern Med* 1986; 31:309–340.

41. Beach KW, Brunzell JD, Strandness DE: Prevalence of severe arteriosclerosis obliterans in patients with diabetes mellitus. Relation to smoking and form of therapy. *Arteriosclerosis* 1982; 2:275–280.

42. Beach KW, Brunzell JD, Conquest LL, et al: The correlation of arteriosclerosis obliterans with lipoproteins in insulin-dependent and non-insulin-dependent diabetes. *Diabetes* 1979; 28:836–840.
43. Lithner F, Tornblom N: Gangrene localized to the feet in diabetic patients. *Acta Med Scand* 1984; 215:75–79.
44. Towne JB: Management of foot lesions in the diabetic patients, in Rutherford RB (ed): *Vascular Surgery.* Philadelphia, WB Saunders, 1984, pp 661–669.
45. Beach KW, Bedford GR, Bergelin RO, et al: Progression of lower-extremity arterial occlusive disease in type II diabetes mellitus. *Diabetes* 1988; 11:464–472.
46. LoGerfo FW, Coffman JD: Vascular and microvascular disease of the foot in diabetes: Implications for foot care. *N Engl J Med* 1984; 311:1615–1619.
47. Faris I, Agerskov K, Henrikson O, et al: Decreased distensibility of a passive vascular bed in diabetes mellitus: An indicator of microangiopathy? *Diabetologia* 1982; 23:411–414.
48. Boulton AJM, Scarpello JHB, Ward JD: Venous oxygenation in the diabetic neuropathic foot: Evidence of arteriovenous shunting? *Diabetologia* 1982; 22:608.
49. Corbin DOC, Young RJ, Morrison DC, et al: Blood flow in the foot, polyneuropathy and foot ulceration in diabetes mellitus. *Diabetologia* 1987; 30:468–473.
50. Bollinger A, Frey J, Jager K, et al: Patterns of diffusion through skin capillaries in patients with long-term diabetes. *N Engl J Med* 1982; 307:1305–1310.
51. Bent-Hansen L, Feldt-Rasmussen B, Kverneland A, et al: Transcapillary escape rate and relative metabolic clearance of glycated and non-glycated albumin in type 1 (insulin-dependent) diabetes mellitus. *Diabetologia* 1987; 30:2–4.
52. Wallberg-Henriksson H, Gunnarsson R, Henriksson J, et al: Influence of physical training on formation of muscle capillaries in type I diabetes. *Diabetes* 1984; 33:851–857.
53. Sapico FL, Witte JL, Canawati HN, et al: The infected foot of the diabetic patient: Quantitative microbiology and analysis of clinical features. *Rev Infect Dis* 1984; 6:S171–S176.
54. Lipsky BA, Pecoraro RE, Larson SA, et al: Outpatient management of uncomplicated lower extremity infections in diabetic patients. *Arch Intern Med* 1990; 150:790–797.
55. Louie TJ, Bartlett JG, Tally FP, et al: Aerobic and anaerobic bacteria in diabetic foot ulcers. *Ann Intern Med* 1976; 85:461–463.
56. Bamberger DM, Daus GP, Gerding DN: Osteomyelitis in the feet of diabetic patients. *Am J Med* 1987; 83:653–660.
57. Leslie CA, Sapico FL, Ginunas VJ, et al: Randomized controlled trial of topical hyperbaric oxygen for treatment of diabetic foot ulcers. *Diabetes Care* 1988; 11:111–115.
58. Sapico FL, Bessman AN, Canawati HN: Bacteremia in diabetic patients with infected lower extremities. *Diabetes Care* 1982; 5:101–104.
59. Hughes CE, Johnson CC, Bamberger DM, et al: Treatment and long-term follow-up of foot infections in patients with diabetes or ischemia: A randomized, prospective, double-blind comparison of cefoxitin and ceftizoxime. *Clin Ther* 1987; 10(suppl A):36–49.
60. Park H-M, Wheat LJ, Siddiqui AR, et al: Scintigraphic evaluation of diabetic osteomyelitis: Concise communication. *J Nucl Med* 1982; 23:569–573.

61. Seldin DW, Heiken JP, Feldman F, et al: Effect of soft-tissue pathology on detection of pedal osteomyelitis in diabetics. *J Nucl Med* 1985; 26:988–993.
62. Baroni G, Porro T, Faglia E, et al: Hyperbaric oxygen in diabetic gangrene treatment. *Diabetes Care* 1987; 10:81–86.
63. Bartlett JG, Finegold SM: Anaerobic pleuropulmonary infections. *Medicine* 1972; 51:413–450.
64. Levison ME, Mangura CT, Lorber B, et al: Clindamycin compared with penicillin for the treatment of anaerobic lung abscess. *Ann Intern Med* 1983; 98:466–471.
65. Reiffel RS, McCarthy JG: Coverage of heel and sole defects: A new subfascial arterialized flap. *Plast Reconstr Surg* 1980; 66:250–260.
66. Masson EA, Cooper MAC, Boulton AJM: Split-skin grafting in the management of extensive neuropathic ulceration. *Diabetic Med* 1989; 6:171–172.
67. Apelqvist J, Castenfors J, Larsson J, et al: Prognostic value of systolic ankle and toe blood pressure levels in outcome of diabetic foot ulcer. *Diabetes Care* 1989; 12:373–350.
68. Vincent DG, Salles-Cunha SX, Bernhard VM, et al: Noninvasive assessment of toe systolic pressures with special reference to diabetes mellitus. *J Cardiovasc Surg* 1983; 24:22–28.
69. Railton R, Newman P, Hislop J, et al: Reduced transcutaneous oxygen tension and impaired vascular response in type I (insulin dependent) diabetes. *Diabetologia* 1983; 25:340–342.
70. Volgelberg KM, Stork W: Measurement of pulse reappearance time in the diagnosis of peripheral vascular disease in diabetes. *Diabetes Care* 1988; 11:345–350.
71. Railton R, Newman P, Hislop J, et al: Reduced transcutaneous oxygen tension and impaired vascular response in type 1 (insulin-dependent) diabetes. *Diabetologia* 1983; 25:340–342.
72. Hauser CJ, Klein SR, Mehringer CM, et al: Assessment of perfusion in the diabetic foot by regional transcutaneous oximetry. *Diabetes* 1984; 33:527–531.
73. Cina C, Katsamouris A, Megerman J, et al: Utility of transcutaneous oxygen tension measurements in peripheral arterial occlusive disease. *J Vasc Surg* 1984; 1:362–369.
74. Wyss CR, Matsen FA III, Simmons CW, et al: Transcutaneous oxygen tension measurements on limbs of diabetic and non-diabetic patients with peripheral vascular disease. *Surgery* 1984; 95:339–345.
75. Osmundson PJ, Rooke TW, Hallett JW: Effect of arterial revascularization on transcutaneous oxygen tension of the ischemic extremity. *Mayo Clin Proc* 1988; 63:897–902.
76. Cruz C, Hricak H, Samhouri F, et al: Contrast media for angiography: Effect on renal function. *Radiology* 1986; 158:109–112.
77. Eisenberg RL, Bank WO, Hedgock MW: Renal failure after major angiography can be avoided with hydration. *Am J Roentgenol* 1981; 136:859–861.
78. Stacul F, Carraro M, Magnald S, et al: Contrast agent nephrotoxicity: Comparison of ionic and nonionic contrast agents. *Am J Roentgenol* 1987; 149:1287–1289.
79. Rooke TW, Stanson AW, Johnson CM, et al: Percutaneous transluminal angioplasty in the lower extremities: A 5 year experience. *Mayo Clin Proc* 1987; 62:85–91.
80. Reichle FA, Rankin KP, Shuman CR: Salvage of extremities with ischemic

necrosis in diabetic patients by infrapopliteal artery bypass. *Diabetes Care* 1979; 2:396–400.

81. Reichle FA, Rankin KP, Tyson RR, et al: Long term results of femoroinfrapopliteal bypass in diabetic patients with severe ischemia of the lower extremity. *Am J Surg* 1979; 137:653–656.

82. Leather RP, Shah DM, Karmody AM: Infrapopliteal arterial bypass for limb salvage: Increased patency and utilization of the saphenous vein used "in situ". *Surgery* 1980; 90:1000–1008.

83. Auer AI, Hurley JJ, Binnington HB, et al: Distal tibial vein grafts for limb salvage. *Arch Surg* 1983; 118:597–602.

84. Cantelmo NL, Snow JR, Menzoian JO, et al: Successful vein bypass in patients with an ischemic limb and palpable popliteal pulse. *Arch Surg* 1986; 121:217–220.

85. Taylor LM, Edwards JM, Phinney ES, et al: Reversed vein bypass to infrapopliteal arteries. Modern results are superior to or equivalent to in-situ bypass for patency and for vein utilization. *Ann Surg* 1987; 205:90–97.

86. Fiessinger JN, Schafer M: Trial of iloprost versus aspirin treatment for critical limb ischaemia of thromboangiitis obliterans. *Lancet* 1990; 335:555–557.

87. Colwell JA, Bingham SF, Abraira C, et al: Veterans Administration Cooperative Study on antiplatelet agents in diabetic patients after amputation for gangrene: II. Effects of aspirin and dipyridamole on atherosclerotic vascular disease rates. *Diabetes Care* 1986; 9:140–148.

88. Mueller MJ, Diamond JE, Sinacore DR, et al: Total contact casting in treatment of diabetic plantar ulcers: Controlled clinical trial. *Diabetes Care* 1989; 12:384–387.

89. Pollard JP, Le Quesne LP: Method of healing diabetic forefoot ulcers. *Br Med J [Clin Res]* 1983; 286:436–437.

90. Coleman WC, Brand PW, Birke JA: The total contact cast: A therapy for plantar ulceration on insensitive feet. *J Am Podiatr Med Assoc* 1984; 74:548–552.

91. Helm PA, Walker SC, Pulliam G: Total contact casting in diabetic patients with neuropathic foot ulcers. *Arch Phys Med Rehabil* 1984; 65:691–693.

92. Boulton AJM, Bowker JH, Gadia M, et al: Use of plaster casts in the management of diabetic neuropathic foot ulcers. *Diabetes Care* 1986; 9:149–152.

93. Sinacore DR, Mueller MJ, Diamond JE, et al: Diabetic neuropathic plantar ulcers treated by total contact casting. *Phys Ther* 1987; 67:1543–1549.

94. Committee on Standards of Care, Council on Foot Care, American Diabetes Association: *Diabetic Foot Care*. Alexandria, Virginia, American Diabetes Association, 1990, pp 1–12.

95. Knighton DR, Ciresi K, Fiegel VD, et al: Stimulation of repair in chronic nonhealing cutaneous ulcers. *Surg Gynecol Obstet* 1990; 170:56–60.

96. Bailey TS, Yu HM, Rayfield EJ: Patterns of foot examination in a diabetes clinic. *Am J Med* 1985; 78:371–374.

97. Davidson JK, Alogna M, Goldsmith M, et al: Assessment of program effectiveness at Grady Memorial Hospital–Atlanta, in Steiner G, Lawrence PA (eds): *Educating Diabetic Patients*. New York, Springer-Verlag, 1981, pp 329–348.

98. Runyan JW: The Memphis Chronic Disease Program. *JAMA* 1975; 231:264–267.

99. Assal JP, Muhlhauser I, Pernat A, et al: Patient education as the basis for diabetes care in clinical practice. *Diabetologia* 1985; 28:602–613.

100. Hampton GJ: Therapeutic footwear for the insensitive foot. *Phys Ther* 1979; 59:23–29.
101. Tovey FI, Moss MJ: Specialist shoes for the diabetic foot, in Connor H, Boulton AJM, Ward JD (eds): *The Foot in Diabetes.* Chichester, J Wiley & Sons, Ltd, 1987, pp 97–108.
102. Soulier SM, Godsey C, Asay ED, et al: The prevention of plantar ulceration in the diabetic foot through the use of running shoes. *Diabetes Educator* 1987; 13:130–132.
103. Coleman WC: Footwear in a management program of injury prevention, in Levin ME, O'Neal LW (eds): *The Diabetic Foot,* 4th ed. St Louis, CV Mosby Co, 1988, pp 293–309.
104. Boulton AJM, Franks CI, Betts RP, et al: Reduction of abnormal foot pressures in diabetic neuropathy using a new polymer insole material. *Diabetes Care* 1984; 7:42–46.
105. Veves A, Masson EA, Fernando DJS, et al: Use of experimental padded hosiery to reduce abnormal foot pressures in diabetic neuropathy. *Diabetes Care* 1989; 12:653–655.
106. Birke JA, Sims Jr DS, Buford WL: Walking casts: Effect on plantar foot pressures. *J Rehabil Res Dev* 1985; 22:18–22.

# Management of the Complications of Human Immunodeficiency Virus Infection

## Sharon Safrin, M.D.

Assistant Clinical Professor of Medicine and Epidemiology and Biostatistics, University of California, San Francisco, School of Medicine, Division of Infectious Diseases, San Francisco General Hospital, San Francisco, California

## Paul Volberding, M.D.

Professor, Department of Medicine, University of California, San Francisco, School of Medicine, Chief, Division of AIDS Oncology, Director, AIDS Program, San Francisco General Hospital, San Francisco, California

## Editor's Introduction

As the epidemic of acquired immunodeficiency syndrome progresses, physicians in every specialty and in every community will be caring for patients with one or several of the complications of AIDS. Moreover, these complications are very frequently the first evidence that a previously unsuspected HIV infection is present.

Awareness of the frequently subtle and insidious nature of these complications therefore becomes the responsibility of every practicing clinician regardless of the patient population in his/her practice. Drs. Safrin and Volberding have in the following review provided a comprehensive discussion of the presentation of both the infections and malignant complications that characterize AIDS. We learn that pneumocystis pneumonia is the commonest clinically important infection and toxoplasmosis is the most frequent agent responsible for an intracerebral mass in the AIDS patient. AIDS has moreover caused the resurgence of tuberculosis, which should be screened for in every patient with AIDS, since it represents an obvious risk to the patient as well as his/her physician. Fortunately treatment is improving for each of the AIDS-related infections and, equally important, hopeful signs of successful prophylaxis, especially directed at preventing pneumocystis pneumonia, are increasingly emerging. There is no longer any question that with its 10-year mean incubation period, AIDS will be a part of our clinical practices for the rest of our professional lives, and every clinician should therefore be familiar with the information in this valuable review.

*Marvin D. Siperstein, M.D., Ph.D*

The worldwide epidemic of infection with the human immunodeficiency virus (HIV) has resulted in a myriad of infectious, oncologic, and systemic complications. The natural history of HIV infection, as well as the most common clinical presentations of the most frequent sequelae, have been reviewed elsewhere. In this article, we discuss the management of the most common acquired immunodeficiency syndrome (AIDS)-associated opportunistic infections and conditions.

## *Pneumocystis carinii* Pneumonia

Although serologic studies have demonstrated that infection with *Pneumocystis carinii* is common in the general population, symptomatic disease is virtually limited to immunocompromised hosts. The most frequent manifestation is pneumonia, although various extrapulmonary sites of infection have been described sporadically as well.[1] The two currently licensed therapies, trimethoprim-sulfamethoxazole (TMP-SMX) and pentamidine, are each effective in 70% to 90% of patients[2, 3]; however, either may be associated with dose-limiting toxicity in up to 50% of patients.[2, 3] Potential side effects of TMP-SMX include rash, nausea and vomiting, leukopenia, thrombocytopenia, and elevated liver function enzymes[2, 3]; side effects of parenteral pentamidine include orthostatic hypotension, hypoglycemia, renal insufficiency, leukopenia, pancreatitis, and diabetes mellitus.[2] Recent studies suggest that lowering the dosage of TMP-SMX from 20 mg/kg/day of the trimethoprim component to 12 to 15 mg/kg/day,[4] and from 4 mg/kg/day of the pentamidine component to 3 mg/kg/day[5] may result in a decreased frequency of major adverse effects without a decrease in efficacy.

Alternative oral therapies for patients with acute *P. carinii* pneumonia (PCP) of mild severity (e.g., arterial $Po_2 \geq 60$ mm Hg) include dapsone in combination with trimethoprim, and clindamycin in combination with primaquine. A recent randomized, double-blind study comparing oral TMP-SMX (20 mg/kg/day) to dapsone (100 mg/day) with trimethoprim (20 mg/kg/day) showed equal efficacy and less frequent toxicity of the latter regimen.[3] Dose-limiting side effects occurred in 30% of patients and included rash, nausea, cytopenias, hepatitis, and methemoglobinemia.[3] Further studies will investigate the possible further lessening of toxicity with a decreased dosage of trimethoprim when administered in combination with dapsone.

Oral dapsone as a single agent in the treatment of acute PCP has been suboptimally effective at dosages of both 100 mg/day[6] and 200 mg/day[7]; in addition, toxicity was increased substantially in patients receiving the higher dose of dapsone.

Clindamycin has been administered successfully in combination with primaquine in the treatment of patients with mild PCP.[8, 9] The dose of clindamycin has ranged from 2,400 to 3,600 mg/day intravenously or 1,200 to 2,400 mg/day orally; primaquine is dosed at 15 to 30 mg/day.[8, 9] Although no controlled studies have been completed yet, the regimen holds promise as an additional option for treating patients with mild PCP, particularly those who have a history of intolerance to sulfonamides or trimethoprim.

Patients with severe PCP continue to have a higher mortality, reaching 40% in some series.[10] Trimetrexate, a potent dihydrofolate reductase enzyme inhibitor that requires adjunctive folinic acid therapy to prevent myelosuppression, showed initial promise in preliminary studies,[11] but failed to show superiority to TMP-SMX in a randomized, double-blind trial (F Sattler, unpublished data, 1989). The addition of systemic corticosteroids to standard anti-*Pneumocystis* treatment recently has been shown to reduce the risk of respiratory failure and to improve survival in patients with moderate to severe PCP (i.e., arterial $Po_2 < 70$ mm Hg) when initiated within 48 to 72 hours of anti-*Pneumocystis* therapy.[10] The recommended dosage is 40 mg twice daily of prednisone for 5 days, followed by 40 mg/day for 5 days, then 20 mg/day for 11 days.[10]

Experimental agents currently under study for the treatment of acute PCP include aerosolized pentamidine, Burroughs Wellcome 566C80, eflu-ornithine (DMFO), recombinant interferon-γ, and 1,3-β glucan inhibitors.

Patients who recover from acute pneumocystosis have a high risk of recurrence, approaching 60% at 12 months.[12] Zidovudine has been shown to prolong survival in such patients, but it only slightly decreases the risk of recurrent PCP.[13] Therefore, specific prophylaxis against *Pneumocystis* is indicated. In addition, patients with CD4 (T helper cell) counts of less than $200/mm^3$ or symptomatic HIV infection should receive primary prophylaxis against *Pneumocystis*, since the risk of infection is substantial.[14] Although the efficacy of anti-*Pneumocystis* prophylaxis has been demonstrated in immunosuppressed rats[15] and in children with malignancies,[16] candidate agents have not been compared directly with one another to date.

Preventive therapy with TMP-SMX (160 to 800 mg twice daily) in combination with leucovorin calcium (5 mg/day) was assessed in a nonblinded, randomized study of 60 patients with Kaposi's sarcoma.[17] No treated patient developed PCP over a period ranging from 1 to 30 months, compared with 53% of untreated patients; a longer mean survival was evident in treated patients as well ($P < .002$). Adverse reactions (rash, nausea, leukopenia) necessitated the discontinuation of treatment in 17% of treated patients. Lower dosages and a decreased interval of administration of TMP-SMX are currently under study for their potential to decrease toxicity while preserving efficacy.

Dapsone is an oral sulfone effective as anti-*Pneumocystis* prophylaxis in the immunosuppressed rat,[18] and in uncontrolled studies in HIV-infected patients.[19] Dosages currently under study range from 50 mg twice daily to 200 mg/wk; combination therapy with pyrimethamine or aerosolized pentamidine is being evaluated as well. Potential toxicities include anemia, methemoglobinemia, rash, fever, nausea, and hepatic dysfunction.[19]

Aerosolized pentamidine is an attractive prophylactic agent because of its selective delivery to the lung and low risk of systemic toxicity. Efficacy has been demonstrated in a placebo-controlled, randomized trial[20] and, on the basis of a large dose-finding study,[21] current recommendations for Pneumocystis prophylaxis are the administration of 300 mg every 4 weeks by Respirgard nebulizer. However, the potential for increased frequency of extrapulmonary pneumocystosis, the possible delay in diagnosis of acute PCP due to atypical radiographic presentations, and a possible increased risk of spontaneous pneumothorax or pancreatitis warrant further study.

Other potential prophylactic agents include pyrimethamine-sulfadoxine and intramuscular pentamidine; neither has been studied in controlled trials. Pyrimethamine-sulfadoxine (Fansidar) administration has been associated with leukopenia and rash; several cases of fatal cutaneous reactions such as erythema multiforme, Stevens-Johnson syndrome, and toxic epidermal necrolysis have been reported.[22] Intermittent parenteral injections of pentamidine may cause sterile abscesses, and the systemic side effects observed with higher daily dosages of the drug for the treatment of acute Pneumocystis infection may occur sporadically as well.

## *Mycobacterium avium* Complex Infection

Disseminated infection with *Mycobacterium avium* complex is frequent and often symptomatic. Infection with this pathogen has been found in up to 53% of patients with AIDS in whom autopsies were performed.[23] Common symptoms include fever, weight loss, diarrhea, abdominal pain, and cytopenias.[23] Obstructive jaundice due to biliary tract compression by enlarged periportal lymph nodes may occur.[23] Other complications in patients with AIDS have included septic arthritis, endobronchial lesions, nodular or pustular skin lesions, and pericarditis. The method of diagnosis is by blood or tissue culture of involved organs (e.g., bone marrow, liver, lymph node). It is likely that both the gastrointestinal tract and the respiratory tract serve as portals of entry for this infection, since the organism frequently may be found in the stools[24] or respiratory secretions[25] of patients with AIDS. However, the duration of colonization prior to dissemination and the effectiveness of administering treatment to prevent dissemination have not been studied.

Some data suggest that the treatment of documented infection may ameliorate symptoms[26] or increase survival.[27, 28] Current choices of treatment are based primarily on data from in vitro studies[29] and animal models,[30] since no controlled studies of therapy have been completed to date. In order to avoid the emergence of resistance, and for additive antimycobacterial effect, combination chemotherapeutic regimens are administered when the decision to institute therapy has been made. In contrast to tuberculosis, duration of therapy for *M. avium* complex infection should be lifelong in AIDS patients. A popular regimen consists of rifampin (600 mg/day), ethambutol (15 to 25 mg/kg/day), ciprofloxacin (750 mg twice daily), and clofazimine (150 to 300 mg/day). Side effects include nausea, skin or body fluid discoloration (clofazimine, rifampin), hepatotoxicity (rifampin, clofazimine), and retrobulbar neuritis (ethambutol). Amikacin (7.5 to 15 mg/kg/day) is often added for the first 4 weeks in view of its high level of antimycobacterial potency in *in vitro* and animal models. However, its potential for nephrotoxicity and requirement for parenteral administration limit its prolonged usage.

Other agents under study for the treatment of disseminated *M. avium* complex infection include macrolide compounds (clarithromycin, azithromycin), quinolone agents (temafloxacin), and rifabutin.

## *Mycobacterium* Tuberculosis

The propensity for active tuberculosis in patients with HIV infection who have been exposed to the organism is increased markedly.[31] Therefore, all patients should be screened with a tuberculin skin test and controls. A chest x-ray should be obtained and collection of sputum specimens for culture considered in all anergic patients and those with symptoms suggestive of active tuberculosis (cough, fever, sweats, weight loss, hemoptysis). The radiographic presentation of pulmonary tuberculosis may be atypical in that there is a higher frequency of negative tuberculin skin tests,[31] increased middle and lower lobe involvement,[32] diffuse rather than localized infiltrates,[31] mediastinal adenopathy, a decreased frequency of cavitation,[32] and a greater frequency of extrapulmonary involvement.[31] Several patients with AIDS and documented pulmonary tuberculosis have been reported to have normal chest x-rays at presentation.[32] Unusual manifestations of extrapulmonary involvement have included endobronchial lesions, vertebral osteomyelitis, intra-abdominal and intramuscular abscess, bacteremia, and central nervous systemic mass lesions. The treatment of pulmonary or extrapulmonary tuberculosis in HIV-infected patients consists of isoniazid (300 mg/day), rifampin (600 mg/day), and pyrazinamide (20 to 30 mg/kg/day); ethambutol (15 to 25 mg/kg/day) may be added if the possibility of resistance to antituberculous medications is present. Pyrazinamide should be discontinued after 2 months of therapy. Ethambutol should be discontinued after 2 months as well, if sputum culture results indicate susceptibility of the organism to both isoniazid and rifampin. Isoniazid and rifampin should be administered for a minimum of 9 months, and at least 6 months beyond conversion of the sputum culture to negative.[33] Since there have been several reports of both therapeutic failure and early relapse in patients with AIDS who receive standard courses of antituberculous therapy,[34, 35] close monitoring during and after completion of therapy is essential. Chest x-ray and sputum culture should be performed at the completion of therapy and again 6 months later. In addition, it should be noted that the administration of ketoconazole in conjunction with rifampin results in decreased serum levels of both drugs[36]; therefore, coadministration of these drugs should be avoided.

Patients with a positive tuberculin skin test and no evidence of active infection should receive isoniazid, 300 mg daily, for a period of 1 year in order to prevent recrudescence.[33] Note that an induration of greater than 5 mm in reaction to the tuberculin skin test is considered positive in patients with HIV infection. Immunization with bacillus Calmette-Guérin should be avoided, because of the possibility of disseminated bacillus Calmette-Guérin disease in patients with HIV infection.[37]

## Toxoplasmosis

Toxoplasma encephalitis is the most common cause of intracerebral mass lesions in patients with AIDS, and represents one of the most common opportunistic infections of the central nervous system in such patients. In the United States, the prevalence of serum antibody to Toxoplasma gondii in HIV-infected populations is 10% to 32%[38, 39]; Toxoplasma encephalitis may develop in up to 40% of seropositives.[38, 39] The diagnosis should be suspected in HIV-infected patients with focal or generalized neurologic abnormalities. Although definitive diagnosis requires a brain biopsy, a presumptive diagnosis may be made in a patient with consistent clinical findings who has ring-enhancing hypodense or isodense lesions (single or multiple) on computerized tomography or magnetic resonance imaging studies. In areas of low endemicity for T. gondii, such as the United States, Toxoplasma encephalitis is usually the result of reactivation of a latent infection, and patients generally will have specific IgG antibody in the absence of serum IgM antibody. In contrast, in countries where toxoplasmosis is more prevalent (e.g., France), as many as 20% of HIV-infected patients with Toxoplasma encephalitis will have an elevated serum IgM antibody level to the organism, indicative of acute infection.[40] Standard therapy consists of the dihydrofolate reductase inhibitor pyrimethamine (75 mg/day) in combination with sulfadiazine (6 to 8 g/day). In many centers, a loading dose of pyrimethamine (200 mg) is administered in order to achieve more rapid therapeutic levels in the serum. Since these agents are active against only the tachyzoite form of the organism rather than the cyst, the infection is suppressed rather than eradicated. Therefore, lifelong therapy is administered in reduced dosages (pyrimethamine 25 mg/day, sulfadiazine 1 to 2 g/day) after clinical and/or radiographic improvement has been documented. Folinic acid (10 to 20 mg/day) may be added to reverse leukopenia. However, in many cases, either bone marrow suppression or cutaneous rash necessitates the alteration of therapy. In addition, sulfadiazine may cause acute renal failure due to crystallization of the drug in the urinary collecting system.[41] One alternative therapy is clindamycin, which has shown efficacy in the murine model of toxoplasmosis.[42] Preliminary studies have suggested effectiveness when clindamycin is administered alone[43] or in combination with pyrimethamine[44, 45]; dosages utilized have ranged from 1,800 to 4,800 mg/day intravenously, in 3 to 4 divided doses daily. Oral doses are generally 600 mg four times daily. Promising new agents include several macrolide compounds, such as azithromycin and clarithromycin, a hydroxynapthoquinone agent called 566C80, and recombinant interferon-γ. Clinical trials currently are ongoing.

## Herpes Simplex Virus

Serologic studies have documented a high frequency of infection with herpes simplex virus (HSV) in patients with HIV infection. In particular, the prevalence of serum antibody to HSV-2 is higher than that seen in the general population.[46, 47, 47a] Some authors have suggested that the frequency and severity of herpetic outbreaks may increase as the level of immunosuppression due to HIV increases,[48] although this has not yet been documented. Chronic cutaneous lesions due to HSV in patients with AIDS have been well described.[49] Oral acyclovir is the standard treatment for acute outbreaks of HSV in HIV-infected patients, in dosages of 200 to 400 mg five times daily; severe episodes may be treated with intravenous acyclovir (5 mg/kg/8 hr). Chemosuppressive therapy with oral acyclovir (400 mg twice daily or 200 mg three times daily) has been shown to decrease the frequency of symptomatic recurrences in immunocompetent patients, and safety has been established in patients receiving suppressive therapy for up to 5 years.[50] Therefore, many HIV-infected patients receive chronic chemosuppression with acyclovir. However, infections that are resistant to treatment with acyclovir clinically and in the laboratory are increasing in incidence.[51, 52] Although it is possible that chronic or recurrent exposure to acyclovir exerts a selection pressure that facilitates the predominance of acyclovir-resistant mutants, risk factors for the development of acyclovir resistance have not yet been defined. The treatment of acyclovir-resistant HSV infection with foscarnet, a parenteral agent that inhibits DNA polymerase,[53] has appeared effective in uncontrolled studies.[52, 54] A recently completed comparative trial of foscarnet vs. vidarabine for the treatment of acyclovir-resistant mucocutaneous HSV infection in patients with AIDS demonstrated superior effect and lesser toxicity of foscarnet.[54a] Potential side effects of foscarnet, used in dosages of 40 mg/kg every 8 hours, include renal insufficiency, anemia, leukopenia, hypocalcemia, hyperphosphatemia, and nausea.[52] However, since acyclovir-resistant HSV is prone to recur once healed,[52, 54a] the investigation of effective secondary prophylactic agents as well as orally bioavailable antiviral agents for the treatment of resistant infection is required.

## Varicella-Zoster Virus

Although infection with varicella-zoster virus infection is common in the general population,[55] symptomatic reactivation manifesting as zoster is uncommon except in immunosuppressed or aged individuals. HIV-infected patients have an increased prevalence of zoster outbreak, particularly as the level of immunosuppression advances.[56] In addition, cutaneous dissemination of zoster and recurrences after healing occur more frequently in

HIV-infected patients than in others.[57] Treatment with oral (800 mg five times daily) or intravenous (10 mg/kg/8 hr) acyclovir has been shown to decrease the rate of dissemination of zoster and to accelerate clinical and virologic cure in immunocompetent[58] and non-HIV immunocompromised[59] patients; because of this, HIV-infected patients with zoster often are treated with acyclovir as well. Although the treatment of localized cutaneous outbreaks has not been proven to be effective in decreasing morbidity in HIV-infected patients, those with zoster in the trigeminal distribution are felt to require therapy in order to prevent ophthalmic complications.

As is the case with HSV infection in HIV-infected patients, reports of acyclovir-resistant zoster recently have begun to appear in the literature.[60, 61] Treatment with foscarnet has been effective in a limited number of patients.[61] Although its efficacy has not been proven, therapy with foscarnet should be considered in circumstances of severe infection that is unresponsive to acyclovir and shows resistance *in vitro*.

## Cytomegalovirus Infection

Greater than 50% of the general population is seropositive for cytomegalovirus (CMV) by the age of 50 years. However, the infection is most often asymptomatic in immunocompetent patients. In contrast, almost one third of the 90% of patients with AIDS who are infected with CMV will manifest disease.[62] Reactivation of latent infection is the usual route of pathogenesis, and occurs with increasing frequency as the level of immunosuppression advances. HIV-infected patients with CMV retinitis typically have CD4 cell counts $<100/mm^3$.

Hematogenous dissemination of CMV infection may result in a variety of clinical presentations, including retinitis, esophagitis, colitis, adrenalitis, hepatitis, and pneumonitis. More rare manifestations include pancreatitis, cutaneous lesions, and appendicitis. Retinal infection, manifested by granular white infiltrates that coalesce, tends to spread along the course of major retinal vessels in the so-called brushfire pattern. Intraretinal hemorrhage may or may not be present. Left untreated, the disease most often progresses within 4 to 6 weeks. Progressive retinal necrosis may cause scotomata, retinal detachment, or infection of the optic nerve, making CMV infection the most common cause of visual loss in patients with AIDS. Other infections that must be considered in the differential diagnosis of retinopathy in patients with AIDS include toxoplasmosis, syphilis, candidal infection, HSV, and varicella-zoster infection. However, accompanying vitreous reaction, the presence of anterior uveitis, and/or the pace of the destructive process help to distinguish these processes from CMV retinitis.

Ganciclovir (formerly DHPG) is a licensed agent for the treatment of CMV retinitis. Two-week induction periods using intravenous dosages of 5 mg/kg/12 hr followed by maintenance therapy (5 mg/kg/day 5 to 7 days a week) have been shown to delay the rate of progression of CMV infection.[63, 64] However, its myelosuppressive side effects, particularly of the white blood cell line, may make it difficult for patients to tolerate chronically and/or to receive the drug in conjunction with the antiretroviral agent zidovudine.[65] The concomitant administration of granulocyte-colony stimulating factor may help to prevent dose-limiting leukopenia in these circumstances.[66] Other potential side effects include thrombocytopenia, the inhibition of spermatogenesis and oocyte maturation, and infections associated with chronic indwelling central venous catheters. An additional concern is the development of resistance to ganciclovir after prolonged exposure to the drug,[67] although the correlation of in vitro resistance in immunosuppressed patients to clinical failure is as yet unclear.

An experimental agent that may hold promise for the treatment of CMV retinitis is foscarnet (phosphonoformic acid). Preliminary studies suggest that foscarnet may effectively decrease the rate of progression of retinal infection.[68] However, like ganciclovir, foscarnet therapy does not appear to be curative. The recommended dosage of this agent is 60 mg/kg/8 hr for 2 to 3 weeks, followed by maintenance therapy of 90 to 120 mg/kg/day. Potential side effects include renal insufficiency, neurologic abnormalities, anemia, hypocalcemia, and gastrointestinal intolerance. The fact that myelosuppression is relatively uncommon with foscarnet administration may enable the concomitant use of zidovudine. Modifications under study for the treatment of CMV retinitis include alternating intravenous ganciclovir with foscarnet to effect a possible synergistic effect and/or prevent the development of resistance, and administering oral ganciclovir.

The diagnosis and treatment of other forms of disseminated CMV infection in patients with AIDS is more controversial. Although uncontrolled studies have reported clinical response of patients with colitis or esophagitis to therapy with ganciclovir,[69] the resolution of ulceration under endoscopic visualization has not been reliably associated with the cessation of viral shedding. In regard to pneumonitis, studies have demonstrated that CMV rarely was found to be the sole pathogen in the bronchoalveolar lavage fluid specimens of AIDS patients with symptoms of pneumonia, and that recovery occurred in the great majority of patients despite the absence of specific anti-CMV treatment.[70] Therefore, more refined diagnostic methods for CMV pneumonia will need to be devised before the effect of therapy can be evaluated.

A polyradiculopathy due to CMV infection has been described in several patients with AIDS, presenting with progressive flaccid paraparesis, urinary retention, and cerebrospinal fluid polymorphonuclear pleocytosis.[71] Ganciclovir therapy, if begun early, holds some potential for success in reversing neurologic deficits. However, once the deficits are fixed, treatment is likely to be ineffective.

## Cryptococcal Infection

Cryptococcal meningitis remains a frequent and potentially severe opportunistic infection in patients with HIV infection. It may present in an indolent manner or as an acute illness. Fever, headache, and malaise are the most common symptoms, and are present in 65% to 90% of patients. Nausea or vomiting and fever, although less specific, are present in 40% to 50% of patients, while alteration in mental status, meningismus, and photophobia are more rare (18% to 28%).[72] Focal neurologic deficits are uncommon, occurring in 10% to 15% of cases.[72, 73] Examination of the cerebrospinal fluid often reveals minimal lymphocytic inflammatory infiltrate, with 20 or more white blood cells present in only 21% of patients in one series.[72] Detectable cryptococcal antigen in the cerebrospinal fluid and a positive India ink test are usually, but not invariably, present, whereas the blood nearly always will have detectable cryptococcal antigen.[72]

Treatment modalities for acute cryptococcal meningitis include intravenous amphotericin B (0.6 to 0.7 mg/kg/day) or fluconazole (200 to 400 mg/day). Flucytosine may be administered in conjunction with amphotericin B, in dosages of 100 to 150 mg/kg/day. Although a synergistic response has been demonstrated in patients not infected with HIV,[74] its benefit has not been proven in patients with AIDS and its use holds a substantial risk of myelosuppression. If flucytosine is administered, therefore, serum levels should be monitored to avoid excessive dosing. Adverse effects of amphotericin B, including a rise in the creatinine level, nausea, fever, and hypokalemia, may be ameliorated partially by symptomatic treatment, but ultimately may cause the discontinuation of therapy. Potential adverse effects of fluconazole are nausea, vomiting, and elevation of liver enzymes; diarrhea, headache, rash, and abdominal pain have been described occasionally as well. However, most patients tolerate therapy with fluconazole quite well. Experimental therapies under study for acute cryptococcal meningitis include triazole compounds (itraconazole), and liposome-encapsulate amphotericin B.

Extraneural involvement with Cryptococcus (e.g., cryptococcemia) tends to be a poor prognosticator.[72] Other factors that may portend a poor prognosis include an abnormal mental status at presentation, a cerebrospinal cryptococcal antigen titer of greater than 1:8, a cerebrospinal white cell count of less than 20 cells per high-power field, age less than or equal to 35 years, and the presence of hyponatremia (Saag M, unpublished data, 1991).

Preliminary results from multicenter studies have shown that cerebrospinal fluid cultures may remain positive in up to 50% of patients after 10 weeks of standard therapy, and that mortality approximates 25%. Therefore, both morbidity and mortality from cryptococcal infection remain substantial in the HIV-infected population. Several studies have demonstrated that maintenance antifungal therapy is required to prevent relapse of cryptococcosis in patients with AIDS; current choices for maintenance therapy include fluconazole (100 to 200 mg/day) or amphotericin B (1 mg/kg/wk).

Pneumonia due to Cryptococcus neoformans may occur in HIV-infected patients without concurrent meningitis. Radiographic presentation is most typically that of nodular interstitial infiltrates. Cavitation or pleural effusion may be present.[75] The isolation of *Cryptococcus* from a respiratory specimen or the detection of cryptococcal antigen in the blood in the absence of meningitis in a patient with HIV infection should be considered an indication for full-dose and prolonged systemic antifungal therapy.

## Kaposi's Sarcoma

Since its recognition in 1981 in previously healthy homosexual men,[76] Kaposi's sarcoma has become the most common neoplasm in HIV-infected patients.[77] For unclear reasons, it remains most prevalent in homosexual men as compared to patients with other risk factors. Recent studies suggest that the percentage of AIDS patients who develop Kaposi's sarcoma is declining, but that the severity of the disease and its prognosis have worsened in recent years compared to those cases diagnosed early in the AIDS epidemic.[78, 79]

AIDS-related Kaposi's sarcoma lesions that occur on the extremities are nodular and subcutaneous, with violaceous pigmentation. Local complications include superficial necrosis, bacterial superinfection, and lymphedema.[77] It has been noted that prognosis is worsened in patients with cutaneous lesions who have concomitant systemic symptoms (e.g., fever, weight loss, night sweats).[80] Other sites of involvement include the peripheral lymph nodes, the mouth (with complications of gingival bleeding or pain), and the visceral organs, particularly the lungs and gastrointestinal tract (with complications of respiratory insufficiency or malabsorption, respectively).

Although the cutaneous lesions of Kaposi's sarcoma generally may be recognized by those familiar with them, obtaining a punch biopsy of the skin to allow differentiation from bacillary epithelioid angiomatosis, an illness that generally responds to treatment with erythromycin, may be prudent.[81] Therapy for Kaposi's sarcoma is palliative rather than curative, and therefore is reserved for patients with painful, cosmetically disfiguring, or systemically symptomatic lesions.[77] Case series of patients receiving either single-agent or multiagent chemotherapy (e.g., vincristine, vinblastine, etoposide, bleomycin, doxorubicin), often in combination with zidovudine, have described varying results; clinical response is generally better in patients with less advanced immunosuppression. Major toxicities have included myelosuppression and peripheral neuropathy. Preliminary reports of topical therapy (e.g., intralesional vinblastine, topical liquid nitrogen, intralesional interferon-α) have been encouraging, but are as yet unconfirmed. Reports of therapeutic trials with the immunomodulators interferon-α and interferon-β have been generally disappointing.[77] Radiation therapy for Kaposi's sarcoma may have good results in specific patients, and is particularly useful when prompt local response is desirable (e.g., in the presence of painful lesions or lymphedema). However, side effects of mucositis and myelosuppression limit the routine use of such therapy.[77] Thus, the selection of therapy for patients with AIDS-associated Kaposi's sarcoma must be individualized according to the degree of dysfunction resulting from the neoplasm in conjunction with the overall clinical and immunologic status of the patient.

## Non-Hodgkin's Lymphoma

Non-Hodgkin's lymphoma appears to occur in all groups at risk for HIV infection, in contrast to Kaposi's sarcoma, and preliminary data suggest that its frequency may be on the rise.[82] Clinical presentation in HIV-infected patients is characterized by widespread disease at the time of diagnosis, with frequent involvement of extranodal sites.[83] The most common sites of involvement are the gastrointestinal tract, the central nervous system or meninges, the bone marrow, the liver, and the lung.[84] In addition, extralymphatic sites such as the anorectal area, the pericardium, and the common bile duct may be involved. Constitutional symptoms are occasionally, but not invariably, present.

The natural history is characterized by B cell phenotypic tumors of intermediate or high-grade histologic subtype that progress rapidly and respond relatively poorly to therapy. In contrast to non–HIV-infected individuals with non-Hodgkin's lymphoma, standard combination chemotherapeutic regimens tend to evoke an incomplete response of short duration. In retrospective studies, the median survival of chemotherapy-treated patients has ranged from 4 to 6 months; deaths were due most frequently to recurrent lymphoma or opportunistic infections. In addition, cytopenic complications of systemic chemotherapy appear to be more frequent in HIV-infected patients than in others.[84] Factors associated with improved prognosis and survival include a CD4 count $> 100/mm^3$, the absence of a prior AIDS diagnosis, Karnofsky performance status $> 70$, and the absence of extranodal sites of disease.[84] Patients with intermediate-grade, large-cell, noncleaved histologic subtypes have longer survival times than do others.[85] Dose-intensive myelosuppressive chemotherapeutic regimens, such as those containing cyclophosphamide, have resulted in shortened survival times in prospective studies of patients with AIDS-related non-Hodgkin's lymphoma.[84] The use of adjunctive recombinant human granulocyte-macrophage colony-stimulating factor to ameliorate the toxicities of systemic chemotherapy is currently under study.

Approximately one third of patients with AIDS lymphoma have central nervous system involvement at diagnosis. However, there have been no prospective studies of therapy for primary central nervous system lymphoma in HIV-infected patients. Although whole-brain irradiation has evoked good initial responses in some,[86] most patients have died shortly after treatment due to opportunistic infections. Therefore, further studies will focus on the use of prophylactic regimens against opportunistic infections in combination with radiation or systemic chemotherapy.

## Immune Thrombocytopenic Purpura

AIDS-related thrombocytopenia may occur as an isolated phenomenon or in combination with other manifestations of HIV infection; its mechanism is poorly understood.[87] Mild thrombocytopenia may respond to the addition of zidovudine therapy.[88] If thrombocytopenia becomes severe, further treatment may be necessary to prevent major bleeding complications. Systemic corticosteroid therapy has seemed to result in an increase in the platelet count when administered to HIV-infected patients with thrombocytopenia in several case series; however, thrombocytopenia tends to recur following the discontinuation of therapy.[89] Splenectomy may be considered in patients who fail to maintain a persistent response. Alternatively, high-dose intravenous immune globulin may be administered.[90] However, elevations in platelet counts generally are transient and the treatment is expensive.

## The Acquired Immunodeficiency Syndrome Dementia Complex

The AIDS dementia complex, also known as HIV encephalopathy, is the most common neurologic problem in AIDS patients, occurring in 40% to 60% of these individuals.[91] It may be the presenting symptom of AIDS, occurring prior to opportunistic infections or malignancies, or it may occur at a later time. Features of the AIDS dementia complex include decreased memory, inability to concentrate, apathy, and psychomotor retardation. Increased ventricular and sulcal size on computerized tomographic scanning is consistent with cerebral atrophy. Progression without treatment is generally slow, but inexorable. However, improvement has been documented in patients treated with zidovudine.[92] It is currently the standard of practice to maintain higher dosages of zidovudine (e.g., 200 mg five times daily) in patients with encephalopathy rather than the lower dosages shown to be effective systemically, in order to ensure adequate central nervous system levels of the drug.

## Neuropathy/Myopathy

Axonal degeneration may cause a sensory polyneuropathy in HIV-infected patients, and typically presents with symmetric distal paresthesias. Although zidovudine therapy has seemed to result in improvement in several case reports, its role in treatment is unclear. Symptomatic treatment with tricyclic antidepressants (amitriptyline, desipramine), phenytoin, or carbamazepine may be effective.

Progressive motor weakness may result from an inflammatory demyelinating polyneuropathy, often seen early in the course of HIV infection. If rapid in onset, it may be indistinguishable from the Guillain-Barré syndrome, and cerebrospinal fluid may show pleocytosis and marked elevation of protein. Although an autoimmune etiology is suspected, effective therapy has not been established; plasmapheresis and/or corticosteroid administration have been advocated by some authors.

An inflammatory myopathy (polymyositis) may occur in the presence of long-term zidovudine usage, with a suggestion of abnormal mitochondria on muscle biopsy ("ragged red fibers"); this is generally reversible upon the discontinuation of zidovudine. Clinical features may include myalgias, proximal muscle weakness, muscle tenderness, and fatigue. In addition, a myopathy in HIV-infected patients who are not receiving zidovudine has been described. Optimal treatment is unclear.

## Wasting

Progressive loss of weight may occur in the late stages of HIV infection, even in the absence of overt malabsorption or diarrhea. Enteral or parenteral nutritional supplementation may have variable success. Experimental therapies under study for the treatment of wasting include appetite stimulants and antiemetics such as megestrol acetate[93] and dronabinol.[94]

## References

1. Northfelt DW, Clement M, Safrin S: Extrapulmonary pneumocystosis: A review of the literature, emphasizing clinical features in human immunodeficiency virus infection. *Medicine* 1990; 69:392–398.
2. Wharton JM, Coleman DL, Wofsy CB, et al: Trimethoprim-sulfamethoxazole or pentamidine for Pneumocystis carinii pneumonia in the acquired immunodeficiency syndrome. *Ann Intern Med* 1986; 105:37–44.
3. Medina I, Mills J, Leoung G, et al: Oral therapy for Pneumocystis carinii pneumonia in the acquired immunodeficiency syndrome. A controlled trial of trimethoprim-sulfamethoxazole versus dapsone-trimethoprim. *N Engl J Med* 1990; 323:776–782.
4. Sattler FR, Cowan R, Nielsen DM, et al: Trimethoprim-sulfamethoxazole compared with pentamidine for treatment of Pneumocystis carinii pneumonia in the acquired immunodeficiency syndrome. A prospective, noncrossover study. *Ann Intern Med* 1989; 110:606–611.
5. Conte JE, Chernoff D, Feigal DW, et al: Intravenous or inhaled pentamidine for treating Pneumocystis carinii pneumonia in AIDS. *Ann Intern Med* 1990; 113:203–209.
6. Mills J, Leoung G, Medina I, et al: Dapsone treatment of Pneumocystis carinii pneumonia in the acquired immunodeficiency syndrome. *Antimicrob Agents Chemother* 1988; 32:1057–1060.
7. Safrin S, Sattler FR, Lee BL, et al: Failure of dapsone as a single agent for therapy of Pneumocystis carinii pneumonia. *JAIDS,* 1991; 4:244-249.
8. Toma E, Fournier S, Poisson M, et al: Clindamycin with primaquine for Pneumocystis carinii pneumonia. *Lancet* 1989; i:1046–1048.
9. Joseph P, Marzouk J, Phelps R: Oral clindamycin plus primaquine for Pneu-

mocystis carinii pneumonia (abstract). Presented at the VIth International Conference on AIDS, San Francisco, California, June 1990.

10. The National Institutes of Health-University of California Expert Panel for Corticosteroids as Adjunctive Therapy for Pneumocystis Pneumonia: Consensus statement on the use of corticosteroids as adjunctive therapy for Pneumocystis pneumonia in the acquired immunodeficiency syndrome. *N Engl J Med* 1990; 323:1500–1504.

11. Allegra CJ, Chabner BA, Tuazon CU, et al: Trimetrexate for the treatment of Pneumocystis carinii pneumonia in patients with the acquired immunodeficiency syndrome. *N Engl J Med* 1987; 317:978–985.

12. U.S. Department of Health and Human Services: Guidelines for prophylaxis against Pneumocystis carinii pneumonia for persons infected with human immunodeficiency virus. *MMWR* 1989; 38(55):1-9.

13. Fischl MA, Richman DD, Grieco MH, et al: The efficacy of azidothymidine (AZT) in the treatment of patients with AIDS and AIDS related complex. *N Engl J Med* 1987; 317:185–191.

14. Phair J, Munoz A, Detels R, et al: The risk of Pneumocystis carinii pneumonia among men infected with human immunodeficiency virus type 1. *N Engl J Med* 1990; 322;161–165.

15. Hughes WT, Rivera GK, Schell MJ, et al: Successful intermittent chemoprophylaxis for Pneumocystis carinii pneumonitis. *N Engl J Med* 1987; 316:1627–1632.

16. Hughes WT, Kuhn S, Chaudhary S, et al: Successful chemoprophylaxis for Pneumocystis carinii pneumonitis. *N Engl J Med* 1977; 297:1419–1426.

17. Fischl MA, Dickinson GM, La Voie L: Safety and efficacy of sulfamethoxazole and trimethoprim chemoprophylaxis for Pneumocystis carinii pneumonia in AIDS. *JAMA* 1988; 259:1185–1189.

18. Hughes WT: Comparison of dosages, intervals and drugs in the prevention of Pneumocystis carinii pneumonia. *Antimicrob Agents Chemother* 1988; 32:623–625.

19. Metroka CE, Braun N, Josefberg H, et al: Successful chemoprophylaxis for Pneumocystis carinii pneumonia with dapsone in patients with AIDS and ARC (abstract). Presented at the IVth International Conference on AIDS, Stockholm, Sweden, June 1988.

20. Girard P-M, Landman R, Gaudebout C, et al: Prevention of Pneumocystis carinii pneumonia relapse by pentamidine aerosol in zidovudine-treated AIDS patients. *Lancet* 1989; ii:1348–1352.

21. Leoung GS, Feigal DW, Montgomery AB, et al: Aerosolized pentamidine for prophylaxis against Pneumocystis carinii pneumonia. The San Francisco community prophylaxis trial. *N Engl J Med* 1990; 323:769.

22. Pearson RD, Hewlett EL: Use of pyrimethamine-sulfadoxine (Fansidar) in prophylaxis against chloroquine-resistant Plasmodium falciparum and Pneumocystis carinii. *Ann Intern Med* 1987; 106:714–718.

23. Hawkins CC, Gold JW, Whimbey E, et al: Mycobacterium avium complex infections in patients with the acquired immunodeficiency syndrome. *Ann Intern Med* 1986; 105:184–188.

24. Stacey AR: Isolation of Mycobacterium avium-intracellulare-scrofulaceum complex from faeces of patients with AIDS. *Br Med J [Clin Res]* 1986; 293:1194.

25. Agins B, Spicehandler D, Zuger A, et al: M. avium-complex infections in AIDS: Significance of respiratory isolates and therapy (abstract). Presented at

the Interscience Conference on Antimicrobial Agents and Chemotherapy, Minneapolis, September 1985.

26. Chiu J, Nussbaum J, Bozzette S, et al: Treatment of disseminated Mycobacterium avium complex infection in AIDS with amikacin, ethambutol, rifampin, and ciprofloxacin. Ann Intern Med 1990; 113:358–361.

27. Cohn J, Holzman RS: Survival of patients with AIDS following M. avium-intracellulare infection: Roles of rifabutin and prior duration of AIDS (abstract). Presented at the Interscience Conference on Antimicrobial Agents and Chemotherapy, New Orleans, September 1986.

28. Horsburgh CR, Havlik JA, Thompson SE: Survival of AIDS patients with disseminated Mycobacterium avium complex infection: A case-controlled study (abstract). Presented at the VIth International Conference on AIDS, San Francisco, California, June 1990.

29. Kiehn TE, Edwards FF, Brannon P, et al: Infections caused by Mycobacterium avium complex in immunocompromised patients: Diagnosis by blood culture and fecal examination, antimicrobial susceptibility tests, and morphological and seroagglutination characteristics. J Clin Microbiol 1985; 21:168–173.

30. Gangadharam PRJ, Perumal VK, Parikh K, et al: Susceptibility of beige mice to Mycobacterium avium complex infections by different routes of challenge. Am Rev Respir Dis 1989; 139:1098–1104.

31. Chaisson RE, Schechter GF, Theuer CP, et al: Tuberculosis in patients with the acquired immunodeficiency syndrome. Am Rev Respir Dis 1987; 136:570–574.

32. Pitchenik AE, Rubinson HA: The radiographic appearance of tuberculosis in patients with the acquired immunodeficiency virus syndrome (AIDS) and pre-AIDS. Am Rev Respir Dis 1985; 131:393–396.

33. Centers for Disease Control: Diagnosis and management of mycobacterial infection and disease in persons with human immunodeficiency virus infection. Ann Intern Med 1987; 106:254–256.

34. Davis I, Acosta A, Lee S: Susceptible M. tuberculosis refractory to standard therapy with progression to central nervous system involvement (abstract). Presented at the VIth International Conference on AIDS, San Francisco, California, June 1990.

35. Sunderam G, Mangura BT, Lombardo JM, et al: Failure of "optimal" four-drug short course tuberculosis chemotherapy in a compliant patient with human immunodeficiency virus. Am Rev Respir Dis 1987; 136:1475–1478.

36. Engelhard D, Stutman HR, Marks MI: Interaction of ketoconazole with rifampin and isoniazid. N Engl J Med 1984; 311:1681–1683.

37. Reynes J, Perez C, Lamaury I, et al: Bacille Calmette-Guerin adenitis 30 years after immunization in a patient with AIDS (letter). J Infect Dis 1989; 160:727.

38. Israelski DM, Byers E, Danneman BR, et al: Prevalence of Toxoplasma gondii in a cohort of homosexual men (abstract). Presented at the 30th Interscience Conference on Antimicrobial Agents and Chemotherapy, Atlanta, Georgia, September 1990.

39. Grant IH, Gold JWM, Rosenblum M, et al: Toxoplasma gondii serology in HIV-infected patients: The development of central nervous system toxoplasmosis in AIDS. Aids 1990; 4:519–521.

40. Luft BJ, Remington JS: Toxoplasmic encephalitis. J Infect Dis 1988; 157:106.

41. Christin S, Baumelou A, Ben Hmida M, et al: Acute renal failure due to sulfadiazine in patients with AIDS. *Nephron* 1990; 55:233–234.

42. Hofflin JM, Remington JS: Clindamycin in a murine model of toxoplasmic encephalitis. *Antimicrob Agents Chemother* 1987; 31:492–496.

43. Danneman BR, Israelski DM, Remington JS: Treatment of toxoplasmic encephalitis with intravenous clindamycin. *Arch Intern Med* 1988; 148:2477–2482.

44. Danneman BR, McCutchan JA, Israelski DM, et al: Treatment of toxoplasma encephalitis in patients with AIDS; a randomized trial comparing pyrimethamine plus clindamycin to pyrimethamine plus sulfonamides (abstract). Presented at the 30th Interscience Conference on Antimicrobial Agents and Chemotherapy, Atlanta, Georgia, September 1990.

45. Leport C, Fdez-Martin J, Morlat P, et al: Combination of pyrimethamine-clindamycin for acute therapy of toxoplasmic encephalitis. A pilot study in 13 AIDS patients (abstract). Presented at the 30th Interscience Conference on Antimicrobial Agents and Chemotherapy, Atlanta, Georgia, September 1990.

46. Holmberg SD, Stewart JA, Gerber AR, et al: Prior herpes simplex virus type 2 infection as a risk factor for HIV infection. *JAMA* 1988; 259:1048–1050.

47. Stamm WE, Handsfield HH, Rompalo AM, et al: The association between genital ulcer disease and acquisition of HIV infection in homosexual men. *JAMA* 1988; 260:1429–1433.

47a. Safrin S, Ashley R, Houlihan C, et al: Clinical and serological features of herpes simplex virus infection in the acquired immunodeficiency syndrome. *AIDS,* in press.

48. Erlich KS, Mills J: Herpes simplex virus, in Cohen PT, Sande MA, Volberding PA, (eds): *The AIDS Knowledge Base.* Waltham, Massachusetts, Massachusetts Medical Society, 1990, pp 6.4.2-1–6.4.2-16.

49. Siegal FP, Lopez C, Hammer GS, et al: Severe acquired immunodeficiency in male homosexuals manifested by chronic perianal ulcerative herpes simplex lesions. *N Engl J Med* 1981; 305:1439–1444.

50. Kurtz TO, Boone GS, and the Acyclovir Study Group: Safety and efficacy of long-term suppressive zovirax treatment of frequently recurring genital herpes: Year 5 results (abstract). Presented at the 30th Interscience Conference on Antimicrobial Agents and Chemotherapy, Atlanta, Georgia, September 1990.

51. Erlich KS, Mills J, Chatis P, et al: Acyclovir-resistant herpes simplex virus infections in patients with the acquired immunodeficiency syndrome. *N Engl J Med* 1989; 320:293–296.

52. Safrin S, Assaykeen T, Follansbee S, et al: Foscarnet therapy for acyclovir-resistant mucocutaneous herpes simplex virus infection in 26 AIDS patients: Preliminary data. *J Infect Dis* 1990; 161:1078–1084.

53. Oberg B: Antiviral effects of phosphonoformate. *Pharmacol Ther* 1983; 19:387–415.

54. Erlich KS, Jacobson MA, Koehler JE, et al: Foscarnet therapy of severe acyclovir-resistant herpes simplex virus infections in patients with the acquired immunodeficiency syndrome. *Ann Intern Med* 1989; 110:710–713.

54a. Safrin S, Crumpacker C, Chatis P, et al: Treatment of acyclovir-resistant mucocutaneous herpes simplex infection in patients with the acquired immunodeficiency syndrome. A randomized multicenter study of foscarnet versus vidarabine. *N Engl J Med,* in press.

55. Weller TH: Varicella and herpes zoster. Changing concepts of the natural his-

tory, control and importance of a not-so-benign virus. N Engl J Med 1983; 309:1362–1368.

56. Friedman-Kien AE, Lafleur FL, Gendler E, et al: Herpes zoster: A possible early clinical sign for development of acquired immunodeficiency syndrome in high-risk individuals. J Am Acad Dermatol 1986; 14:1023–1028.

57. Cohen PR, Beltrani VP, Grossman ME: Disseminated zoster in patients with human immunodeficiency virus infection. Am J Med 1988; 84:1076–1080.

58. Peterslund NA, Seyer-Hansen K, Ipsen J, et al: Acyclovir in herpes zoster. Lancet 1981; ii:827–830.

59. Balfour HH, Bean B, Laskin OL, et al: Acyclovir halts progression of herpes zoster in immunocompromised patients. N Engl J Med 1983; 308:1448–1453.

60. Jacobson MA, Berger TG, Fikrig S, et al: Acyclovir-resistant varicella zoster virus infection after chronic oral acyclovir therapy in patients with the acquired immunodeficiency syndrome. Ann Intern Med 1990; 112:187–191.

61. Safrin S, Berger TG, Gilson I, et al: Foscarnet therapy in five patients with AIDS and acyclovir-resistant varicella zoster infection. Ann Intern Med 1991; 115:19-21.

62. Resta S, Wolitz R, Merigan TC: CMV retinitis in the AIDS patient. AIDS Updates 1990; 3:1–12.

63. Holland GN, Sakamoto MJ, Hardy D, et al: Treatment of cytomegalovirus retinopathy in patients with acquired immunodeficiency syndrome. Arch Ophthalmol 1986; 104:1794–1800.

64. Collaborative DHPG Treatment Study Group: Treatment of serious cytomegalovirus infections with 9-(1,3-dihydroxy-2-propoxymethyl)guanine in patients with AIDS and other immunodeficiencies. N Engl J Med 1986; 314:801–805.

65. Hochster H, Dieterich D, Bozzette S, et al: Toxicity of combined ganciclovir and zidovudine for cytomegalovirus disease associated with AIDS. Ann Intern Med 1990; 113:111–117.

66. Grossberg HS, Bonnem EM, Buhles WC: GM-CSF with ganciclovir for the treatment of CMV retinitis in AIDS. N Engl J Med 1989; 320:1560.

67. Erice A, Chou S, Biron KK, et al: Progressive disease due to ganciclovir-resistant cytomegalovirus in immunocompromised patients. N Engl J Med 1989; 320:289–293.

68. Jacobson MA, O'Donnell JJ, Mills J: Foscarnet treatment of cytomegalovirus retinitis in patients with the acquired immunodeficiency syndrome. Antimicrob Agents Chemother 1989; 33:736–741.

69. Chachoua A, Dieterich D, Krasinksi K, et al: 9-(1,3-dihydroxy-2-propoxymethyl)guanine (ganciclovir) in the treatment of cytomegalovirus gastrointestinal disease with the acquired immunodeficiency syndrome. Ann Intern Med 1987; 107:133–137.

70. Millar AB, Patou G, Miller RF, et al: Cytomegalovirus in the lungs of patients with AIDS. Respiratory pathogen or passenger? Am Rev Respir Dis 1990; 141:1474–1477.

71. Miller RG, Storey JR, Greco CM: Ganciclovir in the treatment of progressive AIDS-related polyradiculopathy. Neurology 1990; 40:569–574.

72. Chuck SL, Sande MA: Infections with Cryptococcus neoformans in the acquired immunodeficiency syndrome. N Engl J Med 1989; 321:794–799.

73. Dismukes WE: Cryptococcal meningitis in patients with AIDS. J Infect Dis 1988; 157:624–628.

74. Bennett JE, Dismukes WE, Duma RJ, et al: A comparison of amphotericin B

alone and combined with flucytosine in the treatment of cryptococcal meningitis. *N Engl J Med* 1979; 301:126–131.

75. Miller WT, Edelman JM, Miller WT: Cryptococcal pulmonary infection in patients with AIDS: Radiographic appearance. *Radiology* 1990; 175:725–728.

76. Friedman-Kien A, Laubenstein L, Marmor M, et al: Kaposi's sarcoma and Pneumocystis pneumonia among homosexual men—New York City and California. *MMWR* 1981; 30:305–308.

77. Northfelt DW, Volberding PA: AIDS-related Kaposi's sarcoma. Clinical presentation, biology, and therapy. *Adv Oncol* 1991; 7:9–17.

78. Rutherford GW, Schwarcz SK, Lemp GF, et al: The epidemiology of AIDS-related Kaposi's sarcoma in San Francisco. *J Infect Dis* 1989; 159:569–571.

79. Cusick PS, Moss AR, Bacchetti P, et al: Serologic variables at diagnosis with Kaposi's sarcoma (KS): Predictors of shortened survival (abstract). Presented at the Vth International Conference on AIDS, Montreal, Canada, June 1989.

80. Volberding PA, Cusick P, Feigal DW: HIV antigenemia at diagnosis with Kaposi's sarcoma. Predictors of shortened survival (abstract). Presented at the IVth International Conference on AIDS, Stockholm, Sweden, June 1988.

81. Koehler JE, LeBoit PE, Egbert BM, et al: Cutaneous vascular lesions and disseminated cat-scratch disease in patients with the acquired immunodeficiency syndrome (AIDS) and AIDS-related complex. *Ann Intern Med* 1988; 109:449–455.

82. Pluda JM, Yarchoan R, Jaffe ES, et al: Development of non-Hodgkin's lymphoma in a cohort of patients with severe human immunodeficiency virus (HIV) infection on long-term antiretroviral therapy. *Ann Intern Med* 1990; 113:276–282.

83. Levine AM: Therapeutic approaches to neoplasms in AIDS. *Rev Infect Dis* 1990; 12:938–943.

84. Kaplan LD, Abrams DI, Feigal E, et al: AIDS-associated non-Hodgkin's lymphoma in San Francisco. *JAMA* 1989; 261:719–724.

85. Knowles DM, Chamulak GA, Subar M, et al: Lymphoid neoplasia associated with the acquired immunodeficiency syndrome (AIDS). *Ann Intern Med* 1988; 108:744–753.

86. Baumgartner JE, Rachlin JR, Beckstead JH, et al: Primary central nervous system lymphomas: Natural history and response to radiation therapy in 55 patients with acquired immunodeficiency syndrome. *J Neurosurg* 1990; 73:206–211.

87. Abrams DI: The persistent lymphadenopathy syndrome and immune thrombocytopenic purpura in HIV-infected individuals, in Levy JA (ed): *AIDS. Pathogenesis and Treatment.* New York, Marcel Dekker Inc, 1989, pp 323–343.

88. The Swiss Group for Clinical Studies on the Acquired Immunodeficiency Syndrome: Zidovudine for the treatment of thrombocytopenia associated with human immunodeficiency virus (HIV). *Ann Intern Med* 1988; 109:718–721.

89. Walsh C, Krigel R, Lennette E, et al: Thrombocytopenia in homosexual patients: Prognosis, response to therapy, and prevalence of antibody to the retrovirus associated with the acquired immunodeficiency syndrome. *Ann Intern Med* 1985; 103:542–545.

90. Pollak AN, Janinis J, Green D: Successful intravenous immune globulin therapy for human immunodeficiency virus-associated thrombocytopenia. *Arch Intern Med* 1988; 148:695–697.

91. Ho DD, Bredesen DE, Vinters HV, et al: The acquired immunodeficiency syndrome (AIDS) dementia complex. Ann Intern Med 1989; 111:400–410.
92. Yarchoan R, Berg G, Brouwers P, et al: Response of human-immunodeficiency-virus-associated neurological disease to 3'-azido-3'-deoxythymidine. Lancet 1987; i:132–135.
93. Von Roenn JH, Murphy RL, Weber KM, et al: Megestrol acetate for treatment of cachexia associated with human immunodeficiency virus infection. Ann Intern Med 1988; 109:840–841.
94. Spaulding M: Recent studies of anorexia and appetite stimulation in the cancer patient. Oncology 1989; 3:17–23.

# The Molecular Genetics of Lung Cancer

## David P. Carbone, M.D., Ph.D.

Assistant Professor of Medical Oncology, University of Texas Southwestern
Medical Center, Dallas, Texas

## John D. Minna, M.D.

Director, Simmons Cancer Center, University of Texas Southwestern Medical
Center, Dallas, Texas

---

### Editor's Introduction

As Drs. Carbone and Minna point out, lung cancer today is the most common type
of cancer in women as well as men. Several environmental factors have been identified such as tobacco smoking, but these authors go on to examine the molecular
genetics of lung cancer, demonstrating that both environmental and familial influence may be related to lung cancer through various patterns of genetic defects.

The knowledge of these patterns of genetic aberration may, in the future, permit
better diagnostic testing for the disease as well as defining molecular-based therapy.

*James J. Leonard, M.D.*

---

An accumulation of genetic mutations within specific genes or their regulatory regions is thought to transform a normal cell into a malignant one. Recent advances in molecular genetics have begun to reveal some of these
lesions. In this chapter, we will review the current state of knowledge concerning the genetic and molecular regulatory lesions that have been found
to be associated with human lung cancer.

Lung cancer is now the most common type of cancer in both men and
women in the United States, accounting for more than 1,000,000 new
cases and 500,000 deaths annually.[1] It has long been known to be associated with exposure to chemical (e.g., tobacco-associated carcinogens) and
physical (e.g., radon) genotoxic agents. Covalent carcinogen-DNA adducts
that may lead to base misincorporation and thus to mutation have been
shown to correlate well with cigarette exposure. These adducts disappear
from the DNA after cessation of smoking,[2] directly linking smoking with
DNA damage.

## Lung Cancer Types

Human lung cancer occurs in several histologic types that, upon molecular analysis, have both similarities and differences. Squamous cell carcinoma and small-cell carcinoma (SCLC) are the types most associated with cigarette smoking; they develop in the proximal airways. Adenocarcinomas and bronchioalveolar carcinomas tend to develop more distally in the terminal bronchioles or alveoli. Mesothelioma develops from the pleura and is particularly associated with asbestos exposure. Last, large-cell carcinomas exhibit few differentiated features visible by light microscopy, and represent those lesions that cannot be otherwise classified. Occasionally, lung cancers occur that are obviously of mixed histology (adenosquamous, for example) and, on detailed examination, many apparently histologically unambiguous cancers display markers typically associated with other types (e.g., non-SCLC with neuroendocrine markers).

A clinical distinction is often drawn between SCLC and non-SCLC, since SCLCs typically are chemoresponsive and highly metastatic early in their course, and non-SCLCs usually are less responsive and more of a local problem. Many molecular studies group results based on this distinction, but it remains to be seen what the most useful molecular groupings will be.

## Dominant vs. Recessive Effects

Genes associated with cancer are called "oncogenes" in the broadest sense. There are several potential classes of genetic lesions involving oncogenes that require different types of molecular analyses for detection (Fig 1). Dominant acting mutations could occur in the coding sequence of genes, resulting in a product that actively causes growth dysregulation. In its simplest form, this type of mutation might occur in only one of the two alleles of a gene. Similarly, a regulatory mutation could occur that would cause overexpression of a normal protein product, also a dominant effect. Another class of genes acts in a recessive manner to suppress growth actively or induce or maintain differentiation. Both alleles would have to be lost or inactivated by mutation for loss of this suppression to occur, as loss of only one would leave a functional gene and gene product. This type of gene is known as a "recessive" oncogene or "tumor suppressor" gene. Dominant oncogenes and tumor suppressor genes will be discussed separately following.

## Dominant Oncogenes

Dominant oncogenes can be especially difficult to uncover without independent information, since the minimal lesion is a single base alteration of one allele. Most of the candidate dominant oncogenes have been found by

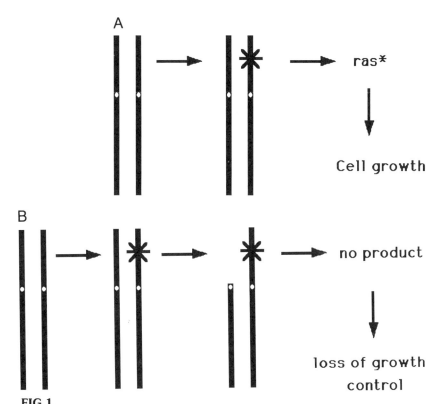

**FIG 1.**
Two classes of oncogenes are depicted: **A,** dominant oncogenes are activated by a mutation in only one of the two chromosomes. The presence of the dominant oncogene product stimulates the tumor cells to grow. **B,** recessive oncogenes ("tumor suppressor" genes) are inactivated by two mutations, one involving each of the two chromosomes. The absence of the recessive oncogene protein product allows the tumor cells to grow without normal controls.

searching for human analogues to viral oncogenic proteins. Retroviruses in particular seem to have the ability to acquire as part of their genomes normal cellular genes that, when mutant or overexpressed, are oncogenic. There are many examples, but *ras* and *myc* have received the most study in human lung cancer and will be discussed in the most detail as follows.

## The *ras* Gene Family

The oncogene *ras* was discovered as the transforming gene coded for by the acutely transforming retroviruses Harvey and Kirsten *rat* sarcoma viruses (hence, the name *ras*). These viruses carried homologous genes that were named v-H-*ras* and v-K-*ras* and caused a high frequency of tumors with a short latent period. Highly conserved normal cellular homologues were found and named H-*ras*-1, K-*ras*-2, and N-*ras*, as well as two pseudogenes. Mutated cellular *ras* genes were the first human genes proven to be oncogenic upon transfection into nonmalignant cells.[3] These genes encode for similar 21-kd proteins that are membrane-associated by virtue of post-translational acylation and are similar in structure to the signaling proteins known as G-proteins. They have been found to bind and hydrolyze guanosine triphosphate (GTP) in concert with another protein known as GAP (guanosine triphosphatase [GTPase] activating protein). The *ras*-GTP-GAP complex appears to be the growth-stimulatory conformation, which converts to a nonstimulating conformation with the hydrolysis of GTP to guanosine diphosphate (GDP).

Rodent viral genes were found to contain point mutations at codons 12 and 59, while mutations in human tumors have been found commonly in codons 12, 13, or 61. These mutations have been shown to render the normal cellular gene much more oncogenic, and to affect GTPase activity or binding affinity.[4, 5] Two studies have examined systematically the transforming efficiency and GTPase activity of all possible *ras* amino acid substitutions at codons 12 and 61.[4, 6] Substitutions at these positions result in similar deficits in GTPase activity, but widely variable in vitro transforming ability, suggesting that GTPase activity contributes only part of the oncogenic potential of these mutant proteins.

Somatic mutations have been found in *ras* genes in human lung cancer.[7, 8] Several large studies in this area are summarized in Table 1. Rodenhius et al.[9] found *ras* mutations in 9 out of 35 lung cancers, only in adenocarcinomas and all in K-*ras* codon 12. Mitsudomi et al.[10] examined 104 human lung

**TABLE 1.**
***ras* Mutations in Lung Cancer***

| Histologic Type | Mutations | Percent |
|---|---|---|
| Adenocarcinoma | 48/153 | 31 |
| Large-cell carcinoma | 7/33 | 21 |
| Squamous cell carcinoma | 3/59 | 5 |
| Adenosquamous carcinoma | 1/10 | 10 |
| Mucoepidermoid carcinoma | 0/1 | 0 |
| Carcinoid | 1/7 | 14 |
| Small-cell lung cancer | 0/52 | 0 |

*Frequency of occurrence of all *ras* mutations in lung cancer histologic subtypes. Data compiled from references 9, 10, and 11.

cancer cell lines and found mutations in 22 out of 65 non-SCLCs, predominantly in adenocarcinomas at K-*ras* codon 12, but also in other histologic types and other *ras* genes. Significantly, they found no *ras* mutations in 42 SCLC cell lines, indicating that these may not be random, unrelated, secondary effects of malignant transformation or growth in tissue culture. In fact, the introduction of a v-H-*ras* gene into SCLC cells in culture can cause their conversion to a phenotype that more closely resembles non-SCLC.[12] Further evidence for the involvement of *ras* genes in the genesis of lung cancer lies in the fact that when a transgenic mouse is produced that carries an activated (i.e., mutated) *ras* gene, lung adenocarcinomas are one of the most frequent tumor types that develop.[13]

The frequency of involvement of the various *ras* genes and codons in these studies of lung cancer is compiled in Table 2. In our experience, human tumors exhibit only those codon 12 and 61 mutants that have high transforming ability in in vitro assays.[10] Interestingly, *ras* mutations are common in colon cancer and rare, if they exist at all, in tumors of the breast and ovary.[14]

The presence of a *ras* mutation also has been reported to be an unfavorable prognostic factor.[15] Slebos et al. examined the status of the *ras* gene in 69 early stage adenocarcinomas of the lung that underwent curative surgical resection, and found highly significantly poorer overall survival ($P = .001$) and disease-free survival ($P = .006$) for the subgroup of patients with K-*ras* mutations. In multivariate analysis, it was the single most important independent prognostic factor for survival. If confirmed by an independent study, this information could be used to identify high-risk patients and as the basis for a prospective clinical trial of adjuvant chemotherapy.

The fact that only about one third of adenocarcinomas have a mutated

**TABLE 2.**
***ras* Codons Involved in Lung Cancer\***

| Codon | K-*ras* | H-*ras* | N-*ras* |
|-------|---------|---------|---------|
| 12 | 30 | 1 | 1 |
| 13 | 8 | 0 | 0 |
| 18 | 1 | 0 | 0 |
| 61 | 7 | 4 | 3 |
| Totals | 46 | 5 | 4 |

\*Frequency of involvement of the different *ras* genes and codons in human lung cancer. Data compiled from references 9, 10, and 11.

ras gene may imply that, in the others, another gene in the ras pathway (i.e., GAP or other G-proteins), may be mutated instead. Recently, the gene associated with neurofibromatosis, NF-1,[16] has been shown to have homology to GAP and to interact directly with ras. The NF-1 gene product stimulates GTPase activity in the normal, but not the mutant forms of ras, and can substitute for defective yeast GAP activity.[17-19] The role of NF-1 or other GAP-related proteins in lung cancer remains to be evaluated.

Finally, as mentioned previously, ras genes are covalently acylated, a property that appears to be essential to their function. It has been found that lovastatin, which is given to humans to lower cholesterol, also inhibits acylation of the ras gene and blocks the ability of an activated ras to transform cells in vitro.[20] Clinical studies of such drugs in human lung cancer patients whose tumors bear activated ras genes are being considered.

## myc Genes in Lung Cancer

The retroviral transforming gene v-myc was isolated from avian myelocytomatosis virus. The normal cellular counterpart was isolated and called c-myc. Two other related, but not identical, genes were isolated and named N-myc (isolated from neuroblastoma) and L-myc (isolated from SCLC). The myc genes code for nuclear phosphoproteins with the ability to bind DNA, and thus are postulated to have a transcriptional regulatory function.

In contrast to the types of mutations found in the ras genes, no coding sequence mutations have been found in myc genes in human cancer. Rather, DNA amplification and/or overexpression is found frequently in SCLC.[21-24] Reported frequencies of amplification in SCLC range from 10% to 100% and seem to be higher in tumors from treated patients than in those from untreated patients, higher in cell lines than in fresh tumors, and higher in the more aggressive and less responsive "variant" SCLC than in the "classic" tumor. In fact, the introduction and overexpression of c-myc into a classic SCLC cell line confers many of the "variant" properties on the recipient cell.[25] Amplification also is associated with poorer clinical outcome.[22] Overexpression is even more frequent than amplification, and was found in 16 out of 18 tumors and 5 out of 6 cell lines in one study.[26] It is interesting to note that the amplification of two different myc family members in the same tumor has not been seen. The reason for this is not known, but it may be because the different myc genes have identical effects and because two overexpressed myc genes add nothing to one, or because they are, in fact, mutually exclusive.

Amplification of the myc gene in non-SCLC is rare, and only 2 cases were found among 47 samples examined in one study.[27] This demonstrates again a molecular specificity to oncogene activation in SCLC vs. non-SCLC. Several mechanisms of transcriptional activation in the absence of amplification have been found, including DNA rearrangement (which places the *myc* gene under the influence of another promoter or enhancer) and point mutations within intron 1 (which seem to increase transcription by an unknown mechanism, possibly by interfering with the binding of a transcription inhibiting factor).[28]

## Her-2/*neu* in Lung Cancer

Some of the oncogenic retroviruses were found to carry oncogenes that subsequently were determined to be homologous to growth factor receptors. c-*erb*B-2 (also called Her-2 or *neu*) is a gene first isolated from rat neuroblastomas that shows sequence homology to the epidermal growth factor receptor. It has been shown that most non-SCLC tumors express significant levels of the receptor, but expression in SCLC lesions is very low or absent.[29, 30] In addition, lung cancer cells have been shown to produce a factor that binds to this receptor, which could produce an autostimulatory autocrine loop, where the cancer cell actively makes a growth factor required for its own growth.

## The Gastrin-Releasing Peptide Receptor in Lung Cancer

SCLC cells in culture have been shown to secrete a peptide factor identified as gastrin-releasing peptide (GRP) into the medium and to stimulate their own growth by its interaction with a specific GRP receptor.[31] Blocking this loop with antibodies to GRP inhibits SCLC growth in culture and in nude mice. The recent cloning of the GRP receptor[32] will allow molecular dissection of this pathway, and provide insight into whether abnormalities of this gene or its regulation contribute to the malignant phenotype.

## Other Oncogenes

C-*myb* has been shown to be overexpressed and amplified in some lung cancer lines,[33] and c-*raf* has been found to be expressed.[34] The *bcl*-1 locus, which has been shown to be rearranged in some chromic B lymphoid malignancies, recently has been determined to be amplified frequently in poorly differentiated squamous cell carcinoma of the lung.[35] The role of these oncogenes is under investigation.

## Searching for Tumor Suppressor Genes Using Cytogenetic and Restriction Fragment Length Polymorphism Analysis in Lung Cancer

In contrast to dominant oncogenes, tumor suppressor genes are defined as those that require the loss of function of both alleles. Homozygous deletion of both alleles is one mechanism of inactivation, and several candidate genes have been isolated by virtue of the discovery of homozygous deletions in a region of tumor DNA. The most common mechanism of inactivation of both alleles, however, is for one allele and surrounding markers to be lost completely and the other to be mutated. The loss of one of the two alleles of a given marker is known as loss of heterozygosity or reduction to hemizygosity. Loss of heterozygosity can be a clue suggesting the presence of a tumor suppressor gene nearby, and can be looked for in one of several ways. In the case of lymphoma-associated translocations and many heritable diseases, gross alterations of the cellular karyotype have been indicators of the involvement of specific genes at the sites of abnormalities. Studies on the karyotypes of lung cancer cells[36, 37] show nearly universal loss of one copy of chromosome 3p in SCLC, and other studies have shown frequent involvement of regions on chromosomes 1, 3p, 11p, 13q, 17p, and others in non-SCLC.[38]

In addition to those lesions visible by karyotypic analysis, restriction fragment length polymorphism analysis has yielded important evidence for loss of heterozygosity in a variety of chromosomal locations in lung cancer. This technique is based on the frequent finding of incidental DNA sequence differences between individual alleles that result in differences in the sequence-specific cuts made by restriction endonucleases. Thus, the same DNA sequence from each of the two alleles will appear as two different-sized bands (one from the maternal and one from the paternal allele) on Southern blots. When probes from specific chromosomal locations are used to examine tumor and normal DNA from the same patient, loss of one of the alleles is indicated by loss of one of the bands in the tumor sample that is present in normal DNA. This is evidence for loss of heterozygosity and suggests that the surrounding chromosome region may contain a tumor suppressor gene with a mutation that has been "uncovered" by deletion of the other allele.

In practice, it has been found that although markers from chromosome 3p have lost heterozygosity almost universally, virtually the entire chromosome arm is involved.[39] In other words, all markers spanning many millions of bases have lost heterozygosity, which is of little use in localizing candidate tumor suppressor genes in that region. The universal finding of loss of nearly all of 3p could indicate that there are several tumor suppressor genes located there, and that they need to be inactivated simultaneously to produce clinical lung cancer. The finding of a homozygous deletion within that region could be the key to pinpointing potential lung cancer tumor suppressor gene(s). No such homozygous deletion has been reported yet in lung cancer, and this remains one of the most active areas of research in lung cancer genetics.

Many other chromosome regions have been reported to have lost heterozygosity, including most of the regions identified by karyotypic analysis.[39–46] Some of the known cancer-associated genes from other systems (such as Wilms', rb, and p53) have been localized to some of these regions.

## *rb* in Lung Cancer

The retinoblastoma susceptibility gene, *rb*, was the first tumor suppressor gene to be isolated. In fact, it was the inheritance pattern of retinoblastoma that led Knudson[47] to propose the existence of tumor suppressor genes. Retinoblastoma occurs in both familial and sporadic forms. The inherited form frequently was multifocal and bilateral with high penetrance, while the sporadic form was unifocal and rare. He proposed that the inherited trait was a defect in one of the two alleles of a suppressor gene, and that infrequent inactivation of the remaining allele produced the cancer. In the sporadic form, somatic inactivation of both alleles was required; thus, it was extremely unlikely to occur. The gene itself was mapped by karyotypic and classical genetic techniques to chromosome band 13q14.11, and cases of homozygous deletion were found for closely linked markers. Since the presumption was that the causative gene was located within the deletion, linked sequences that were present in normal DNA and absent in tumor were examined systematically until a gene that was altered in other cases in a tumor-specific way was found (a chromosome "walk").[48, 49] Introduction of the normal gene into such retinoblastoma tumor cells was shown to revert the malignant phenotype,[50] fulfilling the requirements for a tumor suppressor gene.

The Rb protein product is a 110-kd nuclear phosphoprotein. It undergoes cell cycle–dependent phosphorylation and binding to several viral oncoproteins,[51, 52] and is thought to be involved in cell cycle regulation. Both normal phosphorylation and the ability to bind to the viral oncoproteins SV40 large T, adenovirus E1A, and papillomavirus E7 seem to be associated with normal protein function, as point mutants isolated from tumor cells are found to lack these characteristics, even if they produce a normal-size protein product.[53] The binding of Rb (and p53, to be discussed following) by the oncoproteins of DNA tumor viruses is an exciting observation suggesting the unifying hypothesis that these viruses might transform cells by inactivating recessive oncogene products.

Harbour et al.[54] made the key observation that there were frequent abnormalities in the *rb* gene in SCLC, and much less frequent ones in non-SCLC. Subsequent studies in our laboratory and those of others have shown that the gene is abnormal at the DNA, RNA, or protein level in SCLC as frequently as it is in retinoblastoma, or in >95% of the cases.[55] Non-SCLC seems to have abnormal Rb in about 20% of cases. In contrast to retinoblastoma, where protein is virtually never produced, abnormalities in SCLC may be more subtle, with up to 40% of tumors making Rb protein with subtle abnormalities such as point mutations. These point mutations, however, completely inhibit normal phosphorylation and oncoprotein binding.

The significance of *rb* abnormalities in SCLC is unclear, and tumor suppression after transfection of the normal allele into lung cancer cells has yet to be reported. The fact that it is universally abnormal, however, implies that it has a significant role at some stage of the pathogenesis of SCLC.

## p53 in Lung Cancer

p53 is a 393–amino acid nuclear phosphoprotein discovered because of its ability to bind to viral oncoproteins (SV40 large T,[56] adenovirus E1B,[57] and papillomavirus E6[58]). When it first was cloned, it was found to act as a typical dominant oncogene to cooperate with an activated *ras* in transforming primary rodent cells, but subsequently it was found that what had been cloned was a mutant form. The wild-type form, in fact, was found to suppress transformation[59]; thus, p53 seems to have the ability to act as a dominant oncogene when mutant and as a tumor suppressor when normal. As with Rb, it is only the normal form that complexes with the viral oncoproteins. This suppression appears to function at the level of cell cycle control,[60] and recent evidence shows that p53 may act directly as an activator of transcription.[61, 62]

Takahashi et al. discovered that abnormalities of the p53 gene were frequent events in lung cancer.[63] A recent study of 51 freshly resected early stage non-SCLC,[64] found a 42% overall frequency of p53 mutations, with a statistically significantly greater frequency in squamous cell carcinoma (11 out of 17) and an increased incidence in younger patients. In SCLC, 100% of tumors may have a mutant p53.[65] Survival analyses to determine the prognostic significance of mutations in p53 are in progress.

The most common type of mutation in p53 is a point mutation which, in

TABLE 3.
### Nature of Base Changes in p53 Mutations in Lung Cancer*

| Mutation | Non-SCLC | Nonlung |
|----------|----------|---------|
| G to T | 16 | 0 |
| C to T | 5 | 6 |
| G to C | 5 | 2 |
| G to A | 4 | 11 |
| A to T | 2 | 1 |
| T to G | 2 | 0 |
| C to G | 1 | 0 |
| C to A | 1 | 0 |
| A to C | 1 | 1 |
| A to G | 0 | 2 |
| T to C | 0 | 1 |
| T to A | 0 | 0 |

*Nature of the mutations in non-SCLC[64] compared to those reported in other tumors (predominantly colon, breast, and brain).[66–68]

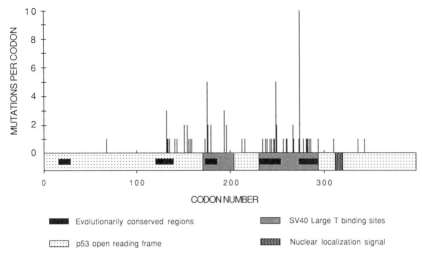

**FIG 2.**
Distribution of the codons involved in 74 mutations in p53 from all tumor types compiled from multiple published and unpublished sources. Highly conserved regions are those described by Soussi T, Caron de Fromental C, May P: *Oncogene* 1990; 5:945–952.

contrast to *ras*, occurs over a wide range of positions in the molecule. Several amino acids are affected more frequently than others, particularly codon 273, and most of them fall within either the evolutionarily conserved regions or the regions known to be involved in viral oncoprotein binding (Fig 2). About 20% of the mutations involve point mutations that result in splicing abnormalities, and there are occasional homozygous deletions of the gene.

Table 3 shows the nature of base changes in p53 mutations in non-SCLC[64] compared with those reported in other tumors. It is interesting to note that G-to-T transversions are the most common in non-SCLC and that G-to-A transversions are most frequent in other tumors. *ras* Mutations in non-SCLC have a similar spectrum of base changes.[10] This may reflect different carcinogen exposures in the lung compared to the colon, breast, or brain.

Additional evidence for this gene's involvement in lung cancer comes from studies of transgenic mice expressing mutant p53 that develop a high incidence of lung tumors.[69] Reintroduction of normal p53 into lung cancer cells drastically inhibits growth of the tumor cells, and those clones that do grow are found to have lost the transfected gene, supporting the role of p53 as a lung cancer tumor suppressor (T. Takahashi and J. Minna, unpublished results).

Many of the different mutants of p53 have a greatly prolonged protein half-life, which leads to greatly increased steady-state p53 protein levels in cells harboring them.[70] This has allowed simple immunohistochemistry to be a screening test for the presence of p53 mutations,[70] as normal cells produce low levels of protein that usually are not detectable and cells with mutant p53 produce easily detectable levels. The mechanism of this prolonged half-life is unclear, and may involve the inability of normal specific degradation machinery (perhaps via ubiquination) to recognize mutant proteins. Some mutations are missed by this screening procedure, however, such as homozygous deletions and those with point mutations resulting in new stop codons and prematurely terminated peptides.

Not only do many different mutations result in a similar prolongation of half-life, but a new common epitope is found that has allowed the production of a monoclonal antibody that will recognize many different mutant proteins, but not normal ones.[71] Recent work has found that p53 (like Rb) undergoes cell cycle–dependent phosphorylation[72] and appears to cycle between two forms, during which the normal p53 transiently assumes the "mutant" configuration. Thus, it is possible that mutations could 'lock" the p53 protein into this presumably growth-permissive form.

## Other Candidate Tumor Suppressor Genes

Several new candidates for tumor suppressor genes have been identified: the WT1 gene thought to play a role in Wilms' tumors, the NF-1 gene in neurofibromatosis, the DCC gene in colon cancer, and others. The roles of these genes in lung cancer are still being evaluated.

## Other Genetic Mechanisms

Many other possible types of genetic lesions exist. As yet undescribed human viral oncogene products could be involved directly, or viral genome integration could insertionally inactivate a gene or, conversely, activate it by promoter proximity. There is some evidence for the involvement of a virus in pulmonary adenomatosis-lung cancer of sheep.[73] Some epidemiologic data on the clustering of cases of bronchioalveolar cancer in humans are consistent with an infectious etiology, but no direct evidence has been published. Another type of lesion could be the production of fusion gene products by DNA rearrangements, resulting in new protein activities or regulation, as is seen in leukemias and lymphomas, but this has not been described yet in lung cancer.

## Evidence for Genetic Predisposition to Lung Cancer

### Family Studies

Clinicians involved with lung cancer have long suspected that different individuals have different susceptibilities to the disease. With the known strong environmental risk factors involved in the development of lung cancer, such as tobacco abuse, radon, and asbestos, it is difficult to prove an inherited predisposition unless it is overwhelming. In addition, any effect is likely to be a summation of effects from multiple genes. Recently, however, a large study supports an inherited predisposition,[74] finding a 2.4-fold overall excess risk to relatives of lung cancer patients after correcting for all known environmental factors. Analysis of these data using various models for patterns of inheritance shows the best fit for a model with autosomal condominant inheritance of a rare allele that, by their analysis, could account for 69% of early onset (<age 50 years) lung cancer.[75] This model predicts an early age of onset of lung cancer for gene carriers and a particularly greatly increased risk for nonsmokers compared to smokers. The authors calculate the risk for nonsmoking homozygous carriers under the age of 50 years to be 2,245-fold greater than for homozygous normal nonsmokers. Heavy smokers under the age of 50 years would have an increased risk of 62-fold when homozygous for the putative high-risk gene. While such a potent human cancer gene has not been identified yet, other genes have been examined for their impact on lung cancer risk, and some of these are described following.

## Specific Genes That May Cause an Inherited Genetic Predisposition to Lung Cancer

### Oncogenes

Tumor suppressor genes are good candidates for inherited cancer genes by definition, as the first one discovered *(rb)* shows clear predispositon to retinoblastoma. Since *rb* is highly associated with SCLC, inherited *rb* defects may lead to an increased inherited predisposition to lung cancer. A study of 4,101 relatives of people with retinoblastoma found a tenfold increased risk of nonocular cancer in carriers of the mutant gene and a 15-fold increased risk of lung cancer, particularly SCLC.[76] While *rb* abnormalities may predispose to lung cancer, they are not likely to be significant on a population basis, due to the gene's high penetrance for retinoblastoma. Inherited mutations of p53 are being looked for actively, and recently there has been a report of germline p53 mutations in five families with the Li-Fraumeni familial cancer syndrome.[77] This syndrome causes very high incidences of many of the cancers independently reported to be associated with p53 mutations, but the incidence of lung cancer in these patients has not been reported. None of the cases of p53 mutations in non-SCLC reported by Chiba[64] were present in normal DNA from those individuals, and thus represented somatic mutations.

Inherited mutations in dominant oncogenes have not been described yet either, but certain types, such as K-*ras* codon 12 mutations, are unlikely to be prevalent, due to the extremely high rates of cancer seen in transgenic mice carrying such mutations. To date, when examined, all mutant K-*ras* alleles have been shown to represent somatic events.

## Debrisoquine Hydroxylase

Tobacco smoke contains a mixture of carcinogens and precarcinogens.[78] Some of these need to be activated metabolically, and a major pathway for hydrocarbon carcinogen activation involves a group of enzymes called p450. One of the p450 enzymes, called CYP2D6 or debrisoquine hydroxylase, has undergone the most study for its association with lung cancer.

Debrisoquine is an antihypertensive drug that was discovered to undergo variable rates of metabolism in different individuals, a trait found to be determined by the inheritance of specific alleles of CYP2D6. An association with lung cancer incidence was discovered by chance and, after adjustment for environmental factors, individuals who were of the extensive-metabolizer phenotype were found to exhibit about a tenfold increased risk of lung cancer.[79] The gene defect resulting in the low-metabolizing allele has been identified,[80] and abnormal gene regulation has been reported in lung cancer.[81] This implies that this enzyme may be involved in the metabolic activation of some unknown carcinogen involved in lung cancer development. As there are many genes involved in the metabolism of hydrocarbon carcinogens, a person's genetic mixture of these genes could account for variable individual susceptibilities to these carcinogens.

## Conclusions

A pattern of genetic defects is emerging from molecular genetic studies of lung cancer where different oncogenes play roles in different histologic types. The cellular pathway involving *ras* oncogenes appears to be activated in non-SCLC, but not in SCLC. Amplifications of *myc* appear to be nearly restricted to SCLC, and to those types most refractory to treatment. The *rb* and p53 genes are almost universally abnormal in SCLC, but less commonly so in non-SCLC. Squamous cell cancers seem to have a disproportionately high frequency of p53 abnormalities, as do younger patients. The significance of these patterns is unclear as yet, but, in the future, it may be possible to define unique molecular patterns and pathways responsible for the distinct malignancies of the lung, and thus begin to be able to assemble rational, molecularly based therapies. While gene replacement therapy for tumor suppression may be impractical, understanding the molecular processes involved may allow intervention elsewhere along the pathway, or use of the mutant oncogene products themselves as the targets for immunotherapy.

## References

1. Minna J, Pass H, Glatstein E, et al: Cancer of the lung, in deVita V, Hellman S, Rosenberg S (eds): *Cancer, Principles and Practice of Oncology.* Philadelphia, JB Lippincott Company, 1989, pp 591–705.

2. Phillips D, Hewer A, Martin C, et al: Correlation of DNA adduct levels in human lung with cigarette smoking. *Nature* 1988; 336:790–792.
3. Shih C, Padhy L, Murray M, et al: Transforming genes of carcinomas and neuroblastomas introduced into mouse fibroblasts. *Nature* 1981; 290:261–264.
4. Der J, Finkel T, Cooper G: Biological and biochemical properties of human rasH genes mutated at codon 61. *Cell* 1986; 44:167–176.
5. Temeles G, Gibbs J, D'Alonzo J, et al: Yeast and mammalian ras proteins have conserved biochemical properties. *Nature* 1985; 313:700–703.
6. Seeburg P, Colby W, Capon D, et al: Biological properties of human c-Haras1 genes mutated at codon 12. *Nature* 1984; 312:71–75.
7. Santos E, Martin-Zanca D, Reddy E, et al: Malignant activation of a K-ras oncogene in lung carcinoma but not in normal tissue of the same patient. *Science* 1984; 223:661–664.
8. Rodenhuis S, van de Wetering M, Mooi W, et al: Mutational activation of the K-*ras* oncogene: A possible pathogenetic factor in adenocarcinoma of the lung. *N Engl J Med* 1987; 317:929–935.
9. Rodenhuis S, Slebos R, Boot AJ, et al: Incidence and possible clinical significance of K-ras oncogene activation in adenocarcinoma of the human lung. *Cancer Res* 1988; 48:5738–5741.
10. Mitsudomi T, Viallet J, Minna J, et al: Mutations of the ras gene distinguish a subset of non-small cell lung cancer cell lines from small cell lung cancer lines. *Oncogene*, in press.
11. Suzuki Y, Orita M, Shiraishi M, et al: Detection of ras gene mutations in human lung cancers by single-strand conformation polymorphism analysis of polymerase chain reaction products. *Oncogene* 1990; 5:1037–1043.
12. Falco J, Baylin S, Lupu R, et al: v-rasH induces non-small cell phenotype, with associated growth factors and receptors, in a small cell lung cancer cell line. *J Clin Invest* 1990; 85:1740–1745.
13. Tremblay P, Pothier F, Hoang T, et al: Transgenic mice carrying the mouse mammary tumor virus ras fusion gene: Distinct effects in various tissues. *Mol Cell Biol* 1989; 9:854–859.
14. Bos J: ras Oncogenes in human cancer: A review. *Cancer Res* 1989; 49:4682–4689.
15. Slebos RJ, Kibbelaar RE, Dalesio O, et al: K-ras oncogene activation as a prognostic marker in adenocarcinoma of the lung. *N Engl J Med* 1990; 323:561–565.
16. Xu G, O'Connell P, Viskochil D, et al: The neurofibromatosis type 1 gene encodes a protein related to GAP. *Cell* 1990; 62:599–608.
17. Ballester R, Marchuk D, Boguski M, et al: The NF1 locus encodes a protein functionally related to mammaliam GAP and yeast IRA proteins. *Cell* 1990; 63:851–859.
18. Martin G, Viskochil D, Bollag G, et al: The GAP-related domain of the neurofibromatosis type 1 gene product interacts with ras p21. *Cell* 1990; 63:843–849.
19. Xu G, Lin B, Tanaka K, et al: The catalytic domain of the neurofibromatosis type 1 gene product stimulates *ras* GTPase and complements *ira* mutants of S. cerevisiae. *Cell* 1990; 63:835-841.
20. Schafer W, Kim R, Sterne R, et al: Genetic and pharmacological suppression of oncogenic mutations in ras genes of yeasts and humans. *Science* 1989; 245:379–385.
21. Little C, Nau M, Carney D, et al: Amplification and expression of the c-*myc* oncogene in human lung cancer cell lines. *Nature* 1983; 306:194–196.

22. Johnson B, Ihde D, Makuch R, et al: myc Family oncogene amplification in tumor cell lines established from small cell lung cancer patients and its relationship to clinical status and course. *J Clin Invest* 1987; 79:1629–1634.

23. Johnson B, Makuch R, Simmons A, et al: myc Family DNA amplification in small cell lung cancer patients' tumors and corresponding cell lines. *Cancer Res* 1988; 48:5163–5166.

24. Kiefer P, Bepler G, Kubassch M, et al: Amplification and expression of protooncogenes in human small cell lung cancer cell lines. *Cancer Res* 1987; 47:6236–6242.

25. Johnson B, Battey J, Linnoila I, et al: Changes in the phenotype of human small cell lung cancer cell lines after transfection and expression of the c-myc proto-oncogene. *J Clin Invest* 1986; 78:525–532.

26. Takahashi T, Obata Y, Sekido Y, et al: Expression and amplification of myc gene family in small cell lung cancer and its relation to biological characteristics. *Cancer Res* 1989; 49:2683–2688.

27. Slebos R, Evers S, Wagenaar S, et al: Cellular protooncogenes are infrequently amplified in untreated non-small cell lung cancer. *Br J Cancer* 1989; 59:76–80.

28. Krystal G, Birrer M, Way J, et al: Multiple mechanisms for transcriptional regulation of the myc gene family in small-cell lung cancer. *Mol Cell Biol* 1988; 8:3373–3381.

29. Sherwin S, Minna J, Gazdar A, et al: Expression of epidermal and nerve growth factor receptors and soft agar growth factor production by human lung cancer cells. *Cancer Res* 1981; 41:3538–3542.

30. Cerney T, Barnes D, Hasleton P, et al: Expression of epidermal growth factor receptor (EGF-R) in human lung tumours. *Br J Cancer* 1986; 54:265–269.

31. Cuttitta F, Fedorko J, Gu J, et al: Gastrin-releasing peptide gene-associated peptides are expressed in normal human fetal lung and small cell lung cancer: A novel peptide family found in man. *J Clin Endocrinol Metab* 1988; 67:576–583.

32. Battey J: Molecular cloning of the GRP receptor. *Proc Natl Acad Sci U S A*, in press.

33. Griffin C, Baylin S: Expression of the c-myb oncogene in human small cell lung carcinoma. *Cancer Res* 1985; 45:272–275.

34. Sithanandam G, Dean M, Brennscheidt U, et al: Loss of heterozygosity at the c-raf locus in small cell lung carcinoma. *Oncogene* 1989; 4:451–455.

35. Berenson J, Koga H, Yang J, et al: Frequent amplification of the bcl-1 locus in poorly differentiated squamous cell carcinoma of the lung. *Oncogene* 1990; 5:1343–1348.

36. Whang-Peng J, Bunn P Jr, Kao-Shan C, et al: A non-random chromosomal abnormality, del 3p(14–23) in human small cell lung cancer. *Cancer Genet Cytogenet* 1982; 6:119–134.

37. Whang-Peng J, Kao-Shan C, Lee E, et al: A specific chromosome defect associated with human small-cell lung cancer: Deletion 3p(14–23). *Science* 1982; 215:181–182.

38. Whang-Peng J, Knutsen T, Gazdar A, et al: Non-random structural and numerical changes in non-small cell lung cancer. *Genes, Chromosomes, and Cancer*, in press.

39. Brauch H, Tory K, Kotler F, et al: Molecular mapping of deletion sites in the short arm of chromosome 3 in human lung cancer. *Genes, Chromosomes, and Cancer* 1990; 1:240–246.

40. Gerber M, Drabkin H, Firnhaber C, et al: Regional localization of chromosome 3-specific DNA fragments by using a hybrid cell deletion mapping panel. *Am J Hum Genet* 1988; 43:442–451.
41. Johnson BE, Sakaguchi AY, Gazdar AF, et al: Restriction fragment length polymorphism studies show consistent loss of chromosome 3p alleles in small cell lung cancer patients' tumors. *J Clin Invest* 1988; 82:502–507.
42. Mori N, Yokota Y, Oshimura M, et al: Concordant deletions of chromosome 3p and loss of heterozygosity for chromosomes 13 and 17 in small cell lung carcinoma. *Cancer Res* 1989; 49:5130–5135.
43. Naylor S, Johnson B, Minna J, et al: Loss of heterozygosity of chromosome 3p markers in small-cell lung cancer. *Nature* 1987; 329:451–454.
44. Shiraishi M, Morinaga S, Noguchi M, et al: Loss of genes on the short arm of chromosome 11 in human lung carcinomas. *Jpn J Cancer Res* 1987; 78:1302–1308.
45. Weston A, Willey J, Modali R, et al: Differential DNA sequence deletions from chromosomes 3, 11, 13, and 17 in squamous-cell carcinoma, large-cell carcinoma, and adenocarcinoma of the human lung. *Proc Natl Acad Sci U S A* 1989; 86:5099–5103.
46. Yokota A, Wad M, Shimosato Y, et al: Loss of heterozygosity on chromosomes 3, 13, 17 in small cell carcinoma and on chromosome 3 in adenocarcinoma of the lung. *Proc Natl Acad Sci U S A* 1987; 84:9252–9256.
47. Knudson AJ, Hethcote HW, Brown BW: Mutation and childhood cancer: A probabilistic model for the incidence of retinoblastoma. *Proc Natl Acad Sci U S A* 1975; 72:5116–5120.
48. Lee WH, Bookstein R, Hong F, et al: Human retinoblastoma susceptibility gene: Cloning, identification, and sequence. *Science* 1987; 235:1394–1399.
49. Friend SH, Bernards R, Rogelj S, et al: A human DNA segment with properties of the gene that predisposes to retinoblastoma and osteosarcoma. *Nature* 1986; 323:643–646.
50. Huang HJ, Yee J-K, Shew J-Y, et al: Suppression of the neoplastic phenotype by replacement of the RB gene in human cancer cells. *Science* 1988; 242:1563–1566.
51. Ludlow J, Shon J, Pipas J, et al: The retinoblastoma susceptibility gene product undergoes cell cycle-dependent dephosphorylation and binding to and release from SV40 Large T. *Cell* 1990; 60:387–396.
52. Mihara K, Cao X-R, Yen A, et al: Cell cycle-dependent regulation of phosphorylation of the human retinoblastoma gene product. *Science* 1989; 246:1300–1303.
53. Kaye F, Kratzke R, Gerster J, et al: A single amino acid substitution results in a retinoblastoma protein defective in phosphorylation and oncoprotein binding. *Proc Natl Acad Sci U S A* 1990; 87:6922–6926.
54. Harbour JW, Lai S-L, Whang-Peng J, et al: Abnormalities in structure and expression of the human retinoblastoma gene in SCLC. *Science* 1988; 241:353–357.
55. Horowitz J, Park S-H, Bogenmann E, et al: Frequent inactivation of the retinoblastoma anti-oncogene is restricted to a subset of human tumor cells. *Proc Natl Acad Sci U S A* 1990; 87:2775–2779.
56. Linzer D, Levine A: Characterization of a 54K dalton cellular SV40 tumor antigen present in SV40-transformed cells and uninfected embryonal carcinoma cells. *Cell* 1979; 17:43–52.
57. Sarnow P, Ho Y, Williams J, et al: Adenovirus E1b-58kd tumor antigen and

SV40 large tumor antigen are physically associated with the same 54kd cellular protein in transformed cells. *Cell* 1982; 28:387–394.

58. Werness B, Levine A, Howley P: Association of human papillomavirus types 16 and 18 E6 proteins with p53. *Science* 1990; 248:76–79.

59. Finlay C, Hinds P, Levine AJ: The p53 protooncogene can act as a suppressor of transformation. *Cell* 1989; 57:1083–1093.

60. Diller L, Kassel J, Nelson C, et al: p53 functions as a cell cycle control protein in osteosarcomas. *Mol Cell Biol* 1990; 10:5772–5781.

61. Fields S, Jang S: Presence of a potent transcription activating sequence in the p53 protein. *Science* 1990; 249:1046–1049.

62. Raycroft L, Wu H, Lozano G: Transcriptional activation by wild-type but not transforming mutants of the p53 anti-oncogene. *Science* 1990; 249: 1049–1051.

63. Takahashi T, Nau M, Chiba I, et al: p53: A frequent target for genetic abnormalities in lung cancer. *Science* 1989; 246:491–494.

64. Chiba I, Takahashi T, Nau M, et al: Mutations in the p53 gene are frequent in primary, resected non-small cell lung cancer. *Oncogene* 1990; 5:1603–1610.

65. D'Amico D, Carbone DP, Mitzudomi T, et al: High frequency of somatically acquired p53 mutations in small cell lung cancer cell lines and tumors. *Oncogene*, in press.

66. Nigro J, Baker S, Preisinger A, et al: Mutations in the p53 gene occur in diverse human tumour types. *Nature* 1989; 342:705–708.

67. Baker S, Fearon E, Nigro J, et al: Chromosome 17 deletions and p53 gene mutations in colorectal carcinomas. *Science* 1989; 244:217–221.

68. Bartek J, Iggo R, Lane D: Genetic and immunochemical analysis of mutant p53 in human breast cancer cell lines. *Oncogene* 1990; 5:893–899.

69. Lavigueur A, Maltby V, Mock D, et al: High incidence of lung, bone, and lymphoid tumors in transgenic mice overexpressing mutant alleles of the p53 oncogene. *Mol Cell Biol* 1989; 9:3982–3991.

70. Iggo R, Gatter K, Bartek J, et al: Increased expression of mutant forms of p53 oncogene in primary lung cancer. *Lancet* 1990; 335:675–679.

71. Gannon J, Greaves R, Iggo R, et al: Activating mutations in p53 produce a common conformational effect. A monoclonal antibody specific for the mutant form. *EMBO J* 1990; 9:1595–1602.

72. Bischoff J, Friedman P, Marshak D, et al: Human p53 is phosphorylated by p60-cdc2 and cyclin B-cdc2. *Proc Natl Acad Sci U S A* 1990; 87:4766–4770.

73. Rosadio R, Sharp J, Lairmore M, et al: Lesions and retroviruses associated with naturally occurring ovine pulmonary carcinoma (sheep pulmonary adenomatosis). *Vet Pathol* 1988; 25:58–66.

74. Ooi WL, Elston RC, Chen VW, et al: Increased familial risk for lung cancer. *J Natl Cancer Inst* 1986; 76:217–222.

75. Sellers TA, Bailey WJ, Elston RC, et al: Evidence for mendelian inheritance in the pathogenesis of lung cancer. *J Natl Cancer Inst* 1990; 82:1272–1279.

76. Sanders B, Jay M, Draper G, et al: Non-ocular cancer in relatives of retinoblastoma patients. *Br J Cancer* 1989; 60:358–365.

77. Malkin D, Li F, Strong L, et al: Germ line p53 mutations in a familial syndrome of breast cancer, sarcomas, and other neoplasms. *Science* 250: 1233–1238.

78. Hecht S, Hoffmann D: Tobacco-specific nitrosamines, an important group of carcinogens in tobacco and tobacco smoke. *Carcinogenesis* 1988; 9:875–884.

79. Caporaso N, Hayes RB, Dosemeci M, et al: Lung cancer risk, occupational ex-

posure, and the debrisoquine metabolic phenotype. *Cancer Res* 1989; 49:3675–3679.

80. Gough A, Miles J, Spurr N, et al: Identification of the primary gene defect at the cytochrome p450 CYP2D locus. *Nature* 1990; 347:773–776.

81. McLemore T, Adelberg S, Czerwinski M, et al: Altered regulation of the cytochrome P4501A1 gene expression in pulmonary carcinoma cell lines. *J Natl Cancer Inst* 1989; 81:1787–1794.

# Hemorrhagic Colitis Associated With Escherichia Coli O157:H7*

## Mitchell B. Cohen, M.D.

Associate Professor of Pediatrics, Division of Pediatric Gastroenterology, University of Cincinnati College of Medicine, Children's Hospital Medical Center, Cincinnati, Ohio

## Ralph A. Giannella, M.D.

Mark Brown Professor of Medicine and Director, Division of Gastroenterology, University of Cincinnati College of Medicine, Veterans Administration Medical Center, Cincinnati, Ohio

## Editor's Introduction

A new and quite virulent dysentery pathogen, *Escherichia coli* O157:H7, emerged in North America during the past decade. This organism produces Shiga-like toxins that are similar or identical to the cytotoxins of *Shigella dysenteriae* type 1, one of the most virulent *Shigella* strains. Hemorrhagic colitis is the usual clinical picture in most patients, but some elderly adults and children infected with this new *E. coli* strain develop hemolytic-uremic syndrome or thrombotic thrombocytopenic purpura. Early recognition of this form of dysentery, especially during outbreaks in nursing homes and day care centers, is essential for diagnosis and treatment. Drs. Cohen and Giannella provide a comprehensive review of this emerging disease, which is quite likely to increase in frequency and importance during the 1990s.

*J. Thomas LaMont, M.D.*

*Escherichia coli* O157:H7 was first identified as a cause of hemorrhagic colitis in 1982, during outbreaks of bloody diarrhea in Oregon and Michigan.[1-3] Epidemiologic investigation of these outbreaks demonstrated that patients with colitis had consumed sandwiches containing a beef patty, rehydrated onions, and pickles at fast-food restaurants of the same national chain.[3] Although no common enteric pathogens were isolated from these patients, laboratory studies identified an unusual *E. coli* serotype (O157:H7)

*Supported by an American Gastroenterological Association/Glaxo Scholar Award, National Institutes of Health grant DK01908, and Veterans Administration grant 539-3108-01.

in 50% of the stool cultures from patients with diarrhea, but in none of the controls. The same strain of *E. coli* also was isolated from a frozen beef patty in Michigan. Following these outbreaks, the Centers for Disease Control conducted a retrospective study of 3,000 *E. coli* strains obtained from clinical isolates in the preceding 10 years. Only one O157:H7 strain was found in this group and it had been isolated in 1975 from a 50-year-old California woman who had self-limited grossly bloody diarrhea.[3] Based on these data, it seemed likely that *E. coli* O157:H7 represented a new pathogen. Subsequent genetic evidence also suggested that *E. coli* O157:H7 was a newly evolved pathogenic serotype.[4]

*E. coli* can be grouped on the basis of their somatic and flagellar antigens. The Kauffman schema recognizes approximately 171 lipopolysaccharide (O) antigens and 56 flagellar (H) serogroups.[5] Since the initial description of this syndrome, many serotypes of *E. coli* other than O157:H7 have been implicated as causes of hemorrhagic colitis (Table 1) and these have been referred to globally as enterohemorrhagic *E. coli* (EHEC).[5] EHEC are now considered to be an important and relatively frequent cause of bloody diarrhea in parts of the United States and Canada.[6, 14] In addition, in the mid-1980s Karmali and coworkers in Toronto reported an association between EHEC infection and the development of hemolytic-

**TABLE 1.**
**Escherichia coli Serotypes Associated With Hemorrhagic Colitis and/or Hemolytic-Uremic Syndrome***

O2:H5
O5:H−
O6:H−
O38:H21
O26:H11
O91:H−
O103:H2
O11:H8
O111:H−
O113:H21
O119:H6
O121:H19
O145:H−
O157:H7
O157:H−
O163:H19

*Data from references 5–13.

uremic syndrome.[15] Many other studies[7, 16-19] have confirmed the association of EHEC infection with this syndrome and also with the related illness, thrombotic thrombocytopenic purpura.[14, 20-22] Thus, E. coli 0157:H7, which at first was thought to be a rare E. coli serotype responsible for two unusual outbreaks of bloody diarrhea, instead has turned out to be the predominant serotype of an important new class of pathogens (EHEC) responsible for hemorrhagic colitis, hemolytic-uremic syndrome, and thrombotic thrombocytopenic purpura.

In this article, we will review the nomenclature, epidemiology, clinical features and sequelae, microbiology, pathogenesis, and treatment of hemorrhagic colitis caused by EHEC.

## Nomenclature

The terminology associated with EHEC has been a source of much confusion. These organisms are differentiated from other diarrheogenic E. coli by their ability to produce one or more cytotoxins for vero cells.[23] As a consequence of this effect on vero cells, these toxins have been called verotoxins or verocytotoxins. These terms are favored by investigators in Canada and England. These toxins are, to varying degrees, similar to Shiga toxin, a cytotoxin produced by Shigella dysenteriae type 1. Therefore, these toxins also have been referred to as Shiga-like toxins (SLT). This term is favored by investigators in the United States. SLT have been divided further into two families of cytotoxins. SLT1 is nearly identical to Shiga toxin[24] and SLT2 and its variant, SLTv, are somewhat less similar.[25] All three toxins have a mechanism of action identical to that of Shiga toxin.[25] Verocytotoxin-producing E. coli refers to all E. coli strains that produce verocytotoxin. EHEC has been used to define E. coli that produce these cytotoxins and also cause the clinical illness of hemorrhagic colitis.

## Epidemiology

Subsequent to the initial outbreaks in 1982, a number of centers began surveillance studies for cases of hemorrhagic colitis associated with E. coli 0157:H7. In the initial prospective studies in Calgary, Canada, E. coli 0157:H7 was isolated from 19 (15%) of 125 patients with grossly bloody diarrhea and from one sibling with nonbloody diarrhea.[26] In other geographic locations, including Japan and the United Kingdom, E. coli 0157:H7 appeared to be a rare pathogen.[20, 27, 28]

The CDC established a surveillance system asking for reports of any illnesses in people with crampy abdominal pain, grossly bloody diarrhea, absent or low-grade fever, and negative stool cultures for Salmonella, Shigella, Campylobacter, and ova and parasites. Between August 1982 and April 1984, 28 persons from 11 states met the clinical criteria and had stool specimens that grew E. coli 0157:H7.[29] This was the first demonstration that hemorrhagic colitis caused by *E. coli* O157:H7 was a sporadic illness distributed widely throughout the United States. Between 1982 and 1986, there were at least eight major outbreaks of *E. coli* O157:H7 infection in North America.[20] Additional outbreaks also were reported in England.[28] More recently, two prospective studies in Calgary, Canada[6] and Washington state[14] have attempted to define the epidemiologic features of EHEC-associated diarrhea. In the Calgary area, EHEC were the most frequent cause of bacterial diarrhea.[6] EHEC infection was most prevalent in the summer months and had the highest incidence in children under 5 years of age. The incidence was also high in geriatric patients. In the Washington state study, infection with *E. coli* O157:H7 was the fourth most common cause of bacterial diarrhea after *Salmonella, Campylobacter,* and *Shigella*.[14] However, there was a similar summertime peak, with 60% of cases occurring between June and September (Fig 1). In addition, the highest attack rate was among children less than 5 years of age and, similar to the findings in the Calgary study, persons over 60 years of age (Fig 2). In contrast to these two studies, surveillance for cases of hemorrhagic colitis during a 12-month period in Chicago yielded only two strains of *E. coli* O157:H7 from 2,552 stool specimens.[30] Thus, it is likely that there is a significant geographic variation in the prevalence of EHEC infection.

In sporadic cases and especially in outbreaks of diarrhea due to *E. coli*

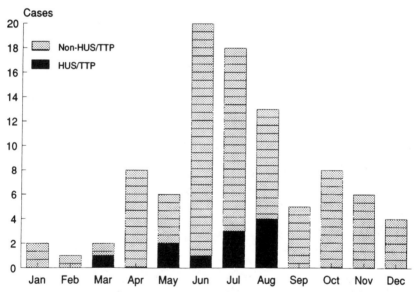

**FIG 1.**
Number of cases of infection with *E. coli* O157:H7 by month in Washington state in 1987. *Solid bars* indicate cases of hemolytic-uremic syndrome (HUS) or thrombotic thrombocytopenic purpura (TTP). *Dotted bars* indicate hemorrhagic colitis without HUS or TTP. (From Ostroff SM, Kobayashi JM, Lewis JH: *JAMA* 1989; 262:356. Used by permission.)

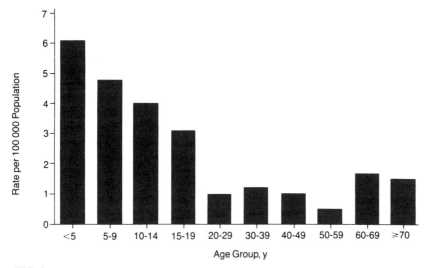

**FIG 2.**
Age-specific rates of infection with *E. coli* 0157:H7 in Washington state in 1987. (From Ostroff SM, Kobayashi JM, Lewis JH: *JAMA* 1989; 262:356. Used by permission.)

0157:H7, there is often an association with improperly cooked ground beef. This was true in the initial community outbreaks reported in 1982 that were associated with eating hamburgers at a fast-food chain.[3] This also has been the case for nursing-home outbreaks in Nebraska and Alberta, Canada.[20, 31] Another outbreak was related to the consumption of unpastuerized milk. In this outbreak, nearly all members of a group of three kindergarten classes who drank unpasteurized milk during a trip to a dairy farm in Ontario, Canada developed hemorrhagic colitis.[32] *E. coli* 0157:H7 was isolated from these children, as well as from two of the dairy cows. Both beef and dairy cattle reservoirs of *E. coli* 0157:H7 have been well documented.[33] In one study, EHEC were isolated from the feces of up to 10% of healthy cattle.[34] EHEC have been isolated also from pork, lamb, and poultry products.[33] In addition, SLT-producing *E. coli* have been isolated from diarrheic cats.[35] Thus, it is likely that there is a wide animal reservoir for these organisms.

There is also strong evidence to suggest that there is significant person-to-person spread of these infections, based on the observation of secondary cases in a nursing-home outbreak[36] and a day-care outbreak.[16] Interestingly, in the day care center, there was sequential movement of the illness from class to class, despite the fact that all children ate the same meals at the site.[16] This sequential pattern of intergroup transmission of disease during an outbreak is strongly suggestive of person-to-person spread. The presence of secondary cases in 5% of households with sporadic *E. coli* 0157:H7 infection is also suggestive of person-to-person spread.[14]

In community outbreaks and sporadic cases, patients have ranged in age from 11 months to 78 years. However, persons in all age groups are not at equal risk for disease.[14] Approximately half of the reported outbreaks have occurred in nursing homes.[20, 31, 36] In the nursing-home outbreaks, the highest attack rate is often in the very old[36] and patients are twice as likely to become ill as staff members.[37, 38] In addition, deaths are more common in the elderly and do not occur in the nursing home employees.[36, 38] A second group at high risk for *E. coli* O157:H7 outbreaks is children in day-care centers or schools. In day-care outbreaks, the highest attack rate is in the youngest children.[16, 39] In one of these outbreaks, there was a four-fold increased attack rate in children under 4 years of age compared with older children.[16] These children are also at greater risk for developing the complication of hemolytic-uremic syndrome.[16]

## Clinical Features

The hallmark of hemorrhagic colitis is the finding of bloody diarrhea. However, in a report of an outbreak in Washington state due to a single strain of *E. coli* O157:H7, Griffin and colleagues detailed the broad clinical spectrum of illnesses associated with this pathogen.[20] In addition to hemorrhagic colitis and bloody diarrhea, they described nonbloody diarrhea, asymptomatic infection, hemolytic-uremic syndrome, and thrombotic thrombocytopenic purpura (Table 2).

## Hemorrhagic Colitis

In a prospective study of infections with *E. coli* O157:H7 in Washington state, Ostroff and coworkers described the clinical findings in 93 patients[14] (Fig 3). The earliest clinical manifestations of infection with *E. coli* O157:H7 were both nonbloody diarrhea and abdominal cramps. Bloody diarrhea usually did not begin until the second or third day of illness. However, 89% of patients developed this symptom by the fifth day of illness. A

TABLE 2.
Illnesses Caused by
Enterohemorrhagic *Escherichia coli*

Hemorrhagic colitis
Nonbloody diarrhea
Asymptomatic infection
Hemolytic-uremic syndrome
Thrombotic thrombocytopenic purpura

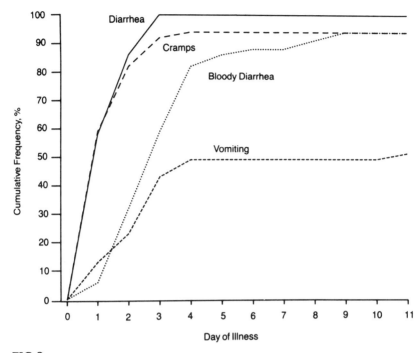

**FIG 3.**
Day of illness on which symptoms appeared during infection with *E. coli* O157:H7 in Washington state in 1987. (From Ostroff SM, Kobayashi JM, Lewis JH: *JAMA* 1989; 262:357. Used by permission.)

similar sequence of events occurs in one third to one half of patients with shigellosis, in which the diarrhea is initially watery and becomes dysenteric after several days of illness.[40] The initial symptoms of watery diarrhea in shigellosis may represent the effects of small-bowel involvement, while the subsequent dysenteric symptoms are the manifestations of colitis.[41] This pattern of "descending infection" from small intestine to colon also might explain the observed clinical findings of nonbloody diarrhea progressing to bloody diarrhea in EHEC infection.

Vomiting occurred in approximately one half of the patients and fever in approximately one third. However, when fever was present, it usually was not high (38 to 38.9° C).[20] This lack of fever distinguishes the illness associated with EHEC from true shigellosis, in which fever is often a prominent component. Also in contrast to shigellosis, fecal leukocytes are typically absent or present in low numbers.[20]

Colonoscopic examinations have revealed a nonuniform distribution of abnormalities, with the ascending and transverse colon being most severely affected. Erythema and edema are the most prominent features.[20, 42] Superficial ulceration has been observed also.[42] Sigmoidoscopic examination may be normal, since the affected areas may be limited to the proximal colon. Abdominal roentgenograms most frequently demonstrate an ileus. A barium enema is not required for the diagnosis of hemorrhagic colitis; however, when this examination is performed, it most often demonstrates a pattern of submucosal edema resembling thumbprinting[3] (Fig 4). As with colonoscopic examination, radiographic evidence of disease appears to be more severe in the ascending and transverse colon. This radiologic finding in the setting of abdominal pain, bloody diarrhea, and low-grade fever may be confused with ischemic colitis. In fact, some of the patients in one nursing-home outbreak initially were thought to have ischemic colitis, and avoided laparotomy only because their illnesses were part of a recogized outbreak of E. coli O157:H7 hemorrhagic colitis.[31] Other patients with sporadic cases of E. coli O157:H7 disease actually have undergone laparotomy with and without colonic resection.[18, 20]

The incubation period of hemorrhagic colitis is approximately 3 to 4 days.[3] The average duration of illness is approximately 7 days,[14] although

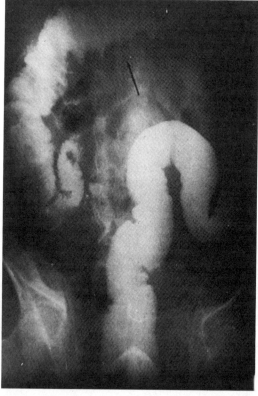

**FIG 4.**
Barium enema demonstrating thumbprinting in ascending and transverse colon of a patient with hemorrhagic colitis. (From Riley LW, Remis RS, Helgerson SD, et al: N Engl J Med 1983; 308:633. Used by permission.)

the range is from 2 to 15 days. Because of the severity of this illness and its predilection for patients at the extremes of age, patients with hemorrhagic colitis are often hospitalized. In the Washington state study, 42% of these patients were hospitalized for a mean of 7.6 days.[14] Most of the patients experienced a self-limiting illness. However, 12% of the patients developed either hemolytic-uremic syndrome or thrombotic thrombocytopenic purpura and these sequelae can be associated with chronic renal disease, neurologic impairment, or death.

## Nonbloody Diarrhea

In most infections, watery diarrhea associated with E. coli 0157:H7 infection progresses to hemorrhagic colitis and bloody diarrhea.[20] However, in various studies, between 17% and 30% of infected persons during outbreaks[20] and 4% and 5% of infected persons during sporadic cases[14, 43] do not follow this progression. Patients with watery diarrhea are more likely to be afebrile and to have a shorter and less severe illness than patients with bloody diarrhea. They also may be less likely to develop the complications of hemolytic-uremic syndrome and thrombotic thrombocytopenic purpura. Nonbloody diarrhea is associated more often with infection with EHEC serotypes other than E. coli 0157:H7.[6, 19] However, nonbloody diarrhea is seen also in sporadic cases and outbreaks of disease caused by E. coli 0157:H7.[16, 20]

## Asymptomatic Infection

E. coli 0157:H7 generally is not isolated from asymptomatic people.[3, 15, 19] However, cases of asymptomatic E. coli 0157:H7 infections have been detected occasionally in the midst of outbreaks. During an outbreak of E. coli 0157:H7 infection in three kindergarten classes who drank raw milk at a dairy, E. coli 0157:H7 was isolated from the stool of an asymptomatic child.[32] Similarly, in nursing-home outbreaks, E. coli 0157:H7 has been isolated from asymptomatic adults.[20, 31] The frequency of asymptomatic infection is likely to be very low. However, pooled human immunoglobulin contains neutralizing antibody to SLT1.[44] Furthermore, antibodies to either SLT1 or SLT2 are present in 14% to 20% of healthy control populations.[19, 45] This is serologic evidence for relatively widespread exposure to EHEC. It is possible that patients with "asymptomatic infection" have had previous, unrecognized illness with EHEC that has rendered them immune and allowed them to become transiently colonized with EHEC during an outbreak, without developing clinical symptoms.

## Hemolytic-Uremic Syndrome

The most important sequela of EHEC infection is the development of hemolytic-uremic syndrome. Idiopathic, nonfamilial hemolytic-uremic syndrome is defined as a syndrome of microangiopathic hemolytic anemia, thrombocytopenia, and acute renal failure. It most commonly affects children between 1 and 4 years of age and may result in persistent renal or neurologic disease. The association of this syndrome with antecedent shigellosis and bloody diarrhea not due to *Shigella* has been well established previously.[46-48] In 1979, Whitington and coworkers reviewed the records of 12 consecutive patients with hemolytic-uremic syndrome and reported that the initial symptoms in all patients were those of enterocolitis.[47] The syndrome was diagnosed anywhere from 2 days to 6 weeks after the onset of symptoms.

In 1983, Karmali and coworkers reported sporadic cases of hemolytic-uremic syndrome associated with EHEC in stools. *E. coli* O157:H7 was the most common *E. coli* serotype identified. Karmali and colleagues also demonstrated that free fecal verotoxin was detectable in the stool of most patients with the syndrome and that these patients demonstrated a fourfold rise in serum verotoxin-neutralizing antibodies.[15]

Recent studies have confirmed the association of hemolytic-uremic syndrome with infections due to *E. coli* O157:H7 as well as other cytotoxin-producing serotypes in both children and adults.[7, 18] Evidence of preexisting infection with EHEC has been found in 75% to 90% of children with the syndrome in North America[7, 15, 49] and in almost 95% of patients in Argentina.[19] However, when stool cultures are obtained at the time of presentation, there is a greatly diminished likelihood of identifying EHEC. Recovery of *E. coli* O157:H7 is highly dependent upon obtaining stool cultures within 6 days of the onset of diarrhea.[3, 50] Since hemolytic-uremic syndrome commonly occurs 7 days (ranging from several days to weeks) after the onset of hemorrhagic colitis, the organism may no longer be present in stool cultures at the time of diagnosis.

In sporadic cases of hemorrhagic colitis, hemolytic-uremic syndrome occurs in approximately 10% of patients.[14, 20] It was reported in 4 (8%) of 48 patients with hemorrhagic colitis in two series[20, 29] and in 9 (10%) of 93 patients in Washington state.[14] The risk of this syndrome following outbreaks of hemorrhagic colitis appears to be higher than that observed in sporadic infections; however, its attack rate has varied greatly in several different studies. In a prospective study in British Columbia, Canada, 9 (36%) out of 25 children with *E. coli* O157:H7 infection developed hemolytic-uremic syndrome.[17] In this outbreak, 2 of the 9 children died. In another day-care outbreak, 3 (8%) cases of this syndrome were associated with 36 cases of diarrhea.[16] In a nursing-home outbreak, 24% of the elderly patients with *E. coli* O157:H7 infection developed hemolytic-uremic syndrome, and more than half of these patients died.[51] In a study involving two institutions for retarded persons in Utah, 8 (40%) cases of the syndrome occurred among 20 residents with *E. coli* O157:H7 infection. Half of these patients died.[38] It appears that the very young and the very old have both an increased rate of developing hemolytic-uremic syndrome as a sequela of EHEC infection and an overall increased incidence of EHEC infection. This age-related difference in the incidence of this syndrome may explain the apparent discrepancy in its attack rates in outbreaks and sporadic cases. For example, in the Washington state surveillance report of sporadic illness, although the overall risk of developing hemolytic-uremic syndrome was 10%, 25% of those less than 10 years old developed it.[14] Other risk factors for the development of this sequela appear to be the presence of bloody diarrhea rather than nonbloody diarrhea,[16] high white blood cell counts or leukemoid reactions,[38] and the use of antimotility or antidiarrheal agents.[39] While antibiotic use appears to be a risk factor for the progression of shigellosis to hemolytic-uremic syndrome,[52] this has not proven to be the case for EHEC-associated diarrhea.[14, 39]

Interestingly, patients with E. coli 0157:H7 infection, but without all of the features of hemolytic-uremic syndrome, may have an abnormal urinalysis or peripheral red blood cell smear.[20] In a survey of patients with E. coli 0157:H7–associated bloody diarrhea but without classic hemolytic-uremic syndrome, Neill and coworkers noted hematuria or proteinuria in 6 of 11 patients, evidence for a microangiopathic hemolysis in 4 of 8 patients, and thrombocytopenia in 3 of 11 patients.[20]

**Thrombotic Thrombocytopenic Purpura**

Thrombotic thrombocytopenic purpura resembles hemolytic-uremic syndrome in many respects, but differs in that it occurs more frequently in adults, is associated more often with fever, and usually does not involve a prodromal illness. The hallmark of this entity is neurologic involvement. Thrombotic thrombocytopenic purpura has been reported to occur after either sporadic cases or outbreaks of E. coli 0157:H7 infection.[20–22] Griffin and coworkers studied an outbreak of E. coli 0157:H7 infection due to a single strain in Washington state and found that both sequelae were associated with this single-strain outbreak.[20] Both the relatedness of the clinical findings of hemolytic-uremic syndrome and thrombotic thrombocytopenic purpura as well as the fact that a single strain can cause both complications suggests that there may be a common mechanism for these two entities.

In the Washington state surveillance report, 2 patients out of 93 with E. coli 0157:H7 infection developed thrombotic thrombocytopenic purpura.[14] Both of these patients were immunocompromised adults. One of these patients was a 56-year-old with multiple myeloma and the other was a 61-year-old with steroid-dependent rheumatoid arthritis. This second patient died after a prolonged hospitalization.

**Microbiology**

The identification of EHEC is made difficult because it is not possible to differentiate disease-producing E. coli from normal enteric flora on the basis of standard microbiologic techniques. There currently are six techniques for the identification of EHEC: cytotoxin production, biochemical markers, serotyping, serum antibody tests, DNA hybridization, and enzyme-linked immunosorbent assays (Table 3).

**TABLE 3.**
**Techniques for Identification of Enterohemorrhagic *Escherichia coli* (EHEC)***

Cytotoxin assays
    Detect the ability of EHEC to produce a cytopathic effect in HeLa or vero cells[7, 23, 53]
Biochemical markers
    Since most *E. coli* O157:H7 do not ferment sorbitol, use of MacConkey-sorbitol agar permits screening for this serotype[1, 55]
Serotyping
    When combined with MacConkey-sorbitol screening assay, permits the detection of *E. coli* O157:H7 with specific "O" and "H" antigen antisera
Serum antibody tests
    Paired sera detect a rise in antibody titer to Shiga-like toxins[15]
DNA hybridization
    Currently available DNA probes detect genes encoding for Shiga-like toxins (SLT1, SLT2) or for specific EHEC fimbrial adhesion[9, 53]
Enzyme-linked immunosorbent assay
    Newly developed assays use monoclonal antibodies or toxin receptor analog to bind and detect cytotoxins[54, 55]

*Adapted from Ashkenazi S, Pickering LK: *Contemporary Pediatrics* 1990; 6:53–74.

## Cytotoxin Production

In the initial report of Konowalchuk and coworkers, a cytotoxin was found in culture filtrates of *E. coli* that differed from heat-stable and heat-labile enterotoxins.[23] This toxin was cytotoxic for vero cells, but not for Y-1 or CHO cells.[23] Subsequent studies have demonstrated that this cytotoxin also causes lysis in HeLa cells.[8] SLT producers can be identified by incubating culture filtrates of suspected organisms with HeLa or vero cells and by observing a cytopathic effect that is neutralized by the addition of anti-SLT1 or anti-SLT2 antisera.[56] In a modification of this cytotoxin assay, Karmali and coworkers, in their initial demonstration of the relationship between hemolytic-uremic syndrome and cytotoxin-producing *E. coli*, measured the presence of free fecal cytotoxin.[15] Still others have modified this technique to detect cytotoxin in stool specimen filtrates by the use of vero cell suspensions rather than vero cell monolayers.[57] Karmali and coworkers also have proposed a screening method involving polymyxin extracts of colony pools or sweeps to detect cytotoxin-producing *E. coli*.[56] Several problems exist with all of these cell culture assays. First, and probably foremost, they are very time-consuming and require a highly specialized laboratory. Second, many *E. coli* produce low levels of cytotoxin and there is no consensus on the interpretation of low titer activity. Additionally, some investigators have noted that the sensitivity of tissue culture cells used in these assays decreases over time,[7] causing assay-to-assay variability.

## Biochemical Markers

In the initial outbreak of hemorrhagic colitis, it was observed that E. coli O157:H7 failed to ferment sorbitol within 24 hours.[1] This differentiates E. coli O157:H7 from approximately 95% of other E. coli strains.[58] The use of sorbitol-MacConkey agar (MacConkey agar containing sorbitol instead of lactose) as a differential medium for the detection of E. coli O157:H7 provides a sensitive but not specific means of detecting this strain.[59] Haldane and coworkers found that 37 (11.3%) of 327 sorbitol-negative E. coli isolates were of the serotype O157:H7.[60] Furthermore, all sorbitol nonfermenting O157:H7 strains decarboxylated both ornithine and lysine in standard identification systems. Inclusion of these decarboxylation tests increased the sensitivity of the sorbitol assay to 33.6%.[60]

## Serotyping

Many clinical laboratories have combined the relatively nonspecific sorbitol screening test with serotyping for E. coli O157:H7 by slide agglutination of those organisms that do not ferment sorbitol. The problem with this method of identification is that it will not detect cytotoxin-producing E. coli other than O157:H7 (see Table 1). In some areas, this serotype is the predominant serotype of EHEC.[14, 61] However, in other geographic locations, this serotype is much less common.[19]

## Serum Antibody Tests

Another method of detecting infection with SLT-producing E. coli has been to determine the presence of anticytotoxin antibodies in serum.[15] In the initial description of the relationship of hemolytic-uremic syndrome to EHEC, 59% of patients who had paired acute and convalescent sera available had a fourfold titer rise to cytotoxin.[16] Of course, this method is limited by the need to obtain convalescent sera.

## DNA Hybridization

A recent strategy for the identification of EHEC is the use of DNA probes to detect either the genes that code for toxin production or a plasmid that encodes for an EHEC-associated attachment factor.[9, 53, 62–65] These techniques are very powerful, but suffer from two limitations. First, these assays require specialized laboratory facilities and are done most efficiently in batch assays. This makes them somewhat less useful on a day-to-day clinical basis, but very useful for assaying large groups of specimens and also for epidemiologic studies. Second, small quantities of SLT1 may be produced by many E. coli and the interpretation of small numbers of gene probe–positive colonies may be difficult. Gene probes also have demonstrated that some strains of E. coli are VT1-positive, some are VT2-positive, and some are positive for both probes.[9, 53, 63, 64]

## Enzyme-Linked Immunosorbent Assays

Two different rapid enzyme-linked immunosorbent assays, based on either binding to antitoxin monoclonal antibodies or to a toxin receptor globotriosyl ceramide (Gb$_3$) analog have been developed recently.[54, 55] In the first method, a sandwich assay based on toxin-specific murine monoclonal capture antibodies and rabbit polyclonal second antibodies specific for SLT1 and SLT2 demonstrated sensitivity to 200 picograms of purified SLT1 and 75 picograms of purified SLT2.[54] This is sufficient to detect high-level toxin producers of either toxin. The second rapid-method enzyme-linked immunosorbent assay detects the ability of Shiga toxin and SLT1 to bind to a Gb$_3$ receptor coated onto microtiter plates.[55] This assay also is able to detect as little as 200 picograms of purified toxin. Although these assays are still research tools, they appear to be sensitive and specific, and may become useful in the clinical laboratory to diagnose EHEC infections.

## Pathogenesis

Both the ability to attach to intestinal epithelia and the ability to produce cytotoxins appear to be important factors in the pathogenesis of EHEC-associated hemorrhagic colitis. Additionally, toxins elaborated by EHEC may have systemic effects outside of the gastrointestinal tract.

## Adherence

The adherence of E. coli O157:H7 to intestinal epithelia is indistinguishable from the attaching and effacing lesions seen for enteropathogenic E. coli[66-68] (Fig 5). Attaching the effacing lesions due to EHEC have been described in the small intestine of calves, the ceca of chickens, and the colon of gnotobiotic pigs and infant rabbits.[69-73] The ability of intestinal pathogens to attach to mucosal surfaces in the gastrointestinal tract is an important step in the process of bacterial colonization. Attachment permits the organism to resist peristaltic clearing of bacteria trapped in mucus and brings elaborated toxins into close contact with the target intestinal cell. It is also likely that damage to the microvilli resulting from the adherence of bacteria interferes with fluid and electrolyte transport and carbohydrate absorption.

Although EHEC and enteropathogenic E. coli share the ability to adhere to HEp-2 cells and intestinal tissue culture cells, these two categories of diarrheogenic E. coli express different genetically determined patterns of adherence to these cells.[67, 74] EHEC do not hybridize with the enteropathogenic E. coli adherence factor gene probe.[9] However, EHEC do possess a 60-MDa plasmid that encodes for a fimbrial antigen and promotes attachment to epithelial cells.[9, 74] The presence of this 60-MDa plasmid is the basis for a gene probe assay for detection of EHEC.[9]

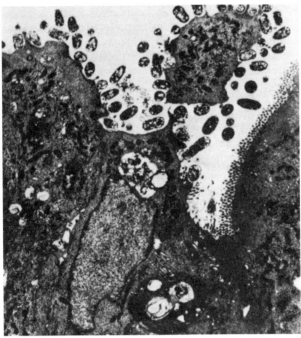

**FIG 5.**
Electron micrograph of distal colon from an infant rabbit infected with *E. coli* 0157:H7. Adherent bacteria form attaching and effacing lesions with loss of microvilli. Microvilli appear normal in the cell on the right where no bacteria are adherent. (From Pai CH, Kelly JK, Meyers GL: *Infect Immun* 1986; 51:20. Used by permission.)

---

## Cytotoxins

The second virulence factor important for the pathogenesis of disease caused by EHEC is the production of one or more cytotoxins. Organisms isolated from the initial outbreak of hemorrhagic colitis were found to produce high levels of toxins that could be neutralized by rabbit anti–Shiga-toxin antisera.[24, 25] On further analysis of cytotoxin-producing organisms, it became apparent that there were at least two families of cytotoxins. These cytotoxins were designated SLT1 and SLT2. Both toxins are composed of two subunits: a single polypeptide A (active) subunit is surrounded by multiple copies of a second polypeptide B (binding) subunit.[25] SLT1 has the same biologic activity and is virtually identical to Shiga toxin. In fact, there are only three nucleotide differences in the genes encoding for Shiga toxin and SLT.[75, 76] These nucleotide differences result in an identical deduced amino acid sequence for both toxins, except at position 45 of the A subunit where a serine is present in SLT1 and a threonine is present in Shiga toxin. As might be expected, these two toxins are also immunologically indistinguishable.

A second group of SLTs including SLT2 and SLT2v are less similar to

Shiga toxin. Both SLT2 and SLT2v are neutralized by polyclonal antisera against SLT2.[25, 77] However, these toxins are not neutralized by anti–Shiga-toxin antibodies. SLT2 has approximately 50% to 60% homology with Shiga toxin, on the basis of deduced amino acid sequence.[64] Nucleotide sequence analysis of the gene encoding for SLT2v has shown that the A and B subunit genes have a 94% and 79% sequence homology to the genes encoding VT2.[78–80] SLT2v is also classified as a variant of SLT2 because it is significantly more cytotoxic for vero cells than for HeLa cells.[77, 81] In fact, there may be several other members of this toxin family that share relatively conserved genetic sequences.[78, 81, 82]

Despite these molecular differences, the mechanisms of action of Shiga toxin, SLT1, SLT2, and SLT2v, as well as the plant toxin ricin, are identical.[25] These toxins interfere with protein synthesis by cleaving an N-glycoside bond at a specific adenine residue located at position 4,324 of 60-S ribosomal RNA in mammalian cells.[25, 82–84] The eukaryotic receptor for the binding (B) units of Shiga toxin, SLT1, and SLT2 is a galactose-$\alpha$-1,4-galactose–containing glycolipid designated $Gb_3$.[85–87] Current evidence suggests that SLT2v does not bind to this $Gb_3$ receptor.[80, 81]

The role of the cytotoxins in the pathogenesis of disease is somewhat less clear. Several animal models have been described. Tzipori and coworkers observed extensive luminal exudation with areas of erosion, ulceration, and necrosis in the gnotobiotic pigs infected with two different strains of *E. coli* O157:H7.[72] The first strain produced what was probably SLT1 and the second strain produced what was probably SLT2. Toxin-containing extracts of *E. coli* O157:H7 caused diarrhea in rabbits and histologic changes in the colon, including apoptosis.[73]

Griffin and coworkers reported a variety of histologic features in patients with *E. coli* O157:H7 infection.[42] All specimens showed hemorrhage and edema in the lamina propria. Furthermore, colonic specimens from 9 out of 11 patients showed focal necrosis, hemorrhage, and acute inflammation in the superficial mucosa, with preservation of the deep crypts.[42] This pattern was suggestive of an ischemic injury. Five of 11 patients showed a neutrophilic infiltration resembling a pattern more commonly seen in infectious colitis. In addition, 4 patients had poorly formed inflammatory pseudomembranes typical of findings in *Clostridium difficile*–associated colitis. There was no difference in the histology in the colonic lesions based on the cytotoxin produced by the *E. coli* O157:H7 isolates.[42]

## Systemic Effects of Cytotoxins

In addition to its cytopathic actions on the intestinal mucosa, SLT may cause systemic illness by directly affecting the extraintestinal vasculature.[88, 89] Shiga toxin has been shown to be directly cytotoxic for human umbilical vein endothelial cells.[89]

SLT2v also is thought to be the "edema disease principle" responsible for edema disease in pigs.[79] In addition, gnotobiotic piglets infected with *E. coli* O157:H7 that produce toxin neutralized by SLT2 antisera developed brain lesions similar to those seen in porcine edema disease.[90] Edema disease of pigs and the sequelae of EHEC infection (hemolytic-uremic syndrome and thrombotic thrombocytopenic purpura) in humans share several common features, including a diarrheal prodrome, central nervous system involvement, and endothelial cell damage, suggesting a common mechanism.[79, 90]

In a study of 3 patients with SLT-producing *E. coli* infections, Richardson and coworkers described a diffuse picture of thrombocytic microangiopathy.[91] This finding was present in both the kidneys and the gastrointestinal tract. Small-vessel thrombolysis was present outside of these two organs also. The widespread microangiopathy seen with hemolytic-uremic syndrome supports the hypothesis that this sequela of EHEC infection is due to damage of capillary endothelial cells by systemic toxemia.

## Treatment

Hemorrhagic colitis has been confused with a number of other conditions, including ischemic colitis, appendicitis, Crohn's disease, ulcerative colitis, cecal polyp, pseudomembranous colitis, and an acute abdomen (ileitis).[20, 47, 92] Therefore, the most important aspect of treating EHEC-associated hemorrhagic colitis is making the correct diagnosis and avoiding angiography and/or laparotomy.

The mainstay of hemorrhagic colitis therapy is the management of dehydration, electrolyte abnormalities, and gastrointestinal blood loss. No controlled trials of antibiotic treatment of EHEC infection have been reported. Although these organisms are uniformly sensitive to antimicrobials in vitro, at present there is no evidence that antimicrobial therapy is helpful in diminishing the severity of illness or the duration of fecal excretion.[20] In one study of a nursing-home outbreak, it appeared that patients who were treated with antibiotics actually had a higher fatality rate.[31] It is unclear whether the antibiotics had an adverse effect or whether the most ill patients were given antibiotics. In more recent studies, the use of antibiotics has not been demonstrated to be a risk factor for more severe illness or progression to hemolytic-uremic syndrome.[14, 39] Commercial preparations of intravenous human immunoglobulin contain antibodies to SLT1.[44] Treatment with these agents has been partially effective in a few patients with hemolytic-uremic syndrome.[93] The use of these preparations as an alternative approach to therapy of hemorrhagic colitis or hemolytic-uremic syndrome needs further study.

## Summary

*E. coli* 0157:H7, the predominant serotype of EHEC, is a cause of both outbreaks and sporadic cases of hemorrhagic colitis. In sporadic cases, and especially in outbreaks, there is an association with the consumption of improperly cooked ground beef. Both young children and geriatric patients have an increased attack rate for EHEC infection as well as an increased incidence of the two sequelae of intestinal infection with EHEC, hemolytic-uremic syndrome, and thrombotic thrombocytopenic purpura. The hallmark of hemorrhagic colitis due to EHEC is the development of bloody diarrhea several days after the onset of nonbloody diarrhea and abdominal pain. Fever is usually absent or low-grade. The pathogenesis of EHEC infection is probably related to at least two bacterial virulence factors: adherence of bacteria to intestinal mucosa and production of one or more cytotoxins. These cytotoxins are closely related to Shiga toxin and therefore are often referred to as Shiga-like toxins. Treatment for hemorrhagic colitis is supportive care; most illnesses are self-limited. At present, there is no evidence that antimicrobial therapy shortens the course of illness or prevents the development of sequelae.

## Acknowledgments

We thank Tamara Shumate for help in preparation of the manuscript.

## References

1. Wells JG, Davis BR, Wachsmuth K, et al: Laboratory investigation of hemorrhagic colitis outbreaks associated with a rare *Escherichia coli* serotype. *J Clin Microbiol* 1983; 18:512–520.
2. Anonymous: Isolation of *E. coli* O157:H7 from sporadic cases of hemorrhagic colitis—United States. *MMWR* 1982; 31:580–585.
3. Riley LW, Remis RS, Helgerson SD, et al: Hemorrhagic colitis associated with a rare *Escherichia coli* serotype. *N Engl J Med* 1983; 308:681–685.
4. Whittam TS, Wachsmuth IK, Wilson RA: Genetic evidence of clonal descent of *Escherichia coli* O157:H7 associated with hemorrhagic colitis and hemolytic uremic syndrome. *J Infect Dis* 1988; 157:1124–1133.
5. Levine M: *Escherichia coli* that cause diarrhea: Enterotoxigenic, enteropathogenic, enteroinvasive, enterohemorrhagic, and enteroadherent. *J Infect Dis* 1987; 155:377–389.
6. Pai CH, Ahmed N, Lior H, et al: Epidemiology of sporadic diarrhea due to verocytotoxin-producing *Escherichia coli:* A two-year study. *J infect Dis* 1988; 157:1054–1057.
7. Cleary TC: Cytotoxin-producing *Escherichia coli* and the hemolytic uremic syndrome. *Pediatr Clin North Am* 1988; 35:485–501.
8. Cleary TG, Mathewson JJ, Faris E, et al: Shiga-like cytotoxin production by enteropathogenic *Escherichia coli* serogroups. *Infect Immun* 1985; 47:335–337.
9. Levine MM, Xu J, Kaper JB, et al: A DNA probe to identify enterohemorrhagic *Escherichia coli* of O157:H7 and other serotypes that cause hemorrhagic colitis and hemolytic uremic syndrome. *J Infect Dis* 1987; 156:175–182.
10. Scotland SM, Day NP, Rowe B: Production of a cytotoxin affecting vero cells by strains of *Escherichia coli* belonging to traditional enteropathogenic serogroups. *FEMS Microbiol Lett* 1980; 7:15–17.
11. Cleary TG, Lopez EL: The shiga-like toxin-producing *Escherichia coli* and hemolytic uremic syndrome. *Pediatr Infect Dis J* 1989; 8:720–724.

12. Bettelheim KA, Brown JE, Lolekha S, et al: Serotypes of *Escherichia coli* that hybridized with DNA probes for genes encoding Shiga-like toxin II, and serogroup O157 enterohemorrhagic *E. coli* fimbriae isolated from adults with diarrhea in Thailand. *J Clin Microbiol* 1990; 28:293–295.
13. Ashkenazi S, Pickering LK: *E. coli* 0157:H7—a new GI pathogen to contend with. *Contemporary Pediatrics* 1990; 6:53–74.
14. Ostroff SM, Kobayashi JM, Lewis JH: Infections with *Escherichia coli* 0157:H7 in Washington state; the first year of statewide surveillance. *JAMA* 1989; 262:355–359.
15. Karmali MA, Petric M, Lim C, et al: The association between idiopathic hemolytic uremic syndrome and infection by verotoxin-producing *Escherichia coli*. *J Infect Dis* 1985; 151:775–782.
16. Spika JS, Parsons JE, Nordenberg D, et al: Hemolytic uremic syndrome and diarrhea associated with *Escherichia coli* 0157:H7 in a day care center. *J Pediatr* 1986; 109:287–291.
17. Gransden WR, Damm S, Anderson JD, et al: Further evidence associating hemolytic uremic syndrome with infection by verotoxin-producing *Escherichia coli* 0157:H7. *J Infect Dis* 1986; 154:522–524.
18. Neill MA, Agosti J, Rosen H: Hemorrhagic colitis with *Escherichia coli* 0157:H7 preceding adult hemolytic uremic syndrome. *Arch Intern Med* 1985; 145:2215–2217.
19. Lopez EL, Diaz M, Grinstein S, et al: Hemolytic uremic syndrome and diarrhea in Argentine children: The role of Shiga-like toxins. *J Infect Dis* 1989; 160:469–475.
20. Griffin PM, Ostroff SM, Tauxe RV, et al: Illnesses associated with *Escherichia coli* 0157:H7 infections; a broad clinical spectrum. *Ann Intern Med* 1988; 109:705–712.
21. Morrison DM, Tyrrell DL, Jewell LD: Colonic biopsy in verotoxin-induced hemorrhagic colitis and thrombotic thrombocytopenic purpura (TTP). *Am J Clin Pathol* 1986; 86:108–112.
22. Anonymous: Thrombotic thrombocytopenic purpura associated with *Escherichia coli* 0157:H7—Washington. *MMWR* 1986; 35:549–551.
23. Konowalchuk J, Speirs JI, Stavric S: Vero response to a cytotoxin of *Escherichia coli*. *Infect Immun* 1977; 18:775–779.
24. O'Brien AD, LaVeck GD: Purification and characterization of a *Shigella dysenteriae* 1-like toxin produced by *Escherichia coli*. *Infect Immun* 1983; 40:675–683.
25. O'Brien AD, Holmes RK: Shiga and Shiga-like toxins. *Microbiol Rev* 1987; 51:206–220.
26. Pai CH, Gordon R, Sims HV, et al: Sporadic cases of hemorrhagic colitis associated with *Escherichia coli* 0157:H7. *Ann Intern Med* 1984; 101:738–742.
27. Smith HR, Gross RJ, Rowe B, et al: Haemorrhagic colitis and verocytotoxin-producing *Escherichia coli* in England and Wales. *Lancet* 1987; 1:1062–1064.
28. Cryan B: Enterohaemorrhagic *Escherichia coli*. *Scand J Infect Dis* 1990; 22:1–4.
29. Remis RS, MacDonald KL, Riley LW, et al: Sporadic cases of hemorrhagic colitis associated with *Escherichia coli* 0157:H7. *Ann Intern Med* 1984; 101:624–626.
30. Harris AA, Kaplan LJ, Goodman LJ, et al: Results of a screening method used in a 12-month survey for *Escherichia coli* 0157:H7. *J Infect Dis* 1985; 152:775–777.
31. Ryan CA, Tauxe RV, Hosek G, et al: *Escherichia coli* 0157:H7 diarrhea in a

nursing home: Clinical, epidemiological, and pathological findings. *J Infect Dis* 1986; 154:631–638.

32. Anonymous: Outbreak of gastrointestinal disease in Sarnia, Ontario. *Ontario Disease Surveillance Report* 1986; 7:604–611.

33. Doyle MP, Schoeni JL: Isolation of *Escherichia coli* O157:H7 from fresh retail meats and poultry. *Appl Environ Microbiol* 1987; 53:2394–2396.

34. Montenegro MA, Bulte M, Trumpf T, et al: Detection and characterization of fecal verotoxin-producing *Escherichia coli* from healthy cattle. *J Clin Microbiol* 1990; 28:1417–1421.

35. Abaas S, Franklin A, Kuhn I, et al: Cytotoxin activity on vero cells among *Escherichia coli* strains associated with diarrhea in cats. *Am J Vet Res* 1989; 50:1294–1296.

36. Carter AO, Borczyk AA, Carlson JAK, et al: A severe outbreak of *Escherichia coli* O157:H7-associated hemorrhagic colitis in a nursing home. *N Engl J Med* 1987; 317:1496–1500.

37. Riley LW: The epidemiologic, clinical, and microbiologic features of hemorrhagic colitis. *Annu Rev Microbiol* 1987; 41:383–407.

38. Pavia AT, Nichols CR, Green DP, et al: Hemolytic-uremic syndrome during an outbreak of *Escherichia coli* O157:H7 infections in institutions for mentally retarded persons: Clinical and epidemiologic observations. *J Pediatr* 1990; 116:544–551.

39. Cimolai N, Carter JE, Morrison BJ, et al: Risk factors for the progression of *Escherichia coli* O157:H7 enteritis to hemolytic-uremic syndrome. *J Pediatr* 1990; 116:589–592.

40. DuPont HL, Hornick RB, Dawkins AT, et al: The response of man to virulent *Shigella flexneri* 2a. *J Infect Dis* 1969; 119:296–299.

41. Rout WR, Formal SB, Giannella RA, et al: Pathophysiology of *Shigella* diarrhea in the rhesus monkey; intestinal transport, morphological and bacteriological studies. *Gastroenterology* 1975; 68:270–278.

42. Griffin PM, Olmstead LC, Petras RE: *Escherichia coli* O157:H7-associated colitis. *Gastroenterology* 1990; 99:142–149.

43. MacDonald KL, O'Leary MJ, Cohen ML, et al: *Escherichia coli* O157:H7, an emerging gastrointestinal pathogen: Results of a one-year prospective, population-based study. *JAMA* 1988; 259:3567–3570.

44. Ashkenazi S, Cleary TG, Lopez E, et al: Anticytotoxin-neutralizing antibodies in immune globulin preparations: Potential use in hemolytic-uremic syndrome. *J Pediatr* 1988; 113:1006–1014.

45. Karmali MA, Petric M, Roscoe M: Neutralizing antibody responses to verocytotoxin 1 ($VR_1$) and VT $_2$ in selected control populations. Abstract LFE11. Presented at the International Symposium and Workshop on Infections Due To Verocytotoxin (Shiga-Like Toxin)–Producing *Escherichia coli*, Toronto, Ontario, July 1987.

46. Koster F, Levin J, Walker L, et al: Hemolytic-uremic syndrome after shigellosis. *N Engl J Med* 1978; 298:927–933.

47. Whitington PF, Friedman AL, Chesney RW: Gastrointestinal disease in the hemolytic-uremic syndrome. *Gastroenterology* 1979; 76:728–733.

48. Anonymous: *Shigella dysenteriae* type 1 in tourists to Cancun, Mexico. *MMWR* 1988; 37:465–466.

49. Tarr PI, Hickman RO: Hemolytic uremic syndrome epidemiology; a population-based study in King County, Washington, 1971 to 1980. *Pediatrics* 1987; 80:41–45.

50. Tarr PI, Neill MA, Clausen CR, et al: *Escherichia coli* O157:H7 and the hemo-

lytic uremic syndrome: Importance of early cultures in establishing the etiology. *J Infect Dis* 1990; 162:553–556.

51. Krishnan C, Fitzgerald VA, Dakin SJ, et al: Laboratory investigation of outbreak of hemorrhagic colitis caused by *Escherichia coli* 0157:H7. *J Clin Microbiol* 1987; 25:1043–1047.

52. Butler T, Islam MR, Azad MAK, et al: Risk factors for development of hemolytic uremic syndrome during shigellosis. *J Pediatr* 1987; 110:894–897.

53. Willshaw GA, Smith HR, Scotland SM, et al: Heterogeneity of *Escherichia coli* phages encoding vero cytotoxins: Comparison of cloned sequences encoding VT1 and VT2 and development of specific gene probes. *J Gen Microbiol* 1987; 133:1309–1317.

54. Downes FP, Green JH, Greene K, et al: Development and evaluation of enzyme-linked immunosorbent assays for detection of shiga-like toxin I and shiga-like toxin II. *J Clin Microbiol* 1989; 27:1292–1297.

55. Ashkenazi S, Cleary TG: Rapid method to detect shiga toxin and shiga-like toxin I based on binding to globotriosyl ceramide ($Gb_3$), their natural receptor. *J Clin Microbiol* 1989; 27:1145–1150.

56. Karmali MA, Petric M, Lim C, et al: Sensitive method for detecting low numbers of verotoxin-producing *Escherichia coli* in mixed cultures by use of colony sweeps and polymyxin extraction of verotoxin. *J Clin Microbiol* 1985; 22:614–619.

57. Maniar AC, Williams T, Anand CM, et al: Detection of verotoxin in stool specimens. *J Clin Microbiol* 1990; 28:134–135.

58. Farmer JJ, Davis BR: H7 antiserum-sorbitol fermentation medium: A single tube screening medium for detecting *Escherichia coli* 0157:H7 associated with hemorrhagic colitis. *J Clin Microbiol* 1985; 22:620–625.

59. March SB, Ratnam S: Sorbitol-MacConkey medium for detection of *Escherichia coli* 0157:H7 associated with hemorrhagic colits. *J Clin Microbiol* 1986; 23:869–872.

60. Haldane DJM, Damm MAS, Anderson JD: Improved biochemical screening procedure for small clinical laboratories for vero (shiga-like)-toxin-producing strains of *Escherichia coli* 0157:H7. *J Clin Microbiol* 1986; 24:652–653.

61. Neill MA, Tarr PI, Clausen CR, et al: *Escherichia coli* 0157:H7 as the predominant pathogen associated with the hemolytic uremic syndrome: A prospective study in the Pacific northwest. *Pediatrics* 1987; 80:37–40.

62. Meyer T, Karch H: Genes coding for Shiga-like toxin and heat-stable enterotoxin in porcine strains of *Escherichia coli*. *FEMS Microbiol Lett* 1989; 58:115–120.

63. Smith HR, Scotland SM, Chart H, et al: Vero cytotoxin production and presence of VT genes in strains of *Escherichia coli* and *Shigella*. *FEMS Microbiol Lett* 1987; 42:173–177.

64. Newland JW, Strockbine NA, Neill RJ: Cloning of genes for production of *Escherichia coli* shiga-like toxin type II. *Infect Immun* 1987; 55:2675–2680.

65. Newland JW, Strockbine NA, Miller SF, et al: Cloning of shiga-like toxin structural genes from a toxin converting phage of *Escherichia coli*. *Science* 1985; 230:179–182.

66. Knutton S, Baldwin T, Williams PH, et al: Actin accumulation at sites of bacterial adhesion to tissue culture cells: Basis of a new diagnostic test for enteropathogenic and enterohemorrhagic *Escherichia coli*. *Infect Immun* 1989; 57:1290–1298.

67. Sherman P, Soni R, Petric M, et al: Surface properties of the vero cytotoxin-producing *Escherichia coli* 0157:H7. *Infect Immun* 1987; 55:1824–1829.

68. Rothbaum R, McAdams AJ, Giannella RA, et al: A clinicopathologic study of enterocyte-adherent *Escherichia coli:* A cause of protracted diarrhea in infants. *Gastroenterology* 1982; 83:441–454.

69. Wray C, McLaren I, Pearson GR: Occurrence of 'attaching and effacing' lesions in the small intestine of calves experimentally infected with bovine isolates of verocytotoxic *E. coli. Vet Rec* 1989; 125:365–368.

70. Berry JT, Doyle MP, Schoeni JL: Colonization of chicken cecae by *Escherichia coli* associated with hemorrhagic colitis. *Appl Environ Microbiol* 1985; 49: 310–315.

71. Hall GA, Chanter N, Bland AP: Comparison in gnotobiotic pigs of lesions caused by verotoxigenic and non-verotoxigenic *Escherichia coli. Vet Pathol* 1988; 25:205–210.

72. Tzipori S, Wachsmuth IK, Chapman C, et al: The pathogenesis of hemorrhagic colitis caused by *Escherichia coli* O157:H7 in gnotobiotic piglets. *J Infect Dis* 1986; 154:712–716.

73. Pai CH, Kelly JK, Meyers GL: Experimental infection of infant rabbits with verotoxin-producing *Escherichia coli. Infect Immun* 1986; 51:16–23.

74. Karch H, Heesemann J, Laufs R, et al: A plasmid of enterohemorrhagic *Escherichia coli* O157:H7 is required for expression of a new fimbrial antigen and for adhesion to epithelial cells. *Infect Immun* 1987; 55:445–461.

75. Jackson MP, Neill RJ, O'Brien AD, et al: Nucleotide sequence analysis and comparison of the structural genes for Shiga-like toxin I and Shiga-like toxin II encoded by bacteriophages from *Escherichia coli* 933. *FEMS Microbiol Lett* 1987; 44:109–114.

76. Strockbine NA, Jackson MP, Sung LM, et al: Cloning and sequencing of the genes for Shiga toxin from *Shigella dysenteriae* type 1. *J Bacteriol* 1988; 170:1116–1122.

77. Marques LR, Moore MA, Wells JG, et al: Production of Shiga-like toxin by *Escherichia coli. J Infect Dis* 1986; 154:338–341.

78. Ito H, Terai A, Kurazono H, et al: Cloning and nucleotide sequencing of vero toxin 2 variant genes from *Escherichia coli* O91:H21 isolated from a patient with the hemolytic uremic syndrome. *Microb Pathog* 1990; 8:47–60.

79. Weinstein DL, Jackson MP, Samuel JE, et al: Cloning and sequencing of Shiga-like toxin II variant from an *Escherichia coli* strain responsible for edema disease of swine. *J Bacteriol* 1988; 170:4223–4230.

80. Gyles CL, DeGrandis SA, MacKenzie C, et al: Cloning and nucleotide sequence analysis of the genes determining verocytotoxin production in a porcine edema disease isolate of *Escherichia coli. Microb Pathog* 1988; 5:419–426.

81. Weinstein DL, Jackson MP, Perera LP, et al: In vivo formation of hybrid toxins comprising shiga toxin and the shiga-like toxins and role of the B subunit in localization and cytotoxin activity. *Infect Immun* 1989; 57:3743–3750.

82. Furutani M, Ito K, Oku Y, et al: Demonstration of RNA N-glycosidase activity of a vero toxin (VT2 variant) produced by *Escherichia coli* O91:H21 from patient with the hemolytic uremic syndrome. *Microbiol Immunol* 1990; 34:387–392.

83. Saxena SK, O'Brien AD, Ackerman EJ: Shiga toxin, Shiga-like toxin II variant, and ricin are all single site RNA N-glycosidases of 28S RNA when microinjected into *Xenopus* oocytes. *J Biol Chem* 1989; 264:596–601.

84. Edelman R, Karmali MA, Fleming PA: Summary of the international symposium and workshop on infections due to verocytotoxin (Shiga-like toxin)-producing *Escherichia coli. J Infect Dis* 1988; 157:1102–1104.

85. Jacewicz M, Clausen H, Nudelman E, et al: Pathogenesis of *Shigella* diarrhea.

XI. Isolation of a *Shigella* toxin-binding glycolipid from rabbit jejunum and Hela cells and its identification as a globotriosylceramide. *J Exp Med* 1986; 163:1391–1404.

86. Lingwood CA, Law H, Richardson S, et al: Glycolipid binding of purified and recombinant *Escherichia coli* produced verotoxin in vitro. *J Biol Chem* 1987; 262:8834–8839.

87. Waddell T, Head S, Petric M, et al: Globotriosyl ceramide is specifically recognized by the *Escherichia coli* verocytotoxin 2. *Biochem Biophys Res Commun* 1988; 153:674–679.

88. Boyd B, Ling C: Verotoxin receptor glycolipid in human renal tissue. *Nephron* 1989; 51:207–210.

89. Obrig TG, Del Vecchio PJ, Brown JE, et al: Direct cytotoxin action of shiga toxin on human vascular endothelial cells. *Infect Immun* 1988; 56:2373–2378.

90. Francis DH, Moxley RA, Andraos CY: Edema disease-like brain lesions in gnotobiotic piglets infected with *Escherichia coli* O157:H7. *Infect Immun* 1989; 57:1339–1342.

91. Richardson SE, Karmali MA, Becker LE, et al: The histopathology of the hemolytic uremic syndrome associated with verocytotoxin-producing *Escherichia coli* infections. *Hum Pathol* 1988; 19:1102–1108.

92. Sonnino RE, Laberge J-M, Mucklow MG, et al: Pathogenic *Escherichia coli:* A new etiology for acute ileitis in children. *J Pediatr Surg* 1989; 24:812–814.

93. Sheth K, Gill JC, Leichter HE, et al: High-dose intravenous gamma globulin infusions in hemolytic-uremic syndrome: A preliminary report. *Am J Dis Child* 1990; 144:268–270.

# Non-A, Non-B Hepatitis: Impact of the Emergence of the Hepatitis C Virus

**Patricia C. Hsia, M.D.**

Fellow in Gastroenterology and Hepatology, Veterans Affairs Medical Center,
Georgetown University School of Medicine, Washington, D.C.

**Leonard B. Seeff, M.D.**

Chief, Gastroenterology and Hepatology, Veterans Affairs Medical Center;
Georgetown University School of Medicine, Washington, DC

## Editor's Introduction

In 1988, the first laboratory test for hepatitis C antibody was introduced into clinical practice. Drs. Hsia and Seeff review the historical background and clinical results obtained so far with this valuable diagnostic tool. Not surprisingly, hepatitis C infection is common in patients who are multiply transfused, in those with cryptogenic cirrhosis, and in intravenous drug addicts. False-positive reactions occur in autoimmune chronic active hepatits, so positive tests in this group need to be interpreted with caution. An important benefit of the antibody test for hepatitis C is the selection of patients for interferon-α therapy. Still in its infancy, this form of immunotherapy holds the promise of slowing or halting the progression of chronic liver disease in millions of hepatitis C patients worldwide.

*J. Thomas LaMont, M.D.*

The term "non-A, non-B" (NANB) hepatitis was first introduced in 1974 to describe acute necroinflammatory disease of the liver that could not be accounted for by either hepatitis A virus (HAV) or hepatitis B virus (HBV) infection.[1-3] This unwieldy label remains in current use to identify acute or chronic hepatitis for which no obvious cause can be determined. Items that need to be excluded for accuracy and consistency of diagnosis consist of the following: infection with HAV, HBV, Epstein-Barr virus (EBV), and cytomegalovirus (CMV); exposure to hepatotoxic drugs; nonalcoholic steatohepatitis; congestive heart failure; severe hypotension; biliary tree disease; and alcoholic liver disease.

Recently, molecular biologic techniques have been used to identify a

*Dr. Hsia currently holds a position in the Gastroenterology Department, Kaiser Permanente Hospital, Fontetane, California.

*Advances in Internal Medicine*, vol. 37
Copyright 1991, Mosby–Year Book, Inc.

single-stranded RNA virus now believed to be the cause of transfusion-associated NANB hepatitis.[4, 5] The agent has been named the "hepatitis C" virus (HCV), joining the ranks of the other established forms—hepatitis A, hepatitis B, hepatitis D, and hepatitis E. The last of these viruses, hepatitis E, previously referred to as epidemic or enteral NANB hepatitis, now is recognized to be the consequence of an agent distinctly different from that of HCV.[6] It is conceivable that there exists a sixth hepatitis virus that may cause some of the cases now referred to as NANB hepatitis. This is deduced from the evidence that not all NANB hepatitis cases can be serologically attributed to HCV infection; further study is required to determine whether these seronegative cases represent low-level HCV carriers not detected by the current relatively insensitive assay. We will review the entity of parenteral and sporadic NANB hepatitis, focusing attention on the evolving data regarding hepatitis C. For information on the fecal-oral form (hepatitis E), which should be regarded no longer as an offshoot of NANB hepatitis, the reader is directed elsewhere to several recent and extensive reviews.[7–12]

## Historic Perspective

Until the mid-1970s, only two types of viral hepatitis were recognized. One of these, originally referred to as "infectious" hepatitis and later as "hepatitis A," was fecally-orally transmitted and produced liver disease after an incubation period of 2 to 6 weeks. The second, labeled initially as "serum" hepatitis and later as "hepatitis B," was believed to be transmitted percutaneously and had a far longer incubation period of 6 weeks to 6 months.[13]

Following the identification of HBV and the development of specific serologic marker tests, however, retrospective evaluation of stored serum samples failed to detect this virus in as many as 50% to 75% of persons with presumed transfusion-associated "serum" hepatitis, even prior to the introduction of routine screening of blood donors for the presence of HBsAg.[14, 15] Indeed, that HBV was not the primary agent of transfusion-related hepatitis was evident from a number of observations. First, serologic assay for HBsAg, after routine screening for this agent had been introduced, demonstrated that HBV accounted for fewer than 10% to 15% of hepatitis cases.[2, 16–21] Second, attack rates calculated for some early studies suggested that had HBV screening been performed and positive units been interdicted, the incidence of type B transfusion-associated hepatitis would have declined by >50%,[22] whereas the overall disease frequency would have fallen by only 25%.[14, 23] Third, it was noted that the presence in donor blood of antibody to the hepatitis B surface antigen (anti-HBs) did not prevent transfusion recipients from developing hepatitis.[24] Fourth, reduced use of commercial blood donors was followed by a lowering of the incidence of not only HBV, but also non–HBV-related transfusion-associated hepatitis.[19, 25–27]

Because only two hepatitis viruses were recognized in the 1970s, it was assumed that HAV infection must have accounted for the non-HBV cases. Still, there was early reluctance to accept this view, because HAV infection was recognized to have an abbreviated viremic phase, making percutaneous transmission unlikely, and a shorter incubation period than the mean of 7 weeks for the transfusion cases. Also, HAV was unassociated with the induction of chronic hepatitis, a common event among the transfusion-associated cases.[10, 11, 21, 28] These misgivings proved well founded after assays for hepatitis A became available.[29] Reanalysis of stored sera from several prospective studies in which it had been found that the incidence of transfusion-associated hepatitis was between 7% and 10% revealed that only 10% of cases could be attributed to hepatitis B and absolutely none to hepatitis A.[2, 16–18, 30] Furthermore, it soon became clear that elderly persons, the group at particularly high risk of developing transfusion-associated hepatitis because of increasing resort to cardiac bypass surgery, have a very high frequency of preexisting, protective antibodies to hepatitis A.[31] Little wonder, then, that there have been only a handful of validated cases of transfusion-associated hepatitis A.[21, 32, 33]

Even prior to the advent of the full spectrum of hepatitis serologic assays, there had been compelling clinical support for the presence of more than two viruses.[20, 21] Multiple episodes of acute hepatitis (as many as four) had been well described quite early on among parenteral drug abusers[34–36] and hemophiliacs.[37] Thus, on the assumption that all hepatitis viruses induce homologous immunity, it was tempting to consider the possibility of the existence of four separate percutaneously transmitted hepatitis viruses.

No serious consideration could be given to other infectious agents as the etiology for NANB hepatitis, such as bacteria, mycobacteria, spirochetes, fungi, rickettsiae, or parasites, since filtration studies established clearly that the size of the putative agent had to correspond to that of viruses.[38] Most known viruses, however, could be excluded by serologic means. Two that warranted at least passing consideration were EBV and CMV, both belonging to the herpes family and known to cause hepatitis. Indeed, EBV infection has been reported after transfusion[39–41] and has been identified as the source of an outbreak of hepatitis in a renal dialysis unit.[42] However, most transfused patients are found to have antibodies to EBV prior to transfusion, and multiple studies have failed to implicate EBV as the etiologic agent of NANB hepatitis.[2, 3, 15, 18, 26, 30]

Determining whether CMV infection might have been responsible for at least some instances of transfusion-transmitted NANB hepatitis also proved difficult for several reasons: (1) antibody levels to CMV (anti-CMV) fluctuate even in normal individuals,[43] (2) multiple CMV serotypes exist,[43] and (3) the validity of serologic test results in earlier studies was questionable because of poor reproducibility.[21] CMV infection has been documented after blood transfusion,[44, 45] as well as among immunosuppressed renal transplant patients.[46–48] Nevertheless, with the exception of one report,[49] most early studies failed to show an association between CMV and transfusion-transmitted hepatitis.[1–3, 15, 18, 21, 44] In the one positive study, performed at the blood bank of the National Institutes of Health, in which a reliable indirect hemagglutination (IHA) test for anti-CMV was used, the virus appeared to account for 15% of the cases.[49] Subsequent studies at this institution failed to identify additional cases of transfusion-related CMV hepatitis, suggesting that the original observations had represented a unique event.

## Abortive Search for Putative Agents and Serologic Tests

The aforementioned considerations notwithstanding, intense efforts were devoted between the years 1975 and 1989 by investigators throughout the world to identify viral particles or serologic markers using techniques that had proved successful in the studies of hepatitis A and B. One important observation was that NANB hepatitis was caused by a transmissible agent that could be passed serially from chimpanzee to chimpanzee.[50-66] Transmission could be accomplished using multiple source inocula (serum, plasma, clotting factor concentrates, liver homogenates) and via different routes (intravenous, intramuscular, subcutaneous, intrahepatic), and was capable of inducing persistent viremia and resultant chronic liver disease.[62-67] In one important chimpanzee inoculation study, it was noted that consistently different ultrastructural responses in the liver could be produced by two separate inocula. One of these, referred to as strain F and later as NANB-1, induced electron-dense tubular structures in the cytoplasm and proliferation of the smooth endoplasmic reticulum, while the other, strain H or NANB-2, induced viral-like intranuclear aggregates.[68] This finding seemed to provide further support for the existence of two separate NANB hepatitis viruses. Strain F now is believed to represent HCV, but the significance of strain H awaits definition. Additional study of the infected chimpanzees established strain F as the predominant cause for transfusion-related hepatitis, and determined it to be chloroform-sensitive and therefore a lipid-coated virus (as opposed to strain H, which was shown to be chloroform-resistant) and to contain virions of a diameter ranging between 30 and 50 nm.[69]

In addition to these studies, the literature during the latter part of the 1980s was replete with reports describing putative viral particles associated with NANB hepatitis. These often were received with skepticism because of the wide variability in particle sizes (ranging from 20 to 85 nm) and the lack of reproducibility.[11, 54, 64, 70-79] Moreover, efforts to develop serologic tests proved unrewarding, even though more than 40 were described,[11, 66] the most promising of which was later discredited through independent evaluation using specially prepared, pedigreed but coded serum panels.[49] Indeed, by the mid-1980s, it seemed unlikely that a specific virus or serologic marker for NANB hepatitis would ever be defined.

## Evaluation of Surrogate Tests

Because of the continuing failure to identify a specific serologic marker for NANB hepatitis, efforts then shifted to the search for surrogate tests that might help identify infectious donor blood. Prompted by early reports that raised alanine aminotransferase (ALT) activity in blood donors appeared to correlate with hepatitis transmission, investigators returned to reexamine the utility of this enzyme as an index of infectivity and to seek other non-specific but useful markers.[80-88] Two that showed promise were the presence of the antibody to the hepatitis B core antigen (anti-HBc) and increased serum guanase activity.[82, 83, 85, 87] Attention focused on ALT and anti-HBc, however, because of the observation that their presence clearly seemed to delineate potential NANB hepatitis infectivity. Indeed, it was estimated from two studies that exclusion of donor blood with raised ALT activity would reduce the incidence of NANB hepatitis by 30%.[80, 81] Analysis of these same studies indicated that 5% of recipients of blood devoid of anti-HBc developed hepatitis, whereas this figure rose to 15% if at least 1 unit transfused tested positive for anti-HBc.[82, 85] Even more compelling was the effect of combining these two indices; the frequency of hepatitis was 6% if all donor units were anti-HBc–negative and ALT was normal, 11% if anti-HBc was present but ALT was normal, 25% if the ALT exceeded 45 IU/L but anti-HBc was negative, and 74% if both anti-HBc positivity and raised ALT were present.[82] Exclusion of donors having these surrogate markers was estimated to lead to a loss of about 1.5% to 5% of donor units.

Promising though this information seemed, it was accepted with guarded enthusiasm because the data had been derived from retrospective analyses rather than prospective studies, the tests were relatively insensitive and nonspecific, and concern was raised that too many potentially noninfectious donors would be lost from the pool.[88] However, decision analysis showed that the increased dollar cost of screening and recruiting to replace lost donors would be offset by the savings of medical care costs from the prevention of NANB hepatitis.[89] Despite the controversy, the American Association of Blood Banks and the American Red Cross in 1987 mandated universal screening of all blood donors for ALT and anti-HBc, hoping to reduce the risk of transfusion-associated NANB hepatitis by 30% to 50%.[11, 86-88]

## Characteristics of Non-A, Non-B Hepatitis

**Demography and Epidemiology.**—NANB hepatitis occurs in two settings—as a percutaneously acquired disease or as one occurring without obvious source (so-called nonpercutaneous, sporadic, or community-acquired hepatitis).[11, 12, 21] Percutaneous transmission of NANB hepatitis occurs in recipients of routine blood transfusions or pooled plasma products (e.g., hemophiliacs), in intravenous drug abusers and hemodialysis and renal transplant patients, and among health care workers, such as may follow an accidental needle-stick exposure. Nonpercutaneous transmission is less well understood, but some cases may derive from intimate sexual contact, a phenomenon that has been difficult to prove.[90, 91] A role for perinatal transmission has not been fully elucidated yet. The disease affects persons of all ages and has an approximately equal sex distribution. It is the predominant form of hepatitis in U.S. adults over 40 years of age[92] and, in one study of acute hepatitis among children, was identified in 6% of the cases.[93]

**Clinical Features.**—The incubation period of NANB transfusion-associated hepatitis extends from 2 to 26 weeks, with the majority of cases appearing between the 5th and 12th post-transfusion weeks.[11, 21] Among recipients of pooled coagulation factors, the disease may begin as early as 4 to 7 days after their receipt.[11] The first evidence of disease is modest elevation (60 to 600 IU/L) of ALT activity. Most patients are totally asymptomatic and would not be identified as ill were enzyme monitoring not conducted. Three enzyme patterns have been seen: monophasic, mulitphasic (fluctuating), or plateau ALT elevations.[94] Most characteristic of NANB hepatitis is the episodic, fluctuating pattern of aminotransferase activity with intervening periods of normal or near-normal levels. Intervals between peaks may be quite variable and sometimes sufficiently protracted that it may be difficult to determine whether or not the acute disease has subsided or chronic NANB hepatitis has evolved. In line with the commonly modest enzyme elevations is the fact that icterus occurs in only about one quarter of cases, although severe and even fulminant NANB hepatitis can develop.[11, 21] This evolution usually appears later in NANB hepatitis than it does in acute hepatitis A or B and is associated with a higher mortality.[11, 12, 21, 95–99] Extrahepatic manifestations, such as a serum-sickness–like syndrome, blood dyscrasias (agranulocytosis, aplastic anemia), and arthritis have been described in persons with acute NANB hepatitis.[11, 12, 21, 100–105] In one study, aplastic anemia was reported to occur in 28% of persons undergoing liver transplantation for acute NANB hepatitis, an outcome not seen in patients receiving a liver transplant for other reasons.[105]

Chronic hepatitis, defined as the persistence of elevated serum enzymes for periods exceeding 6 months, occurs more commonly after acute NANB hepatitis than after acute hepatitis B. This development appears to be slightly more common in patients with transfusion-related hepatitis than in those with sporadic NANB hepatitis.[12, 21, 106–108] The pattern of the ALT elevation may herald the development of chronic hepatitis. In one study, chronic hepatitis developed in 42.5% of those whose acute disease manifested with a monophasic peak, in 86.6% of those with a fluctuating ALT pattern, and in 94.9% of those with a plateau pattern.[109] Alter recently has reviewed six studies of transfusion-associated NANB hepatitis, noting that chronic hepatitis evolved at a rate that ranged in the various studies from 23% to 68%, the mean frequency being 52%.[110] Liver biopsy in 96 patients identified chronic active hepatitis (CAH) in 34% and cirrhosis in 15%. Similar high rates of chronicity have come from other studies.[107, 108, 111–115] One of these consisted of an analysis of 86 patients with chronic hepatitis, 24 of whom had had acute transfusion-related hepatitis and 62 who had experienced acute sporadic NANB hepatitis.[115] Among the former group, liver biopsy revealed chronic persistent hepatitis (CPH) in 55% and CAH progressing over many years to cirrhosis in an additional 16%. Interestingly, among the sporadic hepatitis group, 43% showed the lesion of CPH and 55%

showed progression to CAH and cirrhosis. Chronic NANB hepatitis is a common sequela also among persons with hemophilia and other recipients of pooled plasma products. A recent multicenter study of liver biopsies from over 150 hemophiliacs revealed trivial or mild pathologic features in 64%, CAH in 7%, and cirrhosis in 15%.[116] Another study of 79 hemophiliac patients, of whom 71% had persistent ALT elevations, revealed CAH in 26% and cirrhosis in an additional 12%.[117] In 9 follow-up biopsies among these individuals, 4 of them (2 who had shown initially CPH and 2 who had shown CAH) advanced to cirrhosis, 1 of whom (with CAH) later died from the consequences of portal hypertension.

Prior to the advent of a serologic test for HCV, clinical studies suggested a link between chronic HCV infection and subsequent development of primary hepatocellular carcinoma (HCC).[118–121] Most of these were reports of individual patients with established HCC who had had a previous history of non-B transfusion-associated hepatitis. Data from retrospective studies undertaken in Japan and Italy suggested that NANB hepatitis probably had contributed to two thirds of the cases of HCC that developed among nonalcoholic patients.[122, 123] In another important recent study from Japan, 21 patients were followed from acute transfusion-related NANB hepatitis to the development of HCC; the mean intervals between the time of transfusion and the identification of chronic hepatitis, cirrhosis, and HCC were 10, 21.2, and 29 years, respectively.[124] Indeed, in 2 instances, HCC was identified more than 60 years after the transfusion.

In summary, about one half of persons with acute NANB hepatitis advance to chronic hepatitis and, among those biopsied, CAH will be detected in almost 50% and cirrhosis in nearly 20%. Some individuals with cirrhosis will advance to HCC. Progression to clinically overt or severe disease is insidious over 20 or more years. Clearly, we need more information on the natural history of chronic NANB heptatitis. A large, multicenter, prospective, natural history study is presently in progress to examine this issue in the United States.

## Identification of Hepatitis C Virus

While these epidemiologic and clinical data were being assembled during the 1980s, two recent breakthroughs greatly changed the status and complexion of NANB hepatitis. The first was the report in 1986 by Hoofnagle and colleagues indicating that many patients with NANB hepatitis appeared responsive to certain immunomodulatory drug treatment.[125] The second was the sudden and unexpected announcement in the national press in May 1988 by Houghton and colleagues (Chiron Corporation, California) of the identification of the major NANB virus, followed by publication of the data almost 1 year later.[4, 5] We will discuss the latter item first.

The source material for viral isolation was provided by Dr. Daniel Bradley and colleagues at the Centers for Disease Control in Atlanta. These investigators were conducting cross-inoculation studies using high-titered

NANB-infectious chimpanzee plasma. Bradley had speculated already that the agent of NANB hepatitis was likely to be an RNA virus, and had defined it tentatively as a togarvirus. The Chiron investigators extracted all nucleic acid from the chimpanzee plasma that had been pelleted by ultracentrifugation.[4] The nucleic acid was denatured and both RNA and DNA were used to synthesize complementary DNA (cDNA) through reverse transcription using random primers. The cDNA was fragmented by restriction enzymes, expressed in a bacteriophage vector (GT-11), and the clones were amplified in *Escherichia coli*. A library of over 1 million clones apparently was created and screened, one of which (a 155-base-pair cDNA clone) was detected by using serum from a patient with chronic NANB hepatitis. That this was not the host genome was demonstrated by the fact that it did not hybridize to either control human DNA or DNA derived from plasma or liver from two chimpanzees with NANB hepatitis. A larger 353-base-pair clone then was extracted that hybridized to liver and plasma RNA from the original chimpanzee plasma, showing that it was a component of the infectious serum. Viral antigen from the recombinant clone then was used to develop a radioimmunoassay to detect serum antibody. After ribonuclease and hybridization experiments, it appeared that the clone was derived from a single-stranded RNA. The size of this single-stranded RNA was estimated to be between 5,000 and 10,000 nucleotides, and the agent was named the HCV.

## Diagnostic Assays

The next step was to develop a diagnostic assay for HCV.[5] This was achieved through knowledge that the three overlapping clones isolated from cDNA 5–1–1 contained a common open reading frame that encoded a portion of the NANB viral antigen. The cDNA was expressed in yeast as a fusion polypeptide that was used to coat the wells of microtiter plates to capture and measure circulating HCV antibodies (anti-HCV) by enzyme immunoassay or radioimmunoassay. The specificity and sensitivity of the assay for anti-HCV was tested first in a blinded fashion against a panel of well-pedigreed sera of known infectivity. Of seven NANB hepatitis samples shown to be infectious in chimpanzees, six gave strongly positive results. The sample that gave a negative result came from a patient in the acute phase of post-transfusion NANB hepatitis. In addition, seroconversion could be demonstrated in stored sera from ten well-characterized cases of chronic transfusion-associated hepatitis, although in one of them, seroconversion did not occur until 12 months after transfusion. In most cases, antibody seroconversion was detected within 6 months of transfusion. These results established the usefulness of this assay now marketed by Ortho Diagnostic Systems, Inc. Other test systems from different manufacturers (Abbott Laboratories) have recently been licensed. A similar technique has been reported independently by Arima et al.[126] On the basis of these and other recorded data.[10, 21, 38, 60, 67] this 30- to 50-nm lipid-enveloped virus, clearly the predominant agent of NANB hepatitis, seems to have partial homology with the flaviviruses and pestiviruses, and therefore may be regarded ultimately as belonging to the arbovirus family.[127]

The utility of anti-HCV screening has been well demonstrated in studies of transfusion-associated hepatitis.[128–130] Alter et al. found that, among 15 patients with transfusion-related NANB hepatitis whose disease persisted as chronic hepatitis, all developed anti-HCV, the assay becoming positive a mean of 21.9 weeks after transfusion or 15 weeks after biochemically identified hepatitis.[128] In 14 of these 15 patients, anti-HCV persisted throughout follow-up, which extended beyond 12 years in one instance. In contrast, anti-HCV was detected in only 60% of five patients with acute resolving NANB hepatitis, and disappeared in all three after a mean of 4.1 years. With respect to the blood transfusion donors, 88% were positive for anti-HCV. Interestingly, only one third of these anti-HCV–positive donors had raised ALT activity, while 54% were positive for anti-HBc. The high infectivity of anti-HCV–positive donor blood is supported by data from other studies, although not all recipients of such blood develop hepatitis or seropositivity.[130] In one study, the likelihood of NANB hepatitis transmission from the receipt of anti-HCV–positive donor blood was significantly higher if the donors also had raised ALT activity.[129]

Questions regarding the specificity of the enzyme immunoassay[131, 132] have prompted the development of a recombinant immunoblot assay that incorporates the cloned C100–3 antigen from yeast and the 5–1–1 recombinant antigen from E. coli.[133] A third recombinant antigen, superoxide dismutase (SOD), is also added to the nitrocellulose strip, as well as high and low levels of IgG, as postive control. Test samples are applied to the strips, which subsequently are washed, coated with substrate, washed again, and air-dried. Results are read as "reactive" if both antigens 5–1–1 and C100–3 are positive, "indeterminate" if only one antigen is positive, and "nonreactive" if only SOD or IgG controls respond. This test appears to improve specificity and to be useful in establishing "false-positive" results in the enzyme immunoassay.[133, 134] Newer immunoblot assays containing additional epitopes and other "confirmatory" neutralization tests have also been developed and are currently under investigation.

The tests described are useful immunodiagnostic assays for anti-HCV but do not measure the presence of HCV RNA. Knowledge of the nucleotide sequence of specific HCV cDNA clones, however, has permitted the development of a sensitive, semiquantitative cDNA/polymerase chain reaction assay for HCV RNA in liver or serum.[135] In an initial report, polymerase chain reaction as well as radioimmunoassay testing was used to detect anti-HCV in 15 patients with chronic NANB hepatitis, 1 patient with cryptogenic liver disease, and 1 patient with chronic HBV infection.[135] Nine of the 15 patients with chronic NANB hepatitis and the 1 patient with cryptogenic liver disease were positive for anti-HCV by radioimmunoassay, while 7 of these patients were positive by polymerase chain reaction assay. Two patients who tested negative for anti-HCV by radioimmunoassay were positive by polymerase chain reaction. In additional testing, a sample from a patient during the acute phase of post-transfusion NANB hepatitis had highly positive polymerase chain reaction results, while radioimmuno-assay showed the presence of anti-HCV below the cutoff for positivity. A chimpanzee experiencing an acute episode of post-transfusion NANB hepatitis showed positive results by polymerase chain reaction, but not by radioimmunoassay in serum collected 25 days after infection. Samples from an infected chimpanzee with chronic NANB infection showed similar results—substantial levels of HCV RNA by polymerase chain reaction, with levels of anti-HCV by radioimmunoassay below the cutoff for positivity. These data suggested that the numbers of cases of HCV infection would likely increase with both direct and indirect forms of testing, and that the virus usually is present during the acute phase before the appearance of anti-HCV. Indeed, this assay has been shown to be useful not only in detecting early evidence of acute HCV infection, but also in demonstrating continued infectivity, since anti-HCV is only an indirect marker of HCV replication.[136-138]

## Epidemiology of Hepatitis C Virus Infection

The first reports of anti-HCV prevalence in persons with various liver disorders and volunteer blood donors followed the description of the antibody test, initiating a number of articles on hepatitis C.[91, 139-141] Because of the original focus on transfusion-associated hepatitis, an important early effort was to determine the frequency of anti-HCV among volunteer blood donors. Studies conducted in various countries showed that the prevalence ranged between 0.68% and 1.4%.[140-144] Interestingly, these frequencies exceed the HBsAg-positivity rate among volunteer donors from western countries by a factor of 6 to 10 or more times. Surveys of acute transfusion-associated hepatitis revealed anti-HCV in 15% to 60%, compared to 60% to 90% in chronic NANB hepatitis (Table 1).* Although the anti-HCV–negative cases could represent infection with another as yet undefined virus, other explanations for this finding include the possibility that some or all of the negative cases represent misdiagnoses, or that the currently available assay lacks sensitivity or measures different epitopes of the virus, a problem that might be overcome by the use of polymerase chain reaction amplification or in situ hybridization. The evidence of nonspecificity of the current assay is illustrated by the data of Alter et al.[128] who examined transfusion recipients of recombinant immunoblot assay–positive vs. recombinant immunoblot assay–negative anti-HCV–positive blood. Almost 80% of the former, but only 7% of the latter recipients developed-NANB hepatitis, demonstrating that the recombinant immunoblot assay is highly predictive of infectivity. The unexpected finding that 20% of the recombinant immunoblot assay-positive donors did not transmit the infection suggests that infectious virions are not always present or that some recipients are immune to infection. Conversely, while 75% of recipients who devel-

*References 5, 91, 128, 130, 139, 141, 145–148.

**TABLE 1.**
**Prevalence of Anti-HCV in Transfusion-Associated Hepatitis,**
**Acute and Chronic***

| Author (Reference) | Country | Anti-HCV—Positive (%) Acute | Anti-HCV—Positive (%) Chronic |
|---|---|---|---|
| Alberti[149] | Italy | — | 94 |
| Esteban[130] | Spain | — | 89 |
| Alter[128] | United States | 60 | 88 |
| Miyamura[145] | Japan | 17 | 88 |
| Esteban[91] | Spain | — | 85 |
| Kuo[5] | Italy | — | 84 |
| Roggendorf[141] | Germany | 20 | 79 |
| Kuo[5] | Japan | 15 | 78 |
| McHutchison[146] | United States | 20 | 77 |
| Katkov[147] | United States | — | 70 |
| van der Poel[139] | Netherlands | 25 | 60 |
| Mosley[148] | United States | — | 60 |

*Anti-HCV = hepatitis C virus antibodies.

oped NANB hepatitis had received recombinant immunoblot assay-positive donor blood, one quarter had received anti-HCV—negative blood, again indicating either relative insensitivity of the assay in detecting all HCV carriers or donors in the "window" phase of acute infection who have not yet developed anti-HCV. Strikingly similar data have been accrued by Esteban et al.,[130] although their data do not support the theory of donor transmission during the window period.

The prevalence of anti-HCV among groups known to be at high risk of acquiring HCV infection through parenteral exposure is shown in Table 2).* Not surprisingly, anti-HCV—positivity is common in intravenous drug addicts and multitransfused hemophiliacs, but is unexpectedly infrequent among patients undergoing hemodialysis. With respect to hemophiliacs, transmission derives from the fact that all unheated factor VIII concentrates and most of those treated with dry heat at $60°$ C for 32 hours or with "wet" heat (heptane) may be anti-HCV—positive,[166] whereas those subjected to "superheating" at $80°$ C for 72 hours are antibody-negative[66] and do not transmit HCV.[155] The reason for the lower than anticipated anti-HCV prevalence in hemodialysis units is unclear; perhaps antibody reactivity is blunted in immunocompromised dialysis patients or the incidence of HCV infection has been reduced by careful screening and the proper use of universal precautions.

*References 91, 141, 146, 149, 150, 156, 157.

**TABLE 2.**
**Prevalence of Anti-HCV in Patients With Parenterally Acquired Non-A, Non-B Hepatitis***

| Group | Anti-HCV–Positive (%) | References |
|---|---|---|
| Intravenous drug abusers | 48–86 | 91, 141, 146, 149 |
| Hemophiliacs | 56–85 | 91, 141, 150–155 |
| Hemodialysis patients | 6–24 | 91, 141, 156, 157 |

*Anti-HCV = hepatitis C virus antibodies.

Another unexpected fact is that anti-HCV screening has been unable to confirm intimate sexual contact as a major mode of transmission of HCV infection. Screening of homosexual men has revealed an anti-HCV prevalence of less than 8%,[91, 167] confirming a similarly low prevalence in sexual contacts of intravenous drug abusers or persons with NANB hepatitis.[91, 168] In contrast, a recent serologic survey revealed that anti-HCV was present in 58% of homosexual men who gave no history of any form of parenteral exposure but who had serologic evidence of chronic HBV infection or acute or chronic delta hepatitis infection.[169] Accordingly, the current view, subject to modification in the future, is that sexual transmission probably does occur, but that it is an inefficient means of HCV propagation.

Current data suggest that perinatal transmission from "carrier" mother to newborn infant also is an uncommon mode of HCV spread, in contrast to chronic HBV infection. In several preliminary studies of perinatal transmission of HCV, anti-HCV appears transiently in the newborn infant but disappears generally after the sixth month.[170–173] Since serum transaminases remain normal in these infants, this finding probably represents passive transfer of maternal antibody. In one recent study, however, HCV transmission from mother to infant could be demonstrated by means of polymerase chain reaction amplification.[174] Liver disease rather than simply a serologic response has been reported among newborns infected simultaneously with the human immunodeficiency virus.[175]

An unanswered question is whether sporadic (community-acquired) NANB hepatitis represents the same entity as the percutaneously transmitted form. Because the frequency of progression of acute to chronic hepatitis in these two forms of the disease is quite similar, it has been assumed that HCV is the causative virus in both of them. In a recent seroepidemiologic study, 54% of 115 persons with acute NANB hepatitis of unknown origin, followed for 6 to 48 months, were found to be anti-HCV–positive,[176] suggesting a causative role for HCV in this form of hepatitis.

Particularly disquieting is the fact that the two serious potential sequelae of chronic NANB hepatitis, namely cirrhosis and HCC, show serologic linkage to chronic HCV infection. As shown in Table 3, anti-HCV has been found to be positive in 13% to 89% of persons with cryptogenic cirrhosis and in 29% to 75% of those with HCC.[147, 149, 158–162] As described earlier,[124] 21 anti-HCV–positive patients in Japan have been followed from acute transfusion-associated NANB hepatitis through chronic hepatitis and cirrhosis to HCC, the time period averaging 29 years (range, 15 to 60 years). In this and most of the other reported studies, cirrhosis preceded virtually all instances of HCC, or the prevalence of anti-HCV was very similar in those with cirrhosis and those with HCC,[177, 179] suggesting that HCC derives from the cirrhotic process rather than as a result of the carcinogenic potential of HCV.

The enzyme immunoassay test for anti-HCV has been found to be positive in a number of liver disorders in which its presence would not have been anticipated. Thus, as shown in Table 3, anti-HCV positivity has been noted in 0% to 79% of persons with autoimmune CAH and in 25% to 39% of those with alcoholic liver disease.* This could be interpreted as implying a causal relationship, but additional data tend to dispute this assumption. In one study in which 40% of patients with autoimmune hepatitis were positive by enzyme immunoassay for anti-HCV, antibody levels correlated with serum globulin and IgG concentrations, and tended to disappear when patients were treated.[131] A similiar relationship of anti-HCV to disease activity was noted in another study involving children with autoimmune hepatitis subjected to corticosteroid therapy.[180] These observations suggest that the hypergammaglobulinemic state interfered with the HCV antibody assay, inducing a false-positive test. In support of this view

*References 91, 147, 149, 159, 163–165, 180.

---

**TABLE 3.**
**Prevalence of Anti-HCV in Patients With Various Forms of Chronic Liver Disease ***

| Group | Anti-HCV–Positive (%) | References |
|---|---|---|
| Cryptogenic cirrhosis | 13–89 | 147, 149, 158–160 |
| Hepatocellular carcinoma | 29–75 | 149, 159–162 |
| Autoimmune chronic active hepatitis | 0–79 | 91, 147, 159, 163 |
| Alcoholic liver disease | 25–39 | 149, 159, 164, 165 |

*Anti-HCV = hepatitis C virus antibodies.

is the fact that false-positive tests have been found, using the recombinant immunoblot assay, in other autoimmune or immunologic disorders, such as rheumatoid arthritis[181] and in paraproteinemia.[182] Because the recombinant immunoblot assay also has been reported to demonstrate true positivity in one major study involving patients with type 2 autoimmune hepatitis,[183,184] it is clear that further studies with more specific assays are needed.

## Treatment

Despite the fact that NANB hepatitis has been recognized for well over a decade, early treatment trials have been frustrated by the lack of a specific diagnostic test. The only drug that had received any attention was prednisone, because of its apparent benefit in persons with autoimmune chronic hepatitis. The report in 1986 by Hoofnagle et al. of a pilot treatment trial with recombinant human interferon-α provided some therapeutic promise for the first time.[125] In an open treatment trial of ten patients with parenterally associated chronic NANB hepatitis, subcutaneous doses of 2 to 5 million units of interferon were administered daily for up to 1 year. In eight of these patients, ALT values improved or normalized, generally within 2 months of treatment initiation, and liver biopsies showed improvement in the degree of lobular inflammation, hepatocyte necrosis, and portal infiltration. Five of the eight patients were reported to have sustained normalization of ALT values 2 to 3 years after withdrawing treatment, one showed reduction in enzyme values, and two relapsed.[185]

Supported by similiar results in other uncontrolled treatment trials,[186–188] three controlled studies of interferon were initiated in the late 1980s. The earliest of the three studies, from the United Kingdom, involved a total of 14 patients.[189] Seventy-one percent of the patients treated with lymphoblastoid interferon in a dose of 5 million units three times weekly for 8 weeks were reported to show a complete response (normalization of ALT values), while none of those randomized to receive no treatment responded positively. No follow-up data were presented in this study.

More informative and extensive were two controlled trials (Table 4) conducted subsequently in the United States.[190, 191] The first of these was a double-blind, randomized, controlled trial undertaken at the National Institutes of Health in Bethesda, Maryland.[190] Study subjects had a history of parenteral exposure, ALT elevations at least twice the upper limit of normal for 1 year, and histologic evidence of chronic NANB hepatitis. Hepatitis C serology was not a requirement, since the study initiation predated its availability; nevertheless, over 90% of cases were positive when retrospective testing was performed. Importantly, patients were excluded from the study if they had decompensated liver disease. Treated patients received 1 million units of human interferon-α2b subcutaneously daily for 1 week followed by 2 million units three times weekly for an additional 23 weeks. Control patients received a lyophilized human serum albumin placebo according to the same schedule. As shown in Table 4, after 2 months of treatment, ALT normalized in 48% of interferon recipients (complete re-

**TABLE 4.**
**Controlled Trials of Interferon-α for the Treatment of Chronic Non-A, Non-B Hepatitis**

| Response* | Di Bisceglie[190] | | Davis[191] | | |
|---|---|---|---|---|---|
| | 2 × 10⁶ | Placebo | 3 × 10⁶ | 1 × 10⁶ | Placebo |
| At 2 months | | | | | |
| Complete | 48% | ± | — | — | — |
| Partial | 14% | ± | — | — | — |
| At 6 months | | | | | |
| Complete | 33% | ± | 38% | 16% | 4% |
| Partial | — | — | 7% | 12% | 4% |
| At 1 year | | | | | |
| Complete | 10% | — | 23% | 21% | — |

*Complete = normal alanine aminotransferase; partial = alanine aminotransferase reduced by 50%.
— = Data not reported.

sponse) and improved in an additional 14% (partial response). However, at the end of therapy, normal values were present in 33% of patients, whereas by 1 year (6 months after the cessation of treatment), normal values were present in only 10% of the subjects. Relapse in serum enzyme activity occurred within 2 months of stopping treatment in most instances. In contrast, ALT values declined only minimally in the placebo-treated subjects, there being highly significant differences in average ALT reduction between the two groups. The liver biopsies in the interferon-treated group, but not the placebo-treated group, showed a significant reduction in piecemeal necrosis and lobular injury, but not in hepatic fibrosis and portal inflammation. Side effects consisted of mild fatigue, malaise, weight loss, and slight leukopenia and thrombocytopenia in most of the interferon-treated subjects; two developed hyperthyroidism requiring treatment. No features appeared to predict the likelihood of response. Later study of six patients from this trial (four interferon-treated and two placebo-treated) showed that all had HCV RNA detectable by polymerase chain reaction at the beginning of treatment, while HCV RNA could not be detected in the four treatment responders but was present in the two palcebo-treated patients at the end.[192] HCV RNA reappeared in three of the four treated patients after the discontinuation of therapy.

The second randomized, controlled, but not double-blinded trial was a multicenter study of 166 adults with biopsy-proven chronic hepatitis who had parenteral exposure to blood and whose ALT concentrations had been at least 1.5 times the upper limit of normal for at least 1 year.[191] By random assignment, 57 patients received recombinant interferon-α2b in a subcutaneous dose of 1 million units three times weekly for 24 weeks, 58 received 3 million units according to the same schedule, and 51 received no treatment. Noteworthy is the fact that virtually all of the study subjects had one or another nonspecific symptom. Anti-HCV was present in 90%, 90%, and 78% of the three groups, respectively. The pretreatment liver biopsies showed cirrhosis in 55% of patients, CAH in 27%, and CPH in 18%. Follow-up was maintained for 2 to 46 weeks after treatment discontinuation. At the end of 6 months, complete remission of ALT was present in 38% of the recipients of 3 million units of interferon, in 16% of those treated with 1 million units, and in 4% of the untreated patients, whereas a near-complete response was present in 7%, 12%, and 4% of the three groups, respectively (see Table 4). The response in treated patients occurred invariably within the first 12 weeks of treatment. As in the previous study, relapse after cessation of therapy approached 50% in the two treated groups. Thus, by 6 months after treatment discontinuation, normal values were still present in 23% of the 3-million-unit group and in about 14% of the 1-million-unit interferon recipients. Improvement in the liver biopsies was noted in 52% of the former and 29% of the latter, consisting of regression of lobular inflammation. Side effects requiring a reduction of dosage developed in 14% of the treated patients, and consisted of depression, myalgias, thrombocytopenia, leukopenia, fatigue, and hives. As with the National Institutes of Health study, no factors appeared to determine which patients would respond or relapse, but the majority with relapse who were retreated again responded.[193]

To summarize these studies, treatment with interferon in a dose of 3 million units three times weekly for 6 months appears to induce sustained remission in about 20% to 25% of persons with chronic NANB hepatitis, compared to the spontaneous remission rate of approximately 1%. Whether or not larger doses given for a longer period or maintenance low doses will be more effective is not known, but many additional studies are in progress. Of particular concern if larger doses are administered is the likelihood of increased toxicity, including the induction of immunologic dysfunction and conditions such as thyroiditis.[194] More information is needed on the long-term effects of treatment with respect to the maintenance of remission, reduction in the development of cirrhosis and HCC, and the effect on HCV itself. Additional data are necessary on categories of patients in whom treatment is fully warranted, ranging from the mildest of disease to the most severe. Current data suggest that the use of interferon in patients with HCV-positive autoimmune chronic hepatitis may be dangerous,[194,195] an observation that also requires further study. Finally, it can be anticipated that new drugs or combinations of therapeutic agents will be available for future evaluation.

## References

1. Prince AM, Brotman B, Grady GF, et al: Long-incubation post-tranfusion hepatitis without serological evidence of exposure to hepatitis-B virus. *Lancet* 1974; 2:241–246.

2. Alter HJ, Purcell RH, Holland PV, et al: Clinical and serological analysis of tranfusion-associated hepatitis. *Lancet* 1975; 2:838–841.
3. Feinstone SM, Kapikian AZ, Purcell RH, et al: Transfusion-associated hepatitis not due to viral hepatitis type A or B. *N Engl J Med* 1975; 292:767–770.
4. Choo Q-L, Weiner AJ, Overby LR, et al: Isolation of a cDNA clone derived from a blood-borne non-A, non-B hepatitis genome. *Science* 1989; 244:359–362.
5. Kuo G, Choo Q-L, Alter HJ, et al: An assay for circulating antibodies to a major etiologic virus of human non-A, non-B hepatitis. *Science* 1989; 244:362–364.
6. Reyes GR, Prudy MA, Kim JP, et al: Isolation of a cDNA from the virus responsible for enterically transmitted non-A, non-B hepatitis. *Science* 1990; 247:1335–1339.
7. Wong DC, Purcell RH, Sreenivasan MA, et al: Epidemic and endemic hepatitis in India and evidence for non-A, non-B virus etiology. *Lancet* 1980; 2:876–879.
8. Ramalingaswami V, Purcell RA: Waterborne non-A, non-B hepatitis. *Lancet* 1988; 1:571–573.
9. Khuroo MS: Study of an epidemic form of non-A, non-B hepatitis: Possibility of another human hepatitis virus distinct from post-transfusion non-A, non B type. *Am J Med* 1980; 68:818–824.
10. Bradley DW, Maynard JE: Etiology and natural history of post-transfusion and enterically transmitted non-A, non-B hepatitis. *Semin Liver Dis* 1986; 6:56–66.
11. Dienstag JL, Alter HJ: Non-A, non-B hepatitis: Evolving epidemiologic and clinical perspective. *Semin Liver Dis* 1986; 6:67–81.
12. Seeff LB: Non-A, non-B hepatitis. *Current Opin Gastroenterol* 1989; 5:378–387.
13. Krugman S, Giles JP, Hammond J: Infectious hepatitis: Evidence for two distinctive clinical, epidemiological, and immunological types of infection. *JAMA* 1967; 200:365–373.
14. Gocke DJ: A prospective study of posttransfusion hepatitis: The role of Australia antigen. *JAMA* 1972; 219:1165–1170.
15. Purcell RH, Walsh JH, Holland PV, et al: Seroepidemiological studies of transfusion-associated hepatitis. *J Infect Dis* 1971; 123:406–413.
16. Alter HJ, Holland PV, Purcell RH: The emerging pattern of post-transfusion hepatitis. *Am J Med Sci* 1975; 270:329–334.
17. Goldfield M, Black HC, Bill J, et al: The consequences of administering blood pretested for HBsAg by third generation techniques: A progress report. *Am J Med Sci* 1975; 270:335–342.
18. Knodell RG, Conrad ME, Dienstag JL, et al: Etiological spectrum of post-transfusion hepatitis. *Gastroenterology* 1975; 69:1278–1285.
19. Seeff LB, Zimmerman HJ, Wright EC, et al: A randomized, double-blind controlled trial of the efficacy of immune serum globulin for the prevention of post-transfusion hepatitis: A Veterans Administration cooperative study. *Gastroenterology* 1977; 72:111–121.
20. Dienstag JL: Non-A, non-B hepatitis. *Adv Intern Med* 1980; 26:187–233.
21. Dienstag JL: Non-A, non-B hepatitis: I. Recognition, epidemiology, and clinical features. *Gastroenterology* 1983; 85:439–462.
22. Hollinger FB, Dreesman GR, Fields H, et al: HBcAg, anti-HBc, and DNA polymerase activity in transfused recipients followed prospectively. *Am J Med Sci* 1975; 270:343–348.

23. Gocke DJ, Greenberg HB, Kavey NB: Correlation of Australia antigen with posttransfusion hepatitis. JAMA 1970; 212:877–879.
24. Holland PV, Walsh JH, Morrow AG, et al: Failure of Australia antibody to prevent post-transfusion hepatitis. Lancet 1969; 2:553–555.
25. Grady GF, Chalmers TC, Boston Inter-Hospital Liver Group: Risk of post-transfusion viral hepatitis. N Engl J Med 1964; 271:337–342.
26. Alter HJ, Holland PV, Purcell RH, et al: Post-transfusion hepatitis after exclusion of commercial and hepatitis-B antigen-positive donors. Ann Intern Med 1972; 77:691–699.
27. Walsh JH, Purcell RH, Morrow AG, et al: Posttransfusion hepatitis after open-heart operations: Incidence after the administration of blood from commercial and volunteer donor populations. JAMA 1970; 211:261–265.
28. Dienstag JL, Szmuness W, Stevens CE, et al: Hepatitis A virus infection: New insights from seroepidemiologic studies. J Infect Dis 1978; 137:328–340.
29. Feinstone SM, Kapikian AZ, Purcell RH: Hepatitis A: Detection by immune electron microscopy of a virus-like antigen associated with acute illness. Science 1973; 182:1026–1028.
30. Dienstag JL, Feinstone SM, Purcell RH, et al: Non-A, non-B post-transfusion hepatitis. Lancet 1977; 1:560–562.
31. Szmuness W, Dienstag JL, Purcell RH, et al: Distribution of antibody to hepatitis A antigen in urban adult populations. N Engl J Med 1976; 295:755–759.
32. Seeberg S, Brandberg A, Hermodsson S, et al: Hospital outbreak of hepatitis A secondary to blood exchange in a baby. Lancet 1981; 1:1155–1156.
33. Barbara JA, Howell DR, Briggs M, et al: Post-transfusion hepatitis A (letter). Lancet 1982; 1:738.
34. Havens WP Jr: Viral hepatitis. Multiple attacks in a narcotic addict. Ann Intern Med 1956; 44:199–203.
35. Levine RA, Payne MA: Homologous serum hepatitis in youthful heroin users. Ann Intern Med 1960; 53:164–178.
36. Iwarson S, Lundin P, Holmgram J, et al: Multiple attacks of hepatitis in drug addicts: biochemical, immunochemical, and morphologic characteristics. J Infect Dis 1973; 127:544–550.
37. Craske J, Dilling N, Stern D: An outbreak of hepatitis associated with intravenous injection of factor VII-concentrate. Lancet 1975; 2:221–223.
38. Bradley DW, McCaustland KA, Cook EH, et al: Posttransfusion non-A, non-B hepatitis in chimpanzees. Physicochemical evidence that the tubule-forming agent is a small, enveloped virus. Gastroenterolgoy 1985; 88:773–779.
39. Gerber P, Walsh JH, Rosenblum EN, et al: Association of EB-virus infection with the post-perfusion syndrome. Lancet 1969; 1:593–595.
40. Henle W, Henle G, Scriba M, et al: Antibody responses to the Epstein-Barr virus and cytomegaloviruses after open-heart surgery and other surgery. N Engl J Med 1970; 282:1068–1074.
41. Turner AR, MacDonald RN, Cooper BA: Transmission of infectious mononucleosis by transfusion of pre-illness plasma. Ann Intern Med 1972; 77:751–753.
42. Corey L, Stamm WE, Feorino PM, et al: HBsAg-negative hepatitis in a hemodialysis unit: Relation to Epstein-Barr virus. N Engl J Med 1975; 293:1273–1278.
43. Weller TH: The cytomegaloviruses: Ubiquitous agents with protean clinical manifestations. N Engl J Med 1971; 285:203–214.
44. Prince AM, Szmuness W, Millian SJ, et al: A serologic study of cytomegalo-

virus infections associated with blood transfusions. *N Engl J Med* 1971; 284:1125–1131.

45. Contreras TJ, Lang DJ, Piracek LE, et al: Occurrence of HBsAg, anti-HBs, and anti-CMV following the transfusion of blood products. *Transfusion* 1979; 19:129–136.

46. Luby JP, Burnett W, Hull AR, et al: Relationship between cytomegalovirus and hepatic function abnormalities in the period after renal transplant. *J Infect Dis* 1974; 129:511–518.

47. Fiala M, Payne JE, Berve TV, et al: Epidemiology of cytomegalovirus infection after transplantation and immunosuppression. *J Infect Dis* 1975; 132:421–433.

48. Ware AJ, Luby JP, Hollinger FB, et al: Etiology of liver disease in renal-transplant patients. *Ann Intern Med* 1979; 91:364–371.

49. Alter HJ, Purcell RH, Feinstone SM, et al: Non-A, non-B hepatitis: Its relationship to cytomegalovirus, to chronic hepatitis, and to direct and indirect test methods, in Szmuness W, Alter JH, Maynard JE (eds): *Viral Hepatitis: 1981 International Symposium*. Philadelphia, Franklin Institute Press, 1982, pp 279–294.

50. Tabor E, Gerety RJ, Drucker JA, et al: Transmission of non-A, non-B hepatitis from man to chimpanzee. *Lancet* 1978; 1:463–466.

51. Alter HJ, Purcell RA, Holland PV, et al: Transmissible agent in non-A, non-B hepatitis. *Lancet* 1978; 1:459–463.

52. Yoshizawa H, Akahane Y, Itoh Y, et al: Viruslike particles in plasma fraction (fibrinogen) and in the circulation of apparently healthy blood donors capable of inducing non-A/non-B hepatitis in humans and chimpanzees. *Gastroenterology* 1980; 79:512–520.

53. Wyke RJ, Tsiquaye KN, Thornton A, et al: Transmission of non-A, non-B hepatitis to chimpanzees by factor IX concentrates after fatal complications in patients with chronic liver disease. *Lancet* 1979; 1:520–524.

54. Bradley DW, Cook WH, Maynard KE, et al: Experimental infection of chimpanzees with anti-hemophilic (factor VIII) materials: Recovery of virus-like particles associated with non-A, non-B hepatitis. *J Med Virol* 1979; 3:253–269.

55. Hollinger FB, Gitnick GL, Aach RD, et al: Non-A, non-B hepatitis transmission in chimpanzees: A project of the Transfusion-Transmitted Viruses Study Group. *Intervirology* 1978; 10:60–68.

56. Trepo C, Degos F, Degotte C, et al: Transmission of hepatitis B like non-A, non-B hepatitis and associated markers to chimpanzees successfully immunized against HBV (abstract). *Hepatology* 1982; 2:686.

57. Wands JR, Lieberman HM, Muchmore E, et al: Detection and transmission in chimpanzees of hepatitis B virus-related agents formerly designated "non-A, non-B" hepatitis. *Proc Natl Acad Sci U S A* 1982; 79:7552–7556.

58. Duermeyer W, Stute R, Hellings JA: An enzyme-linked immunosorbent assay for an antigen related to non-A, non-B hepatitis and its antibody: Partial characterization of the antigen and chimpanzee transmission. *J Med Virol* 1983; 11:11–21.

59. Hollinger FB, Mosley JW, Szmuness W, et al: Transfusion-transmitted virus study: Experimental evidence for two non-A, non-B hepatitis agents. *J Infect Dis* 1980; 142:400.

60. Bradley DW, Maynard JE, Cook EH, et al: Non-A/non-B hepatitis in experimentally infected chimpanzees: Cross-challenge and electron microscope studies. *J Med Virol* 1980; 6:185–201.

216 / P.C. Hsia and L.B. Seeff

61. Tabor E, April M, Seeff LB, et al: Acute non-A, non-B hepatitis: Prolonged presence of the infectious agent in blood. *Gastroenterology* 1979; 76:680–684.
62. Bradley DW, Maynard JE, Popper H, et al: Persistent non-A, non-B hepatitis in experimentally infected chimpanzees. *J Infect Dis* 1981; 143:210–218.
63. Feinstone SM, Alter HJ, Dienes HP, et al: Non-A, non-B hepatitis in chimpanzees and marmosets. *J Infect Dis* 1981; 144:588–598.
64. Feinstone SM, Alter HJ, Dienes HP, et al: Studies on non-A, non-B hepatitis in chimpanzees and marmosets, in Szmuness W, Alter HJ, Maynard JE (eds): *Viral Hepatitis: 1981 International Symposium.* Philadelphia, Franklin Institute Press, 1982, pp 295–304.
65. Tabor E, Gerety RJ: The chimpanzee animal model for non-A, non-B hepatitis: New applications, in Szmuness W, Alter HJ, Maynard JE (eds): *Viral Hepatitis: 1981 International Syposium.* Philadelphia, Franklin Institute Press, 1982, pp 305–317.
66. Dienstag JL: Non-A, non-B hepatitis II. Experimental transmission, putative virus agents and markers, and prevention. *Gastroenterology* 1983; 85:743–768.
67. Bradley DW, Krawczynski KZ, Cook EH, et al: Recrudescence of non-A, non-B hepatitis in persistently infected chimpanzees, in Hopkins R, Field S (eds): *Viral Hepatitis: 2nd International Workshop.* Edinburgh, Nuclear Enterprises, 1982, pp 43–48.
68. Shimizu YK, Feinstone SM, Purcell RH, et al: Non-A, non-B hepatitis: Ultrastructural evidence for two agents in experimentally infected chimpanzees. *Science* 1979; 205:197–200.
69. He L-F, Alling D, Popkin T, et al: Determining the size of non-A, non-B hepatitis by filtration. *J Infect Dis* 1987; 156:636–640.
70. Cossart YE, Field AM, Cant B, et al: Parvovirus-like particles in human sera. *Lancet* 1975; 1:72–73.
71. Trepo O, Vitvitski L, Hantz O, et al: Identification and detection of long incubation non-A, non-B hepatitis virus and associated antigens and antibodies. *J Virol Methods* 1980; 2:127–139.
72. Williams AE, Wright JD, Miller JD: Human non-A, non-B hepatitis: Description of a candidate virus (RJ) and a related antigen system in patient sera (abstract). *Gastroenterology* 1980; 79:1066.
73. Marciano-Cabral F, Rublee KL, Carrithers RL Jr, et al: Chronic non-A, non-B hepatitis: Ultrastructural and serologic studies. *Hepatology* 1981; 1:575–582.
74. Mori Y, Ogata S, Ata S, et al: Virus-like particles associated with non-A, non-B hepatitis. *Microbiol Immunol* 1980; 24:1127–1130.
75. Hantz O, Vitvitski L, Trepo O: Non-A, non-B hepatitis: Identification of hepatitis-B-like particles in serum and liver. *J Med Virol* 1980; 5:73–86.
76. Garclin K, Kommerell B, Waldherr R, et al: Intranucleic virus-like particles in a case of sporadic non-A, non-B hepatitis. *J Med Virol* 1980; 5:317–322.
77. Watanabe S, Reddy KR, Jeffers L, et al: Electron microscopic evidence of non-A, non-B hepatitis markers and virus-like particles in immunocompromised humans. *Hepatology* 1984; 4:628–632.
78. Iwarson S, Schaff Z, Seto B, et al: Retrovirus-like particles in hepatocytes of patients with transfusion-acquired non-A, non-B hepatitis. *J Med Virol* 1985; 16:37–45.
79. Bradley DW: The agents of non-A, non-B hepatitis. *J Virol Methods* 1985; 10:307–319.
80. Aach RD, Szmuness W, Mosley JW, et al: Serum alanine aminotransferase of

donors in relation to the risk of non-A, non-B hepatitis in recipients: The transfusion-transmitted viruses study. *N Engl J Med* 1981; 304:989–994.

81. Alter HJ, Purcell RH, Holland PV, et al: Donor transaminase and recipient hepatitis: Impact on blood transfusion services. *JAMA* 1981; 246:630–634.

82. Stevens CE, Aach RD, Hollinger FB, et al: Hepatitis B virus antibody in blood donors and the occurrence of non-A, non-B hepatitis in transfusion recipients: An analysis of the transfusion-transmitted virus study. *Ann Intern Med* 1984; 101:733–738.

83. Ito S, Tsuji Y, Iwasuki A, et al: Relationship between guanase activity in donor blood and the incidence of posttransfusional non-A, non-B hepatitis, and a possible method for preventing posttransfusional hepatitis. *Hepatology* 1986; 5:990–993.

84. Gillon J, Hussey AJ, Howe SP, et al: Post-transfusion non-A, non-B hepatitis: Significance of raised ALT and anti-HBc in blood donors. *Vox Sang* 1988; 54:148–153.

85. Koziol DE, Holland PV, Alling DW, et al: Antibody to hepatitis B core antigen as a paradoxical marker for non-A, non-B hepatitis agents in donated blood. *Ann Intern Med* 1986; 104:488–495.

86. Zuck TF, Sherwood WC, Bove JR: A review of recent events related to surrogate testing of blood to prevent non-A, non-B posttransfusion hepatitis. *Transfusion* 1987; 27:203–206.

87. Sugg V, Schenzle D, Hess G: Antibodies to hepatitis B core antigen in blood donors screened for alanine aminotransferase levels and hepatitis non-A, non-B in recipients. *Transfusion* 1988; 28:386–388.

88. Seeff LB, Dienstag JL: Transfusion-associated non-A, non-B hepatitis. Where do we go from here (editorial)? *Gastroenterology* 1988; 95:530–533.

89. Silverstein MD, Mullery AG, Dienstag JL: Should donor blood be screened for elevated aminotransferase levels? A cost effective analysis. *JAMA* 1984; 252:2839–2845.

90. Alter MJ, Coleman DJ, Alexander WJ, et al: Importance of heterosexual activity in the transmission of hepatitis B and non-A, non-B hepatitis. *JAMA* 1989; 262:1201–1205.

91. Esteban JI, Esteban R, Viladomiu L, et al: Hepatitis C virus antibodies among risk groups in Spain. *Lancet* 1989; 1:294–296.

92. Francis DP, Hadler SC, Prendergast TJ, et al: Occurrence of hepatitis A, B, and non-A/non-B in the United States. *Am J Med* 1984; 76:69–74.

93. Bortolotti F, Cadrobbi P, Armigliatto M, et al: Acute non-A, non-B hepatitis in childhood. *J Pediatr Gastroenterol Nutr* 1988; 7:22–26.

94. Tateda A, Kikuchi K, Numazaki Y, et al: Non-B hepatitis in Japanese recipients of blood transfusions: Clinical and serological studies after the introduction of laboratory screening of donor blood for hepatitis B surface antigen. *J Infect Dis* 1979; 139:511–518.

95. Gimson AES, White YS, Eddleston ALWY, et al: Clinical and prognostic differences in fulminant hepatitis types A, B, and non-A, non-B. *Gut* 1983; 24:1194–1198.

96. Gimson AES, O'Grady J, Ede RS, et al: Late onset hepatic failure: Clinical, serological and histological features. *Hepatology* 1986; 6:288–294.

97. Acute Hepatic Failure Study Group: Etiology and prognosis in fulminant hepatitis (abstract). *Gastroenterology* 1979; 77:33A.

98. Wyke RJ, Williams R: Clinical aspects of non-A, non-B hepatitis infection. *J Virol Methods* 1980; 2:17–29.

99. Papaevangelou G, Tassopoulos N, Rommeliotou-Karayannis A, et al: Etiology of fulminant viral hepatitis in Greece. *Hepatology* 1984; 4:369–372.
100. Dhingra K, Michels SD, Winston EF, et al: Transient bone marrow aplasia associated with non-A, non-B hepatitis. *Am J Hematol* 1988; 29:168–171.
101. Perrillo RP, Pohl DA, Roodman ST, et al: Acute non-A, non-B hepatitis with serum sickness-like syndrome and aplastic anemia. *JAMA* 1981; 245:494–496.
102. van de Stouwe RA, Attia AA, Karanas A, et al: Transient agranulocytosis associated with non-A, non-B hepatitis. *Gastroenterology* 1983; 85:186–189.
103. Carquel A, Vigano P, Davoli C, et al: Sporadic acute non-A, non-B hepatitis complicated by aplastic anemia. *Am J Gastroenterol* 1983; 78:245–247.
104. Zeldis JB, Dienstag JL, Gale RP: Aplastic anemia and non-A, non-B hepatitis. *Am J Med* 1983; 74:64–68.
105. Tzakis AG, Arditi M, Whitington PF, et al: Aplastic anemia complicating orthotopic transplantation for non-A, non-B hepatitis. *N Engl J Med* 1988; 319:393–396.
106. Norkrans A: Clinical, epidemiological and prognostic impact of hepatitis A, B, and "non-A, non-B." *Scand J Infect Dis* 1978; 17:1–44.
107. Jove J, Sanchez-Topias JM, Brugera M, et al: Post-transfusional vs sporadic non-A, non-B chronic hepatitis: A clinicopathological and evolutive study. *Liver* 1988; 8:42–47.
108. Wejstal R, Lindberg J, Lundin P, et al: Chronic non-A, non-B hepatitis: A long-term follow-up study in 49 patients. *Scand J Gastroenterol* 1987; 22:1115–1123.
109. Barcena R, Suarez-Garcia F, Gil LA, et al: Posttransfusion non-A, non-B hepatitis: A prospective study. *Liver* 1985; 5:71–76.
110. Alter HJ: Chronic consequences of non-A, non-B hepatitis, in Seeff LB, Lewis JH (eds): *Current Perspectives in Hepatology: Festschrift for Hyman J Zimmerman, M.D.* New York, Plenum Press, 1989, pp 83–97.
111. Iwarson S, Lindberg J, Lundin P: Progression of hepatitis non-A, non-B to chronic active hepatitis: A histological follow-up of two cases. *J Clin Pathol* 1979; 32:351–355.
112. Realdi G, Alberti A, Rugge M, et al: Long-term follow-up of acute and chronic non-A, non-B post-transfusion hepatitis: Evidence of progression to liver cirrhosis. *Gut* 1982; 23:270–275.
113. Sampliner RE, Woronow DI, Alter MJ, et al: Community-acquired non-A, non-B hepatitis: Clinical characteristics and chronicity. *J Med Virol* 1984; 13:125–130.
114. Mattson L, Weiland O, Glaumann H: Long-term follow-up of chronic post-transfusion non-A, non-B hepatitis: Clinical and pathological outcome. *Liver* 1988; 8:184–188.
115. Hopf V, Moller B, Kuther D, et al: Long-term follow-up of post-transfusion and sporadic chronic hepatitis non-A, non-B and frequency of circulating antibodies to hepatitis C virus (HCV). *J Hepatol* 1990; 10:69–76.
116. Aledort LM, Levine PH, Hilgartner M, et al: A study of liver biopsies and liver disease among hemophiliacs. *Blood* 1985; 66:367–372.
117. Hay CRM, Preston FE, Triger DR, et al: Progressive liver disease in hemophilia: An understated problem? *Lancet* 1985; 1:1495–1497.
118. Resnick RH, Stone K, Antonioli D: Primary hepatocellular carcinoma following non-A, non-B posttransfusion hepatitis. *Dig Dis Sci* 1983; 28:908–911.
119. Kiyosawa K, Akahane Y, Nagata A, et al: Hepatocellular carcinoma after non-A, non-B post-transfusion hepatitis. *Am J Gastroenterol* 1986; 79:777–781.

120. Gilliam JH, Geissinger KR, Richter JE: Primary hepatocellular carcinoma after chronic non-A, non-B post-transfusion hepatitis. *Ann Intern Med* 1984; 101:794–795.

121. Cohen EB, Gang DL, Zeldis JB: Primary hepatocellular carcinoma and nonspecific non-B hepatitis with tumor DNA negative for HBV DNA. *Dig Dis Sci* 1987; 32:1428–1430.

122. Okuda H, Obada H, Motoika Y, et al: Clinicopathological features of hepatocellular carcinoma—comparison of hepatitis B seropositive and seronegative patients. *Hepatogastroenterology* 1984; 31:64–68.

123. Villa E, Baldini GM, Pasquinelli C, et al: Risk factors for hepatocellular carcinoma in Italy: Male sex, hepatitis B virus, non-A, non-B infection, and alcohol. *Cancer* 1988; 62:611–615.

124. Kiyosawa K, Sodeyama T, Tanaka E, et al: Interrelationship of blood transfusion non-A, non-B hepatitis and hepatocellular carcinoma: Analysis by detection of antibody to hepatitis C virus. *Hepatology* 1990; 12:671–675.

125. Hoofnagle JH, Mullen KM, Jones DB, et al: Pilot study of recombinant human alpha interferon in chronic non-A, non-B hepatitis. *N Engl J Med* 1986; 315:1575–1578.

126. Arima T, Shimomura H, Tsuji T, et al: Serum RNA associated with blood-transmitted non-A, non-B hepatitis (abstract). *Hepatology* 1988; 8:1275.

127. Miller R, Purcell RH: Hepatitis C virus shares amino acid sequence similarity with pestiviruses and flaviviruses as well as members of two plant virus subgroups. *Proc Natl Acad Sci U S A* 1990; 87:2051–2061.

128. Alter HJ, Purcell RH, Shih J, et al: Detection of antibody to hepatitic C virus in prospectively followed transfusion recipients with acute and chronic non-A, non-B hepatitis. *N Engl J Med* 1989; 321:1494–1500.

129. van der Poel CL, Reesink HW, Schaasberg W, et al: Infectivity of blood seropositive for hepatitis C virus antibodies. *Lancet* 1990; 1:588–560.

130. Esteban JI, Gonzalez A, Hernandez JM, et al: Evaluation of antibodies to hepatitis C virus in a study of transfusion-associated hepatitis. *N Engl J Med* 1990; 323:1107–1112.

131. McFarlane IG, Smith HM, Johnson PS, et al: Hepatitis C virus antibodies in chronic active hepatitis: Pathogenetic factor or false-positive result? *Lancet* 1990; 335:754–757.

132. Wong DC, Diwan AR, Rosen L, et al: Non-specificity of anti-HCV test for seroepidemiologic analysis (letter). *Lancet* 1990; 2:750–751.

133. Weiner AJ, Truett MA, Rosenblatt J, et al: HCV testing in low-risk populations (letter). *Lancet* 1990; 2:695.

134. Ebeling F, Naukkarmen R, Leikola J: Recombinant immunoblot assay for hepatitis C virus antibody as a predictor of infectivity (letter). *Lancet* 1990; 335:982–983.

135. Weiner A, Kuo G, Bradley DW, et al: Detection of hepatitis C viral sequences in non-A, non-B hepatitis. *Lancet* 1990; 1:1–3.

136. Garson JA, Tedder RS, Briggs M, et al: Detection of hepatitis C viral sequences in blood donations by "nested" polymerase chain reaction and prediction of infectivity. *Lancet* 1990; 1:1419–1422.

137. Zanetti AR, Tanzi E, Zehender A, et al: Hepatitis C virus RNA in symptomless donors implicated in post-transfusion non-A, non-B hepatitis. *Lancet* 1990; 1:448.

138. Farci P, Wong D, Alter HJ, et al: Detection of HCV sequences by PCR in hepatitis C virus infection: Relationship to antibody response and clinical outcome (abstract). *Hepatology* 1990; 12:904.

139. van der Poel CL, Reesink HW, Lelie PN, et al: Anti-hepatitis C antibodies

and non-A, non-B post-transfusion hepatitis in the Netherlands. *Lancet* 1989; 1:297–298.

140. Kuhnl P, Seidl S, Strangel W, et al: Antibody to hepatitis C virus in German blood donors. *Lancet* 1989; 2:324.

141. Roggendorf M, Deinhardt F, Rasshoper R, et al: Antibodies to hepatitis C virus. *Lancet* 1989; 2:324–325.

142. Janot C, Courouce AM, Maniez M: Antibodies to hepatitis C virus in French blood donors. *Lancet* 1982; 2:796–797.

143. Sirchia G, Bellobuono A, Giovanetti A, et al: Antibodies to hepatitis C virus in Italian blood donors. *Lancet* 1989; 2:797.

144. Stevens CE, Taylor PE, Pindyck J. et al: Epidemiology of hepatitis C virus: A preliminary study in volunteer blood donors. *JAMA* 1990; 263:49–53.

145. Miyamura T, Saito I, Katayama T, et al: Detection of antibody against antigen expressed by molecularly cloned hepatitis C virus DNA: Application to diagnosis and blood screening for posttransfusion hepatitis. *Proc Natl Acad Sci U S A* 1990; 87:983–987.

146. McHutchison JG, Kuo G, Houghton M, et al: Circulating antibodies to hepatitis C virus (HCV): A study of 160 cases of acute and chronic NANB hepatitis (abstract). *Hepatology* 1989; 10:645.

147. Katkov WN, Cody H, Evans AA, et al: The role of hepatitis C virus (HCV) in chronic liver disease (abstract). *Hepatology* 1989; 10:644.

148. Mosley JN, Aach RD, Hollinger FB, et al: Non-A, non-B hepatitis and antibody to hepatitis C virus. *JAMA* 1990; 263:77–78.

149. Alberti A, Tremolada F, Bortolotti F, et al: Anti-HCV and liver disease in Italy in the last 10 years (abstract). *Hepatology* 1989; 10:644.

150. Colombo M, Rumi MG, Gringeri A, et al: High prevalence of antibody to hepatitis C virus in multitransfused hemophiliac patients (abstract). *Hepatology* 1989; 10:645.

151. Evans AA, Cody H, Kuo G, et al: Seroepidemiology of hepatitis C virus (HCV) in selected populations (abstract). *Hepatology* 1989; 10:644.

152. Ludlam CA, Chapman D, Cohen B, et al: Antibodies to hepatitis C virus in haemophilia (letter). *Lancet* 1989; 2:560–561.

153. Noel L, Guorois C, Maisonneuve P, et al: Antibodies to hepatitis C virus in haemophilia (letter). *Lancet* 1989; 2:560.

154. Makris M, Preston FC, Triger DR, et al: Hepatitis C antibody and chronic liver disease in haemophilia. *Lancet* 1990; 355:1117–1119.

155. Mannucci PM, Schimpf H, Brettler DB, et al: Low risk for hepatitis C in hemophiliacs given a high purity, pasteurized factor VIII concentrate. *Ann Intern Med* 1990; 113:27–32.

156. Gilli P, Moretti M, Soffritti S, et al: Anti-HCV positive patients in dialysis units (letter)? *Lancet* 1990; 2:243.

157. Mondelli MV, Cristina G, Filice G, et al: Anti-HCV positive patients in dialysis units (letter)? *Lancet* 1990; 2:244.

158. Sanchez-Topias JM, Barrera JM, Costa J, et al: Hepatitis C virus infection in patients with nonalcoholic chronic liver disease. *Ann Intern Med* 1990; 112:921–924.

159. Bruix J, Barrera JM, Calvet X, et al: Prevalence of antibodies to hepatitis C virus in Spanish patients with hepatocellular carcinoma and hepatic cirrhosis. *Lancet* 1989; 2:1004–1006.

160. Colombo M, Kuo G, Choo QL, et al: Prevalence of antibodies to hepatitis C virus in Italian patients with hepatocellular carcinoma. *Lancet* 1989; 2: 1006–1008.

161. Hasan F, Jeffers LJ, De Medina M, et al: Hepatitis C-associated hepatocellular carcinoma. *Hepatology* 1990; 12:589–591.
162. Kew MC, Houghton M, Choo QL, et al: Hepatitis C virus antibodies in southern African blacks with hepatocellular carcinoma. *Lancet* 1990; 335:873–874.
163. Di Bisceglie AM, Alter HJ, Kuo G, et al: Detection of antibody to hepatitic C virus in patients with various chronic liver diseases (abstract). *Hepatology* 1989; 10:581.
164. Brillanti S, Barbara L, Miglioli M, et al: Hepatitis C virus: A possible cause of chronic hepatitis in alcoholics (letter). *Lancet* 1989; 2:1390–1391.
165. Mendenhall CL, Seeff LB, Diehl AM, et al: Hepatitis B and C serologic markers: Relationship to alcoholic hepatitis and cirrhosis. Presented at the 1990 International Symposium on Viral Hepatitis and Liver Disease, Houston, Texas, April 1990.
166. Gardon JA, Preston FE, Makris M, et al: Detection by PCR of hepatitis C virus in factor VIII concentrates (letter). *Lancet* 1990; 1:1473.
167. Melbye M, Biggar RJ, Wantzin P, et al: Sexual transmission of hepatitis C virus: Cohort study (1989–1990) among European homosexual men. *Br Med J [Clin Res]* 1990; 302:210–212.
168. Everhart JE, Di Bisceglie AM, Murray LM, et al: Risk for non-A, non-B (type C) hepatitis through sexual or household contact with chronic carriers. *Ann Intern Med* 1990; 112:54–55.
169. McHutchison JG, Govindarajan S, Valestuck B, et al: Hepatitis C antibodies are commonly detected in intravenous drug abusers (IVDA) and homosexuals (HS) with hepatitis A, B and delta (abstract). *Hepatology* 1990; 12:848.
170. Stevens C: Perinatal and sexual transmission of HCV, in Hollinger FB (ed): *The 1990 International Symposium on Viral Hepatitis and Liver Disease.* New York, Alan Liss, Inc, 1990, in press.
171. Fortuny C, Ercilla MG, Barrera JM, et al: HCV vertical transmission: Prospective study in infants born to HCV seropositive mothers, in Hollinger FB (ed): *The 1990 International Symposium on Viral Hepatitis and Liver Disease.* New York, Alan Liss, Inc, 1990, in press.
172. Reesink HW, Ip HMM, Wang VCW, et al: Lack of evidence for maternal-infant transmission of the hepatitis C virus (HCV), in Hollinger FB (ed): *The 1990 International Symposium on Viral Hepatitis and Liver Disease.* New York, Alan Liss, Inc, 1990, in press.
173. Joung NK, Buskell-Bales Z, Seeff LB: Is HCV transmitted perinatally from Korean mothers to newborns? Presented at the 2nd International Symposium on HCV, Los Angeles, California, November 1990.
174. Thaler MM, Landers DW, Wara DW, et al: Vertical transmission of hepatitis C virus detected by polymerase chain reaction (abstract). *Hepatology* 1990; 12:849.
175. Weintrub PS, Veereman-Waters G, Lowan MJ, et al: Vertically transmitted hepatitis C/HIV co-infection: A case of infantile liver disease (abstract). *Hepatology* 1990; 12:550.
176. Alter MJ, Hadler SC, Judson FN, et al: Risk factors for acute non-A, non-B hepatitis in the United States and association with hepatitis C virus infection. *JAMA* 1990; 264:2231–2235.
177. Dazza M-C, Meneses C-V, Girard P-M, et al: Hepatitis C virus antibody and hepatocellular carcinoma (letter). *Lancet* 1990; 1:1216.
178. Ducreux M, Buffet C, Dussaix E, et al: Antibody to hepatitis C virus in hepatocellular carcinoma (letter). *Lancet* 1990; 335:300.

179. Chiaramonte M, Farinati F, Fagiuolo S, et al: Antibody to hepatitis C virus in hepatocellular carcinoma. *Lancet* 1990; 355:301–302.
180. Lenzi M, Ballardini G, Fusconi M, et al: Type 2 autoimmune hepatitis and hepatitis C virus infection. *Lancet* 1990; 335:258–259.
181. Theilmann L, Blazek, Goeser T, et al: False-positive anti-HCV tests in rheumatoid arthritis (letter). *Lancet* 1990; 1:1346.
182. Bouchart D, Lucas J-C, Muller J-Y, et al: False-positive hepatitis C virus antibody tests in paraproteinaemia (letter). *Lancet* 1990; 335:63–64.
183. Dussaix E, Maggiore G, De Giacomo C, et al: Autoimmune hepatitis in children and hepatitis C virus C testing (letter). *Lancet* 1990; 1:1160–1161.
184. Fusconi M, Lenzi M, Ballardini G, et al: Anti-HCV testing in autoimmune hepatitis and primary biliary cirrhosis (letter). *Lancet* 1990; 2:823–824.
185. Hoofnagle JH: Management of post-transfusion hepatitis. *Transfusion* 1989; 2:215–220.
186. Thomson BJ, Doran M, Lever AML, et al: Alpha-interferon therapy for non-A, non-B hepatitis transmitted by gammaglobulin replacement therapy. *Lancet* 1987; 1:539–541.
187. Kiyosawa S, Sodeyama T, Yoda H, et al: Treatment of chronic non-A, non-B hepatitis with beta-interferon, in Zuckerman AJ (ed): *Viral Hepatitis and Liver Disease*. New York, Alan R Liss, Inc, 1988, pp 895–897.
188. Arima T, Nahkashima H, Shimomura H, et al: Treatment of chronic non-A, non-B hepatitis with human beta-interferon, in Zuckerman AJ (ed): *Viral Hepatitis and Liver Disease*. New York, Alan R Liss, Inc, 1988, pp 898–901.
189. Jacyna MR, Brooks MG, Loke RHT, et al: Randomised controlled trial of interferon alfa (lymphoblastoid interferon) in chronic non-A, non-B hepatitis. *Br Med J [Clin Res]* 1989; 298:80–82.
190. Di Bisceglie AM, Martin P, Kassianides C, et al: Recombinant interferon alfa therapy for chronic hepatitis C. *N Engl J Med* 1989; 321:1506–1510.
191. Davis GL, Balart LA, Schiff E, et al: Treatment of chronic hepatitis C with recombinant interferon alfa. *N Engl J Med* 1989; 321:1501–1506.
192. Shindo M, Di Bisceglie AM, Cheung L, et al: Changes in hepatitis C virus RNA in serum associated with alfa interferon therapy (abstract). *Hepatology* 1990; 12:884.
193. Lindsay KL, Davis GL, Bodenheimer HC, et al: Prediction of relapse and response to retreatment in patients with an initial response to recombinant alfa interferon (rIFN) therapy for chronic hepatitis C (abstract). *Hepatology* 1990; 12:847.
194. Renault PF, Hoofnagle JH: Side effects of alpha interferon. *Semin Liver Dis* 1989; 9:273–277.
195. Vento S, Di Perri G, Garofano T, et al: Hazards of interferon therapy for HBV-seronegative chronic hepatitis (letter). *Lancet* 1989; 2:926.

# Thyroid Dysfunction in Older Persons*

## Clark T. Sawin, M.D.

Professor of Medicine, Tufts University School of Medicine, Chief,
Endocrine-Diabetes Section, Medical Service, Boston Veterans Affairs Medical
Center, Boston, Massachusetts

## Editor's Introduction

The signs and symptoms of thyroid disorders at any age can be extremely subtle, and therefore readily overlooked even by the most sophisticated endocrinologist. The problem of undiagnosed or misdiagnosed thyroid disease, however, is far greater in the elderly, in whom the manifestations of both hyperthyroidism and hypothyroidism can easily go undiagnosed for many years with frequently very serious consequences. As Dr. Sawin's review of this increasingly important topic emphasizes, hyperthyroidism in the elderly may manifest itself by an apathetic affect rather than by the hyperactivity that is typical of the disease in younger individuals, and in this age group atrial fibrillation may represent the only obvious sign of serious hyperthyroidism. On the other hand, the presentations of hypothyroidism in the elderly may likewise be extremely subtle, often mimicking the normal aging process. The following review carefully evaluates the signs and symptoms of thyroid dysfunction in older persons and presents practical and cost-effective methods, making use of the newest laboratory approaches, to diagnosis of these conditions. Finally, therapy for either hypothyroidism or hyperthyroidism in the elderly must be approached with particular attention to the concomitant medical probelms of our increasing aged population.

*Marvin D. Siperstein, M.D, Ph.D.*

Over 100 years ago, Victor Horsley, then 28 years old and later to become famous as a neurosurgeon, thought that ". . . the symptoms of mere senility may be accounted for by the loss of the functions of the thyroid body" because myxedematous monkeys and persons looked much older than they were.[1] While this idea is now passé, some thyroid problems *are* more common in older persons and, when older persons have thyroid dysfunction, they do not have the typical clinical findings seen in younger persons. Therefore, in the aged population, one must look to "subclinical" disease and think about screening and case-finding.

*Supported by the Department of Veterans Affairs Research Service.

## Definitions

"Thyroid dysfunction" as used herein means too little or too much secretion of thyroid hormone. "Older persons" generally means those aged 60 years or more; "older persons" is preferable to "elderly," which, though formerly a term of respect, now has pejorative overtones. "Subclinical" means that an abnormality, however detected, is not seen easily by a practiced physician.

The "sensitivity" of a test assesses how well it detects a disease; one that is 99% sensitive detects 99% of all cases. The "specificity" of a test assesses how well it avoids the diagnosis in those who do not have the disease; one that is 99% "specific" labels as abnormal 1% of those without the disease. But for uncommon disorders, high sensitivity and specificity can be misleading. The "predictive value" is more relevant; the "positive predictive value" tells how often an abnormal test predicts the presence of a disease. If a disease is found in only 1% of 10,000 persons, 100 have the disease and 9,900 do not; of the 100, 99 will have an abnormal test (99% sensitivity) and, of the 9,900, 99 will have an abnormal test (99% specificity). Only 50% of abnormal tests (99/198) will be associated with the disease; the positive predictive value is only 50%.

"Prevalence" is the number of persons in a group who have a finding or condition at a given time. Since "prevalence" sometimes is used to include both those who have the condition and those who used to have it, the term "point prevalence" often is employed to indicate how many have it at a given time. "Incidence" refers to the number of persons in a group who develop a condition *during* a given time, e.g., over 1 year. "Screening" means looking for a finding in a person who is not aware of the abnormality. While the term is used for programs that invite the general public to be tested,[2] thus including a selection bias by the individuals tested, it also is used when everyone in a defined group is tested, e.g., all newborn children or all adults in a community. "Case-finding" means to test for a disorder anyone seeking professional care for another reason[2]; for practicing physicians, it is almost the same as "screening," since physicians generally see only those who come to them for illness or periodic routine examinations. Thus, "case-finding" data can be biased by illness, wherein one might find more of the tested disease, or by health, wherein one might find less of it. The inherent biases in any study, whether it is labeled "screening" or "case-finding," are more important than the label itself in judging the usefulness of the data. A "risk factor" is something associated with a disease, but not necessarily in a known causal manner.

## Age and Thyroid Function

Was Horsley at least partly right? Are there thyroid changes that occur in everyone as they get older? Certainly not all people become hypothyroid, but some thyroid changes are fairly common. Note that the difference between attributing a change to aging and calling it a disease is arbitrary; if a change is judged to be common enough, it is considered a normal part of aging and, if not, it is called a disease.

There is no change in the level of serum thyroxine ($T_4$), free $T_4$, or free $T_4$ index with age.[3] Yet older thyroids take up less radioiodine[4] and secrete less $T_4$.[5] The main reason is the slower degradation of $T_4$,[5] rather than an intrinsic inability of the gland to secrete more $T_4$; why the degradation of $T_4$ should be slower is unknown. Serum triiodothyronine ($T_3$) is often lower in older persons.[6] While age brings with it a lessened conversion of $T_4$ to $T_3$, the lower levels of $T_3$ probably are due more often to nonthyroid disease[7] or perhaps to subtler factors such as dietary changes.

These decreases in $T_4$ secretion and $T_3$ formation do not raise the serum level of thyrotropin (TSH),[8] so the pituitary must sense the ambient level of thyroid hormone as appropriate. If anything, TSH secretion falls slightly with age.[9] Nevertheless, the fall in serum TSH with age should not confuse the diagnosis of hyperthyroidism, provided the most sensitive assay for TSH is used (see later). A clearly raised serum level of TSH is not normal in older persons.

## Thyroid Failure

### Causes and Risk Factors

**Autoimmune Damage.**—A damaged thyroid is fairly common in older persons. Focal lymphocytic thyroiditis occurs more often in this population, especially in women.[10] A more severe degree of lymphocytic infiltration shrinks the gland and is associated with abnormal levels of circulating thyroid autoantibodies.[11] However, these are not a sensitive marker of thyroid failure or damage in older persons, because they may be absent.[12] Conversely, abnormal levels of thyroid autoantibodies occur more often in seemingly normal older persons[12, 13] than in younger ones. Occasionally, a raised level of thyroid autoantibodies reverts to normal.[14]

That thyroid autoantibodies appear more often in older persons is in keeping with an overall change in the immune system with age, as several autoantibodies appear after the age of 60 years.[15] Age alone may not be solely responsible for these changes, because genetic background can play a major role.[16]

The autoimmune destructive process often goes on to cause thyroid failure. When associated with thyroid enlargement or goiter, it is called Hashimoto's disease; when the thyroid has shrunk, it is called atrophic thyroiditis. The latter is by far more common in older persons.[17] Why some get goiter and others develop thyroid atrophy is unknown. Whether there is thyroid atrophy or not, when the damage has gone far enough, $T_4$ secretion falls to a point at which it is noticed by the body's tissues. One of these tissues is the pituitary thyrotrope, which responds by raising the serum level of TSH.

**Other Factors in Thyroid Failure.**—Lymphocytic thyroiditis accounts for most instances of thyroid failure. In addition, certain risk factors, some of which may act only in concert with existing autoimmune damage, increase the probability of thyroid failure. These all can be assessed during an internist's routine examination and are listed in Table 1.

Radiation therapy for head and neck cancer is becoming a common cause of hypothyroidism in older men; probably all of those who receive such treatment should be tested. The same is true for patients who take lithium carbonate, mainly for manic depressive illness. It causes hypothyroidism in some,[18] and whether this phenomenon is more frequent in older persons is unknown.

## Diagnosis

The diagnosis of thyroid failure, once testing is decided upon, is simple. A clearly elevated serum TSH is the most sensitive indicator of primary hypothyroidism.[19] For practical purposes, nothing else consistently raises serum TSH. Thus, one should measure serum TSH and, perhaps, serum $T_4$. Measurement of the latter is not as sensitive, as the value in hypothyroidism, as defined by a clearly elevated TSH level, ranges up to 8 $\mu g/dL$ (103nM). There are, as usual, a few complexities behind this apparently simple statement:

1. What is the relationship of a raised serum TSH to hypothyroidism and clinical findings?
2. What of the entity of subclinical hypothyroidism?
3. How high must the serum TSH be to indicate thyroid failure?
4. Does it matter which assay is used to measure TSH?
5. Are other thyroid tests, such as a serum $T_4$, needed?

The problem of relating a raised serum TSH to hypothyroidism hinges on two concerns, one major and one minor. The major one is when to use the term "hypothyroid." Some would insist that overt clinical findings be present for the patient to be so classified. But the term "hypothyroid" means only that thyroid function is lower than normal; it implies nothing as to its manifestations. Limiting hypothyroidism to only those with overt findings implies that clinical assessment is an accurate detector of thyroid failure, but it is not.[20-22] Since clinical findings are reflections of thyroid deficiency at the tissue level, and since the pituitary's secretion of more TSH is simply one tissue's reflection of that deficiency, a raised serum TSH in the absence of clear-cut clinical findings simply reflects the greater sensitivity of the patient's pituitary compared to the patient's physician. One can equate a raised serum TSH with hypothyroidism. What to do about it is another question (see later).

A minor issue is a possible discrepancy between the thyroid state and the serum TSH. Hypopituitarism can cause hypothyroidism without raising serum TSH. Fortunately, this is rare in adults in the absence of overt pitu-

**TABLE 1.**
**Risk Factors for Thyroid Failure**

I. Past history
  A. Hyperthyroidism.
  B. Subacute
    thyroiditis.
  C. Treated
    head/neck
    cancer.
  D. Autoimmune
    disease.
    1. Addison's
      disease.
    2. Pernicious
      anemia.
  E. Cardiovascular
    disease (?).
II. Family history
  A. Any thyroid
    disease.
III. Current history
  A. Age above 60
    years.
  B. Lithium
    carbonate.
  C. Amiodarone.
  D. Iodine.
IV. Laboratory
  A. Raised serum
    cholesterol.

itary disease. Ninety-eight percent to 99% of thyroid failure in older persons is primary hypothyroidism[23] and, while hypopituitarism should not be forgotten, its prior probability is quite low. Conversely, serum TSH occasionally can be high without hypothyroidism in severely ill patients[24] or those with adrenal insufficiency.[25] In such cases, the serum $T_4$ is high rather than low, as it would be also in the rare pituitary TSH-secreting tumor or the unusual patient with resistance to thyroid hormone. Some assays give falsely high values.[26] It is wise to avoid these.

Subclinical hypothyroidism is not a rigorously defined term, but it is useful. Strictly speaking, it indicates any degree of thyroid failure in the absence of clinical findings. In reality, the term blankets a range of definitions, none of which has been studied prospectively for its effect on patient outcome, although there are some good cross-sectional studies. At present, subclinical hypothyroidism may mean any of 24 different things (choose one part of the definition from each of the four categories in Table 2 to see the possibilities). The potential for taxonomic confusion is obvious. Some of these categories could turn out to have a significant effect on outcome and others could not. When a physician sees a patient, this uncertainty can be dealt with by making an individual judgment, but it also has clear implications for setting health care policy and should be explicit when this is done.

My personal preference is to diagnose subclinical hypothyroidism when the serum TSH is clearly raised (>10 mU/L) and the patient has no signs or symptoms in the usual examination ("routine inquiry"), whether the serum $T_4$ is in the normal range or below it. The use of a clearly raised serum TSH as a diagnostic criterion eliminates the ambivalence of slightly raised levels, so many of which are normal variants. A slightly raised serum TSH does have implications for follow-up, as hypothyroidism can ensue later in both older[27] and younger patients,[28] but I prefer not to attach a diagnosis to such individuals, much as I would not diagnose diabetes mellitus in patients with mild glucose intolerance. Follow-up of those with a clearly raised serum TSH (>10 mU/L) but no symptoms shows that both older and younger adults[27, 29, 30] can develop overt symptoms later.

Routine inquiry as opposed to detailed questioning is all that practically can be done in the usual encounter for a condition that presents vaguely in older persons and that most do not have. No one digs for deep details unless there is a reason. Further, since the correlation of clinical findings with the actual diagnosis is poor, any such symptoms or signs are more useful in monitoring treatment than in making a diagnosis.

Although it is common to label as subclinically hypothyroid only those with a raised serum TSH who have a serum $T_4$ in the "normal" range,[31-34] the raised TSH tells us that that $T_4$ value is too low for those patients. While any taxonomy is reasonable for research purposes if it is clear and

---

**TABLE 2.**
**Possible Definitions of Subclinical Hypothyroidism***

1. Serum TSH clearly above normal (>10 mU/L) or serum TSH above normal (>5 mU/L) or serum TSH hyperresponsive to TRH (any basal value)
2. No signs or symptoms on routine inquiry or no signs or symptoms on close inquiry
3. Serum $T_4$ at any level or serum $T_4$ in the normal range
4. TAB (antimicrosomal) easily detectable or TAB (antimicrosomal) not detectable or not measured

*TSH = thyrotropin; TRH = thyrotropin-releasing hormone; $T_4$ = thyroxine; TAB = thyroid autoantibodies.

consistent, it is physiologically irrational to distinguish clinical from subclinical illness on the basis of whether or not the serum $T_4$ is below the "normal" range. The decrease in $T_4$ secretion may be the same in both instances, but those who end up in the normal range simply may have begun higher in the normal range than those who fall below it. In addition, to limit the diagnosis to those with a normal-range serum $T_4$ implies that all of those with a level below the normal range should be treated. While this may be true, the evidence for benefit actually is better for those with a "normal" serum $T_4$, simply because there are no studies in those with low levels.

It is impractical to lump all patients with TSH values above the normal range into one group. Some have a slightly high value because of the statistics of the normal range: 2.5% of normal persons are, by definition, above the upper limit of "normal." With an upper normal limit of about 4 to 5 mU/L, slightly raised values between 5 and 10 mU/L can be considered a "gray" zone of uncertain significance; some indicate early thyroid failure, but most do not. Values over 10 mU/L indicate hypothyroidism with the aforementioned provisos.

A good assay for TSH is critical. Some assays with an upper limit of 8 to 10 mU/L are still in use; avoid these. Modern sensitive assays (the immunoradiometric assay or the chemiluminescent assay) for serum TSH have a normal range of about 0.2 or 0.4 mU/L to 4 or 5 mU/L. While a very sensitive assay is not needed to diagnose hypothyroidism, it is needed to diagnose hyperthyroidism. It seems sensible to use only the most sensitive test, so that a laboratory can define both types of thyroid dysfunction.

Other thyroid tests are occasionally useful, but not as often as they are used. Most physicians insist on some measure of $T_4$. While this is not unreasonable, a serum $T_4$ measurement would exclude hypothyroidism only if it were greater than 8 μg/dL (103nM). Lower values, which include half the normal population, would require measurement of TSH in any case. A $T_4$ value is also useful in rare instances of otherwise unexplained raised TSH values.

Other common tests include the measurement of thyroid autoantibodies and serum $T_3$, and the performance of a thyrotropin-releasing hormone stimulation test. Thyroid autoantibodies, either as antithyroglobulin or as antimicrosomal antibodies, help define the cause of thyroid failure but, as noted, are neither specific nor sensitive for hypothyroidism. Serum $T_3$ is low less often than is serum $T_4$ and does not help. The thyrotropin-releasing hormone test is too elaborate and expensive. Since autoimmune hypothyroidism is associated with other autoimmune diseases, Addison's disease and diabetes mellitus should be considered in anyone who is hypothyroid.

In summary, the slightest suspicion of hypothyroidism in an older person is enough to justify measurement of the serum TSH and probably the $T_4$; a good case can be made for testing all older persons (as discussed later). Most information will come from the TSH value, and a bit more will be added by the $T_4$ value. Tradition and the cost of the TSH assay permit the serum $T_4$ to continue as the primary test for thyroid failure in many laboratories, but both tradition and cost can and should change. A good compromise for the present is to assay TSH and then assay $T_4$ in the same sample only if the TSH value is out of the normal range.[35]

Hypothyroidism exists whenever the serum TSH is >10 mU/L. The "subclinical" designation can be reserved for those with vague or no symptoms on routine inquiry. The other rare causes of a raised serum TSH usually are identified by a high-normal or raised serum $T_4$. A slightly raised serum TSH (e.g., >5 to <10 mU/L) most often does not indicate hypothyroidism unless there are clear-cut symptoms. However, since the patient could be in an early stage of thyroid failure, careful follow-up is indicated.

## Consequences

Whether or not hypothyroidism causes bodily dysfunction is critical in deciding whether or not to treat the condition. Overt dysfunctions, such as clear-cut symptoms and signs of hypothyroidism, are obvious consequences and require treatment. However, as older persons often do not have clear or specific clinical findings,[20] the efficacy of treatment may depend on showing improvement in less evident findings or other untoward outcomes, such as cardiovascular disease. What, then, are the untoward effects of thyroid failure?

**Cardiovascular and Lipid Changes.**—Poor left ventricular function is a clear consequence of thyroid failure.[36]

Hypothyroidism also has long been considered to cause atherosclerosis and coronary heart disease. The original concept was based on anatomic findings at autopsy,[37] although not all investigators agreed.[38] Most of these data were obtained in retrospect and were not well controlled. More recent anatomic data support the association of coronary heart disease and overt hypothyroidism.[39] Subclinical hypothyroidism may be associated with coronary heart disease in older men[40] and women.[41] While a major epidemiologic survey, using cross-sectional but no longitudinal data, found no association between subclinical hypothyroidism and coronary heart disease in men, most were under the age of 60 years. In women of all ages, there was an association with angina pectoris, possible myocardial infarction, and minor changes in the electrocardiogram.[42]

Clear-cut thyroid failure definitely raises the serum cholesterol,[43] but subclinical hypothyroidism does not, and so might not be related to coronary heart disease.[42] However, a high cholesterol level per se need not be the only mediator of heart disease in hypothyroidism; it might be mediated by the decrease in high-density lipoprotein cholesterol known to occur in subclinical hypothyroidism.[44] Furthermore, there may be an independent connection between thyroid autoantibodies and coronary heart disease, without a change in cholesterol.[41, 45] Hypothyroidism also can be a cause of hypertension,[46] although how often this is so in older persons is unknown.

**Neurologic Changes and Psychiatric Illness.**—Neurologic and psychiatric changes, including myxedema coma and death, clearly occur in overt hypothyroidism.[47] On the other hand, the prevalence of hypothyroidism among those with psychiatric illness, mainly depression or dementia, is variable, ranging from 0.6% to 4.0% in younger adults[48, 49] and from 2% to 7% in older persons.[50, 51] These data are fuzzy at best; many of the series are small and have few older persons, unclear criteria for hypothyroidism, and probably major selection biases. The prevalence rates found among older persons may not differ from those without psychiatric illness. The relationship of mental and neurologic illness to thyroid failure needs better definition.

**Other Changes.**—Poor ventilatory responses[52] and even sleep apnea[53] can be due to overt hypothyroidism; many older persons fall into these groups. Rheumatic symptoms, so common in older individuals, also can be the main complaint in this population.[54]

In summary, the systemic consequences of thyroid failure are not easy to define in older persons. They still require good epidemiologic studies with long-term prospective analysis to get clear answers. For the moment, on balance there is a strong suggestion that hypothyroidism, including the subclinical type, is causally related to cardiac dysfunction and coronary heart disease in older individuals. There also may be subtle effects on vascular, pulmonary, musculoskeletal, and mental function.

---

## Treatment

**Principle.**—Just as the diagnosis of thyroid failure relies on the rise in serum TSH stimulated by a fall in the patient's serum $T_4$, treatment of thyroid failure takes advantage of the same negative feedback system: one gives enough oral $T_4$ to bring the raised serum TSH down to normal.[55] At the same time, one aims to reverse other biologic defects as well, e.g., to remove the symptoms, if present, and to remedy or prevent any untoward effects. I mention normalizing the serum TSH first, a clinician's heresy, not only because clinical assessment is not sensitive to small changes in $T_4$ dose,[56] but also because reversing the raised serum TSH is in fact reversal of a tissue defect, and because those with subclinical disease often have symptomatic improvement only in retrospect. Physicians do not hesitate to treat the clearly raised serum glucose in a patient with asymptomatic diabetes mellitus; there is no reason to hesitate in subclinical hypothyroidism.

**Benefits and Hazards of Treatment.**—A patient with obvious symptoms, a clearly raised serum TSH, a clearly low serum $T_4$, and no other disease should be treated without hesitation and will receive clear benefit. Controversial, however, is whether or not to treat those with subclinical hypothyroidism, particularly older persons. Logically, if enough thyroid hormone fails to reach the body's tissues, all patients with a clearly raised serum TSH should be treated,[57] particularly when the level is high enough to be in the range where some patients do have symptoms, i.e., >10 mU/L. Although older persons with clearly raised serum TSH values are generally without symptoms on routine inquiry,[22, 58] an unknown fraction do have symptoms (usually nonspecific) on closer questioning or in retrospect. About 40% of these individuals with a serum TSH >10 mU/L have a low serum $T_4$.[22] As discussed previously, some would call these persons overtly hypothyroid and treat them. Of great interest is that the treatment of patients with subclinical hypothyroidism, defined as a raised serum TSH and a "normal" serum $T_4$, results in an improvement in symptoms, a response found after close questioning but not initially evident, and that this is so for older[34] as well as younger[32] patients.

Left ventricular dysfunction in overt hypothyroidism clearly improves with $T_4$ therapy.[59] In subclinical hypothyroidism, the data are not as clear, in part because of differing criteria. Most data show a subtle[33, 60] or more overt[31, 34] reversion to normal with treatment, at least in some patients,[32] although one study[61] showed no change. These findings apply to older patients[34] as well as to younger ones,[32] even when limited to those with a "normal" serum $T_4$. Hypertension due to hypothyroidism is at least partly reversible with treatment,[46] as are ventilatory defects and sleep apnea.[52, 53] These data probably apply to older persons.

Unfortunately, there are no data on the benefit of therapy for either overt or subclinical hypothyroidism on long-term outcomes for conditions such as coronary heart disease.

One also can take a "prophylactic" approach and treat all patients, including older ones, who have subclinical hypothyroidism.[62, 63] Such treatment might prevent dementia or cardiovascular disease to some degree, but there is no such evidence as yet.

Balanced against the potential therapeutic benefit in many older persons are the potential hazards of cardiac symptoms or bone loss precipitated by thyroid therapy. Common sense dictates caution in giving thyroid treatment to a patient with known cardiac disease; the initial dose should be small and one may have to accept some degree of hypothyroidism to avoid worsening angina pectoris.[64] Note, however, that treating hypothyroid patients who have angina pectoris decreases their symptoms as often as it worsens them.[65] It also is worth noting that cardiac surgery (including bypass grafting[66]) and other types of surgery[67] can be performed while patients are still hypothyroid without increased morbidity or mortality.

Bone loss occurs in hyperthyroidism if the condition is left untreated long enough.[68] Similarly, overtreatment with thyroid hormone can cause bone loss in both older[69, 70] and younger[71, 72] women. However, some disagree,[73] and even suppressive doses of $T_4$ need not cause bone loss in the spine.[70, 72] Furthermore, there are no studies showing increased fracture rates as a result of physiologic thyroid replacement.[74] Only a few older persons have been studied with modern techniques,[70] and no trial has assessed thyroid therapy's effect relative to the many other risk factors for osteoporosis, particularly with doses of $T_4$ that just normalize the serum TSH. On balance, although more prospective data are needed in older persons, thyroid therapy may not damage bone unless it is given in excess, either inadvertently or intentionally. Its role as a risk factor for fracture is unproven.

**Preparations.**—There is no reason to use anything other than oral sodium L-thyroxine, usually called simply thyroxine or $T_4$.[75] Oral $T_4$ more nearly mimicks the stable serum levels of $T_4$ and $T_3$ seen in normal persons[76] than do other preparations. There seems to be no effect of age on absorption.[77] Since the tablet content of $T_4$ is the main determinant of how much gets into the circulation ("bioavailability"),[78] preparations that contain the stated content of $T_4$ should be used. While this seemingly is self-evident, the actual tablet content of some preparations in the past, including branded ones, has not always reflected the stated content; some have contained too much[79] and others too little.[80, 81] Recent branded preparations now contain what they should;[82, 83] the U.S. Food and Drug Administration periodically spot-checks manufacturers of $T_4$ tablets for accuracy of tablet content. This is particularly important in older persons, who must avoid an inadvertent overdose.

**The Initial Dose.**—The initial dose of oral $T_4$ obviously should not be more than the ultimate dose required or than the patient can take safely. As some older persons require only about 50 μg/day,[84] one should start with 25 μg/day. Some calculate the dose in micrograms per kilogram per day, but this is unnecessary and falsely precise.

**Changing the Dose.**—The aim is to titrate the dose of $T_4$ against the serum TSH until the raised serum TSH goes down into the normal range. A given dose should be taken for at least 1 month before it is increased.[85] It may take that long or longer to establish a stable level of serum TSH. Intervals of 2 or 3 weeks[86] may not be long enough. The dose should be raised by 25 μg/day at no less than monthly intervals until the serum TSH is normal; greater increments may overshoot the goal. In practice, the interval in many patients is 2 or 3 months. Barring some untoward clinical event or patient complaint, *there is no hurry*. Because of the long half-life of $T_4$, this agent need be given only once daily at a time convenient for the patient. Since older patients need less $T_4$ than do younger ones,[84, 87] the dose might be decreased in anyone over 60 years of age who has taken $T_4$ for some years and the serum TSH be monitored to see if less is actually needed.

**Monitoring the Patient.**—Patients in whom the serum TSH becomes normal are euthyroid. The response of the pituitary thyrotrope parallels in general that of other measurable responses to thyroid therapy.[59, 88] Measurement of serum TSH is all that is really needed to monitor patients. The one proviso is that the assay for TSH must separate clearly the lower end of the normal range from the minimum detectable level, so that an overshoot can be detected. Thus, the older radioimmunoassay is not useful, and at least a second-generation immunoradiometric assay must be used.[89] Even better at distinguishing normal from the minimum detectable level is the chemiluminescent assay.[90, 91] It is unclear how often patients should be monitored. Most physicians routinely test once or twice a year, but there are no data that indicate the optimum interval.

Serum $T_4$ is probably measured more often than serum TSH when monitoring the treatment of hypothyroid patients. However, it is usually of little value given a good TSH assay. If the serum $T_4$ is measured, the clinician should be aware that the range of values in properly treated patients (6 to 17 μg/dL) (Sawin, unpublished data, 1983) is wider than that in normal adults (5 to 12 μg/dL). While some have worried that these higher values might mean hyperthyroidism[92] or "tissue thyrotoxicosis,"[93] the "excess" in serum $T_4$ is probably physiologic and replaces metabolically the small amount of $T_3$ that would be secreted were the thyroid gland normal.

Poor compliance may be an issue. Hypothyroid patients may simply stop taking $T_4$ for no particular reason[94] or just not take enough.[22] If this happens, the serum TSH will be high, as expected, and measurement of the serum $T_4$ will help; it will be lower than it was. A common variation on this theme is the patient who takes $T_4$ erratically, allowing the serum TSH to rise, then takes the $T_4$ for a few days before seeing the physician. In this case, both a raised serum TSH *and* a raised serum $T_4$ may be seen, because the $T_4$ has not had time to lower the serum TSH; a careful history can lead to more patient education.

Serum $T_4$ also might be measured when the tablet content is suspect or there is an absorptive problem in a patient who is clearly reliable. The use of $T_4$ preparations known to be compounded accurately usually avoids the former; the latter is solved by awareness of any gastrointestinal disease or co-medication with an agent such as cholestyramine[95] or, rarely, lovastatin,[96] which can raise the serum TSH despite a constant dose of oral $T_4$.

**Inappropriate Thyroid Therapy.**—Overall, 7% of older persons take thyroid hormone (10% of women and 2.3% of men). Most women take it for appropriate reasons (mainly hypothyroidism), but 12% of women and 30% of men take it for apparently poor indications.[23] Furthermore, patients sometimes are treated for hypothyroidism, often for many years, without a certain diagnosis. It is safe to withdraw or decrease $T_4$ therapy to see if the serum TSH rises or not, either confirming or denying that thyroid failure exists. One must wait long enough before measuring the serum TSH; 3 weeks of withdrawal now seem to be used widely,[97, 98] but this interval may not be adequate and could lead prematurely to a poor decision. At least 5 weeks[99] and, in older persons, possibly 3 or 4 months may be needed.[100]

In summary, one can treat older persons who have overt or subclinical thyroid failure (serum TSH >10 μU/L) with oral $T_4$ and reasonably expect net benefit, provided the serum TSH is not suppressed below the normal range. Individual judgment should prevail in each patient, given considerations such as coronary heart disease.

## Prevalence and Incidence

Older estimates of the prevalence of hypothyroidism in older persons did not use serum TSH as a marker. In these studies, about 2% of older individuals were hypothyroid.[21, 101, 102] More recent studies using serum TSH as a marker still show variable data, probably because of differences in the cut-off points used for serum TSH, the selection of patients, and the populations studied. Community studies, which attempted to avoid the selection bias of clinics and hospitals, showed that, in the United Kingdom, about 7% to 8% of the population above 55 years of age had thyroid failure.[103] In the United States, the prevalence was 4% to 7% of individuals above 60 years of age,[22, 58, 104] approximately the same as in Norway[105] and Japan.[106] Elsewhere in Scandinavia, however, only 2% of women above 60 years of age had an elevated serum TSH; this study was unusual as it found more hyperthyroidism than hypothyroidism in the population studied.[107] In an iodine-deficient part of Italy, only 1% of older women had a high serum TSH.[104] Clearly, geography plays some role, perhaps through the iodine content of the diet. These data consistently confirm the greater prevalence of thyroid failure in older women than older men, both of whom have a higher prevalence than do younger adults.

One cannot ignore those already diagnosed and treated as hypothyroid. A substantial fraction (up to one third[23]) are undertreated, as shown by a clearly raised serum TSH, and can be included in hypothyroidism's prevalence.

There are only limited data on the incidence of new thyroid failure in older persons. Our unpublished data indicate that, in normal persons over 60 years of age, about 0.5% per year will develop a clearly raised serum TSH (>10 mU/L). In those with a slightly raised serum TSH (>5 to <10 mU/L) on initial testing, the risk of developing a clearly raised value is ten times higher (5% per year.)

## Screening, Case-Finding, and Recommendations

Neither screening nor case-finding has clinical value unless there is a net benefit to the individual and, even then, the value cannot be judged unless both the prevalence and the incidence are reasonably well known and the individual or the public perceives the benefit to be worth the cost. Even with the best data, one cannot avoid thought and judgment on the question of cost vs. benefit.

Few physicians are involved in community-based screening, but the prevalence and incidence data just discussed help in judging the value of case-finding, whether or not it is more effective than screening.[2] The components of a good case-finding or screening process are (1) a disorder that is not exceedingly rare, is detectable, persists long enough to be present at the time of testing, and is useful for the patient to know about; (2) a test with a reasonably high predictive value (not just a high sensitivity and specificity); (3) a treatment that helps; (4) an approach to follow-up; and (5) a cost that is seen as reasonable. The bulk of hypothyroidism in older persons is subclinical by definition and, for the physician, is uncovered by systematic case-finding. It is not rare, it is easily detectable with a good test, and good follow-up can be planned. The critical issue is whether or not treatment helps. As indicated previously, the data are not complete, particularly for older persons, but physicians must make reasonable judgments in the face of some uncertainty. In those with raised serum TSH and "normal" serum $T_4$ levels, treatment leads to improvement in symptoms, when carefully sought, and in cardiac function. A reasonable extrapolation suggests that there would be at least equal benefit in older persons with a raised serum TSH and a low serum $T_4$. Properly adjusted treatment with $T_4$ is unlikely to cause harm, despite current fears about osteoporosis, provided attention is paid to the cardiovascular system.

This approach implies a commitment to retest at some interval those who initially have normal or equivocal test results. Our preliminary data (given previously) indicate that it takes about 7 to 10 years for a normal older person to develop thyroid failure; retesting a normal person every 5 years or so might be sensible. However, a person with a slightly raised serum TSH probably should be retested annually.

As regards cost, charges for serum TSH and serum $T_4$ levels are major factors and somewhat shifting targets. Current charges are on the order of $10 to $30 for serum $T_4$ and $25 to $60 for serum TSH.[2, 108] It costs more to screen or case-find with the TSH assay than with the $T_4$ assay, but initial testing with serum $T_4$ misses diagnoses in many older patients. Actual costs, which are not the same as charges, need only be a fraction of this.[109] In community-based screening, both tests probably could be done for less than $10, including all overhead and collection costs.[110] In case-finding, costs could be decreased by measuring the serum $T_4$ only when the serum TSH is abnormal; the cost could be even less if the TSH assay were "piggy-backed" on tests already ordered.[111] Calculations of cost per case discovered and treated are usually charge-based,[2] as currently they must be when a physician sees a patient. However, it is not appropriate to apply the same calculation to community-based screening on a large scale. Furthermore, internists could make arrangements for lower charges by organizing large-scale testing with a cooperative laboratory, particularly since there is no need for rapid turnaround. The charge is ultimately negotiable and would be determined by the extent of public commitment. How much society is willing to pay is unclear, but, at present, other screening programs find cases of disease at an apparently acceptable cost of several thousand dollars each[111]; case-finding for hypothyroidism in older persons can cost much less.[109] I believe that the calculation of costs based on quality-adjusted life-years[109] is premature at present because of the need for better quantification of benefit from treatment and the inherent bias of this criterion against older persons.

**What Should the Physician Do?**—As a practical matter for the moment, one can assess everyone over 60 years of age for thyroid failure. Those with a clearly raised serum TSH (>10 mU/L) then could have their serum $T_4$ measured and be examined closely for signs and symptoms. One could treat some or all of these patients. The evidence, though strongly suggestive, is not so overwhelming as to allow one to be dogmatic. Whatever the choice, these patients must be followed at some interval, since many likely will become overtly hypothyroid. Those who have a normal or slightly raised (>5 to <10 mU/L) serum TSH could be retested as previously noted, or more frequently if risk factors were present.

My personal preference is to treat everyone with a serum TSH >10 mU/L who has even vague symptoms unless there is a clinical contraindication such as worsening angina. I am uncertain whether or not to treat those with a serum TSH >10 mU/L who have no findings whatever, but generally lean in favor of therapy. I treat no one with a serum TSH >5 to <10 mU/L unless there are some findings reasonably related to thyroid deficiency.

So that we know better what to do, all of us should encourage further work, remain attuned to journal reports that might define the problem better, or even help in doing some of these badly needed studies, as do physicians in the United Kingdom.

## Hyperthyroidism

### Causes and Risk Factors

Most hyperthyroidism in older persons, as in younger adults, is the result of Graves' disease, another autoimmune disorder. However, autonomously hypersecreting nodules, particularly when multiple, sometimes can cause hyperthyroidism and do so more often in older persons than in younger ones. As with hypothyroidism, there are risk factors for hyperthyroidism that can be obtained from the patient's history (Table 3).

### Diagnosis

One usually must measure serum TSH, because clinical findings in older hyperthyroid persons often are not clear-cut and the serum $T_4$, even when corrected for changes in binding proteins, either may not be clearly raised or may be raised nonspecifically. The only complaint may be weight loss, fatigue, or irritability, and there may be no goiter, tachycardia, tremor, or exophthalmos. Patients may appear placid or depressed in contrast to hyperactive younger patients.[112] Most do not have increased appetite, about one quarter have constipation, and a few of the oldest patients have none of the usual symptoms.[113, 114] A work-up for cancer is usually undertaken, until someone measures the serum $T_4$ or (better) TSH and recognizes hyperthyroidism. This so-called "masked" or "apathetic" hyperthyroidism is really typical in older persons; in a sense, much hyperthyroidism in this population is "subclinical."

Excess secretion of thyroid hormone causes a rise in the serum $T_4$, but it may not always rise out of the normal range of about 5 to 12 μg/dL (64 to 154nM). Nevertheless, hyperthyroidism is quite unlikely if the serum $T_4$ is less than 10 μg/dL (129nM).[114, 115] Furthermore, other factors, particularly those associated with hospitalization and acute or severe illness, can raise the serum $T_4$ in older persons,[116] as can drugs such as propranolol.[117] There may not be a raised serum $T_3$ in older hyperthyroid patients who have other illnesses[118]; hence, the absence of this finding does not exclude the disease.

## TABLE 3.
### Risk Factors for Hyperthyroidism

I. Past history.
  A. Atrial fibrillation.
  B. Multinodular
     goiter.
  C. Osteoporosis.
  D. Congestive
     failure,
     unexplained.
II. Family history.
  A. Any thyroid
     disease.
III. Current history.
  A. Amiodarone.
  B. Iodine.

A serum TSH <0.1 mU/L, usually below 0.05 mU/L, is the most sensitive diagnostic finding; all patients with hyperthyroidism are detected. The original radioimmunoassay cannot measure values this low, so a more sensitive assay is necessary. The immunoradiometric assays have a minimum detectable level of about 0.07 to 0.1 mU/L. Thus, a value around 0.1 mU/L can be measured, albeit often with low precision. The immunoradiometric assay for TSH is also reasonably specific (about 98%), but by itself does not have a high positive predictive value (12%) in older persons because most of those who have a serum TSH <0.1 mU/L with this assay do not have hyperthyroidism.[119] However, the more recent chemiluminescent assay has a minimum detectable level of 0.005 mU/L or less. Precision around 0.1 mU/L is high, and a value of <0.05 or <0.1 mU/L is reliably just that. When a chemiluminescent assay for TSH is used, the positive predictive value of this test alone rises from 12% to 33% and, when then combined with the criterion of a serum $T_4$ >10 μg/dL (129nM), the predictive value rises to 100% in outpatients (Sawin, unpublished data, 1990).

A variation of subclinical hyperthyroidism is the patient with no symptoms but with goiter, who has a serum TSH <0.1 mU/L and a serum $T_4$ in the normal range, sometimes <10 μg/dL.[120] How often this variant occurs in older persons is unknown (we have not yet seen it), and its significance for patient outcome is unclear. Nevertheless, young adults given enough $T_4$ to suppress serum TSH have a significant rise in serum $T_4$ without a fall in serum $T_3$,[121] suggesting that subclinical hyperthyroidism does expose the patient to excess thyroid hormone. There is, for practical purposes, no longer much need to assess the TSH response to thyrotropin-releasing hormone.

In hospitalized or acutely ill patients the serum TSH may be somewhat suppressed, confusing the diagnosis.[122] Use of the chemiluminescent assay helps, as those with nonthyroid illness are less likely to have a serum TSH <0.1 mU/L with this test than with the immunoradiometric assay, and most of those who do are >0.05 mU/L.[91] The use of a lower breakpoint, such as 0.01 mU/L,[91] is reasonable and would eliminate most of the problem, but would miss some hyperthyroid patients who can have values up to 0.06 mU/L[120] (Sawin, unpublished data, 1990).

Thus, in office patients, a serum TSH of >0.05 mU/L, and certainly one of >0.1 mU/L, excludes hyperthyroidism if the chemiluminescent assay is used.[90] A value of <0.05 mU/L, or occasionally >0.05 but <0.1 mU/L, indicates hyperthyroidism if the serum $T_4$ is >10 μg/dL (129nM)[90] (Sawin, unpublished data, 1991). In hospitalized patients, the same criteria can be used, but with a bit more caution.

## Consequences

Most concern about the hazards of hyperthyroidism focuses on the heart, bones, and mind. In extreme cases, untreated hyperthyroidism can kill, particularly older persons with other disease, and sometimes for no known reason,[123] although this should now be a rare event. The effects of hyperthyroidism on the heart are well known. Hyperthyroidism shortens the systolic time intervals[36] and causes tachycardia, which can be uncomfortable, but is less common in older persons. The abnormal systolic time intervals can even progress to an overt cardiomyopathy with congestive failure.[124]

Atrial fibrillation is clearly associated with hyperthyroidism. Note that only a small percentage of older persons with atrial fibrillation are hyperthyroid.[125, 126] On balance, the standard practice of testing all older persons with atrial fibrillation for hyperthyroidism is reasonable; the yield will be small, but there is an effective treatment that may obviate untoward events such as stroke. In addition to osteoporosis, hyperthyroidism occasionally can be related to fracture.[127] No one knows how common this is in older persons.

That hyperthyroidism can cause psychiatric symptoms is clear, but what of the reverse? How often are psychiatric patients found to be hyperthyroid? As with hypothyroidism, older studies used serum $T_4$ as the main marker for the disease. A transiently raised serum $T_4$ is not unusual in acutely ill psychiatric patients.[48] The prevalence of hyperthyroidism is probably not more than 1% to 2% in younger psychiatric patients.[48] It might be higher in older persons, but there are no data to indicate this is so.

## Treatment

The choice of treatment is still open to some discussion; one can use antithyroid drugs (in the United States, propylthiouracil [PTU] or methimazole), radioiodine, or surgery. Since a radioiodine uptake should be done in anyone with hyperthyroidism to rule out spontaneously reversible disease (e.g., iodide-induced disease or thyroiditis), a scan often is done at the same time. This allows discovery of an autonomous nodule(s), if one is present.

Whether the hyperthyroidism is due to Graves' disease or to nodular goiter (and the two are not always easy to separate), therapy can begin with antithyroid drugs. They work fairly quickly and provide a greater chance of avoiding hypothyroidism. While there are no controlled studies to support the practice, most practitioners in the United States prefer to use radioiodine as initial therapy in older persons, particularly if the gland is nodular when larger doses may be needed. A variation is to give larger doses (e.g., 15 mCi or 555 mBq) to all patients to induce hypothyroidism intentionally, and then to give everyone oral $T_4$.[128] Only a rare patient now has thyroidectomy.

If the hyperthyroidism was not evident initially ("subclinical"), but later was thought to be related to a clinical finding such as weight loss or atrial fibrillation, treatment should be provided, since there is good reason to expect benefit. Abnormal systolic time intervals,[129] cardiomyopathy, and tachycardia revert to normal with successful treatment. While atrial fibrillation may not revert to sinus rhythm after therapy of hyperthyroidism in all older persons,[126] it will revert in a substantial fraction.[125] However, if there are no related clinical findings even on close study, most would not treat until clinical evidence appeared. However, because there are no data on the long-term consequences of this variant of subclinical hyperthyroidism, no one really knows what to do. At the least, careful follow-up is needed.

Everyone who is treated must be followed for life. Recurrence or, more commonly, hypothyroidism can appear years later, no matter what therapy is used,[130] and must be found. Note that the serum TSH often remains suppressed long after the patient has become euthyroid, so this is not a good measure of continued hyperthyroidism. One must follow the serum $T_4$ (it should be somewhere in the normal range) and any clinical findings present at diagnosis. Weight gain during the treatment of an older hyperthyroid person, though often unwelcome, is a good indicator of the euthyroid state.

## Prevalence and Incidence

Hyperthyroidism is clearly more common in women than in men, although the actual prevalence is a bit uncertain. Studies based on a raised serum $T_4$ probably give misleadingly high rates, as older persons can have a raised $T_4$ due to causes other than hyperthyroidism.

Prevalence rates of new spontaneous hyperthyroidism in older persons can be as high as 0.8% to 1.9%, based initially on serum TSH values of <0.1 mU/L.[107, 131] These are unusually high rates, several times higher than those of other large-scale surveys, e.g., 0.3% of all adults[103] or 0.1% of older persons (Sawin, unpublished data, 1991). Most likely, the higher rates are due to the inclusion of older individuals with low serum TSH but without hyperthyroidism.[119, 132] Using the chemiluminescent assay for TSH as well as ensuring that the serum $T_4$ is >10 μg/dL (129nM) will clarify the problem. At present, the prevalence of hyperthyroidism in the United States among older persons is at least an order of magnitude less than that of hypothyroidism.

With clinical findings and/or serum protein-bound iodine (PBI) or $T_4$ as the main determinants, the incidence rate of hyperthyroidism in all adults is in the range of 0.02% to 0.06% per year, with women having about three times the rate of men (0.04% to 0.09% per year vs. 0.01 to 0.03% per year). The rate is not substantially higher in older persons, if at all.[133-135] Our own data (unpublished, 1991) are incomplete, but also indicate no increase in incidence above 60 years of age, although the incidence may increase with age in England.[136] The question of whether or not the incidence of hyperthyroidism increases with age is confounded by the fact that, while hyperthyroidism due to Graves' disease does not increase with age, that due to nodular goiter does.[137] Perhaps when nodular goiter is more common in a population, it is more likely that older persons will become hyperthyroid.[138] Data indicating incidence rates in women of 0.2% to 0.3% per year,[103] or in older persons of 1.0% per year[139] seem too high; possibly, the criteria need reexamination or these populations were selected in some way.

## Screening, Case-Finding, and Recommendations

The same criteria for good screening and case-finding in hypothyroidism apply to hyperthyroidism. The main differences are that hyperthyroidism is much less common in older persons and that subclinical hyperthyroidism in the complete absence of symptoms is less well defined as to its bodily effects and thus to its need for treatment.

As both the prevalence and incidence of hyperthyroidism in older persons, as assessed with modern assays, are so low, screening or case-finding seems unjustified. However, if the approach suggested for detecting hypothyroidism in older persons is used, in practice, all individuals above 60 years of age would have serum TSH measured, preferably with a chemiluminescent assay. Those few with a serum TSH of <0.1 mU/L, and certainly those with one of <0.05 mU/L, should be questioned closely, examined, and have a serum $T_4$ measurement performed. If the serum $T_4$ is >10 µg/dL, hyperthyroidism is highly likely. Whether or not these patients are treated, all should be followed carefully.

## References

1. Horsley V: Relation of the thyroid gland to general nutrition. *Lancet* 1886; 1:3–5.
2. Helfand M, Crapo IM: Screening for thyroid disease. *Ann Intern Med* 1990; 112:840–849.
3. Braverman LE, Dawber NA, Ingbar SH: Observations concerning the binding of thyroid hormones in sera of normal subjects of varying ages. *J Clin Invest* 1966; 45:1273–1279.

4. Gaffney GW, Gregerman RI, Shock NW: Relationship of age to the thyroidal accumulation, renal excretion and distribution of radioiodide in euthyroid man. J Clin Endocrinol Metab 1962; 22:784–794.

5. Oddie TH, Meade JH Jr, Fisher DA: An analysis of published data on thyroxine turnover in human subjects. J Clin Endocrinol Metab 1966; 26:425–436.

6. Olsen T, Laurberg P, Weeke J: Low serum triiodothyronine and high serum reverse triiodothyronine in old age: An effect of disease not age. J Clin Endocrinol Metab 1978; 47:1111–1115.

7. Burrows AW, Cooper E, Shakespear RA, et al: Low serum L-T$_3$ levels in the elderly sick: Protein binding, thyroid and pituitary responsiveness, and reverse T$_3$ concentrations. Clin Endocrinol (Oxf) 1977; 7:289–300.

8. Harman SM, Wehmann RE, Blackman MR: Pituitary-thyroid hormone economy in healthy aging men: Basal indices of thyroid function and thyrotropin responses to constant infusions of thyrotropin releasing hormone. J Clin Endocrinol Metab 1984; 58:320–326.

9. van Coevorden A, Laurent E, Decoster C, et al: Decreased basal and stimulated thyrotropin secretion in healthy elderly men. J Clin Endocrinol Metab 1989; 69:177–185.

10. Williams ED, Doniach I: The post-mortem incidence of focal thyroiditis. J Pathol 1962; 83:255–264.

11. Baker BA, Gharib H, Markowitz H: Correlation of thyroid antibodies and cytologic features in suspected autoimmune thyroid disease. Am J Med 1983; 74:941–944.

12. Sawin CT, Bigos S, Land S, et al: The aging thyroid. Relationship between elevated serum thyrotropin level and thyroid antibodies in elderly patients. Am J Med 1985; 79:591–595.

13. Dingle PR, Ferguson A, Horn DB, et al: The incidence of thyroglobulin antibodies and thyroid enlargement in a general practice in north-east England. Clin Exp Immunol 1966; 1:277–284.

14. Hawkins BR, Dawkins RL, Burger HG, et al: Diagnostic significance of thyroid microsomal antibodies in randomly selected population. Lancet 1980; 2:1057–1059.

15. Manoussakis MN, Tzioufas AG, Silis MP, et al: High prevalence of anticardiolipin and other autoantibodies in a healthy elderly population. Clin Exp Immunol 1987; 69:557–565.

16. Hall R, Dingle PR, Roberts DF: Thyroid antibodies: A study of first degree relatives. Clin Genet 1972; 3:319–324.

17. Bastenie PA, Bonnyns M, Neve P, et al: Clinical and pathological significance of asymptomatic atrophic thyroiditis. Lancet 1967; 1:915–919.

18. Hatterer JA, Kocsis JH, Stokes PE: Thyroid function in patients maintained on lithium. Psychiatry Res 1988; 26:249–257.

19. Evered DC, Ormston BJ, Smith PA, et al: Grades of hypothyroidism. Br Med J [Clin Res] 1973; 1:657–673.

20. Barnett DB, Greenfield AA, Howlett PJ, et al: Discriminant value of thyroid function tests. Br Med J [Clin Res] 1973; 2:144–147.

21. Bahemuka M, Hodkinson HM: Screening for hypothyroidism in elderly inpatients. Br Med J [Clin Res] 1975; 2:601–603.

22. Sawin CT, Castelli WP, Hershman JM, et al: The aging thyroid. Thyroid deficiency in the Framingham study. Arch Intern Med 1985; 145:1386–1388.

23. Sawin CT, Geller A, Hershman JM, et al: The aging thyroid. The use of thyroid hormone in older persons. JAMA 1989; 261:2653–2655.

24. Wong ET, Bradley SG, Schultz AL: Elevations of thyroid-stimulating hormone during acute nonthyroidal illness. *Arch Intern Med* 1981; 141:873-875.
25. Stryker TD, Molitch ME: Reversible hyperthyrotropinemia, hyperthyroxinemia, and hyperprolactinemia due to adrenal insufficiency. *Am J Med* 1985; 79:271-276.
26. Hamburger JI, Meier DA, Szpunar WE: Factitious elevation of thyrotropin in euthyroid patients. *N Engl J Med* 1985; 313:267-268.
27. Rosenthal MJ, Hunt WC, Garry PJ, et al: Thyroid failure in the elderly. *JAMA* 1987; 258:209-213.
28. Gordin A, Lamberg B-A: Natural course of symptomless autoimmune thyroiditis. *Lancet* 1975; 2:1234-1238.
29. Nyström E, Bengtsson C, Lindquist O, et al: Thyroid disease and high concentration of serum thyrotrophin in a population sample of women. A four-year follow-up. *Acta Med Scand* 1981; 210:39-46.
30. Lazarus JH, Burr ML, McGregor AM, et al: The prevalence and progression of autoimmune thyroid disease in the elderly. *Acta Endocrinol (Copenh)* 1984; 106:199-202.
31. Ridgway EC, Cooper DS, Walker H, et al: Peripheral responses to thyroid hormone before and after L-thyroxine therapy in patients with subclinical hypothyroidism. *J Clin Endocrinol Metab* 1981; 53:1238-1242.
32. Cooper DS, Halpern R, Wood LC, et al: L-thyroxine therapy in subclinical hypothyroidism. A double-blind, placebo-controlled trial. *Ann Intern Med* 1984; 101:18-24.
33. Bell GM, Todd WTA, Forfar JC, et al: End-organ responses to thyroxine therapy in subclinical hypothyroidism. *Clin Endocrinol (Oxf)* 1985; 22:83-89.
34. Nyström E, Caidahl K, Fager G, et al: A double-blind cross-over 12-month study of L-thyroxine treatment of women with 'subclinical' hypothyroidism. *Clin Endocrinol (Oxf)* 1988; 29:63-76.
35. Caldwell G, Gow SM, Sweeting VM, et al: A new strategy for thyroid function testing. *Lancet* 1985; 1:1117-1119.
36. Young RT, Van Herle AJ, Rodbard D: Improved diagnosis and management of hyper- and hypothyroidism by timing the arterial sounds. *J Clin Endocrinol Metab* 1976; 42:330-340.
37. Higgins WH: The heart in myxedema: Correlation of physical and postmortem findings. *Am J Med Sci* 1936; 191:80-88.
38. Steinberg AD: Myxedema and coronary artery disease. A comparative autopsy study. *Ann Intern Med* 1968; 68:338-344.
39. Vanhaelst L, Neve P, Bastenie PA: Heart and coronary artery disease in hypothyroidism. *Am Heart J* 1968; 76:845-848.
40. Bansal SK, Sahi SP, Basu SK, et al: Hypothyroidism in elderly males—an under diagnosis. *Br J Clin Pract* 1986; 40:17-18.
41. Tièche M, Lupi GA, Gutzwiller F, et al: Borderline low thyroid function and thyroid autoimmunity. Risk factors for coronary heart disease? *Br Heart J* 1981; 46:202-206.
42. Tunbridge WMG, Evered DC, Hall R, et al: Lipid profiles and cardiovascular disease in the Whickham area with particular reference to thyroid failure. *Clin Endocrinol (Oxf)* 1977; 7:495-508.
43. Peters JP, Man EB: The interrelations of serum lipids in patients with thyroid disease. *J Clin Invest* 1943; 22:715-720.
44. Caron Ph, Calazel C, Parra HJ, et al: Decreased HDL cholesterol in subclin-

ical hypothyroidism: The effect of L-thyroxine therapy. *Clin Endocrinol (Oxf)* 1990; 33:519–523.

45. Bastenie PA, Bonnyns M, Vanhaelst L, et al: Preclinical hypothyroidism: A risk factor for coronary heart disease. *Lancet* 1971; 1:203–204.

46. Streeten DHP, Anderson GH Jr, Howland T, et al: Effects of thyroid function on blood pressure. Recognition of hypothyroid hypertension. *Hypertension* 1988; 11:78–83.

47. Sanders V: Neurologic manifestations of myxedema. *N Engl J Med* 1962; 266:547–551, 599–603.

48. Cohen KL, Swigar ME: Thyroid function screening in psychiatric patients. *JAMA* 1979; 242:254–257.

49. Gold MS, Pottash ALC, Extein I: Hypothyroidism and depression. *JAMA* 1981; 245:1919–1922.

50. Smith JS, Kiloh LG: The investigation of dementia: Results in 200 consecutive admissions. *Lancet* 1981; 1:824–827.

51. Sweer L, Martin DC, Ladd RA, et al: The medical evaluation of elderly patients with major depression. *J Gerontol* 1988; 43:M53–M58.

52. Ladenson PW, Goldenheim PD, Ridgway EC: Prediction and reversal of blunted ventilatory responsiveness in patients with hypothyroidism. *Am J Med* 1988; 84:877–883.

53. Grunstein RR, Sullivan CE: Sleep apnea and hypothyroidism: Mechanisms and management. *Am J Med* 1988; 85:775–779.

54. Dorwart BB, Schumacher HR: Joint effusions, chondrocalcinosis and other rheumatic manifestations in hypothyroidism. *Am J Med* 1975; 59:780–790.

55. Evered D, Young ET, Ormston BJ, et al: Treatment of hypothyroidism: A reappraisal of thyroxine therapy. *Br Med J [Clin Res]* 1973; 3:131–134.

56. Carr D, McLeod DT, Parry G, et al: Fine adjustment of thyroxine replacement dosage: Comparison of the thyrotrophin-releasing hormone test using a sensitive thyrotrophin assay with measurement of free thyroid hormones and clinical assessment. *Clin Endocrinol (Oxf)* 1988; 28:325–333.

57. Felicetta JV: The aging thyroid. How it affects diagnosis and treatment in the elderly. *Consultant* 1990; 30:59–71 (Sept).

58. Sawin CT, Chopra D, Azizi F, et al: The aging thyroid. Increased prevalence of elevated serum thyrotropin levels in the elderly. *JAMA* 1979; 242:247–250.

59. Crowley WF, Ridgway EC, Bough EW, et al: Noninvasive evaluation of cardiac function in hypothyroidism. *N Engl J Med* 1977; 296:1–6.

60. Forfar JC, Wathen CG, Todd WTA, et al: Left ventricular performance in subclinical hypothyroidism. *Q J Med* 1985; 57:857–865.

61. Ooi TC, Whitlock RML, Frengley PA, et al: Systolic time intervals and ankle reflex time in patients with minimal serum TSH elevation: Response to triiodothyronine therapy. *Clin Endocrinol (Oxf)* 1980; 13:621–627.

62. Tibaldi J, Barzel US: Thyroxine supplementation. Method for the prevention of clinical hypothyroidism. *Am J Med* 1985; 79:241–244.

63. Drinka PJ, Nolton WE: Subclinical hypothyroidism in the elderly: To treat or not to treat? *Am J Med Sci* 1988; 295:125–128.

64. Levine HD: Compromise therapy in the patient with angina pectoris and hypothyroidism. *Am J Med* 1980; 69:411–418.

65. Keating FR Jr, Parkin TW, Selby JB, et al: Treatment of heart disease associated with myxedema. *Prog Cardiovasc Dis* 1961; 3:364–381.

66. Hay IA, Duick DS, Vlietstra RE, et al: Thyroxine therapy in hypothyroid pa-

tients undergoing coronary revascularization: A retrospective analysis. *Ann Intern Med* 1981; 95:456–457.

67. Weinberg AD, Brennan MD, Gorman CA, et al: Outcome of anesthesia and surgery in hypothyroid patients. *Arch Intern Med* 1983; 143:893–897.

68. Toh SH, Claunch BC, Brown PH: Effect of hyperthyroidism and its treatment on bone mineral content. *Arch Intern Med* 1985; 145:883–886.

69. Coindré J-M, David J-P, Rivière L, et al: Bone loss in hypothyroidism with hormone replacement. A histomorphometric study. *Arch Intern Med* 1986; 146:48–53.

70. Ribot C, Tremollieres F, Pouilles JM, et al: Bone mineral density and thyroid hormone therapy. *Clin Endocrinol (Oxf)* 1990; 33:143–153.

71. Ross DS, Neer RM, Ridgway EC, et al: Subclinical hyperthyroidism and reduced bone density as a possible result of prolonged suppression of the pituitary-thyroid axis with L-thyroxine. *Am J Med* 1987; 82:1167–1170.

72. Paul TL, Kerrigan J, Kelly AM, et al: Long-term L-thyroxine therapy is associated with decreased hip bone density in premenopausal women. *JAMA* 1988; 259:3137–3141.

73. Ahmann AJ, Solomon B, Duncan WE, et al: Normal bone mineral density (BMD) in premenopausal women on suppressive doses of L-thyroxine. *Ann Mtg Amer Thyr Assn* 1987; T-21.

74. Wartofsky L: Osteoporosis: A growing concern for the thyroidologist. *Thyroid Today* 1988; 11(4):1–11.

75. Jackson IMD, Cobb WE: Why does anyone still use desiccated thyroid USP? *Am J Med* 1978; 64:284–288.

76. Surks MI, Schadlow AR, Oppenheimer JH: A new radioimmunoassay for plasma L-triiodothyronine: Measurements in thyroid disease and in patients maintained on hormonal replacement. *J Clin Invest* 1972; 51:3104–3113.

77. Read DG, Hays MT, Hershman JM: Absorption of oral thyroxine in hypothyroid and normal man. *J Clin Endocrinol Metab* 1970; 30:798–799.

78. Fish LH, Schwartz HL, Cavanaugh J, et al: Replacement dose, metabolism, and bioavailability of levothyroxine in the treatment of hypothyroidism. *N Engl J Med* 1987; 316:764–770.

79. Rees-Jones RW, Rolla AR, Larsen PR: Hormonal content of thyroid replacement preparations. *JAMA* 1980; 243:549–550.

80. Stoffer S, Szpunar WE: Potency of levothyroxine products. *JAMA* 1984; 251:635–636.

81. Sawin CT, Surks MI, London M, et al: Oral thyroxine: Variation in biologic action and tablet content. *Ann Intern Med* 1984; 100:641–645.

82. Hennessey JV, Burman KD, Wartofsky L: The equivalency of two 1-thyroxine preparations. *Ann Intern Med* 1985; 102:770–773.

83. Curry SH, Gums JG, Williams LL, et al: Levothyroxine sodium tablets: Chemical equivalence and bioequivalence. *Drug Intell Clin Pharm* 1988; 22:589–591.

84. Sawin CT, Herman T, Molitch ME, et al: Aging and the thyroid. Decreased requirement for thyroid hormone in older hypothyroid patients. *Am J Med* 1983; 75:206–209.

85. England ML, Hershman JM: Serum TSH concentration as an aid to monitoring compliance with thyroid hormone therapy in hypothyroidism. *Am J Med Sci* 1986; 292:264–266.

86. Kabadi UM: Optimal daily levothyroxine dose in primary hypothyroidism. *Arch Intern Med* 1989; 149:2209–2212.

87. Rosenbaum RL, Barzel US: Levothyroxine replacement dose for primary hypothyroidism decreases with age. *Ann Intern Med* 1982; 96:53–55.
88. Gow SM, Caldwell G, Toft AD, et al: Relationship between pituitary and other target organ responsiveness in hypothyroid patients receiving thyroxine replacement. *J Clin Endocrinol Metab* 1987; 64:364–370.
89. Helfand M, Crapo IM: Monitoring therapy in patients taking levothyroxine. *Ann Intern Med* 1990; 113:450–454.
90. Ross DS, Daniels GH, Gouveia D: The use and limitations of a chemiluminescent thyrotropin assay as a single thyroid function test in an outpatient endocrine clinic. *J Clin Endocrinol Metab* 1990; 71:764–769.
91. Spencer CA, LoPresti JS, Patel A, et al: Applications of a new chemiluminometric thyrotropin assay to subnormal measurement. *J Clin Endocrinol Metab* 1990; 70:453–460.
92. Rendell M, Salmon D: 'Chemical hyperthyroidism': The significance of elevated serum thyroxine levels in L-thyroxine treated individuals. *Clin Endocrinol (Oxf)* 1985; 22:693–700.
93. Jennings PE, O'Malley BP, Griffin KE, et al: Relevance of increased serum thyroxine concentrations associated with normal serum triiodothyronine values in hypothyroid patients receiving thyroxine: A case for "tissue thyrotoxicosis." *Br Med J [Clin Res]* 1984; 289:1645–1647.
94. Hedley AJ: Myxoedema. *Practitioner* 1972; 208:349–359.
95. Northcutt RC, Stiel JN, Hollifield JW, et al: The influence of cholestyramine on thyroxine absorption. *JAMA* 1969; 208:1857–1861.
96. Demke DM: Drug interaction between thyroxine and lovastatin. *N Engl J Med* 1989; 321:1341–1342.
97. Rizzolo PJ, Fischer PM: Re-evaluation of thyroid hormone status after long-term hormone therapy. *J Fam Pract* 1982; 6:1017–1021.
98. Jones A: Evaluation of long term thyroid replacement treatment. *Br Med J [Clin Res]* 1985; 291:1476–1478.
99. Krugman LG, Hershman JM, Chopra IJ, et al: Patterns of recovery of the hypothalamic-pituitary-thyroid axis in patients taken off chronic thyroid therapy. *J Clin Endocrinol Metab* 1975; 41:70–80.
100. Molitch ME, Spare SV, Arnold GL, et al: Pituitary-thyroid function after cessation of prolonged thyroid suppression. *N Engl J Med* 1976; 295:231.
101. Lloyd WH, Goldberg IJL: Incidence of hypothyroidism in the elderly. *Br Med J [Clin Res]* 1961; 2:1256–1259.
102. Jefferys PM: The prevalence of thyroid disease in patients admitted to a geriatric department. *Age Ageing* 1972; 1:33–37.
103. Tunbridge WMG, Evered DC, Hall R, et al: The spectrum of thyroid disease in a community: The Whickham survey. *Clin Endocrinol (Oxf)* 1977; 7:481–493.
104. Robuschi G, Safran M, Braverman LE, et al: Hypothyroidism in the elderly. *Endocr Rev* 1987; 8:142–153.
105. Brochmann H, Bjoro T, Gaarder PI, et al: Prevalence of thyroid dysfunction in elderly subjects. A randomized study in a Norwegian rural community (Naeroy). *Acta Endocrinol* 1988; 117:7–12.
106. Okamura K, Ueda K, Sone H, et al: A sensitive thyroid stimulating hormone assay for screening of thyroid functional disorder in elderly Japanese. *J Am Geriatr Soc* 1989; 37:317–322.
107. Falkenberg M, Kagedal B, Norr A: Screening of an elderly female population for hypo- and hyperthyroidism by use of a thyroid hormone panel. *Acta Med Scand* 1983; 214:361–365.

108. de los Santos ET, Starich GL, Mazzaferri EL: Sensitivity, specificity, and cost-effectiveness of the sensitive thyrotropin assay in the diagnosis of thyroid disease in ambulatory patients. *Arch Intern Med* 1989; 149:526–532.

109. Nolan JP, Tarsa NJ, DiBenedetto G: Case-finding for unsuspected thyroid disease: Costs and health benefits. *Am J Clin Pathol* 1985; 83:346–355.

110. Mitchell ML: Personal communication, 1990.

111. Epstein KA, Schneiderman LJ, Bush JW, et al: The 'abnormal' screening serum thyroxine ($T_4$): Analysis of physician response, outcome, cost and health effectiveness. *J Chron Dis* 1981; 34:175–190.

112. Levine SA, Sturgis CC: Hyperthyroidism masked as heart disease. *Bost Med Surg J* 1924; 190:233–237.

113. Davis PJ, Davis FB: Hyperthyroidism in patients over the age of 60 years. *Medicine* 1974; 53:161–181.

114. Tibaldi JM, Barzel US, Albin J, et al: Thyrotoxicosis in the very old. *Am J Med* 1986; 81:619–622.

115. Kaplan MM, Utiger RD: Diagnosis of hyperthyroidism. *Clin Endocrinol Metab* 1978; 7:97–113.

116. Britton KE, Ellis SM, Miralles JM, et al: Is "$T_4$ toxicosis" a normal biochemical finding in elderly women? *Lancet* 1975; 2:141–142.

117. Cooper DS, Daniels GH, Ladenson PW, et al: Hyperthyroxinemia in patients treated with high-dose propranolol. *Am J Med* 1982; 73:867–871.

118. Schlienger JL, Chabrier G, Stephan F, et al: Hyperthyroidie à triiodothyroninémie basse et à $T_3$ inverse élévee. *Nouvelle Presse Méd* 1980; 9:29–30.

119. Sawin CT, Geller A, Kaplan MM, et al: Low serum thyrotropin (thyroid-stimulating hormone) in older persons without hyperthyroidism. *Arch Intern Med* 1991; 151:165–168.

120. Ross DS, Ardisson LJ, Meskell MJ: Measurement of thyrotropin in clinical and subclinical hyperthyroidism using a new chemiluminescent assay. *J Clin Endocrinol Metab* 1989; 69:684–688.

121. Sawin CT, Hershman JM, Chopra IJ: The comparative effect of $T_4$ and $T_3$ on the TSH response to TRH in young adult men. *J Clin Endocrinol Metab* 1977; 44:273–278.

122. Spratt DI, Pont A, Miller MB, et al: Hyperthyroxinemia in patients with acute psychiatric disorders. *Am J Med* 1982; 73:41–48.

123. Parker JLW, Lawson DH: Death from thyrotoxicosis. *Lancet* 1973; 2:894–895.

124. Ikram H: The nature and prognosis of thyrotoxic heart disease. *Q J Med* 1985; 54:19–28.

125. Rohmer V, Hocq R, Galland F, et al: Hyperthyroidie fruste revelée par un trouble du rythme auriculaire. *Presse Méd* 1984; 13:145–148.

126. Tajiri J, Hamasaki S, Shimada T, et al: Masked thyroid dysfunction among elderly patients with atrial fibrillation. *Jpn Heart J* 1986; 27:183–190.

127. Francis RM: Thyrotoxicosis presenting as fracture of femoral neck. *Br Med J [Clin Res]* 1982; 285:97–98.

128. Kendall-Taylor P, Keir MJ, Ross WM: Ablative radioiodine therapy for hyperthyroidism: Long-term follow-up study. *Br Med J [Clin Res]* 1984; 289:361–363.

129. Merillon JP, Passa P, Chastre J, et al: Left ventricular function and hyperthyroidism. *Br Heart J* 1981; 46:137–143.

130. Wood LC, Ingbar SH: Hypothyroidism as a late sequela in patients with

Graves disesase treated with antithyroid agents. *J Clin Invest* 1979; 64:1429-1436.

131. Bagchi N, Brown TR, Parish RF: Thyroid dysfunction in adults over age 55 years. *Arch Intern Med* 1990; 150:785–787.

132. Kirkegaard C, Bregengard C: Assessment of the clinically significant TSH response to TRH in patients with nodular goitre. *Horm Metab Res* 1988; 20:357–359.

133. Furszyfer J, Kurland LT, McConahey WM, et al: Graves' disease in Olmsted County, Minnesota. 1935 through 1967. *Mayo Clin Proc* 1970; 45:636–644.

134. Barker DJP, Phillips DIW: Current incidence of thyrotoxicosis and past prevalence of goitre in 12 British towns. *Lancet* 1984; 2:567–570.

135. Haraldsson A, Gudmundsson ST, Larusson G, et al: Thyrotoxicosis in Iceland 1980–1982. *Acta Med Scand* 1985; 217:253–258.

136. Phillips DIW, Barker DJP, Smith BR, et al: The geographical distribution of thyrotoxicosis in England according to the presence or absence of TSH-receptor antibodies. *Clin Endocrinol (Oxf)* 1985; 23:283–287.

137. Berglund J, Christensen BS, Hallengren B: Total and age-specific incidence of Graves' thyrotoxicosis, toxic nodular goitre and solitary toxic adenoma in Malmo 1970–1974. *J Intern Med* 1990; 227:137–141.

138. Brownlie BEW, Wells JE: The epidemiology of thyrotoxicosis in New Zealand: Incidence and geographical distribution in North Canterbury, 1983–1985. *Clin Endocrinol (Oxf)* 1990; 33:249–259.

139. Ronnov-Jessen V, Kirkegaard C: Hyperthyroidism—a disease of old age? *Br Med J [Clin Res]* 1973; 1:41–43.

# Chylomicronemia Syndrome

## Alan Chait, M.D.

Professor of Medicine, Department of Medicine, Division of Metabolism,
Endocrinology and Nutrition, University of Washington School of Medicine,
Seattle, Washington

## John D. Brunzell, M.D.

Professor of Medicine, Department of Medicine, Division of Metabolism,
Endocrinology and Nutrition, University of Washington School of Medicine,
Seattle, Washington

## Editor's Introduction

The chylomicron syndrome represents one of the most acute and dramatic consequences of any lipid disorder. If misdiagnosed, the pancreatitis that frequently accompanies this syndrome can lead to pancreatic destruction and death. Moreover, the more subtle consequences of hyperchylomicronemia, including the neurologic, psychiatric and dermatologic manifestations, may be similarly misinterpreted for years, leading to confusion and prolonged misdiagnosis. In their review of this important disorder, Drs. Chait and Brunzell present a very up-to-date description of the pathogenesis of the chylomicron syndrome and describe its many clinical manifestations. They discuss their own extensive experience with this disorder and particularly emphasize the important role of secondary factors such as diabetes, estrogen therapy, and alcohol in unmasking one of the underlying genetic defects that is probably required for the chylomicron syndrome to occur. Perhaps most important, as this review documents, it is critical that every clinician be able to recognize this disorder since it is probably the most easily treatable of the hyperlipidemias, almost always responding to the simple institution of a low fat diet.

*Marvin D. Siperstein, M.D., Ph.D.*

Chylomicrons are lipoproteins that transport exogenous triglycerides and cholesterol. They are formed in the intestinal mucosa in response to the consumption of dietary fat and are large, multimolecular complexes that contain triglyceride, cholesterol, phospholipid, and apolipoproteins (apos), primarily apo B-48. Chylomicrons enter the bloodstream via the thoracic duct. In plasma they acquire apo C-II, which shuttles to chylomicrons from high-density lipoproteins (HDL). Apo C-II increases the activity of lipoprotein lipase, an enzyme that hydrolyzes the triglycerides in chylomicrons and very–low-density lipoproteins (VLDL). Chylomicrons and VLDL compete for lipoprotein lipase in situations in which the availability of this enzyme is rate-limiting.[1] When lipoprotein lipase approaches saturation due to VLDL accumulation, chylomicron clearance can be impaired (see later).

Chylomicrons normally start appearing in the bloodstream within 1 to 3 hours after the consumption of a fat-containing meal. Most are cleared from the blood within approximately 8 hours. The rate of clearance is dependent, to some extent, on the baseline triglyceride level; the higher the level, the slower the clearance rate.[1] Plasma obtained after the traditional 12- to 14-hour fast usually does not contain any readily detectable chylomicrons, even in the presence of mild to moderate hypertriglyceridemia. Defects in chylomicron clearance lead to their accumulation in plasma.

A classification system for disorders of lipoprotein metabolism appeared in 1967, based on the separation of plasma lipoprotein classes by paper electrophoresis,[2] in which chylomicrons remain at the origin. The presence of fasting chylomicronemia was described in two lipoprotein patterns. In the type I hyperlipoproteinemia pattern, chylomicrons were the predominant lipoproteins that accumulated in plasma. This pattern was shown to occur when lipoprotein lipase was absent on a genetic basis, but now is known to be also due to apo C-II deficiency. The combined accumulation of chylomicrons and VLDL was designated the type V hyperlipoproteinemia pattern. It originally was described as being either primary (i.e., familial or occurring in the absence of known secondary causes of hyperlipidemia) or secondary to several underlying conditions that could affect plasma lipoprotein metabolism. During the past several years, there has been an emphasis on classifying plasma lipoprotein disorders on the basis of the precise metabolic or molecular defect responsible for the hyperlipidemia.[3] This approach has resulted in an improved understanding of the multiple disorders that are associated with chronic chylomicronemia and the mechanisms responsible for the chylomicron accumulation.

Chronic chylomicronemia is associated with a constellation of symptoms and signs known as the chylomicronemia syndrome.[4, 5] This chapter will (1) review the metabolic abnormalities that can lead to chronic chylomicronemia, (2) discuss their clinical consequences, and (3) provide an approach to the diagnosis and management of patients with this syndrome.

## Definition and Diagnosis

Chronic chylomicronemia is defined as the persistent presence of chylomicrons in plasma, including the fasted state. The chylomicronemia syndrome is present when clinical consequences arise from chronic chylomicronemia.

Chylomicrons are difficult to separate from endogenous VLDL by routine laboratory procedures. The major structural apo in chylomicrons is a truncated form of apo B, termed apo B-48, while apo B-100 is the major structural apo of VLDL. Measurement of these separate forms of apo B in triglyceride-rich lipoproteins is a research procedure and cannot be performed routinely in clinical practice. As mentioned earlier, chylomicrons remain at the origin when electrophoresis of plasma is performed.[2] Although of historic interest, this test is insensitive and has little role in present-day clinical practice. Chylomicrons also have been separated from VLDL using 3% polyvinylpyrrolidone columns.[6] This procedure is time-consuming and is not used in clinical laboratories. Chylomicrons float after overnight storage at 4° C, leading to the appearance of a creamy supernatant over a more turbid infranatant of VLDL. Hence, a simple "refrigerator test," in which plasma is inspected for the presence of a visible chylomicron supernatant fraction after overnight storage in the refrigerator, has been widely used to diagnose the presence of chylomicronemia. Although of some value, this test also is not very specific or sensitive and has limited utility. In addition, the accumulation of chylomicrons sometimes is so marked that no infranatant VLDL fraction is visible.

Chylomicrons have been shown nearly always to be present in plasma when triglyceride levels exceed 1,000 mg/dL[5] (Fig 1). Since other tests for their detection are either unreliable or expensive and time-consuming, determination of the presence of chylomicrons by evaluation of plasma triglyceride levels probably is the most viable method currently available in clinical practice. For practical purposes, chylomicrons can be assumed to present at fasting triglyceride concentrations >1,000 mg/dL. The other simple method of detection that has practical utility is the inspection of plasma. In view of their large size, the triglyceride-rich lipoproteins, chylomicrons, and VLDL scatter light, leading to a turbid, milky, or creamy appearance of plasma. A simple rule of thumb is that plasma having the appearance of nonfat (skim) milk has a triglyceride concentration of approximately 1,000 mg/dL. Plasma with the appearance of regular (4% fat) milk has a triglyceride concentration approximately equal to that of milk (i.e., 4,000 mg/dL). The inspection of plasma for turbidity is useful when clinical decisions need to be made before plasma triglyceride measurements are available (see below).

Thus, no practical, reliable, and sophisticated laboratory tests are routinely available for the detection of chylomicronemia, and reliance must be placed on plasma triglyceride levels and the awareness that chylomicrons always accumulate above certain triglyceride levels. Nonetheless, the plasma triglyceride level provides sufficient information to diagnose chylomicronemia clinically. However, sophisticated tests are available and must be used to determine the precise cause of the chylomicronemia, since the therapeutic approach chosen varies with different causes.

## Causes of the Chylomicronemia Syndrome

### Autosomal Recessive Disorders: Primary Lipoprotein Lipase Deficiency and Apo C-II Deficiency

Familial lipoprotein lipase deficiency is a rare autosomal recessive trait characterized by the complete absence of active enzyme protein in all tis-

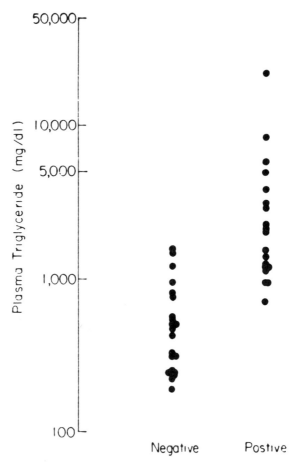

**FIG 1.**
Presence or absence of chylomicronemia as a function of fasting plasma triglyceride levels. (From Brunzell JD, Bierman EL: *Med Clin North Am* 1982; 66:455. Used by permission.)

sues, leading to massive hypertriglyceridemia from birth and recurrent episodes of pancreatitis.[7] Similar syndromes also are caused by inborn defects in other components of the lipoprotein lipase system.

Hydrolysis of triglyceride from chylomicrons and VLDL in vivo requires both lipoprotein lipase and its activator apo C-II. Defects of either of these proteins are associated with severely decreased triglyceride removal and massive hypertriglyceridemia.[8] In infants and young children, the triglyceride accumulates primarily in the form of chylomicrons, which are of dietary origin. In older patients, a defect in the removal of VLDL triglyceride (i.e., endogenous triglyceride) also becomes apparent. Both lipoprotein lipase and apo C-II deficiency are autosomal recessive disorders; often consanguinity can be documented. A number of defects in the genes for lipoprotein lipase[9] (Fig 2) and apo C-II[8] have been described. Individuals with a defect in the secretion of lipoprotein lipase from adipocytes,[10] absent lipoprotein lipase activity in selected tissues only,[11] and an inhibitor of lipoprotein lipase activity on a familial basis[12] also have been described. The latter two groups usually have less severe hypertriglyceridemia and become symptomatic later in life than do those with the classic form of lipoprotein lipase deficiency.

Infants with lipoprotein lipase deficiency usually demonstrate intolerance to fatty foods at an early age. As these children grow, they learn to avoid certain high-fat foods, such as whole milk. Abdominal pain, often with pancreatitis, can occur in association with the accumulation of chylomicron triglyceride. Eruptive xanthomas occur on extensor surfaces, notably the elbows, knees, and buttocks, and are pathognomonic for chronic chylomicronemia. Hepatomegaly and, occasionally, splenomegaly occur because of the accumulation of lipid-laden foam cells. The hepatosplenomegaly rapidly diminishes on a fat-free diet, which clears the chylomicronemia. Eruptive xanthomas also disappear with time after lowering of chylomicron levels. Other signs and symptoms seen with chronic chylomicronemia also may occur (see later).

A young child who presents with abdominal pain and is found to have lactescent plasma should be evaluated for a genetic abnormality in lipoprotein lipase. Other causes of chylomicronemia before adulthood usually are due to the occurrence of a common form of hypertriglyceridemia with di-

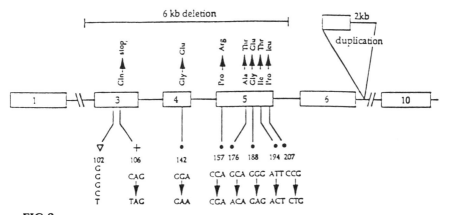

**FIG 2.**
The location and postulated defect of the reported mutations in the lipoprotein lipase gene that result in lipoprotein lipase deficiency. The *closed circles* indicate missense mutation, the *plus signs* indicate a premature stop codon, and the *triangles* indicate frameshift insertion. Also included are a 6-kilobase deletion involving exons 3, 4, and 5, and a 2-kilobase gene reduplication involving exon 6 and the following intron. (From Henderson HE, Ma Y, Hassan MF, et al: *J Clin Invest*, 1991; 87:2005. Used by permission.)

abetes or glucocorticoid therapy. Absent or diminished activity of lipoprotein lipase can be demonstrated in biopsies of adipose tissue or muscle, or in plasma after the administration of intravenous heparin. Apo C-II deficiency or defective apo C-II[8] can be detected by radioimmunoassay, by gel electrophoresis of the plasma apos, or by testing the ability of the patient's plasma to activate purified lipoprotein lipase. These studies need to be performed in a specialized lipoprotein laboratory.

In all of the inborn errors of the lipoprotein lipase–related triglyceride removal system associated with chylomicronemia, a decrease in the total intake of dietary fat is absolutely indicated. A total intake of polyunsaturated and saturated fat as low as 10% of calories often is required. Medium-chain triglycerides can be used to prepare some foods, since their unesterified fatty acids leave the gut via the portal vein rather than the thoracic duct, as does chylomicron triglyceride. The goal is to decrease the amount of dietary fat to a level low enough to eliminate the occurrence of abdominal pain and eruptive xanthomata. These individuals also can be sensitive to agents that raise endogenous VLDL levels, such as alcohol or glucocorticoids, and to the hypertriglyceridemic effects of pregnancy.

## Primary Plus Secondary Forms of Hypertriglyceridemia

Genetic disorders that can cause chylomicronemia independently are rare. By far the most common situation leading to chronic chylomicronemia is the coexistence of one or more secondary causes of hypertriglyceridemia with a common genetic form of hypertriglyceridemia.[13, 14] Most cases of the chylomicronemia syndrome encountered in routine clinical practice are due to the presence of an underlying disease or the use of a drug known to elevate plasma triglyceride levels in a subject with a genetic form of hypertriglyceridemia. When sufficient family members of index patients with chronic chylomicronemia have been available for study, either monogenic familial hypertriglyceridemia (FHTG) or familial combined hyperlipidemia (FCHL) has been shown to exist in these families.[14] The presence of these forms of genetic hyperlipidemia in the absence of secondary factors does not lead to such marked elevations of plasma triglyceride levels. In many instances, insufficient family members have been available to permit the precise diagnosis of a specific genetic disorder, although hyperlipidemia frequently has been detected in those members who were accessible.[14] However, affected family members have markedly lower plasma triglyceride levels than do the index patients (Fig 3), who also have coexisting secondary forms of hypertriglyceridemia.[14] Thus, it seems reasonable to assume that subjects in these families with persistent chylomicronemia have inherited one or the other of these two genetic forms of hypertriglyceridemia and concomitantly have an acquired form of hypertriglyceridemia secondary to an underlying disease (Table 1) or the use of drugs that raise plasma triglyceride levels (Table 2). Thus, it appears that these genetic and secondary forms of hypertriglyceridemia interact to result in marked hypertriglyceridemia and chylomicronemia by mechanisms that will be discussed

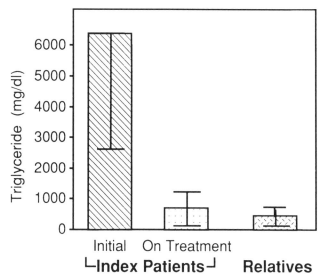

**FIG 3.**
Mean triglyceride levels in index patients with chylomicronemia, before and during lipid-lowering therapy, and in their hyperlipidemic relatives. (Adapted from Chait A, Brunzell JD: *Metabolism* 1983; 32:209.)

later. Rarely, secondary forms of hypertriglyceridemia can interact with remnant removal disease, also known as broad beta disease or type III hyperlipoproteinemia, to lead to marked hypertriglyceridemia and the chylomicronemia syndrome.[14]

Since no molecular, genetic, or biochemical techniques for the diagnosis

**TABLE 1.**
**Diseases That Can Lead to**
**Secondary Hypertriglyceridemia**

| Common | Rare |
|---|---|
| Diabetes mellitus | Cushing's syndrome |
| Hypothyroidism | Acromegaly |
| Uremia and/or dialysis | Systemic lupus erythematosus |
| | |
| Renal transplantation | Dysglobulinemias |
| Nephrotic syndrome | Lipodystrophy |
| Rapid weight gain | Glycogenosis type I |
| | Addison's disease |

**TABLE 2.**
**Drugs That Raise Plasma**
**Triglycerides**

Alcohol
Diuretics
β-Adrenergic blocking agents
Estrogens
Glucocorticoids
Retinoids
Cimetidine (rarely)

of these genetic forms of hypertriglyceridemia are available yet, patients have to be characterized on clinical grounds. A clue to the genetic diagnosis may be obtained by taking a careful family history. The presence of a strongly positive family history of premature atherosclerotic cardiovascular disease suggests the existence of FCHL, whereas a negative history points to FHTG, since the former appears to increase the risk of atherosclerotic disease markedly, while the latter may not.[15] This information is useful in patient management, since the approach to the patient with a presumptive diagnosis of FCHL will include measures to prevent both features of the chylomicronemia syndrome and atherosclerotic complications.

## Usual Secondary Causes

**Diabetes Mellitus.**—The most frequently encountered secondary forms of hypertriglyceridemia in chylomicronemic patients are non–insulin-dependent diabetes and the use of triglyceride-raising drugs, particularly diuretics and β-blockers. In our experience, over one half of patients with plasma triglycerides >2,000 mg/dL have both diabetes and a common genetic form of hypertriglyceridemia.

Mild to moderate hypertriglyceridemia is common in both non–insulin-dependent and insulin-dependent diabetes,[16–19] due to both the impaired clearance and the excessive input[20–25] of triglycerides into plasma. However, chylomicronemia may be more persistent in non–insulin-dependent (type II) diabetes than in the insulin-dependent (type I)[14] form. The observation of marked hypertriglyceridemia or lipemic plasma on routine laboratory testing or presentation with features of the chylomicronemia syndrome can lead to the detection of previously undiagnosed diabetes mellitus. Alternatively, marked hypertriglyceridemia sometimes is detected during the evaluation and follow-up of a known diabetic patient. In such cases, the patient often is untreated, on "diet-therapy" alone, or in poor metabolic control. The institution of treatment, whether with oral hypoglycemic agents or insulin, usually results in the reduction of triglyceride levels, although metabolic disturbances secondary to diabetes may take 6 to 12 weeks to correct.

While chylomicronemia can be observed in insulin-dependent diabetics, especially during ketoacidosis,[26] the hypertriglyceridemia that frequently is encountered in this type of diabetes usually is mild to moderate, rather than severe. One explanation for the difference in prevalence of chylomicronemia between insulin-dependent and non–insulin-dependent diabetes relates to the difference in clinical manifestations of these two distinct disorders. Because of the symptoms associated with its development, insulin-dependent diabetes seldom goes untreated for any length of time. However, patients with non–insulin-dependent diabetes often go undiagnosed and untreated for years when symptoms are absent or mild. Thus, abnormalities of triglyceride metabolism consequent on diabetes (see later) are unlikely to be present for any length of time in insulin-dependent diabetes, but may be present for months or even years in non–insulin-dependent diabetes.

**Drugs.**—The next most common cause of hypertriglyceridemia that interacts with genetic forms of hypertriglyceridemia to lead to chronic chylomicronemia is the use of lipid-raising drugs (Fig 4). The triglyceride-raising effects of diuretics and β-blockers, when administered to normolipidemic

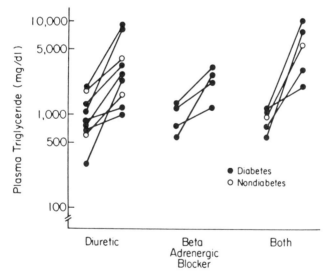

**FIG 4.**
Effect of diuretics and β-adrenergic blocking agents on plasma triglyceride levels in patients who have a familial form of hypertriglyceridemia with *(closed circles)* and without *(open circles)* treated diabetes mellitus. (From Brunzell JD, Chait A: Lipoprotein metabolism, in Rifkin H, Porte D Jr (eds): *Ellenberg and Rifkin's Diabetes Mellitus,* ed 4. New York, Elsevier Science Publishers, 1990, pp 756-767. Used by permission.)

or mildly hyperlipidemic patients, has been documented amply and widely.[27-31] However, the importance of diuretics and β-blockers in interacting with familial forms of hyperlipidemia to result in chronic chylomicronemia has been appreciated only recently. The triglyceride-raising effects of diuretics are observed with both thiazide and loop diuretics. While diuretic-induced hypertriglyceridemia appears to be less common with indapamide in normotriglyceridemic subjects,[28] the presence of an underlying familial form of hypertriglyceridemia may make such individuals more sensitive to the lipid-raising effects of these drugs. Although β-blockers with intrinsic sympathomimetic activity and combined α- and β-blocking agents have fewer adverse effects on plasma lipids and lipoproteins than do the other nonselective and cardioselective β-blocking agents, they also can increase triglycerides further in individuals with genetic forms of hypertriglyceridemia.

Several other drugs that can cause mild to moderate hypertriglyceridemia in normolipidemic individuals can lead to marked hypertriglyceridemia and chylomicronemia in individuals with familial forms of hypertriglyceridemia (see Table 2). Of particular concern, estrogens can interact with familial forms of hypertriglyceridemia and lead to chylomicronemia, even at the low doses used as replacement therapy in the postmenopausal state. In view of the increasingly widespread use of estrogens postmenopausally for the prevention of osteoporosis and cardiovascular disease,[32] it is likely that the incidence of estrogen-induced hypertriglyceridemia will increase. The chylomicronemia syndrome also can occur with the use of birth control pills in susceptible females in their reproductive years.[33, 34] The use of glucocorticoids, even by depot injection, can lead to the development of chylomicronemia.[35] Cis-retinoic acid, which is now used widely for the treatment of acne, is known to cause hypertriglyceridemia[36, 37]; it also can cause chylomicronemia when used by individuals with genetic forms of hypertriglyceridemia.[38] It is of interest that many drugs for which pancreatitis is a reported side effect[5] also raise plasma triglycerides. Since chylomicronemia can cause acute pancreatitis (see later), it would not be surprising if the pancreatitis that has been reported in association with these drugs was due to chylomicronemia induced by their use in genetically susceptible individuals.

**Alcohol.**—Alcohol has long been associated with hypertriglyceridemia, often marked, in certain individuals. The consumption of ethanol leads to an increase in the hepatic output of VLDL in both animals and humans.[39, 40] However, the observations that plasma triglyceride levels frequently are abnormal even after the cessation of alcohol consumption,[14, 41] that it is difficult to induce hypertriglyceridemia by administering alcohol as a replacement for other caloric sources,[42] and that alcohol consumption and abuse is frequent in chylomicronemic subjects with hypertriglyceridemia in their families[14] suggest that alcohol-induced hypertriglyceridemia also is due to the interaction of ethanol with an underlying genetic form of hypertriglyceridemia.[5, 14] It is important to appreciate that the consumption of quantities of alcohol that are considered socially acceptable may be sufficient to raise triglycerides markedly in individuals with familial forms of hypertriglyceridemia. Furthermore, consideration should be given to the possibility that pancreatitis occurring in the face of alcohol use or abuse may be due on occasion to ethanol-induced chylomicronemia rather than to the more commonly observed direct toxic effect of ethanol on the pancreas. Thus, plasma triglycerides should be evaluated before pancreatitis is attributed to alcohol directly.

**Other Acquired Forms of Hypertriglyceridemia.**—Several other acquired forms of hypertriglyceridemia (see Table 1) can interact with familial forms of hypertriglyceridemia and occur in association with the chylomicronemia syndrome. Any condition or drug that increases VLDL input into plasma or inhibits triglyceride clearance can interact with genetic forms of hypertriglyceridemia to saturate triglyceride removal systems and lead to marked hypertriglyceridemia. Other commonly encountered conditions that interact with genetic forms of hypertriglyceridemia to cause chylomicronemia include *hypothyroidism, chronic renal failure, and the nephrotic syndrome*. The role of obesity is controversial; a history of recent weight gain often is obtained at the time of diagnosis of chylomicronemia, although obesity in the absence of acute weight gain is unlikely to be the sole acquired condition that interacts with familial forms of hypertriglyceridemia to lead to chylomicronemia. Sometimes multiple potential causes of hypertriglyceridemia may be present in a single patient, in which case the relative importance and contribution of each may be difficult to gauge. Theoretically, the combination of two or more secondary forms of hypertriglyceridemia or drugs that affect triglyceride metabolism could lead to chylomicronemia and the features of the chylomicronemia syndrome, by mechanisms described later. However, careful evaluation of families of chylomicronemic patients in whom secondary forms of hypertriglyceridemia appear to be playing a contributing role usually reveals hyperlipidemia.[13, 14] We know of no reported case in which secondary forms of hypertriglyceridemia alone account for chronic chylomicronemia where a familial form of hypertriglyceridemia has been excluded with certainty.

## Rare Secondary Causes

A number of rare metabolic and other disorders have been reported to be associated with hypertriglyceridemia and even chylomicronemia. Because of their low frequency, it is difficult to know whether these conditions are chance associations or real causes of hypertriglyceridemia. Several conditions that have been associated with hypertriglyceridemia on occasion are listed in Table 1. In many cases, their mechanism of action on triglyceride metabolism is unknown.

## Causes of Hypertriglyceridemia in Childhood

Marked hypertriglyceridemia rarely presents in childhood. Most individuals with primary lipoprotein lipase deficiency present in the first year of life with symptoms and signs attributable to chylomicronemia, although some occasionally present in their early adult years.[7] Lipemic plasma detected by the clinical laboratory is another frequent mode of presentation in childhood. Sometimes it is due to the infusion of lipid emulsions at the time of or shortly before the blood draw. If lipids are not being infused, the hypertriglyceridemia usually is due to the underlying condition for which the child had blood drawn and is likely to be clinically obvious. Disorders such as diabetes, nephrotic syndrome, renal failure, glycogen storage disease, and liver failure, and the use of drugs such as glucocorticoids, diuretics, and cis-retinoic acid can be associated with hypertriglyceridemia and even chylomicronemia. Mild to moderate hypertriglyceridemia also can occur in childhood, sometimes on a genetic basis, although both FHTG and FCHL usually manifest for the first time in the third decade.[43] Since individuals with these genetic forms of hyperlipidemia tend to be asymptomatic, they are unlikely to be detected unless blood is drawn for some other reason.

## Pathogenesis of the Chylomicronemia

Chylomicrons accumulate in plasma when their clearance is impeded. When lipoprotein lipase is defective as a result of a genetic mutation, or in the rare circumstance in which there is a genetic defect in its cofactor, apo C-II, the hydrolysis of triglycerides in both chylomicrons and VLDL is impaired.[7, 8] Both of these lipoprotein classes accumulate, although the reason for the predominance of chylomicrons is unclear. When lipoprotein lipase is either absent or entirely nonfunctional, the triglyceride-rich lipoproteins must be removed from plasma by alternative mechanisms, including uptake by the reticuloendothelial system.

In most cases of chronic chylomicronemia, i.e., those due to the coexistence of a common familial form of hypertriglyceridemia with a secondary form of the disorder or a triglyceride-raising drug, lipoprotein lipase activity is either normal or only partially impaired.[5] However, the lipoprotein lipase–related triglyceride removal system approaches saturation at triglyceride concentrations of 700 to 1,000 mg/dL.[1] Overproduction of VLDL in both FHTG and FCHL leads to hypertriglyceridemia,[44] although increased VLDL can affect chylomicron removal at much lower triglyceride levels in this curvilinear catabolic process. Chylomicrons that enter plasma after the ingestion of a fat-containing meal then accumulate due to the saturation of triglyceride removal systems and can reside in plasma for days rather than the hours that they do when triglyceride removal systems are functioning normally. Examples of acquired disorders that reversibly impair lipoprotein lipase activity or triglyceride removal are diabetes mellitus,[20, 25, 45] hypothyroidism,[46, 47] chronic renal failure,[48] and the nephrotic syndrome.[49] The overproduction of triglycerides occurs with obesity,[50] ethanol,[39, 40] and the use of estrogens[51] and glucocorticoids.[52] Non–insulin-dependent diabetes can lead to both the overproduction of triglycerides and impaired triglyceride removal.[20–24, 53] The pathogenesis of the hypertriglyceridemia associated with the use of diuretics and β-blockers is not known for certain.

In the rare case in which neither primary defects in lipoprotein lipase nor underlying causes of hypertriglyceridemia are detectable, the chylomicronemia probably results from the saturation of normal triglyceride removal systems by marked VLDL overproduction.

## Incidence and Prevalence

The prevalence of triglyceride levels >2,000 mg/dL is difficult to determine directly. In the Lipid Research Clinics' Prevalence Study, 7 individuals with this magnitude of hypertriglyceridemia were found among a population of 39,090 randomly screened white adults.[54] This represents 1.8 individuals per 10,000 population, or about 20,000 such individuals in the adult white population of the United States. Although no such data are available, it would appear that the prevalence and incidence of marked hypertriglyceridemia is more common in diabetes clinics and in hospitals that care for large numbers of alcoholics.

Of the 123 patients with marked hypertriglyceridemia (defined as plasma triglycerides >2,000 mg/dL) whose families have been studied in our laboratory, all but 13 have a known acquired cause of hypertriglyceridemia. Five of these 13 were found to have a genetic absence of lipoprotein lipase activity. Five other subjects had a genetic form of hypertriglyceridemia in the families of both parents. Thus, these individuals could be homozygous for a common familial form of hypertriglyceridemia or mixed heterozygotes for two disorders. In the remaining 3 cases, the cause of the hypertriglyceridemia remains unknown. One might expect that at least 0.5% of untreated diabetic patients (with low lipoprotein lipase) could have the chylomicronemia syndrome, since they can inherit independently the two common genetic forms of hypertriglyceridemia,[55] which have conservative estimated prevalences of 0.2% for FHTG and 0.3% for FCHL.[43]

Undoubtedly, families exist in which marked hypertriglyceridemia is present in multiple relatives who do not have defects in lipoprotein lipase. The nature of the disorder in these cases remains obscure. Individuals with marked hypertriglyceridemia (many with plasma triglycerides >2,000 mg/dL) and hypertriglyceridemic relatives have been designated as having "familial type V hyperlipoproteinemia."[56, 57] However, a high frequency of secondary forms of hypertriglyceridemia was noted among these individuals. Furthermore, triglyceride levels rarely exceeded 2,000 mg/dL, and acquired disorders were less common among their relatives. This suggests that many of the index patients with familial "type V hyperlipoproteinemia" come from families with one of the common genetic hypertriglyceridemias. Therefore, it is likely that these authors may have been studying the same phenomenon that we are describing here, i.e., chylomicronemia syndrome in the index patient caused by the interaction of a common familial disorder with an acquired form of hyperlipidemia. True "familial type V hyperlipoproteinemia" may be more common in probands who typically have triglyceride levels between 1,000 and 2,000 mg/dL in the absence of acquired causes of hypertriglyceridemia.[2]

## Clinical Manifestations

### Usual Symptoms and Signs

The chylomicronemia syndrome is characterized by a constellation of symptoms and signs that exist singly or in various combinations (Table 3).[4, 5] Their manifestations do not appear to be related to the magnitude of the hypertriglyceridemia, since some individuals with plasma triglyceride levels as high as 30,000 mg/dL can be asymptomatic, while others with much lower levels exhibit marked clinical consequences. Clinical manifestations do not appear to occur at plasma triglyceride levels <2,000 mg/dL.

### Pancreatitis and Chylomicronemia

The most important clinical consequence of chronic chylomicronemia is acute pancreatitis, which can lead to considerable morbidity and even mortality. The association of abdominal pain and pancreatitis in familial lipoprotein lipase deficiency has long been appreciated,[2] suggesting a role for the chylomicronemia in the etiology of the pancreatitis. However, it used to be thought that pancreatitis resulted in the hypertriglyceridemia in most other situations in which the two were associated.[58] The opposite actually appears to be the case.[13, 59, 60] In patients admitted with possible pancre-

TABLE 3.
**Clinical and Laboratory Characteristics of the Chylomicronemia Syndrome**

| Clinical | Laboratory |
|---|---|
| Acute pancreatitis | Lipemic plasma |
| Chronic abdominal pain | Plasma triglycerides >2,000 mg/dL |
| | |
| Hepatosplenomegaly | Low $P_{O_2}$* |
| Eruptive xanthoma | Low hemoglobin* |
| Lipemia retinalis | Increased bilirubin* |
| "Carpal-tunnel–like" syndrome | Low serum sodium |
| Peripheral neuropathy | Abnormal thyroid function tests* |
| | |
| Memory loss/dementia | |
| Dyspnea | |

*Can be due to artifacts associated with marked hypertriglyceridemia.

atitis in whom plasma triglyceride levels were measured, the distribution of triglyceride was bimodal, with one group below 800 mg/dL and the other above 2,000 mg/dL[5] (Fig 5). Individuals in the higher mode were found to have genetic and acquired forms of hypertriglyceridemia, as described earlier. Since these patients had other well-described explanations for their very high triglyceride levels, it is unlikely that the pancreatitis caused them rather than resulted from them. The observation that therapy to maintain lower triglyceride levels resulted in these patients remaining pain-free and having a strikingly reduced incidence of recurrent episodes of pancreatitis[5, 13] provides further evidence that markedly elevated triglycerides cause rather than result from pancreatitis. Further, a plausible mechanism exists by which chylomicronemia can cause pancreatitis (see later).

The pancreatitis caused by the chylomicronemia syndrome may be difficult to distinguish clinically from acute pancreatitis of other causes. It usually has an acute onset and often is recurrent, occasionally leading to total pancreatic necrosis and death. Mild fat malabsorption can occur, but pancreatic calcification does not appear to be common. The abdominal pain of the chylomicronemia syndrome usually is midepigastric and migrates through to the back, but it also can be present in the right or left upper abdominal quadrants or even the mid-anterior chest. The severity of the pain can range from a mild, bothersome ache to pain that causes severe incapacitation. It has been difficult to determine if the pain that occurs in the chylomi-

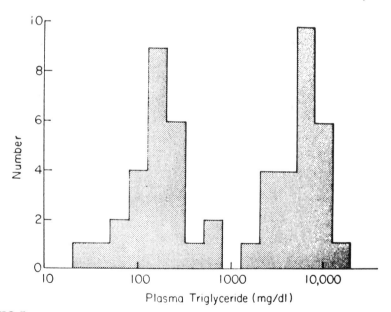

**FIG 5.**
Frequency distribution of plasma triglyceride levels in patients with possible pancreatitis in whom levels were measured during the peak of pain. (From Brunzell JD, Bierman EL: *Med Clin North Am* 1982; 66:455. Used by permission.)

cronemia syndrome always is due to classic pancreatitis, since both serum and urinary amylase levels sometimes are normal. Indeed, amylase levels even have been found to be in the normal range in some patients in whom pancreatitis has been documented at laparotomy.[13, 59, 61] However, many patients with severe pancreatitis due to the chylomicronemia syndrome will have elevated serum or urine amylase levels. Normal amylase levels in the presence of pancreatitis and marked hypertriglyceridemia might be due to interference with the assay by the elevated plasma lipids[62] or to an inhibitor present in the plasma and urine.[63, 64]

The diagnosis of chylomicron-induced pancreatitis can be made at the bedside by inspection of the plasma. Since the pancreatitis is believed to result directly from chronic chylomicronemia, the observation of markedly lipemic plasma in the presence of clinical pancreatitis is sufficient to diagnose chylomicron-induced pancreatitis; clear plasma rules out hypertriglyceridemia as the cause of the abdominal pain. Confirmation can be obtained by subsequent measurement of the plasma triglyceride level. It should be noted that triglyceride levels somewhat less than 2,000 mg/dL may be observed on occasion in patients with chylomicron-induced pancreatitis. In such cases, discontinuation of oral intake as a result of symptoms of the pancreatitis is likely to have resulted in a reduction of the levels from higher values. It is important to distinguish this from other causes of pancreatitis, since recognition and treatment of the hypertriglyceridemia leads to reduced morbidity and mortality from recurrent pancreatitis if plasma triglyceride can be maintained at levels somewhat less than 2,000 mg/dL.[13]

Hepatomegaly is found commonly with chronic chylomicronemia[65] as well as with many milder forms of hypertriglyceridemia. Splenomegaly is present less commonly, but the spleen can be extremely hard. The enlarged spleen can return to normal size with 1 week of lowering of triglyceride levels in patients with lipoprotein lipase deficiency who are placed on a very low fat diet.

Cutaneous manifestation in the form of eruptive xanthomata can occur in isolation or with other features of the syndrome. Eruptive xanthomata are raised, yellow, superficial, papular lesions surrounded by an erythematous base. They sometimes are misdiagnosed as molluscum contagiosum, occur predominantly on extensor surfaces and the buttocks, and rarely are found on the face, soles, or palms. The reason for this distribution is unknown, but may relate to pressure and mild trauma at these sites.

Lipemia retinalis refers to the ophthalmoscopic appearance of the retina in the presence of marked hypertriglyceridemia. Instead of dark vessels standing out against a pink background, the circulating chylomicrons impart a pale appearance to the optic vessels. The discovery of lipemia retinalis during routine ophthalmoscopic examination seldom leads to the diagnosis of chylomicronemia; rather, lipemia retinalis usually is observed with hindsight after the magnitude of the hypertriglyceridemia is known.

Psychoneurologic manifestations also are seen frequently as part of the chylomicronemia syndrome. They include paresthesias of the hands, which may be confused with a "carpal tunnel–like" syndrome, peripheral neuropathy,[66] and a reversible form of dementia that manifests mainly as memory loss, especially for recent events.[4, 67] These neurologic manifestations are all reversible on treatment of the chylomicronemia. Other clinical manifestations that have been described on occasion in association with hypertriglyceridemia are discussed later.

## Pathogenesis of Clinical Manifestations

Chylomicronemic pancreatitis is believed to result from chemical irritation to the pancreas from fatty acids and lysolecithin. These compounds are liberated by pancreatic lipases from the core and surface of chylomicrons circulating at high concentration in the capillaries of the exocrine pancreas. The cause of the more chronic type of abdominal pain that sometimes is seen in the chylomicronemia syndrome is unknown, but it may be chronic inflammatory changes in the pancreas or expansion of the liver capsule caused by fatty infiltration of the liver.

Chylomicrons and their remnants have been demonstrated both extracellularly and in macrophages in eruptive xanthomata.[68] Uptake by macrophages probably represents an alternative mechanism for chylomicron catabolism when lipoprotein lipase activity is either impaired or saturated. However, the reason for the accumulation of macrophages at the sites of distribution of these lesions is unknown.

The pathogenetic mechanisms of the psychoneuropathic manifestations are unknown.

## Rare Manifestations and Associated Artifacts

Both objective and subjective dyspnea have been noted in patients with chylomicronemia,[4] and symptoms resolve with lowering of plasma triglyceride levels. Because of the relationship between hyperlipidemia and angina, it was hypothesized that hypertriglyceridemia might impair both oxygen uptake from the lungs and oxygen delivery to tissues.[69] Subsequent studies concerning oxygenation in hyperlipidemia demonstrated arterial hypoxemia[70] and an increased affinity of hemoglobin for 2,3-diphosphoglycerate levels.[71] It now appears that these abnormalities were artifactual, related to the interference by lipemic plasma with the blood $O_2$ electrode[4] and with the measurement of hemoglobin levels.[72] Thus, the explanation for the dyspnea associated with the chylomicronemia syndrome remains unknown.

Other laboratory tests also can be misleading in the presence of marked hypertriglyceridemia. Chylomicrons may interfere directly with the measurement of amylase and hemoglobin levels, as noted earlier. Bilirubin levels also are artifactually elevated in the chylomicronemia syndrome; this may be a partial explanation for the hyperbilirubinemia seen in Zieve syndrome, in which alcoholism is associated with lipemia, jaundice, hemolytic anemia, and abdominal pain.[73] Chylomicrons also replace water volume, which leads to artifactual decreases in plasma components by dilution. For example, serum sodium levels are decreased from 2 to 4 mEq for each 1,000-mg/dL increase in plasma triglycerides,[74] although osmolality is normal. Thus, a variety of clinical and biochemical findings have been reported in association with the chylomicronemia syndrome, although some may be artifacts. The spectrum of symptoms, signs, and laboratory findings may be quite puzzling and tax the diagnostic acumen of the clinician.

## Therapy

### Treatment of Manifestations of the Chylomicronemia Syndrome

**Chylomicron-Induced Pancreatitis.**—In the acute stages, chylomicron-induced pancreatitis is treated identically to acute pancreatitis resulting from other causes such as alcohol and gallstones. Most important is that the patient should take nothing by mouth, especially fat-containing foods or nutritional supplements, since these will cause additional chylomicrons to enter plasma and delay recovery. Moderate acute caloric restriction will cause a rapid decrease in plasma triglyceride levels. Parenteral nutrition should be commenced early if a prolonged clinical course is anticipated. Lipid emulsions should not be used, since they are metabolized in plasma like chylomicrons. Since they compete with chylomicrons and VLDL for lipoprotein lipase, lipid emulsions could delay clearance of the triglyceride-rich lipoproteins further and thereby exacerbate the pancreatitis. The use of heparin to facilitate chylomicron clearance is not effective and might exacerbate hemorrhage into the pancreatic bed. Also, plasmapheresis to remove chylomicrons from plasma[75] is unnecessary, since it will clear spontaneously over the next few days if no further exogenous triglycerides are administered in the hypocaloric state. Triglycerides should be monitored or the plasma visually inspected at least daily; in most instances, plasma triglycerides fall gradually over a period of a few days, although usually not to normal levels. The residual hypertriglyceridemia often represents that which is due to the underlying genetic cause of hypertriglyceridemia. Plasma triglycerides sometimes fall to well within the normal range, even in the presence of a familial form of hyperlipidemia, presumably due to undernutrition resulting from the catabolic state associated with the acute illness. During the acute phase, treatment of any obvious secondary cause of hyperlipidemia can be commenced.

During the recovery phase, plasma triglycerides must be monitored carefully when foods, especially those containing fats, are reintroduced. During this phase, it is important to evaluate the patient carefully for all secondary forms of hyperlipidemia (see Table 1) and for the use of alcohol or other medications that may have played a contributing role (see Table 2). Laboratory tests should include a fasting blood glucose, thyroid function tests, liver function tests, and an evaluation of renal function, including testing for marked proteinuria. Some laboratory assays, such as thyroid function tests, may be inaccurate when performed on lipemic plasma. It is important to ensure that the clinical laboratory either clarifies the plasma prior to making these measurements or uses an assay that is not affected by marked hypertriglyceridemia. Medications that may have contributed to the development of the hypertriglyceridemia should be discontinued and substituted with lipid-neutral alternatives, where possible (see later).

After discharge, long-term outpatient follow-up is essential, since plasma triglycerides frequently increase again as patients gradually resume their usual habits. Patients usually are compliant with medications and dietary advice for a short while after an admission to the hospital for a serious illness such as pancreatitis. However, bad habits often resume with time, and triglyceride levels tend to increase again. While weight loss will result in a lowering of plasma triglyceride levels, most people regain lost weight with time.[76] A period of rapid weight gain often is observed after a substantial amount of weight loss, during which triglyceride levels can increase markedly and precipitate a further episode of acute pancreatitis. Because of the high recidivism rate following weight loss and occasional recurrent pancreatitis during periods of rapid weight gain, we do not advise patients routinely to attempt to lose substantial amounts of weight. If triglyceride levels remain high (>1,000 mg/dL) at the time of discharge or during outpatient follow-up, as often is the case, then drugs specifically to lower triglyceride levels are indicated (see later).

In the rare patient with primary lipoprotein lipase or apo C-II deficiency, the approach to treatment of the pancreatitis is similar, although a low-fat diet (ideally <10% of calories as fat) will be required.

**Eruptive Xanthomata.**—Eruptive xanthomata regress with correction of the elevated triglyceride levels. Within 6 weeks of triglyceride lowering, lesions appear much flatter and lose their yellow color. They disappear completely within several months. Since they always regress with adequate medical treatment, surgical removal or cryotherapy is not indicated.

**Other.**—The other, less common clinical manifestations of the chylomicronemia syndrome all are reversible with lowering of the markedly elevated plasma triglyceride levels. Thus, abnormal memory loss returns to baseline[4] and paresthesias disappear.

## Secondary Causes

Secondary causes of hypertriglyceridemia that are detected during patient work-up should be treated by whatever means indicated. For example, replacement of thyroid hormones in hypothyroidism will correct the metabolic disorder associated with the underlying disease. The use of insulin in the treatment of insulin-dependent diabetes is quite effective. Insulin should be used if indicated for the treatment of non–insulin-dependent diabetes, but our preference is for the use of oral hypoglycemic agents. Tryglyceride levels will occasionally increase with the use of insulin in patients with non–insulin-dependent diabetes. It is conceivable that patients who demonstrate this response have monogenic FHTG, in which an increase in hepatic triglyceride production[44] occurs, due to a defect in bile acid metabolism.[77] The rise in plasma triglycerides observed with insulin may result from a rapid increase in hepatic production of triglycerides, while the defect in lipoprotein lipase may take several months to revert completely to normal. Alternatively, hypertriglyceridemia following insulin therapy may reflect a unique sensitivity to factors that increase hepatic triglyceride synthesis in FHTG.[78]

These patients often are quite difficult to treat and sometimes have persistent and marked elevation of plasma glucose and triglyceride levels. We have seen 6 patients from a population of over 200 with plasma triglycerides >2,000 mg/dL whose plasma glucose and triglyceride levels are extremely difficult to control, despite seemingly adequate therapy for both the diabetes and the hyperlipidemia. In this situation, we have used phenformin 25 mg three times a day successfully in combination with lipid-lowering drugs. Although phenformin is available in most parts of the world, it is not in the United States and requires special Food and Drug Administration approval for use in this situation. Alternatively, lovastatin 20 mg in combination with insulin, an oral sulfonylurea, and a fibrate can maintain plasma triglycerides and glucose successfully at acceptable levels. Unfortunately, metformin does not seem to work as well as phenformin, despite its reported effect in lowering VLDL secretion.

Diuretic use should be minimized, if feasible. If they must be used, drugs such as indapamide and spironolactone have some advantage over the thiazide and loop diuretics. Lipid-neutral agents such as the calcium channel blockers can be used for the treatment of angina, and drugs such as angiotensin-converting enzyme inhibitors, calcium channel blockers, and α-adrenergic blocking agents can be used for the treatment of hypertension.[29-31]

## Specific Lipid-Lowering Therapy

The fibric acid derivatives are the most effective drugs for lowering lipid levels. Gemfibrozil and clofibrate, which should be administered in doses of 600 mg twice a day and 1,000 mg twice a day, respectively, presently are the only agents available in the United States, although several other fibrates are in widespread use in other parts of the world.

The use of lipid-lowering drugs in patients with primary lipoprotein lipase or apo C-II deficiency is controversial. However, the reduced input of VLDL that occurs with the use of fibrates[79] may lessen the burden on alternative triglyceride removal mechanisms.

Lowering of plasma triglyceride levels usually is associated with an increase in low-density lipoprotein (LDL) concentrations, often to abnormal levels. This may worsen the risk of developing cardiovascular complications, especially in the presence of FCHL. Therefore, particular attention should be given to other cardiovascular risk factors in an attempt to try to prevent atherosclerotic disease in these patients. Smoking should be discouraged vigorously, hypertension should be treated with lipid-neutral or beneficial drugs, and a low saturated fat, low-cholesterol diet should be applied. LDL levels should be monitored; if they rise abnormally, additional drugs specifically to lower them may be required in adult patients.

## Prevention of Recurrent Complications

Recurrent complications can be prevented by ensuring that triglyceride levels remain below 1,000 mg/dL at all times. This can be achieved by continued treatment of any underlying condition, avoidance of drugs known to raise plasma triglycerides, and use of fibrates where indicated. Patients with familial forms of hypertriglyceridemia, especially those known to have been chylomicronemic in the past, should be provided with a list of drugs that should not be used other than under careful medical supervision. Thus, diuretics, β-blockers, estrogens, and cis-retinoic acid should be avoided. Methods of contraception other than the birth control pill may need to be used by at-risk females. Even depot injection of glucocorticoids may elevate triglyceride levels significantly. Alcohol should be avoided entirely by at-risk patients, since even small amounts can raise the plasma triglycerides to a level at which removal systems are saturated.

Avoidance of recurrent complications in the patient with primary lipoprotein lipase or apo C-II deficiency is dependent on long-term compliance with a low-fat diet. The diet recommended, in which not more than 10% of calories come from fat, is difficult to consume long-term. However, patients with these disorders often suffer abdominal discomfort or develop eruptive xanthomata when they consume diets with a higher fat content and thus are relatively compliant. The use of medium-chain triglyceride oils can improve the palatability of the diet. Careful attention should be given to children with these disorders to ensure that nutrient intake is sufficient for optimal growth and development. The assistance of a qualified nutritionist is essential to help get the affected child through the difficult early years, during which peer pressure is an important determinant of eating patterns.

## Summary

This chapter has outlined the reasons for the development of marked elevations of triglycerides that can be associated with the chylomicronemia syndrome. The clinical features of the syndrome have been discussed, with particular emphasis on chylomicron-induced pancreatitis, since this can be life-threatening. An approach to the diagnosis and management of this syndrome has been provided, with emphasis on the need for long-term follow-up and compliance to keep plasma triglycerides to a reasonable level and thereby avoid recurrent clinical complications due to chronic chylomicronemia.

## References

1. Brunzell JD, Hazzard WR, Porte D Jr, et al: Evidence for a common saturable triglyceride removal mechanism for chylomicrons and very low density lipoproteins in man. *J Clin Invest* 1973; 52:1578.

2. Fredrickson DS, Levy RI, Lees RS: Fat transport in lipoproteins—an integrated approach to mechanisms and disorders. N Engl J Med 1967; 276:34.
3. Brunzell JD, Chait A, Bierman EL: Pathophysiology of lipoprotein transport. Metabolism 1978; 27:1109.
4. Chait A, Robertson HT, Brunzell JD: Chylomicronemia syndrome in diabetes mellitus. Diabetes Care 1981; 4:343.
5. Brunzell JD, Bierman EL: Chylomicronemia syndrome. Med Clin North Am 1982; 66:455.
6. O'Hara DD, Porte D Jr, Williams RH: Use of constant composition of polyvinylpyrrolidone columns to study the interaction of fat particles with plasma. J Lipid Res 1966; 7:264.
7. Brunzell JD: Lipoprotein lipase deficiency and other causes of the chylomicronemia syndrome, in Scriver CS, Beaudet AL, Sly WS, et al (eds): Metabolic Basis of Inherited Disease, ed 6. New York, McGraw-Hill, 1989, p 1165.
8. Santamarina-Fojo S, Brewer HB: The familial hyperchylomicronemia syndrome: New insights into underlying genetic defects. JAMA, in press.
9. Henderson HE, Ma Y, Hassan MF, et al: Amino acid substitution (Ile[194]→Thr) in exon 5 of the lipoprotein lipase gene causes lipoprotein lipase deficiency in three unrelated probands: Support for a multicentric origin. J Clin Invest 1991; 87:2005.
10. Fager G, Semb H, Enerbäck S, et al: Hyperlipoproteinemia type I in a patient with active lipoprotein lipase in adipose tissue and indications of defective transport of the enzyme. J Lipid Res 1990; 31:1187.
11. Brunzell JD, Chait A, Nikkila EA, et al: Heterogeneity of primary lipoprotein lipase deficiency. Metabolism 1980; 29:624.
12. Brunzell JD, Miller NE, Alaupovic P, et al: Familial chylomicronemia due to a circulating inhibitor of lipoprotein lipase activity. J Lipid Res 1983; 24:12.
13. Brunzell JD, Schrott HG: The interaction of familial and secondary causes of hypertriglyceridemia: Role in pancreatitis. Trans Assoc Am Physicians 1973; 86:245.
14. Chait A, Brunzell JD: Severe hypertriglyceridemia: Role of familial and acquired disorders. Metabolism 1983; 32:209.
15. Brunzell JD, Schrott HG, Motulsky AG, et al: Myocardial infarction in the familial forms of hypertriglyceridemia. Metabolism 1976; 25:313.
16. Brunzell JD, Chait A: Lipoprotein metabolism, in Rifkin H, Porte D Jr (eds): Ellenberg and Rifkin's Diabetes Mellitus, ed 4. New York, Elsevier Science Publishers, 1990, pp 756-767.
17. Brunzell JD, Chait A, Bierman EL: Plasma lipoproteins in diabetes mellitus. Diabetes Ann 1985; 1:463.
18. Laker MF: Plasma lipids and lipoproteins in diabetes mellitus. Diabetes Annual 1986; 2:267.
19. Laker MF: Plasma lipids and lipoproteins in diabetes mellitus. Diabetes Annual 1987; 3:459.
20. Brunzell JD, Porte D Jr, Bierman EL: Abnormal lipoprotein lipase mediated plasma triglyceride removal in untreated diabetes mellitus associated with hypertriglyceridemia. Metabolism 1979; 28:897.
21. Dunn FL, Raskin P, Bilheimer DW, et al: The effects of diabetic control on very low density lipoprotein triglyceride metabolism in patients with type II diabetes mellitus and marked hypertriglyceridemia. Metabolism 1984; 33:117.
22. Greenfield MS, Doberne L, Rosenthal M, et al: Lipid metabolism in non-insulin-dependent diabetes mellitus: Effects of glipizide therapy. Arch Intern Med 1982; 142:1498.

23. Howard BV, Reitman JS, Vasquez B, et al: Very low density lipoprotein triglyceride metabolism in non-insulin-dependent diabetes mellitus. *Diabetes* 1983; 32:271.

24. Kissebah AH, Alfarsi S, Evans DJ, et al: Integrated regulation of very low density lipoprotein triglyceride and apolipoprotein-B kinetics in non-insulin-dependent diabetes mellitus. *Diabetes* 1982; 31:217.

25. Pykalisto OJ, Smith PH, Brunzell JD: Human adipose tissue lipoprotein lipase: Comparison of assay methods and expression of activity. *J Clin Invest* 1975; 56:1108.

26. Bagdade JD, Bierman EL, Porte D Jr: The significance of basal insulin levels in the evaluation of the insulin response to glucose in diabetic and non-diabetic subjects. *J Clin Invest* 1967; 46:1549.

27. Chait A, Brunzell JD: Acquired hyperlipidemia (secondary dyslipoproteinemia). *Endocrinol Metab Clin North Am* 1990; 19:259.

28. Ames RP: The influence of non-beta-blocking drugs on the lipid profile: Are diuretics outclassed as initial therapy for hypertension? *Am Heart J* 1987; 114:998.

29. Rohlfing JJ, Brunzell JD: The effects of diuretics and adrenergic-blocking agents on plasma lipids. *West J Med* 1986; 145:210.

30. Weinberger MH: Antihypertensive therapy and lipids. *Arch Intern Med* 1985; 145:1102.

31. Weinberger MH: Antihypertensive therapy and lipids. Paradoxical influences on cardiovascular disease risk. *Am J Med* 1986; 80(suppl 2A):64.

32. Notelovitz M: Estrogen replacement therapy: Indications, contraindications and agent selection. *Am J Obstet Gynecol* 1989; 161:1832.

33. Glueck CJ, Scheel D, Fishback J, et al: Estrogen-induced pancreatitis in patients with previously covert familial type V hyperlipoproteinemia. *Metabolism* 1972; 21:657.

34. Molitch ME, Oill P, Odell WD: Massive hyperlipemia during estrogen therapy. *JAMA* 1974; 227:522.

35. El-Shaboury AM, Hayes TM: Hyperlipidaemia in asthmatic patients receiving long-term steroid therapy. *Br Med J* 1973; 1:85.

36. Katz RA, Jorgensen H, Higra TP: Elevation of serum triglyceride levels from oral isotretinoin in disorders of keratinization. *Arch Dermatol* 1980; 116:1369.

37. Marsden J: Hyperlipidemia due to isotretinoin and etretinate: Possible mechanisms and consequences. *Br J Dermatol* 1986; 114:401.

38. Flynn WJ, Freeman PG, Wickboldt LF: Pancreatitis associated with isotretinoin-induced hypertriglyceridemia. *Ann Intern Med* 1987; 107:63.

39. Janus ED, Lewis B: Alcohol and abnormalities of lipid metabolism. *J Clin Endocrinol Metab* 1978; 7:321.

40. Lieber CS, Savolainen M: Ethanol and lipids: Alcoholism. *Clin Exp Res* 1984; 8:409.

41. Chait A, Mancini M, February AW, et al: Clinical and metabolic study of alcoholic hyperlipidaemia. *Lancet* 1972; 2:62.

42. Erkelens DW, Brunzell JD: Effect of alcohol feeding on triglycerides in patients with outpatient hypertriglyceridemia. *J Human Nutr* 1980; 34:370.

43. Goldstein JL, Hazzard WR, Schrott HG, et al: Hyperlipidemia in coronary heart disease. II. Genetic analysis of lipid levels in 176 families and delineation of a new inherited disorder, combined hyperlipidemia. *J Clin Invest* 1973; 52:1533.

44. Chait A, Albers JJ, Brunzell JD: Very low density lipoprotein overproduction in genetic forms of hypertriglyceridemia. *Eur J Clin Invest* 1980; 10:17.

45. Pfeifer MA, Brunzell JD, Best JD, et al: The response of plasma triglyceride, cholesterol, and lipoprotein lipase to treatment in non-insulin-dependent diabetic subjects without familial hypertriglyceridemia. *Diabetes* 1983; 32:525.

46. Lithell H, Boberg J, Hellsing K, et al: Serum lipoprotein and apolipoprotein concentrations and tissue lipoprotein lipase activity in overt and subclinical hypothyroidism: The effects of substitution therapy. *Eur J Clin Invest* 1981; 11:3.

47. Pykalisto O, Goldberg A, Brunzell JD: Reversal of decreased human adipose tissue lipoprotein lipase and hypertriglyceridemia after treatment of hypothyroidism. *J Clin Endocrinol Metab* 1976; 43:549.

48. Goldberg AP, Applebaum-Bowden DM, Bierman EL, et al: Increase in lipoprotein lipase during clofibrate treatment of hypertriglyceridemia in patients on hemodialysis. *N Engl J Med* 1979; 301:1072.

49. Vega GL, Grundy SM: Lovastatin therapy in nephrotic hyperlipidemia: Effects on lipoprotein metabolism. *Kidney Int* 1988; 33:1160.

50. Brunzell JD, Bierman EL: Plasma triglyceride and insulin levels in familial hypertriglyceridemia. *Ann Intern Med* 1977; 87:198.

51. Schaefer EJ, Foster DM, Zech LA, et al: The effect of estrogen administration on plasma lipoprotein metabolism in premenopausal females. *J Clin Endocrinol Metab* 1983; 57:262.

52. Stern MP, Kolterman OG, Fries JF, et al: Adrenocortical steroid treatment of rheumatic diseases: Effects on lipid metabolism. *Arch Intern Med* 1973; 132:97.

53. Greenfield M, Kolterman O, Olefsky J, et al: Mechanism of hypertriglyceridemia in diabetic patients with fasting hyperglycemia. *Diabetologia* 1980; 18:441.

54. *The Lipid Research Clinic's Population Studies Data Book. Volume I, The Prevalence Study.* US Department of Health and Human Services, July 1980.

55. Brunzell JD, Hazzard WR, Motulsky AG, et al: Evidence for diabetes mellitus and genetic forms of hypertriglyceridemia as independent entities. *Metabolism* 1975; 24:1115.

56. Fallat RW, Glueck CJ: Familial and acquired type V hyperlipoproteinemia. *Atherosclerosis* 1976; 23:41.

57. Greenberg BH, Blackwelder WC, Levy RI: Primary type V hyperlipoproteinemia: A descriptive study in 32 families. *Ann Intern Med* 1977; 87:526.

58. Greenberger NJ, Hatch FT, Drummey GD, et al: Pancreatitis and hyperlipemia: A study of serum lipid alterations in 25 patients with acute pancreatitis. *Medicine (Baltimore)* 1966; 45:161.

59. Cameron JL, Capuzzi DM, Zuidema GD, et al: Acute pancreatitis with hyperlipemia: The incidence of lipid abnormalities in acute pancreatitis. *Ann Surg* 1973; 177:483.

60. Farmer RG, Winkelman EI, Brown HB, et al: Hyperlipoproteinemia and pancreatitis. *Am J Med* 1973; 54:161.

61. Howard JM, Ehrlich E, Spitzer JJ, et al: Hyperlipemia in patients with acute pancreatitis. *Ann Surg* 1964; 160:210.

62. Fallat RW, Vestor JW, Glueck CJ: Suppression of amylase activity by hypertriglyceridemia. *JAMA* 1973; 225:1331.

63. Lesser PB, Warshaw AL: Diagnosis of pancreatitis masked by hyperlipemia. *Ann Intern Med* 1975; 82:795.

64. Warshaw AL, Bellini CA, Lesser PB: Inhibition of serum and urine amylase activity in pancreatitis with hyperlipemia. *Ann Surg* 1975; 182:72.

65. Fredrickson DS, Goldstein JL, Brown MS: The familial hyperlipoproteinemias,

in Stanbury JB, Wyngaarden JB, Fredrickson DS (eds): The Metabolic Basis of Inherited Disease. New York, McGraw-Hill, 1978, p 604.

66. Mathew NT, Meyer JS, Achari AN, et al: Hyperlipidemic neuropathy and dementia. *Eur Neurol* 1976; 14:370.

67. Heilman KM, Fisher WR: Hyperlipidemic dementia. *Arch Neurol* 1974; 31:67.

68. Parker F, Bagdade JD, Odland GF, et al: Evidence for the chylomicron origin of lipids accumulating in diabetic eruptive xanthomas: A correlative lipid biochemical, histochemical and electron microscopic study. *J Clin Invest* 1970; 49:2172.

69. Kuo PT, Wherat AF, Horwitz O: The effect of lipemia upon coronary and peripheral arterial circulation in patients with essential hyperlipemia. *Am J Med* 1959; 26:68.

70. Talbot GD, Frayser R: Hyperlipidaemia: A cause of decreased oxygen saturation. *Nature* 1963; 200:684.

71. Ditzel J, Dyerberg J: Hyperlipoproteinemia, diabetes and oxygen affinity of hemoglobin. *Metabolism* 1977; 26:141.

72. Shah PC, Patel AR, Rao KRP: Hyperlipemia and spuriously elevated hemoglobin levels. *Ann Intern Med* 1975; 82:382.

73. Zieve L: Jaundice, hyperlipemia and hemolytic anemia: A heretofore unrecognized syndrome associated with alcoholic fatty liver and cirrhosis. *Ann Intern Med* 1958; 48:471.

74. Steffes MW, Freier EF: A simple and precise method of determining true sodium, potassium and chloride concentrations in hyperlipemia. *J Lab Clin Med* 1976; 88:683.

75. Kollef MH, McCormack MT, Caras WE, et al: The fat overload syndrome: Successful treatment with plasma exchange. *Ann Intern Med* 1990; 112:545.

76. Johnson D, Drenick EJ: Therapeutic fasting in morbid obesity: Long-term follow-up. *Arch Intern Med* 1977; 137:1381.

77. Angelin B, Hershon KS, Brunzell JD: Bile acid metabolism in hereditary forms of hypertriglyceridemia: Evidence for an increased synthesis rate in monogenic familial hypertriglyceridemia. *Proc Natl Acad Sci USA* 1987; 84:5434.

78. Brunzell JD, Bierman EL: Plasma triglyceride and insulin levels in familial hypertriglyceridemia. *Ann Intern Med* 1977; 87:198.

79. Bierman EL, Brunzell JD, Bagdade JD, et al: On the mechanism of action of Atromid-S on triglyceride transport in man. *Trans Assoc Am Physicians* 1970; 83:211.

# Primary Hyperparathyroidism: Recent Advances in Pathogenesis, Diagnosis, and Management

## Hunter Heath III, M.D.

Professor of Medicine, Endocrine Research Unit, Mayo Medical School,
Consultant in Endocrinology, Metabolism, and Internal Medicine, Mayo
Foundation and Clinic, Rochester, Minnesota*

## Editor's Introduction

The routine screening of patients for hypercalcemia has caused a radical change in our estimates of the frequency of hyperparathyroidism. Hyperparathyroidism, as Dr. Heath's review documents, is now known to occur in .2% of Caucasian women over age 60, a frequency that assures that almost every internist will have the opportunity of seeing patients with this condition. However, screening for hypercalcemia has also changed the clinical presentation of hyperparathyroidism. Rather than waiting for the severe symptoms of renal stones and crippling bone disease that characterize prolonged hyperparathyroidism, patients are now diagnosed while symptoms are usually quite subtle, consisting of hypertension, very mild osteopenia, nonspecific mental depression, forgetfulness, and often loss of muscle strength. The nonspecificity of these symptoms makes it important that the clinician maintain a high index of suspicion for hyperparathyroidism and make use of readily available, relatively specific parathormone immunoassays that have only recently become available. These tests also permit rapid differential diagnosis of hyperparathyroidism from the several other causes of hypercalcemia ranging from sarcoidosis to familial hypocalciuric hypercalcemia. As this review emphasizes, the question of how aggressively to treat mild hyperthyroidism remains a matter of clinical judgment, with surgery clearly being indicated in cases with severe symptoms, and careful medical follow-up often being adequate in the more elderly with major surgical risk factors. It is apparent that despite these major advances in our ability to diagnose hyperparathyroidism, there remains an important role for wise clinical judgment in the management of this now relatively common condition.

*Marvin D. Siperstein, M.D., Ph.D.*

*Dr. Heath is currently Chairman, Division of Endocrinology and Metabolism, University of Utah Medical Center, Salt Lake City, Utah.

Physicians' concepts of, diagnostic methods for, and treatment approaches to primary hyperparathyroidism (PHPT) have undergone considerable evolution in the last decade. This article is not an encyclopedic review of PHPT, but instead focuses on some specific advances in understanding the pathogenesis, effects, diagnosis, and treatment of the disease. The most important advances have been in understanding the actual spectrum of severity of the disorder, developing vastly improved diagnostic tools, improving noninvasive parathyroid localization, and discovering some nonsurgical therapeutic approaches that may offer benefit in selected cases. One section will offer a provisional strategy for diagnosis and therapeutic decision-making that, in general, reflects the thoughts of a recent Consensus Development Conference on mild PHPT impaneled by the National Institutes of Health.[1] Finally, a number of outstanding questions about PHPT will be outlined that reflect continuing uncertainties regarding the optimal management for all cases.

## The Clinical Spectrum of Primary Hyperparathyroidism

As has been detailed elsewhere,[2, 3] the once-"classical" picture of PHPT as a severe disorder accompanied by symptoms of hypercalcemia, bone pain, and renal lithiasis was questioned for decades,[4, 5] but has been firmly discarded over only the last 10 to 15 years. Population-based epidemiologic studies in three countries have found similar incidence rates for PHPT, in the range of 25 to 28 cases per 100,000 population annually.[6-8] These overall incidence figures obscure the true picture, wherein PHPT is clearly a disorder of middle age and late life that primarily affects women (Table 1). Average annual incidence rates for PHPT in white women over 60 years of age are almost 190 cases per 100,000 persons per year.[7] Although absolute numbers of cases seen in a given setting decline in late life,[8] this is an artifact of survivorship and not an accurate reflection of incidence rate.

The incidence rates for PHPT have been affected strongly by changing clinical laboratory technology. The coming of relatively inexpensive, accurate serum calcium determination with automated analyzers in the late 1960s was responsible for a greater than fivefold increase in case ascertainment everywhere in the western world (see Table 1).[6-10] Predictably, this kind of case-finding by screening for hypercalcemia brought forth many cases of PHPT in asymptomatic patients, or patients with unpredicted symptoms or complications. Most patients found to have PHPT today have only mild hypercalcemia, with the majority having serum calcium values less than 11 mg/dL (2.75 mmol/L), as shown in Table 2. Patients with severe, symptomatic PHPT are still seen, of course, but in numbers similar to those before the era of automated serum chemistry analyzers.

Several detailed studies of symptoms and complications in PHPT have clarified the distribution of accompanying problems; the results of three such studies are summarized in Table 3. In essence, PHPT today is char-

## TABLE 1.
Average Age- and Sex-Specific Annual Incidence Rates (New Cases per 100,000 Population Yearly) for Primary Hyperparathyroidism in Rochester, Minnesota*

| Period of Observation† | Age (yr) | Incidence Rate | |
| | | Men | Women |
| --- | --- | --- | --- |
| Before screening | ≤39 | 2.5 | 1.6 |
| | 40–59 | 12.0 | 20.4 |
| | ≥60 | 16.7 | 30.7 |
| After screening | ≤39 | 4.5 | 8.0 |
| | 40–59 | 25.9 | 103.6 |
| | ≥60 | 92.2 | 188.5 |

*From Heath H III, Hodgson SF, Kennedy MA: N Engl J Med 1980; 302:189–193. Used by permission.
†In the initial period of observation (before screening), serum calcium measurement was not included on the serum chemistry panels used locally, but in the second period (after screening), it was.

## TABLE 2.
Percentage Distribution of Serum Total Calcium Values in 90 Unselected Patients With Primary Hyperparathyroidism*

| Serum Calcium (mg/dL) | Percent of Total Cases |
| --- | --- |
| ≤10.1 | 6 |
| 10.2–10.5 | 36 } 78 |
| 10.6–11.0 | 36 |
| 11.1–11.5 | 8 |
| 11.6–12.0 | 8 |
| 12.1–13.0 | 6 |
| ≥13.1 | 0 |

*From Heath H III, Hodgson SF, Kennedy MA: N Engl J Med 1980; 302:189–193. Used by permission.

**TABLE 3.**
**Percentage of Unselected Patients With Primary**
**Hyperparathyroidism Manifesting Various Symptoms and Signs**
**in the "Postscreening" Era**

| Symptom or Sign | Heath et al.[7]* | Mundy et al.[8]* |
|---|---|---|
| No symptoms | 51 | 57 |
| Urolithiasis | 4 | 7 |
| Hypercalciuria† | 22 | NR |
| Hyperparathyroid bone disease | 8 | 0 |
| Osteoporosis | 12 | NR |
| Decreased renal function | 14 | NR |
| Peptic ulcer disease/gastrointestinal symptoms | 8 | 4 |
| Arterial hypertension | 48 | 5 |
| Pancreatitis | 0 | NR |
| Psychiatric problems | 20 | 5 |
| Acute hypercalcemic syndrome | 0 | 14 |
| Symptoms of hypercalcemia (lethargy, polyuria, etc.) | NR | 8 |

*NR = not reported.
†>250 mg or 6.2 mmol/day.

acterized by a much lower prevalence of urolithiasis, hyperparathyroid bone disease, and other severe complications than in the past, and by a much higher likelihood of either no symptoms or ones previously not considered typical of the disorder. Symptoms and signs may include vague malaise, muscular weakness, mental depression, arterial hypertension, and bland osteoporosis. Most available studies have been small, and many have had insufficient controls, so it is unclear to what extent such concomitant conditions as hypertension or neuromuscular dysfunction are consequences of PHPT or of hypercalcemia. It is also unclear to what extent such problems are resolved or mitigated by surgical cure of the hyperparathyroidism,[1] and the effect this uncertainty has on treatment decisions is discussed as follows.

An issue of considerable practical importance is the relative likelihood of PHPT vs. humoral hypercalcemia of malignancy or other causes of elevated blood calcium in a given patient found to have persistent, true hypercalcemia. The likelihood depends upon the clinical setting and whether or not the patient is symptomatic. Among hospitalized patients in one study, hypercalcemia was most likely to result from a malignant tumor (54%), although PHPT was still common (31%).[11] The remaining 15% of cases resulted from a wide variety of causes. In contrast, among ambulatory persons, persistent hypercalcemia resulted from PHPT in over 85% of cases.[12] The physician, therefore, must adjust likelihood estimates for PHPT vs. other causes of hypercalcemia depending on the circumstances: if the individual is an asymptomatic or oligosymptomatic outpatient, persistent hypercalcemia most likely results from PHPT; if the patient is symptomatic enough to be in a hospital, the chance of cancer-associated hypercalcemia is greatly increased. These considerations, of course, do not take into account various specific symptoms, historic findings, or physical signs that may point to definite causes of hypercalcemia.

Thus, in the 1990s, the typical patient with PHPT is a woman over the age of 40 years, often elderly, who has few or no symptoms clearly referable to the parathyroid disorder, but perhaps some vague symptoms, hypertension, or osteoporosis.[13] Her serum calcium level will be modestly elevated, perhaps to 10.5 to 11.0 mg/dL (2.62 to 2.75 mmol/L), and other biochemical findings will be mild or absent. As an example, hypophosphatemia occurs in only about half of all cases. Elevations of urine calcium excretion also occur in perhaps half of these patients, and raised serum alkaline phosphatase levels from the effects of parathyroid hormone (PTH) on bone are uncommon (less than 10%). However, the diagnosis usually will be secured by the finding of an elevated blood level of PTH using modern assay methods, as in discussed following sections.

## Pathogenesis of Parathyroid Gland Tumors

The causes of most parathyroid tumors remain obscure. However, ionizing radiation to the parathyroid region clearly is associated with later development of typical parathyroid adenomas, often after delays of more than 20 years.[14, 15] Case-control studies place the increase in risk at 2 to 3 times that of the general population,[16, 17] but the net impact of past irradiation on the incidence rate of PHPT is probably small, and other factors related to aging and tumorigenesis in general probably are involved.

The incidence of PHPT is highest in women after the menopause,[6–8] which suggests a role for estrogen deficiency in the emergence of hyperparathyroidism. Indeed, the administration of estrogen to postmenopausal women with mild to moderate PHPT lowers serum calcium levels, sometimes to normal.[18–20] While there is no evidence to link estrogen deficiency with causation of parathyroid tumors, one suspects that estrogen lack may "expose" the effects of small preexisting tumors.

There has been controversy about whether parathyroid adenomas arise from prolonged parathyroid hyperplasia, with the emergence of a "dominant nodule" that is taken clinically to be a solitary adenoma. While earlier studies of isoenzymes had suggested polyclonal origins for adenomas, consistent with the hyperplasia theory,[21] more recent work using the tools of molecular biology led to the opposite conclusion. In these more recent studies,[22-24] examination of chromosomes and DNA extracted from parathyroid adenomas suggested that most such tumors are monoclonal in origin. Thus, it seems likely that parathyroid adenomas arise from acquired genetic abnormalities in one or a few cells, which in turn transmit those abnormalities to their progeny. These results support the belief that primary parathyroid hyperplasia and adenomas result from different causes. There is a useful clinical effect of this information; if all or most "adenomas" were really manifestations of diffuse parathyroid hyperplasia, then it would not be rational to remove only obviously enlarged parathyroid glands. Some authors in the past suggested that routine subtotal parathyroidectomy was indicated in most cases,[25] but such an approach may result in unacceptable rates of postsurgical hypoparathyroidism.[26] Moreover, the late results of removing only enlarged parathyroid tissue show that recurrence is not an issue.[27, 28] Thus, a monoclonal origin of parathyroid adenomas bolsters the case for removal of only obviously enlarged parathyroid tissue, when surgery is indicated.

At a more basic level, studies of DNA in parathyroid tumors suggest a variety of defects in the genetic material.[22-24, 29] This work and similar studies with other tumors suggest that tumors may arise in part because mutations occur that deprive the cells of certain genes needed to regulate the replication of cells normally (often termed "tumor suppressor genes").[30] Especially when multiple areas of the genome are lost, unrestrained growth and malignant behavior ensue. While of great interest in the understanding of how tumors begin, this information has not yet provided new leads in tumor therapy.

A final issue in the pathogenesis of hyperparathyroidism concerns so-called "ectopic PHPT" in patients with certain malignant tumors. True blood PTH levels are seldom increased in patients with hypercalcemia accompanying malignancy.[31-33] Most such patients instead have excessive tumor secretion of parathyroid hormone–related peptide (PTHrP),[34, 35] a compound that closely mimics the actions of PTH on bone, kidney, and blood calcium regulation (Fig 1).[36-39] A review of humoral hypercalcemia of malignancy is beyond the scope of this article, but additional information may be found elsewhere.[40] After the discovery of PTHrP, some physicians concluded that true ectopic secretion of PTH did not occur, but several recent case studies have shown otherwise.[41-43] Rarely, malignant tumors may secrete PTH alone or in combination with PTHrP.[42] This could pose great difficulties in diagnosis, as a patient might have an obvious cancer, hypercalcemia, and an elevated blood PTH level. The most likely explanation would be concurrent PHPT and cancer, but the clinician should be alert for the other possibilities. In a patient with cancer and suspected PHPT, an attempt to visualize the parathyroid tumor by high-resolution ultrasonography[44, 45] might be in order. Failure to visualize the tumor would prove nothing, but seeing it would make the diagnosis clearer.

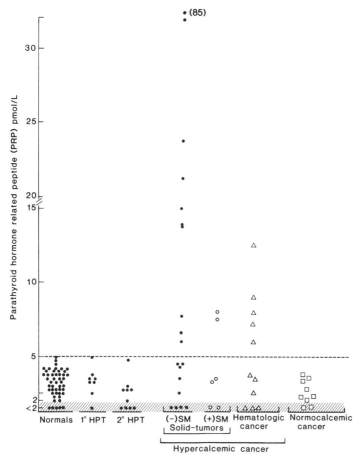

**FIG 1.**
Plasma parathyroid hormone–related peptide immunoreactivity in various conditions. Plasma parathyroid hormone–related peptide was determined in normal volunteers and patients with primary hyperparathyroidism *(1° HPT)*, secondary hyperparathyroidism *(2° HPT)*, hypercalcemia and solid tumors with *(+)* or without *(−)* skeletal metastatic lesions *(SM)*, hematogenous cancer and hypercalcemia, and normocalcemia and cancer. The *dashed horizontal line* indicates the upper limit of normal for parathyroid hormone–related peptide; the *hatched area* indicates the region of undetectability. (From Kao PC, Klee GG, Taylor RL, et al: *Mayo Clin Proc* 1990; 65:1399–1407. Used by permission.)

# New Diagnostic Tests in Hypercalcemia

**Measurement of Serum Calcium.**—Hypercalcemia itself is easily detected, and most laboratories today offer accurate and reproducible calcium measurements. The slowly growing availability of serum ionized calcium determination promises further improvements in assessing calcemic status, especially when abnormal binding of calcium to serum proteins is suspected.[46] However, clinicians need to be aware of the limitations of serum total calcium measurements,[47] and the fact that many laboratories have not made accurate determinations of population normal ranges. Until recently, some laboratories still cited upper limits of normal for serum calcium as high as 11.0 to 11.5 mg/dL (2.75 to 2.88 mmol/L), and many continue to report upper normal calcium values of 10.5 to 10.8 mg/dL (2.62 to 2.70 mmol/L) despite extensive studies showing the proper adult upper limit to be 10.1 to 10.4 mg/dL (2.52 to 2.60 mmol/L).[48, 49] In my experience, most laboratories report measured serum calcium values accurately; they simply publish an incorrect upper limit of normal. The clinician faced with such a report usually may assume safely that serum calcium values over 10.2 to 10.4 mg/dL (2.55 to 2.60 mmol/L) are abnormal. Hypercalcemia also may be verified by measuring ionized calcium.

**Measurements of Parathyroid Hormone.**—The first radioimmunoassay for PTH was developed over 22 years ago, and subsequent incremental improvements in technique brought about a revolution in the differential diagnosis of hypercalcemia. Nonetheless, even the best radioimmunoassays for PTH had serious limitations in sensitivity, specificity, and technical demands, and those limitations sometimes led to uncertainty about diagnosis. The newest generation of PTH assay also uses antibodies against the PTH molecule, but in a way that bypasses many of the prior difficulties. In the immunometric assays,[50] antibodies specific for one region of the PTH molecule are immobilized by attachment to a solid substrate, such as a plastic bead. Other antibodies, specific for a different region of the PTH molecule, are labeled either with a radioactive tracer or with a compound capable of giving off light in a chemical reaction. Serum containing an unknown amount of PTH is added to the immobilized antibodies and allowed to bind. Then, the dissolved, labeled antibodies are added and bind to free portions of the PTH molecules. (Alternatively, serum may be added to the free labeled antibodies first.) After washing away the serum and excess antibody, the amount of PTH is determined by counting the radioactivity or quantifying light output from the second antibodies. Because such assays depend upon the binding of antibody molecules to at least two sites on the PTH molecule, they are termed "two-site" assays, thus, the term "two-site immunoradiometric assay" (IRMA) or "two-site immunochemiluminometric assay" (ICMA).[31-33] Two-site immunometric assays are now available from a number of major national reference laboratories.

What are the advantages of two-site immunometric assays? There are many.[31-33, 50] First is ease and rapidity of performance; in contrast to the many hours to days required for the most sensitive radioimmunoassays for PTH, results from IRMA or ICMA methods are usually available the same or next day. Second, and ultimately more important, is the specificity of the measurements. PTH circulates not just as the intact peptide, but as a complex mixture of abbreviated peptides ("fragments"), most of which are not biologically active, and which tend to accumulate when renal function is decreased. Detection of these fragments in conventional radioimmunoassays obscures many details about PTH levels in various diseases. Two-site assays can recognize only the bioactive intact peptide and, thus, give an accurate representation of PTH secretion at the time of sampling. Finally, the newer assays for the first time are capable of measuring the full range of normal values, and can distinguish among low, normal, and high PTH levels. Taking the sensitivity and specificity together, the new PTH assays permit much more confident distinction between hyperparathyroid states and nonparathyroidal hypercalcemia (such as humoral hypercalcemia of malignancy), and clarify the diagnosis of hypoparathyroidism as well.[31–33] Figure 2 shows the degree of separation among clinical syndromes achievable with a two-site ICMA.

The effect of the newer PTH assays is to reduce considerably the need for other blood or urine tests in the differential diagnosis of hypercalcemia. Table 4 illustrates the use of several modern tests to differentiate among

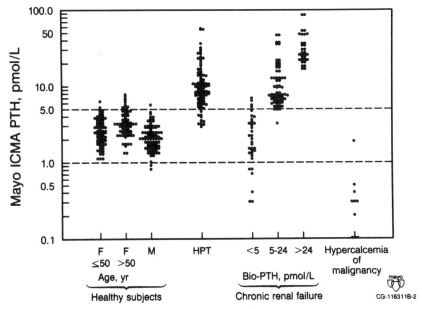

**FIG 2.**
Plasma concentration of parathyroid hormone (*PTH*) by two-site immunochemiluminometric assay (*ICMA*) in healthy adults, with results in women separated at age 50 (left three columns), in patients with surgically proved primary hyperparathyroidism (*HPT*, fourth column from left), and in patients with hypercalcemia of malignancy (rightmost column). Note suppression of PTH in patients with cancer. In addition, results of plasma PTH *bioactivity* are shown for patients with varying degrees of renal failure; results by ICMA are similar. (Courtesy of Drs. G.G. Klee and P.-C. Kao, Mayo Clinic.)

# TABLE 4.
## Findings With Selected Current Serum or Plasma Laboratory Tests Useful in the Differential Diagnosis of Hypercalcemia*

| Disorder | Calcium | Phosphorus | Test PTH | PTHrP | 25(OH)D | 1,25(OH)$_2$D |
|---|---|---|---|---|---|---|
| PHPT | ↑ | ↓ (50%) | ↑ (80% to 90%) | N | N | N/↑ (50%) |
| HHM | ↑ | ↑/N/↓ | → | ↑ (50% to 70%) | N | ↓/N |
| Sarcoidosis | ↑ | N/↑ | → | N? | N | ↑ |
| Hypervitaminosis D | ↑ | N/↓ | → | N? | ↑ | N/↑ |
| FBH | ↑ | N/↓ | N(80% to 90%) | N | N | N |

*N = normal; ↑ = increased; ↓ = decreased; PTH = parathyroid hormone measured by 2-site immunometric assay; PTHrP = PTH-related peptide; 25(OH)D = 25-hydroxyvitamin D; 1,25(OH)$_2$D = 1,25-dihydroxyvitamin D; PHPT = primary hyperparathyroidism; HHM = humoral hypercalcemia of malignancy; FBH = familial benign hypercalcemia (also called hypocalciuric hypercalcemia or FHH). Percentages indicate approximate fraction of cases with the stated finding.

PHPT, humoral hypercalcemia of malignancy, vitamin D intoxication, and other forms of nonparathyroidal hypercalcemia. As a practical matter, it is seldom necessary to obtain all these measurements. In the majority of cases, once persistent hypercalcemia is established, measurement of PTH in serum by a quality two-site IRMA or ICMA will verify that the patient has PHPT. If the PTH level is low, then other possibilities must be excluded, and other tests may be needed.

## Localization of Abnormal Parathyroid Tissue

Tremendous effort has been expended to develop both invasive and non-invasive techniques for locating abnormal parathyroid tissue,[44, 45] because the natural variation in location of the parathyroids has given many surgeons difficulty. Early methods were primitive (e.g., esophagography) or invasive (regional arteriography and venous sampling for PTH measurement). More recently, small-parts ultrasonography has achieved impressive results in the detection of parathyroid adenomas,[44] locating most of those that weigh 1 g or more, and many smaller ones, and finding particular usefulness in patients with persistent or recurrent PHPT after operation.[51] However, ultrasonography has several limitations. For example, the presence of thyroid nodules often obscures parathyroid tumors; if there is parathyroid hyperplasia, the examiner may see only one of the enlarged glands; and mediastinal tumors cannot be seen by ultrasonography. Another recent approach is sequential scanning with technetium 99m and thallium-201 wherein the thyroid and parathyroids both take up thallium, but only the thyroid concentrates technetium; by subtracting the technetium image from the thallium image, parathyroid tissue may be seen. Numerous reports show the effectiveness of this technique for localizing intrathoracic as well as cervical adenomas. The scan technique also has marked limitations; it often cannot detect the usual small adenoma (<1,000 mg), may be confounded by enlargement or nodularity of the thyroid, and is expensive. Computed tomography and magnetic resonance imaging also have been effective for locating abnormal parathyroid tissue[52-54]; however, these are expensive, time-consuming techniques. Thus far, there is no one localization technique for parathyroid gland tumors with the desired combination of low cost, noninvasiveness, sensitivity, and specificity.

Most experienced endocrinologists and parathyroid surgeons believe that preoperative localization procedures are unnecessary before primary explorations done by experienced parathyroid surgeons, and generally reserve such tests for special situations (especially patients who have had prior neck exploration).[44, 45, 51-55] The physician also should recognize that the effectiveness of parathyroid localization procedures is related strongly to operator experience, and centers doing few such procedures are unlikely to find many tumors.

## Newer Approaches to Treatment

At present, surgical removal of abnormal parathyroid tissue remains the treatment of choice for PHPT, when treatment is indicated. There are, however, some nonsurgical options either in use or under exploration.

**Inhibitors of PTH Secretion or Action: Synthetic PTH Analogues.**—Analogues of the PTH molecule that lack the first few amino acid residues, such as the 3-34 or 7-34 peptides, or ones with various alterations of sequence, are competitive antagonists of PTH action; they bind to the PTH receptor, but are weak or impotent in activating cells normally.[56] In animal studies, such peptides have been shown to block PTH action, but the cost of the peptide quantities needed for human studies has so far prevented them from being performed. While such peptides are attractive in theory, parathyroid tumors probably would respond to the blockade of PTH action simply by secreting more PTH until the drug's effect was overcome. *WR-2721*, or S-2(3-aminopropylamino)ethylphosphorothioic acid, is a remarkable compound that has several actions tending to lower plasma calcium levels. It not only inhibits PTH secretion by an unknown mechanism, but decreases bone resorption and renal tubular reabsorption of calcium directly.[57, 58] While WR-2721 must be given parenterally,[59] compounds that can be taken orally may be under development, and I have high hopes for this class of drugs. If they prove to be tolerated chronically, they may provide the first highly effective medical therapy for PHPT. *Gallium nitrate* is effective in any hypercalcemia associated with increased bone resorption, by blocking osteoclast activity. This drug, too, shows great promise, although its role in therapy is still unclear.[60, 61] The *bisphosphonates* also act primarily to inhibit osteoclastic bone resorption. While etidronate, the form currently available in the United States, is not highly effective in PHPT, newer, more powerful bisphosphonates may have a role in treating this disorder.[62-65] I have some reservations about the long-term utility of drugs that only block bone resorption; lowering plasma calcium levels will cause most parathyroid tumors to secrete more PTH, and the drugs do not address the increased renal tubular reabsorption of calcium induced by PTH. In any case, such drugs may have a role in short-term treatment.[66]

**Nonsurgical Ablation of Parathyroid Adenomas.**—Parathyroid tumors have been damaged or destroyed by obstructing their arterial supply under arteriographic guidance,[67-70] but this technique is invasive and requires considerable experience to be safe and successful. More recently, adenomatous and hyperplastic parathyroid tissue has been attacked by the injection of concentrated ethanol under ultrasonographic guidance,[71-73] with some success. However, there are concerns about injecting a sclerosing agent so near the recurrent laryngeal nerves. Complications of the procedure have been relatively common, and recurrent hyperparathyroidism is possible. In selected cases, the procedure may be worth consideration, but it does not provide a commonly usable alternative to surgery.

**Estrogen Administration.**—As mentioned previously, estrogen therapy often lowers serum calcium levels in women with PHPT, sometimes to normal, and may retard bone loss.[18–20] However, the numbers of patients studied have been small and the duration of treatment short, so, in my view, the evidence is not strong for long-term benefit from estrogen treatment. Nonetheless, some investigators advocate such treatment as an alternative to surgery in selected women with mild PHPT,[19, 20, 74] and I certainly have used that option myself in a few instances. Needless to say, a serious limitation of estrogen therapy for PHPT is its inapplicability to male patients.

## Clinical Strategy for Diagnosis and Treatment of Primary Hyperparathyroidism

An approach to diagnosis based on the use of up-to-date laboratory tests is outlined in Figure 3. The key test is the measurement of PTH with a high-quality two-site immunometric assay done by a major reference laboratory. This approach assumes that a thorough history has been taken, a complete physical examination performed, and other basic blood and urine tests done. In most cases, these measures will suffice to make a diagnosis of

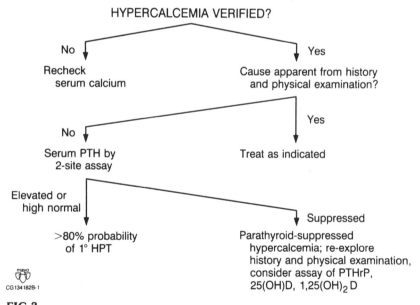

**FIG 3.**
Schematic of approach to differential diagnosis in an outpatient setting. See also Table 4. *PTH* = parathyroid hormone; *HPT* = hyperparathyroidism; *PTHrP* = parathyroid hormone–related peptide; *25(OH)D* = 25-hydroxyvitamin D; *1,25(OH) 2D* = 1,25-dihydroxyvitamin D.

PHPT. However, there are pitfalls. For example, PTH values are within normal limits in 10% to 20% of *unselected* hyperparathyroid patients, even with the best methods. In such cases, interpretation as "inappropriately elevated" may be correct, but should dictate caution. Familial benign hypercalcemia (also called hypocalciuric hypercalcemia) most commonly presents as asymptomatic hypercalcemia with normal serum PTH.[75] Patients with cancer may have multifactorial hypercalcemia.

If the diagnosis remains uncertain after PTH is measured, other tests may be required. If cancer is suspected, measurement of PTHrP in the blood may be diagnostic.[36-39] If vitamin D intoxication is possible, and not excluded by history, assay of serum 25-hydroxyvitamin D will help confirm the diagnosis. Rarely, ingestion of 1,25-dihydroxyvitamin D would require measurement of that metabolite for a specific diagnosis. Except when cancer is strongly suspected, the extensive multisystem testing that used to be done in most hypercalcemic patients is seldom needed today.

## Remaining Uncertainties

Despite the progress described above in understanding the pathogenesis of PHPT, diagnosing it, and recognizing its changed clinical spectrum, there remain a number of problems that nag clinicians caring for hyperparathyroid patients. First, there is the large question of whether the increased discovery of mild or asymptomatic hyperparathyroidism because of frequent serum calcium measurement has been of benefit. Some students of PHPT believe that many (perhaps most) such patients would have done well without discovery; others believe that all such patients need definitive treatment,[1, 3, 13] but most thoughtful physicians' opinions fall somewhere in between. I think that even mild PHPT is a *disease*. However, there are grades of disease severity and, for most people, PHPT is a mild affliction. Some probably suffer no conscious ill effects from it. On the other hand, there is abundant, although not wholly convincing, evidence for multisystem, nontraditional effects of PHPT, including osteopenia (bone loss), arterial hypertension, altered mentation, depression, and decreased muscular strength. These issues have been reviewed in detail by the aforementioned Consensus Development Conference.[1]

Obviously, patients with PHPT who are severely hypercalcemic, have symptoms likely to arise from the disease, have obvious complications (e.g., urolithiasis or bone disease), or will have difficulty with medical follow-up (e.g., they are moving to a medically primitive area) need definitive surgical treatment. Others, especially fragile elderly persons, often can tolerate mild PHPT for extended periods without gross harm, and careful follow-up probably is justified. Again, these issues have been discussed extensively elsewhere.[1, 3, 13]

Major questions remain to be addressed. Is arterial hypertension caused by PHPT, and does cure of the latter benefit the former? Is mild PHPT a cause of accelerated or excessive bone loss? If so, does it contribute to osteoporotic fractures? Does mild PHPT result in meaningful reduction in quality of life for most who have it, and is that quality restored after surgery? What is the most cost-effective way to diagnose and manage mild PHPT? Is estrogen therapy of PHPT effective in the long term, and does it protect bone? Are any other medical options able to supplant surgery for mild PHPT? It is likely that the Consensus Development Conference[1] will spur a number of major studies of PHPT that should provide useful answers to these and many other questions in the next 5 years.

## Acknowledgments

I wish to acknowledge the many contributions of my colleagues in the Division of Endocrinology, Metabolism, and Internal Medicine, and the Department of Surgery at the Mayo Clinic to my education about PHPT. They shared their patients and their insights generously over more than 15 years. I also wish to acknowledge the support of the National Institutes of Health in the form of several research grants over those years, most recently DK-38855.

## References

1. Consensus Development Conference on the Diagnosis and Management of Asymptomatic Primary Hyperparathyroidism. *J Bone Miner Res,* in press.
2. Adami S, Milroy EJG, O'Riordan JLH: Primary hyperparathyroidism, in Nordin BEC (ed): *Metabolic Bone and Stone Disease.* New York, Churchill Livingstone, 1984, pp 112–142.
3. Heath DA: Primary hyperparathyroidism. Clinical presentation and factors influencing clinical management. *Endocrinol Metab Clin North Am* 1989; 18:631–646.
4. Keating FR Jr, Cook EN: The recognition of primary hyperparathyroidism. An analysis of twenty-four cases. *JAMA* 1945; 129:994–1002.
5. Gordan GS, Goldman L: Hyperparathyroidism. *Mod Treatm* 1970; 7:649–661.
6. Stenstrom G, Heedman P-A: Clinical findings in patients with hypercalcemia. A final investigation based on biochemical screening. *Acta Med Scand* 1974; 195:473–477.
7. Heath H III, Hodgson SF, Kennedy MA: Primary hyperparathyroidism. Incidence, morbidity, and potential economic impact in a community. *N Engl J Med* 1980; 302:189–193.
8. Mundy GR, Cove DH, Fisken R: Primary hyperparathyroidism: Changes in the pattern of clinical presentation. *Lancet* 1980; 1:1317–1320.
9. Britton DC, Johnston IDA, Thompson MH, et al: The outcome of treatment and changes in presentation of primary hyperparathyroidism. *Br J Surg* 1973; 60:782–785.
10. Aitken RE, Bartley PC, Bryant SJ, et al: The effect of multiphasic biochemical screening on the diagnosis of primary hyperparathyroidism. *Aust N Z J Med* 1975; 5:224–226.
11. Fisken RA, Heath DA, Somers S, et al: Hypercalcaemia in hospital patients. Clinical and diagnostic aspects. *Lancet* 1981; 1:202–207.

12. Christensson T, Hellstrom K, Wengle B, et al: Prevalence of hypercalcaemia in a health screening in Stockholm. *Acta Med Scand* 1976; 200:131–137.
13. Heath H III, Purnell DC: Asymptomatic hypercalcemia and primary hyperparathyroidism, in Heath D, Marx JJ (eds): *Butterworth's International Medical Reviews, Clinical Endocrinology 1, Calcium Disorders.* London, Butterworth Scientific, 1982, pp 189–215.
14. Christensson T: Hyperparathyroidism and radiation therapy. *Ann Intern Med* 1978; 89:216–217.
15. Hedman I, Tisell L-E: Associated hyperparathyroidism and nonmedullary thyroid carcinoma: The etiologic role of radiation. *Surgery* 1984; 95:392–397.
16. Beard CM, Heath H III, O'Fallon WM, et al: Therapeutic radiation and hyperparathyroidism. A case-control study in Rochester, Minn. *Arch Intern Med* 1989; 149:1887–1890.
17. Cohen J, Gierlowski TC, Schneider AB: A prospective study of hyperparathyroidism in individuals exposed to radiation in childhood. *JAMA* 1990; 264:581–584.
18. Herbai G, Ljunghall S: Normalization of hypercalcaemia of primary hyperparathyroidism by treatment with methallenestril, a synthetic oestrogen with low oestrogenicity. *Urol Int* 1983; 38:371–373.
19. Marcus R, Madvig P, Crim M, et al: Conjugated estrogens in the treatment of postmenopausal women with hyperparathyroidism. *Ann Intern Med* 1984; 100:633–640.
20. Selby PL, Peacock M: Ethinyl estradiol and norethindrone in the treatment of primary hyperparathyroidism in postmenopausal women. *N Engl J Med* 1986; 314:1481–1485.
21. Fialkow PJ, Jackson CE, Block MA, et al: Multicellular origin of parathyroid "adenomas." *N Engl J Med* 1977; 297:696–698.
22. Arnold A, Staunton CE, Kim HG, et al: Monoclonality and abnormal parathyroid hormone genes in parathyroid adenomas. *N Engl J Med* 1988; 318:658–662.
23. Friedman E, Bale AE, Marx SJ, et al: Genetic abnormalities in sporadic parathyroid adenomas. *J Clin Endocrinol Metab* 1990; 71:293–297.
24. Orndal C, Johansson M, Heim S, et al: Parathyroid adenoma with t(1;5)(p22;q32) as the sole clonal chromosome abnormality. *Cancer Genet Cytogenet* 1990; 48:225–228.
25. Paloyan E, Lawrence AM, Oslapas R, et al: Subtotal parathyroidectomy for primary hyperparathyroidism. Long-term results in 292 patients. *Arch Surg* 1983; 118:425–431.
26. Edis AJ, Beahrs OH, van Heerden JA, et al: "Conservative" versus "liberal" approach to parathyroid neck exploration. *Surgery* 1977; 82:466–473.
27. Attie JN, Wise L, Mir R, et al: The rationale against routine subtotal parathyroidectomy for primary hyperparathyroidism. *Am J Surg* 1978; 136:437–444.
28. Rudberg C, Akerstrom G, Palmer M, et al: Late results of operation for primary hyperparathyroidism in 441 patients. *Surgery* 1986; 99:643–651.
29. Marx SJ: Familial multiple endocrine neoplasia type 1. Mutation of a tumor suppressor gene. *Trends Endocrinol Metab* 1989; 1:76–82.
30. Benedict WF, Xu H-J, Hu S-X, et al: Role of the retinoblastoma gene in the initiation and progression of human cancer. *J Clin Invest* 1990; 85:988–993.
31. Brown RC, Aston JP, Weeks I, et al: Circulating intact parathyroid hormone measured by a two-site immunochemiluminometric assay. *J Clin Endocrinol Metab* 1987; 65:407–414.

32. Nussbaum SR, Zahradnik RJ, Lavigne JR, et al: Highly sensitive two-site immunoradiometric assay of parathyrin, and its clinical utility in evaluating patients with hypercalcemia *Clin Chem* 1987; 33:1364–1367.
33. Blind E, Schmidt-Gayk H, Scharla S, et al: Two-site assay of intact parathyroid hormone in the investigation of primary hyperparathyroidism and other disorders of calcium metabolism compared with a midregion assay. *J Clin Endocrinol Metab* 1988; 67:353–360.
34. Martin TJ: Properties of parathyroid hormone-related protein and its role in malignant hypercalcemia. *Q J Med* 1983; 76:771–786.
35. Stewart AF, Broadus AE: Clinical review 16: Parathyroid hormone-related proteins: Coming of age in the 1990s. *J Clin Endocrinol Metab* 1990; 71:1410–1414.
36. Budayr AA, Nissenson RA, Klein RF, et al: Increased serum levels of a parathyroid hormone-like protein in malignancy-associated hypercalcemia. *Ann Intern Med* 1989; 111:807–812.
37. Henderson JE, Shustik C, Kremer R, et al: Circulating concentrations of parathyroid hormone-like peptide in malignancy and in hyperparathyroidism. *J Bone Miner Res* 1990; 5:105–113.
38. Burtis WJ, Brady TG, Orloff JJ, et al: Immunochemical characterization of circulating parathyroid hormone-related protein in patients with humoral hypercalcemia of cancer. *N Engl J Med* 1990; 322:1106–1112.
39. Kao PC, Klee GG, Taylor RL, et al: Parathyroid hormone-related peptide in plasma of patients with hypercalcemia and malignant lesions. *Mayo Clin Proc* 1990; 65:1399–1407.
40. Ralston SH: The pathogenesis of humoral hypercalcaemia of malignancy. *Lancet* 1987; 2:1443–1446.
41. Yoshimoto K, Yamasaki R, Sakai H, et al: Ectopic production of parathyroid hormone by small cell lung cancer in a patient with hypercalcemia. *J Clin Endocrinol Metab* 1989; 68:976–981.
42. Budayr AA, Bruce RJ, Clark OH, et al: Secretion of authentic parathyroid hormone by a malignant tumor. *Clin Res* 1990; 38:462A.
43. Nussbaum SR, Gaz RD, Arnold AA: Hypercalcemia and ectopic secretion of parathyroid hormone by an ovarian carcinoma with rearrangement of the gene for parathyroid hormone. *N Engl J Med* 1990; 323:1324–1328.
44. Reading CC, Charboneau JW, James EM, et al: High-resolution parathyroid sonography. *AJR* 1982; 139:539–546.
45. Winzelberg GG: Parathyroid imaging. *Ann Intern Med* 1987; 107:64–70.
46. Buckley BM, Russell LJ: The measurement of ionised calcium in blood plasma. *Ann Clin Biochem* 1988; 25:447–465.
47. Robertson WG, Marshall RW: Calcium measurements in serum and plasma—total and ionized. *CRC Crit Rev Clin Lab Sci* 1979; 15:271–304.
48. Keating FR Jr, Jones JD, Elveback LR, et al: The relation of age and sex to distribution of values in healthy adults of serum calcium, inorganic phosphorus, magnesium, alkaline phosphatase, total proteins, albumin, and blood urea. *J Lab Clin Med* 1969; 73:825–834.
49. Humphrey KR, Gruemer H-D, Lott JA: Impact of posture on the "reference range" for serum proteins and calcium. *Clin Chem* 1977; 23:1343–1345.
50. Segre GV: Advances in techniques for measurement of parathyroid hormone. Current applications in clinical medicine and directions for future research. *Trends Endocrinol Metab* 1990; 1:243–247.
51. Reading CC, Charboneau JW, James EM, et al: Postoperative parathyroid

high-frequency sonography: Evaluation of persistent or recurrent hyperpara-thyroidism. *AJR* 1985; 144:399–402.

52. Auffermann W, Gooding GAW, Okerlund MD, et al: Diagnosis of recurrent hyperparathyroidism: Comparison of MR imaging and other imaging tech-niques. *AJR* 1988; 150:1027–1033.

53. Higgins CB, Auffermann W: MR imaging of thyroid and parathyroid glands: A review of current status. *AJR* 1988; 151:1095–1106.

54. Krubsack AJ, Wilson SD, Lawson TL, et al: Prospective comparison of radio-nuclide, computed tomographic, sonographic, and magnetic resonance local-ization of parathyroid tumors. *Surgery* 1989; 106:639–646.

55. Whelan PJ, Rotstein LE, Rosen IB, et al: Do we really need another localizing technique for parathyroid glands? *Am J Surg* 1989; 158:382–384.

56. Rosenblatt M: Peptide hormone antagonists that are effective in vivo. *N Engl J Med* 1986; 315:1004–1013.

57. Attie MF, Fallon MD, Spar B, et al: Bone and parathyroid inhibitory effects of S-2(3-aminopropylamino)ethylphosphorothioic acid. Studies in experimental animals and cultured bone cells. *J Clin Invest* 1985; 75:1191–1197.

58. Hirschel-Scholz S, Caverzasio J, Bonjour J-P: Inhibition of parathyroid hor-mone secretion and parathyroid hormone-independent diminution of tubular calcium reabsorption by WR-2721, a unique hypocalcemic agent. *J Clin Invest* 1985; 76:1851–1856.

59. Morita M, Higashi K, Tajiri J, et al: S-2 (3-aminopropylamino)ethylphospho-rothioic acid (WR-2721) in primary hyperparathyroidism (letter). *Ann Intern Med* 1985; 103:961.

60. Warrell RP Jr, Issacs M, Alcock NW, et al: Gallium nitrate for treatment of re-fractory hypercalcemia from parathyroid carcinoma. *Ann Intern Med* 1987; 107:683–686.

61. Warrell RP Jr, Israel R, Frisone M, Snyder T, et al: Gallium nitrate for acute treatment of cancer-related hypercalcemia. A randomized, double-blind com-parison to calcitonin. *Ann Intern Med* 1988; 108:669–674.

62. van Breukelen FJM, Bijvoet OLM, Frijlink WB, et al: Efficacy of amino-hy-droxypropylidene bisphosphonate in hypercalcemia: Observations on regula-tion of serum calcium. *Calcif Tissue Int* 1982; 34:321–327.

63. Shane E, Baquiran DC, Bilezikian JP: Effects of dichloromethylene diphospho-nate on serum and urinary calcium in primary hyperparathyroidism. *Ann In-tern Med* 1981; 95:23–27.

64. Douglas DL, Kanis JA, Paterson AD, et al: Drug treatment of primary hyper-parathyroidism: Use of clodronate sodium. *Br Med J* 1983; 286:587–590.

65. Schmidli RS, Wilson I, Espiner EA, et al: Aminopropylidine diphosphonate (APD) in mild primary hyperparathyroidism: Effect on clinical status. *Clin En-docrinol (Oxf)* 1990; 32:293–300.

66. Bilezikian JP: The medical management of primary hyperparathyroidism. *Ann Intern Med* 1982; 96:198–202.

67. Doppman JL: The localization and treatment of parathyroid adenomas by an-giographic techniques. *Ann Radiol (Paris)* 1980; 23:253–258.

68. Doppman JL: The treatment of hyperparathyroidism by transcatheter tech-niques. *Cardiovasc Intervent Radiol* 1980; 3:268–281.

69. Miller DL, Doppman JL, Chang R, et al: Angiographic ablation of parathyroid adenomas: Lessons from a 10-year experience. *Radiology* 1987; 165:601–607.

70. Eisenberg H, Pallotta J, Sacks B, et al: Parathyroid localization, three-dimen-

sional modeling, and percutaneous ablation techniques. *Endocrinol Clin North Am* 1989; 18:659–700.

71. Solbiati L, Giangrande A, De Pra L, et al: Percutaneous ethanol injection of parathyroid tumors under US guidance: Treatment for secondary hyperpara-thyroidism. *Radiology* 1985; 155:607–610.

72. Charboneau JW, Hay ID, van Heerden JA: Persistent primary hyperparathy-roidism: Successful ultrasound-guided percutaneous ethanol ablation of an oc-cult adenoma. *Mayo Clin Proc* 1988; 63:913–917.

73. Tomic-Brzac H, Pavlovic D, Bence-Zigman Z, et al: Ultrasound guided percu-taneous ethanol injection into parathyroid tumor. *Periodicum Biologorum* 1989; 91:463–464.

74. Coe FL, Favus MJ, Parks JH: Is estrogen preferable to surgery for postmeno-pausal women with primary hyperparathyroidism? *N Engl J Med* 1986; 314:1508–1509.

75. Heath H III: Familial benign (hypocalciuric) hypercalcemia: A troublesome mimic of mild primary hyperparathyroidism. *Endocrinol Clin North Am* 1989; 18:723–740.

# Autoimmunity to hsp65 and the Immunologic Paradigm*

## Irun R. Cohen, M.D.

Mauerberger Chair of Immunology, Department of Cell Biology, The Weizmann Institute of Science, Rehovot, Israel

## Editor's Introduction

Dr. Irun Cohen's review of autoimmunity 8 years ago in volume 29 of this series introduced what was then a dawning concept, namely that autoimmunity is primarily physiological and only when aberrant is it pathological. Since then, an avalanche of studies with the powerful tools of recombinant DNA technology has put autoimmunity research on a molecular basis. T-cell receptors and their ligands have been structurally defined in the quest to decipher the complex process of self and nonself recognition. Dr. Cohen reminds us that lymphocyte recognition of antigens should trigger a reflex attack on antigen-bearing cells, whether self or foreign. Burnet's clonal selection theory by which T cells capable of recognition of self antigens are deleted before birth, is, however, only one of several possible explanations of immunologic self-tolerance. Other mechanisms include active suppression of the process, one which for a long time we have called anergy (and still do). What Dr. Cohen now specifically reviews is his recent work and that of others on autoimmunity related to the heat shock protein hsp65. This 65-kd protein antigen produced by heat-stressed cells of all species, bacterial and animal, appears to be intimately involved in autoimmune disease in man and mouse, because suppression of autoimmune responses to hsp can abort autoimmune injury. The impact of heat-shock protein immunology on current concepts of suppression of autoimmunity is the subject of Dr. Cohen's brilliant avant garde review.

*Gene H. Stollerman, M.D.*

## The Reflex Paradigm of Immunity

In most walks of life, unfulfilled expectations are a misfortune; in science, they can be providential. Expectations are preconceived notions. Their

*The investigations done in my laboratory were supported in part by grants from the National Institutes of Health (AR32192), the Juvenile Diabetes Foundation International, the Merieux Foundation, the Minerva Foundation, the Tauro Foundation, and Mr. Rowland Schaefer.

frustration by controlled observation is an opportunity to discard an inadequate idea and draw a better mental approximation of nature. Orthodox ideas about autoimmunity rest on the premise, described by Burnet in his theory of clonal selection,[1] that the etiology of autoimmune disease is self-recognition: the binding of lymphocyte receptors (or antibodies) to self-antigens. Recognition is central to immunology. Clonal selection posits that the immune response to an antigen is triggered by the fit between a preformed lymphocyte receptor and an antigen (the receptor's ligand). The consequences of recognition, to use a neurologic metaphor, are as inexorable as a reflex[2]: sensory input (reception of the antigen signal) automatically leads to an effector output (the immune attack mediated by activated lymphocytes and antibodies). Recognition, according to notions of classic clonal selection, is both the means and the aim of the immune system. The job of the system is to distinguish between self and foreign. The foreign, upon recognition, is designated for attack. The self obviously must not be attacked. Since recognition induces reflex attack, the self is best protected by not being recognized, i.e., by being a nonstimulus.

In a simple reflex, the strength of the output often is linked to the strength of the input: foreign antigens elicit a strong protective response when they are quantitatively present in high concentration and intrinsically immunogenic. How can self-antigens avoid being recognized? Clearly, self-antigens that float freely in body fluids or are attached to exposed surfaces are accessible for recognition. Moreover, even those molecules that exist in the interiors of cells are processed and brought to the surface as peptide epitopes in the clasp of major histocompatibility complex (MHC) gene products.[3] So, for self-antigens not to be recognized, the logic of clonal selection requires that there be no receptors in the system capable of recognizing them. Burnet reasoned that the immune system might rid itself of self-recognizing lymphocytes at an early stage in lymphocyte maturation when contact with antigen induces programmed death.[4] Self-antigens, he proposed, might contact developing lymphocytes and kill the self-recognizers. The lymphocytes with receptors for foreign antigens mature safe from antigen contact and meet their antigens late, when contact induces reflex activation.

An alternative to clonal deletion as the mechanism controlling autoimmunity can be derived from the evidence that nonresponsiveness of lymphocytes to some foreign antigens might be caused by active suppression.[5] Tolerance to self-antigens too might be realized by suppressor lymphocytes that regulate the activities of self-recognizing effector lymphocytes. However, unlike helper T cells, suppressor T cells for specific antigens have evaded cloning and characterization and, therefore, many investigators have been led to doubt their existence.[6]

Recently, experiments have shown that T cells with receptors for certain antigens present in the thymus actually are deleted.[7] In addition, T cells also have been shown to become unresponsive, or anergic, upon contact with antigens outside of the thymus.[8] The mechanisms of clonal deletion and clonal anergy can be viewed together as the experimental vindication of the idea that self-tolerance may arise from the death or functional inactivation of self-recognizing lymphocytes.[6] A collection of papers on the subject under the heading "Tolerance in the Immune System" appears in volume 248 of the 1990 issue of *Science,* pages 1335 to 1393.

The reflex paradigm of the immune response can be phrased thus: molecules that are recognized by immunologically competent cells are operationally defined as foreign. Conversely, the self is operationally defined as that which is not recognized by immunologically competent cells. The mechanisms responsible for creating this difference between the self and the foreign are clonal deletion and anergy. Hence, the sensory world perceived by the immune system is fashioned out of the visible (the foreign) and the invisible (the self); the visible constitute the subjects of recognition and the invisible form the ground (Fig 1).

Autoimmune diseases develop, according to this way of thinking, when self-antigens that should be invisible become visible through the illegitimate emergence of competent self-recognizing lymphocytes.[4] The transformation of ground into subject triggers reflex attack. A number of expectations about autoimmunity arise from this reflex paradigm of the immune response:

1. Self-recognition should not occur in healthy persons.
2. Antigens that resemble self-molecules should be poor immunogens.
3. Autoimmune reactions develop by accident and should have no bias toward any particular set of self-antigens.

This chapter has two objectives: to review new information about the immunology and autoimmunology of a molecule recently discovered to be a specific antigen and to ask whether this information fits the reflex paradigm of immunity. The specific antigen is the 65-kd heat shock protein (hsp65), and what we are learning about its immunology appears to contradict our expectations. But nature was interested in hsp65 before she invented lymphocytes, and we shall first consider the physiology of hsp65 before we explore its immunology.

## A Molecular Chaperone: hsp65

Molecules of hsp constitute a family of proteins divided into subfamilies named for their approximate molecular masses in kilodaltons: hsp90, hsp70, hsp65 (also termed hsp60), and other, lower–molecular-weight proteins.[9] Members of each hsp subfamily are produced by widely different creatures. Nevertheless, they are characterized by high degrees of sequence homology. Molecules of hsp are among the most conserved proteins in evolution. The human and bacterial versions of hsp65 are identical in about 50% of their amino acid residues,[10] despite their divergence from a common ancestor cell at the dawn of life. This remarkable conservation implies that hsp molecules must be essential for the survival of all cells,

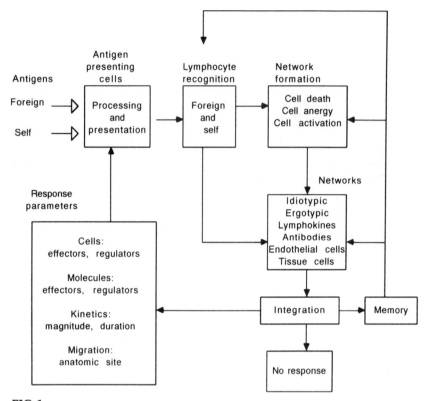

**FIG 1.**
The reflex paradigm of the immune response. According to this view of the immune system, the immune response is regulated by the act of lymphocyte recognition. A sharp distinction is proposed to exist between the T and B cells that recognize foreign antigens and those that recognize self-antigens. The lymphocytes that recognize self-antigens are either killed or inactivated (anergy) by contact with the self-antigen. In contrast, the lymphocytes that recognize foreign antigens are not inactivated. They constitute the mature repertoire and, by contact with their foreign antigens, become activated to mediate an effector response. Activation also generates memory lymphocytes that feed back into the pool of foreign-recognizers. This scheme shows that antigen-presenting cells, which process the antigens, limit the numbers of antigens available for recognition by lymphocytes (denoted by the transition from *open arrowheads* to *closed arrowheads*).

prokaryotic and eukaryotic. One would expect that the functions of hsp molecules should be transparently clear if these functions were so elemental that the existence of cells without them could not be contrived by nature. Alas, we are only beginning to see a hazy outline of hsp functions. One problem is that the few hsp molecules seem to do too many things.

The term hsp is a misnomer, due to the fact that the hsp family was discovered when their production by cells of fruit flies was noted to be augmented upon heating the cells.[11] It soon became evident that all cells produced hsp molecules when heated. The temperature required to trigger augmented hsp production varies according to the life-style of the cell. Mammalian cells used to living at 37° C respond when exposed to temperatures reached during a high fever, thermophilic bacteria that grow at 65° C respond at 76 to 85° C, and blood parasites such as leishmania produce hsp molecules as they experience the sudden transition from insect vector (about 20° C) to mammalian host (37° C). Thus, the heat shock stimulus can be defined as an elevation of temperature above that to which the molecules currently operating in the particular cell are best adapted.

Heat is not the only inducer of augmented hsp production. Almost any type of metabolic, toxic, or physical stress will do. For this reason, hsp proteins also are called stress proteins.[12] Stress for a multicellular organism usually refers to a perceived threat to survival that elicits a "fight-or-flight" response mediated by the endocrine and nervous systems. Stress at the level of the cell is molecular. Thermal, metabolic, or osmotic stress can produce the unfolding of a cell's molecules called denaturation. An important job of hsp molecules must be to deal with denatured proteins, because hsp molecules are produced in large amounts when cells are threatened by denaturing conditions. It is likely that hsp production is universal, because molecular disorder is a constant feature of cellular life: biology must contend with the laws of thermodynamics.

Disorder is not confined to the disorderly molecule. Unfolding exposes otherwise buried hydrophobic and electrostatic forces so that an unfolded polypeptide can stick to other molecules and in turn denature them. Denaturation of molecules can become epidemic and threaten the whole cell. Molecules of hsp are thought to operate as scavengers that trap disorderly polypeptides and protect the stressed cell from cascading denaturation.[9]

However, unfolded polypeptide chains are generated also during orderly cellular life independent of stress.[9] Proteins are synthesized as linear polypeptide chains; in other words, proteins are born unfolded. The unfolded polypeptides can fold into well-natured proteins only after synthesis has been completed. Only the whole polypeptide chain furnishes all the forces necessary to make the proper intramolecular bridges for shaping the mature protein. Molecular disorder (linearity) is a prerequisite for molecular order (folding).

Moreover, even mature, well-folded proteins become unfolded physiologically, for example, when transported across membranes.[9] Once through the membrane, the unfolded polypeptide must refold to the protein's functional shape. It is believed that hsp molecules play a role in the unfolding and refolding required for protein transport.

To summarize, hsp molecules probably function physiologically at baseline levels in protein synthesis, assembly, and transport. In addition, hsp molecules are produced in augmented amounts to combat the denaturation produced by stress. Because the binding of hsp molecules to unfolded polypeptides prevents dangerous liaisons with other molecules, this binding has been called the chaperone function.[9] Hence, hsp65 (hsp60) molecules also are named chaperonins. The idea of the hsp molecular chaperone is attractive; it explains the universal importance of hsp molecules and hence their conservation throughout evolution. The molecular questions are being investigated now. How can the few chaperonins interact with the thousands of different unfolded or denatured proteins? What is the canonical signal that marks molecules for hsp intervention? What do chaperonins recognize? How do chaperonins bind, and how does binding effect both unfolding and folding? How does the cell sense stress so as to express augmented hsp production? Beyond the basic molecular biology of chaperonins, their likely role in the pathophysiology of disease awaits discovery. The subject of their immunology,[12, 13] to which we shall turn now, only touches the surface of what is in store for the physician.

## A Proving Ground for Self-Tolerance

The hsp65 molecule confronts the immune system with a problem in distinguishing between self and foreign. Because of preservation throughout evolution, the hsp65 molecules of all cells, prokaryotes and eukaryotes, are identical in some highly conserved stretches of their amino acid sequence and dissimilar in other variable stretches. Hence, the hsp65 molecule of any invading bacterium or higher parasite confronts the host with a combination of both self and foreign epitopes.[14] Can the immune system respond to such a hybrid between self and foreign? Which hsp65 epitopes are recognized? How is the danger of autoimmunity controlled? These questions can be explored by investigating immunity to hsp65 in three contexts: immune responses to overt infection, natural immunity in the healthy, and immunity in individuals afflicted with autoimmune disease.

## hsp65 Is a Dominant Bacterial Antigen

Antigenic dominance refers to the capacity of a particular molecule to arouse a strong immune response in the face of competing antigenic molecules. Infection with bacteria or other cellular parasites exposes the immune system to a large number of invader antigens simultaneously. Which antigens draw immunologic attention? The clonal selection paradigm predicts that the dominant antigen would be the one with the greatest number of foreign epitopes capable of engaging the greatest number of lymphocyte clones. The hsp65 molecule, studded with self-epitopes, would not be expected to attract much attention.

Despite this reasoning, Table 1 shows that the hsp65 molecules of many different infectious agents are dominant antigens. Humans responding to mycobacteria, enteric bacteria, or higher parasites mount major responses to hsp65 molecules.[15] In mice immunized with whole mycobacteria, 20% of all the T cells aroused to respond are directed to hsp65.[16] The hsp65 molecule has been called the common bacterial antigen.[17]

**TABLE 1.**
**Immunologic Dominance of hsp65 in Microbial Immunity***

| Immune Response to hsp65 | |
|---|---|
| Pathogens | Diseases |
| Borrelia burgdorferi | Lyme disease |
| Chlamydia trachomatis | Trachoma |
| Coxiella burnetii | Q fever |
| Legionella pneumophila | Legionnaires' disease |
| Mycobacterium leprae | Leprosy |
| Mycobacterium tuberculosis | Tuberculosis |
| Treponema pallidum | Syphilis |

*The hsp65 molecules of the above microbes are the targets of immune responses. Reference list appears in reference 15.

Molecular biology has made it technically possible to clone and sequence the genes of antigens recognized by antibodies or T cells. Protein antigens now can be defined by their primary amino acid sequences and not merely by their molecular weight, charge, or mode of preparation. This revolution in microbial immunology has revealed the immunologic dominance of hsp65. It also has revealed the dominance of other microbial antigens that share very high degrees of homology to host molecules, such as the other hsp subfamilies and certain highly conserved essential enzymes. Douglas Young and I have documented and discussed this paradox elsewhere in greater detail.[15] In this article, it need be noted only that microbial antigens selected for major immune responses include protein antigens such as hsp65 that are very much like self to the responding host; the familiar, contrary to the expectations of clonal deletion, is not only recognized but preferred.

## Healthy hsp65 Immunity

Because healthy people are commonly in contact with microbial parasites, and because hsp65 is a common bacterial antigen, we would expect healthy people to exhibit immune reactivity to hsp65, but only to epitopes of hsp65 specific for common bacteria. The reflex paradigm of immunity would lead us to predict that healthy people would have no natural immunity to the conserved epitopes of hsp65 shared by human hosts and their parasites. This prediction is not borne out by experimental results. Munk and associates synthesized four peptides of the hsp65 sequence identical or almost identical in humans and mycobacteria and tested the T cell responses in vitro of healthy people to these peptides: eight of the nine people tested showed T cell immunity.[18] If T cell immunity to self-epitopes of hsp65 can be detected in the healthy, we may conclude that T cells reactive to at least some self-epitopes escape deletion and are not permanently anergic. We may push this line of reasoning forward. If T cell autoimmunity to hsp65 is compatible with health, then either autoimmunity to hsp65 is incapable of causing clinical disease, or there must exist immune mechanisms other than deletion or anergy for regulating the consequences of hsp65 autoimmunity.

## hsp65 and Autoimmune Arthritis

My colleagues and I stumbled into the labyrinth of hsp65 autoimmunity while tracking down T cells responsible for adjuvant arthritis, an autoimmune disease of rats induced by immunization to killed *Mycobacterium tuberculosis* organisms. Adjuvant arthritis was described over 30 years ago by Pearson and associates.[19] Whether or not adjuvant arthritis is a good model of human rheumatoid arthritis,[20] it has served as a useful model of progressive inflammation of the joints produced by the immune system. The problem confronting us was to understand the connection between immunity to a bacterial antigen and what appeared to be an autoimmune disease of the joints.

The approach developed in my laboratory for investigating experimental autoimmune diseases is to isolate as long-term lines or clones the autoimmune T cells responsible for producing the particular disease.[21] The key for unlocking the complexities of pathogenesis is to isolate the etiologic agent itself, whether it be a gene, a toxin, a parasite, or an autoimmune lymphocyte. From a rat with adjuvant arthritis, a T cell clone capable of transmitting arthritis was isolated.[22] This clone, called A2b, was found to respond to an antigen present in both *M tuberculosis* and joint cartilage.[23] We could conclude that immunization to the microbe stimulated the rat to develop an immune response to a microbial antigen that looked like a self-antigen of the joints. The arthritis produced by the T cells was the result of antigenic cross-reactivity between host and mycobacterial immunogen.[24]

Progress subsequently was made in identifying the mycobacterial antigen by investigating the reactivity of the arthritogenic T cell clone to mycobacterial antigens that had been genetically engineered into *Escherichia coli*. The target antigen of the arthritogenic T cell clone turned out to be hsp65.[25] The key epitope of hsp65 was identified as the nine amino acids at positions 180 through 188 in the mycobacterial hsp65 sequence.[25] Surprisingly, this part of the hsp65 sequence was in an unconserved segment of the molecule. There was no sequence similarity between the mycobacterial and mammalian epitopes at this site.[10] Thus, the arthritis could not be due to an attack of the T cell clones against the rats' own hsp65 expressed in joints. In agreement with our earlier finding of T cell cross-reactivity between the mycobacterial antigen and cartilage,[23] we noted a slight homology between the 180 through 188 peptide and a segment of the link protein of cartilage proteoglycan.[26] However, we now know that our T cell clone does not respond in vitro to the proposed peptide sequence of the link protein (unpublished observation, 1990), so the chemical connection between mycobacterial hsp65 and cartilage is yet unresolved.

Our investigations of rat arthritis pointed out a new element for study in human arthritis: does immunity to hsp65 occur in rheumatoid or reactive arthritides? If so, which epitopes are recognized: the 180 through 188 peptide of the mycobacterial hsp65 sequence or other hsp65 epitopes, foreign or self? The experiments done to date clearly show that human arthritis patients manifest T cell responses to hsp65; however, the meaning of the reactivity is obscure. The first investigations indicated that synovial fluid T cells recovered from rheumatoid arthritis joints did respond to hsp65.[27-29] Patients with juvenile rheumatoid arthritis were found to respond to the mycobacterial hsp65 molecule and to its 180 through 188 peptide epitope.[30] However, adult rheumatoid arthritis patients did not show immunity to the 180 through 188 epitope.[30] These differences in immunologic reactivity could result from a real difference in etiology between the juvenile and adult forms of rheumatoid arthritis or they might reflect merely the evolution in time of a single disease entity.

A further complication is the finding that immunity to the mycobacterial hsp65 molecule also accompanies other chronic immunologic diseases, such as scleroderma.[31] Moreover, it was reported that T cell immunity to mycobacterial antigens, including hsp65, may be detected in plural exudates associated with tumors or other causes unrelated to mycobacterial infection.[32] Thus, immunity to mycobacterial hsp65 may accompany various forms of chronic inflammation, not only arthritis.

Another enigma is that many of the T cells responding to mycobacterial hsp65 seem to bear the γδ T cell receptor for antigen.[33] The function of such T cells is not clear.[34] Perhaps the meaning of hsp65 immunity will become clearer when the target epitopes involved in the different diseases are clarified. Nevertheless, the fact that arthritis can be produced by a rat T cell recognizing a defined epitope of hsp65 suggests that hsp65 immunity may have an intimate relationship to the arthritogenic process, at least in rats. Note, however, that the autoimmune process responsible for the arthritis is not hsp65 autoimmunity but an apparent cross-reactivity between the 180 through 188 peptide of mycobacterial hsp65 and some epitope in joint cartilage.[26] True autoimmunity to a mammalian hsp65 molecule does seem to cause a spontaneous autoimmune disease in mice, i.e., type 1 or insulin-dependent diabetes mellitus (IDDM).

## hsp65 and Autoimmune Diabetes

Mice of the nonobese diabetic (NOD) strain spontaneously develop IDDM that mimics the disorder developing in humans.[35] At an early stage in life (4 to 6 weeks of age) NOD mice spontaneously develop inflammation of the islets. The insulitis persists and progressively damages the beta cells. The cumulative loss of beta cells causes a deficiency of insulin production that becomes manifest as overt diabetes at 4 to 6 months of age. Since T cells can transfer diabetes,[36] it seems likely that the IDDM process involves a T cell response to a specific peptide epitope. Unexpectedly, that epitope turned out to be a fragment of the self-hsp65 molecule.

This observation was made when we employed mycobacterial hsp65, our arthritis antigen, as a "control" antigen for the immune reactivity to insulin that we had been studying in NOD mice.[37] We have discovered since that the most active epitope is not in mycobacterial hsp65, but in the mammalian hsp65 sequence. T cell reactivity to human hsp65 is about fivefold greater than it is to the mycobacterial hsp65.[38]

The evidence implicating human-hsp65 as a target antigen in mouse IDDM can be summarized thus:

1. The spontaneous development of insulitis is accompanied by autoimmune T cells and autoantibodies to hsp65.[37] These autoimmune phenomena precede overt diabetes by several months. NOD mice that fail to develop IDDM do not manifest hsp65 autoimmunity.

2. T cell clones (CD4$^+$, CD8$^-$) responsive to a 24-amino-acid peptide in the human hsp65 sequence can transfer insulitis and hyperglycemia to prediabetic NOD mice. The T clones also can cause diabetes in an MHC-compatible strain of mice that does not otherwise develop diabetes, the NON-H-2$^{NOD}$ strain. Active immunization of nondiabetic NOD or NON-H-2$^{NOD}$ mice induces diabetes.[38]

3. The autoimmune destruction of beta cells and the development of IDDM can be aborted by specifically reducing the autoimmune response to the hsp65 peptide.[38] (How we can control reactivity to hsp65 will be explained later.)

We now have cloned and sequenced the hsp65 gene from a mouse insulinoma cell and have found that the mouse and human hsp65 molecules are 97% identical; they differ by only one amino acid in the key epitope.[39] Thus, the response to human hsp65 probably reflects autoimmunity to mouse hsp65. In other words, hsp65 autoimmunity is both necessary and sufficient for the development of IDDM in NOD mice. Inducing the immunity induces the disease and preventing the immunity prevents the disease.

Although the immunologic results are crystal clear, their relationship to the pathophysiology of beta cell destruction is perplexing. An organ-specific autoimmune disease is expected to have an organ-specific target antigen. The hsp65 molecule is inducible in all cells; why should anti-hsp65 T cells target to the islets? It is conceivable that hsp65 has a physiologic role in the assembly or secretion of insulin, which is unique to beta cells. If so, the T cells must have a way of detecting this unique form of hsp65 expression. It also is possible that hsp65 autoimmunity is a critical cofactor to an additional immune response more specifically focused on beta cells.

Note that the 64-kd antigen, another autoantigen related to IDDM, has been identified as the enzyme glutamic acid decarboxylase.[40] Similar to hsp65, the expression of glutamic acid decarboxylase is not unique to beta cells. Thus, there is much to learn about the association between reactivity to particular autoantigens and the expression of autoimmune disease. Be that as it may, the importance of hsp65 autoimmunity is not limited to NOD mice. A preliminary study of T cells from newly diagnosed IDDM patients showed strong reactivity to the very same 24-amino-acid peptide discovered in the NOD model.[41]

## Paradoxes

The results of the investigations of arthritis in rats and IDDM in mice indicate that epitopes of hsp65, bacterial as well as self, can be involved in autoimmune disease. Is it not dangerous for hsp65 to be a dominant antigen in microbial disease and a natural self-antigen in health? Clearly, the immunology of hsp65 cannot be explained by the reflex paradigm or by the mechanisms of deletion or anergy as the guardians of self-tolerance.[2, 6] Whether or not an autoimmune disease develops is not determined only by whether or not self-epitopes are recognized; hsp65 is recognized universally. The determination of health or disease is made distal to the act of recognition. It depends on how the immune system behaves subsequent to recognition. Recognition is only the first step; it merely defines the raw material upon which the immune system then acts. The nature of the immune response to hsp65 can dominate the responses to other antigens, it can be physiologically useful to the host in the host-parasite relationship, or it can be perniciously destructive in an autoimmune disease. How are these diverse programs implemented? Who decides which program to load? The hardware of the system is ready—the T cells and B cells have receptors for hsp65 epitopes; the antigen-presenting cells can process the epitopes; and the phagocytes, inflammatory cells, and complement are available. The outcome of hsp65 recognition depends on the software—the particular organizational program for implementation.

## An Immunologic Brain

To return to the nervous system metaphor, what we are learning about immunity to hsp65 is not compatible with a view of the immune response as a stereotyped undiversified reflex. The diverse outcome of hsp65 immunity and its complexity supports a view of the immune system as a brain. The first step in the transition from reflex to brain is the interposition of an interneuron between sensory input and motor output, between recognition and response. The interneuron is the seed from which sprout the neural networks whose complexities create the integration of information within the nervous system leading to the behavioral repertoire, learning, memory, and adaptation. It should be clear to anyone who observes immune behavior that the immune system too can express a wide range of actions, learn, remember, and adapt. To attribute all this to variations of primary recognition is to seriously oversimplify the system.

## Lymphocyte Networks and T Cell Vaccination

If the immune system acts like an integrating brain rather than like a monotonic reflex, where are its interneurons, its lymphocyte networks? Experimental investigation of immune networks is in an early stage. Nevertheless, lymphocyte networks have been described by several groups, and the work of Coutinho[42] and Rajewsky[43] and their colleagues may be consulted. My appreciation of the power of T cell networks has come about through my work and that of my colleagues aimed at controlling autoimmune diseases by T cell vaccination. The term "T cell vaccination" was coined by us to describe the prevention and therapy of an autoimmune disease by the administration of attenuated autoimmune effector T lymphocytes.[44] Our success in isolating and growing the virulent T cells responsible for an autoimmune disease, experimental autoimmune encephalomyelitis,[45] led us immediately to try to prevent this disease by vaccinating rats with the same T cells, attenuated by irradiation.[46]

Since then, T cell vaccination has been applied successfully to prevent and even to treat a variety of experimental autoimmune diseases such as thyroiditis,[47] adjuvant arthritis,[48] and IDDM.[38] The vaccination effect can be induced by synthetic peptides comprising parts of the sequence of the T cell receptor,[49] indicating that anti-idiotypic immunity to the autoimmune T cell receptors is involved in controlling the autoimmune process. Indeed, anti-idiotypic T cells of both the CD4+ and CD8+ types have been isolated[50] and an anti-idiotypic CD8+ T clone was shown to prevent experimental autoimmune encephalomyelitis in vivo.[51]

The general success of T cell vaccination in the animal models has justified preliminary phase I trials in multiple sclerosis and rheumatoid arthritis.[6] Distinct from the potential value of medicinal T cell vaccination as a therapeutic maneuver in clincal autoimmunity, study of the antiautoimmune mechanisms aroused by T cell vaccination has provided evidence for the existence of natural T cell networks. It seems that animals may respond to T cell vaccination by activating or amplifying T cell networks that already exist before vaccination. In other words, T cell vaccination exploits natural regulatory networks whose physiologic function is to control the expression of autoimmunity.

The evidence for natural networks has been discussed elsewhere.[2, 44, 52, 53] What we know specifically about hsp65 networks can be stated briefly. Both adjuvant arthritis in rats[48] and IDDM in mice[38] can be cured by administering T cells responsive to the epitopes of hsp65 involved in the particular disease. Freedom from disease can be attributed to anti-idiotypic networks of T cells (unpublished data, 1991). Recognition of hsp65 itself is a given in both health and disease; disease or health depends on the behavior of the network of anti-idiotypic T cells organized around hsp65 and the T cells that recognize it.

It has been reported that administration of the 180 through 188 peptide of mycobacterial hsp65 can ameliorate adjuvant arthritis.[54] Moreover, we have found that IDDM too can be treated by vaccinating NOD mice with the 24-amino-acid peptide specific for IDDM.[38] Interestingly, we find that peptide vaccination induces the same immune regulation of the response to human hsp65 as does T cell vaccination with anti-hsp65 T cells.[38] Indeed, peptide vaccination seems to activate anti-idiotypic T cells responsive to the anti-hsp65 T cells that cause IDDM (unpublished observation, 1991). This is what would be expected of an immune network.[53]

Immunologic networks are not only anti-idiotypic. There is evidence that T cells can regulate other T cells through recognition of their state of activation.[55] Moreover, it is becoming clear that networks of lymphokines and cytokines have a great influence on the quantity and quality of the effector cells and molecules deployed by the immune system.[56] These elements integrate to determine the biologic meaning of the response (Fig 2).

The nervous system processes information about the self using a series of neural networks that encode in the brain a functional representation of the body. Recall the neurologic homunculus pictured in neurology textbooks. It now seems that the immune system too processes information about self-molecules such as hsp65 using lymphocyte networks that encode a representation of the self-antigen, a type of immunologic homunculus.[2, 15, 52] This encoding of hsp65 within the networks of the immunologic homunculus may be the cause of the immunologic dominance of this antigen.

Recent research in immunology has advanced greatly our knowledge of the chemistry of the processing, presentation, and recognition of antigen. It was hoped that an understanding of the molecular basis of recognition would suffice to explain the behavior of the immune system. It should not be surprising that this hope will go unfulfilled. The behavior of the nervous system, the other system we use to process information, also cannot be predicted merely by knowing the chemistry of receptors and synapses.

Recognition is only the beginning of the story. The immune system has been selected during evolution, not to recognize the difference between self and nonself, but rather to adapt the individual to the environment in a way that promotes survival. The test of the appropriateness of an immune response is whether the response is beneficial, irrespective of whether the molecule recognized is self or foreign. For example, if a well-regulated response to a self-hsp65 epitope will help rid the person of a microbial infection or a tumor cell, then the autoimmune response is beneficial. In contrast, an immune response to a harmless foreign antigen can trigger an allergy that may damage health and handicap survival. The immune system decides how best to respond to what it recognizes on the basis of what it has learned from past experience. The immunologic networks that encode experience and weigh decisions constitute the immune system's brain.

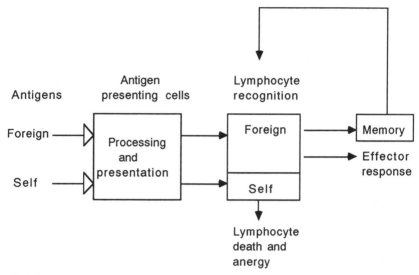

**FIG 2.**
Brain paradigm of the immune system. This paradigm differs from the reflex paradigm in Figure 1 in that lymphocyte recognition of processed antigens is merely the gateway into the system and there is no absolute difference between the lymphocytes that recognize foreign or self-antigens. Lymphocyte recognition of antigen accomplishes two ends: it forms cell networks by cell activation, death and anergy; and it activates these networks to produce an immune response. The networks include lymphocytes (idiotypic and ergotypic), factors (lymphokines and antibodies), and other cell types (endothelial and tissue cells that communicate with lymphocytes by way of cytokines and adhesion molecules). The output of the networks is the integration of information that directs the responses to the antigens. There may be no response to some antigens. Responses to other antigens may include memory (adaptations of the existing networks, the formation of new networks, and changes in the numbers of lymphocytes with receptors for the antigens). Integration of the various networks modifies the parameters of the response, including effector and regulatory T and B cells, effector and regulatory antibody and lymphokine molecules, and the kinetics of the response and traffic of the cells to various sites. The immune response also can feed back to influence the processing and presentation of antigens. According to the brain paradigm, the pressures of natural selection have molded an immune system whose primary job is not to distinguish between self and non-self, but to aid survival of the organism in a changing environment.

## Acknowledgments

I thank Doris Ohayon and Malvine Baer for helping me prepare this article.

## References

1. Burnet FM: *The Clonal Selection Theory of Acquired Immunity.* Nashville, Vanderbilt University Press, 1959.

2. Cohen IR: The immunological homunculus and autoimmune disease, in Talal N (ed): *Molecular Autoimmunity.* New York, Academic Press, in press.

3. Townsend A, Bodmer H: Antigen recognition by class I-restricted T lymphocytes. *Annu Rev Immunol* 1989; 7:601.

4. Burnet M: *Self and Not-Self.* Cambridge, England, Cambridge University Press, 1969.

5. Gershon RK, Kondo K: Infectious immunological tolerance. *Immunology* 1971; 21:903.

6. Rennie J: The body against itself. *Sci Am* 1990; 263:76.

7. Kappler JW, Roehm N, Marrack P: T cell tolerance by clonal elimination in the thymus. *Cell* 1987; 49:273.

8. Goodnow CC, Adelstein S, Basten A: The need for central and peripheral tolerance in the B cell repertoire. *Science* 1990; 248:1373.

9. Ellis RJ: The molecular chaperone concept. *Seminars in Cell Biology* 1990; 1:1.

10. Jindal S, Dudani AK, Harley CB, et al: Primary structure of a human mitochondrial protein homologous to bacterial and plant chaperonins and to hsp65 K D mycobacterial antigen. *Mol Cell Biol* 1989; 9:2279.

11. Lindquist S, Craig EA: The heat-shock proteins. *Annu Rev Genet* 1988; 22:631.

12. Young RA: Stress proteins and immunology. *Annu Rev Immunol* 1990; 8:401.

13. Young DB: Chaperonins and the immune response. *Seminars in Cell Biology* 1990; 1:27.

14. Cohen IR: Autoimmunity to chaperonins in the pathogenesis of arthritis and diabetes. *Annu Rev Immunol,* 1991; 9:567.

15. Cohen IR, Young DB: Autoimmunity, microbial immunity and the immunological homunculus. *Immunology Today,* 1991; 12:105.

16. Kaufmann SHE, Vath U, Thole JER, et al: Enumeration of T cells reactive with Mycobacterium tuberculosis organisms and specific for the recombinant mycobacterial 64 kilodalton protein. *Eur J Immunol* 1987; 17:351.

17. Young DB, Ivanyi J, Cox JH, et al: The 65kD antigen of mycobacteria — a common bacterial protein? *Immunology Today* 1987; 8:215.

18. Munk ME, Schoel B, Modrow S, et al: T lymphocytes from healthy individuals with specificity to self epitopes shared by the mycobacterial and human 65kDa heat shock protein. *J Immunol* 1989; 143:2844.

19. Pearson CM: Development of arthritis, periarthritis and periostitis in rats given adjuvants. *Proc Soc Exp Biol Med* 1956; 91:95.

20. Pearson CM: Experimental models in rheumatoid disease. *Arthritis Rheum* 1964; 7:80.

21. Cohen IR: Regulation of autoimmune disease: Physiological and therapeutic. *Immunol Rev* 1986; 94:5.

22. Holoshitz J, Matitau A, Cohen IR: Arthritis induced in rats by cloned T lymphocytes responsive to mycobacteria but not to collagen type II. *J Clin Invest* 1984; 73:211.

23. van Eden W, Holoshitz J, Nevo Z, et al: Arthritis induced by a T lymphocyte clone that responds to mycobacterium tuberculosis and to cartilage proteoglycans. *Proc Natl Acad Sci U S A* 1985; 82:5117.

24. Cohen IR, Holoshitz J, van Eden W, et al: T lymphocyte clones illuminate pathogenesis and effect therapy of experimental arthritis. *Arthritis Rheum* 1985; 28:841.

25. van Eden W, Thole J, van der Zee R, et al: Cloning of the mycobacterial

epitope recognized by T lymphocytes in adjuvant arthritis. *Nature* 1988; 331:171–173.

26. Cohen IR: The self, the world and autoimmunity. *Sci Am* 1988; 258:52.

27. Res PCM, Schaar CG, Breedveld FC, et al: Synovial fluid T cell reactivity against 65kD heat shock protein of mycobacteria in early chronic arthritis. *Lancet* 1988; 2:478.

28. Gaston JSH, Life PF, Bailey LC, et al: In vitro responses to a 65-kilodalton mycobacterial protein by synovial T cells from inflammatory arthritis patients. *J Immunol* 1989; 143:2494.

29. Gaston JSH, Lif PF, Jenner PJ, et al: Recognition of a mycobacteria-specific epitope in the 65-kD heat-shock protein by synovial fluid-derived T cell clones. *J Exp Med* 1990; 171:831.

30. Danieli MG, Markovits D, Gabrielli A, et al: Juvenile rheumatoid arthritis patients manifest immune reactivity to the mycobacterial 65kD heat shock protein, to its 180-188 peptide and to a partially homologous peptide of the proteoglycan link protein. Submitted for publication.

31. Danieli MG, Gabrielli A, Candela M, et al: Antibodies to mycobacterial 65kD heat shock protein in systemic sclerosis (scleroderma). Submitted for publication.

32. Res PCM, Telgt D, van Laar JM, et al: High antigen reactivity in mononuclear cells from sites of chronic inflammation. *Lancet* 1990; 336:1406.

33. Haregewoin A, Soman G, Hom RC, et al: Human gamma-delta T cells respond to mycobacterial heat-shock protein. *Nature* 1989; 340:309.

34. Raulet DH: The structure, function, and molecular genetics of the γδ T cell receptor. *Annu Rev Immunol* 1989; 7:175.

35. Castano L, Eisenbarth GS: Type-1 diabetes: A chronic autoimmune disease of human, mouse, and rat. *Annu Rev Imunol* 1990; 8:647.

36. Bendelac A, Carnaud C, Boitard C, et al: Syngeneic transfer of autoimmune diabetes from diabetic NOD mice to healthy neonates. Requirement for both L3T4+ and Lyt-2+ T cells. *J Exp Med* 1987; 166:823.

37. Elias D, Markovits D, Reshef T, et al: Induction and therapy of autoimmune diabetes in the non-obese diabetic (NOD/LT) mouse by a 65-kDa heat shock protein. *Proc Natl Acad Sci U S A* 1990; 87:1576.

38. Elias D, Reshef T, Birk OS, et al: Vaccination against autoimmune mouse diabetes using a T cell epitope of the human 65kDa heat shock protein. *Proc Natl Acad Sci U S A,* 1991; 88:3088.

39. Birk OS, Rosen A, Weiss A, et al: A β cell cDNA encoding the mouse heat shock protein 65. Submitted for publication.

40. Baekkeskov S, Aanstoot HJ, Christgau S, et al: Identification of the 64k autoantigen in insulin-dependent diabetes as the GABA-synthesizing enzyme glutamic acid decarboxylase. *Nature* 1990; 347:151.

41. Chatenoud L, Volpini W, Birk OS, et al: Patients with insulin dependent diabetes mellitus of recent onset manifest T cell immunity to the human 65kDa heat shock protein and to its p277 peptide. *J Autoimmun,* in press.

42. Pereira P, Bandeira A, Coutinho A, et al: V-region connectivity in T-cell repertoires. *Annu Rev Immunol* 1989; 7:209.

43. Kocks C, Rajewsky K: Stable expression and somatic hypermutation of antibody V regions in B-cell developmental pathways. *Annu Rev Immunol* 1989; 7:537.

44. Cohen IR: The physiological basis of T cell vaccination against autoimmune diseases. *Cold Spring Harbor Symposia on Quantitative Biology* 1989; 59:879.

45. Ben-Nun A, Wekerle H, Cohen IR: The rapid isolation of clonable antigen-specific T lymphocyte lines capable of mediating autoimmune encephalomyelitis. *Eur J Immunol* 1981; 11:195.
46. Ben Nun A, Wekerle H, Cohen IR: Vaccination against autoimmune encephalomyelitis using attenuated cells of a T lymphocyte line reactive against myelin basic protein. *Nature* 1981; 292:60.
47. Maron R, Zerubavel R, Friedman A, et al: T lymphocyte line specific for thyroglobulin produces or vaccinates against autoimmune thyroiditis in mice. *J Immunol* 1983; 131:2316.
48. Lider O, Karin N, Shinitzky M, et al: Therapeutic vaccination against adjuvant arthritis using autoimmune T lymphocytes treated with hydrostatic pressure. *Proc Natl Acad Sci U S A* 1987; 84:4577.
49. Vandenbark AA, Hashim G, Offner H: Immunization with a synthetic T-cell receptor V-region peptide protects against experimental autoimmune encephalomyelitis. *Nature* 1989; 341:541.
50. Lider O, Reshef T, Beraud E, et al: Anti-idiotypic network induced by T cell vaccination against experimental autoimmune encephalomyelitis. *Science* 1988; 239:181.
51. Sun D, Qin Y, Chluba J, et al: Suppression of experimentally induced autoimmune encephalomyelitis by cytolytic T-T interactions. *Nature* 1988; 332:843.
52. Cohen IR: Natural id-anti-id networks and the immunological homunculus, in Atlan H, Cohen IR (eds): *Theories of Immune Networks*. Berlin, Springer-Verlag, 1989, p 6.
53. Cohen IR, Atlan H: Network regulation of autoimmunity: An automaton model. *J Autoimmun* 1989; 2:613.
54. Yang XD, Gasser J, Riniker B, et al: Treatment of adjuvant arthritis in rats: Vaccination potential of a synthetic nonapeptide from the 65kDa heat shock protein of mycobacteria. *J Autoimmun* 1990; 3:11.
55. Lohse A, Mor F, Karin N, et al: Control of experimental autoimmune encephalomyelitis by T cells responding to activated T cells. *Science* 1989; 244:820.
56. Mosmann TR, Coffman RL: TH1 and TH2 cells: Different patterns of lymphokine secretion lead to different functional properties. *Annu Rev Immunol* 1989; 7:145.

# C-Reactive Protein and the Acute Phase Response*

### Stanley P. Ballou, M.D.

Associate Professor of Medicine, Case Western Reserve University at MetroHealth Medical Center, Cleveland, Ohio

### Irving Kushner, M.D.

Professor of Medicine and Pathology, Case Western Reserve University at MetroHealth Medical Center, Cleveland, Ohio

## Editor's Introduction

In the decade that has elapsed since C-reactive protein and the acute phase response was last reviewed by Gewurz and his colleagues in vol. 27 of *Advances in Internal Medicine*, the research of the host's exudative response to acute cellular injury has largely involved transforming phenomenology into the molecular biology of the cellular hormones (cytokines) that orchestrate the events of inflammation. C-reactive protein has joined a more narrowly defined phase of the acute response, namely the synthesis and release from the liver of the plasma proteins needed to expedite the acute defense, such as, in addition to CRP, fibrinogen and serum amyloid. Whereas the role of serum amyloid remains obscure, that of fibrinogen is well defined. CRP, however, seems to be involved in a real busy-body role of activation of phagocytes, complement, platelets, and other cells, presumably by its direct attachment to its widely distributed phophocholine receptor. The clinical applications of CRP measurement have yet to be fully appreciated. But to those of us who avidly studied the inflammation of rheumatic fever in the 1950s by this most sensitive clinical measure of persistent exudative inflammation (see reference 6), Drs. Ballou and Kushner's review is very gratifying. It illuminates much of what has previously been clinically and biologically intuitively perceived, and delineates how CRP's measurement may be better applied in the future diagnosis and management of inflammatory processes.

*Gene H. Stollerman, M.D.*

All living organisms manifest the ability to respond to external threats with adaptive mechanisms that presumably are important for survival. These mechanisms range from the increased intracellular synthesis of heat shock

*This work was supported in part by National Institutes of Health grant 5 RO1 AG02467-09.

or stress proteins by prokaryotes to a vast array of more complex responses that occur in vertebrates. The changes in vertebrates represent a departure from the homeostatic mechanisms that normally maintain physiologic stability, and include biochemical, hormonal, physiologic, and immunologic responses of a systemic nature that accompany the localized inflammatory response.[1] This systemic response of a vertebrate organism to tissue injury, whether caused by chemical, physical, immunologic, or infectious agents, has been termed the "acute phase response," and is presumed to play an important defensive and adaptive role. It may be relatively transient, reverting to normal with recovery, or persistent in chronic disease.

In recent years, both clinical and basic research interests have focused on a more narrowly defined "acute phase response": the changes in concentration of a number of plasma proteins that result largely from reorchestration of the pattern of plasma protein synthesis in hepatocytes. The proteins that manifest substantial change in concentration are referred to as the acute phase proteins. Since the last review of this subject in these pages by Gewurz et al.,[2] there has been increasing interest in clarification of the mechanisms that regulate these changes and elucidation of the biologic function and clinical significance of this response. Some of these issues have been the subject of recent reviews.[3-5]

The initial recognition of the acute phase response probably can be attributed to the ancient Greeks, who observed that the blood of healthy individuals formed a homogeneous clot upon standing, while the blood of sick persons rapidly sedimented into four relatively distinct layers before clotting. They hypothesized that the failure of these four blood elements, or humors, to blend was responsible for disease. This belief governed medical thought for over 2,000 years, until it was appreciated gradually that rapid sedimentation of the red blood cells was the result, rather than the cause, of disease. The potential clinical usefulness of determining the erythrocyte sedimentation rate was recognized by Fahraeus, who in 1921 quantitated the rate of blood sedimentation in normal individuals, in pregnancy, and in various disease states. Subsequent studies have revealed that a rapid erythrocyte sedimentation rate reflects elevated concentrations of some acute phase proteins, particularly fibrinogen.

The discovery of C-reactive protein (CRP) less than a decade after the clinical studies of Fahraeus was the first specific clue that the body's chemistry is altered substantially during inflammatory states. The circumstances of the discovery of this prototypical acute phase protein, which normally is present in serum in only trace amounts, but whose concentration may rise markedly with inflammatory stimuli, have been reviewed by McCarty.[6]

It now is apparent that the acute phase response is remarkably heterogeneous in a number of respects. First, there are differences in the proteins that participate in the acute phase response in different species. Although some plasma proteins, such as fibrinogen and haptoglobin, behave as acute phase reactants in all species studied, other plasma proteins display acute phase behavior in some species, but not in other, even closely related, species. Second, there are differences in the magnitude and rapidity of change in plasma concentrations of the various structurally and functionally diverse acute phase proteins during the human acute phase response.[1] Ceruloplasmin and the complement components C3 and C4 typically display modest acute phase behavior (about 50% elevation in humans), while concentrations of proteins such as haptoglobin and fibrinogen may increase twofold to fivefold. Most strikingly, plasma concentrations of the two major human acute phase proteins, CRP and serum amyloid A SAA), may increase 1,000-fold or more within a few days after stimulus. In contrast, some plasma proteins, such as albumin and transferrin, consistently demonstrate reduction in plasma concentration during the acute phase response in humans and often are referred to as "negative" acute phase proteins. Third, it has become clear quite recently that the mechanisms that regulate the acute phase response are remarkably diverse, as discussed later. Finally, it appears that the functional consequences of the acute phase response, when known, may be either beneficial or deleterious. Thus, the administration of CRP affords protection against experimentally induced pneumococcal infection in mice,[7, 8] whereas chronically elevated levels of SAA may lead to the injurious accumulation of amyloid in parenchymal tissues in some individuals.[9]

Although the following discussion will focus on CRP, the best-studied major acute phase protein in humans, broader aspects of the acute phase response will be addressed also where appropriate. In addition, we will review briefly the usefulness of assessing CRP and other constituents of the acute phase response in current clinical practice.

## C-Reactive Protein: Structure and Evolution

Human CRP is a pentameric protein comprised of five identical, noncovalently bound subunits, arranged in cyclic symmetry in a single plane[10] (Fig 1). The gene for the CRP subunit in humans is encoded on chromosome 1,[11] and sequence analysis of genomic clones has shown each subunit to consist of a linear chain of 206 polypeptides with a single intrachain disulfide bond and a calculated molecular weight (Mr) of 23,017.[12, 13] The protein is nonglycosylated and nonphosphorylated. Neither polymorphic forms nor isolated subunits have been observed in humans in vivo.

It is of interest that proteins that share structural homology, immunologic cross-reactivity, and phosphorylcholine (PC)-binding capacity (see later) with human CRP have been identified in virtually all mammals tested, as well as in chickens and fish.[14] Indeed, such a protein has been identified in limulus polyphemus, the horseshoe crab, a "living fossil" that has existed on earth for nearly one half billion years.[15] These observations indicate both a primitive origin and great evolutionary conservation of this protein. Nonetheless, there is remarkable diversity in the plasma level and acute phase behavior of these CRPs in various species. For example, normal levels of CRP may be less than 0.02 μg/mL in the mouse, but more than 500

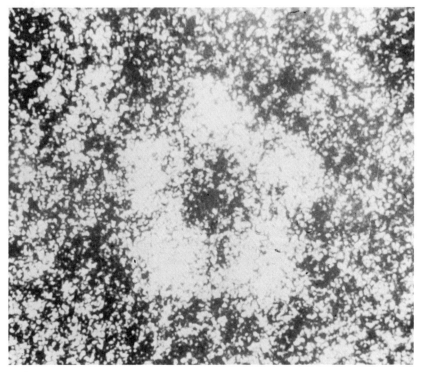

**FIG 1.**
The pentagonal structure of CRP, comprised of five subunits, is depicted in this photograph of five CRP molecules superimposed (× 3,000,000). (From Osmand AP, Friedenson B, Gewurz H, et al: *Proc Natl Acad Sci U S A* 1977; 74:739. Used by permission.)

µg/mL in the rat. Furthermore, in response to inflammatory stimuli, CRP displays dramatic acute phase behavior in humans, monkey, and rabbit, only modest increases in concentration in the mouse, and virtually no acute phase behavior in some species, such as the cow. In the rat, increases in CRP levels are relatively small when expressed as a percent of normal levels, but substantial when expressed quantitatively.

## Function of C-Reactive Protein

### Binding Reactivities of C-Reactive Protein

While the dramatic acute phase behavior and evolutionary conservation of CRP suggest that this protein plays an important physiologic role, its precise in vivo function is uncertain. Nonetheless, two major and potentially important types of biologic activity of CRP have been well defined. First,

CRP has a number of recognition capabilities, i.e., it is able to bind several biologic substrates that are distributed widely in nature. Second, it has significant activation capabilities; in particular, it has the capacity to activate the complement system and to bind to and modulate the function of phagocytic leukocytes.

The discovery of CRP as a molecule that precipitated pneumococcal C-polysaccharide provided the initial evidence for a recognition capacity of this protein. Subsequent studies have established that PC, an integral component of the C-polysaccharide, constitutes a major binding specificity for CRP.[16] Indeed, the calcium-dependent binding of CRP to PC is employed as an operational definition of this protein at the functional level,[17] and this characteristic interaction has been investigated extensively. Biochemical,[18] physical,[19] and electron microscopic techniques[20] have disclosed a single binding site for PC on each CRP subunit, located in a plane perpendicular to that of a distinct calcium binding site,[21] and have suggested that both the phosphate group and the cationic trimethyl-ammonium groups of the MPC molecule are important in the binding interaction.[22] The binding affinity ($K_d$) is approximately $5 \times 10^{-6}$[23] and the interaction between CRP and MPC can be inhibited competitively by other phosphate monoesters, although such compounds bind CRP with lower affinity than does PC.[16] The ubiquitous presence of PC within cell walls of bacteria, fungi, and parasites, and as a component of eukaryotic cell membrane phospholipids such as lecithin and sphingomyelin, has suggested a potentially important role for CRP in the clearance of exogenous infectious agents and endogenous damaged cells.[5] Further support for such a role has been provided by the observation that CRP is localized at sites of damaged tissue in vivo in both experimentally induced[24, 25] and naturally occurring inflammation.[26]

Other binding reactivities of CRP have been studied less well but are potentially of equal biologic significance. Foremost among these are calcium-dependent binding specificities for two constituents of cell nuclei. An interaction of CRP with an affinity constant even greater than that of the CRP-PC interaction is that with rabbit nuclear chromatin.[27] The precise basis of this interaction is not entirely clear. It does not appear to be due to CRP binding to individual histones,[27a] even though CRP is capable of binding to several purified nuclear histones, and histone H1 appears to be necessary for binding to native chromatin.[28] This capacity of CRP to bind nuclear chromatin in physiologic conditions recently has been questioned based on studies employing chicken chromatin.[29] In addition, the ability of CRP to bind the U1 small nuclear ribonucleoprotein has been reported recently.[30] These reactivities of CRP with nuclear ligands may involve the PC binding site of the CRP molecule (or a closely related site), since both interactions can be inhibited by PC. Other reports have demonstrated that CRP is capable of similar binding in a calcium-dependent, PC-inhibiting manner to the extracellular matrix adhesion proteins fibronectin[31, 32] and laminin,[32] and, in certain circumstances, to lipoproteins.[33] Possible implications of these interactions for wound healing and repair and in the pathogenesis of atherosclerosis have been discussed.[32-34] A calcium-dependent binding reactivity of CRP for polysaccharides containing galactose and for other carbohydrates also has been described[35]; the significance of these observations is unclear, and may be related to the presence of phosphate moieties in some of the materials.[36]

In contrast to these interactions, which require calcium, CRP has been reported to bind several biologic polycations, such as protamine, poly L-lysine, and myelin basic protein, in the absence of calcium.[37] These binding reactivities were reported to be inhibited by calcium, but were restored following the addition of both PC and calcium to CRP.[38] One interpretation of these findings is that the polycationic binding site on CRP either is associated physically with or modulated by the PC binding site.

Two other binding specificities of CRP are associated with important activation functions and probably are of considerable biologic significance: (1) ligand-complexed CRP is able to activate complement, and (2) CRP is able to bind to and modulate the function of phagocytic cells. Kaplan and Volanakis initially reported that ligand-complexed CRP bound human C1q, with subsequent activation of the classic complement pathway.[39] Most biologic ligands of CRP studied thus far, including phosphate monoesters,[35] nuclear chromatin,[40] and polycations[41] have been associated with CRP-mediated complement activation. Whether CRP has a similar capacity to activate the alternate complement pathway is not clear; ligand-complexed CRP was reported to inhibit alternate pathway activation in vitro,[42] but in vivo studies have suggested the enhancement of alternate pathway activation by CRP.[43] It is not certain that CRP-induced complement activation occurs in all species.

The most recently recognized binding reactivity of CRP that also is associated with activation functions is its capacity to interact with phagocytic leukocytes. The attachment of heat-aggregated or ligand-complexed CRP to neutrophils and monocytes had been described by several workers.[44, 45] More recently, radioligand binding studies have confirmed the presence of specific receptors for CRP on both human neutrophils[46, 47] and monocytes.[48] The binding to each cell type was observed to be rapid ($T_{1/2}$ for an association <5 minutes) and calcium-dependent, with an estimated $K_d$ of 3 to 10 $\times$ $10^{-8}$M for neutrophils and 1 $\times$ $10^{-7}$M for monocytes. Studies using flow cytometry have confirmed specific, calcium-dependent binding of CRP to about 60% of human peripheral blood monocytes[49, 50] and 40% of neutrophils.[45] The preliminary isolation of two CRP-receptor proteins of approximately 40 kd and 60 kd from the human myelomonocytic cell line U-937 has been reported recently.[51] This group also has identified two human CRP-binding proteins from solubilized mouse macrophages.[52]

There has been confusion regarding a potential relation of the CRP receptors of phagocytic cells with the better-characterized IgG Fc receptors (FcγR) present on these cells. Initial reports of binding of CRP to neutrophils described inhibition by heat-aggregated IgG,[46, 47] but other workers found no such inhibition by monoclonal IgG or by anti-FcγR antibodies,[53] and binding of CRP was not inhibited by IgG in studies of monocytes.[48] Moreover, CRP-binding proteins isolated from solubilized mouse macrophages and U-937 cells have been shown to be distinct from FcγR on these cells.[51, 52] Finally, recent studies of CRP-monocyte binding using both fluid phase and surface-immobilized IgG have suggested that CRP binds to a receptor that is distinct from, but possibly physically associated with, FcγR on these cells.[54] The best-defined binding specificities of CRP are summarized in Table 1.

## Effects of C-Reactive Protein on Phagocytic Cells

The ability of CRP to bind various biologic substrates, activate the complement pathway, and directly bind phagocytic cells has suggested that a major function of this acute phase protein may be to opsonize exogenous or endogenous substrates and modulate phagocytic cell activities. Such a role would be consistent with the previously noted capacity of CRP to protect against experimentally induced pneumococcal infection.[7, 8] However, studies of the effects of CRP on the chemotaxis, phagocytosis, and respiratory burst activity of phagocytic cells have not yielded consistent findings. Chemotaxis of both monocytes and neutrophils was reported to be enhanced by low concentrations of CRP,[55, 56] but that of neutrophils was reported to be either unaffected[57, 58] or inhibited[59] by CRP. While most investigators have reported the enhancement of leukocyte phagocytosis by CRP,[53, 56, 60] others have detected no effect of CRP on the phagocytosis of a variety of bacteria.[61] Finally, native CRP either reduced[56] or had no effect on neutrophil superoxide production,[57, 58] but aggregated CRP significantly enhanced IgG-initiated respiratory burst activity in both neutrophils and monocytes.[62] These apparent discrepancies may be attributed to a number of factors, including variation in experimental methodology, the use of diverse cell populations (total leukocytes, neutrophils, monocytes, or macrophages), and the use of varying forms of CRP, including native, ligand-complexed, and heat-aggregated types.

In recent years, interest has focused on a possible physiologic role for several types of fragments of CRP, including free subunits,[63] proteolytically degraded fragments,[64] and chemically or physically modified forms.[65] There has been particular interest in the possible effects of short polypeptide fragments derived from the CRP molecule, which closely resemble the immunomodulatory tetrapeptide tuftsin.[58, 66] Such peptides, whether synthesized de novo or derived from the native molecule by proteolytic degradation, have been reported to both stimulate and inhibit phagocytic cell functions.[58, 64, 66] It is possible that these divergent findings may be explained by differences of even single amino acids within these peptides.[67] Unfortunately, it is not clear which form of CRP (native pentamer, ligand-complexed molecule, polypeptide fragment, or even subunit) is most physiologically relevant. It is possible that the various forms of CRP may have differing effects on phagocytic cells in vivo. These uncertainties and inconsistent experimental findings preclude an overall consensus regarding the effects of CRP on the chemotaxis, phagocytosis, and superoxide production of phagocytic cells.

**TABLE 1.**
**Reported Binding Reactivities of Human C-Reactive Protein**

| Ligands | Binding Characteristics* | Possible Physiologic Role | Reference |
|---|---|---|---|
| Recognition Functions | | | |
| Phosphocholine† | $k_d = 5 \times 10^{-6}$M; one site per subunit | Opsonization of bacteria and damaged cells | 16, 18–23, 35 |
| Chromatin | $k_d = 8 \times 10^{-7}$M | Opsonization of nuclear debris from damaged cells | 27, 28 |
| U1 SnRNP‡ | | Modulation of autoantibody responses (?) | 30 |
| Fibronectin | $k_d = 10^{-7} - 10^{-8}$M | Tissue repair (?) | 31, 32 |
| Lipoproteins | | ? | 33 |
| Polysaccharides | Secondary to phosphate groups (?) | ? | 35, 36 |
| Polycations | Modulated by phosphorylcholine binding | Clearance of biologic substrates (?) | 37, 38 |
| Activation Functions | | | |
| Complement C1q | Requires prior ligand binding | Activation of classic complement pathway | 39, 41 |
| Phagocytic cells | | | |
| Neutrophils | $k_d = 3 - 10 \times 10^{-8}$M | Modulation of chemotaxis, phagocytosis, superoxide production | 46, 47 |
| Monocytes | $k_d = 1 \times 10^{-7}$M | As for neutrophils above; induction of cytokine release | 48–52 |

*All binding reactivities are calcium-dependent except the one with polycations.
†Includes other phosphate monoesters (lower-affinity binding).
‡U1 SnRNP = U1 small nuclear ribonucleoprotein.

An effect of CRP on two other important functions of mononuclear phagocytes, tumoricidal activity and cytokine production, also has been reported. Several investigators have observed CRP to enhance the tumoricidal activity of macrophages.[68, 69] This effect was independent of lymphokines,[68] but was complement-dependent.[69] The exact mechanism and specificity of this phenomenon remain unclear. More recent reports have described increased synthesis of the cytokines interleukin-1[49, 63, 70] and tumor necrosis factor-α[70, 71] by human monocytes cultured in the presence of CRP. In view of recent information concerning the induction by cytokines of hepatic synthesis of CRP (and other acute phase proteins), a potential effect of CRP on cytokine production may have important implications for positive (or negative) feedback mechanisms regulating acute phase protein synthesis.

## Effects of C-Reactive Protein on Lymphocytes and Platelets

While there has been considerable interest in a possible effect of CRP on lymphocytes, few consistent data have emerged to support such a role. Flow cytometry studies have demonstrated the attachment of aggregated CRP to a small proportion (8%) of lymphocytes,[62] but no attachment of native CRP to various lymphocyte subpopulations was detected,[50] and radioligand binding studies have been unable to detect specific binding of CRP to these cells.[48] Although highly purified CRP appears to have little consistent effect on a range of lymphocyte functions,[72] it has been reported to induce the proliferation of resting lymphocytes and lymphocytes stimulated in mixed lymphocyte culture[72] and to enhance the cytotoxicity of lymphocytes[72] and natural killer (NK) cells.[73]

The effect of CRP on platelets also has been examined. Peptide fragments derived from CRP have been reported to inhibit platelet aggregation.[74] The induction of platelet-mediated cytotoxicity by CRP has been reported also.[75] In addition, CRP may be capable of binding and blocking the activity of the potent lipid autocoid mediator, platelet activity factor.[76, 77] Such binding would not be unexpected, since PC is a prominent constituent of this molecule.

The mechanisms whereby CRP exerts its effects on cells, i.e., the pathways of membrane signal transduction following ligand-receptor interaction, are largely unknown. Buchta et al.[56] observed a rapid and marked rise in cyclic adenosine monophosphate levels in neutrophils following CRP binding. Shephard et al.[64] found that intracellular calcium mobilization in these cells was unaffected by native CRP, but was altered by proteolytically degraded CRP peptide fragments.

In summary, the ability of CRP to bind multiple biologic substrates, activate the complement system, and modulate the activity of phagocytic cells supports an opsonic role for this acute phase protein. This view is supported by recent studies of the effects of CRP on the phagocytosis of heat-injured cells.[78] Taken together, these recognition and activation capabilities of CRP suggest that a major function of this protein is to recognize foreign pathogens and membrane or nuclear constituents of damaged cells and to set in motion a sequence of responses that lead to their containment or elimination.[5] Other reported effects of CRP described earlier hint that there may be additional potentially important biologic activities of this acute phase protein.

## Regulation of Synthesis and Secretion of C-Reactive Protein

The dramatic acute phase behavior of CRP has aroused considerable interest in the regulation of the synthesis and secretion of this protein during the acute phase response. Elevated plasma concentrations of CRP are detectable as early as 4 hours following tissue injury, and peak levels are attained within 24 to 72 hours.[79] The major source of plasma CRP is the liver,[80] and progressive recruitment of hepatocytes to CRP synthesis was found following experimental injury in the rabbit.[81]

The capacity of tissue injury at a distant site to lead to acute changes in the synthesis of proteins by hepatocytes suggested humoral mechanisms for induction of the acute phase response. It is now clear that cytokines, the peptide regulatory molecules produced by a variety of activated cells, are major mediators of acute phase protein induction. Interleukin-6 currently is felt to be the major cytokine influencing acute phase protein changes, while interleukin-1, tumor necrosis factor-$\alpha$, transforming growth factor $\beta$-1, and $\gamma$-interferon also are capable of influencing the synthesis of some plasma proteins in liver cells, and interactive effects of combinations of these cytokines have been shown.[82-84]

Interleukin-6 plays a critical role in CRP induction, although other cytokines may participate in this process under certain circumstances. Thus, CRP induction has been accomplished in human primary hepatocyte culture[85] and in the human hepatoma cell line NPLC/PRF/5[86] by interleukin-6 alone, but not by other cytokines. In contrast, both interleukin-1 and interleukin-6 were required for CRP induction in the Hep 3B cell line. Other studies have indicated that interleukin-1 and transforming growth factor $\beta$-1 also may be capable of influencing CRP synthesis in some human hepatoma cell lines.[86, 87] In addition, corticosteroids can modulate acute phase protein regulation. For example, our own studies have shown that dexamethasone potentiated the induction of both CRP and SAA by cytokines in Hep 3B cells.[84a]

More recent observations have demonstrated that the various acute phase proteins differ in their responses to combinations of cytokines, suggesting that the potential exists for highly specific regulation of each plasma protein by particular combinations of cytokines. These findings suggest that the acute phase response is not a unitary, global phenomenon, but rather that it represents the integrated sum of multiple, separately regulated changes in gene expression. Previous clinical studies have revealed that the various acute phase reactants do not always respond in unison in disease states, suggesting heterogeneous induction mechanisms.[88, 89] The relative proportions of cytokines released by various activated cells could well vary in different pathophysiologic states, leading to different patterns of acute phase protein changes. These observations suggest an in vivo scenario in which the hepatocyte receives a complex mixture of endocrine or paracrine signals that are integrated by multiple interacting postreceptor mechanisms to cause a finely regulated set of changes in plasma protein gene expression.

The specific signal transduction events that mediate acute phase protein induction have not been studied intensively as yet. Several recognized second messenger systems have been implicated in the regulation of the synthesis of different proteins, but an integrated picture has not emerged yet, perhaps reflecting heterogeneity in the effects of different cytokines or combinations of cytokines on different genes. The induction of acute phase proteins is accompanied by increased transcription of acute phase protein genes, mediated by a number of transacting nuclear factors, many of which have been recognized previously as genetic regulatory factors. In addition, post-transcriptional events are felt to participate in acute phase protein induction. Both in vivo and in vitro studies have suggested that the stabilization of messenger RNAs for various acute phase proteins may play a role in the induction of some of these proteins. Recently, the induction of hepatocellular ferritin by interleukin-1 was found to be regulated at the level of messenger RNA translation.[90]

In addition, the process of CRP secretion, as distinct from CRP synthesis, appears to be regulated separately during the course of the acute phase response. The intracellular transport of newly synthesized rabbit CRP has been examined in a series of pulse-chase radiolabeling experiments, which showed that the intact CRP pentamer traverses the secretory pathway from the endoplasmic reticulum to the extracellular space more rapidly in rabbits undergoing an acute phase response than in normal, uninflamed animals.[91] These observations imply that a retention mechanism for the intact pentamer may be operative within the endoplasmic reticulum in the unstimulated state. They raise the possibility that the rate of secretion of newly synthesized CRP may be regulated by specific receptors in the endoplasmic reticulum whose number or affinity for binding of CRP is decreased during the inflammatory response by an undefined regulatory mechanism. Subsequent preliminary studies employing techniques of radioligand binding and immunoelectron microscopy have lent support to this possibility.[92]

Following secretion, CRP appears to display a rapid rate of plasma turnover in the rabbit, with a half-time in the circulation of approximately 4 to 5 hours.[93] Unpublished studies in humans suggest a half-life of 18 hours (M. B. Pepys, personal communication, 1990). During inflammatory states, clearance may be slightly more rapid.[94] The histologic observation that CRP is deposited at local inflammatory sites[24, 25] is consistent with the possibility that there is enhanced clearance at sites of inflammation.

Post-translational glycosylation of a number of acute phase proteins also has been found to be regulated by cytokines during the acute phase response.[95, 96] The mechanisms responsible for this phenomenon are unknown, although it is presumed that alteration in the activity of various glycosylating enzymes may play a role.

## Clinical Value of Assessment of the Acute Phase Response

The major clinical value of assessing the acute phase response today is substantially the same as was recognized by the ancient Greeks over 2,000 years ago, i.e., it allows us, in a general way, to differentiate "sick" from "nonsick." Although a large number of acute phase proteins have been identified, clinical assessment of the acute phase response currently makes use of two measurements, the erythrocyte sedimentation rate and serum levels of CRP. In general, these studies may be of value in evaluating patients for the presence of active inflammatory states. The advantages and disadvantages of these two laboratory tests and a summary of their clinical usefulness are discussed briefly as follows.

## The Erythrocyte Sedimentation Rate

The rate at which red blood cells form sediment is related directly to the concentrations of certain acute phase proteins (particularly fibrinogen) that cause red cells to aggregate and thus to fall through plasma more rapidly.[97] Thus, the erythrocyte sedimentation rate is an indirect way of detecting elevated levels of fibrinogen and other acute phase proteins, an extremely valuable determination when this test was introduced in 1921. However, now that it is possible to measure concentrations of acute phase proteins directly, the usefulness of this indirect test has been questioned.[97] The rate of red cell sedimentation is influenced by factors intrinsic to the cells, such as their size, shape, and concentration, so that anisocytosis, poikilocytosis, anemia, and polycythemia may affect the erythrocyte sedimentation rate and cannot be corrected for accurately. In addition, the rate is affected by other serum proteins, such as monoclonal immunoglobulins and lipoproteins, which generally do not participate in the acute phase response. Thus, monoclonal gammopathies cause a high erythrocyte sedimentation rate in the absence of an inflammatory state. Other disadvantages of this test are that the erythrocyte sedimentation rate rises and falls relatively slowly with the onset and resolution of inflammatory states, reflecting the slower induction of synthesis and longer plasma half-life of fibrinogen compared to the rapidly responsive CRP. The CRP concentration reflects relatively current events, while the erythrocyte sedimentation rate reflects "stale news," a concern more relevant to acute disease than to chronic inflammatory states. In addition, the range of abnormal determinations is much greater for CRP than for the erythrocyte sedimentation rate, and different degrees of CRP elevation may have different clinical implications, as discussed below. Finally, the precise "normal" value of the erythrocyte sedimentation rate is unclear. Although there is widespread recognition that the mean rate increases with age,[98] the magnitude of this change in presumably healthy individuals is not certain. Despite these problems, this test has the advantages of widespread familiarity, low cost, and ease of performance.

In clinical practice, the erythrocyte sedimentation rate has limited application as a diagnostic tool. Extreme elevation of this rate (greater than 100) has some diagnostic value in polymyalgia rheumatica, giant cell arteritis, and multiple myeloma, by increasing the clinical probability of these diagnoses. Although an erythrocyte sedimentation rate over 100 has a high degree of sensitivity for these disorders, it is not 100%; many examples of polymyalgia rheumatica and giant cell arteritis with normal values have been reported.[97] Such elevations more often suggest the need to consider other disorders, such as occult malignancy or, most frequently, infection.[99] While a single test of the erythrocyte sedimentation rate has no prognostic value, persistent elevation in patients without a rheumatic disease or paraproteinemia has been associated with poor prognosis.[99] The test is most useful, however, as a guide to the ongoing management of certain inflammatory diseases, such as polymyalgia rheumatica and rheumatoid arthritis, in which a declining erythrocyte sedimentation rate usually is reassuring and an elevation indicates the need for careful follow-up and perhaps more aggressive therapy.

## Clinical Value of C-Reactive Protein Measurement

The value of CRP determinations for monitoring clinical disease activity has recently been reviewed.[99a] Measurement of CRP may be more generally useful than the erythrocyte sedimentation rate in clinical circumstances, since this test permits precise, direct quantitation of a single acute phase protein, levels of this protein rise extremely rapidly following tissue injury and decline equally rapidly with recovery, and a large range of elevated CRP concentrations can be detected in various clinical situations, reflecting different degrees of severity (Fig 2). Levels of CRP can be quantitated precisely and rapidly by any of several techniques, including radioimmunoassay, enzyme immunoassay, and laser nephelometry. Recently, a simple, semiquantitative, solid phase immunoassay has been developed for use in the physician's office. The normal CRP level in adults is not precisely defined, since relatively minor events during the course of daily living, such as stubbing one's toe or vigorous physical exercise, may be associated with minor elevations of CRP. Thus, while most adults have plasma levels of CRP less than 0.2 mg/dL, levels up to 1 mg/dL (minor or "insignificant" elevations) may be found occasionally in apparently healthy individuals.[100, 101] For purposes of simplicity, CRP levels of 1 to 10 mg/dL conveniently can be regarded as moderate elevations and levels greater than 10 mg/dL are considered to be marked elevations. In markedly inflamed individuals, almost always with severe infections, CRP concentrations of even 50 mg/dL may be seen. Table 2 lists examples of conditions typically associated with differing degrees of CRP secretion.

The diagnostic value of a CRP measurement is related to the level of

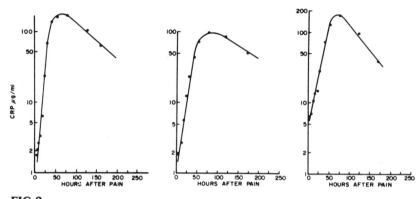

**FIG 2.**
Semilogarithmic plot of serum CRP concentrations after the onset of chest pain in three patients with acute myocardial infarction. (From Kushner I, Broder ML, Karp D: *J Clin Invest* 1978; 61:235. Used by permission.)

CRP detected. For example, insignificant CRP elevations (less than 1 mg/dL) generally are not useful for clinical purposes. The lack of specificity associated with moderate levels of CRP elevation (1 to 10 mg/dL) precludes any consistent diagnostic value of such measurements, although they do suggest the presence of an inflammatory process. Marked elevations of CRP, however, are relatively specific for acute bacterial infections, which are present in 80% to 85% of individuals displaying levels over 10 mg/dL.[102, 103]

Recent studies of the possible differential diagnostic value of assessing

**TABLE 2.**
**Examples of Conditions Associated With Elevated C-Reactive Protein Levels**

| Normal or Insignificant Elevation (<1 mg/dL) | Moderate Elevation (1–10 mg/dL) | Marked Elevation (>10 mg/dL) |
|---|---|---|
| Vigorous exercise | Myocardial infarction | Acute bacterial infection |
| Common cold | Malignancies | (80% to 85%) |
| Pregnancy | Pancreatitis | Major trauma |
| Gingivitis | Mucosal infection | Systemic vasculitis |
| Cerebrovascular | (bronchitis, cystitis) | |
| accident | Most connective tissue | |
| Seizures | diseases | |
| Angina | | |
| Asthma | | |

CRP levels in various acute infectious disease states are tabulated in Table 3. A number of reports have suggested that CRP measurements are of clinical value in differentiating cystitis from pyelonephritis,[102, 104] bronchitis from acute bacterial pneumonia,[102] pulmonary sarcoidosis from tuberculosis,[105] and viral meningitis from acute bacterial meningitis.[102, 106] In addi-

---

**TABLE 3.**
**Disorders in Which Measurement of C-Reactive Protein Has Been Reported To Be of Clinical Value**

---

I. Differential diagnosis.*
   A. Pyelonephritis vs. cystitis.[102, 104]
   B. Pneumonia vs. bronchitis.[102]
   C. Rheumatoid arthritis vs. osteoarthritis.[113, 114]
   D. Myocardial infarction vs. angina.[79]
   E. Bacterial vs. aseptic meningitis.[102, 106]
   F. Acute appendicitis.[115]
   G. Deep vein thrombosis.[116]
   H. Pulmonary tuberculosis vs. sarcoidosis.[105]
   I. Presence of occult infection.
      1. In neonates.[107, 108]
      2. In postoperative patients.[112]
      3. Superimposed on chronic disease.[109–111, 119]
II. Follow-up of disease activity.
   A. Rheumatic diseases.
      1. Gout.[118]
      2. Rheumatoid arthritis.[120]
      3. Polymyalgia rheumatica/giant cell arteritis.[121, 122]
      4. Systemic lupus erythematosus.[110, 119]
      5. Ankylosing spondylitis.[123]
      6. Reiter's syndrome.[123]
      7. Juvenile arthritis.[124]
   B. Other diseases.
      1. Inflammatory bowel disease.[125, 126]
      2. Pancreatitis.[117]

*The precise sensitivity and specificity of elevated C-reactive protein levels for diagnosis in these disorders is uncertain.

---

tion, CRP determination may be helpful in suggesting the presence of bacterial infection in neonates[107, 108]; patients with malignancy,[102, 109] systemic lupus erythematosus,[110] and other chronic diseases[111]; and postoperative patients.[112] It has been suggested that moderate to marked elevations of CRP are also helpful in the differential diagnosis of noninfectious disorders such as angina vs. acute myocardial infarction,[79] osteoarthritis vs. rheumatoid arthritis,[113, 114] acute appendicitis,[115] and deep vein thrombosis.[116] These observations suggest a clinically useful degree of diagnostic specificity associated with high levels of CRP in certain disease states. However, additional studies employing large, well-defined patient populations and repeated determinations of CRP levels over defined time periods are necessary before definitive conclusions regarding the precise sensitivities and specificities of this test can be obtained.

There also has been considerable interest in the potential clinical value of CRP measurements for the follow-up of inflammatory diseases. In general, the resolution of acute traumatic or inflammatory processes such as surgery,[117] gout,[118] pancreatitis,[127] myocardial infarction,[79] or infection[103, 128, 129] is accompanied by declines in CRP levels; persistent elevations of varying degree have been associated with postoperative complications[112] and inadequate treatment.[130] It has been suggested, moreover, that monitoring of CRP levels over time may be useful in the management of chronic inflammatory disorders such as inflammatory bowel disease,[125, 126] polymyalgia rheumatica,[121, 122] ankylosing spondylitis and Reiter's syndrome,[123] juvenile chronic arthritis,[124] and rheumatoid arthritis.[120] It will be of interest to learn whether repeated measurement of CRP levels in other chronic inflammatory disorders has prognostic value or implications for continuing therapy.

## Clinical Value of Measurement of Other Components of the Acute Phase Response

With the exception of SAA, the human acute phase proteins other than CRP display only relatively modest changes in concentration after inflammatory stimuli and have not been employed widely for differential diagnosis or clinical management. Studies of serum SAA levels in various disorders suggest that their measurement may rival the clinical value of CRP, and indeed may be even more sensitive to minor inflammatory states.[88, 114, 125, 131] At present, SAA determinations are not available for widespread clinical use.

A recent and innovative approach to the clinical assessment of a different component of the acute phase response involves measurement of the microheterogeneity patterns of glycosylation of several of the acute phase proteins, notably $\alpha_1$-proteinase inhibitor ($\alpha_1$-antitrypsin) and $\alpha_1$-acid glycoprotein (orosomucoid). Affinity electrophoretic techniques have demonstrated that differences in the glycosylation patterns of these plasma proteins occur during the acute phase response,[95] and may be unrelated to serum levels of these proteins. For example, differences in the glycosylation of $\alpha_1$-acid glycoprotein have been used to distinguish lupus patients with superimposed infection from those with active lupus alone.[119] Changes in the patterns of glycosylation of various proteins during the acute phase response potentially are of both biologic and clinical interest. Further studies of these changes in inflammatory disease states not only may elucidate the mechanisms and significance of post-translational modification of secretory proteins during the acute phase response, but also may define a role for such determinations in the diagnosis and management of disease.

---

## References

1. Kushner I: The phenomenon of the acute phase response. *Ann N Y Acad Sci* 1982; 389:39–48.
2. Gewurz H, Mold C, Siegel J, et al: C-reactive protein and the acute phase response. *Adv Intern Med* 1982; 27:345–372.
3. Gotschlich EC: C-reactive protein. A historical overview. *Ann N Y Acad Sci* 1989; 557:9–18.
4. Kushner I, Ganapathi MK, Schultz D: The acute phase response is mediated by heterogeneous mechanisms. *Ann N Y Acad Sci* 1989; 557:19–30.
5. Volanakis JE, Xu Y, Macon KJ: Human C-reactive protein and host defense, in Marchalonis JJ, Reinisch CL (eds): *Defense Molecules.* New York, Wiley-Liss, Inc, 1990, pp 161–175.
6. McCarty M: Historical perspective on C-reactive protein. *Ann N Y Acad Sci* 1982; 389:1–10.
7. Mold C, Nakayama S, Holzer TJ, et al: C-reactive protein is protective against fatal *Streptococcus pneumoniae* infection in mice. *J Exp Med* 1981; 154:1703–1708.
8. Yother J, Volanakis JE, Briles DE: Human C-reactive protein is protective against fatal *Streptococcus pneumoniae* infection in mice. *J Immunol* 1982; 128:2374–2376.
9. McAdam KPWJ, Sipe JD: Murine model for human secondary amyloidosis: Genetic variability of the acute-phase serum protein SAA response to endotoxins and casein. *J Exp Med* 1976; 144:1121–1127.
10. Osmand AP, Friedenson B, Gewurz H, et al: Characterization of C-reactive protein and the complement subcomponent C1t as homologous proteins displaying cyclic pentameric symmetry (pentraxins). *Proc Natl Acad Sci U S A* 1977; 74:739–743.
11. Whitehead AS, Bruns GAP, Markham AF, et al: Isolation of human C-reactive protein complementary DNA and localization of the gene to chromosome 1. *Science* 1983; 221:69–71.
12. Lei KJ, Liu T, Zon G, et al: Genomic DNA sequence for human C-reactive protein. *J Biol Chem* 1985; 260:13377–13383.
13. Woo P, Korenberg JR, Whitehead AS: Characterization of genomic and complementary DNA sequence of human C-reactive protein, and comparison with complementary DNA sequence of serum amyloid P component. *J Biol Chem* 1985; 260:13384–13388.
14. Baltz ML, de Beer FC, Feinstein A, et al: Phylogenetic aspects of C-reactive protein and related proteins. *Ann N Y Acad Sci* 1982; 389:49–75.
15. Robey F, Liu T-Y: Limulin: A C-reactive protein from *Limulus polyphemus. J Biol Chem* 1981; 256:969–975.

16. Volanakis JE, Kaplan MH: Specificity of C-reactive protein for choline phosphate residues of pneumococcal c-polysaccharide. *Proc Soc Exp Biol Med* 1971; 163:612–614.
17. Kushner I: How C-reactive protein has evolved, in Peeters H (ed): *Protides of the Biological Fluids*, vol 34. Oxford, Pergamon Press, 1986, pp 259–261.
18. Volanakis JE, Kearney JF: Cross-reactivity between C-reactive protein and idiotypic determinants on a phosphocholine-binding murine myeloma protein. *J Exp Med* 1981; 153:1604–1614.
19. Robey FA, Liu T-Y: Synthesis and use of new spin labeled derivatives of phosphorylcholine in a comparative study of human, dogfish and *Limulus* C-reactive proteins. *J Biol Chem* 1983; 258:3895–3900.
20. Roux KH, Kilpatrick JM, Volanakis JE, et al: Localization of the phosphocholine-binding sites on C-reactive protein by immunoelectron microscopy. *J Immunol* 1983; 131:2411–2415.
21. Kilpatrick JM, Kearney JF, Volanakis JE: Demonstration of calcium-induced conformational change(s) in C-reactive protein by using monoclonal antibodies. *Mol Immunol* 1982; 19:1159–1165.
22. Oliveira EB, Gotschlich EC, Liu T-Y: Comparative studies on the binding properties of human and rabbit C-reactive proteins. *J Immunol* 1980; 124:1396–1402.
23. Anderson JK, Stroud RM, Volanakis JE: Studies on the binding specificity of human C-reactive protein for phosphorylcholine. *Federation Proceedings* 1970; 37:1495.
24. Kushner I, Kaplan MH: Studies of acute phase protein. I. An immunohistochemical method for the localization of Cx-reactive protein in rabbits. Association with necrosis in local inflammatory lesions. *J Exp Med* 1961; 114:961–974.
25. Du Clos TW, Mold C, Paterson PY, et al: Localization of C-reactive protein in inflammatory lesions of experimental allergic encephalomyelitis. *Clin Exp Immunol* 1981; 43:565–573.
26. Gitlin JD, Gitlin JI, Gitlin D: Localization of C-reactive protein in synovium of patients with rheumatoid arthritis. *Arthritis Rheum* 1977; 20:1491–1499.
27. Robey FA, Jones KD, Tanaka T, et al: Binding of C-reactive protein to chromatin and nucleosome core particles. *J Biol Chem* 1984; 259:7311–7316.
27a. Du Clos TW, Marnell L, Zlock LR, et al: Analysis of the binding of C-reactive protein to chromatin subunits. *J Immunol* 1991; 146:1220-1225.
28. Du Clos TW, Zlock LT, Rubin RL: Analysis of the binding of C-reactive protein to histones and chromatin. *J Immunol* 1988; 141:4266–4270.
29. Butler PJG, Tennent GA, Pepys MB: Pentraxin-chromatin interactions: Serum amyloid P component specifically displaces H1-type histones and solubilizes native long chromatin. *J Exp Med* 1990; 172:13–18.
30. Du Clos TW: C-reactive protein reacts with the U1 small nuclear ribonucleoprotein *J Immunol* 1989; 143:2553–2559.
31. Salonen E-M, Vartio T, Hedman K, et al: Binding of fibronectin by the acute phase reactant C-reactive protein. *J Biol Chem* 1984; 259:1496–1501.
32. Tseng J, Mortensen RF: The effect of human C-reactive protein on the cell-attachment activity of fibronectin and laminin. *Exp Cell Res* 1989; 180:303–313.
33. Pepys MB, Rowe IF, Baltz ML: C-reactive protein: Binding to lipids and lipoproteins. *Int Rev Exp Pathol* 1985; 27:83–111.
34. Reynolds GD, Vance RP: C-reactive protein immunohistochemical localiza-

tion in normal and atherosclerotic human aortas. *Arch Pathol Lab Med* 1987; 111:265–269.

35. Volanakis JE, Narkates AJ: Interaction of C-reactive protein with artificial phosphatidylcholine bilayers and complement. *J Immunol* 1981; 126:1820–1825.

36. Soelter J, Uhlenbruck G: The role of phosphate groups in the interaction of human C-reactive protein with galactan polysaccharides. *Immunology* 1986; 58:139–144.

37. DiCamelli R, Potempa LA, Siegel J, et al: Binding reactivity of C-reactive protein for polycations. *J Immunol* 1980; 125:1933–1938.

38. Potempa LA, Siegel JN, Gewurz H: Binding reactivity of C-reactive protein for polycations. II. Modulatory effects of calcium and phosphocholine. *J Immunol* 1981; 127:1509–1514.

39. Kaplan MH, Volanakis JE: Interaction of C-reactive protein complexes with the complement system. I. Consumption of human complement associated with reaction of C-reactive protein with pneumococcal C-polysaccharide and with choline phosphatides, lecithin and sphingomyelin. *J Immunol* 1974; 112:2135–2147.

40. Robey FA, Jones KD, Steinberg AD: C-reactive protein mediates the solubilization of nuclear DNA by complement *in vitro*. *J Exp Med* 1985; 161:1344–1356.

41. Siegel J, Osmand AP, Wilson MF: Interactions of C-reactive protein with the complement system. II. C-reactive protein-mediated consumption by poly-L-lysine polymers and other polycations. *J Exp Med* 1975; 142:709–712.

42. Mold C, Kingzette M, Gewurz H: C-reactive protein inhibits pneumococcal activation of the alternative pathway by increasing the interaction between factor H and C3b. *J Immunol* 1984; 133:882–885.

43. Rabinovitch RA, Koethe SM, Kalbfleisch JH: Relationships between alternative complement pathway activation, C-reactive protein, and pneumococcal infection. *J Clin Microbiol* 1986; 23:56–61.

44. Mortensen RF, Osmand AP, Lint TF: Interaction of C-reactive protein with lymphocytes and monocytes: Complement-dependent adherence and phagocytosis. *J Immunol* 1976; 119:774–781.

45. Zeller JM, Landay AL, Lint TF: Aggregated C-reactive protein binds to human polymorphonuclear leukocytes and potentiates Fc receptor-mediated chemiluminescence. *J Lab Clin Med* 1986; 108:567–576.

46. Müller H, Fehr J: Binding of C-reactive protein to human polymorphonuclear leukocytes: Evidence for association of binding sites with Fc receptors. *J Immunol* 1986; 136:2202–2207.

47. Buchta R, Pontet M, Fridkin M: Binding of C-reactive protein to human neutrophils. *FEBS Lett* 1987; 211:165–168.

48. Ballou SP, Buniel J, Macintyre SS: Specific binding of human C-reactive protein to human monocytes *in vitro*. *J Immunol* 1989; 142:2708–2713.

49. Terada KY, Honda SAA, Hanakahi LA, et al: Direct CRP binding to human monocytes and enhanced IL-1 synthesis induced by CRP-PAF complexes. *FASEB J* 1988; 2:A685.

50. Ballou SP, Cleveland RP: Binding of human C-reactive protein to monocytes: Analysis by flow cytometry. *Clin Exp Immunol* 1991; 84:329–335.

51. Tebo JM, Mortensen RF: Characterization and isolation of a C-reactive protein receptor from the human monocytic cell line U-937. *J Immunol* 1990; 144:231–238.

52. Zahedi K, Tebo JM, Siripont J, et al: Binding of human C-reactive protein to mouse macrophages is mediated by distinct receptors. J Immunol 1989; 142:2384–2392.
53. Kilpatrick JM, Volanakis JE: Opsonic properties of C-reactive protein. Stimulation by phorbol myrisate acetate enables human neutrophils to phagocytize C-reactive protein-coated cells. J Immunol 1985; 134:3364–3370.
54. Zeller M, Kubak BM, Gewurz H: Binding sites for C-reactive protein on human monocytes are distinct from IgG Fc receptors. Immunology 1989; 67:51–55.
55. Whisler RL, Proctor VK, Downs EC, et al: Modulation of human monocyte chemotaxis and procoagulant activity by human C-reactive protein (CRP). Lymphokine Res 1986; 5:223–228.
56. Buchta R, Fridkin M, Pontet M, et al: Modulation of human neutrophil function by C-reactive protein. Eur J Biochem 1987; 163:141–146.
57. Shephard EG, Anderson R, Strachan AF, et al: CRP and neutrophils: Functional effects and complex uptake. Clin Exp Immunol 1986; 63:718–727.
58. Robey FA, Ohura K, Futaki S, et al: Proteolysis of human C-reactive protein produces peptides with potent immunomodulating activity. J Biol Chem 1987; 262:7053–7057.
59. Kew RR, Hyers TM, Webster RO: Human C-reactive protein inhibits neutrophil chemotaxis in vitro: Possible implications for the adult respiratory distress syndrome. J Lab Clin Med 1990; 115:339–345.
60. Kindmark C-O: Stimulating effect of C-reactive protein on phagocytosis of various species of pathogenic bacteria. Clin Exp Immunol 1971; 8:941–948.
61. Williams RC, Quie PG: Studies of human C-reactive protein in an in vitro phagocytic system. J Immunology 1968; 101:426–432.
62. Zeller JM, Landay AL, Lint TF: Enhancement of human peripheral blood monocyte respiratory burst activity by aggregated C-reactive protein. J Leukoc Biol 1986; 40:769–783.
63. Potempa LA, Gewurz H, Harris JE, et al: Stimulatory effects of the C-reactive protein subunit on monocyte function, including release of IL-1, in Peeters H (ed): Protides of the Biological Fluids, vol 34. Oxford, Pergamon Press, 1986, pp 287–290.
64. Shephard EG, Anderson R, Beer SM, et al: Neutrophil lysosomal degradation of human CRP: CRP-derived peptides modulate neutrophil function. Clin Exp Immunol 1988; 73:139–145.
65. Potempa LA, Zeller JM, Fiedel BA, et al: Stimulation of human neutrophils, monocytes and platelets by modified C-reactive protein expressing a neoantigenic specificity. Inflammation 1988; 12:391–405.
66. Buchta R, Fridkin M, Pontet M, et al: Synthetic peptides from C-reactive protein containing tuftsin-related sequences. Peptides 1986; 7:961–968.
67. Shephard EG, Anderson R, Rosen O, et al: Peptides generated from C-reactive protein by a neutrophil membrane protease. J Immunol 1990; 145:1469–1476.
68. Zahedi K, Mortensen RF: Macrophage tumoricidal activity induced by human C-reactive protein. Cancer Res 1986; 46:5077–5083.
69. Gautam S, James K, Deodhar SD: Macrophage-mediated tumoricidal activity generated by human C-reactive protein (CRP) encapsulated in liposomes is complement-dependent. Clev Clin Q 1986; 53:235–239.
70. Barna BP, Thomassen MJ, Clements M, et al: Cytokine induction associated with human C-reactive protein. FASEB J 1989; 3:A824.

71. Suthun PA, Katsura K, Hokama Y: Effect of C-reactive protein (CRP) and platelet activating factor (PAF) on tumor necrosis factor (TNF) synthesis in monocytes. FASEB J 1990; 4:A1037.
72. Vetter ML, Gewurz H, Hansen B, et al: Effects of C-reactive protein on human lymphocyte responsiveness. J Immunol 1983; 130:2121–2126.
73. Hamoudi W, Baum LL: C-reactive protein is involved in calcium dependent programming of natural killer cells. Federation Proceedings 1986; 45:489.
74. Fiedel BA, Gewurz H: Cleaved forms of C-reactive protein are associated with platelet inhibition. J Immunol 1986; 136:2551–2555.
75. Bout D, Joseph M, Pontet M, et al: Rat resistance to schistosomiasis: Platelet-mediated cytotoxicity induced by C-reactive protein. Science 1986; 231:153–156.
76. Vigo C: Effect of C-reactive protein on platelet-activating factor-induced platelet aggregation and membrane stabilization. J Biol Chem 1985; 260:3418–3422.
77. Kilpatrick JM, Virella G: Inhibition of platelet activating factor by rabbit C-reactive protein. Clin Immunol Immunopathol 1985; 37:276–281.
78. Yamada Y, Kimball K, Okusawa S, et al: Cytokines, acute phase proteins, and tissue injury. Ann N Y Acad Sci 1990; 587:351–361.
79. Kushner I, Broder ML, Karp D: Control of the acute phase response. Serum C-reactive protein kinetics after acute myocardial infarction. J Clin Invest 1978; 61:235–242.
80. Hurliman J, Thorbecke GJ, Hochwald GM: The liver as the site of C-reactive protein formation. J Exp Med 1966; 123:365–378.
81. Kushner I, Feldman G: Control of the acute phase response. Demonstration of C-reactive protein synthesis and secretion by hepatocytes during acute inflammation in the rabbit. J Exp Med 1978; 148:466–477.
82. Baumann H, Richards C, Gauldie J: Interaction among hepatocyte-stimulating factors, interleukin 1, and glucocorticoids for regulation of acute phase plasma proteins in human hepatoma (Hep G2) cells. J Immunol 1987; 139:4122–4128.
83. Mackiewicz A, Ganapathi MK, Schultz D, et al: Transforming growth factor β1 regulates synthesis of acute phase proteins. Proc Natl Acad Sci U S A 1990; 87:1491–1495.
84. Mackiewicz A, Speroff T, Ganapathi MK, et al: Effects of cytokine combinations on acute phase protein production in two human hepatoma cell lines. J Immunol 1991; 146:3032-3037.
84a. Ganapathi MK, Rzewnick D, Samols D, et al: Effect of combinations of cytokines and hormones on synthesis of serum amyloid A and C-reactive protein in Hep 3B cells. J Immunol 1991, in press.
85. Castell JV, Gomez-Lechon MJ, David M, et al: Recombinant human interleukin-6 (IL-6/BSF-2/HSF) regulates the synthesis of acute phase proteins in human hepatocytes. FEBS Lett 1988; 232:347–350.
86. Ganapathi MK, May LT, Schultz D, et al: Role of interleukin-6 in regulating synthesis of C-reactive protein and serum amyloid A in human hepatoma cell lines. Biochem Biophys Res Commun 1988; 157:271–277.
87. Taylor AW, Ku NO, Mortensen RF: Regulation of cytokine-induced human C-reactive protein production by transforming growth factor-β1. J Immunol 1990; 145:2507–2513.
88. Maury CP: Comparative study of serum amyloid A protein and C-reactive protein in disease. Clin Sci 1985; 68:233–238.

89. Pereira Da Silva JA, Elkon KB, Hughes GR, et al: C-reactive protein levels in systemic lupus erythematosus: A classification criterion? *Arthritis Rheum* 1990; 23:770–771.
90. Rogers JT, Bridges KR, Durmowicz GP, et al: Translational control during the acute phase response. Ferritin synthesis in response to interleukin 1. *J Biol Chem* 1990; 265:14572–14578.
91. Macintyre SS, Samols D, Kushner I: Secretion of C-reactive protein becomes more efficient during the course of the acute phase response. *J Biol Chem* 1985; 260:4169–4193.
92. Macintyre SS, Samols D, Ballou SP: Release of newly synthesized C-reactive protein from the endoplasmic reticulum is regulated during the acute phase response. *J Cell Biol* 1989; 109:98a.
93. Chelladurai M, Macintyre SS, Kushner I: In vivo studies of serum C-reactive protein turnover in rabbits. *J Clin Invest* 1983; 71:604–610.
94. Rowe IF, Baltz ML, Soutar AK, et al: In vivo turnover studies of C-reactive protein and lipoproteins in the rabbit. *Clin Exp Immunol* 1984; 58:245–252.
95. Mackiewicz A, Ganapathi MK, Schultz D, et al: Monokines regulate glycosylation of acute phase proteins. *J Exp Med* 1987; 166:253–258.
96. Mackiewicz A, Kushner I: Transforming growth factor β1 influences glycosylation of α1-protease inhibitor in human hepatoma cell lines. *Inflammation* 1990; 14:485–497.
97. Kushner I: The acute phase reactants, in Kelley W, Harris E, Ruddy S, et al. (eds): *Textbook of Rheumatology*, 2nd ed. Philadelphia, WB Saunders, 1985, pp 653–664.
98. Shearn MA, Kang IY: Effect of age and sex on the erythrocyte sedimentation rate. *J Rheumatol* 1986; 13:297–298.
99. Ford MJ, Innes JA, Parrish FM, et al: The significance of gross elevations of the erythrocyte sedimentation rate in a general medical unit. *Eur J Clin Invest* 1979; 9:191–194.
99a. Deodhar SD: C-reactive protein: The best laboratory indicator available for monitoring disease activity. *Cleve Clin J Med* 1989; 56:126–130.
100. Claus DR, Osmand AP, Gewurz H: Radioimmunoassay of human C-reactive proteins and levels in normal sera. *J Lab Clin Med* 1976; 87:120–128.
101. Palosuo T, Husman T, Koistinen J, et al: C-reactive protein in population samples. *Acta Med Scand* 1986; 220:175–179.
102. Morley JJ, Kushner I: Serum C-reactive protein levels in disease. *Ann N Y Acad Sci* 1982; 389:406–418.
103. Cox ML, Rudd AG, Gallimore R, et al: Real-time measurement of serum C-reactive protein in the management of infection in the elderly. *Age Ageing* 1986; 15:257–266.
104. Hellerstein S, Duggan E, Welchert E, et al: Serum C-reactive protein and the site of urinary tract infections. *J Pediatr* 1982; 100:21–25.
105. Hind CRK, Flint KC, Hudspith BN, et al: Serum C-reactive protein concentrations in patients with pulmonary sarcoidosis. *Thorax* 1987; 42:332–335.
106. Valmari P: White blood cell count, erythrocyte sedimentation rate and serum C-reactive protein in meningitis: Magnitude of the response related to bacterial species. *Infection* 1984; 12:328–330.
107. McCord FB, Jenkins JG, Lim HHK: C-reactive protein concentration as screening test for bacterial infection in febrile children. *Br Med J [Clin Res]* 1985; 291:1685–1686.
108. Forest JC, Lariviere F, Dolce P, et al: C-reactive protein as biochemical indicator of bacterial infection in neonates. *Clin Biochem* 1986; 19:192–194.

109. Venditti M, Brandimarte C, Trobiani P, et al: Serial study of C-reactive protein for the diagnosis of bacterial and fungal infections in neutropenic patients with hematologic malignancies. *Haematologica* (Pavia) 1988; 73: 285–291.

110. Becker GJ, Waldenburger M, Hughes GRV, et al: Value of serum C-reactive protein measurement in the investigation of fever in systemic lupus erythematosus. *Ann Rheum Dis* 1980; 39:50–52.

111. Hind CRK, Thomson SP, Winearls CG, et al: Serum C-reactive protein concentration in the management of infection in patients treated by continuous ambulatory peritoneal dialysis. *J Clin Pathol* 1985; 38:459–463.

112. Fischer CL, Gill C, Forrester MG, et al: Quantitation of "acute phase proteins" postoperatively. Value in detection and monitoring of complications. *Am J Clin Pathol* 1976; 66:840–846.

113. Rowe IF, Sheldon J, Riches PG, et al: Comparative studies of serum and synovial fluid C-reactive protein concentrations. *Ann Rheum Dis* 1987; 46:721–726.

114. Sukenik S, Henkin J, Zimlichman S, et al: Serum and synovial fluid levels of serum amyloid A protein and C-reactive protein in inflammatory and noninflammatory arthritis. *J Rheumatol* 1988; 15:942–945.

115. Dueholm S, Bagi P, Bud M: Laboratory aid in the diagnosis of acute appendicitis. A blinded, prospective trial concerning diagnostic value of leukocyte count, neutrophil differential count and C-reactive protein. *Dis Colon Rectum* 1989; 32:855–859.

116. Thomas EA, Cobby MJ, Rhys Davies E, et al: Liquid crystal thermography and C-reactive protein in the detection of deep venous thrombosis. *Br Med J* [Clin Res] 1989; 299:951–952.

117. Fleck A, Myers MA, Nagendran V: The time course of the acute phase response after surgery: Contrast with exercise. *Br J Rheumatol* 1985; 24 (suppl 1):209–212.

118. Roseff R, Wohlgethan JR, Sipe JD, et al: The acute phase response in gout. *J Rheumatol* 1987; 14:974–977.

119. Mackiewicz A, Marcinkowska-Pieta R, Mackiewicz S, et al: Microheterogeneity of alpha$_1$-acid glycoprotein in the detection of intercurrent infection in systemic lupus erythematosus. *Arthritis Rheum* 1987; 30:513–518.

120. Dixon JS, Pickup ME, Lowe JR, et al: Discriminatory indices of response of patients with rheumatoid arthritis treated with D-penicillamine. *Ann Rheum Dis* 1980; 39:301–311.

121. Mallya RK, Hind CRK, Berry H, et al: Serum C-reactive protein in polymyalgia rheumatica: A prospective serial study. *Arthritis Rheum* 1985; 28:383–387.

122. Kyle V, Cawston TE, Hazleman BL: Erythrocyte sedimentation rate and C-reactive protein in the assessment of polymyalgia rheumatica/giant cell arteritis on presentation and during follow-up. *Ann Rheum Dis* 1989; 48:667–671.

123. Nashel DJ, Petrone DL, Ulmer CC, et al: C-reactive protein: A marker for disease activity in ankylosing spondylitis and Reiter's syndrome. *J Rheumatol* 1986; 13:364–367.

124. Gwyther M, Schwarz H, Howard A, et al: C-reactive protein in juvenile chronic arthritis: An indicator of disease activity and possibly amyloidosis. *Ann Rheum Dis* 1982; 41:259–262.

125. Chambers RE, Stross P, Barry RE, et al: Serum amyloid A protein compared with C-reactive protein, alpha 1-antichymotrypsin and alpha 1-acid glycopro-

tein as a monitor of inflammatory bowel disease. *Eur J Clin Invest* 1987; 17:460–467.

126. Prantera C, Davoli M, Lorenzetti R, et al: Clinical and laboratory indicators of extent of ulcerative colitis. Serum C-reactive protein helps the most. *J Clin Gastroenterol* 1988; 10:41–45.

127. Wilson C, Heads A, Shenkin A, et al: C-reactive protein, antiproteases and complement factors as objective markers of severity in acute pancreatitis. *Br J Surg* 1989; 76:177–181.

128. McCabe RE, Remington JS: C-reactive protein in patients with bacteremia. *J Clin Microbiol* 1984; 20:317–319.

129. McCartney AC, Orange GV, Pringle SD, et al: Serum C reactive protein in infective endocarditis. *J Clin Pathol* 1988; 41:44–48.

130. Angerman NS, Evans MI, Moravec WD: C-reactive protein in the evaluation of antibiotic therapy for pelvic infections. *J Reprod Med* 1980; 25:63–66.

131. Grindulis KA, Scott DL, Robinson MW, et al: Serum amyloid A protein during the treatment of rheumatoid arthritis with second-line drugs. *Br J Rheumatol* 1985; 24:158–163.

# Lung Biopsy

## James P. Utz, M.D.

Consultant, Division of Internal Medicine and Thoracic Diseases, The Mayo
Foundation and Clinic, Rochester, Minnesota

## Mark A. Perrella, M.D.

Fellow, Division of Internal Medicine and Thoracic Diseases, The Mayo
Foundation and Clinic, Rochester, Minnesota

## Edward C. Rosenow, III, M.D.

Arthur M. and Gladys D. Gray Professor of Medicine, Division of Internal
Medicine and Thoracic Diseases, The Mayo Foundation and Clinic, Rochester,
Minnesota

## Editor's Introduction

The internist, through consultation with the pulmonary physician, has an entire
armamentarium of biopsy techniques available for the more definitive diagnosis of
pulmonary parenchymal disease. Drs. Utz, Perrella, and Rosenow point out what
the various biopsy techniques have to offer and when and how each may be used,
assessing the yields and risks of each procedure and whether they are used separately, in combination, or in sequence.

These techniques are being used with increasing frequency in immunocompromised patients, especially those with AIDS, for which they offer special help in
prompt and definitive diagnosis and, therefore, in planning treatment.

*James J. Leonard, M.D.*

Lung biopsy often is required during the evaluation of pulmonary disease.
A variety of techniques are used; these are outlined in Table 1. Every effort
should be made to choose the least invasive method necessary to establish
a diagnosis, thereby limiting risk, discomfort, and expense for the patient.
Unfortunately, less invasive techniques may not provide a diagnosis. The
selection of a biopsy technique depends upon several factors, including the
type of lesion present and the immune status of the patient. A framework
for a discussion of lung biopsy is outlined in Table 2.

## TABLE 1.
### Lung Biopsy Techniques

Expectorated or induced sputum analysis
Bronchoscopic techniques
  Bronchial washings and brushings
  Bronchial biopsy
  Transbronchoscopic lung biopsy
  Transbronchoscopic needle aspiration
Transthoracic needle aspiration
Mediastinoscopy
Mediastinotomy
Thoracotomy

## TABLE 2.
### Lung Biopsy

Lung biopsy in focal pulmonary disease (nonimmunocompromised host)
  Bronchoscopic biopsy techniques
  Percutaneous biopsy techniques
  Staging of mediastinal and hilar lymph nodes in cancer
Lung biopsy in diffuse pulmonary disease (nonimmunocompromised host)
  Transbronchoscopic lung biopsy
  Open lung biopsy
Lung biopsy in the immunocompromised host
  Percutaneous biopsy techniques
  Bronchoscopy
  Open lung biopsy

## Lung Biopsy in Focal Pulmonary Disease in the Nonimmunocompromised Host

Focal pulmonary disease encompasses various types of lesions, including focal infiltrates, small nodules, and larger, masslike lesions. The charge of the physician often is to delineate benignity from malignancy, and that distinction usually requires biopsy. The biopsy technique used depends upon many factors, including the size and position of the lesion, the presence of relative contraindications to a particular technique, the experience and skill of the physician performing the biopsy and interpreting the specimen, and whether the lesion likely would lend itself to cytologic diagnosis or whether a histologic specimen is likely to be required.

A variety of techniques are available for lung biopsy. The most accurate procedure is open lung biopsy, which most often provides a definitive diagnosis and treatment if the lesion is simple. Less invasive biopsy techniques have been developed and are often effective in identifying disease, thereby avoiding a thoracotomy with its attendant morbidity and infrequent mortality. At times, a simple expectorated or induced sputum examination may be helpful in establishing a diagnosis. Unfortunately, less invasive biopsy techniques sometimes fail to yield a specific diagnosis. Frequently, more than one technique will provide useful diagnostic information, and the selection of a particular procedure depends on weighing its relative yields and risks.

Apart from open lung biopsy, techniques for lung biopsy in focal pulmonary disease can be categorized broadly into bronchoscopic and percutaneous procedures.

## Bronchoscopic Biopsy Techniques in Focal Pulmonary Disease

Bronchoscopy has been the primary nonsurgical technique used to biopsy pulmonary lesions. The introduction of the fiberoptic bronchoscope in the late 1960s expanded bronchoscopy's use, making it one of the most common diagnostic procedures in pulmonary medicine today. Histologic and cytologic specimens can be obtained by bronchoscopy in several ways, including endobronchial washing and brushing, forceps biopsy of visible endobronchial lesions, transbronchial forceps biopsy of parenchymal lesions without visible endobronchial involvement, and transbronchial needle aspiration and biopsy of parenchymal and mediastinal lesions. These techniques are often complimentary in obtaining a diagnosis, and their use is based on the radiographic appearance and position of the lesion(s) and the endobronchial findings at the time of bronchoscopy. Suspicion of cancer is often the most important reason for biopsying the lung in this manner, although bronchoscopy also can be used to diagnose pulmonary infections and, in a more limited way, noninfectious benign diseases.

When endobronchial lesions are seen, the diagnostic yield of direct forceps biopsy is high, approaching 90% to 100%[1-4]; endobronchial washings and brushings add little to the diagnostic yield under these circumstances.

Peripheral lung lesions not visible bronchoscopically still may be diagnosed by bronchoscopic techniques, although this is more difficult. Bronchial washings may provide a cytologic diagnosis of peripheral cancer. However, brushings and transbronchial lung biopsy (TBBx) with biplane fluoroscopic guidance have a higher yield. All three of these sampling techniques are complimentary and have been reported to provide a diagnosis in 60% of peripheral lung cancers.[5]

The yield of TBBx in the diagnosis of peripheral masses is dependent upon a number of factors, most importantly the size of the lesion. The yield in lesions less than 2 cm in diameter falls to 15% to 35%.[5-8] TBBx yield is higher for primary bronchogenic carcinoma compared to metastatic lesions,[6, 9, 10] and for malignant vs. benign lesions.[6, 7] Multiple TBBxs increase the yield in peripheral lesions.[2] Success in diagnosing peripheral lung cancers with brushings and TBBx also appears to be dependent on the cellular type,[5] the location of the lesion by bronchopulmonary segment,[5] and its distance from the hilum,[5, 8] though these results have been variable.[11]

The risk of bronchoscopy is low and largely dependent on TBBx, when it is added. The incidence of pneumothorax with TBBx has decreased from that reported when the technique was first described, and now is about 1% to 4%.[3, 12-15] Hemoptysis may be seen following TBBx, but usually is not significant.[13, 14, 16-18]

More recently, transbronchial needle aspiration (TBNA) has been used, and this technique may increase further the diagnostic yield in peripheral lung cancers.[19-21] In TBNA, a needle is passed through the working channel of the bronchoscope into the airway. Under direct vision, the needle then is passed through the bronchial wall into the area to be sampled. As with TBBx, the success of TBNA is greatest for lesions greater than 2 cm in diameter.[19, 20] Similarly, the yield of TBNA of peripheral lung lesions is enhanced when brushings and washings are done also.[20-22] In properly selected patients with peripheral lung masses, TBNA may have a higher diagnostic yield than TBBx.[19, 20] TBNA has been advocated in situations where standard forceps biopsy is difficult, including cases of suspected submucosal spread of tumor and cases of extrinsic compression by peribronchial tumor.[21, 23, 24] Occasionally, TBBx, TBNA, and brushings are all performed to maximize the diagnostic yield. The relative diagnostic yields of lung biopsy techniques in the nonimmunocompromised host are summarized in Table 3.

Whether used for sampling pulmonary parenchymal lesions or staging mediastinal lymph nodes (see later), TBNA appears to be a safe procedure, although the combined experience with TBNA is smaller than that with TBBx. To date, few significant complications have been reported.[19-23]

## Percutaneous Biopsy Techniques in Focal Pulmonary Disease

Percutaneous needle aspiration biopsy of the lung has been used as a diagnostic tool since the late 19th century. Several types of percutaneous biopsy needles have been employed, including cutting needles, high-speed drills, and fine aspiration needles. The cutting needle and high-speed drill needle (trephine biopsy technique) have been largely abandoned because of their unacceptably high complication rates.[25-29] The fine-needle aspiration (FNA) technique has become the percutaneous biopsy procedure of choice.

## TABLE 3.
## Relative Yields of Lung Biopsy Techniques in the Nonimmunocompromised Host

I. Focal disease.
  A. Bronchoscopy.
    1. Endobronchially visible lesion. Yield = 90% to 100%.[1-4]
    2. Lesion not endobronchially visible.
      a. Washings, brushings, transbronchial biopsy. Yield = 48% to 64%.[5, 20, 21]
      b. Washings, brushings, transbronchial biopsy, transbronchial needle aspiration. Yield = 55% to 71%.[19-21]
    3. Peripheral lesion <2 cm in diameter. Yield = 15% to 35%.[5-8]
  B. Percutaneous fine-needle aspiration.
    1. All lesions. Yield = 75% to 93%.[32-35]
    2. Malignant lesions. Yield = 81.5% to 96%.[34, 36-38]
II. Diffuse disease.
  A. Transbronchial lung biopsy. Yield = 38% to 85%.[14, 17, 18, 78-83*]
  B. Open lung biopsy. Yield = 80% to 94%.[76, 77-79]

*May be overestimated by including nonspecific findings as "diagnostic."

Percutaneous FNA in a useful form was developed by Dahlgren and Nordenstrom,[30] and its success was based on the introduction of thin-walled 18- or 20-gauge needles, biplane fluoroscopy, and improved cytologic techniques. Percutaneous FNA provides primarily cytologic specimens, although small fragments of tissue are sometimes available for histologic examination, and samples can be cultured. Contraindications to transthoracic FNA (Table 4) include uncorrectable coagulation abnormalities, severe pulmonary hypertension, a suspected vascular lesion, inability to visualize the lesion at the time of biopsy, and inability or unwillingness on the part of the patient to remain still and control breathing and coughing on command.[31] Increased risk for transthoracic FNA exists in patients with bullous emphysema or cysts within or adjacent to the area to be biopsied, hypercarbia or hypoxemia, uremia, pulmonary hypertension, coagulation disorders, more central lesions, recent myocardial infarction, unstable angina, cardiac decompensation, uncontrolled cardiac arrhythmia, superior vena cava obstruction, advanced stage of cancer, debility, malnutrition, and lung disease significant enough that a pneumothorax would likely cause severe respiratory distress.[31] Transthoracic FNA also is contraindicated in situations in which a positive or negative result is unlikely to have an impact upon a patient's management or prognosis.[31]

The reported diagnostic yield of transthoracic FNA ranges from 75% to 93%, including some patients who have undergone multiple biopsy at-

## TABLE 4.
### Transthoracic Fine-Needle Aspiration*

Contraindications
  Uncorrectable coagulation abnormalities
  Severe pulmonary hypertension
  Suspected vascular lesion
  Inability to visualize lesion at time of biopsy
  Patient unable or unwilling to remain still and control breathing and coughing
    on command
  Result unlikely to have impact on patient's management or prognosis
Increased risk
  Bullous emphysema or cysts within or adjacent to area to be biopsied
  Lung disease severe enough that pneumothorax is likely to cause severe
    respiratory distress
  Hypercarbia, hypoxemia, uremia
  Pulmonary hypertension
  Coagulation disorder
  Recent myocardial infarction, unstable angina, uncontrolled arrhythmia, cardiac
    decompensation
  Superior vena cava obstruction
  Advanced stage of cancer, debility, malnutrition

*Adapted from Sokolowski JW, Burgher LW, Jones FL Jr, et al: *Am Rev Respir Dis* 1989; 140:255–256.

---

tempts.[32-35] For malignant lesions, the reported diagnostic yield ranges from 81.5% to 96%.[34, 36-38] The yield is increased when multiple attempts at biopsy are made, although this likely increases the complication rate. The ability to visualize the lesion fluoroscopically seems to have more to do with successful biopsy than does lesion size.[32, 34] When a malignant lesion is not visible bronchoscopically, transthoracic FNA has a significantly higher diagnostic yield compared to bronchial brushings, washings, and blind biopsy.[39, 40] These reported yields have led some to recommend enthusiastically the use of transthoracic FNA in the diagnostic work-up of focal pulmonary disease.[33, 34, 36-38, 41, 42] Some have endorsed it as the procedure of choice in virtually all cases of such disease.[43]

The widespread acceptance of transthoracic FNA has been constrained, however, by concerns related to the degree of skill needed to perform the procedure, the skill needed in cytopathologic interpretation, the complications of the procedure, false-negative findings in malignant disease, and the failure of the procedure to affect ultimate management in a significant number of patients.

The success of transthoracic FNA depends largely on the skill of the operator. As experience is gained by groups performing large numbers of these procedures, the diagnostic yield and accuracy have increased and complication rates have decreased.[33, 34, 42] This makes it difficult to extend this technique widely to centers that lack these skilled operators or the large number of patients needed to acquire that skill.

Complications from transthoracic FNA are not trivial, and the decision to employ this technique in an individual patient must take these risks into consideration. The incidence of pneumothorax has been reported to range from 4.4% to 31.9%, with most reporting a rate of approximately 20% to 30%.[32–34, 36, 37, 41, 42, 44, 45] Chest tube drainage has been reported to be necessary in 1.5% to 14% of patients biopsied, with most authors reporting a rate of approximately 10%.[34, 36, 37, 41, 42, 44, 45] A small-bore tube attached to a Heimlich valve apparatus often is utilized, and is relatively well tolerated by patients.[34, 41, 42, 46, 47] Interestingly, when computed tomographic guidance is used, the pneumothorax rate may be increased significantly, which may relate to the use of such guidance for lesions more difficult to biopsy and prolongation of the time the needle traverses the pleura when it is employed.[47] It is not unusual for minor hemoptysis to occur after the procedure.[32–34, 36, 37, 41, 44, 45, 47] Although significant hemoptysis is quite unusual, fatal pulmonary hemorrhage has been reported.[48–50] Malignant seeding of the needle tract also has been reported, although it is decidedly unusual.[51–54]

A potential advantage of transthoracic FNA is the identification of benign disease, which would obviate the need for thoracotomy. A specific benign diagnosis may be made by transthoracic FNA.[40] A major concern with this technique is the false-negative rate of biopsy in disease eventually proven to be malignant, which has been reported to be 2% to 18%.[32–37, 44] This is of obvious concern, since a false-negative biopsy may delay potentially curative surgery. It can be argued effectively that, when the likelihood of malignancy is substantial and the lesion otherwise appears resectable, a thoracotomy should be performed, regardless of the result of transthoracic FNA. Given the false-negative rate of transthoracic FNA in malignant disease, one may not be able to eliminate the diagnosis of malignancy confidently, and a thoracotomy may be warranted. Given a positive diagnosis of malignancy, thoracotomy is necessary. Therefore, thoracotomy is indicated in both scenarios, and transthoracic FNA should be avoided.

Some argue that it is helpful to establish the presence of malignancy by transthoracic FNA preoperatively, since thoracotomy may be recommended and planned more confidently.[37, 45] When the clinical history or radiologic appearance suggests that the risk of malignancy is high, this practice merely substitutes a therapeutic thoracotomy for one that is diagnostic and therapeutic, and adds an additional preoperative procedure. Furthermore, since bronchoscopy is considered in some patients preoperatively to rule out a second occult carcinoma, it is often preferable to proceed with a diagnostic bronchoscopy rather than a transthoracic FNA, since it adds information relating to resectability in addition to providing a histologic diagnosis.

The distinction between small-cell lung cancer and non–small-cell lung cancer is important, since the former generally is considered to be a non-surgical disease. The ability to identify small-cell lung cancer by less invasive means may make a thoracotomy unnecessary. Peripheral nodular lesions are less likely to be small-cell lung cancer; therefore, the likelihood of identifying this nonsurgical lesion by transthoracic FNA is low. Furthermore, while some have found that it is difficult to distinguish small-cell lung carcinoma from the non–small-cell form on cytologic specimens,[35, 37, 44] others have not found this to be a problem.[36, 43, 47] Transthoracic FNA biopsy also is considered to be less dependable in other conditions in which a cytologic specimen or tiny fragment of tissue may be misleading, such as thymoma, lymphoma, or mesothelioma.[31] It should be performed only when highly skilled cytopathologic interpretation is available.

Transthoracic FNA should not be performed when an endobronchial lesion is suspected.[31, 34, 40, 41] Under these circumstances, a bronchoscopic examination is the procedure of choice, because the false-negative rate of FNA may be increased, especially if a postobstructive pneumonitis is sampled inadvertently instead of the endobronchial lesion.

Most importantly, transthoracic FNA should not be used when a positive or negative result will not impact upon management.[31] The position that transthoracic FNA ought to be undertaken in virtually any case of focal pulmonary disease seems untenable. It is a useful procedure in carefully selected patients. The American Thoracic Society has recommended that transthoracic FNA be used to biopsy suspected metastatic lesions, to diagnose cancer in a patient who is not a candidate for resection of a lesion unless it is definitely malignant (e.g., a solitary lung nodule in a patient with advanced chronic obstructive pulmonary disease), to identify and histologically classify a pulmonary cancer that is clearly nonresectable, and to biopsy a lesion that is likely to be malignant in a patient who will not undergo a thoracotomy unless the lesion is definitely proven to be malignant prior to that surgery.[31]

## Staging of Mediastinal and Hilar Lymph Nodes in Lung Cancer

Not all patients with lung cancer benefit from surgical resection. Small-cell lung cancer generally is considered a nonsurgical disease. Whether a patient with non–small cell cancer is likely to benefit from surgery depends upon a variety of factors, including tumor size, the involvement of surrounding structures, the presence or absence of lymph node involvement and nodal location, and the presence or absence of metastatic lesions. The staging of lung cancer is based upon radiographic and bronchoscopic criteria, as well as surgical and nonsurgical histologic and cytologic sampling.

Mediastinal and hilar lymph nodes may be staged at the time of thoracotomy. Techniques to identify patients with unresectable cancer are desirable in that they may make thoracotomy unnecessary in these individuals. Mediastinoscopy or mediastinotomy through a small parasternal incision often is used for this purpose. Other methods of preoperative lymph node staging in primary lung cancer have been evaluated. Radiologic assessment has not been able to supplant pathologic staging. Computed tomographic scanning is more sensitive than plain tomography or chest radiography in detecting hilar or mediastinal lymphadenopathy,[55] but it cannot be relied upon exclusively, since enlarged nodes by tomographic criteria may be uninvolved by cancer and normal-sized nodes by the same criteria may be involved.[55-59] Radiologic techniques, including computed tomographic scanning, appear to be most useful in identifying a population of patients with suspicious lymph nodes that may be evaluated with other techniques short of thoracotomy in order to demonstrate unresectability. In each case, unresectability should be based on pathologic sampling. If radiologic techniques, including computed tomographic scanning, do not suggest adenopathy and the lesion otherwise appears resectable, a thoracotomy should be undertaken to resect the lesion and surgically sample accessible lymph nodes for staging purposes.

The transbronchoscopic FNA technique has been used to sample accessible mediastinal and hilar lymph nodes enlarged by radiographic criteria.[60-65] The use of transbronchoscopic FNA of mediastinal and hilar nodes usually is directed by a chest computed tomogram. Enthusiasm for this staging technique must be tempered by recognition of the possibility of false-positive aspirations of lymph nodes related to endobronchial mucosal contamination of the sampling or inadvertent sampling of areas other than lymph nodes.[65-68] A negative result on needle aspiration does not ensure uninvolved lymph nodes. However, this is not a serious problem, since the patient will undergo surgical staging at the time of thoracotomy. Transbronchial FNA may be a particularly useful technique in sampling the hilum in cases of suspected small-cell carcinoma, since these lesions are often central and difficult to detect endobronchially. This identification could direct a patient away from unhelpful thoracotomy and toward more effective nonsurgical therapy.

Percutaneous transthoracic FNA and biopsy of mediastinal and hilar lymph nodes has been advocated by some,[69-72] but has not been utilized widely. Limited experience with this technique has suggested a favorable diagnostic yield, although it shares with other percutaneous techniques a higher incidence of complications than is seen with bronchoscopic techniques.[69-72]

## Lung Biopsy in Diffuse Pulmonary Disease in the Nonimmunocompromised Host

Diffuse lung disease in the nonimmunocompromised host comprises a dizzying array of conditions manifested by widespread chronic interstitial or alveolar infiltrates. The decision to biopsy the lung in this setting often stems from an inability to render a specific diagnosis with confidence in light of relatively nonspecific, noninvasive findings.

For practical purposes, open biopsy and TBBx are the only useful methods of lung biopsy in diffuse lung disease. Open lung biopsy is certainly the "gold standard" against which all other biopsy techniques are compared. The advent of the TBBx technique has sparked great interest, since it offers the possibility of obtaining lung tissue without a thoracotomy and its attendant morbidity. Transthoracic FNA has not been an effective biopsy technique in diffuse disease, since only cytologic specimens (or tiny fragments of tissue) are obtained. The drill core or trephine needle biopsy techniques do provide larger biopsy samples, but these have been largely abandoned because of the previously mentioned unacceptably high complication rates.

The decision to biopsy the lung in diffuse lung disease fundamentally relates to the need to make a specific diagnosis in order to provide a specific treatment, withhold useless and potentially harmful therapy, and provide important information to the physician and patient regarding prognosis.

Open lung biopsy by a limited thoracotomy for diagnostic purposes has been refined throughout the years and now usually involves a small anterolateral exploratory thoracotomy in the fourth to fifth interspace. This technique provides the greatest chance of obtaining a specific diagnosis in diffuse lung disease and is the standard to which TBBx is compared. The enthusiasm for open lung biopsy is tempered, of course, by the morbidity and mortality (albeit low) associated with the procedure, the physician's and patient's level of comfort in diagnostic uncertainty, the perceived urgency of diagnosis and treatment, and the recognition that no consistently effective treatment exists for a variety of diffuse lung disorders.

TBBx was described first in 1965 by Andersen et al.[73] After noting that normal lung tissue was obtained occasionally by a flexible forceps without pneumothorax or other untoward reaction, they were able to obtain small samples of pulmonary parenchyma regularly while evaluating parenchymal disease. Their experience was updated in 1978 to include 939 cases.[18] TBBx has been embraced by many and is a common and sometimes useful biopsy technique in diffuse lung disease.

Both open lung biopsy and TBBx are safe procedures. TBBx is well tolerated. Pneumothorax and hemorrhage are the most common complications. The incidence of pneumothorax after TBBx has decreased as experience has been gained and now occurs in 1% to 4% of patients.[3, 12, 13-15] Andersen and colleagues reported the largest series in TBBx, and only 6 of their 939 patients (less than 1%) had greater than 50 mL of associated bleeding.[18] A review of several series comprising 1,289 cases of TBBx disclosed only 3 deaths (0.2%).[74]

The risks of open lung biopsy also are relatively small. Ray and colleagues reported 2 deaths among 270 patients (0.4%) undergoing open lung biopsy that were thought to be related directly to the procedure.[75] Gaensler and Carrington reported 1 death among 360 patients (0.3%) undergoing open lung biopsy.[76] That death occurred in a severely ill 60-year-old man who proved to have a bronchoalveolar cell carcinoma and multiple pulmonary emboli. A review of several series comprising 2,290 open lung biopsies revealed a 1% 30-day mortality rate (excluding terminal cancer).[74] Consequently, lung biopsy by open or transbronchial techniques should not be viewed as inherently dangerous and should not be withheld if indicated.

The usefulness of a diagnostic technique is predicated not only on its safety, but on its ability to provide useful information that impacts on the care of the patient. When considering the relative diagnostic yields of open lung biopsy and TBBx, it must be understood that most of the diffuse lung diseases are idiopathic and require clinical-pathologic correlation for diagnosis. The pathologic diagnosis of many diffuse lung diseases depends on the histologic pattern, heterogeneity, and distribution of abnormalities, correlated with historic and other clinical information, rather than on the identification of a specific organism or cell type. Often, the small biopsy sample afforded by the TBBx technique is inadequate for this purpose.

The reported diagnostic yield of open lung biopsy in diffuse lung disease ranges from 80% to 94%.[76-79] It is important to realize that open lung biopsy will not provide a specific diagnosis in a small proportion of patients, despite an adequate biopsy specimen.

The reported diagnostic yield of TBBx ranges from 38% to 85%.[14, 17, 18, 78-83] These relatively higher yields include many patients in whom nonspecific findings result, including "fibrosis" and "interstitial pneumonitis." When specific diagnostic criteria are applied to patients prospectively undergoing TBBx and open lung biopsy, the relative yields of these procedures have been reported to be 37.7% and 92%, respectively.[78]

TBBxs are inherently tiny and unselected. The tissue may not be representative of the overall disease process; it may be unhelpful at best, and actually may be misleading.[78, 81-84] The finding of fibrosis and interstitial pneumonitis on a small TBBx might be attributed unwisely to idiopathic pulmonary fibrosis, while an open lung biopsy might show an entirely different process. TBBxs therefore, need to be interpreted with caution in view of the significant potential for sampling error.

Since the tissue from a TBBx essentially is avulsed from the surrounding parenchyma by a forceps, crush artifact may make interpretation difficult. The tissue also comes from regions immediately adjacent to the bronchi, which may exhibit nonspecific changes unrepresentative of the parenchymal disease. Multiple TBBxs often are obtained in order to try and reduce the potential for sampling error, although this practice likely increases the risk of complications.

It seems prudent to avoid certain areas when performing a biopsy on patients with diffuse lung disease. Areas of greatest involvement traditionally have been targeted for biopsy, but it may be better to sample an area of "average" involvement, since the most severely diseased areas may show only end-stage fibrosis, often the "final common pathway" of a variety of conditions. It also has been suggested that biopsy of the lingula be avoided in diffuse lung disease, since it may be a common site of chronic nonspecific inflammation.[74, 85] Although this has been challenged by others,[86] it seems wise to avoid these areas.

Because TBBx is subject to sampling error, claims of diagnostic "accuracy" are difficult to evaluate, particularly since most series have not compared TBBx results directly with open lung biopsy results in the same patients. TBBx, therefore, has been taken as the diagnostic endpoint and not compared with the diagnostic "gold standard." When TBBx and open lung biopsy were compared in a retrospective fashion in patients with nonspecific diagnostic findings on TBBx, one half of the patients were found to have "specific" findings on open lung biopsy.[83] In a prospective study, a more diagnostic biopsy was obtained with open lung biopsy in the majority of patients with nonspecific findings on TBBx.[78] Furthermore, nonspecific findings on TBBx sometimes were felt to be unreliable and often entirely misleading when compared to the eventual diagnosis obtained by open sampling.

The use of TBBx in diffuse lung disease must be tailored to the individual patient. If an individual likely suffers from a disease amenable to accurate TBBx assessment (e.g., lymphangitic spread of carcinoma, sarcoidosis, histiocytosis X), then TBBx is warranted. Even under these circumstances, however, a nonspecific TBBx result should not preclude moving on to a more definitive open lung biopsy. TBBx should be viewed as a less invasive way of obtaining a diagnosis in a subset of patients with diffuse lung disease, but open lung biopsy should be obtained when the TBBx results are not helpful, or are unlikely to be helpful.

Lung biopsy is indicated in cases of diffuse lung disease when diagnostic uncertainty exists. There are occasions when the results of biopsy are unlikely to be of any consequence to the patient's management, and biopsy might best be avoided. Under most circumstances, lung biopsy has diagnostic worth in patients with diffuse lung disease. The value of the procedure may be measured also in terms of its effect on therapy or patient outcome. In a retrospective series looking at patients with diffuse lung disease, open lung biopsy led to a change in therapy in a substantial number of patients in whom less invasive studies had failed to yield a diagnosis.[87] Under those conditions, open lung biopsy appeared to offer therapeutic worth.

Although it would seem that lung biopsy ought to have a beneficial effect on outcome in patients with diffuse lung disease, this has not been shown in any prospective fashion and attempting to do so may be a quixotic exercise. Much of the difficulty stems from the unfortunate practice of grouping diverse lung diseases under one umbrella, thereby obscuring any insight that might be gained regarding individual disorders. It seems prudent to abandon this futile practice and rediscover the trees within the forest.

## Lung Biopsy in the Immunocompromised Host

The decisions to be made concerning invasive diagnostic tests, such as lung biopsy, in the immunocompromised host are much different than in the patient with an intact immune system. While the pulmonary processes requiring a lung biopsy for diagnosis in the immunocompetent patient are often chronic in nature and may be evaluated at a more leisurely pace, those in the immunocompromised often proceed at a rapid rate and require more immediate diagnosis. Studies have suggested that patient outcome in the immunocompromised state may be related to the rapidity with which a specific diagnosis is made.[88–91] When contemplating direct sampling techniques in such patients, factors such as severity of the illness, progression of the disease, type of abnormality on chest radiograph, and expertise of those performing the sampling techniques must be taken into account.

Several diagnostic possibilities must be considered in the evaluation of an immunocompromised host with a new or recurrent pulmonary process (Table 5), including infection, recurrence or extension of the basic underlying disease process, adverse pulmonary reaction to therapy, a new unrelated disease, or any combination of these.[92] Infection, commonly with opportunistic organisms, is the most common cause of morbidity and mortality in the immunocompromised.[93, 94] Noninvasive procedures, such as sputum evaluation, are often unrewarding. In the immunocompromised patient with neutropenia, sputum production is often minimal, and examination of the sputum may not reveal common bacterial pathogens.[95] In patients in whom sputum may be induced, markers of infection such as polymorphonuclear leukocytes and identifiable organisms on gram stain may be absent, even in those who ultimately have a proven pneumonia.[96] Also, more invasive procedures to acquire respiratory secretions, such as transtracheal aspiration, are not used in the majority of institutions, and serious complications of these may arise in the hands of an inexperienced operator.[97] Frequently, direct sampling of a pulmonary lesion is necessary

---

**TABLE 5.**
**Pulmonary Diseases in the**
**Immunocompromised Host**

---

Opportunistic infection(s)
Extension of the basic underlying disease
    process to involve the lungs
Pulmonary reaction to therapy
    Drugs
    Radiation
A new, unrelated disease process
    New or second neoplasm
    Hemorrhage
    Adult respiratory distress syndrome
    Oxygen toxicity
    Aspiration
    Pulmonary embolism
    Cardiac pulmonary edema
Any combination of the above processes

---

to distinguish infection from extension of the primary disease into the lung parenchyma, or complications of a therapeutic drug or radiation.[92, 94] The following section will review more frequently used techniques to acquire pulmonary secretions and tissue in the immunocompromised host, and examine their diagnostic and therapeutic utility. The specific procedures to be discussed will include transthoracic needle biopsy (FNA and large-gauge needle biopsy), bronchoscopy (bronchial brushings, TBBx, and bronchoalveolar lavage), and open lung biopsy.

## Percutaneous Biopsy Techniques

FNA has been shown to be particularly useful in the evaluation of peripheral, focal, and cavitary lesions of >1.0 cm in diameter, with diagnostic yields ranging from 60% to 80% in the immunocompromised patient with a suspected pneumonia.[36, 98, 99] FNA is not as useful in diffuse lung disease in which tissue histology is necessary to make a specific diagnosis,[89, 100] such as lymphangitic spread of an underlying malignancy, leukemic infiltration of the lung parenchyma, and drug- or radiation-induced pneumonitis. In an attempt to provide larger tissue specimens, large-gauge needles (such as cutting needles and trephine air drills) have been devised. However, biopsy procedures with these needles have been associated with high complication rates (up to 60% pneumothorax, 35% hemorrhage, and an occasional death), without significant improvement in diagnostic yield, especially in patients with a diffuse pulmonary process.[27, 100–102] Consequently, transthoracic biopsies with large-gauge needles are almost never used.

## Bronchoscopy

Procedures performed via the fiberoptic bronchoscope provide secretions and tissue for culture and histopathologic identification of the pulmonary processes that afflict the immunocompromised patient. Bronchoscopic procedures are most beneficial in the evaluation of diffuse pulmonary diseases and peripheral localized processes ≥2 cm in diameter. Secretions from the lower respiratory tract may be obtained with bronchial brush catheters. These are particularly useful in the diagnosis of opportunistic pathogens such as pneumocystic, viral, and fungal infections.[102–105] Bronchial brushings are not as useful in the diagnosis of bacterial pneumonia, due to the possible contamination of the catheter with oropharyngeal secretions. Protected brush catheters have been devised to prevent oropharyngeal contamination, although quantitative cultures of the secretions may be necessary to distinguish pathogens from nonpathogens (contaminants or colonizers).[106, 107] Bronchial brushing is a rapid and safe way to obtain lower respiratory secretions via the fiberoptic bronchoscope with a minimal risk of pneumothorax, hemorrhage, or exacerbation of respiratory failure in the immunocompromised patient. However, brushings are unable to provide tissue for histopathologic examination.

TBBx via the fiberoptic bronchoscope provides not only material for culture, but also tissue for histopathologic examination. In the immunocompromised host without acquired immune deficiency syndrome (AIDS), the diagnostic yield of TBBx ranges from 30% to 60%,[102-104, 108-110] while in AIDS patients, it ranges from 60% to 90%.[111, 112] By providing tissue for histopathologic examination, TBBx adds to the diagnostic yield of bronchial brushings[102-104, 108] and is particularly useful in disease states that may require tissue for diagnosis, such as neoplasms and drug- or radiation-induced pneumonitis.

Bronchoalveolar lavage via the fiberoptic bronchoscope is an excellent diagnostic tool in the immunocompromised patient with suspected infection. It is very useful in the diagnosis of opportunistic infections[111-119] and pulmonary hemorrhage.[113, 120] However, diagnosing pulmonary hemorrhage requires the identification of hemosiderin-laden macrophages, which may not be present within the first 24 hours. Bronchoalveolar lavage is not as useful in the diagnosis of pulmonary neoplasms and drug- or radiation-induced pneumonitis, which often require histopathologic delineation. The overall diagnostic yield of bronchoalveolar lavage in non-AIDS patients is 50% to 60%,[113-116] and increases to 80% to 90% in non-AIDS patients with infectious pulmonary processes. The overall diagnostic yield of the procedure in infected AIDS patients is 85% to 95%.[111, 112, 119] The diagnostic yield of bronchoalveolar lavage may be increased to 95% to 98% in AIDS patients with the addition of TBBx, which helps in detecting non-pneumocystic infections such as mycobacteria and fungi. Diseases typically missed by bronchoscopy in AIDS patients are Kaposi's sarcoma and lymphocytic interstitial pneumonitis.[111, 112, 119, 121] Studies have suggested that open lung biopsy is necessary for their diagnosis.[122-124] Since the majority of the pulmonary processes in AIDS patients have an infectious etiology, and bronchoalveolar lavage has a very high diagnostic yield, TBBx can be avoided if a risk of hemorrhage is present in the patient.[111] The diagnostic yield of bronchoalveolar lavage tends to decrease if it is performed beyond 48 hours after the initiation of therapy, especially in infected patients. Complications associated with the procedure are minimal. Studies have shown that it may be performed safely in thrombocytopenic patients (<50,000 platelets).[113, 114, 119] The most recognized complications of bronchoalveolar lavage are slight temperature elevation with an increased pulmonary infiltrate in the location of the lavage[113, 119] and the exacerbation of respiratory failure requiring transient mechanical ventilation (<5% of patients).[114] Although bronchoalveolar lavage is limited in its ability to detect neoplastic disease, recent studies have suggested that it may be useful in the diagnosis of lymphangitic carcinomatosis by cytologic examination,[125] and pulmonary lymphoma by the use of Southern blot analysis.[126]

## Open Lung Biopsy

Open lung biopsy is the "gold standard" procedure for the diagnosis of pulmonary processes in the immunocompromised host, and is particularly useful in detecting noninfectious pulmonary diseases, including neoplasms (Kaposi's sarcoma in the AIDS patient) and drug- or radiation-induced pneumonitis. Typically, open lung biopsy is used when less invasive procedures are unable to provide an acceptable diagnosis, or when a definitive diagnosis is needed immediately in a rapidly deteriorating patient. Table 6 compares the diagnostic yield and complications of open lung biopsy, TBBx, and bronchoalveolar lavage in the immunocompromised patient. Open lung biopsy provides a specific diagnosis in 55% to 85% of cases.[90, 91, 127–130] However, when considering the diagnostic yield of open lung biopsy, it is important to realize that the patients analyzed in many of these studies have failed empiric antibiotics and diagnosis by other invasive techniques, such as TBBx. Thus, patients who typically would have a specific diagnosis made by open lung biopsy are excluded. Despite this, investigations have shown open lung biopsy to be a useful diagnostic test in patients with a prior nondiagnostic TBBx.[90, 127] Even though open lung biopsy is the "gold standard" procedure, studies have suggested that it may not reveal diagnoses in certain patient populations,[132] and that empiric antibiotics may be just as efficacious.[133]

Open lung biopsy is performed infrequently in individuals with AIDS, due to the very high diagnostic yield of bronchoscopy in these patients.[93, 111, 112, 121, 131] The most common pulmonary disease missed by bronchoscopy in the AIDS population is Kaposi's sarcoma; after diagnosis of this disease, even with the initiation of therapy, the median survival is less than 6 months.[122, 123] A recent study retrospectively assessed the efficacy of open lung biopsy in 66 patients with AIDS and found that therapy was altered due to the biopsy result in only 1.5% of patients.[131]

## TABLE 6.
### Diagnostic Yield and Complications of Bronchoscopy and Open Lung Biopsy in the Immunocompromised Host

| Type of Procedure* | Number of Procedures | Specific Diagnosis, % | Complications,† % |
|---|---|---|---|
| Transbronchial biopsy | | | |
| Non-AIDS[102–104, 108–110] | 188 | 37 | 13 |
| AIDS[111, 119, 124] | 289 | 71‡ | 6 |
| Bronchoalveolar lavage | | | |
| Non-AIDS[113–116] | 357 | 58 | 1 |
| AIDS[111, 119, 124] | 300 | 85‡ | 0 |
| Open lung biopsy | | | |
| Non-AIDS[91, 127–130] | 366 | 70 | 10 |
| AIDS[112, 119, 124, 131] | 134 | 87 | — |

*AIDS = acquired immune deficiency syndrome.
†Pneumothorax requiring chest tube placement or hemorrhage.
‡Diagnostic yield in AIDS patients with infection; diagnostic yield of bronchoscopy is 65% to 85% with the inclusion of Kaposi's sarcoma patients.[119, 124]

Open lung biopsy has both disadvantages and advantages when compared to other diagnostic procedures, such as TBBx. It requires general anesthesia and a thoracotomy, and involves a certain amount of postoperative incisional pain. However, open lung biopsy allows direct visualization of the biopsy site and the acquisition of a larger tissue specimen; therefore, the number of tests that can be done on or with the tissue is not limited, as it is with TBBx. Also, in the thrombocytopenic patient, hemostasis can be obtained better with direct visualization of the biopsy site, compared to a blind procedure such as TBBx. Overall, serious complications due to open lung biosy are minimal.

A pivotal question remains as to whether a specific diagnosis by open lung biopsy changes therapy and outcome for the patient. In the non-AIDS immunocompromised host, studies conflict in regard to this question. A specific diagnosis should allow a directed therapeutic approach to the patient, but this does not assure a beneficial clinical outcome. Studies have suggested that patient outcome may be related to the rapidity with which a specific diagnosis is made.[88–91, 127] If patients with multiorgan failure are referred late in their disease course, a specific diagnosis by open lung biopsy does not alter the mortality rate compared to patients with a nonspecific diagnosis.[129] As mentioned previously, open lung biopsy in AIDS patients has little influence on therapy or patient outcome,[131] especially when therapy has been directed by a previous bronchoscopy.

## Noninvasive Radiologic Tests

Noninvasive radiologic tests, such as routine chest radiography and computerized tomography, are unable to provide specific diagnoses, but do provide diagnostic clues. In an immunocompromised patient whose clinical course suggests infection, a focal cavitary lesion more likely represents a bacterial or fungal infection, while a diffuse infiltrate suggests a viral or pneumocystic infection.[94] Also, in patients with a history of lymphoma, lymphadenopathy with a subacute clinical course would suggest recurrent lymphoma. Clues such as these provide guidance for therapy and direction in selecting the appropriate diagnostic procedure in an immunocompromised patient with an unknown lung process.

## General Approach to the Immunocompromised Host

Table 7 outlines a general approach to the immunocompromised patient when considering a lung biopsy for an unknown pulmonary process. Initially, noninvasive tests such as sputum examination, blood cultures, and a chest radiograph should be obtained, and empiric antibiotics should be initiated if the clinical scenario dictates the need. If no diagnosis is made and the patient does not improve, more invasive testing needs to be undertaken. FNA may be considered when a focal, peripheral, and/or cavitary infiltrate is present on the chest radiograph, as long as no contraindications are present. If the FNA is nondiagnostic, the patient has AIDS, or the pulmonary process is diffuse, bronchoscopy is useful. TBBx may be per-

**TABLE 7.**
**Approach to the Immunocompromised Host With Pulmonary Disease**

Noninvasive testing including sputum examination, blood cultures, and chest radiography; initiate empiric antibiotics if the clinical scenario dictates
If no diagnosis or improvement, and the lesion is focal, peripheral, and/or cavitary, consider fine-needle aspiration if no contraindications
If the fine-needle aspiration is nondiagnostic, the patient has the acquired immune deficiency syndrome, or the pulmonary process is diffuse, proceed to bronchoscopy
    If there are no contraindications, perform transbronchial biopsy along with bronchoalveolar lavage and bronchial brushings to increase the diagnostic yield
    If transbronchial biopsy is contraindicated, perform bronchoalveolar lavage and brushings without a biopsy
    If possible, proceed to bronchoalveolar lavage within 48 hours of initiating therapy to improve the diagnostic yield
If the patient is deteriorating rapidly and an immediate diagnosis is needed, or the above procedures are nondiagnostic, proceed to open lung biopsy (do not perform open lung biopsy prior to bronchoscopy in acquired immune deficiency syndrome patients)
    If possible, perform open lung biopsy prior to severe clinical deterioration and multiorgan failure

---

formed, as well as bronchoalveolar lavage and bronchial brushings to increase the diagnostic yield. If TBBx is contraindicated, bronchoalveolar lavage and brushings may be used without a biopsy, considering their high diagnostic yield in patients with an infection and/or AIDS. The diagnostic yield of bronchoscopy is best when it is performed within 48 hours of the initiation of therapy (i.e., empiric antibiotics). If the patient is deteriorating rapidly and an immediate diagnosis is needed, or if the aforementioned procedures are nondiagnostic, open lung biopsy is indicated. However, bronchoscopy always should be performed prior to open lung biopsy in the AIDS patient. Bronchoscopy will diagnose the majority of disease processes in the AIDS patient, other than Kaposi's sarcoma. To maximize the chance that open lung biopsy will improve the clinical course of the patient, it should be performed prior to severe clinical deterioration and multiorgan failure.

# References

1. Shure D, Astarita RW: Bronchogenic carcinoma presenting as an endobronchial mass. *Chest* 1983; 6:865–867.

2. Popovich J, Kvale PA, Eichenhorn MS, et al: Diagnostic accuracy of multiple biopsies from flexible fiberoptic bronchoscopy. *Am Rev Respir Dis* 1982; 125:521–523.

3. Zavala DC: Diagnostic fiberoptic bronchoscopy: Techniques and results of biopsy in 600 patients. *Chest* 1975; 68:12–19.

4. Martini N, McCormick PM: Assessment of endoscopically visible bronchial carcinomas. *Chest* 1978; 73:718–720.

5. Cortese DA, McDougall JC: Biopsy and brushing of peripheral lung cancer with fluoroscopic guidance. *Chest* 1979; 75:141–145.

6. Fletcher EC, Levin DC: Flexible fiberoptic bronchoscopy and fluoroscopically guided transbronchial biopsy in the management of solitary pulmonary nodules. *West J Med* 1982; 136:477–483.

7. Wallace JM, Deutsch AL: Flexible fiberoptic bronchoscopy and percutaneous needle lung aspiration for evaluating the solitary pulmonary nodule. *Chest* 1982; 81:665–671.

8. Stringfield JT, Markowitz DJ, Bentz RR, et al: The effect of tumor size and location on diagnosis by fiberoptic bronchoscopy. *Chest* 1977; 72:474–476.

9. Cortese DA, McDougall JC: Bronchoscopic biopsy and brushing with fluoroscopic guidance in nodular metastatic lung cancer. *Chest* 1981; 79:610–611.

10. Poe RH, Ortiz C, Israel RH, et al: Sensitivity, specificity, and predictive values of bronchoscopy in neoplasm metastatic to lung. *Chest* 1985; 88:84–88.

11. Radke JR, Conway WA, Eyler WR, et al: Diagnostic accuracy in peripheral lung lesions. *Chest* 1979; 76:176–179.

12. Hanson R, Zavala DC, Rhodes ML, et al: Transbronchial biopsy via flexible fiberoptic bronchoscope: Results in 164 patients. *Am Rev Respir Dis* 1976; 114:67–72.

13. Anders GT, Johnson JE, Bush BA, et al: Transbronchial biopsy without fluoroscopy. *Chest* 1988; 94:557–560.

14. Joyner LR, Scheinhorn DJ: Transbronchial forceps lung biopsy through the fiberoptic bronchoscope. *Chest* 1975; 67:532–535.

15. Shure D: Transbronchial biopsy and needle aspiration. *Chest* 1989; 95:1130–1138.

16. Ellis JH: Transbronchial lung biopsy via the fiberoptic bronchoscope. *Chest* 1975; 68:524–532.

17. Levin DC, Wicks AB, Ellis JH Jr: Transbronchial lung biopsy via the fiberoptic bronchoscope. *Am Rev Respir Dis* 1974; 110:4–12.

18. Andersen HA: Transbronchoscopic lung biopsy for diffuse pulmonary disease. *Chest* 1978; 73:734–736.

19. Wang Ko-Pen, Haponik EF, Britt EJ, et al: Transbronchial needle aspiration of peripheral pulmonary nodules. *Chest* 1984; 86:819–823.

20. Shure D, Fedullo PF: Transbronchial needle aspiration of peripheral masses. *Am Rev Respir Dis* 1983; 128:1090–1092.

21. Schenk DA, Bryan CL, Bower JH, et al: Transbronchial needle aspiration in the diagnosis of bronchogenic carcinoma. *Chest* 1987; 92:83–85.

22. Bhat N, Bhagat P, Pearlman ES, et al: Transbronchial needle aspiration biopsy in the diagnosis of pulmonary neoplasms. *Diagn Cytopathol* 1990; 6:14–17.

23. Shure D, Fedullo PE: Transbronchial needle aspiration in the diagnosis of submucosal and peribronchial bronchogenic carcinoma. *Chest* 1985; 88:49–51.

24. Gay PC, Brutinel WM: Transbronchial needle aspiration in the practice of bronchoscopy. *Mayo Clin Proc* 1989; 64:158–162.

25. Forrest JV, Sagel SS: Cutting needle biopsies. *Chest* 1976; 69:244–245.
26. Norenberg R, Claxton CP Jr, Takaro T: Percutaneous needle biopsy of the lung: Report of two fatal complications. *Chest* 1974; 66:216–218.
27. Zavala DC, Bedell GN: Percutaneous lung biopsy with a cutting needle: An analysis of 40 cases and comparison with other biopsy techniques. *Am Rev Respir Dis* 1972; 106:186–193.
28. Vitums VC: Percutaneous needle biopsy of the lung with a new disposable needle. *Chest* 1972; 62:717–719.
29. Mehnert JH, Brown MJ: Percutaneous needle core biopsy of peripheral pulmonary masses. *Am J Surg* 1978; 136:151–156.
30. Dahlgren S, Nordenstrom B: *Transthoracic Needle Biopsy.* Chicago, Year Book Medical Publishers, 1966.
31. Sokolowski JW, Burgher LW, Jones FL Jr, et al: Guidelines for percutaneous transthoracic needle biopsy. *Am Rev Respir Dis* 1989; 140:255–256.
32. Jereb M: The usefulness of needle biopsy in chest lesions of different sizes and locations. *Radiology* 1980; 134:13–15.
33. Kaufman M, Schwartz I, Weissberg D: Fine needle aspiration biopsy in diagnosis of pulmonary masses. *Am Surg* 1987; 53:339–341.
34. Khouri NF, Stitik FP, Erozan YS et al: Transthoracic needle aspiration biopsy of benign and malignant lung lesions. *Am J Roentgenol* 1985; 144: 281–288.
35. Penketh C, Robinson AA, Barker V, et al: Use of percutaneous needle biopsy in the investigation of solitary pulmonary nodules. *Thorax* 1987; 42:967–971.
36. Sagel SS, Ferguson TB, Forrest JV, et al: Percutaneous transthoracic aspiration needle biopsy. *Ann Thorac Surg* 1978; 26:399–405.
37. Todd TRJ, Weisbrod G, Tao LC, et al: Aspiration needle biopsy of thoracic lesions. *Ann Thorac Surg* 1982; 32:154–161.
38. Francis D: Aspiration biopsies from diagnostically difficult pulmonary lesions: A consecutive case material. *Acta Pathol Microbiol Scand* 1977; 85: 235–239.
39. Borgeskov S, Francis D: A comparison between fine-needle biopsy and fiberoptic bronchoscopy in patients with lung lesions. *Thorax* 1974; 29:352–354.
40. Levine MS, Weiss JM, Harrell JH, et al: Transthoracic needle aspiration biopsy following negative fiberoptic bronchoscopy in solitary pulmonary nodules. *Chest* 1988; 93:1152–1155.
41. Westcott JL: Direct percutaneous needle aspiration of localized pulmonary lesions: Results in 422 patients. *Radiology* 1980; 137:31–35.
42. Tao LC, Pearson FG, Delarue NC, et al: Percutaneous fine-needle aspiration biopsy. *Cancer* 1980; 45:1480–1485.
43. Khouri NF, Meziane MA: Transthoracic needle aspiration biopsy-optimizing the yield. *J Thorac Imaging* 1987; 2:18–26.
44. McEvoy RD, Begley MD, Antic R: Percutaneous biopsy of intrapulmonary mass lesions. *Cancer* 1983; 51:2321–2326.
45. Mark JBD, Marglin SI, Castellino RA: The role of bronchoscopy and needle aspiration in the diagnosis of peripheral lung masses. *J Thorac Cardiovasc Surg* 1978; 76:266–268.
46. Westcott JL: Percutaneous transthoracic needle biopsy. *Radiology* 1988; 169:593–601.
47. Weisbrod GL: Transthoracic percutaneous lung biopsy. *Radiol Clin North Am* 1990; 28:647–655.

48. Milner LB, Ryan K, Gullo J: Fatal intrathoracic hemorrhage after percutaneous aspiration lung biopsy. *AJR* 1979; 132:280–281.
49. Pearce JG, Patt NL: Fatal pulmonary hemorrhage after percutaneous aspiration lung biopsy. *Am Rev Respir Dis* 1974; 110:346–349.
50. Norenberg R, Claxton CP Jr, Takaro T: Percutaneous needle biopsy of the lung: Report of two fatal complications. *Chest* 1974; 66:216–218.
51. Ferrucci JT, Wittenberg J, Margolies MN, et al: Malignant seeding of the tract after thin-needle aspiration biopsy. *Radiology* 1979; 130:345–346.
52. Sinner WN, Zajicek J: Implantation metastasis after percutaneous transthoracic needle aspiration biopsy. *Acta Radiol* 1976; 17:473–480.
53. Redwood N, Beggs D, Morgan WE: Dissemination of tumour cells from fine needle biopsy. *Thorax* 1989; 44:826–827.
54. Sacchini V, Galimberti V, Marchini S, et al: Percutaneous transthoracic needle aspiration biopsy: A case report of implantation metastasis. *Eur J Surg Oncol* 1989; 15:179–183.
55. Osborne DR, Korobkin M, Racin CE, et al: Comparison of plain radiography, conventional tomography, and computed tomography in detecting intrathoracic lymph node metastases from lung carcinoma. *Radiology* 1982; 142:157–161.
56. Ekholm S, Albrechtsson U, Kugelberg J, et al: Computed tomography in preoperative staging of bronchogenic carcinoma. *J Comput Assist Tomogr* 1980; 4:763–765.
57. Richey HM, Matthews JI, Helsel RA, et al: Thoracic CT scanning in the staging of bronchogenic carcinoma. *Chest* 1984; 85:218–221.
58. Faling LJ, Pugatch RD, Jung-Legg Y, et al: Computed tomographic scanning of the mediastinum in the staging of bronchogenic carcinoma. *Am Rev Respir Dis* 1981; 124:690–695.
59. Ratto GB, Mereu C, Motta G: The prognostic significance of preoperative assessment of mediastinal lymph nodes in patients with lung cancer. *Chest* 1988; 93:807–813.
60. Wang Ko-Pen, Brower R, Haponik EF, et al: Flexible transbronchial needle aspiration for staging of bronchogenic carcinoma. *Chest* 1983; 84:571–576.
61. Wang Ko-Pen: Flexible transbronchial needle aspiration biopsy for histologic specimens. *Chest* 1985; 88:860–863.
62. Mehta AC, Kavuru MS, Meeker DP, et al: Transbronchial needle aspiration for histology specimens. *Chest* 1989; 96:1228–1232.
63. Shure D, Fedullo PF: The role of transcarinal needle aspiration in the staging of bronchogenic carcinoma. *Chest* 1984; 86:693–696.
64. Schenk DA, Strollo PJ, Pickard JS, et al: Utility of the Wang 18-gauge transbronchial histology needle in the staging of bronchogenic carcinoma. *Chest* 1989; 96:272–274.
65. Harrow EM, Oldenburg FA, Lingenfelter MS, et al: Transbronchial needle aspiration in clinical practice. *Chest* 1989; 96:1268–1272.
66. Schenk DA, Bower JH, Bryan CL, et al: Transbronchial needle aspiration staging of bronchogenic carcinoma. *Am Rev Respir Dis* 1986; 134:146–148.
67. Cropp AJ, DiMarco AF, Lankerani M: False-positive transbronchial needle aspiration in bronchogenic carcinoma. *Chest* 1984; 85:696–697.
68. Schenk DA, Chasen MH, McCarthy MJ, et al: Potential false positive mediastinal transbronchial needle aspiration in bronchogenic carcinoma. *Chest* 1984; 86:649–650.
69. Westcott JL: Transthoracic needle biopsy of the hilum and mediastinum. *J Thorac Imaging* 1987; 2:41–48.

70. Weisbrod GL, Lyons DJ, Tao LC, et al: Percutaneous fine-needle aspiration biopsy of mediastinal lesions. *AJR* 1984; 143:525–529.
71. Goblen RP, Skucas J, Paris BS: CT-assisted fluoroscopically guided aspiration biopsy of central hilar and mediastinal masses. *Radiology* 1981; 141:443–447.
72. Adler OB, Rosenberger A, Peleg H: Fine-needle aspiration biopsy of mediastinal masses: Evaluation of 136 experiences. *AJR* 1983; 140:893–896.
73. Andersen HA, Fontana RS, Harrison EG Jr: Transbronchoscopic lung biopsy in diffuse pulmonary disease. *Diseases of the Chest* 1965; 48:187–192.
74. Gaensler EA: Open and closed lung biopsy, in Sackner MA (ed): *Diagnostic Techniques in Pulmonary Disease, Part II.* New York, Marcel Dekker, 1980, pp 579–622.
75. Ray JF, Lawton BR, Myers WO, et al: Open pulmonary biopsy—nineteen-year experience with 416 consecutive operations. *Chest* 1976; 69:43–47.
76. Gaensler EA, Carrington CB: Open biopsy for chronic diffuse infiltrative lung disease: Clinical, roentgenographic, and physiological correlations in 502 patients. *Ann Thorac Surg* 1980; 30:411–426.
77. Scadding JG: Lung biopsy in the diagnosis of diffuse lung disease. *Br Med J [Clin Res]* 1970; 2:557–564.
78. Wall CP, Gaensler EA, Carrington CB, et al: Comparison of transbronchial and open biopsies in chronic infiltrative lung diseases. *Am Rev Respir Dis* 1981; 123:280–285.
79. Burt ME, Flye MW, Webber BL, et al: Prospective evaluation of aspiration needle, cutting needle, transbronchial, and open lung biopsy in patients with pulmonary infiltrates. *Ann Thorac Surg* 1981; 32:146–153.
80. Hanson RR, Zavala DC, Rhodes ML, et al: Transbronchial biopsy via flexible fiberoptic bronchoscope: results in 164 patients. *Am Rev Respir Dis* 1976; 114:67-72.
81. Joyner LR, Scheinhorn DJ: Transbronchial forceps lung biopsy through the fiberoptic bronchoscope. *Chest* 1975; 67:532–535.
82. Poe RH, Utell MJ, Israel RH, et al: Sensitivity and specificity of the nonspecific transbronchial lung biopsy. *Am Rev Respir Dis* 1979; 119:25–31.
83. Smith CW, Murray GF, Wilcox BR, et al: The role of transbronchial lung biopsy in diffuse pulmonary disease. *Ann Thorac Surg* 1977; 24:54–58.
84. Chuang MT, Krellenstein DJ, Raskin J, et al: Bronchoscopy in diffuse lung disease: Evaluation by open lung biopsy in nondiagnostic transbronchial lung biopsy. *Ann Otol Rhinol Laryngol* 1987; 96:654–657.
85. Wilson RK, Fechner RE, Greenberg SD, et al: Clinical implications of a "nonspecific" transbronchial biopsy. *Am J Med* 1978; 65:252–256.
86. Newman SL, Michel RP, Wang Nai-San: Lingular lung biopsy: Is it representative? *Am Rev Respir Dis* 1985; 132:1084–1086.
87. Miller RR, Nelems B, Müller NL, et al: Lingular and right middle lobe biopsy in the assessment of diffuse lung disease. *Ann Thorac Surg* 1987; 44:269–273.
88. Walker WA, Cole FH Jr, Khandekar A, et al: Does open lung biopsy affect treatment in patients with diffuse pulmonary infiltrates? *J Thorac Cardiovasc Surg* 1989; 97:534–540.
89. Palmer DL, Davidson M, Lusk R: Needle aspiration of the lung in complex pneumonias. *Chest* 1980; 78:16–21.
90. Cockerill FR, Wilson WR, Carpenter HA, et al: Open lung biopsy in immunocompromised patients. *Arch Intern Med* 1985; 145:1398–1404.
91. Toledo-Pereyra LH, DeMeester TR, Kinealey A, et al: The benefits of open

lung biopsy in patients with previous non-diagnostic transbronchial lung biopsy. A guide to appropriate therapy. Chest 1980; 77:647–650.
92. McCabe RE: Diagnosis of pulmonary infections in immunocompromised patients. Med Clin North Am 1988; 72:1067–1089.
93. Ramsey PG, Robin RH, Tolkoff-Rubin NE, et al: The renal transplant patient with fever and pulmonary infiltrates: Etiology, clinical manifestations, and management. Medicine 1980; 59:206–222.
94. Worthington M: Viral, opportunistic and fungal infections in the lung in the intensive care unit, in Disease States and Their Management in the Respiratory Intensive Care Unit, first ed. Little, Brown & Company, 1987, pp 283–311.
95. Rosenow EC, Wilson WR, Cockerill FR: Pulmonary disease in the immunocompromised host. Mayo Clin Proc 1985; 60:473–487.
96. Barrett-Conner E: The nonvalue of sputum culture in the diagnosis of pneumococcal pneumonia. Am Rev Respir Dis 1972; 103:845–848.
97. Sickles EA, Young VM, Greene WH, et al: Pneumonia in acute leukemia. Ann Intern Med 1973; 79:528–534.
98. Cunningham JH, Zavala DC, Corry RJ, et al: Trephine air drill, bronchial brush, and fiberoptic transbronchial lung biopsies in immunosuppressed patients. Am Rev Respir Dis 1977; 115:213–220.
99. Bandt PD, Blank N, Castellino RA: Needle diagnosis of pneumonitis. Value in high-risk patients. JAMA 1972; 220:1578–1580.
100. Spencer CD, Beaty HN: Complications of transtracheal aspiration. N Engl J Med 1972; 286:304–306.
101. Youmans CR, deGroot WJ, Marshall R, et al: Needle biopsy in the lung in diffuse parenchymal disease. An analysis of 151 cases. Am J Surg 1970; 120:637–643.
102. Neff TA: Percutaneous trephine biopsy of the lung. Chest 1972; 61:18–23.
103. Greenman RL, Goodall PT, King D: Lung biopsy in immunocompromised hosts. Am J Med 1975; 59:488–496.
104. Matthay RA, Farmer WC, Odero D: Diagnostic fiberoptic bronchoscopy in the immunocompromised host with pulmonary infiltrates. Thorax 1977; 32:539–545.
105. Lauver GL, Hasan FM, Morgan RB, et al: The usefulness of fiberoptic bronchoscopy in evaluating new pulmonary lesions in the compromised host. Am J Med 1979; 66:580–585.
106. Nishio JN, Lynch JP: Fiberoptic bronchoscopy in the immunocompromised host: The significance of a "nonspecific" transbronchial biopsy. Am Rev Respir Dis 1980; 121:307–312.
107. Wimberley N, Faling LJ, Bartlett JG: A fiberoptic bronchoscopy technique to obtain uncontaminated lower airway secretions for bacterial culture. Am Rev Respir Dis 1979; 119:337–343.
108. Albelda SM, Talbot GH, Gerson SL, et al: Role of fiberoptic bronchoscopy in the diagnosis of invasive pulmonary aspergillosis in patients with acute leukemia. Am J Med 1984; 76:1027–1034.
109. Wimberley NW, Bass JB, Boyd BW, et al: Use of a bronchoscopic protected catheter brush for the diagnosis of pulmonary infections. Chest 1982; 81:556–562.
110. Pennington JE, Feldman NT: Pulmonary infiltrates and fever in patient with hematologic malignancy. Assessment of transbronchial biopsy. Am J Med 1977; 62:581–587.
111. Haponik EF, Summer WR, Terry PB, et al: Clinical decision making with

transbronchial lung biopsies. The value of nonspecific histologic examination. *Am Rev Respir Dis* 1982; 125:524–529.

112. Broaddus C, Dake MD, Stulbarg MS, et al: Bronchoalveolar lavage and transbronchial biopsy for the diagnosis of pulmonary infections in the acquired immunodeficiency syndrome. *Ann Intern Med* 1985; 102:747–752.

113. Murray JF, Felton CP, Garay SM, et al: Pulmonary complications of the acquired immunodeficiency syndrome. Report of a National Heart, Lung, and Blood Institute workshop. *N Engl J Med* 1984; 310:1682–1688.

114. Stover DE, Zaman MB, Hajdu SI, et al: Bronchoalveolar lavage in the diagnosis of diffuse pulmonary infiltrates in the immunosuppressed host. *Ann Intern Med* 1984; 101:1–7.

115. Martin WJ, Smith TF, Brutinel WM, et al: Role of bronchoalveolar lavage in the assessment of opportunistic pulmonary infections: Utility and complications. *Mayo Clin Proc* 1987; 62:549–557.

116. Cordonnier C, Bernaudin JF, Fleury J, et al: Diagnostic yield of bronchoalveolar lavage in pneumonitis occurring after allogeneic bone marrow transplantation. *Am Rev Respir Dis* 1985; 132:1118–1123.

117. Xaubet A, Torres A, Marco F, et al: Pulmonary infiltrates in immunocompromised patients. Diagnostic value of telescoping plugged catheter and bronchoalveolar lavage. *Chest* 1989; 95:130–135.

118. Springmeyer SC, Hackman RC, Holle R, et al: Use of bronchoalveolar lavage to diagnose acute diffuse pneumonia in the immunocompromised host. *J Infect Dis* 1986; 154:604–610.

119. McCabe RE, Brooks RG, Mark JBD, et al: Open lung biopsy in patients with acute leukemia. *Am J Med* 1985; 78:609–616.

120. Young JA, Hopkin JM, Cuthbertson WP: Pulmonary infiltrates in immunocompromised patients: Diagnosis by cytological examination of bronchoalveolar lavage fluid. *J Clin Pathol* 1984; 37:390–397.

121. Kahn FW, Jones JM, England DM: Diagnosis of pulmonary hemorrhage in the immunocompromised host. *Am Rev Respir Dis* 1987; 136:155–160.

122. Cohn DL, Stover DE, O'Brien RF, et al: Pulmonary complications of AIDS: Advances in diagnosis and treatment. *Am Rev Respir Dis* 1988; 138:1051–1052.

123. Ognibene FP, Steis RG, Macher AM, et al: Kaposi's sarcoma causing pulmonary infiltrates and respiratory failure in the acquired immunodeficiency syndrome. *Ann Intern Med* 1985; 102:471–475.

124. Stover DE, White DA, Romano PA, et al: Diagnosis of pulmonary disease in acquired immune deficiency syndrome (AIDS). Role of bronchoscopy and bronchoalveolar lavage. *Am Rev Respir Dis* 1984; 130:659–662.

125. Ognibene FP, Shelhamer JH: Kaposi's sarcoma. *Clin Chest Med* 1988; 9:459–465.

126. Levy H, Horak DA, Lewis M: The value of bronchial washings and bronchoalveolar lavage in the diagnosis of lymphangitic carcinomatosis. *Chest* 1988; 94:1028–1030.

127. Pisani RJ, Witzig RE, Li Ci-Y, et al: Confirmation of lymphomatous pulmonary involvement by immunophenotypic and gene rearrangement analysis of bronchoalveolar lavage fluid. *Mayo Clin Proc* 1990; 65:651–656.

128. Cheson BD, Samlowski WE, Tang TT, et al: Value of open-lung biopsy in 87 immunocompromised patients with pulmonary infiltrates. *Cancer* 1985; 55:453–459.

129. Leight GS, Michaelis LL: Open lung biopsy for the diagnosis of acute, diffuse

pulmonary infiltrates in the immunosuppressed patient. *Chest* 1978; 73:477–482.

130. Rossiter SJ, Miller DC, Churg AM, et al: Open lung biopsy in the immuno-suppressed patient. Is it really beneficial? *J Thorac Cardiovasc Surg* 1979; 77:338–345.

131. Haverkos HW, Cowling JN, Pasculle AW, et al: Diagnosis of pneumonitis in immunocompromised patients by open lung biopsy. *Cancer* 1983; 52:1093–1097.

132. Potter D, Pass HI, Brower S, et al: Prospective randomized study of open lung biopsy versus empirical antibiotic therapy for acute pneumonitis in non-neutropenic cancer patients. *Ann Thorac Surg* 1985; 40:422–428.

133. Bonfils-Roberts EA, Nickodem A, Nealon TF: Retrospective analysis of the efficacy of open lung biopsy in acquired immunodeficiency syndrome. *Ann Thorac Surg* 1990; 49:115–117.

134. McKenna RJ, Campbell A, McMurtrey MJ, et al: Diagnosis for interstitial lung disease in patients with acquired immunodeficiency syndrome (AIDS): A pro-spective comparison of bronchial washing, alveolar lavage, transbronchial lung biopsy, and open-lung biopsy. *Ann Thorac Surg* 1986; 41:318–321.

# Balloon Valvuloplasty

## David R. Holmes, Jr., M.D.

Consultant, Division of Cardiovascular Diseases and Internal Medicine, Mayo Clinic and Mayo Foundation; Professor of Medicine, Mayo Medical School, Rochester, Minnesota

## Rick A. Nishimura, M.D.

Consultant, Division of Cardiovascular Diseases and Internal Medicine, Mayo Clinic and Mayo Foundation; Associate Professor of Medicine, Mayo Medical School, Rochester, Minnesota

## Editor's Introduction

Balloon valvuloplasty is being used extensively for patients with valvular stenosis, especially pulmonic, aortic, and mitral stenosis. The exact place of this noninvasive procedure in the physician's armamentarium is still being worked out. Drs. Holmes and Nishimura point out that this is emerging as the procedure of choice in congenital pulmonic stenosis. Mitral balloon valvuloplasty also gives excellent results in patients with pliable valves with little or no calcification, and as such may offer the best choice in extremely high risk patients. The authors further point out that aortic balloon valvuloplasty has been used primarily in relatively high risk patients. As such, it offers some palliation of symptoms and may buy time to improve the patient's status to the point where he or she may become a more reasonable surgical candidate. Aortic balloon valvuloplasty, because of its high restenosis rate over a short term follow-up, is not usually considered definitive therapy for aortic stenosis.

*James J. Leonard, M.D.*

Attempts at identifying the optimal treatment strategy for patients with valvular heart disease continue. The requirements for each specific group of patients with symptomatic valvular heart disease vary; what is needed for a 21-year-old patient with symptomatic aortic stenosis may be quite different from what is required for an 85-year-old patient with the same degree of aortic stenosis. Attempts to develop ideal treatment strategies have led to improved prosthetic devices and new surgical approaches, such as CUSA (Cavitron Ultrasonic Surgical Aspirator, Cavitron Surgical Systems) decalcification.[1–4] None of these approaches has solved all the problems. Some techniques, such as aortic valve decalcification, have traded stenosis for aortic regurgitation. Other approaches, such as the use of certain types of tissue valves, have traded longevity for the need for anticoagulation therapy. Attempts to develop optimal treatment strategies also have led to the evaluation of nonsurgical methods, such as balloon valvuloplasty. This approach has revisited older surgical efforts, including the aortic valvuloplasty operation of the early 1950s and the mitral commissurotomy procedure of the 1950s and 1960s.[5-7] Balloon valvuloplasty has been used extensively for treating adult patients who have aortic and mitral stenosis. It also has been used for a small number of patients with tricuspid stenoses and occasionally for patients with prosthetic stenoses. Finally, it has become the treatment of choice for patients with isolated pulmonic stenosis.

## Aortic Valvuloplasty

Aortic valvuloplasty performed with various dilators during open chest cardiac operation was evaluated in the early 1950s and abandoned because thromboembolic events and aortic regurgitation resulted from the procedure.[5-7] Valvuloplasty was reintroduced in 1986 by Cribier et al.[8] to treat three adult patients (68, 69, and 77 years old) who had severe symptomatic aortic stenosis. Either aortic valve replacement was not possible in these patients or they declined the operation. Valvuloplasty produced hemodynamic and symptomatic improvement in all three patients.

The rationale for the reintroduction of valvuloplasty was related to several factors. The most important factor concerned the risks of aortic valve replacement in the increasing number of elderly patients with severe symptomatic aortic stenosis.[9-18] This growing population was the result of an increase in the number of elderly individuals and the availability and use of M-mode and two-dimensional Doppler echocardiography to screen patients with cardiac murmurs.[19] The morbidity and mortality of aortic valve replacement are substantially increased in elderly patients. Advanced age is a significant factor for operative and perioperative risks,[9, 12, 15, 16, 18] particularly in combination with left ventricular dysfunction, hemodynamic instability, and associated diseases such as coexistent coronary artery and pulmonary disease. Not only is perioperative mortality increased in this population, but also convalescence may be prolonged and neurologic complications are a significant problem.[15]

## Mechanism

The mechanism of aortic valvuloplasty depends on the cause of the aortic stenosis.[20-23] The most common cause in the elderly patients (>70 years old) who have been treated with aortic valvuloplasty is senile calcific aortic stenosis,[20] which is seen in approximately 50% of these individuals. The stenosis results from heaped up nodules of calcium in the valve cusps and thickened, rigid hinge motion of the cusps. The valve commissures are normal. Balloon inflation in these patients fractures the calcific plates, thereby improving hinge mobility. In approximately 25% of elderly patients, the stenosis is related to a bicuspid valve, and in another 25%, it is related to rheumatic heart disease. In patients with rheumatic aortic stenosis, balloon inflation may split the fused commissures.

## Methods

A retrograde transfemoral approach has been used most commonly in the past and, by virtue of its ease, continues to be the most popular method.[24–26] Other approaches have been described, including a transvenous transseptal technique.[27, 28] With this approach, a transseptal puncture is created and a long exchange wire is positioned across the mitral valve into the left ventricle and out the aortic valve into the aorta. Various dilating balloons then can be advanced over this wire for aortic valve dilatation. Another method that has been described is a cutdown brachial approach. This has been used when arterial access from the leg is difficult. However, the small size of the brachial artery limits the size of the balloon catheters that can be used. Also, several approaches using multiple balloons have been described. The balloons are placed from both femoral arteries or from a combination of femoral and brachial arteries.[29–33] Smaller balloons can be used with this technique in an attempt to decrease peripheral vascular complications. Although some data suggest that multiple balloons may be useful when a single balloon is ineffective, data do not suggest that one technique is better than the other for producing significant long-term improvement.[29, 32]

Arterial access is achieved by using either standard percutaneous or cutdown approaches. Previously, the cutdown method was used with valvuloplasty to decrease vascular complications. Currently, the percutaneous approach generally is used. The aortic valve is crossed retrogradely and a long exchange wire is used for positioning the balloons. The wire is preshaped to facilitate stable positioning of the balloons and to reduce the chance of left ventricular perforation or sustained ventricular arrhythmias.

Balloons of various shapes and sizes (8 to 25 mm) are available.[24, 34, 35] They are generally large and have 8-French or 9-French shaft sizes. Some balloons have straight tips, while others have a pigtail configuration. In the National Heart, Lung, and Blood Institute (NHLBI) Valvuloplasty Registry of 674 patients who underwent aortic valvuloplasty, a single 20-mm balloon was used in 56% of patients and a 23-mm balloon was used in 37%.[36] Selection of the initial balloon size depends on the size of the patient, the severity of the aortic stenosis, and the experience and approach of the operator. Oversized balloons should be avoided because they may cause rupture of the aortic annulus.[37–39]

Balloon construction varies. The most commonly used devices are single balloons that have a cylindrical shape. Bifoil or trefoil balloons are used frequently in Europe and, because they permit central blood flow during inflation, inflation may be tolerated better. Balloons also have various shaft designs. Some shafts have two lumens, one for inflation of the balloon and one for the guide wire. Other shafts have three lumens, one for inflation of the balloon and two for measuring the pressures across the aortic valve simultaneously to assess the effect of valvuloplasty.

After baseline hemodynamics are measured (preferably by using simultaneous left ventricular and ascending aortic pressures with measurement of cardiac output), the balloon is advanced over the guide wire positioned in the left ventricle. After the balloon is positioned across the aortic valve, it is inflated under fluoroscopic guidance. During inflation, the balloon may migrate either forward into the left ventricle or backward into the aorta. Usually, the plane of the aortic valve is identified easily by dense calcification. If the balloon migrates, its position must be adjusted.

The approach to inflation duration depends on the clinical situation. Hypotension occurs in most patients and may be profound.[25, 40–43] It is especially a problem in patients who have left ventricular dysfunction initially. Depression of left ventricular function during inflation commonly is related to the marked increase in afterload, the decrease in left ventricular compliance and severe aortic regurgitation, the exacerbation of any preexistent mitral regurgitation, and the decrease in coronary perfusion. For these reasons, inflations usually are limited to ≤1 minute. The shortest inflations possible are used in patients with significant hypotension.

After inflation, the condition of the patient is allowed to stabilize and then hemodynamics are reassessed. It is best to measure left ventricular and ascending aortic pressures simultaneously. Aortic root angiography is performed whenever possible to assess the degree of aortic regurgitation. If the hemodynamic result is satisfactory, the catheters are withdrawn and local bleeding is arrested. Because of the large size of the catheters, local arterial problems—hematoma, persistent bleeding, or pseudoaneurysm formation—are seen in 10% to 15% of patients.[26, 36, 43–45]

## Outcome

The immediate results of aortic balloon valvuloplasty are very similar in most reported studies (Table 1).[26, 36, 42, 43, 46–49] The definition of a successful procedure usually includes (1) a 50% reduction in the peak-to-peak transvalvular gradient, (2) a residual gradient <40 mm Hg, and (3) a 25% or greater increase in aortic valve area. In the patient series reported, the gradient typically decreased from 60 to 80 mm Hg to 30 to 40 mm Hg (see Table 1). This was associated with an increase in aortic valve area from 0.5 to 0.6 cm$^2$ to 0.75 to 0.90 cm$^2$. This hemodynamic outcome depends heavily on the initial hemodynamics. Only a moderate improvement in hemodynamics usually is obtained. Therefore, if a patient has very severe aortic stenosis and an aortic valve area of 0.4 cm$^2$ before the procedure, there are likely to be significant aortic stenosis and a valve area of ≤0.7 cm$^2$ at the end of the procedure. If the initial degree of severity is only moderate, the aortic valve area may be approximately 1.0 cm$^2$ or more at the end of the procedure.

Among the 674 patients enrolled in the multicenter NHLBI Valvuloplasty Registry from November 1987 to November 1989, aortic valve dilatation was successful in 87%.[36] The mean aortic valve gradient decreased from 55 ± 21 to 29 ± 13 mm Hg, and the aortic valve area increased

## TABLE 1.
## Outcome of Aortic Balloon Valvuloplasty in Selected Series of Patients

| Series | Year | Number of Patients | Aortic Valve Area (cm$^2$, Mean ± Standard Deviation) | | Gradient | |
|--------|------|--------------------|--------|--------|--------|--------|
| | | | Before | After | Before | After |
| Bashore[36] | * | 674 | 0.5 ± 0.2 | 0.8 ± 0.3 | 55 ± 21 | 29 ± 13 |
| Holmes[46]† | 1991 | 455 | 0.51 ± 0.01 | 0.83 ± 0.01 | 60 ± 11 | 29.5 ± 6 |
| Lewin[47] | 1989 | 125 | 0.6 ± 0.2 | 1.0 ± 0.3 | 70 ± 26 | 30 ± 13 |
| Letac[48] | 1988 | 218 | 0.52 ± 0.18 | 0.93 ± 0.33 | 72 ± 25 | 29 ± 14 |
| Safian[26] | 1988 | 170 | 0.6 ± 0.2 | 0.9 ± 0.3 | 56 ± 19 | 31 ± 12 |

*In press.
†Data on survivors of percutaneous aortic balloon valvuloplasty.

from 0.5 ± 0.2 cm$^2$ to 0.8 ± 0.3 cm$^2$. The increase in aortic valve area was <0.4 cm$^2$ in approximately 80% of the patients. At the end of the procedure, the aortic valve area was <0.8 cm$^2$ in 45% of the patients and ≥ 0.8 cm$^2$ in the rest. The final outcome was excellent in 29% of patients, who had an aortic valve area ≥1.0 cm$^2$.

## Complications

Significant cardiac and noncardiac complications can occur with percutaneous aortic balloon valvuloplasty. The pattern of complications depends in part on the technique used and the experience of the operator, but probably more on patient selection. The complications in patients with inoperable end-stage disease may be quite different from those in low-risk patients.

In an early multicenter registry experience, the in-hospital mortality rate was 7.5% (Table 2).[43] In this study, there were significant differences in the initial clinical and hemodynamic characteristics between hospital survivors and nonsurvivors. Among the patients who died, the initial left ventricular systolic pressure and cardiac output were lower and the initial and final aortic valve areas were less.

In the NHLBI Valvuloplasty Registry,[36] the in-hospital cardiac mortality was 8% and 23 additional patients died within the first month, resulting in a cumulative 30-day mortality rate of 14%. As was true in the Mansfield Registry, the patients who died had been more impaired and, as a group, had a significantly greater frequency of myocardial infarction, hepatic or renal disease, decreased ejection fraction and cardiac output, and severe aortic stenosis. Among the patients who died within the first month, there

**TABLE 2.**
Rate of Complications and Mortality in Five Series of Patients Who Underwent Balloon Valvuloplasty

| Series | Year | Number of Patients | Procedure-Related Death (%) | In-Hospital Death (%) | Embolic Event, % | Myocardial Infarction, % | Vascular Complication, % | Tamponade, % | Severe Aortic Regurgitation, % |
|---|---|---|---|---|---|---|---|---|---|
| Mansfield[43] | * | 492 | 4.9 | 7.5 | 2.2 | 0.2 | 11.0 | 1.4 | 1.0 |
| NHLBI† Valvuloplasty Registry[36] | * | 674 | 3.0 | 8.0 | 3.0 | 2.0 | 7.0 | 1.0 | 1.0 |
| Safian[26] | 1988 | 170 | — | 3.5 | — | 0.6 | 10.0 | 1.8 | 1.1 |
| Lewin[47] | 1989 | 125 | 2.4 | 10.4 | 3.2 | 1.6 | 9.6 | — | 1.6 |
| Letac[48] | 1988 | 218 | 0.5 | 4.0 | 2.0 | 0.5 | 13.0 | — | — |

*In press.
†NHLBI = National Heart, Lung, and Blood Institute.

was a very high-risk group identified by blood pressure values <100 mm Hg and functional class IV congestive heart failure, blood urea nitrogen concentration >30 mg/dL, need for antiarrhythmia medication, or cardiac output ≤3.0 L/min.

A substantial number of other complications have been reported. A significant complication occurred in 17% of patients in the Mansfield Registry and 25% in the NHLBI Balloon Valvuloplasty Registry. The most common complications have involved vascular problems related to the arterial entry site; these occurred in 10% to 15% of patients. In some of these individuals, conservative treatment was indicated, but in others (up to 5% of series), vascular surgery was required, which increased the potential for morbidity and mortality.[50]

Although embolic events were a problem in the early valvuloplasty operations, they are uncommon with a percutaneous balloon dilatation procedure. Acute focal neurologic deficits were reported in only 2% to 3% of patients.[46, 51] This incidence is not unexpected, given coexisting cerebrovascular disease and the hypotension that occurs during dilatation. Asymptomatic embolic events have been documented; thus, the incidence of emboli may be underreported.[51]

Concerns about the potential for creating severe aortic regurgitation led to selection criteria that excluded patients with significant or moderate aortic regurgitation. With the use of these selection criteria, severe aortic regurgitation has been uncommon and has been reported in only about 2% of patients.* Severe aortic regurgitation may result from annular disruption, aortic wall laceration, leaflet disruption, or leaflet eversion. On the other hand, a mild increase in aortic regurgitation is relatively common and is seen in 10% to 15% of patients.

Other complications include ventricular arrhythmias, atrial ventricular block, prolonged angina or infarction, myocardial perforation, and acute renal dysfunction.

---

## Follow-Up

The rate of follow-up events in patients who have undergone aortic balloon valvuloplasty is relatively high.[26, 36, 45, 54–57] This is related partly to the initial condition of the patient. Depressed left ventricular function is associated with both poor short-term and long-term outcome. The significant incidence of both short-term and long-term mortality may be due to various factors, including inadequate dilatation, irreversible left ventricular dysfunction, and restenosis. The relative importance of each factor is not clear; it is probable that several interact.

In the Mansfield Registry experience, 492 patients underwent aortic balloon valvuloplasty from 1986 to 1987.[54] Vital status was available in 488 of these patients for a mean of 7 months. During this follow-up, 81 patients (16.6%) required either repeat valvuloplasty or aortic valve replacement. One hundred seventeen patients died. The 1-year survival rate was

*References 25, 26, 36, 39, 43, 47, 48, 52, 53.

only 64%. Only 43% were alive and free of aortic valve replacement or repeat valvuloplasty. Patients who died had significantly more impairment initially.

Eight variables that are associated independently and significantly with improved survival (Table 3) are higher left ventricular systolic pressure, absence of coronary artery disease, higher initial cardiac output, better functional class initially (according to the New York Heart Association classification), greater final aortic valve area, lower left ventricular end-diastolic pressure, younger age, and fewer balloon inflations. With these data, a discriminate score was developed that could predict survival probability accurately by patient groups.

The effect of aortic valvuloplasty on long-term mortality compared to other interventions in similar groups of patients is difficult to determine. O'Keefe et al.[58] reported on a series of unoperated patients with severe aortic stenosis seen at the Mayo Clinic. During follow-up, the mortality rate of these patients was 3.8% per month, and at the end of 2 years, only 25% of the medically treated patients were alive. The survival rate for aortic valvuloplasty appears to be better. The experience with surgical treatment of patients is somewhat variable. Increased surgical mortality and greater postoperative morbidity in very elderly patients has been documented clearly. However, despite the increased postoperative mortality and morbidity, the posthospital survival rate is relatively encouraging.[59, 60] Acar et al.[59] documented a 5-year survival of 67.5% in patients over the

## TABLE 3.
### Survival Probability After Aortic Valvuloplasty*†

| Discriminant Score | Probability of 1-Year Survival (%) |
| --- | --- |
| −2.75 to −0.80 | 80 |
| −0.79 to −0.30 | 66 |
| −0.29 to 0.25 | 55 |
| 0.26 to 0.95 | 42 |
| 0.96 to 3.20 | 25 |

*Data from O'Neill WW for the Mansifeld Scientific Aortic Valvuloplasty Registry Investigators: *J Am Coll Cardiol* 1991; 17:193–198.

†Eight variables were identified that were associated independently and significantly with survival. These included initial left ventricular end systolic pressure (LVESP), absence of coronary artery disease, higher baseline cardiac output, better functional class according to the New York Heart Association (NYHA) classification, lower left ventricular end-diastolic pressure (LVEDP), greater final aortic valve area, younger age, and fewer balloon inflations. By using these factors, discriminate analysis allowed formulation of the following survival probability equation: discriminate score = 0.612 + 0.020 (age in years) + 0.023 (LVEDP) + 0.881 (coronary artery disease present = 1 and absent = 0) + 3.371 (NYHA class at baseline) + 0.014 (LVESP) − 0.782 (final aortic valve area).

age of 70 years. In addition, most patients have excellent palliation of their symptoms. Levinson et al.[61] documented an operation mortality of 9.4% in 64 octogenarian patients. The 5-year actuarial survival was 67 ± 10%, and survivors typically were asymptomatic or had only mild symptoms.

Symptomatic improvement following aortic balloon valvuloplasty is seen in most survivors, at least in the short term.[8, 25, 26, 48, 49, 56] In the Mansfield Registry, 66% of patients had symptomatic improvement and 26% were asymptomatic at short-term follow-up.[54] However, restenosis rates are high; in fact, restenosis develops in most patients if follow-up is long enough. In some of these patients, the restenosis may not be severe enough to cause symptoms. However, given the increased morbidity and mortality, restenosis continues to cause significant problems.

Enthusiasm for aortic balloon valvuloplasty has waned because of only moderate hemodynamic improvement, the high event rate during follow-up, and the high rate of restenosis. Whether advances in technology will improve the outlook remains to be seen. Currently, aortic balloon valvuloplasty should be limited to very selected patients. One obvious patient group is those with severe symptomatic aortic stenosis in whom aortic valve replacement is not possible because of either severe associated diseases or advanced left ventricular dysfunction making them inoperable. Valvuloplasty may improve symptomatic outcome in these patients, although a high event rate remains.[36, 55, 60, 62, 63] In addition, patients at very high risk for surgery are candidates for valvuloplasty. Other patients also may benefit, including those with significant aortic stenosis who need to undergo noncardiac operation. In these individuals, the risks of noncardiac operation may be increased and perioperative care may be more difficult.[64–68] Aortic balloon valvuloplasty may decrease their surgical risk and improve their outcome. Patients with limited life expectancy from noncardiac causes but with significant symptomatic aortic stenosis also may benefit. There has been growing interest in performing aortic balloon valvuloplasty in young patients with congenital aortic stenosis. Initial short-term results are encouraging, but longer follow-up is required to determine the role of balloon valvuloplasty in this subgroup of patients. For other individuals with significant symptomatic aortic stenosis, conventional aortic valve replacement remains the treatment of choice. More effective means for improving the early outcome and limiting restenosis are being developed and evaluated.

## Mitral Valvuloplasty

Mitral balloon valvuloplasty, introduced in 1984 by Inoue and his associates,[69] has become an alternative to surgical mitral commissurotomy in selected patients with symptomatic mitral stenosis.[40] In the United States, mitral balloon valvuloplasty was performed initially in elderly patients who were high operative risks.[70, 71] However, it became apparent that the heavily calcified, rigid valves of these patients posed an increased risk for the valvuloplasty procedure. Therefore, mitral balloon valvuloplasty has been reserved for younger patients with pliable, noncalcified valves. Results with this procedure in these patients have been excellent and are comparable to the results of surgical commissurotomy. At many medical centers, percutaneous mitral balloon valvuloplasty is the preferred treatment for selected patients with severe symptomatic mitral stenosis.[40, 72, 73] For patients at high risk for surgical treatment—those with severe calcification and thickening of the mitral valve apparatus—balloon valvuloplasty may be indicated if open heart operation is not an option, but the initial and short-term results are not as favorable.

## Mechanism

In adults, isolated mitral stenosis is nearly always the result of rheumatic heart disease.[74, 75] The rheumatic process causes fusion of mitral commissures, stiff and rigid mitral leaflets, and fusion and shortening of the subchordal apparatus. There is commissural fusion in 75% of cases of stenosis of the mitral valve.

Surgical treatment of mitral stenosis has centered on methods that split the fused commissures. Closed commissurotomy was preferred initially. Either a transseptal finger fracture or a transventricular dilator was used to dilate the stenotic mitral valve, thereby causing commissural splitting.[76, 77] With the advent of cardiopulmonary bypass, open commissurotomy done under direct visualization has become the operation of choice.[78, 79] With open commissurotomy, atrial thrombi can be removed and the commissures can be incised under direct visual guidance. If necessary, fused chordae or papillary muscles also may be separated. It was discovered that commissurotomy usually produced suboptimal hemodynamics in patients with calcified, rigid valves and subvalvular fusion. Therefore, replacement of the mitral valve with a valve prosthesis was recommended for these patients.

The mechanism of percutaneous mitral balloon valvuloplasty is similar to that of surgical commissurotomy. In vitro studies on excised mitral valves[80-82] and studies performed intraoperatively[69] have demonstrated that balloon inflation across a stenotic valve causes splitting of fused commissures rather than remolding of valve leaflets. Two-dimensional echocardiograms have shown an increase in the angle of the anterior or lateral commissures after balloon valvuloplasty.[83, 84] Fracturing of nodular calcifications within the leaflets also may lead to increased valve mobility.[80] As with surgical commissurotomy, commissural splitting may not occur in patients with calcified, rigid mitral leaflets. In addition, the obstruction caused by fusion and shortening of the subchordal apparatus is not relieved by either balloon dilatation or surgical commissurotomy.

## Preoperative Assessment

The preoperative assessment of patients with mitral stenosis who are to undergo percutaneous mitral balloon valvuloplasty is important. As with surgical commissurotomy and percutaneous balloon valvuloplasty, thickening and fusion of the subvalvular apparatus and heavy calcification and rigidity of valve leaflets portend suboptimal immediate results and complications.[40, 73, 85–87] In addition, the long-term results for patients with heavily calcified mitral valves frequently are unsatisfactory, and these patients often require surgical treatment later.[86, 88, 89] Therefore, it is essential to identify the morphology of the mitral valve apparatus before undertaking percutaneous mitral balloon valvuloplasty.

Two-dimensional echocardiography is an ideal, noninvasive method for examining the mitral valve apparatus. A mitral valve echocardiographic score has been developed that represents the degree of leaflet mobility, leaflet thickening, subvalvular thickening, and calcification.[90] The specific grading of the score is shown in Table 4. It is our experience and that of others[40, 73, 85–87] that for patients who score less than 8, the immediate

**TABLE 4.**
**Mitral Valve Echocardiography Score Based on Morphologic Features***

| Grade | Definition |
|---|---|
| | Mobility |
| 1 | Highly mobile valve with only leaflet tips restricted |
| 2 | Normal mobility of midportion and base of leaflet |
| 3 | Valve moving forward in diastole, mainly from the base |
| 4 | No or minimal forward movement of leaflets in diastole |
| | Leaflet thickening |
| 1 | Leaflets nearly normal in thickness (4 to 5 mm) |
| 2 | Midportion of leaflets normal; marked thickening of margins (5 to 8 mm) |
| 3 | Thickening extending through entire leaflet (5 to 8 mm) |
| 4 | Marked thickening of all leaflet tissue (>8 to 10 mm) |
| | Subvalvular thickening |
| 1 | Minimal thickening just below mitral leaflets |
| 2 | Thickening of chordal structures extending up to one third of the chordal length |
| 3 | Thickening extending to distal third of the chords |
| 4 | Extensive thickening and shortening of all chordal structures extending down to papillary muscles |
| | Calcification |
| 1 | Single area of increased echocardiographic brightness |
| 2 | Scattered areas of brightness confined to leaflet margins |
| 3 | Brightness extending into midportion of leaflets |
| 4 | Extensive brightness throughout much of the leaflet tissue |

*From Abascal VM, Wilkins GT, Choong CY, et al: *J Am Coll Cardiol* 1988; 11:257–263. Used by permission.

results usually are excellent and there is a low incidence of complications after mitral valvuloplasty. However, if the echocardiographic score is greater than 10, the results are less than optimal and the risk for complications is higher.

Coexistent mitral regurgitation of at least moderate severity is a contraindication for mitral balloon valvuloplasty. Color-flow imaging with two-dimensional echocardiography allows a semiquantitative estimate of the severity of mitral regurgitation.[91] If the color-flow jet occupies less than 20% of the left atrial area, mitral regurgitation is considered mild in severity. If the physical examination does not reveal a loud systolic murmur in a patient with these echocardiographic findings, the patient may be considered for mitral balloon valvuloplasty. If the results of the physical examination and echocardiography are discrepant about the degree of mitral regurgitation, left ventriculography is required. If mitral regurgitation is 2+ or greater, mitral balloon valvuloplasty should not be performed.

There may be an atrial thrombus in patients with mitral stenosis, especially those in atrial fibrillation. Balloon valvuloplasty can dislodge atrial thrombi and cause systemic embolization. Although it is important in evaluating mitral valve morphology, precordial echocardiography is not sensitive enough to detect thrombi in the left atrium, especially those localized to the left atrial appendage. Therefore, at our institution, transesophageal echocardiography is performed before each procedure to determine whether there are thrombi in either the left atrial cavity or the left atrial appendage. If thrombi are visible, percutaneous mitral balloon valvuloplasty is contraindicated. Anticoagulation therapy for 3 months before the procedure is recommended for patients who have had embolic events, even if thrombi are not seen on transesophageal examination.

## Methodology

There are several methods for performing mitral balloon valvuloplasty.[40, 70, 71, 74, 92–97] A transseptal approach through the right femoral vein is used at our institution. This is done with a specially designed 8-French Mullins catheter to create a puncture in the area of the fossa ovalis. Biplane fluoroscopy is important for ensuring that the puncture is posterior and for avoiding complications such as aortic puncture and pericardial tamponade. After the Mullins sheath is introduced into the left atrium, a 7-French balloon-wedge catheter is passed into the left ventricle. Left atrial and left ventricular pressures are recorded simultaneously to determine the mean transmitral gradient. Cardiac output is estimated from green dye-dilution curves, and mitral valve area is calculated with the Gorlin equation.[98]

After hemodynamics are assessed, the Mullins sheath is passed through the mitral valve into the left ventricle. The balloon-wedge catheter is withdrawn from the sheath, and two long, 0.038 in. exchange guide wires are placed in the sheath. The guide wires are specifically preformed with coils at the distal tip that will curl in the apex of the left ventricle. The Mullins sheath then is withdrawn, and the guide wires are left in place across the fossa ovalis, across the mitral valve, and in the apex of the left ventricle. After introduction of the guide wires, a 6- or 8-mm dilatation balloon is advanced across the atrial septum along one of the guide wires to enlarge the opening so that larger balloons can be introduced to dilate the subcutaneous tissue at the site of the venous entry (Fig 1).

After dilatation of the venous entry and the atrial septum, two large balloons are passed along the guide wires. In instances of critical mitral stenosis, an initial inflation is performed with one balloon, and then both balloons are inflated simultaneously across the mitral valve (Fig 2). The optimal balloon size for dual-balloon technique depends on the size of the patient and the morphology of the mitral valve apparatus.[88, 96, 99] In patients

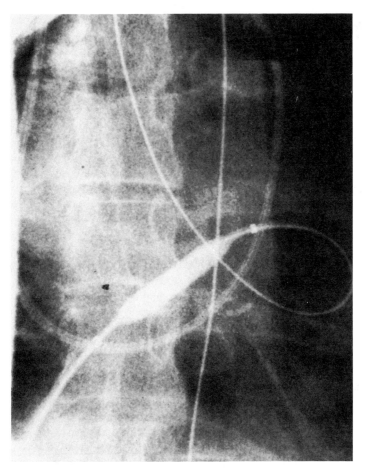

**FIG 1.**
Radiograph of an 8-mm balloon inflated across the atrial septum to enlarge the opening so that larger balloons can be introduced.

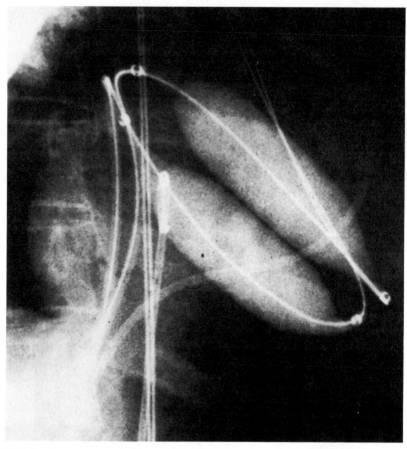

**FIG 2.**
Radiograph of two balloons inflated simultaneously across the mitral valve.

with high mitral valve echocardiography scores, smaller balloons are used initially.

Because forward flow is decreased during balloon inflation, there frequently is severe hypotension. In addition, ventricular arrhythmias are common during balloon manipulation and inflation. This necessitates short periods of inflation, usually less than 5 to 10 seconds. The prophylactic administration of β-blockers intravenously before balloon dilatation results in less ventricular ectopy and a more stable position of the balloon. After balloon dilatation, hemodynamic measurements are performed again and, if the results are not optimum, large balloons are introduced.

Single conventional balloons also may be used to dilate the mitral valve. The largest size available is 25 mm; this limits the final size of the mitral valve area. In addition, a single large balloon may cause more damage to the atrial septum during withdrawal after deflation than would two smaller balloons that are withdrawn sequentially.

An alternative technique involves a unique self-positioning balloon (the Inoue balloon) that has a "pillow-shaped" configuration. It allows inflations to be performed in a more stable position than do conventional balloons.[69, 100] Also, it has the advantage of using preformed wires and a flow-directed balloon tip that decrease catheter motion in the left atrium and avoid dislodging thrombi.

The Inoue balloon requires a transseptal puncture similar to the dual-balloon technique. However, after the puncture is created and the Mullins sheath is introduced into the left atrium, a stiff wire that has several circular loops is put in the left atrium to prevent catheter movement into the left atrial appendage (Fig 3). A dilator used to dilate the atrial septum and fem-

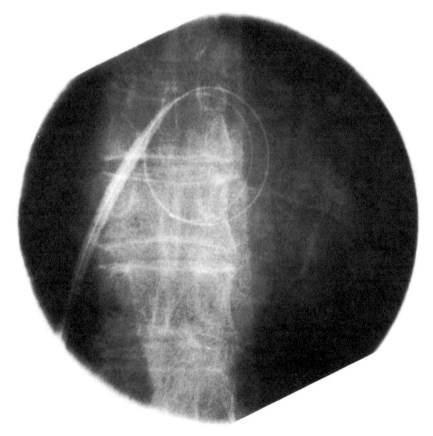

**FIG 3.**
A wire with several circular loops is used with the Inoue balloon technique to avoid catheter movement into the left atrial appendage.

oral vein is introduced around the guide wire, after which the Inoue balloon is extended ("slenderized") and placed through the atrial septum into the left atrium. The balloon then is returned to its original shape, and carbon dioxide is used to inflate its distal end. This results in "flow directing" the catheter through the mitral valve into the left ventricle. After placement of the balloon across the mitral valve, the balloon is inflated. The balloon is designed specifically so that the distal end in the left ventricle is inflated first. Afterward, the balloon is pulled back so that the inflated portion is adjacent to the ventricular surface of the mitral valve (Fig 4,A). Additional inflation causes the proximal end of the balloon to inflate, and this stabilizes the balloon across the mitral valve (see Fig 4,B). Finally, additional injection inflates the middle portion of the balloon and dilates the mitral valve (see Fig 4,C).

The advantage of the Inoue balloon is that inflation is more stable. Therefore, there is less motion of the balloon during dilatation, which decreases the incidence of perforation of the left ventricle, tears of the mitral leaflets, and tearing of the atrial septum. Use of the Inoue balloon may produce lower event rates for cerebrovascular events, atrial septal defects, and severe mitral regurgitation.[100]

It is controversial whether the use of a single Inoue balloon gives less satisfactory results than the dual-balloon technique. The use of the two balloons may cause a greater degree of commissural splitting than would a single large balloon because of either a larger "effective balloon area"[96, 99] or improved orientation of the balloons within the oval orifice of the mitral valve.[99] Studies are needed to determine which technique ultimately provides better results.

Another variation of percutaneous balloon valvuloplasty is the use of a retrograde approach, in which guide wires are snared and brought out through the femoral artery.[93] This allows the balloons to be introduced through the femoral artery. Other approaches include using long transseptal sheaths through which the balloons are placed,[94] and placing guide wires across the aortic valve into the aorta to decrease the possibility of perforation.[99]

## Acute Results

The immediate results of percutaneous mitral balloon valvuloplasty are comparable to the results of surgical open commissurotomy (Figs 5 and 6).[69, 80, 92–97, 99, 101] The mean gradient across the mitral valve decreases by 50% to 60%. Because of increased cardiac output, the mitral valve area usually is doubled. In patients who had a pliable, noncalcified valve and a severe mitral stenosis before the procedure, the mean gradient after the procedure is usually $<5$ mm Hg and the valve area is $\geq 2$ cm$^2$. These changes are associated with rapid decreases in pulmonary artery pressure and pulmonary vascular resistance during the 24 hours after the procedure.[92] Plasma levels of atrial natriuretic factor, antidiuretic hormone, and cyclic adenosine monophosphate increase after dilation and then de-

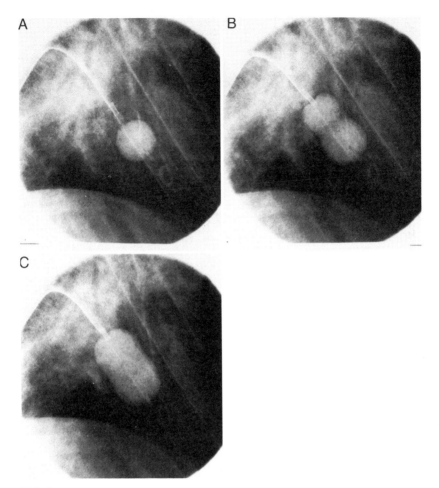

**FIG 4.**
**A,** the distal end of the Inoue balloon is inflated and snug against the ventricular surface of the mitral valve. **B,** additional inflation stabilizes the balloon across the mitral valve by causing the proximal end to inflate. **C,** additional injection inflates the middle portion of the balloon and dilates the mitral valve. (From Nishimura RA, Holmes DR Jr, Reeder GS: *Mayo Clin Proc* 1991; 66:276–282. Used by permission.)

crease to levels lower than those obtained before the procedure.[102–104]

The acute outcome of mitral balloon valvuloplasty depends on the underlying mitral valve morphology.[73, 83, 85] Patients with a mitral valve echocardiography score less than 8 usually have excellent results. However, if the echocardiographic score is greater than 10, the results are suboptimal and there is a higher risk of complications.

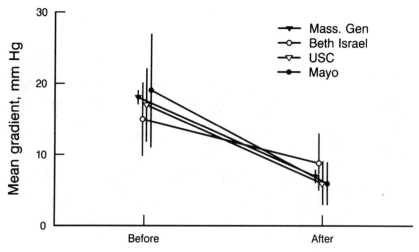

**FIG 5.**
Results of percutaneous mitral balloon valvuloplasty. An acute decrease in the mean gradient across the mitral valve was found in a series of patients studied at Massachusetts General Hospital *(Mass. Gen)*, Beth Israel Hospital, the University of Southern California *(USC)*, and Mayo Clinic *(Mayo)*. *Vertical lines* indicate the standard deviation. (From Nishimura RA, Holmes DR Jr, Reeder GS: *Mayo Clin Proc* 1990; 65:198–220. Used by permission.)

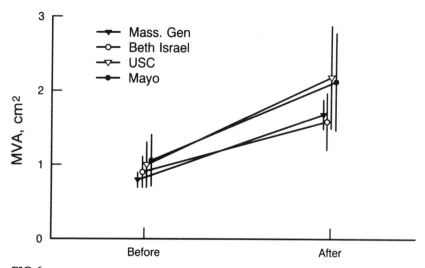

**FIG 6.**
Results of percutaneous mitral balloon valvuloplasty. An acute increase in the mitral valve area *(MVA)* was seen in several series of patients. *Mass. Gen* = Massachusetts General Hospital; *USC* = the University of Southern California; *Mayo* = Mayo Clinic. *Vertical lines* represent the standard deviation. (From Nishimura RA, Holmes DR Jr, Reeder GS: *Mayo Clin Proc* 1990; 65:198–220. Used by permission.)

## Complications

The complications of mitral balloon valvuloplasty are listed in Table 5. Cardiac tamponade and hemopericardium may be caused by perforation of either the left atrium or the aorta during transseptal puncture or by perforation of the left ventricle during balloon dilatation. Mitral regurgitation may increase by one grade after balloon valvuloplasty in about 30% to 40% of patients and by two grades in about 10%.[80, 90, 92, 99] Severe mitral regurgitation develops in fewer than 5% of patients. It usually occurs in patients with a high echocardiographic score in whom balloon inflation tears the leaflets rather than separates the commissures.

Atrial septal defects may occur from placing large balloons across the atrial septum. The reported incidence of atrial septal defects seems to depend primarily on the sensitivity of the diagnostic technique.[107, 108] When transesophageal echocardiography is used, as many as 87% of patients have an atrial septal defect.[107] However, the shunt usually is less than a Qp/Qs of 1.5 to 1.0 and progressively decreases during the follow-up period because of a gradual reduction in left atrial pressure.[85, 99] Larger defects may occur if a balloon is not deflated completely on withdrawal or if it slides back during inflation. Acute right heart failure caused by left-to-right shunting is rare.[109]

## TABLE 5.
### Reported Complications of Mitral Valvuloplasty in Three Studies*

| Complication | McKay[105] (n = 63) | | NHLBI[106†] (n = 72) | | Babic et al.[97] (n = 76) | |
|---|---|---|---|---|---|---|
| | Number | Percent | Number | Percent | Number | Percent |
| Cerebrovascular accident | 2 | 3.2 | 3 | 4.2 | 3 | 3.9 |
| Cardiac tamponade | 0 | 0 | 4 | 5.6 | — | — |
| Death | 1 | 1.6 | 1 | 1.4 | 1 | 1.3 |
| Severe mitral regurgitation | 0 | 0 | 2 | 2.8 | 2 | 2.6 |
| Prolonged hypotension | — | — | 7 | 9.7 | — | — |
| Local vascular complication | — | — | — | — | 3 | 3.9 |
| Atrial septal defect | 13 | 20.6 | — | — | — | — |

*From Nishimua RA, Holmes DR Jr, Reeder GS: *Mayo Clin Proc* 1990; 65:198–220. Used by permission.
†National Heart, Lung, and Blood Institute.

Mitral balloon valvuloplasty can produce systemic embolization if a left atrial thrombus is dislodged. In several large series, the incidence of cerebral embolic events was as high as 4%.[97, 106] At our institution, transesophageal echocardiography is performed before each procedure to determine whether thrombi are in either the atrium or the atrial appendage. If there is an atrial thrombus, the patient is treated with anticoagulation medication for 3 months and the transesophageal echocardiogram is repeated. If there is no atrial thrombus at follow-up, it is our experience that the procedure can be performed without the occurrence of embolic events. In cases of heavily calcified mitral valve leaflets, calcific embolus may occur after balloon inflation; however, this rarely occurs.

## Follow-up

Follow-up of patients after percutaneous mitral balloon valvuloplasty is limited, ranging from 6 to 27 months.[86, 96, 97, 110–112] Functional capacity is improved markedly in most patients and the majority who were in functional class III to IV (according to the New York Heart Association classification) before valvuloplasty, are in class I to II at short-term follow-up. A 50% improvement in exercise capacity also is noted.[110]

The rates of recurrent symptoms and restenosis at follow-up are related to mitral valve morphology. In patients with pliable, noncalcified valves, these rates are less than 10%.[86, 100] However, in patients with heavily calcified, nonpliable valves, the incidence of symptom recurrence is 30% to 40% and the rate of restenosis is more than 40%.[86, 100]

Follow-up over a 10-year period will be necessary to assess fully the efficacy of percutaneous mitral balloon valvuloplasty and to compare it with surgical commissurotomy.

## Current Patient Selection

Percutaneous mitral balloon valvuloplasty is a well-accepted treatment for severe symptomatic mitral stenosis in selected patients, but long-term follow-up is necessary to determine the optimal role for this procedure. The technique is more complicated than either aortic or pulmonic valvuloplasty, and it should be performed only at medical centers that have extensive experience with the procedure. Balloon valvuloplasty may be the treatment of choice for patients with noncalcified, pliable valves, because it can be performed at low risk and can produce excellent immediate and short-term results. In patients with calcified valves and subvalvular fusion, there are higher complication risks, less satisfactory results, and higher rates of restenosis. Balloon valvuloplasty is a reasonable procedure to consider for these patients, provided they are not surgical candidates because of coexistent medical conditions.

# References

1. Freeman WK, Schaff HV, Orszulak TA, et al: Ultrasonic aortic valve decalcification: Serial Doppler echocardiographic follow-up. *J Am Coll Cardiol* 1990; 16:623–630.
2. Campbell DB, Waldhausen JA: "Conservative" aortic valve intervention: Thwarted again (editorial)! *J Am Coll Cardiol* 1990; 16:631–632.
3. Rahimtoola SH: Perspective on valvular heart disease: An update. *J Am Coll Cardiol* 1989; 14:1–23.
4. Pierce WS, Pae WE, Myers JL, et al: Cardiac surgery: A glimpse into the future. *J Am Coll Cardiol* 1989; 14:265–275.
5. Cutler EC, Beck CS: The present status of the surgical procedures in chronic valvular disease of the heart: Final report of all surgical cases. *Arch Surg* 1929; 18:403–416.
6. Bailey CP, Bolton HE, Nichols HT, et al: The surgical treatment of aortic stenosis. *J Thorac Surg* 1956; 31:375–437.
7. Harken DE, Black H, Taylor WJ, et al: The surgical correction of calcific aortic stenosis in adults; results in the first 100 consecutive transaortic valvuloplasties. *J Thorac Surg* 1958; 36:759–773.
8. Cribier A, Savin T, Saoudi N, et al: Percutaneous transluminal valvuloplasty of acquired aortic stenosis in elderly patients: An alternative to valve replacement? *Lancet* 1986; 1:63–67.
9. Mullany CJ, Elveback LR, Frye RL, et al: Coronary artery disease and its management: Influence on survival in patients undergoing aortic valve replacement. *J Am Coll Cardiol* 1987; 10:66–72.
10. Teply JF, Grunkemeier GL, Starr A: Cardiac valve replacement in patients over 75 years of age. *Thorac Cardiovasc Surg* 1981; 29:47–50.
11. Pelletier LC, Castonguay YR, Chaitman BR: Open-heart surgery in elderly patients. *Can Med Assoc J* 1983; 128:409–412.
12. Edmunds LH Jr, Stephenson LW, Edie RN, et al: Open-heart surgery in octogenarians. *N Engl J Med* 1988; 319:131–136.
13. Rahimtoola SH: Outcome of aortic valve surgery. *Circulation* 1979; 60:1191–1195.
14. Craver JM, Goldstein J, Jones EL, et al: Clinical, hemodynamic, and operative descriptors affecting outcome of aortic valve replacement in elderly versus young patients. *Ann Surg* 1984; 199:733–740.
15. Craver JM, Weintraub WS, Jones EL, et al: Predictors of mortality, complications, and length of stay in aortic valve replacement for aortic stenosis. *Circulation* 1988; 78(suppl I):85–90.
16. Magovern JA, Pennock JL, Campbell DB, et al: Aortic valve replacement and combined aortic valve replacement and coronary artery bypass grafting: Predicting high risk groups. *J Am Coll Cardiol* 1987; 9:38–43.
17. Kirklin JK, Naftel DC, Blackstone EH, et al: Risk factors for mortality after primary combined valvular and coronary artery surgery. *Circulation* 1989; 79(suppl):I-185–I-190.
18. Tsai TP, Matloff JM, Chaux A, et al: Combined valve and coronary artery bypass procedures in septuagenarians and octogenarians: Results in 120 patients. *Ann Thorac Surg* 1986; 42:681–684.
19. Olson LJ, Edwards WD, Tajik AJ: Aortic valve stenosis: Etiology, pathophysiology, evaluation, and management. *Curr Probl Cardiol* 1987; 12:455–508.

20. Passik CS, Ackermann DM, Pluth JR, et al: Temporal changes in the causes of aortic stenosis: A surgical pathologic study of 646 cases. *Mayo Clin Proc* 1987; 62:119–123.

21. Kennedy KD, Hauck AJ, Edwards WD, et al: Mechanism of reduction of aortic valvular stenosis by percutaneous transluminal ballon valvuloplasty: Report of five cases and review of literature. *Mayo Clin Proc* 1988; 63:769–776.

22. Isner JM, Samuels DA, Slovenkai GA, et al: Mechanism of aortic balloon valvuloplasty: Fracture of valvular calcific deposits. *Ann Intern Med* 1988; 108:377–380.

23. Safian RD, Mandell VS, Thurer RE, et al: Postmortem and intraoperative balloon valvuloplasty of calcific aortic stenosis in elderly patients: Mechanisms of successful dilation. *J Am Coll Cardiol* 1987; 9:655–660.

24. Holmes DR, Nishimura RA: Catheter balloon valvuloplasty in adults with aortic stenosis, in Kulick DL, Rahimtoola SH (eds): *Techniques and Applications in Interventional Cardiology*. Chicago, Mosby-Year Book, 1991.

25. Cribier A, Savin T, Berland J, et al: Percutaneous transluminal balloon valvuloplasty of adult aortic stenosis: Report of 92 cases. *J Am Coll Cardiol* 1987; 9:381–386.

26. Safian RD, Berman AD, Diver DJ, et al: Balloon aortic valvuloplasty in 170 consecutive patients. *N Engl J Med* 1988; 319:125–130.

27. Grollier G, Commeau P, Agostini D, et al: Anterograde percutaneous transseptal valvuloplasty in a case of severe calcific aortic stenosis. *Eur Heart J* 1987; 8:190–193.

28. Block PC, Palacios IF: Comparison of hemodynamic results of anterograde versus retrograde percutaneous balloon aortic valvuloplasty. *Am J Cardiol* 1987; 60:659–662.

29. Midei MG, Brennan M, Walford GD, et al: Double vs single balloon technique for aortic balloon valvuloplasty. *Chest* 1988; 94:245–250.

30. Dorros G, Lewin RF, King JF, et al: Percutaneous transluminal valvuloplasty in calcific aortic stenosis: The double balloon technique. *Cathet Cardiovasc Diagn* 1987; 13:151–156.

31. Isner JM, Salem DN, Desnoyers MR, et al: Dual balloon technique for valvuloplasty of aortic stenosis in adults. *Am J Cardiol* 1988; 61:583–589.

32. Orme EC, Wray RB, Barry WH, et al: Comparison of three techniques for percutaneous balloon aortic valvuloplasty of aortic stenosis in adults. *Am Heart J* 1989; 117:11–17.

33. Voudris V, Drobinski G, L'Epine Y, et al: Results of percutaneous valvuloplasty for calcific aortic stenosis with different balloon catheters. *Cathet Cardiovasc Diagn* 1989; 17:80–83.

34. Meier B, Friedli B, Oberhänsli I: Trefoil balloon for aortic valvuloplasty. *Br Heart J* 1986; 56:292–293.

35. Meier B, Friedli B, Oberhaensli I, et al: Trefoil balloon for percutaneous valvuloplasty. *Cathet Cardiovasc Diagn* 1986; 12:277–281.

36. Bashore TM for the NHLBI Balloon Valvuloplasty Registry Participants: Percutaneous balloon aortic valvuloplasty. The acute and 30 day follow-up results in 674 patients from the NHLBI Balloon Valvuloplasty Registry. *Circulation,* in press.

37. Lewin RF, Dorros G, King JF, et al: Aortic annular tear after valvuloplasty: The role of aortic annulus echocardiographic measurement. *Cathet Cardiovasc Diagn* 1989; 16:123–129.

38. Waller BF, Girod DA, Dillon JC: Transverse aortic wall tears in infants after

balloon angioplasty for aortic valve stenosis: Relation of aortic wall damage to diameter of inflated angioplasty balloon and aortic lumen in seven necropsy cases. *J Am Coll Cardiol* 1984; 4:1235–1241.

39. Lembo NJ, King SB III, Roubin GS, et al: Fatal aortic rupture during percutaneous balloon valvuloplasty for valvular aortic stenosis. *Am J Cardiol* 1987; 60:733–736.

40. Nishimura RA, Holmes DR Jr, Reeder GS: Percutaneous balloon valvuloplasty. *Mayo Clin Proc* 1990; 65:198–220.

41. McKay RG, Safian RD, Lock JE, et al: Assessment of left ventricular and aortic valve function after aortic balloon valvuloplasty in adult patients with critical aortic stenosis. *Circulation* 1987; 75:192–203.

42. Nishimura RA, Holmes DR Jr, Reeder GS, et al: Doppler echocardiographic observations during percutaneous aortic balloon valvuloplasty. *J Am Coll Cardiol* 1988; 11:1219–1226.

43. McKay RG for the Mansfield Scientific Aortic Valvuloplasty Registry Investigators: The Mansfield Scientific Balloon Aortic Valvuloplasty Registry: Overview of acute hemodynamic results and procedural complications. *J Am Coll Cardiol*, in press.

44. Nishimura RA, Holmes DR Jr, Reeder GS, et al: Doppler evaluation of results of percutaneous aortic balloon valvuloplasty in calcific aortic stenosis. *Circulation* 1988; 78:791–799.

45. Litvack F, Jakubowski AT, Buchbinder NA, et al: Lack of sustained clinical improvement in an elderly population after percutaneous aortic valvuloplasty. *Am J Cardiol* 1988; 62:270–275.

46. Holmes DR Jr, Nishimura RA, Reeder GS: In-hospital mortality after balloon aortic valvuloplasty: Frequency and associated factors. *J Am Coll Cardiol* 1991; 17:189–192.

47. Lewin RF, Dorros G, King JF, et al: Percutaneous transluminal aortic valvuloplasty: Acute outcome and follow-up of 125 patients. *J Am Coll Cardiol* 1989; 14:1210–1217.

48. Letac B, Cribier A, Koning R, et al: Results of percutaneous transluminal valvuloplasty in 218 adults with valvular aortic stenosis. *Am J Cardiol* 1988; 62:598–605.

49. Letac B, Cribier A, Koning R, et al: Aortic stenosis in elderly patients aged 80 or older: Treatment by percutaneous balloon valvuloplasty in a series of 92 cases. *Circulation* 1989; 80:1514–1520.

50. Hallett JW Jr, Wolk SW, Cherry KJ Jr, et al: The femoral neuralgia syndrome after arterial catheter trauma. *J Vasc Surg* 1990; 11:702–706.

51. Davidson CJ, Skelton TN, Kisslo KB, et al: The risk for systemic embolization associated with percutaneous balloon valvuloplasty in adults: A prospective comprehensive evaluation. *Ann Intern Med* 1988; 108:557–560.

52. Treasure CB, Schoen FJ, Treseler PA, et al: Leaflet entrapment causing acute severe aortic insufficiency during balloon aortic valvuloplasty. *Clin Cardiol* 1989; 12:405–408.

53. Phillips RR, Gerlis LM, Wilson N, et al: Aortic valve damage caused by operative balloon dilatation of critical aortic valve stenosis. *Br Heart J* 1987; 57:168–170.

54. O'Neill WW for the Mansfield Scientific Aortic Valvuloplasty Registry Investigators: Predictors of long-term survival after percutaneous aortic valvuloplasty: Report of the Mansfield Scientific Balloon Aortic Valvuloplasty Registry. *J Am Coll Cardiol* 1991; 17:193–198.

55. Nishimura RA, Holmes DR Jr, Michela MA, et al: Follow-up of patients with

low output, low gradient hemodynamics after percutaneous balloon aortic valvuloplasty: The Mansfield Scientific Balloon Aortic Valvuloplasty Registry. *J Am Coll Cardiol* 1991; 17:828–833.

56. Holmes DR Jr, Nishimura RA, Reeder GS, et al: Clinical follow-up after percutaneous aortic balloon valvuloplasty. *Arch Intern Med* 1989; 149:1405–1409.

57. Block PC, Palacios IF: Clinical and hemodynamic follow-up after percutaneous aortic valvuloplasty in the elderly. *Am J Cardiol* 1988; 62:760–763.

58. O'Keefe JH Jr, Vlietstra RE, Bailey KR, et al: Natural history of candidates for balloon aortic valvuloplasty. *Mayo Clin Proc* 1987; 62:986–991.

59. Acar J, Vahanian A, Slama M, et al: Treatment of calcified aortic stenosis: Surgery or percutaneous transluminal aortic valvuloplasty? *Eur Heart J* 1988; 9(suppl E):163–168.

60. Desnoyers MR, Salem DN, Rosenfield K, et al: Treatment of cardiogenic shock by emergency aortic balloon valvuloplasty. *Ann Intern Med* 1988; 108:833–835.

61. Levinson JR, Akins CW, Buckley MJ, et al: Octogenarians with aortic stenosis: Outcome after aortic valve replacement. *Circulation* 1989; 80(suppl): I-49–I-56.

62. Davidson CJ, Harrison JK, Leithe ME, et al: Failure of balloon aortic valvuloplasty to result in sustained clinical improvement in patients with depressed left ventricular function. *Am J Cardiol* 1990; 65:72–77.

63. Berland J, Cribier A, Savin T, et al: Percutaneous balloon valvuloplasty in patients with severe aortic stenosis and low ejection fraction: Immediate results and 1-year follow-up. *Circulation* 1989; 79:1189–1196.

64. Goldman L, Caldera DL, Nussbaum SR, et al: Multifactorial index of cardiac risk in noncardiac surgical procedures. *N Engl J Med* 1977; 297:845–850.

65. Hayes SH, Holmes DR Jr, Nishimura RA, et al: Palliative percutaneous aortic balloon valvuloplasty before noncardiac operations and invasive diagnostic procedures. *Mayo Clin Proc* 1989; 64:753–757.

66. Roth RB, Palacios IF, Block PC: Percutaneous aortic balloon valvuloplasty: Its role in the management of patients with aortic stenosis requiring major noncardiac surgery. *J Am Coll Cardiol* 1989; 13:1039–1041.

67. O'Keefe JH, Shub C, Rettke SR: Risk of noncardiac surgical procedures in patients with aortic stenosis. *Mayo Clin Proc* 1989; 64:400–405.

68. Levine MJ, Berman AD, Safian RD, et al: Palliation of valvular aortic stenosis by balloon valvuloplasty as preoperative preparation for noncardiac surgery. *Am J Cardiol* 1988; 62:1309–1310.

69. Inoue K, Owaki T, Nakamura T, et al: Clinical application of transvenous mitral commissurotomy by a new balloon catheter. *J Thorac Cardiovasc Surg* 1984; 87:394–402.

70. McKay RG, Lock JE, Keane JF, et al: Percutaneous mitral valvuloplasty in an adult patient with calcific rheumatic mitral stenosis. *J Am Coll Cardiol* 1986; 7:1410–1415.

71. Palacios IF, Lock JE, Keane JF, et al: Percutaneous transvenous balloon valvotomy in a patient with severe calcific mitral stenosis. *J Am Coll Cardiol* 1986; 7:1416–1419.

72. Rahimtoola SH: Catheter balloon valvuloplasty of aortic and mitral stenosis in adults: 1987. *Circulation* 1987; 75:895–901.

73. Block PC: Who is suitable for percutaneous balloon mitral valvotomy (editorial)? *Int J Cardiol* 1988; 20:9–14.

74. Rusted IE, Scheifley CH, Edwards JE: Studies of the mitral valve. II. Certain anatomic features of the mitral valve and associated structures in mitral stenosis. *Circulation* 1956; 14:398–406.
75. Harken DE, Dexter L, Ellis LB, et al: The surgery of mitral stenosis. III. Finger-fracture valvuloplasty. *Ann Surg* 1951; 134:722–741.
76. Baker C, Brock RC, Campbell M: Valvulotomy for mitral stenosis: Report of six successful cases. *Br Med J [Clin Res]* 1950; 1:1283–1293.
77. Ellis LB, Harken DE, Black H: A clinical study of 1,000 consecutive cases of mitral stenosis two to nine years after mitral valvuloplasty. *Circulation* 1959; 19:803–820.
78. Roe BB, Edmunds LH Jr, Fishman NH, et al: Open mitral valvulotomy. *Ann Thorac Surg* 1971; 12:483–489.
79. Mullin MJ, Engelman RM, Isom OW, et al: Experience with open mitral commissurotomy in 100 consecutive patients. *Surgery* 1974; 76:974–982.
80. McKay RG, Lock JE, Safian RD, et al: Balloon dilation of mitral stenosis in adult patients: Postmortem and percutaneous mitral valvuloplasty studies. *J Am Coll Cardiol* 1987; 9:723–731.
81. Kaplan JD, Isner JM, Karas RH, et al: In vitro analysis of mechanisms of balloon valvuloplasty of stenotic mitral valves. *Am J Cardiol* 1987; 59:318–323.
82. Block PC, Palacios IF, Jacobs ML, et al: Mechanism of percutaneous mitral valvotomy. *Am J Cardiol* 1987; 59:178–179.
83. Reid CL, McKay CR, Chandraratna PAN, et al: Mechanisms of increase in mitral valve area and influence of anatomic features in double-balloon, catheter balloon valvuloplasty in adults with rheumatic mitral stenosis: A Doppler and two-dimensional echocardiographic study. *Circulation* 1987; 76:628–636.
84. Come PC, Riley MF, Diver DJ, et al: Noninvasive assessment of mitral stenosis before and after percutaneous balloon mitral valvuloplasty. *Am J Cardiol* 1988; 61:817–825.
85. Abascal VM, Wilkins GT, Choong CY, et al: Echocardiographic evaluation of mitral valve structure and function in patients followed for at least six months after percutaneous balloon mitral valvuloplasty. *J Am Coll Cardiol* 1988; 12:606–615.
86. Palacios IF, Block PC, Wilkins GT, et al: Follow-up of patients undergoing percutaneous mitral balloon valvotomy: Analysis of factors determining restenosis. *Circulation* 1989; 79:573–579.
87. Wilkins GT, Weyman AE, Abascal VM, et al: Percutaneous balloon dilatation of the mitral valve: An analysis of echocardiographic variables related to outcome and the mechanism of dilatation. *Br Heart J* 1988; 60:299–308.
88. Reid CL, Chandraratna PAN, Kawanishi DT, et al: Influence of mitral valve morphology on double-balloon catheter balloon valvuloplasty in patients with mitral stenosis: Analysis of factors predicting immediate and 3-month results. *Circulation* 1989; 80:515–524.
89. Abascal VM, Wilkins GT, O'Shea JP, et al: Prediction of successful outcome in 130 patients undergoing percutaneous balloon mitral valvotomy. *Circulation* 1990; 82:448–456.
90. Abascal VM, Wilkins GT, Choong CY, et al: Mitral regurgitation after percutaneous balloon mitral valvuloplasty in adults: Evaluation by pulsed Doppler echocardiography. *J Am Coll Cardiol* 1988; 11:257–263.
91. Helmcke F, Nanda NC, Hsiung MC, et al: Color Doppler assessment of mitral regurgitation with orthogonal planes. *Circulation* 1987; 75:175–183.

92. McKay CR, Kawanishi DT, Rahimtoola SH: Catheter balloon valvuloplasty of the mitral valve in adults using a double-balloon technique: Early hemodynamic results. *JAMA* 1987; 257:1753–1761.

93. Babic UU, Pejcic P, Djurisic Z, et al: Percutaneous transarterial balloon valvuloplasty for mitral valve stenosis. *Am J Cardiol* 1986; 57:1101–1104.

94. Al-Zaibag M, Ribeiro PA, Al-Kasab S, et al: Percutaneous double-balloon mitral valvotomy for rheumatic mitral valve stenosis. *Lancet* 1986; 1:757–761.

95. Babic UU, Pejcic P, Djurisic Z, et al: Transarterial balloon mitral valvuloplasty. *Z Kardiol* 1987; 76(suppl 6):111–117.

96. Chen C, Lo Z, Huang Z, et al: Percutaneous transseptal balloon mitral valvuloplasty: The Chinese experience in 30 patients. *Am Heart J* 1988; 115:937–947.

97. Babic UU, Pejcic P, Djurisic Z, et al: Percutaneous transarterial balloon mitral valvuloplasty: 30 months' experience. *Herz* 1988; 13:91–99.

98. Gorlin R, Gorlin SG: Hydraulic formula for calculation of the area of the stenotic mitral valve, other cardiac valves, and central circulatory shunts. I. *Am Heart J* 1951:41:1–29.

99. Palacios I, Block PC, Brandi S, et al: Percutaneous balloon valvotomy for patients with severe mitral stenosis. *Circulation* 1987; 75:778–784.

100. Nobuyoshi M, Hamasaki N, Kimura T, et al: Indications, complications, and short-term clinical outcome of percutaneous transvenous mitral commissurotomy. *Circulation* 1989; 80:782–792.

101. Lock JE, Khalilullah M, Shrivastava S, et al: Percutaneous catheter commissurotomy in rheumatic mitral stenosis. *N Engl J Med* 1985; 313:1515–1518.

102. Dussaule J-C, Vahanian A, Michel P-L, et al: Plasma atrial natriuretic factor and cyclic GMP in mitral stenosis treated by balloon valvulotomy: Effect of atrial fibrillation. *Circulation* 1988; 78:276–285.

103. Tsai R-C, Yamaji T, Ishibashi M, et al: Atrial natriuretic peptide and vasopressin during percutaneous transvenous mitral valvuloplasty and relation to renin-angiotensin-aldosterone system and renal function. *Am J Cardiol* 1990; 65:882–886.

104. Waldman HM, Palacios IF, Block PC, et al: Responsiveness of plasma atrial natriuretic factor to short-term changes in left atrial hemodynamics after percutaneous balloon mitral valvuloplasty. *J Am Coll Cardiol* 1988; 12:649–655.

105. McKay RG: Balloon valvuloplasty for treating pulmonic mitral and aortic valve stenosis. *Am J Cardiol* May 1988; 61:102G–108G.

106. Block PC: Early results of mitral balloon valvuloplasty (MBV) for mitral stenosis: Report from the NHLBI Registry (abstract). *Circulation* 1988; 78(suppl):II-489.

107. Yoshida K, Yoshikawa J, Akasaka T, et al: Assessment of left-to-right atrial shunting after percutaneous mitral valvuloplasty by transesophageal color Doppler flow-mapping. *Circulation* 1989; 80:1521–1526.

108. Fields CD, Slovenkai GA, Isner JM: Atrial septal defect resulting from mitral balloon valvuloplasty: Relation of defect morphology to transseptal balloon catheter delivery. *Am Heart J* 1990; 119:568–576.

109. Acar C, Deloche A, Tibi PR, et al: Operative findings after percutaneous mitral dilation. *Ann Thorac Surg* 1990; 49:959–963.

110. McKay CR, Kawanishi DT, Kotlewski A, et al: Improvement in exercise capacity and exercise hemodynamics 3 months after double-balloon, catheter balloon valvuloplasty treatment of patients with symptomatic mitral stenosis. *Circulation* 1988; 77:1013–1021.

111. Al Zaibag M, Ribeiro PA, Al Kasab S, et al: One-year follow-up after percutaneous double balloon mitral valvotomy. *Am J Cardiol* 1989; 63:126–127.
112. Chen CR, Hu SW, Chen JY, et al: Percutaneous mitral valvuloplasty with a single rubber-nylon balloon (Inoue balloon): Long-term results in 71 patients. *Am Heart J* 1990; 120:561–568.

# Diagnostic Paracentesis

## John C. Hoefs, M.D.

Associate Professor, Department of Medicine, University of California, Irvine, School of Medicine, Orange County, California

## Gavin M. Jonas, M.D.

Clinical Instructor, Gastroenterology, Southern California Permanente Medical Group, Anaheim, California

## Editor's Introduction

What laboratory tests to perform on ascites fluid has always been a somewhat confusing issue. Drs. Hoefs and Jonas critically analyze the literature plus their own wide experience in diagnostic paracentesis, and provide us with logical and precise guidelines. By calculating the gradient between serum and ascites albumin, the authors are able to predict which patients with ascites are likely to have chronic liver disease and portal hypertension vs. heart failure or infection. Helpful diagnostic features to differentiate spontaneous bacterial peritonitis from secondary bacterial peritonitis are also provided. The guidelines outlined below should increase the diagnostic efficiency of paracentesis by careful analysis of laboratory tests available in every hospital.

*J. Thomas La Mont, M.D.*

The importance of paracentesis as a diagnostic tool in the clinical evaluation of ascitic patients has been re-emphasized for the following reasons: (1) a 10% to 25% incidence of spontaneous bacterial peritonitis (SBP), a reversible cause of deterioration in cirrhotic patients with ascites[1, 2]; (2) the safety of the procedure, even in very ill patients with coagulopathy[3]; (3) easily available tests for rapid differential diagnosis; and (4) a better understanding of ascites formation and SBP. Paracentesis should be performed in any patient with new-onset ascites, in all patients with ascites who are admitted to the hospital (because of the high incidence of SBP), and in the presence of clinical deterioration in patients with underlying liver disease and ascites. Although the initial paracentesis may not yield a definitive diagnosis, it will reveal the presence or absence of portal hypertension, which is a key to the evaluation of ascitic patients; identify most cases of peritonitis; and distinguish secondary bacterial peritonitis from SBP. Hence, a significant part of the work-up will have been initiated. This review will define these features and provide an approach to the evaluation of ascitic patients.

*Advances in Internal Medicine*®, vol. 37
Copyright 1992, Mosby–Year Book, Inc.

## Diagnostic Approach to the Assessment of Ascitic Patients

A thorough clinical assessment prior to performing paracentesis is essential, as it will identify the most likely diagnosis and, by so doing, influence the tests ordered on the ascitic fluid and set the stage for the interpretation of these tests. Paracentesis serves to confirm the cause thought to be most likely clinically based on the history and physical examination approximately 80% of the time.

The most common cause of ascites is chronic liver disease (CLD) (Table 1), which is usually obvious on history, physical examination, and blood tests (Table 2). Ninety-nine percent of patients will have a portal pressure >10 mm Hg at the time of initial presentation with new-onset ascites. The risk factors for CLD include long-standing alcohol intake, previous blood transfusions, intravenous drug abuse with shared needles, previous hepatitis infection, intimate contact with a person infected with hepatitis, a carrier of hepatitis B, Oriental background, or a family history of liver disease. The first presentation of liver disease may be with jaundice, abnormal liver tests, or the complications of portal hypertension, such as bleeding esophageal varices, hepatic encephalopathy, and ascites. On physical examination, patients with advanced liver disease and ascites have wasting of their extremities and faces with a protuberant abdomen. Jaundice and pallor are clues to the presence of severe underlying liver disease and anemia. Extra-abdominal stigmata of CLD (SCLD) include spider angiomata, gynecomastia, testicular atrophy, Dupuytren's contracture, parotid enlargement, liver nails, clubbing of the nails, and palmar erythema. Abdominal wall collaterals may be visible and are often palpable. Prominent, palpable collaterals around the umbilicus (i.e., caput medusae) are found in less than 20% of patients. The presence of ascites is usually obvious, but must be confirmed clinically by bilateral flank dullness, shifting dullness as the patient is turned, and eventually by paracentesis. The presence of an enlarged spleen in the left upper quadrant suggests long-standing portal hypertension. The liver may be enlarged with subacute liver disease or small with advanced cirrhosis. In either case, it is mild to moderately firm when palpable. Peripheral edema may vary from ankle edema to anasarca.

A firm liver, splenomegaly, icterus, or one of the SCLD is found in 98% of patients with ascites due to CLD; 75% to 80% will have all of these at presentation. If ascites interferes with the evaluation of splenomegaly or liver firmness, 5 to 6 L of fluid can be removed to access the abdominal contents better. The absence of physical evidence of liver disease, even in an alcoholic, raises the suspicion of an etiology other than liver disease.

Most other causes for ascites related to portal hypertension have their own natural history and predisposing factors, the details of which would be inappropriate to this chapter. However, it is reasonable to emphasize cardiac ascites, which frequently is preceded by symptoms of congestive heart failure and often occurs in the setting of known cardiac disease. Furthermore, all non–liver-disease causes for portal hypertensive ascites also produce hepatomegaly, firmness of the liver, and splenomegaly (except for

## TABLE 1.
## Wide and Narrow Albumin Gradient Ascites*

I. Portal hypertensive, wide gradient (>1.1 g/dL).

   A. Chronic liver disease (80%).
   B. Cardiac (3%).
   C. Massive hepatic metastases (3%).
   D. Veno-occlusive disease.
   E. Budd-Chiari syndrome with or without inferior vena cava block.
   F. Myxedema.
   G. Hemodialysis with fluid overload (1%).

II. Nonportal hypertensive, narrow gradient (<1.2 g/dL).

   A. Peritoneal carcinomatosis (6%).
   B. Peritoneal inflammation (increased white blood cell count, 2%).
      1. Infection.
         a. Permeability plus lymphatic obstruction.
            (1) Tuberculoous.
            (2) Fungal.
         b. Permeability alone.
            (1) Cytomegalovirus.
            (2) Viral.
            (3) Chlamydia.
            (4) Bacterial.
      2. Serositis.
   C. Hollow organ leak.
      1. Leak of low-protein fluid.
         a. Pancreatic.
         b. Ureteric.
         c. Bilious.
         d. Post renal transplant.
      2. Leak of high-protein fluid.
         a. Lymphatic rupture.
            (1) Chylous.
            (2) Nonchylous.
         b. Peritoneal hemorrhage.
   D. Oncotic
      1. Nephrotic syndrome.
      2. Protein-losing enteropathy.
      3. Kwashiorkor.
   E. Idiopathic.
   F. Peritoneal permeability increase without inflammation(?).
      1. Post peritoneal dialysis.
      2. Hemodialysis without fluid overload.

*The percent of all causes is shown in parentheses, except those accounting for <1%.

**TABLE 2.**
**Features on Physical Examination That Should Be Sought Initially in All Patients With Ascites***

| | | | | Portal Hypertension | | | | |
| | Present | | | | | Absent | | |
| Clinical Feature | CLD, % | CHF, % | MHM, % | VOD BCS-1, % | VOD BCS-2, % | MYX, % | ONC, % | Rest, % |
|---|---|---|---|---|---|---|---|---|
| Predisposing cause for CLD | 90 | 5–10 | 5 | 5 | 5 | 5 | 5 | 5 |
| Physical examination | | | | | | | | |
| Jaundice (icterus only) | *60 (90)‡* | 1 (30) | 1 (10) | 5 (60) | 0 (60) | 0 (0) | 0 (0) | 0 (0) |
| Stigmata of chronic liver disease | 90 | 5 | 5 | 5 | 5 | 5 | 5 | 5 |
| Abnormal liver size | | | | | | | | |
| Small | 40 | 0 | 0 | 5 | 5 | 0 | 0 | 0 |
| Large | 40 | 80 | 80 | 80 | 80 | 60 | 0 | 0 |
| Liver firmness (mild to moderate) | 90 | 90 | 90† | 90 | 90 | 50 | 0 | 0 |
| Splenomegaly | 70 | 50 | 5 | 80 | 80 | 0 | 0 | 0 |
| Edema | 50 | 80 | 20 | 50 | 80 | 70 | 100 | 5–10 |
| Abdomen wall collaterals | 20 | 0 | 0 | 20 | 50 | 0 | 0 | 0 |
| Jugular venous distention | 0 | 95 | 0 | 0 | 0 | 0 | 0 | 0 |
| Anasarca | 5–10 | 5–25 | 0 | 0 | 0 | 0 | 50–80 | 0 |
| Large back veins | 0 | 0 | 0 | 0 | 95 | 0 | 0 | 0 |
| Pulse <60/bpm | 0 | 5 | 0 | 0 | 0 | 95 | 0 | 0 |

*Unique features for a given cause are italicized for emphasis. CLD = chronic liver disease; CHF = congestive heart failure; MHM = massive hepatic metastasis; VOD = veno-occlusive disease; BCS-1 = Budd-Chiari syndrome; BCS-2 = Budd-Chiari syndrome with inferior vena cava obstruction above the hepatic veins; MYX = myxedema; ONC = oncotic ascites.
†Moderate to severe firmness.
‡The incidence of scleral icterus.

massive hepatic metastases) on physical examination, but rarely cause deep jaundice (although icterus is not uncommon) or SCLD (see Table 1). Distended neck veins almost invariably are present in patients with cardiac ascites at the initial presentation (although they may be absent before the resolution of ascites after effective therapy of congestive heart failure). Large paravertebral back veins are found in patients with chronic IVC obstruction above the hepatic veins; a large, very firm liver is found with massive hepatic metastases; and a pulse of <60 bpm is found with myxedematous ascites.

Ascites not associated with portal hypertension lacks the above clinical features. The presence of anasarca in the absence of distended neck veins or hepatomegaly is suggestive of oncotic ascites (i.e., that due to a very low serum colloid osmotic pressure, usually with an albumin level of 1.5 g%). Most other nonportal hypertensive causes for ascites lack specific suggestive features on the clinical evaluation (see Table 2); these are listed in Table 1.

Overall, the clinical evaluation of ascitic patients is very helpful in suggesting the probable cause of the ascites, but a simple means of confirming the clinical impression and directing the work-up is necessary when the usual causes seem less likely. Furthermore, peritonitis must be excluded, since it occurs in 10% to 25% of patients with ascites due to CLD. The majority of these patients are minimally symptomatic, and peritonitis cannot be excluded by clinical features. Therefore, a diagnostic paracentesis is required on all patients with ascites.

## Portal Hypertensive vs. Nonportal Hypertensive Ascites

A useful initial step in establishing the etiology of ascitic fluid is to separate the causes into those that are associated with portal hypertension and those that are not (see Table 1). Prior use of a transudate vs. an exudate base on the ascitic fluid total protein concentration is no longer reliable for the following reasons: (1) since the normal peritoneal fluid total protein concentration is >4 g/dL, "exudative" etiologies would form peritoneal fluid with a normal total protein concentration[4-6]; (2) the ascitic total protein concentration increases in cirrhotics to >3 g/dL during diuresis and albumin infusion[7-10]; (3) some transudative etiologies, such as congestive cardiac failure, have a characteristically high total protein concentration in the ascitic fluid[11-13]; and (4) cirrhosis may be the most common cause of high-protein ascites.[11-13] Attempts to use the lactic dehydrogenase levels in ascites as well as total protein with or without the ascites-to-serum ratio are marginally better than protein alone.[11]

The serum-to-ascites albumin gradient (A-GRAD, serum albumin minus ascites albumin) has been shown to correlate closely with portal pressure.[14, 15] The following relationship has been established:

$$PP - Pa \sim (S)_A - (Asc)_A = (A\text{-}GRAD),$$

where PP is the portal pressure, Pa is the ascites hydrostatic pressure, $(S)_A$ is the serum albumin concentration, $(Asc)_A$ is the ascites albumin concentration, and (A-GRAD) is the serum-to-ascites albumin gradient. Physiologically, this relationship of portal pressure to the albumin gradient can be understood as the result of the passive dilution of peritoneal fluid protein until the colloid osmotic pressure gradient due to proteins in ascites and serum is in hemodynamic balance with the hydrostatic gradient between portal capillaries and ascites, per the equation

$$CHP - IAP = \frac{BPx + PP}{1 + x} - IAP = \sigma d(\pi s - \pi a) + FF,$$

where CHP is capillary hydrostatic pressure, BP is mean blood pressure, x is the ratio of precapillary to postcapillary resistance, $\sigma d$ is the osmotic reflection coefficient, $\pi s$ is the colloid osmotic pressure of serum, $\pi a$ is the colloid osmotic pressure of ascites, IAP is intra-abdominal pressure, and FF is fluid formation factors. In humans, IAP is generally within 1 to 2 mm Hg of inferior vena cava pressure. Since x is usually <.05, BPx is similar between patients and 1+x is close to 1. Studies in man have confirmed a relationship of the portal pressure gradient to the colloid osmotic pressure gradient,[16] as well as the albumin gradient.[14, 15] Thus, the A-GRAD widens proportional to the portal pressure gradient to intra-abdominal pressure (Pa) or inferior vena cava pressure. The formula, estimated PP gradient (in mm Hg) = (AGRAD) × 7.08 + 3.62 can be used to estimate the portal pressure and is usually within 2 mm Hg for portal pressure gradient (portal pressure minus inferior vena cava pressure) if ascites and blood are drawn simultaneously.[15] Hence, the A-GRAD can be used to detect those patients with portal hypertension. A wide A-GRAD of >1.1 g/dL differentiates causes of ascites due to portal hypertension from cases of normal portal pressure ascites with a narrow A-GRAD of <1.1 g/dL (see Table 1).

The A-GRAD has been found to be the most effective test to distinguish CLD and massive hepatic metastasis from peritoneal carcinomatosis (93% to 96% accuracy).[13, 17-20] Chylous ascites could be variable, depending on the etiology (Table 3).[21] Cardiac ascites[22] has a wide A-GRAD and total ascitic protein >3.0 g/dL, compared to CLD, which has a wide A-GRAD and a protein in the ascites fluid <1.5 g/dL. However, 20% of patients with CLD have a protein >3.0% as well.

Some clinical difficulties in using the A-GRAD should be appreciated. The A-GRAD remains wide in those patients with portal hypertension who develop another cause for ascites that usually would give a narrow A-GRAD, since it reflects portal pressure regardless of the cause.[13, 19] Furthermore, the A-GRAD is dependent on the patient being hemodynamically stable.[14] It also has been reported to narrow (potentially into a nondiagnostic range) by diuresis, a serum albumin concentration <1.2 g/dL, and a high serum globulin concentration.[14] Lack of simultaneous blood sampling, leaving the tourniquet on too long, and sampling downstream from an intravenous infusion site are common technical errors that affect the A-GRAD and decrease its value.[23] Thus, the A-GRAD should be used in conjunction with the clinical evaluation and other tests to make the diagnosis.

**TABLE 3.**
**Syndromes With Multiple Mechanisms or Etiologies**

I. Malignant ascites.
  A. Massive hepatic metastasis (30%).
  B. Peritoneal carcinomatosis (67%).
  C. Budd-Chiari syndrome (<1%).
  D. Chylous (<1%).
II. Chylous.
  A. Obstruction of the thoracic duct.
    1. Malignancy (80%).
    2. Tuberculosis (14%).
  B. Local lymphatic leak.
    1. Chronic liver disease (5%).
    2. Cardiac (<1%).
    3. Lymphangiectasia (<1%).
III. Renal-related.
  A. Nephrotic syndrome.
  B. Hemodialysis.
    1. Fluid overload.
    2. Not fluid overload.
  C. Peritoneal dialysis.
  D. Post renal transplant.
  E. Serositis (i.e., systemic lupus erythematosus).
  F. Ureteric.
IV. Narrow serum-to-ascites albumin gradient with an elevated neutrophil count.
  A. Pancreatic, biliary, perforated peptic ulcer.
  B. Serositis (systemic lupus erythematosus, rheumatoid arthritis, eosinophilic enteritis).
  C. Acute infectious peritonitis.
    1. Secondary bacterial peritonitis.
    2. Cytomegalovirus.
    3. Chlamydia.
  D. Peritoneal carcinomatosis.
V. Intra-peritoneal hemorrhage
  A. Trauma.
  B. Hepatocellular carcinoma.
  C. Oral contraceptives adenoma.
  D. Peritoneal carcinomatosis.
  E. Fistula to a blood vessel.

Once the cause for ascites has been evaluated regarding the presence or absence of portal hypertension, other studies of the fluid, such as a cell count and differential, cytology, and chemistries, will aid in the final diagnosis. A lymphocytic predominance is seen in tuberculosis,[24] fungal infections, and peritoneal lymphoma,[17, 19, 23, 25] and a polymorphonuclear predominance is evident with acute peritonitis or serositis.[1] Ascites fluid pH, lactate, glucose, and lactic dehydrogenase frequently are abnormal with infiltrative and inflammatory conditions within the peritoneal cavity.[11, 19, 26–28] Cytology is postiive in 73% to 95% of patients with peritoneal carcinomatosis.[19, 20] Special chemistries, such as amylase, bilirubin, and triglycerides, are increased above the serum levels in pancreatitis, pancreatic or biliary leaks, and chylous ascites, respectively.[17, 19, 21] The ascitic fibronectin[29] and cholesterol[30] also can be used to distinguish CLD from peritoneal carcinomatosis (collectively, 97% accurate), but are less helpful in differentiating it from other etiologies.[31]

Syndromes with multiple mechanisms or etiologies are listed in Table 3. In cases in which the etiology remains unclear or blind liver biopsy is hazardous because of the presence of ascitic fluid, laparoscopy allows ascitic fluid to be obtained for investigation, liver biopsy to be performed under direct vision, and the peritoneal cavity to be examined for evidence of peritoneal carcinomatosis, serositis, or tuberculosis.

## Peritonitis

The diagnosis of peritonitis at the time of presentation is important because of the high associated morbidity and mortality. SBP should be suspected in all patients with underlying liver disease who are presenting for the first time (there is a 10% to 25% incidence of SBP in cirrhotics with ascites[1, 2, 17]), have clinical features suggestive of peritonitis, or have experienced a change in the clinical state. SBP needs to be distinguished from other causes of peritonitis, as the investigation and treatment of these conditions are different. Eighty-five percent of peritonitis is due to a primary cause, while the remaining 15% is due to a secondary cause. Since SBP occurs almost always in patients with CLD, secondary peritonitis should be suspected when peritonitis is documented in patients with any other cause for ascites, particularly in those with a narrow A-GRAD.

Conn and colleagues[27, 32, 33] were the first to emphasize the importance of SBP in patients with CLD. There are two variants of SBP that behave identically and appear to occur in the same population of patients: (1) culture-negative neutrocytic ascites, in which the ascitic neutrophil count is elevated (polymorphonuclear neutrophil leukocyte count >250 cells per milliliter); and (2) bacterascites, in which only the culture is positive. Although SBP and culture-negative neutrocytic ascites will be defined separately, they will be combined as "SBP" for the purpose of this discussion, in which only the polymorphonuclear neutrophil leukocyte concentration is likely to be available. Early diagnosis is based on an elevated ascitic fluid neutrophil count detected by initial paracentesis.

Peritonitis, detected in the initial paracentesis by an elevated ascitic fluid neutrophil count, also may be due to a contained intra-abdominal infection or bowel perforation. In the first instance, the peritonitis usually evolves more rapidly because of the large number of organisms entering the peritoneal cavity. Thus, severe peritonitis as indicated by abnormal lactic dehydrogenase or glucose requires immediate evaluation for bowel perforation, and urgent laparotomy if this is confirmed.

## Definitions

### Primary Bacterial Peritonitis

SBP is an infectious process of the peritoneal cavity, usually in cirrhotic patients with ascites, in the absence of a contiguous local source. Because the number of organisms present is low, lactic dehydrogenase and glucose levels are normal and response to treatment is rapid. The diagnosis requires a positive ascitic fluid culture, an ascitic fluid neutrophil count >250/mm$^3$, and the absence of an obvious intra-abdominal source of infection such as abscess or perforation.[1]

Culture-negative neutrocytic ascites has a total ascitic neutrophil count >250/mm$^3$, but a negative culture,[34] no recent antibiotic therapy, and the absence of an alternate cause for the elevated neutrophils, such as peritoneal carcinomatosis,[26] pancreatitis, penetrating duodenal ulcer,[35] bleeding into the peritoneum,[26] serositis due to conditions such as systemic lupus erythematosus, or an infectious process such as tuberculosis.[26, 34] Careful study indicates that patients with culture-negative neutrocytic ascites are clinically indistinguishable from those with SBP in regard to symptomatology, laboratory evaluation, response to antibiotics, and mortality.[34] Twenty-four percent of survivors either have had a previously documented episode of SBP, or will develop SBP in the future. Possible explanations for culture-negativity include spontaneous resolution of SBP and inadequate routine culture techniques. The use of bedside inoculation of ascitic fluid into blood culture bottles has decreased the incidence of culture-negative neutrocytic ascites from 50% to 10% of patients with an elevated ascitic neutrophil count.

Bacterascites is culture-positive ascites with an ascitic fluid neutrophil count of <250 mm$^3$.[36] Polymicrobial bacterascites is infrequent and usually represents puncture of the bowel at paracentesis. Monomicrobial bacterascites is colonization of ascites without a host response. Thus, it may represent an early stage of infection prior to the inflammatory response, or a poor host response to infection. Patients with bacterascites have the same mortality as do those with SBP. Bacterascites almost never is suspected at the time of paracentesis, since the neutrophil count is low, and will be detected only when cultures are positive.

### Secondary Bacterial Peritonitis

Secondary bacterial peritonitis[37–39] is infection of the peritoneal cavity with positive ascitic fluid bacterial cultures, an ascitic fluid neutrophil count of >250 mm$^3$, and evidence of an intra-abdominal source of infection. Seconary infection may result from a nearby "contained" infection, such as an abscess, or from perforation of the colon or small intestine. Secondary bacterial peritonitis initially may be similar to SBP, but it evolves more rapidly and does not respond as well to antibiotics, especially in the presence of perforation. Due to the large number of organisms initially entering the peritoneal cavity, secondary peritonitis usually can be distinguished from SBP by the number and type of infecting organisms, ascitic fluid analysis, the presence of a contiguous source of infection, air under the diaphragm, and a poor response to antibiotic therapy. The importance of the differentiation is that patients with secondary peritonitis may require an emergent operation or percutaneous drainage of an abscess in addition to antibiotics for effective treatment.

## Incidence

Eighty-five percent of cirrhotic patients presenting with peritonitis will have the primary bacterial form; the remaining 15% will have the secondary form. At the time of presentation to the hospital, 25% of cirrhotic patients will have SBP.[40] An additional 10% to 15% may develop SBP at some time during their hospitalization. SBP has been known to occur rarely in ascites from causes other than cirrhosis, namely, nephrotic syndrome in children,[41] severe viral hepatitis,[42] congestive cardiac failure,[22, 43] and massive hepatic metastasis.[20, 44] All of these conditions have an ascites total protein concentration under 1.5 g%.

## Etiology

SBP is rare in the absence of ascites. Ascitic fluid infection is found more commonly in cirrhosis, alcoholic hepatitis,[42] fulminant hepatic failure, and childhood nephrotic syndrome,[41] and is uncommon in physiologic peritoneal fluid, peritoneal carcinomatosis, and cardiac ascites.[22, 43] The unifying feature of the former type of ascites is a low protein concentration.[20, 44] In fact, even cirrhotic ascites rarely becomes infected spontaneously if the protein concentration is >1.5 g%.[45] The opsonic activity of ascitic fluid correlates closely with the protein concentration.[46] Phagocytic cells are ineffective in phagocytosing bacteria in the absence of specific and nonspecific opsonins such as complement, fibronectin, and immunoglobulins.[19] Peritonitis in a patient with a protein concentration >1.5 g% is more consistent with secondary peritonitis, in which a low protein concentration is not a predisposing factor.

Spontaneous bacteremia in cirrhotic patients is three times more common than SBP, and similar organisms are found.[47] Positive blood cultures are noted in more than half of all patients with SBP, and in one third of those with culture-negative neutrocytic ascites.[1, 34] This is evidenced further by the frequency with which distant sources of infection, such as pneumonia, cystitis, and dental abscess, are documented in patients with SBP.[1, 40, 48] Gastrointestinal hemorrhage has been shown to predispose cirrhotics to bacteremia.[49] The mechanisms for this is unknown.

## Evaluation of Spontaneous Bacterial Peritonitis

Signs and symptoms are not required to make the diagnosis of SBP, because there may be no clinical manifestations of the infection.[1, 40, 48] In general, the signs and symptoms of SBP are mild and do not differentiate clearly between infected and uninfected patients[40] or between SBP and secondary peritonitis.[37-39] The emergency room physician often will be the first medical contact with the patient. It is important that the ascites removed be sent for the relevant tests (Table 4) along with simultaneously obtained serum, whether the ascites is thought to be related to liver disease or not.

Paracentesis should be performed in patients with new-onset ascites and in those with known ascites who are exhibiting clinical deterioration of any kind. Paracentesis in these patients is a safe procedure, provided certain precautions are taken.[3] These include accurate localization of ascitic fluid by percussion or ultrasound, the use of small-gauge metal needles (22-gauge), and the avoidance of abdominal surgical scars (which frequently have bowel firmly adherent to their peritoneal surface). Coagulopathy does not contraindicate paracentesis, especially if the needle is inserted through the avascular midline. In fact, SBP is the major cause of disseminated intravascular coagulation in patients with liver disease.

Ascitic fluid should be obtained for (see Table 3) cell count and differential, total protein, albumin, glucose, lactic dehydrogenase, amylase, Gram stain, and bacterial cultures. Depending on the index of suspicion, tuberculosis smears and cultures, and cytology can be obtained also. Serum should be drawn simultaneously and measured for total protein, albumin, lactic dehydrogenase, glucose, and amylase.

A rapid means of making the diagnosis of SBP is to centrifuge 10 to 20 mL of ascitic fluid and observe the size of the pellet. A Gram stain should be performed on the pellet. If there is more than a thin film of white sediment, the white cell count probably is increased. The Gram stain will demonstrate organisms in 10% to 55% of cases of SBP[37, 40] and in nearly all patients with secondary peritonitis.[37-39] The presence of multiple organisms should prompt evaluation for possible secondary bacterial peritonitis, particularly bowel or gallbladder perforation. At the same time, the white cell count and differential can be estimated.

The ascitic fluid neutrophil count is the most reliable parameter in making the diagnosis of peritonitis. The neutrophil count is calculated by multiplying the white blood cell count times the percent of neutrophils in the differential count, divided by 100. It has been established that the mean number of neutrophils in "normal," uninfected ascites is $60/mm^3$, and that <1% have a value >$500/mm^3$.[7] More than 90% of patients with SBP and 100% of those with secondary peritonitis have an ascitic fluid neutrophil count of >$1,000/mm^3$.[1]

Ascitic fluid chemical analysis is important in identifying those patients prone to develop SBP and determining the severity of peritonitis. The as-

**TABLE 4.**
**Laboratory Tests To Be Obtained on Ascitic Fluid and Serum Simultaneously at the Time of Presentation**

I. Ascitic fluid
  A. Microscopy.
    1. Cell count.
    2. Differential.
  B. Chemistry.
    1. Total protein.
    2. Albumin.
    3. Glucose.
    4. Lactic dehydrogenase.
    5. Amylase.
  C. Microbiology.
    1. Ten cubic centimeters inoculated into blood culture bottles at the bedside.
    2. Gram stain (10 to 20 cc centrifuged × 10 minutes at 500 rpm).
    3. Tuberculosis smears and cultures.*
  D. Cytology.*
II. Serum.
  A. Chemistry.
    1. Total protein.
    2. Albumin.
    3. Glucose.
    4. Lactic dehydrogenase.
    5. Amylase.
  B. Microbiology.
    1. Blood cultures.

*Optional depending on index of suspicion.

cites total protein concentration is inversely related to the risk of SBP. Most patients with SBP will have a total protein concentration <1.5 g%.[36] Since secondary peritonitis can occur in patients with either high- or low-protein ascites, peritonitis in a patient with high-protein ascites should suggest secondary peritonitis. An albumin gradient of >1.1 g/dL, determined by subtracting the ascitic fluid albumin concentration from the serum albumin concentration measured on blood obtained at the time of paracentesis, correlates closely with portal hypertension by direct measurement.[14] Patients with a low gradient generally do not have portal hypertension and cirrhosis as the cause of ascites, or SBP as the cause of a white blood cell count increase. Furthermore, the absence of portal hypertension as shown by a low gradient suggests a noncirrhotic cause of ascites, such as pancreatic ascites, tuberculosis, or peritoneal carcinomatosis (see Table 1).[18, 20] The concentration of glucose in ascitic fluid does not decrease with the advent of SBP, although the ascites-to-serum ratio may be lower.[50] The level of lactic dehydrogenase does increase in a significant percentage of patients with SBP, but not to the extent that it is elevated in patients with secondary bacterial peritonitis.[37-39, 50] Ascitic fluid pH and lactate concentration have not been found to be of additional value in the early diagnosis of SBP.[1, 27]

Severe peritonitis in patients with ascites is due to a high bacterial load in the peritoneal cavity and may be caused by SBP as well as intra-abdominal abscess or bowel perforation.[1] Severe peritonitis is defined as bacterial peritonitis with at least two of the following criteria: (1) an ascitic fluid total protein concentration >1 g/dL, (2) an ascitic glucose concentration <50 mg/dL, and (3) a lactic dehydrogenase concentration greater than the upper limit of normal for serum.[27, 37-39, 51] The neutrophil concentration does not differentiate severe from less severe peritonitis, although there is a tendency toward a higher count in the former. The Gram stain usually is positive with severe peritonitis. A single organism is typical of SBP or an abscess, while multiple organisms suggest bowel perforation. Severe peritonitis is found in 100% of patients with a ruptured viscus and 50% of those with a contained intraperitoneal source of infection, but in only 5% of those with SBP.[27] Hence, ascitic fluid findings that tend to distinguish secondary peritonitis from SBP are a Gram stain demonstrating multiple organisms,[33, 48, 52] an ascites glucose level <50 mg/dL,[27, 51] a lactic dehydrogenase level greater than the serum upper limit of normal,[51] an ascitic fluid protein concentration >1.0 g/dL,[51] continued culture positivity during antibiotic therapy,[51] and failure of ascites neutrophil count to decrease quickly with antibiotic treatment.[51] Patients treated successfully for SBP have an exponential decline in the ascites neutrophil count when it is measured by repeat paracentesis 48 hours after the initiation of antibiotic treatment.[51, 53] Continued culture positivity when ascitic fluid is recultured at 48 hours is specific and sensitive for secondary peritonitis, especially if the organism is sensitive to the antibiotic used.[51, 53]

The preferred method for obtaining ascitic fluid cultures is to inoculate aerobic blood culture bottles with 10 mL of ascitic fluid at the bedside.[1, 54, 55] This method has increased the percentage of positive cultures from 43% to 93%.[54, 55] The inoculation of 10 mL has been found to be more sensitive than that of smaller volumes.[55] Table 5 shows the organisms seen most commonly in SBP.[1] Anaerobes are cultured in less than 6% of cases. Five percent of cultures in SBP are polymicrobial. These usually include one or more isolates typical of SBP, plus one or more peculiar organisms, such as *Staphylococcus aureus, Candida* species, or anaerobes.

It is important to obtain blood cultures in all patients in whom SBP is suspected. Fifty-four percent of ascites culture-positive patients with SBP also have positive blood cultures.[1] The majority grow out the same organism in the blood and the ascitic fluid. One third of patients with culture-negative neutrocytic ascites have positive blood cultures, from which antibiotic sensitivity of the ascites organism can be obtained.[34]

**TABLE 5.**
**Bacteria Isolated From Ascitic**
**Fluid in Patients With**
**Spontaneous Bacterial Peritonitis**

| Type of Bacteria Isolated | Percentage |
|---|---|
| Escherichia coli | 43 |
| Klebsiella pneumoniae | 8 |
| Streptococcus pneumoniae | 8 |
| α-Hemolytic streptococcus | 5 |
| Group D streptococcus | 5 |
| Unclassified streptococcus | 4 |
| β-Hemolytic streptococcus | 4 |
| Enterobacteriaceae | 3 |
| Staphylococcus aureus | 2 |
| Miscellaneous | 16 |
| | |
| Anaerobes | <6 |
| Polymicrobial | <10 |

## An Approach to the Assessment of Ascites

Summary of important steps:

1. Paracentesis should be performed in all patients with new-onset ascites, in all those with ascites who are admitted to the hospital (because of the high incidence of SBP), and in the presence of clinical deterioration in those with underlying liver disease and ascites.

2. Ascitic fluid should be sent for total protein, albumin, glucose, lactic dehydrogenase, and a cell count with differential. If clinically appropriate, amylase, triglyceride, bilirubin, cytology, and tuberculosis cultures and stains should be obtained.

3. A Gram stain should be performed on the pellet from 20 cc of spun fluid. Ten cubic centimeters of ascitic fluid should be inoculated into each of two blood culture bottles, one aerobic and one anaerobic, at the bedside.

4. Serum drawn simultaneously should be sent for total protein, albumin, lactic dehydrogenase, glucose, amylase, and a cell count with differential. Patients also should have serum sent for liver function tests and any additional studies as indicated by the clinical picture.

5. An ascites neutrophil count (total ascitic white cell count multiplied by the percentage of polymorphos present) greater than 250/mL or clinical signs of peritonitis are keys to the presence of peritonitis.

**TABLE 6.**
**Ascitic Fluid Findings To Distinguish Spontaneous Bacterial Peritonitis vs. Secondary Peritonitis**

| Finding | Primary Peritonitis | | Secondary Peritonitis | |
| | SBP* | CNNA* | BA* | Perforated Viscus | Contained Infection |
|---|---|---|---|---|---|
| Total protein (g/dL) | <1.0 | <1.0 | <1.0 | >3.0 | >3.0 |
| A-GRAD* | >1.1 | >1.1 | >1.1 | <1.1 | <1.1 |
| Neutrophil count (cells/cc) | >250 | >250 | <250 | >250 | >250 |
| Positive cultures | Yes | No | Yes | Yes | Yes |
| Monomicrobial | >90% | — | >90% | Rarely | Usually |
| Polymicrobial | <10% | — | <10% | >90% | Rarely |
| Anaerobes | <6% | — | Rarely | >90% | ? |
| Severe peritonitis† | 5% | 5% | 0% | 100% | 50% |
| Culture positive after 48 hours of antibiotics | Rarely | — | Rarely | Usually | Frequently |
| Neutrophil count after 48 hours of antibiotics <50% of initial count | Usually | Usually | Usually | Rarely | 50% |

*SBP = spontaneous bacterial peritonitis; CNNA = culture negative neutrocytic ascites; BA = bacterascites; A-GRAD = serum-to-ascites albumin gradient.
†Severe peritonitis is characterized by two or more of the following: a total ascitic fluid protein concentration >1 g/dL, a lactic dehydrogenase level greater than the upper range of normal for the serum, and an ascites glucose concentration <50 mg/dL.

6. SBP is suggested by the presence of an A-GRAD >1.1 g/dL, the absence of a contained intraperitoneal source of infection, a single organism on Gram stain or culture, an ascites total protein concentration <1.0 g/dL, an ascites lactic dehydrogenase less than that of serum, an ascites glucose >50 mg/dL, and underlying chronic liver disease (Table 6).

7. Secondary peritonitis from abscess or perforation should be suspected when the A-GRAD is <1.1 g/dL and multiple organisms are seen on the Gram stain, or if two of three of the following are present: (1) an ascites total protein >1 g/dL, (2) an ascites lactic dehydrogenase greater than the upper limit of normal in the serum, and (3) an ascites glucose <50 mg/dL (see Table 6). These patients should be evaluated for a perforated viscus or a contained intra-abdominal source of infection with an acute abdominal series, a meglumine diatrizoate (Gastrografin) swallow or enema to rule out a perforation, and a surgical consultation.

8. Those patients suspected of having SBP should be treated immediately with the appropriate antibiotic pending results of the cultures. The paracentesis should be repeated after 48 hours to assess antibiotic responsiveness as indicated by a decrease in the ascites neutrophil count and negative repeat ascitic fluid cultures. Multiple organisms on the initial culture, a persistently elevated ascites neutrophil count equal to or greater than the initial count, or persistently positive ascitic fluid cultures suggests a secondary peritonitis.

9. In the absence of peritonitis, patients can be subdivided into those with and those without a wide A-GRAD. Those patients with an A-GRAD >1.1 g/dL and an ascites total protein <1.5 g/dL should be evaluated for liver disease. Those with an A-GRAD >1.1 g/dL and an ascites total protein >3 g/dL should be evaluated for a posthepatic obstructive cause. Malignancy, serositis, tuberculosis, etc., should be suspected in patients with a narrow A-GRAD (<1.1 g/dL).

## Conclusion

The importance of timely paracentesis and the appropriate choice of ascitic fluid and serum tests cannot be overemphasized. The A-GRAD has replaced the ascites total protein as a means of differentiating portal hypertensive vs. non-portal hypertensive ascites. The failure to diagnose peritonitis carries a high morbidity and mortality. SBP needs to be distinguished from secondary peritonitis, since the latter requires more immediate and more aggressive intervention.

## References

1. Hoefs JC, Runyon BA: Spontaneous bacterial peritonitis. Dis Mon 1985; 31:3–48.
2. Almad TP, Skinhoj P: Spontaneous bacterial peritonitis in cirrhosis: Incidence, diagnosis, and prognosis. Scand J Gastroenterol 1987; 22:295–300.

3. Runyon BA: Paracentesis of ascitic fluid, a safe procedure. *Arch Intern Med* 1986; 146:2259–2261.
4. Simberkoff M, Moldover N, Weiss G: Bactericidal and opsonic activity of cirrhotic ascites and nonascitic peritoneal fluid. *J Lab Clin Med* 1978; 91:831–839.
5. Maathuis JB, VanLook PFA, Michie EA: Changes in volume, total protein and ovarian steroid concentrations of peritoneal fluid throughout the human menstrual cycle. *J Endocrinol* 1978; 76:123–133.
6. Bouckaert PJM, Evers JLH, Doesberg WH, et al: Patterns of change in protein in the peritoneal fluid of women during the periovulatory phase of the menstrual cycle. *J Reprod Fertil* 1986; 77:329.
7. Hoefs JC: Increase in ascites white blood count and protein concentrations during diuresis in patients with chronic liver disease. *Hepatology* 1981; 1:249.
8. Hoefs JC: The mechanism of ascitic fluid protein concentration increase during diuresis in patients with chronic liver disease. *Am J Gastroenterol* 1981; 76:423–431.
9. Patek AJ Jr, Mankin H, Colcher N, et al: The effect of intravenous injection of concentrated human serum albumin upon blood plasma, ascites and renal function in three patients with cirrhosis of the liver. *J Clin Invest* 1948; 27:135.
10. Dykes PW: A study of the effects of albumin infusions in patients with cirrhosis of the liver. *Q J Med* 1961; 119:297.
11. Boyer TD, Kahn AM, Reynolds TB: Diagnostic value of ascitic fluid lactic dehydrogenase, protein and WBC levels. *Arch Intern Med* 1978; 138:1103.
12. Sampliner RE, Iber FL: High protein ascites in patients with uncomplicated hepatic cirrhosis. *Am J Med Sci* 1974; 267:275.
13. Rector WG, Reynolds TB: Superiority of the serum-to-ascites albumin difference over the total protein concentration in preparation of transudative and exudative ascites. *Am J Med* 1984; 77:83–85.
14. Hoefs JC: Serum protein concentration and portal pressure determines the ascitic fluid protein concentration in patients with chronic liver disease. *J Lab Clin Med* 1983; 102:260–273.
15. Amra S, Elie R, Kronborg I: Factors that determine refractoriness of ascites to conventional therapy. *Can Med Assoc J* 1986; 135:481–484.
16. Hendiksen JH: Colloid osmotic pressure in decompensated cirrhosis. *Scand J Gastroenterol* 1985; 20:170–174.
17. Albillos A, Cuervas-Mons V, Millan I, et al: Ascitic fluid polymorphonuclear cell count and serum to ascites albumin gradient in the diagnosis of bacterial peritonitis. *Gastroenterology* 1990; 98:134–140.
18. Pare P, Talbot J, Hoefs JC: Serum-ascites albumin concentration gradient: A physiological approach to differential diagnosis of ascites. *Gastroenterology* 1983; 85:240–244.
19. Mauer K, Manzione N: Usefulness of serum-ascites albumin difference in separating transudative from exudative ascites—another look. *Dig Dis Sci* 1988; 33:1208–1213.
20. Runyon BA, Hoefs JC, Morgan T: Ascitic fluid analysis in malignancy-related ascites. *Hepatology* 1988; 8:1104–1109.
21. Rector WG: Spontaneous chylous ascites of cirrhosis. *J Clin Gastroenterol* 1984; 6:369–372.
22. Runyon BA: Cardiac ascites: A characterization. *J Clin Gastroenterol* 1988; 10:410–412.
23. Losowsky EM, Alltree EM, Atkinson M: Plasma colloid osmotic pressure and its relation to protein fractions. *Clin Sci* 1962; 22:249–257.

24. Marshall JB, Vogele KA: Serum-ascites albumin difference in tuberculous peritonitis. *Am J Gastroenterol* 1988; 83:1259–1261.
25. Runyon BA: Peritoneal lymphomatosis with ascites. *Arch Intern Med* 1986; 146:887–888.
26. Yang CY, Liae YF, Chu CM, et al: White count, pH and lactate in ascites in the diagnosis of spontaneous bacterial peritonitis. *Hepatology* 1985; 5:85–90.
27. Garcia-Tsao G, Conn HO, Lerner E: The diagnosis of bacterial peritonitis: Comparison of pH, lactate concentration and leukocyte count. *Hepatology* 1985; 5:91–96.
28. Attali P, Turner K, Pelletier G, et al: pH of ascitic fluid: Diagnostic and prognostic value in cirrhotic and noncirrhotic patients. *Gastroenterology* 1986; 90:1255–1265.
29. Runyon BA: Elevated ascitic fluid fibronectin concentration; a non-specific finding. *J Hepatol* 1986; 3:219–222.
30. Jungst D, Gerbes AL, Martin R, et al: Value of ascitic lipids in the differentiation between cirrhotic and malignant ascites. *Hepatology* 1986; 6:239–243.
31. Prieto M, Gomea-Lechon MJ, Melchor H, et al: Diagnosis of malignant ascites. Comparison of ascitic fibronectin, cholesterol, and serum-ascites albumin difference. *Dig Dis Sci* 1988; 33:833–838.
32. Bar-Meir S, Lerner E, Conn HO: Analysis of ascitic fluid in cirrhosis. *Dig Dis Sci* 1979; 24:135.
33. Correia JP, Conn HO: Spontaneous bacterial peritonitis in cirrhosis: Endemic or epidemic? *Med Clin North Am* 1975; 59:963–981.
34. Runyon BA, Hoefs JC: Culture-negative neutrocytic ascites: A variant of spontaneous bacterial peritonitis. *Hepatology* 1984; 4:1209–1211.
35. Harty RF, Steinberg WM: Noninfectious ascitic fluid leukocytosis associated with penetrating duodenal ulcer. *Dig Dis Sci* 1978; 23:1132–1136.
36. Runyon BA: Monomicrobial bacterascites. A potentially lethal variant of spontaneous bacterial peritonitis (abstract). *Hepatology* 1986; 6:1140.
37. Runyon BA, Hoefs JC: Ascitic fluid analysis in the differentiation of spontaneous bacterial peritonitis from gastrointestinal tract perforation into ascitic fluid. *Hepatology* 1984; 4:447–450.
38. Runyon BA: Bacterial peritonitis secondary to a perinephric abscess: Case report and differentiation from spontaneous bacterial peritonitis. *Am J Med* 1986; 80:997–998.
39. Runyon BA, Hoefs JC: Spontaneous vs secondary bacterial peritonitis: Differentiation by response of ascitic fluid neutrophil count to antimicrobial therapy. *Arch Intern Med* 1986; 146:1563–1565.
40. Pinzello G, Simonetti RG, Craxi A, et al: Spontaneous bacterial peritonitis: A prospective investigation in predominantly nonalcoholic cirrhotic patients. *Hepatology* 1983; 3:545–549.
41. Barness LA, Moll GH, Janeway CA: Nephrotic syndrome. I. Natural history of the disease. *Pediatrics* 1950; 5:486–503.
42. Thomas FB, Fromkes JJ: Spontaneous bacterial peritonitis associated with viral hepatitis. *J Clin Gastroenterol* 1982; 4:259–262.
43. Runyon BA: Spontaneous peritonitis associated with cardiac disease. *Am J Gastroenterol* 1984; 79:796.
44. Isner JI, MacDonald JS, Schein PS: Spontaneous streptococcus pneumonia peritonitis in a patient with metastatic gastric cancer. *Cancer* 1977; 39:2306–2309.
45. Runyon BA: Low-protein-concentration ascitic fluid is predisposed to spontaneous bacterial peritonitis. *Gastroenterology* 1986; 91:1343–1346.

46. Runyon BA, Morrissey R, Hoefs JC, et al: Opsonic activity of human ascitic fluid: A potentially important protective mechanism against spontaneous bacterial peritonitis. *Hepatology* 1985; 5:634–637.
47. Weinstein MP, Iannini PB, Stratton CW, et al: Spontaneous bacterial peritonitis. A review of 28 cases with emphasis on improved survival and factors influencing prognosis. *Am J Med* 1979; 64:592–598.
48. Hoefs JC, Canawati HN, Sapico FL, et al: Spontaneous bacterial peritonitis. *Hepatology* 1982; 2:399–407.
49. Runyon BA: Gastrointestinal hemorrhage markedly increases the risk development of spontaneous bacterial peritonitis (abstract). *Gastroenterology* 1986; 90:1763.
50. Runyon BA, Hoefs JC: Ascitic fluid chemical analysis before, during and after spontaneous bacterial peritonitis. *Hepatology* 1985; 5:257–259.
51. Akriviadis EA, Runyon BA: Utility of an algorithm in differentiating spontaneous from secondary bacterial peritonitis. *Gastroenterology* 1990; 98:127–133.
52. Runyon BA, Hoefs JC, Canawati HN: Polymicrobial bacterascites: A unique entity in the spectrum of infected ascitic fluid. *Arch Intern Med* 1986; 146:2173–2175.
53. Akriviadis EA, Runyon BA: When should paracentesis be repeated to assess the response of infected ascites to antimicrobial therapy (abstract). *Hepatology* 1987; 7:1030.
54. Runyon BA, Umland ET, Merlin T: Inoculation of blood culture bottles with ascitic fluid: Improved detection of spontaneous bacterial peritonitis. *Arch Intern Med* 1987; 147:7375.
55. Runyon BA, Canawati HN, Akriviadis AE: Optimization of ascitic fluid culture techniques. *Gastroenterology* 1988; 95:1351–1355.

# Coxsackievirus Myocarditis*

## Noel R. Rose, M.D., Ph.D.

Professor and Chairman, Department of Immunology and Infectious Diseases; Professor, Department of Medicine, The Johns Hopkins Medical Institutions, Baltimore, Maryland

## David A. Neumann, Ph.D.

Research Associate, Department of Immunology and Infectious Diseases, The Johns Hopkins Medical Institutions, Baltimore, Maryland

## Ahvie Herskowitz, M.D.

Assistant Professor of Medicine, Department of Medicine, Department of Immunology and Infectious Diseases, The Johns Hopkins Medical Institutions, Baltimore, Maryland

## Editor's Introduction

For some four decades since the isolation of coxsackie virus in suckling mice, its affinity for cardiac muscle has made it a leading candidate for an etiological role in myocarditis. The frustration, however, of the inability to isolate the virus from immunologically mature patients with promising epidemiological, clinical, and serological evidence supporting its probable causative role, has left Koch's postulates unfulfilled. The powerful new methodology of recombinant DNA technology and defined peptide epitopes have made it possible to identify viral antigens by DNA probes. With these tools and excellent experimental models in mice, it begins to look much more convincingly that much of human myocarditis and even dilated myocardiopathy may be due to autoimmune responses to virally transformed cardiac proteins in genetically susceptible hosts. A leading authority of this subject, Dr. Noel Rose, and his associates, Drs. Neumann and Herskowitz, review both experimental and clinical data in support of these arguments and point to the future opportunities to advance diagnosis, treatment, and perhaps even prevention of viral myocarditis.

*Gene H. Stollerman, M.D.*

*The authors' original investigations are supported by National Institutes of Health grant HL 33878.

Myocarditis, inflammation of the myocardium, accompanies many acute generalized infectious diseases. Ordinarily, significant clinical findings are not evident. Sometimes, fulminant infection may cause myocardial failure; in other instances, myocarditis may take a chronic course, leading eventually to weakening of the heart muscle, impairment of function, and dilatation. Viral studies have shown that in North America and Europe many cases of myocarditis are associated with strains of coxsackievirus group B. The viral infection may precede the onset of cardiac manifestations by a significant period, possibly years, so that their relationship often is overlooked. Moreover, the sequence of events has raised the suspicion that myocarditis is an immunopathic sequela rather than a direct effect of the viral damage.

In this chapter, we will weigh the evidence for and against the concept that coxsackievirus myocarditis is an immunopathic consequence of the initial viral infection. The issues raised have immediate implications for the diagnosis and treatment of the disease as well as for longer-range questions of prevention and identifying individuals at risk. Of special concern is the relationship of viral myocarditis to idiopathic dilated cardiomyopathy, a major cause of cardiac failure, especially among younger individuals. The question arises whether there are clues to identify individuals who are likely to progress from acute, self-limited myocarditis to ongoing heart disease, leading to cardiomyopathy.

Because it frequently is inapparent clinically, the incidence and prevalence of myocarditis in the United States are unknown. Recent studies in Great Britain[1] have shown, however, that the incidence of dilated cardiomyopathy is approximately 7.5/100,000/yr, and the prevalence is about 8,300/100,000. The prevalence varied greatly from region to region. If these figures can be generalized, they imply an annual incidence in the United States of over 18,000 potential cases of cardiomyopathy, representing a significant public health problem.

Attendant issues of public health policy are raised by these figures. Many patients with idiopathic dilated cardiomyopathy become candidates for cardiac transplantation. They are frequently younger individuals in generally good health, except for their cardiac failure. As a regular modality of treatment, however, transplantation involves serious questions of availability of appropriate organs and intrinsic problems of protracted immunosuppression. Generalized immunosuppression necessarily involves increased susceptibility to infection and activation of latent viruses. In fact, recent reports have attributed the high incidence of atherosclerotic heart disease in transplant recipients to the reactivation of cytomegalovirus.[2] Inadequate immunosuppression, on the other hand, entails dangers of rejection and recurrence of an underlying immunopathic state. Finally, the costs of cardiac transplantation and its effect on the nation's health budget are not insignificant.

# Lessons Learned From Studies of Experimental Myocarditis

## Virus-Induced Myocarditis in Mice

Myocarditis can be produced in experimental animals by several viral agents, including group B coxsackieviruses, encephalomyocarditis virus, and cytomegalovirus. The animals used include monkeys, minipigs, guinea pigs, rats, and hamsters, but mice have been the most useful because of the great variety of inbred strains available. Viruses may be isolated directly from human subjects for use in animal studies; most, however, are carried out with well-characterized isolates known to produce cardiac disease. In the case of coxsackievirus B3 (CB3), complementary myocarditogenic and nonmyocarditogenic isolates have been valuable for comparative studies.

A valuable model of coxsackievirus-induced cardiac disease in mice was developed by Lerner and colleagues.[3-6] They demonstrated that 14-day-old mice of several strains developed severe inflammatory heart disease following the intraperitoneal injection of CB3. The disease was intensified if the animals were forced to swim daily following viral inoculation.[7] A striking finding was the lack of mononuclear cell infiltrates in the hearts of infected athymic nu/nu mice.[8] This observation suggested that the inflammatory response was related to an immune response. Similar findings were reported by Woodruff and Huber,[9-11] who used a slightly different model of CB3-induced myocarditis in mice.

The lesions in mice closely resembled those seen in the human disease. The primary lesion consisted of scattered necrotic foci surrounded by mononuclear cells throughout the ventricles and, to a lesser extent, in the atria. Adjacent interstitial areas of the myocardium were spared. Later, the necrotic foci were replaced with connective tissue and calcification, and the number of mononuclear cells diminished. A few strains of mice developed a chronic disease, in which inflammation continued beyond day 9. The inflammatory cells comprised primarily macrophages and included CD4 and CD8 T cells, B cells, and natural killer (NK) cells. The number of both T cell subsets increased during the course of disease, but the proportion of CD8 cells increased.

## Genetics of Susceptibility to Myocarditis

In order to analyze the mechanisms involved in myocardial injury, we[12-14] infected a variety of inbred mice with CB3 and systematically evaluated the content of virus in various organs, the production of neutralizing antibody in the serum, and the appearance of pathologic changes in the heart. Mouse strains were selected because they were genetically identical, except for the major histocompatibility complex (MHC), or because they were identical at the MHC but differed in background genotype. We discovered that some strains of mice produce an acute, self-limited disease, whereas others develop progressive, ongoing myocarditis. The two phases of the disease differed histologically. The early phase was characterized by focal myocyte necrosis, together with polymorphonuclear and mononuclear infiltration. In most strains of mice, this inflammatory myocarditis began to recede about the seventh day after infection and completely subsided by day 21. In the few strains of mice that developed onging myocarditis, the histologic appearance was quite different after day 9. Lesions were disseminated throughout the ventricle and consisted primarily of diffuse mononuclear infiltrates between separated myocardial fibers. Despite the presence of this ongoing disease, no infectious virus could be isolated from the hearts of the mice after day 9.

## The Role of Cardiac Myosin

Sera from all mice were studied for the presence of autoantibody to mouse heart.[12] Initially, heart-reactive antibodies were found in all of the mice, whether they developed ongoing myocarditis or not. On closer examination, only mice with progressive myocarditis had significant titers of IgG antibody to mouse heart. Moreover, absorption experiments showed that this antibody was specific for heart muscle and failed to cross-react with skeletal muscle. Immunochemical studies revealed that the most prominent antigen to which the autoantibodies were directed was the heavy chain of cardiac myosin.[15] Further characterization of the major antigenic determinants on the myosin molecule are under way.

The IgG autoantibodies specific for cardiac myosin were found only in strains of mice with the characteristics of progressive myocarditis. Other strains of mice produced mainly IgM antibodies that reacted equally well with skeletal and cardiac myosin. It was hypothesized, therefore, that the progressing form of myocarditis represents an autoimmune response to cardiac myosin. Therefore, mice of a number of inbred strains were immunized with purified cardiac myosin or, for comparison, skeletal muscle myosin.[16, 17] Antibodies specific for cardiac myosin were found only in the strains of mice that developed ongoing myocarditis following CB3 infection. Moreover, all of the mice developed a myocarditis that resembled histologically the late phase of the disease. The inference was drawn, therefore, that progressive myocarditis in genetically predisposed mice is due to autoimmunization to the cardiac isoform of myosin.

## Pathogenetic Mechanisms

The genetic experiments just described allow a discerning analysis of the pathogenetic mechanisms involved in myocardial injury. During the early stage of disease, when virus can still be obtained from heart tissue, it is likely that virus itself induces significant cytopathic alterations in the myocytes. Since this form of injury depends upon virus replication, one critical factor is the genetically determined tempo of neutralizing antibody production. Our studies[13, 18] showed that the mouse strains most susceptible to early disease had no demonstrable neutralizing antibody on the third day after infection, whereas the more resistant strains were all positive for neutralizing antibody at that time. This genetic trait depended primarily upon non-MHC background genes. Perhaps interferon production is related to the severity of early phase disease, although evidence on this point is still lacking. NK cell activity is clearly important. Mice treated with antiasialo GM-1 to decrease NK activity show increased viral content and extensive necrosis in the heart.[19, 20] As mentioned previously, exercise aggravates myocarditis, perhaps by reducing the immune response, as do such environmental stresses as hypothermia and dietary deprivation.

The inflammatory response itself is not responsible for initial myocardial damage, since extensive myocyte necrosis occurs even after the inflammatory response is blocked by the administration of cortisone to CB3-infected mice.[21] It seems unlikely, therefore, that cardiac injury during the early stages of CB3 infection results from host responses.

In the later stages of early phase myocarditis, as well as in the second phase, host response appears to be decisive in determining myocardial damage. The inoculation of T lymphocyte–deficient mice with CB3 results in virus production in the heart equivalent to that of nonimmunocompromised infected controls, but only minimal myocarditis develops.[22, 23] Severe damage becomes evident only 5 days after infection, when lymphocytic infiltration begins.

The increased proportion of CD8 lymphocytes during the evolution of chronic myocarditis suggests that cytotoxic T cells are involved in the pathologic process. The studies of Huber and her colleagues[24–28] have shown that two distinct populations of cytotoxic T lymphocytes are produced following CB3 infection of mice. One population is virus-specific, since it acts upon cardiocytes that are expressing antigenic determinants of the virus. An unexpected finding is that the cytotoxic T cells are CD4+ rather than CD8+, and are MHC class II–restricted. A second population of T cells reacts to glycoproteins induced after infection but not encoded by the viral genome. This newly expressed antigen reacts with the lectin *Ulex europaeus* agglutinin, as shown by Gauntt and his colleagues.[29, 30] Since picornavirus proteins normally are not glycosylated, this new antigen must be of cellular rather than viral origin.

The immunopathic changes induced by these T lymphocytes are a product of the body's immune response to the virus. They are directed either to a viral antigen or to a cellular antigen produced as a consequence of virus infection. They represent, then, part of the protective immunologic responses resulting from the host's effort to remove virus-infected cells.

Autoimmunity has been implicated as another immunopathic mechanism in those strains of mice that develop ongoing myocarditis. The most persuasive evidence is the finding that CB3-infected mice produce autoantibodies specific for cardiac myosin, and that cardiac myosin can induce inflammatory myocarditic changes in the same mouse strains. Genetic susceptibility to autoimmune myocarditis is conferred by a number of genes outside of the MHC. At least one gene appears to be linked to the locus of the α chain of the T cell receptor.[31] Yet, the MHC is important to the autoimmune response, since it seems to determine the magnitude of the histologic damage.

The mechanism of myocardial damage following autoimmunization is still uncertain. In general, the presence of IgG antibodies correlates with the degree of myocarditis, although exceptions have been noted. Huber and her colleagues[32, 33] have reported that DBA/2 mice inoculated with CB3 developed high titers of heart-specific autoantibodies, and that these antibodies could be detected in the hearts of infected mice by immunofluorescence. Myocardial injury can be prevented in this strain by depletion either of complement or of CD4 T-helper cells. In other strains of mice, cell-mediated autoimmunity is more significant. Cytotoxic T cells capable of lysing uninfected myocytes can be selected by adherence to uninfected myocytes. These effector cells are capable of recognizing normally expressed antigens of uninfected myocytes. These cytotoxic T cells are CD8+ and depletion of this subset in vivo, using monoclonal antibodies, abrogates cardiac inflammation in infected mice. In addition, these same T cell populations are capable of transferring myocarditis, indicating that they are both autoimmune and pathogenic.

In addition to direct cytotoxic effects, T cells may produce injury by the production of cytokines. Recent experiments in our laboratory[34] have shown that CB3-induced myocarditis is greatly enhanced when bacterial lipopolysaccharide is administered along with the viral inoculum. In fact, severe myocarditis occurred even in strains of mice that normally are not susceptible to the onging form of the disease. Since a major action of lipopolysaccharide is the induction of γ-interferon and tumor necrosis factor, an attractive possibility is that cytokine production induces or augments myocardial damage.

## Unanswered Questions

An unanswered question concerns the relationship of myocarditis and dilated cardiomyopathy. Dilated cardiomyopathy is defined by the dilatation of one or both ventricles that impairs cardiac output. If such a disease is a sequela of earlier myocarditis, it is likely related to the genetic constitution of the host. A number of environmental factors, including specific nutritional deficiencies, drug hypersensitivity and/or toxicity, pregnancy, and enforced exercise, may contribute to the development of the disease. The interrelationship of these two diseases is an important subject for future investigation using experimental models.

A related topic requiring clarification is the persistence of virus after infection. As noted previously, infectious virus cannot be isolated from the hearts of mice inoculated with CB3 after 9 days. Experiments by Kandolf and colleagues,[35, 36] however, have suggested that viral genomic RNA can be detected in heart tissue long after that time. The possibility then arises that some myocytes or other infected cells continue to produce viral antigen, perhaps at a low, undetectable level. The continued presence of viral antigen may well be an important factor in the persistence of an immunopathic reaction.

The role of CB3 in the subsequent development of autoimmune myocarditis also requires clarification. Studies carried out in our laboratory[37] failed to find any evidence of a serologic cross-reaction between antibodies to cardiac myosin and viral capsid proteins. These experiments, however, do not rule out the possibility that there may be sequence homologies between myosin and one of the capsid proteins, which can be recognized by T cells. In the absence of positive evidence of such cross-reaction, an attractive possibility is that the virus damages myocytes, causing the release or increased expression of myosin determinants on the surface of the cell. Should myosin be released during the course of viral infection, it may be taken up by neighboring dendritic cells as well as by macrophages invading the inflamed heart. These cells are able to process myosin and present it in conjunction with class II MHC products to CD4 T cells. Recent experiments have shown that class II MHC determinants are expressed on cardiac myocytes during myocarditis.[34] An alternative possibility, therefore, is that the expressed myosin determinants join with newly expressed MHC determinants to form the bimolecular complex recognized by myosin-specific T cells.

Finally, it should be pointed out that autoimmune myocarditis may represent a final common pathway of myocardial damage rather than a unique relationship between CB3 and this autoimmune disease. A recent study by Price et al.[38] has documented the role of cytomegalovirus in producing myocarditis in newborn and adult mice. They reported that the severity of myocarditis varied greatly from strain to strain and depended on both MHC and non-MHC traits. A few strains, such as Balb/c and Balb.b and Balb.k mice developed persistent myocarditis. O'Donoghue et al.[39] reported that mice of the susceptible Balb/c strain had high titers of autoantibodies reacting specifically with the cardiac isoform of myosin. In contrast, strains such as C57/B10 showed only a slight transient increase in antimyosin titer. The finding that unrelated viruses can produce such similar pictures of autoimmune myocarditis strengthens the view that the antigenic stimulus may arise from the host's own cells rather than from the specific virus. Huber et al.[40] report that heart-reactive T cells from CB3-infected mice also recognize cardiac myocytes treated with the cardiotoxic drug actinomycin D, suggesting that virus-induced and drug-induced changes in myocyte metabolism may lead to the induction of common antigens.

This critical role of myosin has been supported by recent studies of acute rheumatic fever, a form of myocarditis associated with prior infection by group A streptococci. Using a panel of murine monoclonal antibodies from animals immunized with streptococcal membranes, Cunningham and her colleagues[41, 42] have demonstrated a cross-reaction with cardiac myosin heavy chain. It is not yet known, however, whether the antigenic determinants of myosin responsible for streptococcal cross-reactions are the same as those involved in CB3-induced myocarditis.

## Human Myocarditis

### Diagnosis

In all publications about heart diseases, there is agreement with regard to the diagnosis of myocarditis: it is quite uncertain, i.e., not possible inasmuch as an uncertain diagnosis is no diagnosis. This may be due to the failure of postmortem examinations to confirm the clinical diagnosis or to the demonstration of myocarditis which had not been diagnosed clinically.

*Rühle, 1878*

The foregoing quotation, obtained through the courtesy of Dr. J. Mason of the University of Utah, epitomizes the problem with respect to the diagnosis of myocarditis. Until autopsy examination, the diagnosis frequently is uncertain, even to this day.

The classic clinical signs of myocarditis are malaise, fever, persistent tachycardia, and, occasionally, evidence of ventricular failure. The characteristic electrocardiographic changes include nonspecific ST-T wave abnormalities, conduction and voltage disturbances, and Q wave abnormalities, all changes that may mimic myocardial infarction. Sometimes a pericardial rub indicates pericarditis. In most cases, though, patients cannot clearly associate the symptoms with a preceding febrile illness, and most present with unexplained congestive heart failure or arrhythmias as their only signs.

**Endomyocardial Biopsy.**—The diagnosis of myocarditis was greatly improved by the introduction of endomyocardial biopsy by Sakakibara and Konno in 1962,[43] permitting for the first time histologic confirmation of the clinical diagnosis ante mortem. Unfortunately, discrepancies have continued between the histologic and clinical diagnoses. In patients with a clinical diagnosis of myocarditis or unexplained heart failure, the frequency of positive findings in biopsies ranges from 10% to 65%.[44-46] In patients with dilated cardiomyopathy, the frequency varies from 0% to 63%. This wide range of variability likely reflects the random character of the tissue sampling as well as center-to-center differences in evaluating the histologic findings.

In connection with a multicenter trial of immunosuppressive treatment of myocarditis, a group of pathologists gathered in Dallas in 1984 to establish some standards, generally referred to as the Dallas criteria.[47] For the diagnosis of acute myocarditis, they required the presence of a process characterized by an inflammatory infiltrate of the myocardium with necrosis or degeneration of the adjacent myocytes not typical of the ischemic damage associated with coronary artery disease. A histologic diagnosis of borderline myocarditis was based on the presence of a myocardial inflammatory infiltrate without evidence of concomitant myocyte damage.

Despite widespread acceptance of the Dallas criteria, the diagnosis of myocarditis has remained problematic. One of the major difficulties is the inherent insensitivity of the biopsy technique. The Dallas panel recommended that 3 to 5 biopsy samples be obtained in order to minimize the likelihood of sampling error. The focal nature of the inflammatory process, however, still limits the possibility that myocardial lesions will be detected. A recent study by Hauck et al.[48] utilized hearts taken at autopsy from patients with proven myocarditis. Endomyocardial biopsy specimens were obtained from various sites along the apical and septal surfaces of the right and left ventricles in order to simulate as accurately as possible biopsies of living patients. False-negative biopsy results (that is, a diagnosis of either

no myocarditis or borderline myocarditis) were obtained in the right ventricular biopsy specimens of 14 out of 38 cases (37%) and in the left ventricular specimens in 17 cases (45%). These results suggest that inflammatory infiltrates occurred in locations inaccessible to the bioptome. In fact, all
tissues from the usual biopsy sites in living patients were negative for myocarditis in 5 out of 38 cases (13%). No matter how many samples were
taken, these cases would have been considered negative. Thus, endomyocardial biopsy may miss a significant portion of myocarditis cases.

The value of repeated endomyocardial biopsies was evaluated by Dec et
al.[49] They studied 28 patients with dilated cardiomyopathy of greater than
12 months' duration and either symptomatic heart failure or life-threatening ventricular arrhythmia. Myocarditis was strongly suspected in all cases,
but was not confirmed on the initial biopsy. Myocarditis was confirmed on
repeat biopsy in 4 out of 6 patients whose initial biopsy revealed borderline myocarditis, compared with none of 22 patients whose initial biopsy
showed either myocyte hypertrophy or interstitial fibrosis.

The relative insensitivity of endomyocardial biopsy has encouraged investigations of other diagnostic methods that promise to be more sensitive
and specific. One approach has been the demonstration of abnormal expression of MHC antigens on biopsy specimens.[50, 51] A sensitive radioim-
munosassay was developed, using monoclonal antibodies to human MHC
class I and class II gene products to quantitate the expression of these antigens within the biopsy. Increased MHC antigen expression was found in
11 of 13 myocarditis specimens and 1 of 8 control samples (specificity
88%, sensitivity 84.6%). Active myocarditis samples had approximately a
tenfold increase in MHC expression. Concurrent immunohistochemical
studies demonstrated increased MHC expression within the microvascular
endothelium and along myocyte surfaces. This study points to the possible
value of assessing MHC antigen expression within an endomyocardial biopsy as a useful adjunct to the histologic diagnosis of myocarditis.

In studies not yet published (1990), Herskowitz and his colleagues employed fluorescein-labeled rabbit antisera to adenine nucleotide transloca-
ter (ANT) and branch-chain alpha ketoacid dehydrogenase (BCKD) to
study the distribution of these mitochondrial enzymes in normal and diseased cardiac tissue. Using an indirect immunoperoxidase system, small
deposits of colored product indicating intracellular localization were observed in normal biopsies, whereas cardiac tissues from patients with dilated cardiomyopathy showed intense reactivity with the myocyte membrane. The same rabbit antisera failed to show significant cell surface activity with cardiac tissue of patients with ischemic disease, valvular disease,
hypertensive cardiomyopathy, or alcoholic cardiomyopathy.

Myosin is another intracellular constituent that may be abnormally expressed on the myocyte surface after injury. Monoclonal antibodies to myosin labeled with [111]indium were injected into patients in order to image
cardiac injury. Obrador et al.[52] injected labeled antimyosin antibody into
17 patients with chronic idiopathic dilated cardiomyopathy, 12 patients
with large hearts not due to dilated cardiomyopathy, and 8 normal controls. Abnormal myosin uptake was seen in 12 (70%) of the 17 patients

with cardiomyopathy and in only 1 (8%) of the 12 control patients. Similar investigations were reported by Yasuda et al.,[53] who injected labeled antimyosin antibody into 28 patients clinically suspected of having myocarditis. Antimyosin scans were positive in 9 myocarditis patients and negative in 11 controls who had no evidence of myocarditis by biopsy. An additional 8 patients had positive antimyosin scans, but showed no biopsy evidence of myocarditis. Using endomyocardial biopsy as the standard, the sensitivity of this method was estimated to be 100% and the specificity 58%. A later study[54] was performed on 82 patients with suspected myocarditis, 74 patients with dilated myocardiopathy of greater than 1 year in duration, and 8 patients with normal ventricular function. In this study, antimyosin imaging gave a sensitivity of 83%, a specificity of 53%, and an overall predictive value of 92%. Furthermore, improvement in cardiac function occurred within 6 months of treatment in 54% of patients with an abnormal antimyosin scan compared to 18% of those with a normal scan. The authors concluded that antimyosin-based cardiac imaging may be useful in the initial evaluation of patients with dilated and nondilated cardiomyopathy, as well as clinically suspected myocarditis.

**Heart-Specific Autoantibodies.**—The use of serologic tests for the diagnosis of myocarditis and dilated cardiomyopathy was pioneered by Maisch and his colleagues.[55-57] Using indirect immunofluorescence, they compared the staining of normal cardiac tissue by the sera of patients with the sera from control subjects. Antibodies reactive with the sarcolemma were demonstrated in 94% of patients with postmyocarditic dilated cardiomyopathy, but in only 25% of 30 patients with other forms of dilated cardiomyopathy, and in 25% of healthy control subjects. The antibodies may have functional significance, since antisarcolemmic antibodies were eluted from biopsy specimens and postmortem specimens from patients with cardiomyopathy. Furthermore, the sera of patients, who had elevated titers of antisarcolemmic antibody, produced complement-mediated cytolysis with isolated cardiocytes. In another study, Maisch et al.[58] found that 91% of patients with coxsackievirus B, influenza, or mumps myocarditis gave positive reactions with human or rat cardiocytes, whereas only 31% to 35% of healthy controls showed similar reactions.

In our own studies,[59] in which more conservative criteria for immunofluorescence were employed, 40% of patients with biopsy-proven myocarditis were positive, as were 20% of patients with dilated cardiomyopathy. In contrast, none of the healthy controls were positive by indirect immunofluorescence.

In our hands,[59] Western immunoblots are somewhat more sensitive than indirect immunofluorescence for the demonstration of heart-reactive autoantibodies. Such antibodies were detected in 48 of 103 samples by immunofluorescence, whereas 97 samples were reactive in immunoblots. No single pattern of antigen reactivity was unique to patients with myocarditis or dilated cardiomyopathy. Myocarditis sera reacted predominantly with higher molecular-weight proteins, whereas cardiomyopathy sera exhibited greater prevalence of antibody to lower molecular-weight antigens.

Although the individual antigens have not been identified yet, it is likely that the 190- to 199-kd class represents the heavy chain of cardiac myosin and the 40- to 49-kd class represents actin.

Immunoassays to individual constituents of the myocardium potentially offer serologic tests of greater sensitivity and specificity than tests carried out with whole heart tissue. Schultheiss et al.[60] studied autoantibodies directed to ANT, the adenosine diphosphate/adenosine triphosphate carrier protein, and found that titers were elevated significantly in 24 of 32 patients with dilated cardiomyopathy. Controls with coronary heart disease, alcoholic cardiomyopathy, and hypetrophic obstructive cardiomyopathy were within normal limits. Furthermore, purified IgG fractions of the sera were found to inhibit nucleotide exchange in myocytes, suggesting that the antibodies are functionally effective.

In our own studies, autoantibodies to BCKD, another example of a mitochondrial enzyme, were found in 93% of patients with acute myocarditis and 73% of patients with dilated cardiomyopathy.

Limas et al.[61, 62] demonstrated autoantibodies against β-adrenergic receptors in patients wtih idiopathic dilated cardiomyopathy by measuring the ability of the sera to inhibit the binding of dihydroalprenolol to rat cardiac membranes. Although there was considerable scatter in values, the cardiomyopathy group showed significantly greater inhibitory effect than did normal controls or patients with ischemic or valvular heart disease.

Autoantibodies to laminin are also prominent in patients with dilated cardiomyopathy and myocarditis. Seventy-eight percent of 41 dilated cardiomyopathy cases were found to be positive by Wolff et al.,[63] as were 75% of myocarditis patients. In contrast, only 5% of 65 controls were positive.

Based on our experimental studies in mice described previously, we carried out tests for antibody to myosin. Using an enzyme immunoassay, 40% of patients with cardiomyopathy and 60% of patients with myocarditis were positive, in contrast to 7% of controls with ischemic heart disease.

The use of serologic tests to assist in the diagnosis of myocarditis and cardiomyopathy shows great promise. At the moment, no single antigen appears to be sufficiently sensitive and selective to stand by itself. However, a panel of antigens, such as ANT, β-adrenergic receptor, and myosin, may prove to be a valuable diagnostic tool. In addition, the measurement of circulating antibodies may be useful in monitoring treatment. Preliminary studies in our laboratory have shown that the patients who respond best to immunosuppressive therapy show a marked drop in their ANT antibody titers. Since therapy remains a major problem in dealing with myocarditis, the availability of a predictive test would be invaluable.

**Virus Infection.**—An etiologic diagnosis of viral myocarditis ultimately depends on demonstrating the causative agent. At present, viral diagnosis generally relies on showing a rising titer of virus-specific neutralizing antibody. For example, at least a fourfold increase in neutralizing antibody to CB3 is taken as evidence of recent infection. Since myocarditis is generally evident well after the virus infection, however, this means of viral identification is rarely adequate.

An alternative strategy is to demonstrate virus in the cardiac tissue itself. Isolation of viable virus is rarely feasible in the diagnostic laboratory, and few examples have been reported. Some attempts have been made, however, to demonstrate viral antigen in cardiac tissue. In a study by Poulis et al.,[64] cardiac myocytes were positive for capsid protein VP-1 in 12 out of 20 cases of coxsackievirus B myocarditis, using an immunocytochemical technique with virus-specific antiserum.

Werner et al.[65] used CB3 complementary DNA as molecular probes for in situ hybridization. Because of the high degree of nucleic acid sequence homology among the enteroviruses, the probe was not specific for CB3. Enterovirus-specific nucleic acid sequences were demonstrated in the heart tissue of patients with active myocarditis, as well as in a small number of patients with dilated cardiomyopathy, using in situ hybridization. Future studies using the polymerase chain reaction undoubtedly will raise the sensitivity of this technique and allow the demonstration of virus-specific sequences in a greater proportion of biopsy specimens.

## Treatment

The appropriate treatments of myocarditis and dilated cardiomyopathy represent continuing clinical challenges. According to the concepts described above, acute viral myocarditis resolves spontaneously in most patients, unless they are subjected to unusual stress. Thus, only supportive treatment is appropriate. In a few patients, progressive inflammatory myocarditis and, eventually, dilated cardiomyopathy develop. If the immunopathic concept is valid, these continuing pathologic changes are attributable to a continuing immune response to viral products expressed by the myocardial cells or to autoimmunity to normal myocardial constituents, or both. In the latter case, the rational treatment of autoimmune manifestations of continuing myocarditis and cardiomyopathy is immunosuppression. On the other hand, immunosuppressive treatment would have unpredictable or even unfavorable results if a causative virus is persistent or latent.

As would be predicted from the foregoing concepts, a recent study by Parrillo et al.[66] has shown that prednisone treatment of dilated cardiomyopathy gives the full spectrum of consequences. They randomly assigned 102 patients to either treatment or control groups. After 3 months of prednisone therapy, clinical improvement was observed in 53% of the treatment group and 27% of the controls. Even more striking, 67% of the patients who showed lymphocytic infiltration or deposits of immunoglobulins on endomyocardial biopsy improved compared with only 27% of the controls. The authors concluded that high-dose prednisone treatment of selected patients with dilated cardiomyopathy may lead to some temporary improvement. The beneficial effect is most likely to occur in patients with obvious inflammatory heart muscle disease. However, prednisone should not be considered standard therapy for dilated cardiomyopathy.

A more searching clinical pathologic classification of myocarditis was suggested by Lieberman et al.[67] as a basis for designing therapy. Four distinct subgroups were identified. Patients with fulminant myocarditis became acutely ill following a definite virus infection. They developed severe signs of cardiovascular impairment and, on biopsy, showed multiple foci of active myocarditis. If patients did not die at an early stage, the disease resolved spontaneously. Patients with an acute form of myocarditis presented with obvious ventricular dysfunction. They responded to immunosuppressive treatment or progressed to dilated cardiomyopathy. Patients with chronic active myocarditis responded initially to immunosuppressive treatment, but often showed clinical and histologic evidence of relapse. Finally, chronic persistent myocarditis was characterized by persistent histologic infiltrates, often with foci of myocyte necrosis, but without ventricular dysfunction other than symptoms such as chest pain or arrhythmias. Their clinical course was not altered by immunosuppressive therapy. In brief, then, these authors' experience suggests that immunosuppression appears to be of greatest benefit in patients who fall within the clinical category of acute myocarditis.

The uncertainties of diagnosing and treating myocarditis have stimulated a large multicenter treatment trial. Patients are being admitted on the basis of the Dallas criteria of acute myocarditis and are being randomized into treatment and control groups. Treated patients are receiving cyclosporine and prednisone, whereas the controls are being given a placebo. In addition to clinical data, extensive immunologic studies are being performed on these patients in the search for clues that will predict a favorable response to immunosuppression.

## Future Research

### Risk Factors

Based on evidence from studies of the murine models of myocarditis, we can predict that patients who develop ongoing or persistent myocarditis are genetically predisposed to an immunopathic response. Two categories of genetic traits are involved. Non-MHC genes appear to control susceptibility to the autoimmune phase of myocarditis, whereas MHC genes determine the degree of response. The localization of a non-MHC gene depends upon its linkage to a well-defined and easily measurable, heritable characteristic. There is suggestive evidence from studies in mice that one of the non-MHC genes responsible for susceptibility to autoimmune myocarditis is linked to a gene encoding the T cell receptor.[68] In addition to providing an important prognostic tool, this finding, if confirmed, would give a clue to the immunologic basis of autoimmune susceptibility.

Considerable effort has been devoted to identifying human histocompatibility types defined by human leukocyte antigen expression (HLA) with susceptibility to dilated cardiomyopathy. Anderson et al.[69] found that HLA-DR4 was overrepresented in cardiomyopathy patients compared with normal subjects, giving a relative risk of 2.2. HLA-DR6Y was underrepresented and may offer protection against this sequela. These initial findings require confirmation, but suggest that genetically determined immune response genes may play a role in the pathogenesis of dilated cardiomyopathy and myocarditis.

Another explanation for the variable outcomes of early viral myocarditis rests with the differences among strains of virus. Although the isolation of living virus from later phases of myocarditis and cardiomyopathy does not appear to be feasible, molecular and immunocytochemical probes may be adapted to the detection of persistent virus in cardiac biopsies. Monoclonal antibodies to the viral capsid proteins also may uncover strain-specific differences associated with myocarditogenic strains. In situ detection of enterovirus RNA in infected cardiac cells has been demonstrated using complementary DNA probes. This technique will be invaluable for examining the concept that virus persistence is responsible for chronic myocarditis and cardiomyopathy. Eventually, examination of precise nucleic acid sequences may make it possible to identify strains of virus that are likely to give rise to persistent disease.

## Etiology and Pathogenesis

Better understanding of the etiology and pathogenesis of myocarditis and dilated cardiomyopathy will guide future therapies. Immunosuppressive treatment clearly would not be indicated in the presence of replicating viral RNA, since increased viral replication as well as inhibition of the endogenous interferon system may result. In the case of chronically infected heart cells, antiviral treatment may be beneficial, possibly using interferon.

In view of the inherent difficulties in distinguishing viral from immunopathic phases of myocarditis in the clinical setting, global immunosuppression may not be the treatment of choice. Rather, antigen-specific immunosuppression is less likely to lead to unfavorable consequences. Assuming that an autoimmune form of myocarditis is instigated by particular antigenic determinants of myosin heavy chain, several methods can be envisioned to arrest this autoimmune response. Binding of the pathogenic epitopes to particular MHC class II determinants can be blocked by monoclonal antibodies to the MHC determinants. Binding to the MHC product also may be blocked by administering a counterfeit peptide. An alternative approach is to determine the variable regions of the T cell receptor responsible for binding the pathogenic epitopes and to block their reaction with an appropriate monoclonal antibody. These methods, although visionary at present, are being explored with other autoimmune diseases.

The actual mechanisms of tissue injury need to be considered. The presence of antibody to the β-adrenergic receptor or to ANT may be necessary and sufficient for the development of disease. Production of these antibodies might be arrested by anti-idiotypic therapy. On the other hand, cytotoxic T cells may be more important than antibody. In experimental models, it has been possible to overcome the effects of cytotoxic T cells by injecting the animal with inactivated T cells. Under these conditions, it is postulated that the host develops an immune response to the specific T cell receptor. The unique peptide of the T cell receptor variable region has been used in experimental models of autoimmune diseases to arrest the induction of disease.

Finally, there is evidence that the cardiac damage may be due in part to the production of cytokines, such as tumor necrosis factor and $\gamma$-interferon. If such proves to be the case, the use of anticytokine antisera becomes rational.

## Prevention

The ultimate goal of all of the basic and clinical investigations of myocarditis is the prevention of ongoing myocarditis and dilated cardiomyopathy following acute viral myocarditis. The steps outlined earlier represent logical progress in that direction. If individuals with definable risk factors and virus strains with myocarditogenic propensity can be identified during the early stages of disease, later progression may be prevented. It might involve the earlier institution of antiviral or specific immunosuppressive treatment as indicated. In this way, the most serious cardiologic consequences of viral myocarditis can be avoided.

## Acknowledgments

The authors wish to thank Dr. Kenneth Baughman for reviewing the manuscript and Mrs. Hermine Bongers for her valued editorial assistance.

## References

1. Williams DG, Olsen EGL: Prevalence of overt dilated cardiomyopathy in two regions of England. *Br Heart J* 1985; 54:153–155.
2. Grattan MT, Moreno-Cabral CE, Starnes VA, et al: Cytomegalovirus infection is associated with cardiac allograft rejection and atherosclerosis. *JAMA* 1989; 261:3561–3566.
3. Lerner A, Wilson FM, Reyes MP: Enteroviruses and the heart (with special emphasis on the probable role of coxsackieviruses, group B, types 1–5). II. Observations in humans. *Cardiovasc Dis* 1975; 44:11–15.
4. Khatib R, Chason JL, Silberberg BK, et al: Age-dependent pathogenicity of group B coxsackieviruses in Swiss-Webster mice: Infectivity for myocardium and pancreas. *J Infect Dis* 1980; 141:394–403.
5. Khatib R, Chason JL, Lerner AM: A mouse model of transmural necrosis due to coxsackievirus B4: Observations over 12 months. *Intervirology* 1982; 18:197–202.
6. Reyes MP, Lerner AM: Coxsackievirus myocarditis—with special reference to acute and chronic effects. *Prog Cardiovasc Dis* 1985; 27:373–394.
7. Gatmaitan BG, Chason JL, Lerner AM: Augmentation of the virulence of murine coxsackievirus B-3 myocardiopathy by exercise. *J Exp Med* 1969; 131:1121–1136.
8. Gomez MP, Reyes MP, Smith F, et al: Coxsackievirus B3-positive mononuclear leukocytes in peripheral blood of Swiss and athymic mice during infection. *Proc Soc Exp Biol Med* 1980; 165:107–113.
9. Huber SA, Job LP, Woodruff JF: Lysis of infected myofibers by coxsackievirus B-3-immune T lymphocytes. *Am J Pathol* 1980; 98:681–694.

10. Huber SA, Job LP, Auld KR, et al: Sex-related differences in the rapid production of cytotoxic spleen cells active against uninfected myofibers during coxsackievirus B-3 infection. J Immunol 1981; 126:1336–1340.

11. Huber SA, Job LP, Woodruff JF: In vitro culture of coxsackievirus group B, type 3 immune spleen cells on infected endothelial cells and biological activity of the cultured cells in vivo. Infect Immun 1984; 43:567–573.

12. Wolfgram LJ, Beisel KW, Rose NR: Heart-specific autoantibodies following murine coxsackievirus B3 myocarditis. J Exp Med 1985; 161:1112–1121.

13. Wolfgram LJ, Beisel KW, Herskowitz A, et al: Variations in the susceptibility to coxsackievirus B3-induced myocarditis among different strains of mice. J Immunol 1986; 136:1846–1852.

14. Herskowitz A, Wolfgram LJ, Rose NR, et al: Coxsackievirus B3 murine myocarditis: A pathologic spectrum of myocarditis in genetically defined inbred strains. J Am Coll Cardiol 1987; 9:1311–1319.

15. Alvarez FL, Neu N, Rose NR, et al: Heart-specific autoantibodies induced by coxsackievirus B3: Identification of heart autoantigens. Clin Immunol Immunopathol 1987; 43:129–139.

16. Neu N, Rose NR, Beisel KW, et al: Cardiac myosin induces myocarditis in genetically predisposed mice. J Immunol 1987; 139:3630–3636.

17. Neu N, Beisel KW, Traystman MD, et al: Autoantibodies specific for the cardiac myosin isoform are found in mice susceptible to coxsackievirus B3-induced myocarditis. J Immunol 1987; 138:2488–2492.

18. Rose NR, Wolfgram LJ, Herskowitz A, et al: Postinfectious autoimmunity: Two distinct phases of coxsackievirus B3-induced myocarditis. Ann N Y Acad Sci 1986; 475:146–156.

19. Godeny EK, Gauntt CJ: Involvement of natural killer cells in coxsackievirus B3-induced murine myocarditis. J Immunol 1986; 137:1695–1702.

20. Godeny EK, Gauntt CJ: Murine natural killer cells limit coxsackievirus B3 replication. J Immunol 1987; 139:913–918.

21. Woodruff JF: Lack of correlation between neutralizing antibody production and suppression of coxsackievirus B-3 replication in target organs: Evidence for involvement of mononuclear inflammatory cells in defense. J Immunol 1979; 123:31–36.

22. Hashimoto I, Komatsu T: Myocardial changes after infection with coxsackie virus B3 in nude mice. Br J Exp Pathol 1978; 59:13–20.

23. Hashimoto I, Tatsumi M, Nakagawa M: The role of T lymphocytes in the pathogenesis of Coxsackie virus B3 heart disease. Br J Exp Pathol 1983; 64:497–504.

24. Huber SA, Job LP: Cellular immune mechanisms in coxsackievirus group B, type 3 induced myocarditis in Balb/C mice. Adv Exp Med Biol 1983; 161:491–508.

25. Guthrie M, Lodge PA, Huber SA: Cardiac injury in myocarditis induced by coxsackievirus group B, type 3 in Balb/c mice is mediated by Lyt 2+ cytolytic lymphocytes. Cell Immunol 1984; 88:558–567.

26. Huber SA, Job LP: Differences in cytotoxic T cell response of Balb/c mice infected with myocarditic and non-myocarditic strains of coxsackievirus group B, type 3. Infect Immun 1983; 39:1419–1427.

27. Huber SA, Lyden DC, Lodge PA: Immunopathogenesis of experimental coxsackievirus induced myocarditis: Role of autoimmunity. Herz 1985; 10:1–7.

28. Estrin M, Huber SA: Coxsackievirus B3-induced myocarditis. Autoimmunity is L3T4+ T helper cell and IL-2 independent in BALB/c mice. Am J Pathol 1987; 127:335–341.

29. Lutton CW, Gauntt CJ: Coxsackievirus B3 infection alters plasma membrane of neonatal skin fibroblasts. *J Virol* 1986; 60:294–296.

30. Godeny EK, Gauntt CJ: In situ immune autoradiographic identification of cells in heart tissues of mice with coxsackievirus B3-induced myocarditis. *Am J Pathol* 1987; 129:267–276.

31. Beisel KW, Traystman MD: Viral myocarditis: Immunogenetic and autoimmune aspects, in Schultheiss H-P (ed): *New Concepts in Viral Heart Disease.* Berlin, Springer-Verlag, 1988, pp 148–159.

32. Huber SA, Lodge PA: Coxsackievirus B-3 myocarditis. Identification of different pathogenic mechanisms in DBA/2 and Balb/c mice. *Am J Pathol* 1986; 122:284–291.

33. Lodge PA, Herzum M, Olszewski J, et al: Coxsackievirus B-3 myocarditis. Acute and chronic forms of the disease caused by different immunopathogenic mechanisms. *Am J Pathol* 1987; 128:455–463.

34. Lane JE, Neumann DA, LaFond-Walker A, et al: LPS promotes CB3-induced myocarditis in resistant B10.A mice. *Cell Immunol,* in press.

35. Kandolf R, Ameis D, Kirschner P, et al: In situ detection of enteroviral genomes in myocardital cells by nucleic acid hybridization: An approach to the diagnosis of viral heart disease. *Proc Natl Acad Sci U S A* 1987; 84:6272–6276.

36. Mall G, Klingel K, Seemann M, et al: The natural history of coxsackievirus B3-induced myocarditis in ACA/SN mice: Viral persistence demonstrated by quantitative in situ hybridization histochemistry. *Eur Heart J,* in press.

37. Neu N, Craig SW, Rose NR, et al: Coxsackievirus induced myocarditis in mice: Cardiac myosin autoantibodies do not cross-react with the virus. *Clin Exp Immunol* 1987; 69:566–574.

38. Price P, Winter JG, Eddy KS, et al: Inflammatory and immunological responses to murine cytomegalovirus in resistant CBA mice. *Arch Virol* 1989; 104:35–51.

39. O'Donoghue HL, Lawson CM, Reed WD: Autoantibodies to cardiac myosin in mouse cytomegalovirus myocarditis. *Immunology* 1990; 71:20–28.

40. Huber SA, Heintz N, Tracy R: Coxsackievirus B-3-induced myocarditis. Virus and actinomycin D treatment of myocytes induces novel antigens recognized by cytolytic T lymphocytes. *J Immunol* 1988; 141:3214–3219.

41. Cunningham MW, Hall NK, Krisher KK, et al: A study of anti-group A streptococcal monoclonal antibodies cross-reactive with myosin. *J Immunol* 1986; 136:293–298.

42. Ayakawa GY, Bleiweis AS, Crowley PJ, et al: Heart cross-reactive antigens of mutans streptococci share epitopes with group A streptococci and myosin. *J Immunol* 1988; 140:253–257.

43. Sakakibara S, Konno S: Endomyocardial biopsy. *Jpn Heart J* 1962; 3:537–543.

44. Edwards WD: Current problems in establishing quantitative histopathologic criteria for the diagnosis of lymphocytic myocarditis by endomyocardial biopsy. *Heart Vessels* 1985; 1(suppl):138–142.

45. Tazelaar HD, Billingham ME: Myocardial lymphocytes. Fact, fancy, or myocarditis. *Am J Cardiovasc Pathol* 1987; 1:47–50.

46. Lie JT: Myocarditis and endomyocardial biopsy in unexplained heart failure: A diagnosis in search of a disease. *Ann Intern Med* 1988; 109:525–528.

47. Aretz HT, Billingham ME, Edwards WD, et al: Myocarditis. A histopathologic definition and classification. *Am J Cardiovasc Pathol* 1986; 1:3–14.

48. Hauck AJ, Kearney DL, Edwards WD: Evaluation of postmortem endomyo-

cardial biopsy specimens from 38 patients wtih lymphocytic myocarditis: Implications for role of sampling error. *Mayo Clin Proc* 1989; 64:1235–1245.

49. Dec GW, Fallon JT, Southern JF, et al: "Borderline" myocarditis: An indication for repeat endomyocardial biopsy. *J Am Coll Cardiol* 1990; 15: 283–289.

50. Herskowitz A, Baughman KL, Rose NR, et al: Induction of major histocompatibility antigens on myocardial cells in patients with active myocarditis and idiopathic cardiomyopathy, in Schultheiss H-P (ed): *New Concepts in Viral Heart Disease.* Berlin, Springer-Verlag, 1988, pp 312–324.

51. Herskowitz A, Ahmed-Ansari A, Neumann DA: Induction of major histocompatibility complex (MHC) antigens with the myocardium of patients with active myocarditis: A nonhistologic marker of myocarditis. *J Am Coll Cardiol* 1990; 15:624–632.

52. Obrador D, Ballester M, Carrio I, et al: High prevalence of myocardial monoclonal antimyosin antibody uptake in patients with chronic idiopathic dilated cardiomyopathy. *J Am Coll Cardiol* 1989; 13:1289–1293.

53. Yasuda T, Palacios IF, Dec GW, et al: Indium 111-monoclonal antimyosin antibody imaging in the diagnosis of acute myocarditis. *Circulation* 1987; 76:306–311.

54. Dec GW, Palacios I, Yasuda T, et al: Antimyosin antibody cardiac imaging: Its role in the diagnosis of myocarditis. *J Am Coll Cardiol* 1990; 16:97–104.

55. Maisch B, Berg PA, Kochsiek K: Immunological parameters in patients with congestive cardiomyopathy. *Basic Res Cardiol* 1980; 75:221–222.

56. Maisch B, Trostel-Soeder R, Stechemesser E, et al: Diagnostic relevance of humoral and cell-mediated immune reactions in patients with acute viral myocarditis. *Clin Exp Immunol* 1982; 48:533–545.

57. Maisch B, Deeg P, Liebau G, et al: Diagnostic relevance of humoral and cytotoxic immune reactions in primary and secondary dilated cardiomyopathy. *Am J Cardiol* 1983; 52:1072–1078.

58. Maisch B, Herzum M, Izumi T, et al: The importance of humoral and cellular immunological parameters for the pathogenesis of viral myocarditis, in Schultheiss H-P (ed): *New Concepts in Viral Heart Disease.* Berlin, Springer-Verlag, 1988, pp 259–273.

59. Neumann DA, Burek CL, Baughman KL, et al: Circulating heart-reactive antibodies in patients with myocarditis or cardiomyopathy. *J Am Coll Cardiol* 1990; 16:839–846.

60. Schultheiss H-P, Schulze K, Kuhl U, et al: The ADP/ATP carrier as a mitochondrial auto-antigen—facts and perspectives. *Ann N Y Acad Sci* 1986; 488:44–63.

61. Limas CJ, Limas C: Beta-adrenoreceptor autoantibodies in idiopathic dilated cardiomyopathy, in Schultheiss H-P (ed): *New Concepts in Viral Heart Disease.* Berlin, Springer-Verlag, 1988, pp 217–224.

62. Limas CJ, Goldenberg IF, Limas C: Autoantibodies against beta-adrenoreceptors in human idiopathic dilated cardiomyopathy. *Circ Res* 1989; 64:97–103.

63. Wolff PG, Kuhl U, Schultheiss H-P: Laminin distribution and autoantibodies to laminin in dilated cardiomyopathy and myocarditis. *Am Heart J* 1989; 117:1303–1309.

64. Poulis AK, Farquharson MA, Cameron SO, et al: A search for the presence of the enteroviral capsid protein VP1 in pancreases of patients with type 1 (insulin-dependent) diabetes and pancreases and hearts of infants who died of coxsackieviral myocarditis. *Diabetologia* 1990; 33:290–298.

65. Werner S, Schönke H, Klump W, et al: Generation of enterovirus group-spe-

cific antisera using bacterially synthesized coxsackievirus B3 proteins, in Schultheiss H-P (ed): *New Concepts in Viral Heart Disease.* Berlin, Springer-Verlag, 1988, pp 125–136.

66. Parrillo JE, Cunnion RE, Eptstein SE: A prospective, randomized, controlled trial of prednisone for dilated cardiomyopathy. *N Engl J Med* 1989; 321:1061–1068.

67. Lieberman EB, Herskowitz A, Hutchins GM, et al: A clinicopathologic description of myocarditis. *J Am Coll Cardiol*, in press.

68. Rose NR, Neumann DA, Herskowitz A: Genetics of susceptibility to viral myocarditis in mice. *Pathol Immunopathol Res* 1988; 7:266–278.

69. Anderson JL, Carlquist JF, Lutz JR, et al: HLA A, B and DR typing in idiopathic dilated cardiomyopathy: A search for immune response factors. *Am J Cardiol* 1984; 53:1326–1330.

# Parvovirus B19 and Human Disease

## Thomas J. Török, M.D.

Chief, Epidemiology Section, Respiratory and Enterovirus Branch, Division of
Viral and Rickettsial Diseases, National Center for Infectious Diseases, Centers for
Disease Control, Atlanta, Georgia

## Editor's Introduction

Human parvovirus B19 caused relatively little excitement when it was discovered in the mid-1970s during blood screening studies for hepatitis, because it was identified as the cause of a self-limited childhood febrile illness with a rash, namely erythema infectiosum or fifth disease. In the early 1980s, however, it was discovered to be the cause of aplastic crises in sickle cell anemia and other chronic anemias, because of its affinity for erythroid progenitor cells. Since then, the spectrum of illness with which it is associated is growing. Neurologic, polyarthritic, vasculitic, and myocarditic syndromes have all come under strong suspicion, reflecting the broad tissue tropism of this virus and its propensity to cause illness by a variety of immunopathologic mechanisms. Dr. Thomas Török reviews for us the current state of knowledge about parvovirus B19 microbiology, epidemiology, and clinical manifestations. We should take careful note of this infection, because the powerful technologies of the polymerase chain reaction in the construction of DNA probes will no doubt be vigorously applied to the spectrum of autoimmune diseases that are in eager search of an infectious etiology. Within the coming year or two, we may need a follow-up article, much as we have needed in the past after introductory reviews like this were presented in these volumes for such "new infections" as legionnaires' disease, non-A non-B hepatitis, *Helicobacter* (alias *Campylobacter*) *pylori* gastritis, and HIV (alias HLTV-III)—to name a few!

*Gene H. Stollerman, M.D.*

Human parvovirus B19 is the etiologic agent of the common rash illness erythema infectiosum (EI), also known as fifth disease. In addition to this mild, self-limited infection, B19 has been shown to cause an acute symmetrical peripheral polyarthropathy, is the primary cause of aplastic crisis in patients with chronic hematologic disorders, may cause chronic anemia in immunocompromised patients, and may result in fetal hydrops. B19 infection also has been linked with other hematologic manifestations, including neutropenia, thrombocytopenia, and hemophagocytic syndrome, and there are reports that suggest that B19 may be linked etiologically with some neuropathies and vasculitides (Table 1). The full spectrum of clinical

*Advances in Internal Medicine*®, vol. 37
Copyright 1992, Mosby–Year Book, Inc.

**TABLE 1.**
**Clinical Manifestations of B19 Infection and Populations at Risk**

I. Infection in the normal host.
   A. Arthropathy; adults > children.
   B. Asymptomatic infection; all.
   C. Erythema infectiosum (fifth disease); children > adults.
II. Infection in special hosts.
   1. Chronic anemia; congenital and acquired immunodeficiency
      syndromes, lymphoproliferative disorders, organ transplant recipients.
   2. Hydrops fetalis and fetal death; fetus, especially <20 wk.
III. Conditions possibly caused by B19 infection.
   A. Neurologic disease.
      1. Brachial plexus neuropathy.
      2. Encephalitis/meningitis.
   B. Hematologic disorders.
      1. Aplastic anemia.
      2. Idiopathic thrombocytopenic purpura.
      3. Transient erythroblastopenia of childhood.
      4. Virus-associated hemophagocytic syndrome.
   C. Systemic vasculitis.
   D. Acute myocarditis.

associations still may be incomplete because the limited availability of diagnostic testing has constrained research into B19 significantly. As testing becomes more widespread during the next several years, it seems likely that this remarkable list of clinical manifestations will continue to grow in size and importance.

The history of B19 is brief. It was discovered by chance in 1974 while screening healthy blood donors for hepatitis B.[1] Seroprevalence studies suggested that human infection was common, and a systematic search of blood samples was undertaken to identify infected patients and a possible clinical correlate. This work resulted, in 1981, in the discovery of B19 in the serum of patients with aplastic crises and sickle cell disease.[2] This work soon was confirmed in population-based studies of sickle cell disease patients,[3] and then was found to be generalizable to patients with other causes of chronic anemia.[4] The next major association was made in 1983, when recent B19 infection was diagnosed in the majority of cases of EI in a school outbreak.[5] This was confirmed by a retrospective analysis of specimens collected from an earlier, intensively studied outbreak.[6] The association of B19 with fetal disease and arthropathy was made in 1984 and 1985, respectively, following community outbreaks of EI.[7-9] Chronic B19 infection with anemia was identified in a patient with a congenital immunodeficiency syndrome and reported in 1987.[10] Subsequent investigations have shown that patients with human immunodeficiency virus infections, patients being treated with chemotherapeutic agents for cancer, and organ transplant recipients also are at risk for chronic B19 infection.

One additional historic point deserves comment. The selection of the name "B19" for this virus refers to the specimen designation of the first isolate.[11, 12] A more logical choice might have been "HPV," for human parvovirus, but this acronym was already in widespread use for human papillomavirus, and it was thought that "B19" would lead to less confusion. It does beg the question about what happened to B1 through B18. And it is reminiscent of the designation "fifth disease" for EI, where an irrelevant and obsolete nomenclature continues to provoke questions nearly 100 years later and provides no insight into the etiologic agent, clinical manifestations, or pathogenesis of the disease.

To date, B19 is the only parvovirus well documented to be pathogenic in man. Parvovirus-like particles have been seen in fecal specimens taken during outbreaks of gastroenteritis. These seem to be antigenically distinct from B19, but preliminary investigations show that the nucleotide sequences may be similar to B19 in some regions of the genome.[13] The RA-1 virus has been reported as a possible human pathogen, but this has not been confirmed.[14] This review will be limited to a discussion of B19 and its associated clinical manifestations.

## Etiology

B19 is a small (23-nm), nonenveloped, 5.5-kilobase, single-stranded DNA virus belonging to the family Parvoviridae.[12, 15] It is a member of the genus *Parvovirus*, which includes autonomously replicating parvoviruses such as canine parvovirus and feline panleukopenia virus. Members of the genus *Dependovirus* require a helper virus, such as adenovirus or herpesvirus, for replication; the nonpathogenic human adeno-associated viruses are included in this group. Parvoviruses generally are species-specific, and no animal model has been identified that permits the replication of B19. B19 has two capsid proteins, VP-1 (83 kd) and VP-2 (58 kd); VP-2 predominates.[16] The capsid proteins are transcribed from overlapping messenger RNA (mRNA) and the amino acid sequence of VP-2 is contained entirely within the amino acid sequence of VP-1. There is a nonstructural protein, NS-1, that is associated with virulence. The nucleotide sequence of B19 has been determined,[17] and B19 shows very limited heterogeneity at the nucleotide level.[18] B19 is a heat-stable virus and can survive at 56° C for 30 minutes.[19]

There is no practical in vitro system for the isolation of B19 from clinical specimens. The virus has been grown in fresh human bone marrow cells,[20] erythroid cells derived from fetal liver,[21] and erythroid leukemic cells.[22] While these systems have been valuable for characterizing the virus, they are not available for specimen isolation studies.

## Epidemiology

The distribution of B19 is worldwide. Cases may occur year-round, but outbreaks of EI in North America are most common in the spring.[23] The level of EI activity in a community may vary from year to year, but there are insufficient data to document trends or establish the periodicity in the United States. Most infections occur among school-aged children. The reported prevalence of IgG antibodies ranges from 2% to 15% in children 1 to 5 years old, 15% to 60% in children 5 to 19 years old, and 30% to 60% in adults.[24]

B19 DNA may be found in the respiratory secretions of viremic patients, suggesting that direct contact with these secretions is the most likely mode of transmission.[19, 25] Outbreaks of EI in schools may be prolonged over months, which suggests close contact rather than aerosol transmission. There are no data on transmission by fomites. Vertical transmission may occur from mother to fetus in about one third of cases with serologically confirmed maternal infection.[26]

Parenteral transmission may occur by transfusion of contaminated blood products. The risk would be low for single-donor blood products (prevalence of virus antigen 1 in 40,000 to 1 in 50,000), but may be common following treatment with clotting-factor concentrates.[27–29] In one study, 5 (29%) of 17 susceptible hemophiliacs seroconverted following the first infusion of stream- or dry-heat–treated concentrate.[28] In one study, B19 DNA was demonstrated in an implicated lot of factor IX concentrate.[29] High-temperature, dry-heat treatment of concentrates may be an effective method of inactivating parvoviruses.[30, 31] Immunoglobulin products have not been associated with B19 transmission and may present a low risk because they contain B19 antibodies. At this time, there are insufficient data to state that these products are risk-free. Tattooing was the probable source of infection in two patients.[32]

Secondary spread to susceptible (IgG-negative) household contacts is common; in one outbreak investigation, it was 50%.[19] In school outbreaks, from 10% to 60% of students will develop EI. In outbreaks in which student involvement is widespread, approximately 20% to 30% of susceptible staff members develop serologic evidence of B19 infection.[33]

The incubation period will be variable, depending on the clinical manifestation. From volunteer studies, the incubation period can be estimated at approximately 9 days for symptoms associated with red cell aplasia, and approximately 17 to 19 days for immunologically mediated conditions like EI or arthropathy.[34] In studies of secondary cases in households, the majority will become symptomatic 6 to 12 days following the index case[35–37]; these findings are consistent with the peak in infectivity being during the peak of viremia. In transfusion-associated cases, the time from infusion to rash onset was 12 to 14 days in two adults and 35 days in a 1-year-old.[29] Two patients reported a febrile illness 9 days following tattooing and were noted to have B19 viremia.[32]

Transmission of B19 in hospital and laboratory settings is reported infrequently.[38–41] Most patients with EI are beyond their period of infectiousness, present a low risk for further transmission, and do not need to be isolated. The principal risk in clinical settings appears to come from patients with high-titer viremia, such as inpatients with acute (e.g., sickle cell anemia with aplastic crisis) or chronic pure red cell aplasia (e.g., human immunodeficiency virus–infected patients with B19-associated red cell aplasia). These patients should be placed in isolation precautions for the duration of the illness.[42] According to the Centers for Disease Control[43]:

> Patients with transient aplastic crisis or chronic B19 infection should be admitted to private rooms, masks should be worn by persons in close contact with the patients, gloves are necessary for persons likely to touch infective material such as respiratory secretions, and gowns are necessary when soiling is anticipated (contact isolation). Hands should be washed after touching the patient or potentially contaminated articles and before taking care of another patient. B19-infected patients may share a room with another B19-infected patient unless other potentially transmissible infections are present and require a single room.

Recommendations concerning high-risk personnel such as pregnant health care workers are controversial. The American Academy of Pediatrics also has recommended that pregnant personnel not care for patients with aplastic crisis.[44]

## Pathogenesis and Pathology

B19 infects, replicates in, and then lyses erythroid progenitor cells, including the erythroid colony-forming unit and burst-forming unit.[36, 45–48] The varied clinical manifestations result either directly from the subsequent erythroid aplasia or from the host immune response. In the normal host, infection results in a self-limited red cell aplasia that is clinically inapparent, followed a by rash illness or arthropathy that is presumed to be mediated immunologically. Recovery is associated with the production of specific antibodies and immunity. In patients with hematologic disorders characterized by decreased red cell production or increased red cell destruction, B19 infection may result in a dramatic decrease in hemoglobin and symptoms associated with severe anemia. In immunocompromised patients, infection may become persistent and result in chronic anemia.[49] The fetus presents an extreme example of vulnerability to both severe anemia and chronic infection. The fetus has a rapidly expanding red cell volume, its red cell survival is about half that of a normal adult, and it may be unable to mount an effective immune response to clear the infection.

The course of acute infection has been characterized in several volunteer studies in the normal host[34, 48] and in careful clinical observations in patients with chronic hemolytic anemias.[50] Virus is detectable in the serum beginning about 5 days after intranasal inoculation and peaks at approximately 9 days; virus may be detected in nasal washes and gargles during the time the patient is viremic. The illness is biphasic. Symptoms associated with viremia include fever, malaise, headache, myalgia, and mild itching. The second phase begins 15 to 17 days after inoculation and may include an erythematous rash, arthropathy, and pruritus.

Reticulocytes disappear between days 8 and 10, and reappear 5 days to 2 weeks later. In the normal host, the hemoglobin may fall by 2 to 3 g/dL in the intervening period. Neutropenia, lymphocytopenia, and thrombocytopenia (as low as 30% of baseline values) also occur and follow a time course similar to that of the reticulocyte count. In the bone marrow there is almost a total loss of erythroid cells at all developmental stages by day 10, and abnormal giant proerythroblasts may be present. These cells are typically >35 μm in diameter and have basophilic cytoplasm, fine chromatin, prominent irregular nucleoli, or viral inclusions.[10, 25, 50, 51] Vacuoles and pseudopod formation also may be seen.

Recovery from acute infection characteristically begins with an IgM response first detectable about 10 days following inoculation, followed by IgG several days later. The IgG is first predominantly to VP-2, and then to VP-1.[52] Antibodies to both VP-1 and VP-2 are neutralizing. The presence of IgG antibody correlates with a decreased risk of infection.[34]

The cause of the transient neutropenia has not been adequately defined. B19 does not inhibit granulocyte-macrophage progenitor cells. However, replicative forms of B19 DNA have been found in granulocyte-enriched fractions of human serum, suggesting that direct infection by B19 may play some role.[53] The thrombocytopenia seen in many patients with acute infection is probably multifactorial. B19 has not been shown to replicate in megakaryocytes, but it inhibits megakaryocyte colony formation in vitro, suggesting that B19 infection leads to a decrease in platelet production.[54] The effect presumably is due to NS-1 protein, because altering the gene that encodes this protein will diminish the effect. Hypersplenism in patients with chronic hemolytic anemias will increase the peripheral destruction of platelets and may increase the apparent effect. Finally, platelet destruction may be immunologically mediated in part, as discussed as follows.

## Clinical Manifestations in the Normal Host

### Asymptomatic Infection

Asymptomatic infection is common in children and adults. In outbreak investigations, asymptomatic infection has been reported in approximately 20% of children and adults.[6, 19] In studies of IgM-positive pregnant women selected for exposure to symptomatic persons, fewer than half reported symptoms of rash or arthropathy[55] (CDC, unpublished observations, 1987-1990). In patients with chronic hemolytic anemias, asymptomatic seroconversion has been reported in association with recent transfusion, suggesting that symptoms may be masked by the transfusion of red cells with a longer survival time than the patient's own cells.[56]

### Erythema Infectiosum (Fifth Disease)

Erythema infectiosum, also known as fifth disease, is the most commonly recognized manifestation of B19 infection. The etiologic agent first was identified as B19 during an outbreak investigation among schoolchildren in

London in 1983[5, 57] and confirmed by analysis of specimens collected in 1980 during an outbreak investigation in Canada.[6]

The distinctive features of the rash include marked erythema of the cheeks sparing the circumoral region and bridge of the nose, a lacy rash on the trunk and extremities, and the tendency for the rash to fade and then reappear abruptly following either heat or cold exposure for periods of several weeks. Either the facial or the body rash may be inapparent in any individual case. Some reports have suggested a typical progression of the rash from face to body, but data from outbreak investigations suggest that, in most cases, both occur at about the same time.[58] The rash also may involve the palms and soles.[6] Prodromal symptoms generally are mild, nonspecific, and frequently overlooked. Pruritus is common in some outbreaks, affecting as many as 70% of reported cases.[37, 58] The diagnosis of EI is made on clinical grounds and, in the setting of community outbreaks and typical features, is easy; sporadic cases or atypical rash illnesses are likely to be misdiagnosed. Other rashes occasionally are reported in patients with acute B19 infection, including vesicular, petechial, purpuric, and desquamative rashes.[24, 59–65]

## Arthropathy

In some reported outbreaks of EI, cases of arthralgias and arthritis have been common, especially among adults, with as many as 60% reporting joint swelling and pain.[37] Ten percent or less of children with EI will have joint pains or swelling.[66] Although B19 was identified as the etiologic agent of EI in 1983,[5] it was not until 1985 that B19 first was linked directly to joint disease; 12% of 193 patients evaluated for early synovitis were found to be B19-IgM–positive.[8, 9] The HLA antigen DR4 has been associated with rheumatoid arthritis and, in one study, was present in 12 (67%) of 18 patients with B19-associated arthropathy.[67] Further studies are necessary to determine whether or not HLA type can be used to identify patients at risk for B19-associated arthropathy.

The arthropathy presumably is immunologically mediated, because its onset is coincident with the first appearance of circulating antibodies. B19 was detected in synovial cells by in situ hybridization in one patient with acute arthropathy,[68] but this finding has not been confirmed by others. Duration of symptoms has not been shown to correlate with prolonged viremia or persistence of viral DNA in synovial membrane, cells, or fluid.[69]

The characteristic clinical presentation is the sudden onset of a symmetrical peripheral polyarthropathy. The joints most commonly affected and the approximate frequency of involvement are the metacarpophalangeal joints (75%), proximal interphalangeal joints (75%), knees (65%), wrists (55%), and ankles (40%). A prior history of rash illness may be reported in less than half of all patients. Improvement generally is noted within 2 weeks, but some symptoms may remain for months or, rarely, years. Some cases may meet American Rheumatism Association criteria for rheumatoid arthritis. Joint fluid analysis has been reported infrequently, but is consistent with inflammation.[70, 71]

Some studies suggest that B19 infection results in a subclinical autoimmune disorder.[72, 73] In a series of 48 B19-IgM–positive serum samples, 35 (73%) were positive for anti-double-stranded DNA (anti-ds-DNA), 28 (58%) were positive for anti-single-stranded DNA (anti-ss-DNA), and 43 (90%) were positive for antilymphocyte IgM antibody.[73] Some patients also may be positive for rheumatoid factor or antinuclear antibodies transiently.[74, 75]

When serologic tests become commercially available, it should be routine practice to look for IgM in adult patients presenting with an acute symmetric polyarthropathy. The role of B19 in chronic arthropathies is unclear at this time, and will be difficult to study. For symptoms persisting longer than several months, IgM may no longer be detectable, and no specific biologic markers have been identified. Treatment is supportive, with anti-inflammatory drugs and reassurance.

# B19 Infections in Special Hosts

## B19 Infection in Patients With Anemia

Transient aplastic crisis (TAC) was the first significant clinical illness linked to B19 infection. TAC refers to an acute, self-limited episode of pure red cell aplasia (PRCA) in patients with underlying chronic hemolytic disorders. In 1981, Pattison and his colleagues described six children with sickle cell disease and TAC who had evidence of recent B19 infection.[2] All had B19 antibody, viral antigen was detected in three serum samples, and virus particles were seen by immune electron microscopy in two serum samples. Since that time, B19 has been associated with acute, self-limited PRCA in patients with a variety of underlying hematologic disorders, not just chronic hemolytic anemia (Table 2).

Among patients in known risk groups presenting with TAC, 80% to 93% will have evidence of recent B19 infection.[19, 79, 92, 101] The majority of patients are infected in childhood. The incidence of TAC in patients with chronic hemolytic anemias has varied from 1.7% to 5% per year[3, 19, 80, 56] during community outbreaks. In family studies, the majority of secondary cases of TAC will become symptomatic 6 to 12 days following the index case.[35]

Most patients will report pallor, fever, headache, and malaise for 2 to 3 days prior to presentation. Nonproductive cough, coryza, and sore throat are less common. Vomiting, nausea, and abdominal pain may be reported in about one third of cases. Skin rash is reported very uncommonly. Clinically inapparent infection also may occur. In some patients with chronic hemolytic anemias, red cell transfusions prior to infection may have caused them to be clinically inapparent.[56, 92]

At the time of presentation, the patient is severely anemic and the reticulocyte count is low. In the bone marrow there will be a near absence of red cell precursors, and those that are present may include giant forms; other cell lines generally will be unaffected. Bone marrow necrosis may be extensive in some cases.[91] Transient thrombocytopenia and neutropenia are

## TABLE 2.
## Hematologic Disorders Shown to Predispose Patients to B19-Associated Acute Pure Red Cell Aplasia.

Functional classification.
 Hematologic disorder.
I. Anemias associated with decreased red cell production.
  A. Ineffective erythropoiesis.
    1. Congenital dyserythropoietic anemia (HEMPAS).[76]
  B. Decreased hemoglobin synthesis.
    1. Iron deficiency.[77, 78]
    2. Thalassemia.[60, 79–82]
II. Anemias associated with increased red cell destruction or loss.
  A. Membrane defects.
    1. Hereditary spherocytosis.[35, 36, 79, 83, 84]
    2. Hereditary stomatocytosis.[85]
  B. Enzyme deficiencies.
    1. Glucose-6-phosphate dehydrogenase deficiency.[86, 87]
    2. Pyruvate kinase deficiency.[88]
    3. Pyrimidine-5'-nucleotidase deficiency.[89]
  C. Hemoglobinopathies.
    1. Sickle cell disease and related disorders.[36, 56, 79, 80, 82, 90–92]
  D. Paroxysmal nocturnal hemoglobinuria.[93]
  E. Infections.
    1. Malaria.[94]
  F. Antibody-mediated.
    1. Chronic autoimmune hemolytic anemia.[79, 80, 95–98]
    2. Cold antibody-mediated autoimmune hemolytic disease.[99]
  G. Blood loss.[100]

---

reported commonly,* but have not been associated with bleeding complications or secondary infections. In the recovery phase, 10 to 12 days following symptom onset, the peripheral smear will show reticulocytosis, leukocytosis, thrombocytosis, along with a hypererythroblastic bone marrow.[35]

Management of the patient with PRCA is based on symptomatic treatment of the associated anemia and may require blood transfusion. B19-associated PRCA may be fatal if untreated.[85, 101] Patients should be presumed infectious and placed in contact isolation, generally for the duration of hospitalization.[38, 43]

### B19 Infection in Pregnancy and Fetal Disease

Some animal parvoviruses are known to be embryocidal and teratogenic.[102] In humans, maternal infection with B19 during pregnancy is associated with an increased risk of fetal death and nonimmunologic hydrops,[43, 103] but

*References 56, 76–81, 84, 86, 87, 89, 91, 93, 96, 100.

there is no evidence that B19 infection in utero results in an increased risk of birth defects among liveborn infants, or that B19 is a major cause of spontaneous abortions in women not selected for exposure to, or with symptoms suggestive of B19 infection.[104-106] There have been several reports concerning one case of an abortus with eye anomalies and histologic evidence of B19 infection in other tissues; the most complete report of this case is included in the references.[107]

The reported prevalence of IgG antibodies among pregnant women and women of reproductive age is roughly 50% (range 25% to 75%),[55, 104, 108] suggesting that many women are immune and therefore not at risk for B19-associated fetal disease. However, maternal exposure to B19 may be common during pregnancy. The annual incidence of infection in women of reproductive age was 1.5% in one longitudinal study.[108] The prevalence of B19 IgM antibodies in pregnant women has been about 1% in studies that did not preselect subjects on the basis of exposure or symptoms suggestive of B19 infection.[106] During a community outbreak of EI, the prevalence of B19 IgM was 1.7% among pregnant patients not selected for B19 exposure or symptoms (2.6% of susceptibles), and 2.9% (6% of susceptibles) among women with perceived exposure.[55] The risk of exposure and infection may be increased for women in some occupations, such as elementary school teachers.[33]

There have been only two studies reported to date that have followed prospectively to term cohorts of B19-infected women without evidence of fetal disease at the time of diagnosis.[26, 109] These studies suggest that the risk of an adverse outcome in women with serologically confirmed B19 infection is less than 10% overall, and that it is greatest in the first 20 weeks of pregnancy. The Public Health Laboratory Service Working Party on Fifth Disease in the United Kingdom identified 193 IgM-positive pregnant women and followed 190 of them to term.[26] Four had therapeutic abortions. Among those remaining, there were 30 (16%) fetal deaths, and as many as 17 (9%) were estimated to be attributable to B19 infection on the basis of DNA studies of a sample of abortuses. Most fetal deaths occurred before 20 weeks. One-year follow-up of liveborn infants has not revealed any adverse effects attributable to intrauterine B19 infection. In a study of 39 pregnancies complicated by maternal B19-infection, there were 2 fetal deaths, only 1 (3%) of which could be attributed to B19, and it occurred at 10 weeks' gestation.[109] Preliminary data from controlled studies in progress at the Centers for Disease Control are in agreement with these two studies (CDC, unpublished data. 1987-1990).

The pathogenesis of B19-associated fetal hydrops has not been elucidated completely. In the fetus, B19 lytically infects red cell precursors, producing a profound anemia and hypoxemia. The anemia may precipitate congestive heart failure with the accumulation of fluid in body cavities, generalized edema, and finally death. The fetus may not be able to produce an effective immune response, and the infection may become chronic[110]; viral DNA often can be demonstrated in the absence of fetal IgM.[111] Hemolysis with hemosiderin deposition may lead to hepatic fibrosis[112] and varices.[113] Infection of cardiac muscle by B19 has been demonstrated occasionally and may contribute to the development of hydrops,[114, 115] although fetal death may occur in the absence of heart failure.[116] In fetal tissues, the pathologic findings typically include a leukoerythroblastic reaction, with hemosiderin deposition and eosinophilic nuclear inclusions in erythroblasts.[7, 117] By electron microscopy, these inclusions have been shown to contain viral particles, and B19 DNA is demonstrable in fetal tissues.[118, 119]

The optimal management of a pregnancy complicated by maternal B19 infection has not been determined in controlled clinical trials, and the risks of any interventions must be weighed carefully against uncertain benefits. Serial determinations of maternal serum α-fetoprotein levels have been advocated by some based on reports of increased levels in the case of affected fetuses.[120] However, levels also may be normal in affected fetuses[111] and may not predict adverse outcomes. Serial ultrasound examinations have been recommended for patient follow-up, but in the only prospective study to date, no cases of fetal hydrops were identified or prevented.[109] It seems likely that the routine use of ultrasound is unwarranted in this patient group. Intrauterine blood transfusion is a high-risk procedure that has been used for the treatment of fetal hydrops and anemia.[121, 122] But it has been recognized recently that B19-associated fetal hydrops also may resolve spontaneously,[111, 123, 124] which leaves the question of when to intervene with intrauterine blood transfusion unresolved. At this point, it should not be considered as routine treatment for B19-related hydrops.

## Congenital and Acquired Immunodeficiency Syndromes

Chronic bone marrow failure has been reported in several patients with proven or suspected congenital immunodeficiency syndromes.[10, 125, 126] Infection occurs in the absence of the usual manifestations of rash or arthropathy. The first report was of a child with combined immunodeficiency with immunoglobulins (Nezelof syndrome).[10] The patient presented acutely with anemia, reticulocytopenia, and neutropenia, and was shown to improve and relapse spontaneously over the ensuing months. B19 DNA and antigen were demonstrated in bone marrow and serum, along with the characteristic giant proerythroblasts in bone marrow. IgM and IgG antibodies were detected by radioimmunoassay, but poorly by immunoblotting, and did not neutralize virus well, suggesting a qualitative defect in antibody production. Another case occurred in a child with common variable immunodeficiency (predominantly T cell, CD4+, lymphopenia). The child remained transfusion-dependent for months and then the red cell aplasia resolved spontaneously. In a subsequent febrile illness, the patient became neutropenic and giant erythroblasts were seen again in his bone marrow aspirate, despite the presence of B19-specific antibodies.

B19 also has been described as an opportunistic pathogen in patients with human immunodeficiency virus type 1 infection and the acquired immunodeficiency syndrome.[25, 127] Infection is probably uncommon, but may be difficult to detect unless there is strong suspicion. In one study, investigators screened sera from 50 patients with the acquired immunodeficiency syndrome and 20 with lymphadenopathy, and none contained B19 DNA.[128]

Patients present with symptoms caused by anemia and have findings consistent with PRCA. In published reports, the hemoglobin has been <5 g/dL, reticulocytes have been absent, granulocyte and platelet counts have been normal, and lymphocyte counts have been consistent with the degree of immunosuppression present due to human immunodeficiency virus type 1 infection. Bone marrow examination shows erythroid hypoplasia and occasional large proerythroblasts (0.5% of nucleated cells).

Treatment with intravenous immunoglobulin has been associated with a reduction in serum virus concentration and improvement in hematologic indices. The amount and duration of therapy should be based on response. Relapses have been documented, even following treatment with high doses.

## Lymphoproliferative Disorders

There are no data indicating how often B19 infection may complicate the treatment of leukemia. Since the peak incidence of EI occurs in childhood, exposure to B19 may be a common occurrence for children with leukemia. Chronic B19 infection associated with severe anemia has been reported in 13 patients with acute lymphoblastic leukemia receiving induction[129] or maintenance chemotherapy,[51, 98, 130–136] in 1 patient receiving maintenance treatment for chronic myelomonocytic leukemia,[137] and in 2 patients following allogeneic bone marrow transplantation for acute myelogenous leukemia.[138, 139] Among the 16 patients described in these reports, all were anemic (hemoglobin range 4.7 g/dL to 9.6 g/dL) and, in most cases, the anemia was detected in the course of routine follow-up. Erythroid hypoplasia was noted in all cases reporting results of bone marrow studies, and giant proerythroblasts were noted in 11 cases. Six patients were neutropenic (<1.5 × 10^9/L) and 6 were thrombocytopenic (range 2 × 10^9/L to 158 × 10^9/L). Eleven patients recovered when chemotherapy was completed or interrupted temporarily, 2 recovered despite continued chemotherapy, 1 had persistent anemia 2 months following the discontinuation of chemotherapy but recovered following intravenous immune globulin therapy, and 2 died. Specific IgM was noted rarely during the illness and in only some of the cases during recovery.

The diagnosis in these cases was made on the basis of unexpected anemia, reticulocytopenia, erythroid hypoplasia, and giant proerythroblasts, with confirmatory laboratory studies demonstrating B19 antigen or DNA. The typical manifestations of EI or arthropathy were absent. Three patients had rash illnesses during the recovery phase, but only 1 had a history of a rash prior to hematologic recovery.

Patients with lymphoproliferative disorders are at risk for chronic infection because immunosuppressive therapy probably precludes an adequate humoral immune response. This has been shown by low levels of immunoglobulins,[51, 131] improvement following the completion or temporary cessation of chemotherapy, and improvement following the administration of plasma or immune globulin containing specific B19 antibodies. These patients may be treated by interrupting or modifying chemotherapy regimens, if it would not compromise treatment of the underlying disease, or by administering intravenous immune globulin. Since these patients are viremic, they may present a risk of nosocomial transmission, and hospitalized patients should be placed in contact isolation for the duration of the illness.

There have been a few reports of patients with acute B19 infection complicating the treatment of other malignancies, including Burkitt's lymphosarcoma,[140] lymphoblastic lymphoma, astrocytoma, and Wilms' tumor.[134] These reports suggest a similar clinical picture of anemia, neutropenia, thrombocytopenia, impaired antibody response, and improvement after the interruption of chemotherapy schedules.

## Organ Transplant Recipients

Chronic infection with B19 also has been documented following organ transplantation.[1, 141] The original report describing B19 viremia included a patient 1 week following renal transplantation.[1] No additional clinical information was provided in that case, but in another renal transplant patient, B19 infection resulted in a self-limited infection.[141] Chronic B19 infection with pancytopenia also has been documented in cardiac and liver transplant patients[142] (CDC, unpublished data, 1990-1991). The risk of B19 infection and its natural history in transplant recipients has not been determined. In a preliminary report, 4 of 20 recent transplant patients had B19 DNA detected in serum specimens.[142]

Pancytopenia has been the most commonly noted abnormality. The diagnostic evaluation should include a careful search for giant proerythroblasts in bone marrow aspirate material (which would be presumptive evidence of B19 infection), serologic studies to identify B19 IgM, and studies for B19 DNA. The only reliable measures of recovery would be clinical improvement in association with failure to recover viral DNA from clinical samples. IgM and IgG antibodies may wax and wane over the course of chronic infection, and the presence of IgG antibodies alone may not be reliable evidence of recovery. Patients can improve spontaneously, but they may respond more rapidly to a reduction in immunosuppressive drug therapy or the administration of intravenous immune globulin.

## Other Clinical Manifestations

### Neurologic Disease

Prior to the identification of B19 as the causative agent of EI, two cases of encephalitis were reported in patients clinically diagnosed with EI.[143, 144] In both cases, extensive evaluations were undertaken to identify other potential etiologic agents of encephalitis, but these studies were unproductive. Also, in both instances, there were cases of EI in the community coincident with the patients' illnesses, suggesting that they probably were infected recently with B19. In several recent reports, serologically confirmed B19 has been associated with extremity numbness and tingling, and brachial plexus neuropathy.[145–147] The onset of symptoms occurred coincident with rash and arthralgias, suggesting that the neuropathy is immunologically mediated.

## Other Hematologic Manifestations

**Aplastic Anemia.**—Since B19 produces a lytic infection in bone marrow cells and, in the setting of PRCA, has been associated with other transient cytopenias, there has been considerable interest in a potential etiologic role for B19 in some of the other syndromes associated with bone marrow failure. Aplastic anemia in one patient was associated with B19 IgM antibodies, suggesting recent infection.[148] However, B19 is unlikely to be a common cause of aplastic anemia. In a series of patients with aplastic anemia, none of 11 had B19 antigen in serum samples, and 3 of 28 had very low levels of B19 IgM that the authors thought were nonspecific.[15]

**Idiopathic Thrombocytopenic Purpura.**—Although a transient, mild thrombocytopenia is noted commonly in patients with B19-associated PRCA, B19 probably is an uncommon cause of idiopathic thrombocytopenic purpura, but it may occur occasionally in patients with no known underlying hematologic disease. In a series of 61 patients with the disorder, 3 (5%) had IgM, suggesting recent infection.[149] The few reported cases have been characterized by the acute onset of a petechial rash, an increase in megakaryocytes in the bone marrow, and B19 IgM antibodies in serum.[150, 151] In one case, the patient improved spontaneously; in the other case, the patient did not improve after intravenous immune globulin, but did improve coincident with glucocorticoid treatment.

**Transient Erythroblastopenia of Childhood.**—B19 infection has not been shown to be the etiologic agent responsible for transient erythroblastopenia of childhood, a PRCA of children without known underlying hematologic disorders. In a series of 21 patients, none had B19 antigen or IgM antibody.[15] In a second study, none of 5 such patients tested had IgM antibody, but the seasonality of transient erythroblastopenia of childhood and TAC cases was similar.[82] However, there have been several case reports of probable transient erythroblastopenia of childhood associated with B19 IgM antibody.[152, 153] Whether some of these cases are due to B19 is still unresolved at this time. A much more common occurrence is that an episode of TAC is the sentinel event that leads to the discovery of a previously unrecognized hematologic disorder in the patient and family members.[79]

**Virus-Associated Hemophagocytic Syndrome.**—There have been two reports of B19-associated hemophagocytic syndrome.[98, 154] The first occurred in a child on maintenance chemotherapy for acute lymphoblastic anemia. Neutropenia and histiocytic infiltration of the bone marrow with erythrophagocytosis were the most striking findings; his serum contained B19 DNA. His chemotherapy was discontinued temporarily, he improved spontaneously, and specific IgM and IgG were detected in his serum. The second case occurred in a child with no known underlying disease. He developed an acute febrile illness with pancytopenia; his bone marrow aspirate revealed leukophagocytosis and hemophagocytosis. To differentiate between malignant histiocytosis and virus-associated hemophagocytic syndrome, he underwent splenectomy, liver biopsy, and lymph node biopsy. Necrotic nodules composed of T cells and macrophages were noted in the spleen, and well-differentiated histiocytes exhibiting erythrophagocytosis were present in all the tissues. Spleen tissue was positive for B19 DNA by the polymerase chain reaction (CDC, unpublished observations, 1990), and a serum sample from the time of admission was positive for IgM and IgG antibodies. The patient recovered and remained well when last seen 3 months later. Although a variety of pathogenic agents previously have been linked to virus-associated hemophagocytic syndrome, B19-infected red cells would be an attractive target for phagocytic cells. Further studies are needed to determine the extent to which B19 is involved with this syndrome.

## Systemic Vasculitis

There have been a number of reports of serologically confirmed B19 and nonthrombocytopenic purpura, including Henoch-Schönlein purpura.[60–64] In contrast to patients with thrombocytopenia, who generally are antibody-positive at the time of presentation, patients with nonthrombocytopenic purpura may be viremic, and B19 IgM antibody is detected only in convalescent specimens. Most of the reported patients have not had an underlying hematologic disorder and have not been anemic. A skin biopsy was reported in one case and showed a leukocytoclastic vasculitis and C3 deposition, but no IgG, IgA, or IgM.[64] A preliminary report of chronic B19 infection in a patient with polyarteritis nodosa is of considerable interest.[155] The patient was not anemic, and signs and symptoms of inflammation disappeared when he was treated with intravenous immunoglobulin, allowing tapering of his immunosuppressive therapy. Whether B19 was important in the pathogenesis of this patient's underlying disease or was an opportunistic pathogen may never be resolved, but it deserves further study as a potential etiologic agent or trigger of vasculitis.

## Acute Myocarditis

Animal parvoviruses may result in myocarditis. There has been one fatal case of B19-associated myocarditis reported in a 1-year-old.[156] The patient died with biventricular failure several weeks following EI. The histopathologic findings were typical of myocarditis, B19 was shown by immunocytochemical techniques in myocardial tissue sections, and B19 IgM was present in patient serum. B19 has been found in myocardial cells in the fetus and may play a role in the pathogenesis of fetal hydrops in some cases.[114, 115]

## Laboratory Diagnosis

Specific laboratory diagnosis of B19 infection depends on the identification of B19 antibodies, antigen, or DNA. Histopathologic findings may be sufficiently characteristic to make the presumptive diagnosis of B19 infection in some cases, even in the absence of specific laboratory tests, and may be the only practical recourse until widespread testing is available. To use the diagnostic studies optimally, it is important to take into consideration the patients' clinical manifestations, time course in illness, and underlying conditions.

In the normal host, the only test necessary for the diagnosis of recent B19 infection is an IgM antibody assay. IgM generally is detectable by radioimmunoassay or enzyme immunoassay within 3 days after symptom onset, peaks in 2 to 3 weeks, and then begins to decline over the following 1 to 2 months.[157, 158] IgG becomes detectable within several days after IgM, and persists for years and probably for life. Patients with EI or acute arthropathy are almost always IgM-positive at the time of presentation, and the collection of a single serum sample for serologic testing is sufficient to make a diagnosis. The inability to propagate B19 in vitro to produce viral antigens for test kits has limited severely the availability of serologic testing for B19. The development of recombinant cell lines that express B19 capsid proteins promises a renewable source of antigen suitable for commercial kits.[159] Synthetic peptides also have been developed for serologic testing.[160]

The interpretation of serologic results is more difficult in other patient populations. Patients with chronic hematologic disorders may present with aplastic crises before IgM or IgG antibodies are detectable, and immunocompromised patients (including the fetus) with chronic infections may have an unpredictable antibody response. Tests for B19 DNA or viral antigens are most useful in these patients. The most sensitive assays for detecting B19 DNA are hybridization assays and the polymerase chain reaction. Both techniques have been applied successfully to a variety of clinical specimens, including amniotic fluid, fetal blood, serum, leukocytes, respiratory secretions, fresh tissues, and paraffin-embedded tissues.[10, 18, 124, 161–166] The polymerase chain reaction is the more sensitive of the two techniques, and B19 DNA may be detectable in serum for several months, even after an uncomplicated infection.[165] Both techniques require meticulous care and adequate controls to ensure reliable results. A major limitation is that these techniques are not widely available outside of research laboratories.

Light and electron microscopy may be very helpful in diagnosing B19 infection. In anemic patients, bone marrow aspirates should be examined carefully for giant proerythroblasts; if present, they constitute strong evidence of B19 infection. In the majority of women with hydropic fetuses, maternal IgM will suggest the diagnosis, but in some cases, IgM may become undetectable by the time fetal disease is recognized. Examination of fetal tissues, including the placenta, for the characteristic inclusions in nucleated red cells may suggest the diagnosis in these cases. In situ hybridization and immunohistochemical studies can confirm the diagnosis, but are not generally available. Electron microscopy may reveal virus particles in the serum of some infected patients[1, 167] and hydropic fetuses.

## Coda

In the 10 years since B19 first was identified as the etiologic agent of aplastic crises in patients with sickle cell disease, there has been a great increase in our understanding of the many clinical entities associated with B19 infection and of the extraordinary way in which the virus-host interaction results in these varied manifestations. These achievements were made despite the difficulties caused by working with a fastidious organism, with no practical in vitro culture system, no animal model, and no easy access to viral antigens for serologic tests. Because of these constraints, it seems likely that the spectrum of clinical manifestations is still incompletely catalogued. Some of these obstacles will be resolved in the near future and will greatly facilitate the further study of B19.

There are a number of areas that should be high priorities for future study. The risk of infection to the fetus needs to be characterized better and controlled studies of treatment for the affected fetus need to be undertaken. The importance of B19 as an opportunistic pathogen in immuno-compromised patients needs to be determined and the role of intravenous immune globulins further evaluated as treatment. It still needs to be resolved whether or not B19 is an important cause of chronic arthritis and whether or not there are other pathogenic parvoviruses of man that may be arthritogenic. Does B19 play an etiologic role in systemic vasculitis, or act solely as an opportunistic pathogen in patients on immunosuppressive therapy? The answers to these questions will help to decide whether sufficient morbidity and mortality are associated with B19 to warrant the development and use of B19 immune globulins or vaccines.

## References

1. Cossart YE, Field AM, Cant B, et al: Parvovirus-like particles in human sera. *Lancet* 1975; 1:72–73.
2. Pattison JR, Jones SE, Hodgson J, et al: Parvovirus infections and hypoplastic crisis in sickle-cell anaemia (letter). *Lancet* 1981; 1:664–665.
3. Serjeant GR, Topley JM, Mason K, et al: Outbreak of aplastic crises in sickle cell anaemia associated with parvovirus-like agent. *Lancet* 1981; 2:595–597.
4. Young N: Hematologic and hematopoietic consequences of B19 parvovirus infection. *Semin Hematol* 1988; 25:159–172.
5. Anderson MJ, Jones SE, Fisher-Hoch SP, et al: Human parvovirus, the cause of erythema infectiosum (fifth disease) (letter)? *Lancet* 1983; 1:1378.
6. Plummer FA, Hammond GW, Forward K, et al: An erythema infectiosum-like illness caused by human parvovirus infection. *N Engl J Med* 1985; 313:74–79.
7. Anand A, Gray ES, Brown T, et al: Human parvovirus infection in pregnancy and hydrops fetalis. *N Engl J Med* 1987; 316:183–186.

8. Reid DM, Reid TMS, Brown T, et al: Human parvovirus-associated with arthritis: A clinical and laboratory description. *Lancet* 1985; 1:422–425.
9. White DG, Woolf AD, Mortimer PP, et al: Human parvovirus arthropathy. *Lancet* 1985; 1:419–421.
10. Kurtzman GJ, Ozawa K, Cohen B, et al: Chronic bone marrow failure due to persistent B19 parvovirus infection. *N Engl J Med* 1987; 317:287–294.
11. Pattison JR: The discovery of human parvoviruses, in Pattison JR (ed): *Parvoviruses and Human Disease*. Boca Raton, Florida, CRC Press, 1988, pp 1–4.
12. Siegl G, Bates RC, Berns KI, et al: Characteristics and taxonomy of Parvoviridae. *Intervirology* 1985; 23:61–73.
13. Turton J, Appleton H, Clewley JP: Similarities in nucleotide sequence between serum and faecal human parvovirus DNA. *Epidemiol Infect* 1990; 105:197–201.
14. Simpson RW, McGinty L, Simon L, et al: Association of parvoviruses with rheumatoid arthritis of humans. *Science* 1984; 223:1425–1428.
15. Young NS, Mortimer PP, Moore JG, et al: Characterization of a virus that causes transient aplastic crisis. *J Clin Invest* 1984; 73:224–230.
16. Cotmore SF, McKie VC, Anderson LJ, et al: Identification of the major structural and nonstructural proteins encoded by human parvovirus B19 and mapping of their genes by procaryotic expression of isolated genomic fragments. *J Virol* 1986; 60:548–557.
17. Shade RO, Blundell MC, Cotmore SF, et al: Nucleotide sequence and genome organization of human parvovirus B19 isolated from the serum of a child during aplastic crisis. *J Virol* 1986; 58:921–936.
18. Frickhofen N, Young NS: Polymerase chain reaction for detection of parvovirus B19 in immunodeficient patients with anemia. *Behring Inst Mitt* 1990; 85:46–54.
19. Chorba T, Coccia P, Holman RC, et al: The role of parvovirus B19 in aplastic crisis and erythema infectiosum (fifth disease). *J Infect Dis* 1986; 154:383–393.
20. Ozawa K, Kurtzman G, Young N: Repliction of the B19 parvovirus in human bone marrow cell cultures. *Science* 1986; 233:883–886.
21. Yaegashi N, Shiraishi H, Takeshita T, et al: Propagation of human parvovirus B19 in primary culture of erythroid lineage cells derived from fetal liver. *J Virol* 1989; 63:2422–2426.
22. Takahashi T, Ozawa K, Mitani K, et al: B19 parvovirus replicates in erythroid leukemic cells in vitro (letter). *J Infect Dis* 1989; 160:548–549.
23. Anderson MJ, Cherry JD: Parvoviruses, in Feigin RD, Cherry JD (eds): *Textbook of Pediatric Infectious Diseases*, 2nd ed. Philadelphia, WB Saunders, 1987, pp 1646–1653.
24. Anderson LJ: Role of parvovirus B19 in human disease. *Pediatr Infect Dis J* 1987; 6:711–718.
25. Frickhofen N, Abkowitz JL, Safford M, et al: Persistent B19 parvovirus infection in patients infected with human immunodeficiency virus type 1 (HIV-1): A treatable cause of anemia in AIDS. *Ann Intern Med* 1990; 113:926–933.
26. Public Health Laboratory Service Working Party on Fifth Disease: Prospective study of human parvovirus (B19) infection in pregnancy. *Br Med J* 1990; 300:1166–1170.
27. Mortimer PP, Luban NLC, Kelleher JF, et al: Transmission of serum parvovirus-like virus by clotting-factor concentrates. *Lancet* 1983; 2:482–484.
28. Bartolomei Corsi O, Assi A, Morfini M, et al: Human parvovirus infection in

haemophiliacs first infused with treated clotting factor concentrates. *J Med Virol* 1988; 25:165–170.

29. Lyon DJ, Chapman CS, Martin C, et al: Symptomatic parvovirus B19 infection and heat-treated factor IX concentrate (letter). *Lancet* 1989; 1:1085.

30. Williams MD, Cohen BJ, Beddall AC, et al: Transmission of human parvovirus B19 by coagulation factor concentrates. *Vox Sang* 1990; 58:177–181.

31. Rubinstein AI, Rubinstein DB: Inability of solvent-detergent (S-D) treated factor VIII concentrate to inactivate parvoviruses and non-lipid enveloped non-A, non-B hepatitis virus in factor VIII concentrate: Advantages to using sterilizing 100° C dry heat treatment. *Am J Hematol* 1990; 35:142.

32. Shneerson JM, Mortimer PP, Vandervelde EM: Febrile illness due to a parvovirus. *Br Med J [Clin Res]* 1980; 1:1580.

33. Gillespie SM, Cartter ML, Asch S, et al: Occupational risk of human parvovirus B19 infection for school and day-care personnel during an outbreak of erythema infectiosum. *JAMA* 1990; 263:2061–2065.

34. Anderson MJ, Higgins PG, Davis LR, et al: Experimental parvoviral infection in humans. *J Infect Dis* 1985; 152:257–265.

35. Mortimer PP: Hypothesis: The aplastic crisis of hereditary spherocytosis is due to a single transmissible agent. *J Clin Pathol* 1983; 36:445–448.

36. Saarinen Ua, Chorba TL, Tattersall P, et al: Human parvovirus B19 induced epidemic red-cell aplasia in patients with hereditary hemolytic anemia. *Blood* 1986; 67:1411–1417.

37. Ager EA, Chin TDY, Poland JD: Epidemic erythema infectiosum. *N Engl J Med* 1966; 275:1326–1331.

38. Evans JPM, Rossiter MA, Kumaran TO, et al: Human parvovirus aplasia: Case due to cross infection in a ward. *Br Med J [Clin Res]* 1984; 288:681.

39. Ueda K, Akeda H, Tokugawa K, et al: Human parvovirus infection (letter). *N Engl J Med* 1986; 314:645–646.

40. Bell LM, Naides SJ, Stoffman P, et al: Human parvovirus B19 infection among hospital staff members after contact with infected patients. *N Engl J Med* 1989; 321:485–491.

41. Cohen BJ, Courouce AM, Schwarz TF, et al: Laboratory infection with parvovirus B19 (letter). *J Clin Pathol* 1988; 41:1027–1028.

42. Garner JS, Simmons BP: Guideline for isolation precautions in hospitals. *Infect Control Hosp Epidemiol* 1983; 4(suppl):245–325.

43. Centers for Disease Control: Risks associated with human parvovirus B19 infection. *MMWR* 1989; 38:81–88.

44. American Academy of Pediatrics Committee on Infectious Diseases: Parvovirus, erythema infectiosum, and pregnancy. *Pediatrics* 1990; 85:131–133.

45. Mortimer PP, Humphries RK, Moore JG, et al: A human parvovirus-like virus inhibits haematopoietic colony formation "in vitro." *Nature* 1983; 302:426–429.

46. Young N, Harrison M, Moore J, et al: Direct demonstration of the human parvovirus in erythroid progenitor cells infected in vitro. *J Clin Invest* 1984; 74:2024–2032.

47. Ozawa K, Kurtzman G, Young N: Productive infection of B19 parvovirus of human erythroid bone marrow cells in vitro. *Blood* 1987; 70:384–391.

48. Potter CG, Potter AC, Hatton CSR, et al: Variation of erythroid and myeloid precursors in the marrow of volunteer subjects infected with human parvovirus (B19). *J Clin Invest* 1987; 79:1486–1492.

49. Frickhofen N, Young NS: Persistent parvovirus B19 infections in humans. *Microbial Pathogenesis* 1989; 7:319–327.

50. Owren PA: Congenital hemolytic jaundice. The pathogenesis of the "hemolytic crisis." *Blood* 1948; 3:231–248.
51. Kurtzman GJ, Cohen B, Meyers P, et al: Persistent B19 parvovirus infection as a cause of severe chronic anemia in children with acute lymphocytic leukemia. *Lancet* 1988; 2:1159–1162.
52. Kurtzman GJ, Cohen BJ, Field AM, et al: Immune response to B19 parvovirus and an antibody defect in persistent viral infection. *J Clin Invest* 1989; 84:114–123.
53. Kurtzman GJ, Gascon P, Caras M, et al: B19 parvovirus replicates in circulating cells of acutely infected patients. *Blood* 1988; 71:1448–1454.
54. Srivastava A, Bruno E, Briddell R, et al: Parvovirus B19-induced perturbation of human megakaryocytopoiesis in vitro. *Blood* 1990; 10:1997–2004.
55. Cartter ML, Farley TA, Rosengren S, et al: Occupational risk factors for infection with parvovirus B19 among pregnant women. *J Infect Dis* 1991; 163:282–285.
56. Anderson MJ, Davis LR, Hodgson J, et al: Occurrence of infection with a parvovirus-like agent in children with sickle cell anaemia during a two-year period. *J Clin Pathol* 1982; 35:744–749.
57. Anderson MJ, Lewis E, Kidd IM, et al: An outbreak of erythema infectiosum associated with human parvovirus infection. *J Hyg Epidemiol Mirobiol Immunol* 1984; 93:85–93.
58. Lauer BA, MacCormack JN, Wilfert C: Erythema infectiosum. An elementary school outbreak. *Am J Dis Child* 1976; 130:252–254.
59. Naides SJ, Piette W, Veach LA, et al: Human parvovirus B19-induced vesiculopustular skin eruption. *Am J Med* 1988; 84:968–972.
60. Lefrere JJ, Courouce AM, Muller JY, et al: Human parvovirus and purpura (letter). *Lancet* 1985; 2:730.
61. Mortimer PP, Cohen BJ, Rossiter MA, et al: Human parvovirus and purpura (letter). *Lancet* 1985; 2:730–731.
62. Lefrere JJ, Courouce AM, Soulier JP, et al: Henoch-Schönlein purpura and human parvovirus infection. *Pediatrics* 1986; 78:183–184.
63. Li Loong TC, Coyle PV, Anderson MJ, et al: Human serum parvovirus associated vasculitis. *Postgrad Med J* 1986; 62:493–494.
64. Lassen C, Bonneau D, Berthier M, et al: Purpura vasculaire fébrile dû à un parvovirus (letter). *Arch Fr Pediatr* 1987; 44:619.
65. Dinerman JL, Corman LC: Human parvovirus B19 arthropathy associated with desquamation. *Am J Med* 1990; 89:826–828.
66. Joseph PR: Fifth disease: The frequency of joint involvement in adults. *N Y State J Med* 1986; 86:560–563.
67. Klouda PT, Corbin SA, Bradley BA, et al: HLA and acute arthritis following human parvovirus infection. *Tissue Antigens* 1986; 28:318–319.
68. Kandolf R, Kirschner P, Hofschneider PH, et al: Detection of parvovirus in a patient with "reactive arthritis" by in situ hybridization. *Clin Rheumatol* 1989; 8:398–401.
69. Woolf AD: Human parvovirus B19 and arthritis. *Behring Inst Mitt* 1990; 85:64–68.
70. Semble EL, Agudelo CA, Pegram PS: Human parvovirus B19 arthropathy in two adults after contact with childhood erythema infectiosum. *Am J Med* 1987; 83:560–562.
71. Aussedat R, Fener P, Pourel J: Coxite aiguë de l'adolescent, manifestation unique d'une infection par le parvovirus B19 (letter). *Presse Med* 1987; 16:1978.

72. Soloninka CA, Anderson MJ, Laskin CA: Anti-DNA and antilymphocyte antibodies during acute infection with human parvovirus B19. *J Rheumatol* 1989; 16:777–781.
73. Soloninka CA, Anderson MJ, Laskin CA: Autoantibodies in sera from patients with parvovirus B19 infection (letter). *J Rheumatol* 1990; 17:416.
74. Naides SJ, Field EH: Transient rheumatoid factor positivity in acute human parvovirus B19 infection. *Arch Intern Med* 1988; 148:2587–2589.
75. Sasaki T, Takahashi Y, Yoshinaga K, et al: An association between human parvovirus B-19 infection and autoantibody production (letter). *J Rheumatol* 1989; 16:708–709.
76. West NC, Meigh RE, Mackie M, et al: Parvovirus infection associated with aplastic crisis in a patient with HEMPAS. *J Clin Pathol* 1986; 39:1019–1020.
77. Lefrere JJ, Bourgeois H: Human parvovirus associated with erythroblastopenia in iron deficiency anaemia (letter). *J Clin Pathol* 1986; 39:1277–1278.
78. Kojima S, Matsuyama K, Ishii E: High serum iron in human parvovirus-induced aplastic crisis in iron deficiency anemia. *Acta Haematol (Basel)* 1988; 80:171–172.
79. Lefrere JJ, Courouce AM, Bertrand Y, et al: Human parvovirus and aplastic crisis in chronic hemolytic anemias: A study of 24 observations. *Am J Hematol* 1986; 23:271–275.
80. Rao KRP, Patel AR, Anderson MJ, et al: Infection with parvovirus-like virus and aplastic crisis in chronic hemolytic anemia. *Ann Intern Med* 1983; 98:930–932.
81. Doran HM, Teall AJ: Neutropenia accompanying erythroid aplasia in human parvovirus infection. *Br J Haematol* 1988; 69:287–288.
82. Bhambhani K, Inoue S, Sarnaik SA: Seasonal clustering of transient erythroblastopenia of childhood. *Am J Dis Child* 1988; 142:175–177.
83. Kelleher JF, Luban NLC, Mortimer PP, et al: Human serum "parvovirus": A specific cause of aplastic crisis in children with hereditary spherocytosis. *J Pediatr* 1983; 102:720–722.
84. Saunders PWG, Reid MM, Cohen BJ: Human parvovirus induced cytopenias: A report of five cases (letter). *Br J Haematol* 1986; 63:407–410.
85. Mabin DC, Chowdhury V: Aplastic crisis caused by human parvovirus in two patients with hereditary stomatocytosis. *Br J Haematol* 1990; 76:153–154.
86. Nibu K, Matsumot I, Yanai F, et al: Aplastic crisis due to human parvovirus B19 infection in glucose-6-phosphate dehydrogenase deficiency. *Nippon Ketsueki Gakkai Zasshi* 1989; 52:1117–1121.
87. Goldman F, Rotbart H, Gutierrez K, et al: Parvovirus-associated aplastic crisis in a patient with red blood cell glucose-6-phosphate dehydrogenase deficiency. *Pediatr Infect Dis J* 1990; 9:593–594.
88. Duncan Jr, Potter CG, Cappellini MD, et al: Aplastic crisis due to parvovirus infection in pyruvate kinase deficiency. *Lancet* 1983; 2:14–16.
89. Rechavi G, Vonsover A, Manor Y, et al: Aplastic crisis due to human B19 parvovirus infection in red cell pyrimidine-5′-nucleotidase deficiency. *Acta Haematol (Basel)* 1989; 82:46–49.
90. Serjeant GR, Goldstein AR: B19 virus infection and the aplastic crisis, in Pattison JR (ed): *Parvoviruses and Human Disease.* Boca Raton, Florida, CRC Press, 1988, pp 85–92.
91. Conrad ME, Studdard H, Anderson LJ: Case report: Aplastic crisis in sickle cell disorders: Bone marrow necrosis and human parvovirus infection. *Am J Med Sci* 1988; 295:212–215.
92. Gowda N, Rao SP, Cohen B, et al: Human parvovirus infection in patients

with sickle cell disease with and without hypoplastic crisis. *J Pediatr* 1987; 110:81–84.

93. Lakhani AK, Malkovska V, Bevan DH, et al: Transient pancytopenia associated with parvovirus infection in paroxysmal nocturnal haemoglobinuria. *Postgrad Med J* 1987; 63:483–484.

94. Jones PH, Pickett LC, Anderson MJ, et al: Human parvovirus infection in children and severe anaemia seen in an area endemic for malaria. *J Trop Med Hyg* 1990; 93:67–70.

95. Bertrand Y, Lefrere JJ, Leverger G, et al: Autoimmune haemolytic anaemia revealed by human parvovirus linked erythroblastopenia (letter). *Lancet* 1985; 2:382–383.

96. Tomiyama J, Adachi Y, Hanada T, et al: Human parvovirus B19-induced aplastic crisis in autoimmune haemolytic anaemia. *Br J Haematol* 1988; 69:288–289.

97. Smith MA, Shah NS, Lobel JS: Parvovirus B19 infection associated with reticulocytopenia and chronic autoimmune hemolytic anemia. *Am J Pediatr Hematol Oncol* 1989; 11:167–169.

98. Koch WC, Massey G, Russell CE, et al: Manifestations and treatment of human parvovirus B19 infection in immunocompromised patients. *J Pediatr* 1990; 116:355–359.

99. Chitnavis VN, Patou G, Makar YF, et al: B19 parvovirus induced red cell aplasia complication acute cold antibody mediated haemolytic anemia. *Br J Haematol* 1990; 76:433–434.

100. Frickhofen N, Raghavachar A, Heit H, et al: Human parvovirus infection (letter). *N Engl J Med* 1986; 314:646.

101. Goldstein AR, Anderson MJ, Serjeant GR: Parvovirus associated aplastic crisis in homozygous sickle cell disease. *Arch Dis Child* 1987; 62:585–588.

102. Siegl G: Biology and pathogenicity of autonomous parvoviruses, in Berns KI (ed): *The Parvoviruses*. New York, Plenum Press, 1984, pp 297–362.

103. Anderson LJ, Hurwitz ES: Human parvovirus B19 and pregnancy. *Clin Perinatol* 1988; 15:273–286.

104. Mortimer PP, Cohen BJ, Buckley MM, et al: Human parvovirus and the fetus (letter). *Lancet* 1985; 2:1012.

105. Lefrere JJ, Dumez Y, Courouce AM, et al: Intrauterine infection with human parvovirus (letter). *Lancet* 1986; 1:449.

106. Kinney JS, Anderson LJ, Farrar J, et al: Risk of adverse outcomes of pregnancy after human parvovirus B19 infection. *J Infect Dis* 1988; 157: 663–667.

107. Hartwig NG, Vermeij-Keers C, Van Elsacker-Niele AMW, et al: Embryonic malformations in a case of intrauterine parvovirus B19 infection. *Teratology* 1989; 39:295–302.

108. Koch WC, Adler SP: Human parvovirus V19 infections in women of childbearing age and within families. *Pediatr Infect Dis J* 1989; 8:83–87.

109. Rodis JF, Quinn DL, Gary GW, et al: Management and outcomes of pregnancies complicated by human B19 parvovirus infection: A prospective study. *Am J Obstet Gynecol* 1990; 163:1168–1171.

110. Anderson MJ, Khousam MN, Maxwell DJ, et al: Human parvovirus B19 and hydrops fetalis (letter). *Lancet* 1988; 1:535.

111. Morey AL, Nicolini U, Welch CR, et al: Parvovirus B19 infection and transient fetal hydrops (letter). *Lancet* 1991; 337:496.

112. Metzman R, Anand A, DeGiulio PA, et al: Hepatic disease associated with

intrauterine parvovirus B19 infection in a newborn premature infant. *J Pediatr Gastroenterol Nutr* 1989; 9:112–114.

113. Franciosi RA, Tattersall P: Fetal infection with human parvovirus B19. *Hum Pathol* 1988; 19:489–491.

114. Porter HJ, Quantrill AM, Fleming KA: B19 parvovirus infection of myocardial cells (letter). *Lancet* 1988; 1:535–536.

115. Naides SJ, Weiner CP: Antenatal diagnosis and palliative treatment of nonimmune hydrops fetalis secondary to fetal parvovirus B19 infection. *Prenat Diagn* 1989; 9:105–114.

116. Maeda H, Shimokawa H, Satoh S, et al: Nonimmunologic hydrops fetalis resulting from intrauterine human parvovirus B-19 infection: Report of two cases. *Obstet Gynecol* 1988; 72:482–485.

117. Caul EO, Usher MJ, Burton PA: Intrauterine infection with human parvovirus B19: A light and electron microscopy study. *J Med Virol* 1988; 24:55–66.

118. Clewley JP, Cohen BJ, Field AM: Detection of parvovirus B19 DNA, antigen, and particles in the human fetus. *J Med Virol* 1987; 23:367–376.

119. Porter HJ, Khong TY, Evans MF, et al: Parvovirus as a cause of hydrops fetalis: Detection by in situ DNA hybridisation. *J Clin Pathol* 1988; 41:381–383.

120. Carrington D, Gilmore DH, Whittle MJ, et al: Maternal serum alpha-fetoprotein—a marker of fetal aplastic crisis during intrauterine human parvovirus infection. *Lancet* 1987; 1:433–435.

121. Schwarz TF, Roggendorf M, Hottentrager B, et al: Human parvovirus B19 infection in pregnancy (letter). *Lancet* 1988; 2:566–567.

122. Peters MT, Nicolaides KH: Cordocentesis for the diagnosis and treatment of human fetal parvovirus infection. *Obstet Gynecol* 1990; 75:501–504.

123. Gloning KP, Schramm T, Brusis E, et al: Successful intrauterine treatment of fetal hydrops caused by parvovirus B19 infection. *Behring Inst Mitt* 1990; 85:79-85.

124. Török TJ, Wang Q-Y, Gary GW, et al: Prenatal diagnosis of intrauterine parvovirus B19 infection by the polymerase chain reaction technique. *Rev Infect Dis,* in press.

125. Davidson JE, Gibson B, Gibson A, et al: Parvovirus infection, leukemia, and immunodeficiency (letter). *Lancet* 1989; 1:102.

126. Kurtzman G, Frickhofen N, Kimball J, et al: Pure red-cell aplasia of 10 years' duration due to persistent parvovirus B19 infection and its cure with immunoglobulin therapy. *N Engl J Med* 1989; 321:519–523.

127. Mitchell SA, Welch JM, Weston-Smith S, et al: Parvovirus infection and anaemia in a patient with AIDS: Case report. *Genitourin Med* 1990; 66:95–96.

128. Anderson MJ, Kidd IM, Jones SE, et al: Parvovirus infection and the acquired immunodeficiency syndrome. *Ann Intern Med* 1985; 102:275.

129. Azzi A, Macchia PA, Favre C, et al: Aplastic crisis caused by B19 virus in a child during induction therapy for acute lymphoblastic leukemia. *Haematologica (Pavia)* 1989; 74:191–194.

130. Van Horn DK, Mortimer PP, Young N, et al: Human parvovirus-associated red cell aplasia in the absence of underlying hemolytic anemia. *Am J Pediatr Hematol Oncol* 1986; 8:235–239.

131. Smith MA, Shah NR, Lobel JS, et al: Severe anemia caused by human parvovirus in a leukemia patient on maintenance chemotherapy. *Clin Pediatr* 1988; 27:383–386.

132. Coulombel L, Morinet F, Mielot F, et al: Parvovirus infection, leukaemia, and immunodeficiency (letter). *Lancet* 1989; 1:101–102.

133. Carstensen H, Cohen BJ: Human parvovirus B19 infection associated with prolonged erythroblastopenia in a leukemic child (letter). *Pediatr Infect Dis J* 1989; 8:56.

134. Graeve JLA, de Alarcon PA, Naides SJ: Parvovirus B19 infection in patients receiving cancer chemotherapy: The expanding spectrum of disease. *Am J Pediatr Hematol Oncol* 1989; 11:441–444.

135. Rao SP, Miller ST, Cohen BJ: Severe anemia due to B19 parvovirus infection in children with acute leukemia in remission. *Am J Pediatr Hematol Oncol* 1990; 12:194–197.

136. Takahashi M, Moriyama Y, Shibata A, et al: Anemia caused by parvovirus in an adult patient with acute lymphoblastic leukemia in complete remission (letter). *Eur J Haematol* 1991; 46:47.

137. Malarme M, Vandervelde D, Brasseur M: Parvovirus infection, leukemia, and immunodeficiency (letter). *Lancet* 1989; 1:1457.

138. Weiland HT, Salimans MMM, Fibbe WE, et al: Prolonged parvovirus B19 infection with severe anemia in a bone marrow transplant recipient (letter). *Br J Haematol* 1989; 71:300.

139. Niitsu H, Takatsu H, Miura I, et al: Pure red cell aplasia induced by B19 parvovirus during allogeneic bone marrow transplantation. *Rinsho Ketsueki* 1990; 31:1566–1571.

140. Courouce AM, Ferchal F, Morinet F, et al: Human parvovirus infections in France (letter). *Lancet* 1984; 1:160.

141. Neild G, Anderson M, Hawes S, et al: Parvovirus infection after renal transplant (letter). *Lancet* 1986; 2:1226–1227.

142. Marshall WF, Telenti A, Smith TF: Polymerase chain reaction detection of parvovirus B19 viremia after organ transplantation (abstract), in *Program and Abstracts of the 30th Interscience Conference on Antimicrobial Agents and Chemotherapy*. Atlanta, Georgia, 1990, p 292.

143. Balfour HH Jr, Schiff GM, Bloom JE: Encephalitis associated with erythema infectiosum. *JAMA* 1970; 77:133–136.

144. Hall CB, Horner FA: Encephalopathy with erythema infectiosum. *Am J Dis Child* 1977; 131:65–67.

145. Denning DW, Amos A, Rudge P, et al: Neuralgic amyotrophy due to parvovirus infection (letter). *J Neurol Neurosurg Psychiatry* 1987; 50:641–642.

146. Walsh KJ, Armstrong RD, Turner AM: Brachial plexus neuropathy associated with human parvovirus infection. *Br Med J [Clin Res]* 1988; 296:896.

147. Faden H, Gary GW, Korman M: Numbness and tingling of fingers associated with parvovirus B19 infection (letter). *J Infect Dis* 1990; 161:354–355.

148. Hamon MD, Newland AC, Anderson MJ: Severe aplastic anaemia after parvovirus infection in the absence of underlying haemolytic anaemia. *J Clin Pathol* 1988; 41:1242–1246.

149. Lefrere JJ, Courouce AM, Kaplan C: Parvovirus and idiopathic thrombocytopenic purpura (letter). *Lancet* 1989; 1:279.

150. Lefrere JJ, Got D: Peripheral thrombocytopenia in human parvovirus infection (letter). *J Clin Pathol* 1987; 40:469.

151. Foreman NK, Oakhill A, Caul EO: Parvovirus-associated thrombocytopenic purpura (letter). *Lancet* 1988; 2:1426–1427.

152. Guillot M, Lefrere JJ, Raventet N, et al: Acute anaemia and aplastic crisis without haemolysis in human parvovirus infection (letter). *J Clin Pathol* 1987; 40:1264–1265.

153. Wodzinski MA, Lilleyman JS: Transient erythroblastopenia of childhood due to parvovirus B19 infection. *Br J Haematol* 1989; 73:127–131.
154. Boruchoff SE, Woda BA, Pihan GA, et al: Parvovirus B19-associated hemophagocytic syndrome. *Arch Intern Med* 1990; 150:897–899.
155. Finkel TH, Gelfand EW, Harveck R, et al: Chronic parvovirus infection presenting as juvenile polyarteritis nodosum. Presented at the 54th Annual Meeting, American College of Rheumatology, Seattle, Washington, October/November, 1990.
156. Saint-Martin J, Choulot JJ, Bonnaud E, et al: Myocarditis caused by parvovirus (letter). *J Pediatr* 1990; 116:1007–1008.
157. Anderson MJ, Davis LR, Jones SE, et al: The development and use of an antibody capture radioimmunoassay for specific IgM to a human parvovirus-like agent. *J Hyg Epidemiol Microbiol Immunol* 1982; 88:309–324.
158. Anderson LJ, Tsou C, Parker RA, et al: Detection of antibodies and antigens of human parvovirus B19 by enzyme-linked immunosorbent assay. *J Clin Microbiol* 1986; 24:522–526.
159. Kajigaya S, Shimada T, Fujita S, et al: A genetically engineered cell line that produces empty capsids of B19 (human) parvovirus. *Proc Natl Acad Sci U S A* 1989; 86:7601–7605.
160. Fridell E, Trojnar J, Wahren B: A new peptide for human parvovirus B19 antibody detection. *Scand J Infect Dis* 1989; 21:597–603.
161. Anderson MJ, Jones SE, Minson AC: Diagnosis of human parvovirus infection by dot-blot hybridization using cloned viral DNA. *J Med Virol* 1985; 15:163–172.
162. Clewley JP: Detection of human parvovirus using a molecular cloned probe. *J Med Virol* 1985; 15:173–181.
163. Salimans MMM, Holsappel S, van de Rijke FM, et al: Rapid detection of human parvovirus B19 DNA by dot-hybridization and the polymerase chain reaction. *J Virol Methods* 1989; 23:19–28.
164. Salimans MMM, van de Rijke FM, Raap AK, et al: Detection of parvovirus B19 DNA in fetal tissues by in situ hybridisation and polymerase chain reaction. *J Clin Pathol* 1989; 42:525–530.
165. Clewley JP: Polymerase chain reaction assay of parvovirus B19 DNA in clinical specimens. *J Clin Microbiol* 1989; 27:2647–2651.
166. Koch WC, Adler SP: Detection of human parvovirus B19 DNA by using the polymerase chain reaction. *J Clin Microbiol* 1990; 28:65–69.
167. Chrystie IL, Almeida JD, Welch J: Case report: Electron microscopic detection of human parvovirus (B19) in a patient with HIV infection. *J Med Virol* 1990; 30:249–252.

# Advances in Internal Medicine Cumulative Index Volumes 33–37

*(The numbers in italics indicate the volume)*

## A

Abdomen
  acute, in pheochromocytoma, *35*, 204
  pain in AIDS, *34*, 65
Abuse
  cocaine, *37*, 21–35
  drug, for athletic enhancement (*see*
    Athletic enhancement, drugs for)
Acarbose: in obesity, *34*, 142
Acetaminophen
  hypoglycemia due to, *33*, 223
  overdose in pregnancy, and liver
    disease, *35*, 304
Acetylcholine
  in atherosclerotic arteries
    coronary, *34*, 370
    iliac (in monkey), *34*, 368
  -induced endothelium-dependent
    relaxation, discovery of, *34*,
    358–359
Achalasia: causing esophageal chest pain,
  *33*, 314
Achlorhydria: causing delayed gastric
  emptying, *33*, 367–369
Acid perfusion test: in esophageal chest
  pain, *33*, 320
Acidosis: lactic, in pheochromocytoma, *35*,
  204
Acquired immune deficiency syndrome
  (*see* AIDS)
ACTH
  activities in normal tissues, *34*, 332
  production by cancers, *34*, 326–332
Acute phase response, *37*, 313–336; *34*,
  3–5
  assessment, clinical value of, *37*,
    324–329
  components, clinical value of
    measurement of, *37*, 328–329
  C-reactive protein and, *37*, 313–336
  erythrocyte sedimentation rate and, *37*,
    324–325
  interleukin-1 and, *34*, 5–6

physiologic components of, *34*, 4
Acutrim: in obesity, *34*, 141
Acyclovir
  in Epstein-Barr virus infection,
    gastrointestinal, in AIDS, *34*, 52
  in herpes simplex disease in AIDS, *37*,
    139; *34*, 64
    gastrointestinal, *34*, 52
  in varicella-zoster virus infection in AIDS,
    *37*, 140
Acyl coenzyme A dehydrogenase
  deficiency: and fatty liver of
  pregnancy, *35*, 293
Addison's disease: and hypoglycemia, *33*,
  223
Adenoma, parathyroid
  nonsurgical ablation, *37*, 286
  origin, *37*, 279–280
S-Adenosyl-L-methionine: in intrahepatic
  cholestasis of pregnancy, *35*, 297
Adenovirus
  gastrointestinal symptoms in AIDS due
    to, *34*, 53
  in pathogenesis of celiac disease, *35*,
    358
Adhesins: of
  *Escherichia coli*, *33*, 241
Adolescent: diabetic, growth rate, and
  insulin pump therapy, *35*, 126
Adrenal
  cortex (*see* Adrenocortical)
  hypothalamic-pituitary-adrenal axis and
    withdrawal of glucocorticoid
    therapy, *35*, 184–186
  mass, differential diagnosis of, *35*, 211
Adrenergic
  antagonists, central, in pregnancy, *35*,
    280
  beta-adrenergic (*see* Beta-adrenergic)
Adrenocortical
  carcinoma, chorionic gonadotropin
    production by, *34*, 332
  cortisol, and glucose counterregulation,
    *33*, 209

# A Simple, Once-a-Year Dose!

Review the partial list of titles below. And then request your own FREE 30-day preview. When you purchase a Year Book, we'll also send you an automatic notice of future volumes about two months before they publish.

This system was designed for your convenience and to take up as little of your time as possible. If you do not want the Year Book, the advance notice makes it easy for you to let us know. And if you elect to receive the new Year Book, you need do nothing. We will send it on publication.

No worry. No wasted motion. And, of course, every Year Book is yours to examine FREE of charge for thirty days.

Year Book of **Anesthesia**® (22137)
Year Book of **Cardiology**® (22114)
Year Book of **Critical Care Medicine**® (22091)
Year Book of **Dermatology**® (22108)
Year Book of **Diagnostic Radiology**® (22132)
Year Book of **Digestive Diseases**® (22081)
Year Book of **Drug Therapy**® (22139)
Year Book of **Emergency Medicine**® (22085)
Year Book of **Endocrinology**® (22107)
Year Book of **Family Practice**® (20801)
Year Book of **Geriatrics and Gerontology** (22121)
Year Book of **Hand Surgery**® (22096)
Year Book of **Hematology**® (22604)
Year Book of **Health Care Management**® (21145)
Year Book of **Infectious Diseases**® (22606)
Year Book of **Infertility** (22093)
Year Book of **Medicine**® (22087)
Year Book of **Neonatal-Perinatal Medicine** (22117)
Year Book of **Neurology and Neurosurgery**® (22120)
Year Book of **Nuclear Medicine**® (22140)
Year Book of **Obstetrics and Gynecology**® (22118)
Year Book of **Occupational and Environmental Medicine** (22092)
Year Book of **Oncology** (22128)
Year Book of **Ophthalmology**® (22135)
Year Book of **Orthopedics**® (22116)
Year Book of **Otolaryngology – Head and Neck Surgery**® (22086)
Year Book of **Pathology and Clinical Pathology**® (22104)
Year Book of **Pediatrics**® (22088)
Year Book of **Plastic and Reconstructive Surgery**® (22112)
Year Book of **Psychiatry and Applied Mental Health**® (22110)
Year Book of **Pulmonary Disease**® (22109)
Year Book of **Sports Medicine**® (22115)
Year Book of **Surgery**® (22084)
Year Book of **Ultrasound** (21170)
Year Book of **Urology**® (22094)
Year Book of **Vascular Surgery**® (22105)

Mosby-Year Book, Inc. • 11830 Westline Industrial Drive • St. Louis, MO 63146